HARVARD ECONOMIC STUDIES

HARVARD UNIVERSITY PRESS
CAMBRIDGE, MASS., U.S.A.

LONDON : HUMPHREY MILFORD

OXFORD UNIVERSITY PRESS

HARVARD ECONOMIC STUDIES

VOLUME XLIII

THE STUDIES IN THIS SERIES ARE PUBLISHED BY THE DEPARTMENT OF
ECONOMICS OF HARVARD UNIVERSITY, WHICH, HOWEVER, ASSUMES
NO RESPONSIBILITY FOR THE VIEWS EXPRESSED

THE LOCK OF THE GREEN TREASURE CHEST

Probably the "Arca Verde," often mentioned in the sixteenth- and seventeenth-century accounts of the Casa de la Contratación as a strong box for American treasure. The chest now rests at the head of the stairway in the Archivo General de Indias, which occupies the building of the old Casa Lonja in Seville. As was true of other public safes of the day, three keys, held individually by the officials of the Casa de la Contratación (contador, factor, and tesorero), were required to open the green chest. Another receptacle for Indian treasure, the "Arca de Tres Llaves," received frequent mention in the Contratación papers.

AMERICAN TREASURE AND THE PRICE REVOLUTION IN SPAIN, 1501–1650

BY

EARL J. HAMILTON, Ph.D.

PROFESSOR OF ECONOMICS IN DUKE UNIVERSITY

CAMBRIDGE, MASSACHUSETTS

HARVARD UNIVERSITY PRESS

1934

HB
235
S75
H3

HC

330.8
H 67
v. 43

To

SITA

**WHO CROSSED THE ATLANTIC AT THE AGE OF
SIX WEEKS AND RAMBLED OVER SPAIN
THE NEXT TWO YEARS ON THE
TRAIL OF OLD PAPER**

PREFACE

No OTHER period in history has witnessed so great a proportional increase in the production of the precious metals as occurred in the wake of the Mexican and Peruvian conquests. A modicum of treasure was obtained in the Antilles before 1520, but not until the fabulous mines were discovered on the mainland — in New Spain, Peru, and New Granada — did the harvest of the precious metals transcend the wildest dreams of the *conquistadores*. Pouring into Europe in a mammoth stream, American gold and silver precipitated the Price Revolution, which in turn played a significant rôle in the transformation of social and economic institutions in the first two centuries of the modern era. Thoroughly imbued with mercantilist principles, the rulers of Castile spared no pains to attract the largest possible flow of specie to the motherland, and to obstruct its outward passage. To further these ends and to facilitate the collection of royal dues, the Catholic Kings and the Hapsburgs bestowed upon Seville the monopoly of American trade and navigation and required all the gold and silver of the Indies that legally entered Europe to pass through the coffers of the *Casa de la Contratación* (India House). Presumably the Price Revolution was more abrupt and transcendent in Spain than in any other European country, and *a priori* one would suppose that the phenomenon spread over Spain in concentric waves from Seville, the fountainhead.

Precise measurement of the effect of American treasure upon Spanish prices and wages presupposed accurate information concerning the quantity of gold and silver imports from the Indies; and the data could be obtained only from the contemporary documents deposited in the Archivo General de Indias at Seville. Although one could not foresee the contingency, it proved equally indispensable to study Castilian and Valencian money anew from the manuscript sources of the national and leading municipal archives. The search for price and wage statistics, absolutely all of which have been taken from contemporary documents and account-books, carried the writer into more than a hundred towns, scattered from the highlands of León to the Mediterranean coast and from the plains of Extremadura to the foothills of the Pyrenees.

Research on the scale required by the present project was rendered possible by a Frederick Sheldon Traveling Fellowship from Harvard University in 1926–1927, which financed the collection of data on treasure imports and a preliminary investigation of Andalusian prices; a Social Science Research Council Fellowship for 1929–1930, which supported the study of Castilian money and Old Castilian and Andalusian prices and wages; and a liberal grant for 1930–1934 from the funds supplied the International Scientific Committee on Price History by the Laura Spelman Rockefeller Foundation, which carried forward the research on prices and wages in New Castile and on money, prices, and wages in Valencia. I welcome this opportunity to express gratitude for the generosity of the benefactors who have supported forty-two months' research in Spanish archives and have never imposed restrictions upon freedom of thought or action. To the administration of Duke University I am indebted for three years' leave of absence, sympathetic interest in my research, and the exaction of the minimum of routine duties compatible with my academic post.

The number of individuals who have assisted me in one way or another is legion. Professor Abbott Payson Usher of Harvard University, who directed my doctoral thesis on "A History of Money and Prices in Andalusia, 1503–1660" and whose teaching awakened my initial interest in economic history, offered much constructive criticism; and his paternal interest in my subsequent research has been a source of delight and inspiration. For numerous courtesies beyond what could be expected in the complete discharge of their official duties I am indebted to the following Directors of Spanish archives and libraries: Don Miguel Artigas of the Biblioteca Nacional, Don Fernando Ferraz Penelas of the Archivo Regional de Valencia, Don Miguel Gómez del Campillo of the Archivo Histórico Nacional, Don Angel Plaza y Bores of the Archivo General de Simancas, Don Juan Tamayo y Francisco of the Archivo General de Indias, and Don Fernando Valls y Taberner of the Archivo de la Corona de Aragón. The members of the Cuerpo de Archiveros to whom I am indebted are too numerous to name; but at the risk of being unfair to others, I feel duty bound to mention Don Pedro Longás y Bartibás of the Sección de Manuscritos of the Biblioteca Nacional, Don Samuel Ventura y Solsona of the Archivo General de Indias, Don Antonio Torres y Gasión of the Archivo Histórico Nacional, Don Cristóbal Bermúdez Plata of the Biblioteca Universitaria de Sevilla, and Don Ricardo Magdaleno, formerly of the Archivo General de Simancas. Don José de la Peña y Cámara of the Archivo General de Indias placed his profound knowledge of the Archive unstintedly at my disposal and assisted me in countless ways toward a better understanding and appreciation of things Spanish, both past and present. Of the local archivists Don Adolfo García Olmedo of the Archivo del Ayuntamiento of Valladolid and Don Luis Cebrián Ibor of the Archivo de la Diputación Provincial of Valencia deserve special mention.

Don Agustín Rodriguez, Superintendent of the Hospital de Tavera, Don Mariano Morate, Superintendent of the Hospital de San Bernabé y San Antolín, and Don Lorenzo Casas Martínez, Trustee of the Hospital de Antezana, not only gave me free access to the account-books of their respective institutions, but did everything within their power to expedite my work. The Asociación General de Ganaderos del Reino generously permitted me to use the Archivo de la Mesta. Without the cheerful and effective intervention of Don Pedro Serrano, then President of the Diputación Provincial of Valencia, it would have been impossible to utilize the invaluable papers of the Hospital dels Inocents, containing one of the longest series of price statistics in existence, more than four hours a week! Many other Presidents of Diputaciones Provinciales and Civil Governors authorized the use of documents not open to the public.

Don Ramón Paz Remolar and Don Federico Navarro Franco, young members of the Cuerpo de Archiveros, rendered valuable aid in the collection of price and wage statistics for New Castile. The energy and skill of the following clerical workers employed at one time or another deserve special mention: Sres. Manuel Medina, José María Esteve, and Ángel González López; Srtas. Josefina Díaz and Maruja Arellano; and Miss Josephine Hawley. My colleague, Dr. B. F. Lemert, constructed the map of Spain, and Sr. Luis Suances Pascual drew the charts. Mrs. Eveline A. Green, who typed the manuscript, detected many mechanical errors and made few.

My colleagues, Drs. John Tate Lanning and Robert S. Smith, and my former student, Mr. E. S. Wallace, have read most of the manuscript and offered helpful criticism. Mr. W. H. Delaplane, Fellow in Economics at Duke, rendered valuable service in averaging and tabulating wages; and Dr. Smith calculated the annual averages for about half the commodities included in the Old Castilian-Leonese indices. Mr. Warren C. Scoville has been remarkably efficient and faithful in computing index numbers and reading proof. Don Ramón Carande, formerly President of the University of Seville and now economic adviser to the Spanish government, has assisted me in the location of important documents.

To the superior intelligence, good judgment, and industry of Don Miguel Bordonau y Mas, sometime Director of the Archivo General de Simancas and now attached to the Sección de Manuscritos of the Biblioteca Nacional, much of whatever merit the present study may possess is due. His fertile mind has devised many schemes for enhancing the efficiency of the work in archives, and his super-personality has smoothed the path to several invaluable private collections of institutional records. Throughout the two years that Don Miguel has assisted me, my conviction that few men ever attain similar perfection has constantly grown.

I am indebted to four scientific journals for permission to reproduce, wholly or partially, the following articles they have published:

1. *Journal of Economic and Business History* for "American Treasure and Andalusian Prices, 1503–1660," vol. I, pp. 1–35.

2. *Quarterly Journal of Economics* for "Imports of American Gold and Silver into Spain, 1503–1660," vol. XLIII, pp. 436–472.

3. *Economic History* for "Monetary Inflation in Castile, 1598–1660," vol. II, pp. 177–212.

4. *Annales d'Histoire Économique et Sociale* for "La Monnaie en Castille, 1501–1650," Mars et Mai, 1932.

In all cases I have added many data unknown to me when the articles were written and have made substantial corrections.

The present study has benefited greatly from the experience, embodied in written reports and oral discussions at biennial meetings, of the members of the International Scientific Committee on Price History — including Professor Arthur H. Cole, the Financial Representative —, all eminent scholars engaged in price research in their respective countries.

I find no words adequate to express my obligation to Professor Edwin F. Gay of Harvard University, at whose suggestion the present study was undertaken. Notwithstanding the pressure of manifold duties, he has always found time to criticise, instruct, and inspire in a manner seldom equaled and never excelled.

Most of all I owe to my wife, Gladys Dallas Hamilton, who collected at least half the data on treasure imports, computed almost all the averages, constructed all the tables, performed the mental work and supervised the mechanical labor involved in the calculation of index numbers and the preparation of charts, and (through criticism of the text) eliminated many faults of style and content. Furthermore, she has made countless economic and social sacrifices in the interest of our study and research and has cheerfully executed more than her part of every undertaking in the years that we have been one.

Few readers are likely to form a correct impression of the quantity of labor required to produce a history of prices for the sixteenth and the first half of the seventeenth century entirely from manuscript material.[1] Mrs. Hamilton and I have spent more than six years, during half of which we were not free from

---

[1] Thorold Rogers devoted more than a quarter of a century to his study of English prices (*A History of Agriculture and Prices in England*, VI [1887], xvii), and thirty-two years elapsed between the publication of the first and the last volume of Vicomte d'Avenel's investigation of French prices (*Histoire Économique de la Propriété, des Salaires, des Denreês et de Tous les Prix en Général*, I–VII [1894–1926]).

other occupation, on the present study, working jointly about 30,750 hours; and we have had approximately 12,500 hours of assistance. Not less than three million computations have been made. But there has been a significant waste of effort through uneconomical procedure and mistaken attempts at super-refinement. Present indications are that the studies of Spanish money, prices, and wages in the periods 1351–1500 and 1651–1800, now well advanced, will require considerably less labor.

EARL J. HAMILTON

SAN LORENZO DEL ESCORIAL, SPAIN
        March 18, 1933

CONTENTS

TABLES

CHARTS

ILLUSTRATIONS

BIBLIOGRAPHY

Since the catalogues of Spanish archives and libraries have been designed largely to facilitate research in political history and have given scant attention to matters economic, it has seemed desirable to include in the present Bibliography numerous titles of miscellaneous pamphlets and manuscripts. For instance, the virtually uncatalogued *Sección de Varios* of the Biblioteca Nacional, which consists of some 467 boxes of pamphlets and royal ordinances, proved rich in material for economic history; and several weeks were required to ferret out the data relating to money and prices. To conserve the results of the laborious search in the *Sección de Varios*, much of the material found there has been listed below, along with the library references (V. 1–158–66, for instance). Most of the invaluable collections of the *Sección de Manuscritos* of the Biblioteca Nacional, which have been largely neglected by economic historians, are well catalogued. But the titles in the *Manuscritos* inventories, too long to reproduce here, have been greatly abridged and the reference numbers listed after each item. Titles and dates have been given in Spanish when it seemed that this procedure conduced to clarity.

The sources of price and wage statistics have been divided into *used* and *not used* categories. For the most part, the "used" sections contain the data on which the index numbers are based. Most of the documents utilized only as controls, along with series too short or incomplete to be of value for the present study (but which may conceivably be utilized in future research projects), have been relegated to the "not used" category. Inasmuch as relatively few of the documents that have yielded price and wage statistics are deposited in archives and since most of them are completely devoid of inventories and orderly arrangement, it is not possible to cite catalogue numbers nor to identify the material satisfactorily. In the main, however, sixteenth- and seventeenth-century account-books are bound in parchment; and most of the documents listed below as sources of price and wage data can be located without a prohibitive search.

The inventories of the vast collection of ecclesiastical papers in the Archivo Histórico Nacional give only the points of origin and the number of *legajos* from each institution. Had not Don Miguel Bordonau, who, as a member of the Cuerpo de Archiveros, was able to obtain stack privileges, made a catalogue of the documents relating to prices and wages for the purpose of the present study, it would have proved utterly impossible to utilize these invaluable papers. Hence it seems desirable to list some of the most important sources of prices unearthed by Sr. Bordonau.[1]

I have divided the Bibliography into sections corresponding to the two main divisions of the text; but certain items relating to both Parts, such as legal codes and parliamentary proceedings, have been listed under Money and Treasure and not repeated.

Critical discussions of the manuscript sources have been reserved for the appropriate chapters of the text.

The key to frequently recurring abbreviations follows.

ABBREVIATIONS

AH	Academia de la Historia.
Actas	Actas de las Cortes de Castilla.
Burriel	Andrés Marcos Burriel.
AA	Archivo del Ayuntamiento.
A. de I.	Archivo General de Indias.
AS	Archivo General de Simancas.
AHN	Archivo Histórico Nacional.
AR	Archivo Regional de Valencia.
BN	Biblioteca Nacional.
BUV	Biblioteca Universitaria de Valencia.
BAH	Boletín de la Real Academia de la Historia.
Cortes	Cortes de los Antiguos Reinos de León y Castilla.
HS	Hospital de la Sangre, Seville.
Quaderno de Leyes	Quaderno de Leyes Añadidas a la Nueva Recopilación.
Recopilación	Recopilación de Leyes de España.
Recopilación de Indias	Recopilación de Leyes de los Reinos de las Indias.
RABM	Revista de Archivos, Bibliotecas y Museos.
V.	Sección de Varios, BN.

---

[1] *Vide infra*, p. 141.

I. MONEY AND TREASURE

A. PRINTED SOURCES

1 Acosta, José. *Historia Natural y Moral de las Indias.* Barcelona, 1591.

2 *Actas de las Cortes de Castilla, 1563–1632.* Madrid, 1861–1929. 51 vols.

3 Aguiar y Acuña, R. de. *Sumarios de la Recopilación General de las Leyes y Ordenanzas, Provisiones . . . para las Indias Occidentales.* Madrid, 1626.

4 Aingo de Ezpeleta, Pedro. *Resoluciones de las Dudas Ocasionadas de la Baxa de la Moneda de Vellón.* Cordova, 1643.

5 Alba, Duque de. "La Hacienda Real de España en el Siglo XVI." In BAH, LXXX, 146–184.

6 Antúnez y Acevedo, Rafael. *Memorias Históricas sobre la Legislación y Gobierno del Comercio de los Españoles con sus Colonias en las Indias Occidentales.* Madrid, 1797.

7 Arphe y Villafañe, Juan de. *Quilatador de la Plata, Oro y Piedras Preciosas.* Valladolid, 1572.

8 Artíñano, Gervasio de. *Historia del Comercio con las Indias.* Barcelona, 1917.

9 *Aureum Opus Regalium Privilegiorum Ciuitatis et Regni Valentiae.* Valencia, 1515.

10 Babelon, J. "A propos de la Monnaie de Segovie." In *Bulletin Hispanique*, XXIII, 304–317.

11 Barbón y Castañeda, Guillén. *Provechosos Arbitrios al Consumo del Vellón.* Madrid, 1628 (V. 1–124–3).

12 Barthé, Bautista. *Colección de Documentos para la Historia Monetaria de España.* Madrid, 1843.

13 Basso, Gerardo. *Arbitrio sobre la Mudanza de la Moneda.* 4 Septiembre 1631 (V. 1–145–29).

14 Bécker y González, Jerónimo. *La Política Española en las Indias.* Madrid, 1920.

15 Belveder, Juan. *Libro General de las Reducciones de Plata y Oro de Diferentes Leyes y Pesos.* Lima, 1597.

16 Benítez, Sebastián. *Medios para Impedir la Entrada de Vellón en estos Reinos.* 24 Junio 1625 (V. 1–158–66).

17 Blanchet, A. "Fabrication de Fausses Monnaies d'Espagne au Temps de la Ligue (1583–1590)." In *Revue Numismatique*, Second trimestre, 1906.

18 Bonneville, Pierre-Frédéric. *Traité des Monnaies d'Or et d'Argent.* Paris, 1806.

19 Calvo, Ignacio. "Los Reales de a Cuatro." In RABM, 3ª Época, XLVI, 420–442.

20 Campos y González, Vicente de. *Defensorio de las Monedas Antiguas de Oro y Plata de España.* Madrid, 1759.

21 Canga Argüelles, José. *De la Ley, el Peso y Valor de las Monedas que Circularon en el Reino de Valencia durante el Gobierno de sus Fueros.* Madrid, 1838.

22   Cantos y Benítez, Pedro de. *Escrutinio de Maravedises y Monedas de Oro Antiguas*. Madrid, 1763.

23   Cardona, Tomás de. *Discurso Tocante a la Moneda de Vellón*. About 1619.

24   Cardona, Tomás de. *Memorial sobre el Crecimiento de la Plata y Moneda de Cobre*. Madrid, 27 Septiembre 1622 (V. 1-124-38).

25   Carranza, Alonso. *El Ajustamiento i Proporción de las Monedas de Oro, Plata i Cobre*. Madrid, 1629.

26   Chavarría, Fernando de. *Advertimiento para Consumir la Moneda de Vellón*. Murcia, 31 Diciembre 1624 (V. 1-158-72).

27   Chavarría, Fernando de. *Segundo Advertimiento para el Consumo de la Moneda de Vellón y de la Causa de Haberse Encarecido los Precios de Todas las Cosas*. Murcia, 15 Noviembre 1625 (V. 1-158-73).

28   Chavarría, Fernando de. *Tercero Advertimiento para el Consumo de la Moneda de Vellón*. Murcia, 15 Febrero 1627 (V. 1-158-71).

29   Clemencín, Diego. "Elógio de la Réina Católica Doña Isabel." In *Memorias de la Real Academia de la Historia*, vi (Madrid, 1821), 235-303, 507-555.

30   *Colección de Documentos Inéditos Relativos al Descubrimiento, Conquista y Organización de las Antiguas Posesiones Españolas de Ultramar*. Madrid, 1885-1900. 13 vols.

31   *Nueva Colección de Documentos Inéditos para la Historia de España y sus Indias*. Madrid, 1892-1896. 6 vols.

32   Colmeiro y Penido, Manuel. *Historia de la Economía Política en España*. Madrid, 1863. 2 vols.

33   *Cortes de los Antiguos Reinos de León y de Castilla, 1020-1559*. Madrid, 1861-1903. 7 vols.

34   Covarrubias, Diego de. *Veterum Numismatum Collatio cum his quae Modo Expenduntur Publica et Regia Auctoritate Recusa*. 1550.

35   Dávila y Lugo, Francisco. *Desengaños a las Proposiciones de Gerardo Basso en Razón de las Monedas Ligadas de 9 y 3 Dineros de Ley, y Medios de Consumir el Vellón de España*. 1632 (V. 1-124-32).

36   Deza, Andrés de. *Arbitrio sobre la Conveniencia de Llevar al Perú y Nueva España Moneda de Vellón de la Fabricada en Segovia*. Madrid, 12 Noviembre 1626. BN, *Raros*, 17,270.

37   "Discurso en que se Prueba la Forma para que Hubiese Moneda en Castilla y sus Dominios." In *Semanario Erudito*, xxxiv, 245-252.

38   Espejo, Cristóbal. "Sobre Organización de la Hacienda Española en el Siglo XVI." In *Cultura Española*, 1907, pp. 402-426, 687-904.

39   Espejo, Cristóbal. "El Interés del Dinero en los Reinos Españoles bajo los tres Austrias." In *Boletín Sociedad Castellana Excursiones Valladolid*, v, 336-340, 359-363, 408-415, 449-452, 510-516.

40   Espínola, Bartolomé. *Sobre el Consumo y Reducción de la Moneda de Vellón*. Undated, but posterior to 1616 (V. 1-12-93).

41   Espinosa, Lucio de. *Tratado de la Moneda*. Madrid, 1626 (V. 1-158-67).

42   Estacio da Silveira, Simón. *Discurso sobre Traer por el Marañón la Plata del Perú*. Madrid, 15 Junio 1626.

43 Fernández Duro, Cesáreo. *La Armada Española desde la Unión de los Reinos de Castilla y Aragón.* Madrid, 1895–1903. 9 vols.

44 *Furs de Valencia.* Colección Formada por D. Vicente Salvá. 5 vols.

45 García Caballero, José. *Breve Cotejo y Valance de las Pesas y Medidas.* Madrid, 1731.

46 Gil Ayuso, Faustino. *Noticia Bibliográfica de Textos y Disposiciones Legales de los Siglos XVI y XVII.* To be published soon by the Biblioteca Nacional.

47 Gil y Pablos, Francisco. *Estudios sobre la Moneda y los Cambios.* Madrid, 1906.

48 González de Castro, Sebastián. *Declaración del Valor de la Plata, Ley y Peso de las Monedas Antiguas de Plata Ligada de Castilla y Aragón.* Madrid, 1658.

49 González Palencia, Ángel, and Varón Vallejo, Eudosio. *Archivo Histórico Nacional . . . Sala de Alcaldes de Casa y Corte. Catálogo.* Madrid, 1925.

50 Gounon-Loubens, Jules. *Essai sur l'Administration de la Castille au XVIe Siècle.* Paris, 1860.

51 Goury du Roslan. *Essai sur l'Histoire Économique de l'Espagne.* Paris, 1888.

52 Hamilton, Earl J. "American Treasure and the Rise of Capitalism (1500–1700)." In *Economica,* November, 1929, pp. 338–357.

53 Haring, Clarence Henry. "American Gold and Silver Production in the First Half of the Sixteenth Century." In *Quarterly Journal of Economics,* XXIX, 433–479.

54 Heiss, Aloïs. *Descripción General de las Monedas Hispano-Cristianas desde la Invasión de los Árabes.* Madrid, 1865–1869. 6 vols.

55 Heriz, Enrique. *Memoria sobre la Unidad Monetaria.* Barcelona, 1873.

56 Herrera, Antonio de. *Décadas de Indias.* Madrid, 1730.

57 Humboldt, Alexandre de. *Essai Politique sur le Royaume de la Nouvelle-Espagne.* Paris, 1811. 2 vols.

58 Institut d'Estudis Catalans. *Follets Bonsoms.*

59 Keynes, John Maynard. *A Treatise on Money.* London, 1931. II, 152–163.

60 Laiglesia y Auset, Francisco de. *Estudios Históricos 1515–1555.* II (Madrid, 1918), 225–251, 299–345.

61 Lexis, W. "Beiträge zur Statistik der Edelmetalle." In *Jahrbücher für Nationalökonomie und Statistik,* XXXIV, 361–417.

62 Lisón y Biedma, Mateo. *Memorial de la Ciudad de Granada sobre el Consumo de la Moneda de Vellón.* 1622. BN, Raros, 13,174.

63 Llanos, F. *Apuros de la Hacienda y Enfermedad de la Moneda Española en Tiempo de Cervantes.* Madrid, 1905.

64 Lonchay, H. "Recherches sur l'Origine et la Valeur des Ducats et des Écus Epagnoles." In *B. L. Ac. Belgique,* 1906, no. 11.

65 Mariana, Juan de. "Tratado y Discurso sobre la Moneda de Vellón que al Presente se Labra en Castilla." In *Biblioteca de Autores Españoles de Rivadeneyra,* XXXI, 577–593.

66 Marien y Arróspide, Tomás Antonio. *Tratado General de Monedas, Pesos, Medidas y Cambios de todas las Naciones Reducidas a las que se Usan en España.* Madrid, 1789.

67 Mateu y Llopis, Felipe. *La Ceca de Valencia y las Acuñaciones Valencianas de los Siglos XIII al XVIII.* Valencia, 1929.

? √ 68 Moncada, Sancho de. *España con Moneda y Plata.* Madrid, 1619 (V. 1–70–34).

69 Morgado, Alonso de. *Historia de Sevilla.* Seville, 1587.

70 Núñez, Cristóbal. *Sobre el Consumo de la Moneda de Vellón.* Undated, but posterior to 1606 (V. 1–12–94).

71 Ortiz, José Mariano. "Cathálogo Chronológico de las Monedas que Corrieron en el Reyno desde el Año 1238 hasta el de 1737 con Expresión del Valor, Aumento y Baxa." In *Compendio de la Vida de D. Francisco Fernández Pérez de Aranda.* Madrid, 1777.

72 Palmireno, Juan Lorenzo. *Vocabulario del Humanista . . . donde se Trata de Aves, Peces . . . Monedas. . . .* Valencia, 1569.

73 "Papel que se Presentó al Señor Rey D. Felipe IV sobre Crecer el Valor de la Moneda, en el Año 1620." In *Semanario Erudito,* XXXIV, 80–88.

74 Paz, Julián. *Catálogo de la Colección de Documentos Inéditos para la Historia de España.* Madrid, 1930–1931. 2 vols.

75 Pérez, Diego. *Pragmáticas y Leyes Hechas y Recopiladas.* Medina del Campo, 1549.

76 Pérez Manrique, Francisco. *Baja de la Moneda de Vellón.* Seville, 23 Diciembre 1642 (V. 1–155–64).

77 Peris y Fuentes, Manuel. "La Taula de Valencia." In *III Congrés d'Historia de la Corona d'Aragó,* I, 503–517.

78 Portillo, Bernardo. *Sobre que no se Labre Moneda de Cobre.* Toledo, 24 Octubre 1624 and 26 Marzo 1625 (V. 1–124–37).

79 *Pragmáticas del Reino de Valencia.* BUV, Ms. 168.

80 *Pragmáticas del Reyno . . . Recopilación de Algunas Bulas.* Alcalá de Henares, 1528.

81 Pragmatics pertaining to: *Extracción de Oro y Plata,* 1522; *Prohibición que las Tarjas corran por Moneda,* 1537 (V. 1–1–4); *Crecimiento del Valor de la Moneda de Oro,* 1566 (V. 1–49–32 and 1–54–48); *Prohibición de Cambios,* 1598 (V. 1–1–39); *Establecimiento de Bancos y sus Quiebras,* 1602; *Establecimiento del Valor del Escudo de Oro,* 1609 (V. 1–58–28); *Premio por Reducción de Vellón a Plata y Oro,* 1625, 1636, 1637, 1638, 1640, and 1641 (V. 1–60–70; 1–157–40; 1–60–84; 1–60–89; 1–60–93); *Reducción de la Moneda de Vellón a su Justo Valor,* 1627 (V. 1–60–73 and 74); *Prohibición de Sacar Moneda de Plata y Oro,* 1628 (V. 1–60–78); *Reducción de Toda la Moneda de Vellón a la Mitad de su Precio,* 1628 (V. 1–60–77 and 1–157–115); *Consumo de la Moneda de Vellón,* 1638 (V. 1–60–85); *Recogida de las Piezas de Vellón de a 4 Maravedises,* 1641 (V. 1–60–92 and 1–157–41); *Establecimiento del Valor de los Reales de a Ocho de Plata para que se Tomen por 10 Reales Vellón,* 1647 (Archivo del Ayuntamiento de Burgos, *Sección Histórica,* 1032); *Reducción de la Moneda de Plata Labrada en el Perú,* 1650 (V. 1–60–98).

82 *Provisiones, Cédulas, Capítulos de Ordenanzas . . . Tocantes al Buen Gobierno de las Indias. . . .* Madrid, 1596. 4 vols.

83 Recio de León, Manuel. *Discursos Acerca del Transporte de la Plata del Perú a Través del Marañón.* 1625 y 1626. BN, *Raros*, 17,270.

84 *Recopilación de Leyes de los Reinos de las Indias, Mandadas Imprimir y Publicar por D. Carlos II.* Madrid, 1681. 4 vols.

85 *Recopilación*[1] *de las Leyes destos Reynos Hecha por Mandado del Rey Don Phillipe Segundo.* Alcalá de Henares, 1569. 2 vols.

86 Riberos de León, Manuel. *Discursos Primero y Tercero sobre Moneda de Vellón y Plata.* 12 Septiembre 1622 (V. 1–145–38 and 39).

87 Rivero, Casto Maria del. "Ingenio de la Moneda de Segovia." In RABM, 3ª Época, XXXVIII, 20–31, 191–206; XXXIX, 28–36, 288–306; XL, 141–156.

88 Rojas, Antonio de. *Extinción y Consumo de la Moneda de Vellón.* 20 Mayo 1623 (V. 1–145–21).

89 Rojas, Antonio de, and Levanto, Oracio. *Discursos sobre la Introducción de la Nueva Moneda de Plata y Cobre.* 1623 (?). BN, 2/63,044.

90 Román, Fr. Gaspar. *Resolución Moral y Apoyo de que es Culpa Mortal Resellar con Sello Falso Moneda de Vellón contra Algunos Teólogos que Aseguran lo Contrario.* Granada, 1652.

91 Roscher, Wilhelm. *The Spanish Colonial System.* Translation by E. G. Bourne. New York, 1904.

92 Royal Cédulas concerning: *Tarjas,* 1533 and 1569 (Archivo del Ayuntamiento de Burgos, *Sección Histórica,* 3738 and 3741); *Saca de Moneda,* 1549 (V. 1–1–7); *El Premio que se ha de Llevar por los Truecos de Plata y Oro,* 1627 (V. 1–159–40); *Recogida del Vellón Resellado y que se Reselle de Nuevo Aumentando su Valor,* 1627 (V. 1–149–2 and 1–149–9); *La Labor del Oro en Escudos Sencillos y la de Plata en Reales de a Dos, Sencillos y Medios Reales,* 1627 (V. 1–157–39); *Recogida de Moneda Falsa para Resellar,* Auto de 1641 (V. 1–1–66); *Trueque de Vellón a Plata,* 1638 (V. 1–60–24); *Excesivos Precios de los Premios,* 1642 (V. 1–149–21).

93 Salas, Javier, and Rada y Delgado, Juan de Dios de la. "Informe de los Académicos . . . sobre Reducción de Antiguos Maravedises a la Moneda Corriente." In BAH, I, 366–368.

94 Sánchez del Castellar, Jaume. *Llibre de Reals Pragmatiques Publicades en la Present Ciutat de Valencia.* BUV, *Var.* 167.

95 Sandoval y Guzmán, Sebastián. *Pretensiones de la Villa Imperial de Potosí Propuestas en el Real Consejo de las Indias.* Madrid, 1634.

96 Sanz Arizmendi, C. "Las Primeras Acuñaciones de los Reyes Católicos." In RABM, 3ª Época, XLI, 68–80.

97 Sentenach, Narciso. "El Maravedí. Su Grandeza y Decadencia." In RABM, 3ª Época, XII, 195–220.

---

[1] Subsequent editions, with revisions and accretions, appeared under the titles *Recopilación, Nueva Recopilación,* and *Novísima Recopilación.* The editions of 1640 and 1775 proved particularly valuable for money and legal maximum prices respectively.

98 Sentenach, Narciso. "Monedas de Oro Castellanas; La Dobla, el Excelente o Ducado, el Escudo." In RABM, 3ª Época, XIII, 180–199.

99 Sentenach, Narciso. "Monedas de Vellón Castellanas." In RABM, 3ª Época, XIV, 329–345.

100 Shaw, W. A. *The History of Currency 1252 to 1894.* London, 1896. Pp. 23–25, 61–153.

101 Soetbeer, Adolf. *Edelmetall-Produktion und Werthverhältniss zwischen Gold und Silber seit der Entdeckung Amerikas bis zur Gegenwart.* Gotha, 1879.

102 Somoza y Quiroga, Juan. *Discurso Tocante a la Estabilidad, Medios y Dificultades que se Consideran en la Moneda desta Corona de Castilla.* Madrid, 1671.

103 Surrá y Rull, Juan. *Breve Reseña Histórico-Crítica de la Moneda Española y Reducción de sus Valores a los del Sistema Métrico Vigente.* Madrid, 1862 (published anonymously).

104 Surrá y Rull, Juan. *Breve Reseña Histórica de la Organización y Régimen de las Casas de Moneda de España.* Madrid, 1869.

105 *Tratado de la Reducción de las Monedas.* 1 Agosto 1622 (V. 1–145–12).

106 Ulloa, Antonio. *Noticias Americanas.* Madrid, 1792.

107 Vadillo, José Manuel de. *Discursos Económico-Políticos y Sumario de la España Económica de los Siglos XVI y XVII.* Cádiz, 1844.

108 Vallejera Mardones, Francisco. *Aviso y Discursos Tocantes al Repercutir que Conviene a esta Monarquía sobre la Moneda de Plata y Vellón que se ha de Labrar.* 1619.

109 Vallejera Mardones, Francisco. *Discurso sobre Tener la Moneda de Vellón tan Crecido Valor y para que se Abaxen todos los Quartos de a Ocho Maravedís por la Mitad de su Valor dentro de un Año.* Madrid, 19 Febrero 1625 (V. 1–124–34).

110 Vallejera Mardones, Francisco. *Memorial al Rey sobre la Baja de la Moneda de Vellón sin Perjuicio de Tercero.* 1623.

111 Vallejera Mardones, Francisco. *Memorial a S. M. sobre Premio de Monedas.* 3 Febrero 1628 (V. 1–124–44).

112 Veitia Linaje, José de.[1] *Norte de la Contratación de las Indias Occidentales.* Seville, 1672.

113 Vives y Escudero, Antonio. *Moneda Castellana.* Madrid, 1901.

114 Vives y Escudero, Antonio. *Reforma Monetaria de los Reyes Católicos.* Madrid, 1897.

---

[1] The title page is signed Joseph de Veitia Linage. While Treasurer of the House of Trade, Veitia's signature was often Joseph de Veytia Linage. It is interesting to note that on March 29, 1673, he received permission to send a ship of "250 tons of domestic manufacture" to the Indies "in order to aid in the expenses of publication of the book entitled *Norte de la Contratación de las Indias*" (A. de I., *Contratación*, 5183). The purpose of the subsidy, granted the year after the publication of the book, was apparently to recoup a loss which the author, or possibly the publisher, had incurred.

B. MANUSCRIPTS

1. ARCHIVES

a A. de I., *Registros de Oro, Plata y Mercaderías para Su Magestad y Particulares; Cuenta y Razón; Cargo y Data; Patronato; Audiencia de Méjico; Libros de Asientos del Recibo y Venta del Oro y Plata que Venían de Indias; Relaciones de los Caudales y Efectos que Venían de Indias en Armadas, Flotas y Naos Sueltas; Contratación; Indiferente General.*

b AA, Burgos, *Sección Histórica.*

c AA, Cordova, *Moneda.*

d AA, Cuenca, *Moneda.*

e AA, León, *Sección Primera.*

f AA, Madrid, *Moneda.*

g AA, Valencia, *Llibres de Cartes Reals; Crides; Manuals de Consells.*

h AA, Valladolid, *Esgueva Papers.*

i Archivos de los Hospitales de: la Resurrección (Valladolid), Simón Ruiz (Medina del Campo), Tavera (Toledo), Antezana (Alcalá de Henares), Nuestra Señora de la Caridad (Illescas), la Sangre (Seville), el Cardenal (Seville), Inocents (Valencia).

j AS, *Contadurías Generales: Razón y Relaciones; Tribunal Mayor de Cuentas; Contaduría Mayor; Diversos de Castilla; Casa Real (E.M.).*

k Archivo General Central de Alcalá de Henares, *Hacienda.*

l AHN, *Clero; Colección de Reales Cédulas; Universidades y Colegios.*

m AR, *Maestre Racional, Tesorería; Conventos.*

2. BN, SECCIÓN DE MANUSCRITOS

a *Arbitristas.* Mss. 20217[29], 11268[11], 6734, 11268[12], 1092, 6389, 6731, 18633[88], 9372.

b Argüello, Fray Tomás de. *Tratado sobre el Consumo de la Moneda de Vellón, Ley, Peso y Valor de la Moneda de Plata y del Oro Traido de las Indias y Medios para el Renacimiento de las Manufacturas.* Madrid, 24 Mayo 1681. Ms. 9475.

c *Baja de Moneda.* Mss. 18203, 6731.

d *Colección de Documentos ... sobre Monedas Antiguas y su Alteración y Valor en Diferentes Reinados hasta el Año 1660.* Ms. 11203.

e *Extracción de Moneda.* Mss. 6731, 18653[53].

f Lisón y Biedma, Mateo. *Fundación de Erarios y Consumo del Vellón.* 1627. Ms. 10913.

g *Moneda de Plata.* Ms. 11268.

h *Moneda de Vellón.* Mss. 14497[14], 6734, 10913, 3207, 6731, 1092, 7971, 2367.

i *Pareceres del Consejo sobre Mudanza de Moneda.* 1583. Ms. 904.

j *Premios.* Mss. 12052, 18433[9].

k *Salida de Oro y Plata de Aragón.* 1617. Ms. 13295.

l Struzzi, Luis. *Advertencias sobre Moneda de Vellón, Trueco de Plata.* Ms. 10441.

m *Tarjas.* Ms. 18670[4].

II. PRICES

A. PRINTED MATERIAL

1   Abensalero, Pascual de. *Libro de Almutazafes*. Zaragoza, 1609.
2   Alcalá, Fray Luis de. *Tractado de los Préstamos que Passan entre Mercaderes y Tractantes y por Consiguiente de los Logros*. Toledo, 1546.
3   Alvarez Osorio, Miguel. "Extensión Política y Económica." In *Educación Popular*, Parte 1ª, Apéndice A. Madrid, 1775.
4   Ansiaux, Maurice. "Histoire Économique de la Prospérité et de la Décadence de l'Espagne au XVIᵉ et au XVIIᵉ Siècles." In *Revue d'Économie Politique*, VII, 509-566, 1025-1054.
5   Artíñano, Gervasio de. *La Producción Española en la Edad Moderna*. Madrid, 1914.
6   Asso, Ignacio de. *Historia de la Economía Política de Aragón*. Zaragoza, 1798.
7   Bodin, Jean. "Response au Paradoxe de Malestroit Touchant l'Encherissement de toutes Choses et le Moyen d'y Remedier" (Henri Hauser Ed.). Paris, 1932.
8   Boix, Vicente. *Historia de la Ciudad y Reino de Valencia*. Valencia, 1845-1847. 3 vols.
9   Bona, Raymond. *Essai sur le Problème Mercantiliste en Espagne au XVIIᵉ Siècle*. Bordeaux, 1911.
10 Bonn, Julius Moritz. *Spaniens Niedergang während der Preisrevolution des 16. Jahrhunderts*. Stuttgart, 1896.
11 Burriel, Andrés Marcos. *Informe de Toledo sobre Pesos y Medidas*. Madrid, 1758.
12 Campillo y Cosío, José del. *Nuevo Sistema de Gobierno Económico para la América*. Madrid, 1789.
13 Cangas Inclán, Vicente. "Carta a Felipe Quinto sobre . . . Motivos de las Carestías y Baraturas." In *Semanario Erudito*, III, 237-269.
14 Castelot, E. "Coup d'oeil sur la Litterature Économique de l'Espagne au XVIᵉ et XVIIᵉ Siècles." In *Journal des Économistes*, 5ᵉ Serie, XLV, 189-203.
15 Caxa de Leruela, Miguel. *Discurso sobre la Principal Causa y Reparo de la Necesidad Común, Carestía General y Despoblación destos Reynos*. Madrid, 1627.
16 Caxa de Leruela, Miguel. *Restauración de la Abundancia de España*. Naples, 1631.
17 Cid, C. "Un Bando sobre Subsistencias en el Siglo XVI." In *Boletín de la Comisión de Monumentos de Orense*. Mayo-Junio, 1924.
18 Danvila y Villarrasa, Bernardo Joaquín. *Lecciones de Economía Civil o del Comercio*. Madrid, 1779.
19 Escolano, Gaspar. *Décadas de la Historia de Valencia*. Valencia, 1878-1880. 3 vols.
20 Espejo, Cristóbal. "Arbitrio sobre Imposición Tributaria en el Trigo y en la Cebada." In RABM, 3ª Época, XLIV, 258-264.

21 Espejo, Cristóbal. "La Carestía de la Vida en el Siglo XVI y Medios de Abaratarla." In RABM, 3ª Época, XLI, 36–54, 169–204, 329–354; XLII, 1–18, 199–225.

22 Espejo, Cristóbal. "Precio de los Principales Artículos en San Sebastián y Valladolid en Tiempo de Felipe II." In RABM, 3ª Época, XVI, 389–404.

23 Espejo, Cristóbal, and Paz, Julián. *Las Antiguas Ferias de Medina del Campo.* Valladolid, 1912.

24 Fernández Navarrete, Pedro. *Conservación de Monarquías y Discursos Políticos.* Madrid, 1626.

25 Gaitán de Torres, Manuel. *Reglas para el Govierno destos Reinos.* Jerez de la Frontera, 1625. BN, 3/3532.

26 Gil Sanz, Alvaro. "Situación Económica de España durante la Dominación Austriaca." In *Revista de España*, IX, 489–510.

27 González, Tomás. *Censo de Población de las Provincias y Partidos de la Corona de Castilla en el Siglo XVI.* Madrid, 1829.

28 Guiard Larrauri, Teófilo. *Historia de la Noble Villa de Bilbao.* Bilbao, 1905. I, 505–529.

29 Haebler, Konrad. *Die Wirtschaftliche Blüte Spaniens im 16. Jahrhundert und ihr Verfall.* Berlin, 1888.

30 Hamilton, Earl J. "American Treasure and Andalusian Prices, 1503–1660." In *Journal of Economic and Business History*, I, 1–35.

31 Hamilton, Earl J. "Wages and Subsistence on Spanish Treasure Ships, 1503–1660." In *The Journal of Political Economy*, XXXVII, 430–450.

32 Hume, Martin. *La Cour de Philippe IV et la Décadence de l'Espagne.* Paris, 1912.

33 Ibarra y Rodriguez, Eduardo. *Documentos de Asunto Económico Correspondientes al Reinado de los Reyes Católicos (1475–1516).* Madrid, 1917.

34 Ibarra y Rodriguez, Eduardo. "El Problema de las Subsistencias en España al Comenzar la Edad Moderna." In *Nuestro Tiempo*, Marzo, 1926, pp. 222–250.

35 Larruga, Eugenio. *Memorias Políticas y Económicas sobre los Frutos, Comercio, Fábricas y Minas de España.* Madrid, 1787–1800. 45 vols.

36 Leyes, Ordenanzas, Premáticas y Declaraciones de las Ordenanzas Antiguas que Hablan del Obraje de las Lanas y Paños, desde el Comienzo del Apartar y del Vender. 1528 (V. 1–49–60).

37 Lisón y Biedma, Mateo de. *Sobre la Entrada en estos Reynos de Mercaderías Fabricadas en los Estraños con que Sacan la Moneda y Quitan las Artes y Oficios.* 1621 (V. 1–123–33).

38 Llorente y Lannas, Alejandro. "La Primera Crisis de Hacienda en Tiempo de Felipe II." In *Revista de España*, I, 317–361.

39 Manojo de la Corte, Fernando. *Pruébase que Conviene Reformar los Precios de las Cosas.* BN, 2/65025.

40 Mantilla, C. "Precios de algunos Sueldos, Jornales y Artículos a Mediados del Siglo XVI." In *Revista Histórica de Valladolid*, Enero–Marzo, 1914.

41 Mercado, Tomás de. *Suma de Tratos y Contratos.* Seville, 1569.

42 Moncada, Sancho de. *Censura de las Causas que se Carga el Daño General de España.* 1619 (V. 1–70–35).

43 Moncada, Sancho de. *Restauración Política de España.* Madrid, 1746.

44 Moses, Bernard. "Economic Condition of Spain, 1500–1600." In *Journal of Political Economy*, I, 513–534.

45 "Observaciones Dirigidas a Averiguar las Medidas y Pesos Corrientes ó Imaginarios que Están en Uso en las Diferentes Provincias de España." In BAH, XXXIII, 202–217.

46 *Ordenanzas para el Gobierno de León.* León, 1669.

47 *Ordenanzas de Sevilla.* Seville, 1632.

48 *Ordenanzas de Valladolid.* Valladolid, 1737.

49 Orellana, Marcos Antonio de. *Valencia Antigua y Moderna.* Valencia, 1921–1924. 3 vols.

50 Pragmatics pertaining to: *Paños,* 1549 (V. 1–58–10); *Precios a que han de Venderse el Pan, Trigo, Cebada, Centeno y Panizo,* 1558 (V. 1–49–64); *Tasa de las Aves que se Toman para la Real Casa,* 1560 (V. 1–55–3); *Igualdad de las Varas de Medir,* 1568 (V. 1–49–7); *Como Han de Venderse el Trigo, Harina y Pan Cocido,* 1571 (V. 1–49–29); *Subida del Precio del Pan,* 1587 (V. 1–1–19); *Labor de las Sedas,* 1593 (V. 1–1–43); *Prohibición de Matar Terneras y Terneros,* 1598 (V. 1–1–35); *Subida del Precio de la Fanega de Cebada,* 1598 (V. 1–1–37); *Prohibición de Matar Corderos,* 1598 and 1605 (V. 1–50–2 and 1–58–20); *Subida del Precio del Trigo,* 1605 (V. 1–58–19); *Reformación de las Causas de la Carestía General, Moderación en los Precios y Tasa General de los Precios de las Mercaderías,* 1627 (V. 1–60–72); *Que se Guarde la Tasa del Trigo y Cebada,* 1628 (V. 1–60–79); *Administració del Almodí de Valencia,* 1645 (V. 1–12–137).

51 *Pregón sobre las Terneras Hembras por la Escasez de Carne y Excesivos Precios.* Toledo, 6 Septiembre 1525 (V. 1–1–1).

52 Pulgar, Fernando del. *Discurso por el qual se Declara la Causa de la General Carestía que ay en el Reyno así en los Bastimentos como en Todas las demás Cosas y el Medio para Reduzirlas a Precios Moderados.*

53 Rahola, Federico. *Economistas Españoles de los Siglos XVI y XVII.* Barcelona, 1885.

54 Ramírez de Arellano, Rafael. "Ordenanzas de Aljabiles, Sastres, Calceteros, Juboneros" [En Córdoba, Siglo XVI]. In RABM, 3ª Época, IV, 723–735.

55 Royal Cédulas concerning: *Las Carnes y que no Haya Revendedores,* 1561; *Servicio Otorgado por el Reyno que se Imponga en la Sisa del Vino y Aceite,* 1601.

56 Saigey, J. F. *Traité de Métrologie Ancienne et Moderne.* Paris, 1834.

57 Saravia de la Calle, Luis. *Instrucción de los Mercaderes.* Medina del Campo, 1544.

58 Sempere y Guarinos, Juan. *Biblioteca Española Económico-Política.* Madrid, 1801–1821. 4 vols.

59 Teixidor, José. *Antigüedades de Valencia.* Valencia, 1895. 2 vols.

60 Ulloa, Bernardo de. *Restablecimiento de las Fábricas y Comercio Español, Errores que se Padecen en los Causales de su Decadencia.* Madrid, 1740.
61 Villalón, Cristóbal de. *Tratado de Cambios y Contrataciones de Mercaderes y Reprobación de Usura.* Valladolid, 1546.
62 Viñas Mey, Carmelo. "Felipe II y el Problema Económico Español." In *Revista Nacional de Economía*, 1921, pp. 349-383.
63 Wiebe, Georg. *Zur Geschichte der Preisrevolution des XVI. und XVII. Jahrhunderts.* Leipzig, 1895.

B. MANUSCRIPTS [1]

1 *Cartas de Jerónimo Burgos sobre Carestía y Escasez de Pan.* Siglo XVI. Ms. 1761.
2 *Carta Original de Diego Morlán a Gil Morlán Residente en Zaragoza en que se Disculpa del Mayor Gasto Causado aquel Año por la Carestía de los Granos.* Salamanca, 13 Agosto 1546. Ms. 1869[81].
3 *Carta Original de S. M. al Corregidor de Palencia para que Informe acerca de las Causas de la Despoblación de los Lugares de su Jurisdicción y Remedios Oportunos.* 22 Diciembre 1626. Ms. 11265[71].
4 *Gasto de cada Dia de una Familia de Ocho Personas.* 1631. Ms. 6389.
5 *Libros de Cuentas de Gastos, Salarios y Jornales de la Casa de Pastrana.* 1562-1672. Mss. 8736, 8991, 7266, 8725-8727, 11015.
6 *Pragmáticas y Reales Cédulas sobre Trigo:* 1503, 1530, 1558, 1568, and 1598. Ms. 11374.
7 *Tasa de Gallinas y Pollos.* 1535. Ms. 904, fol. 246.

C. SOURCES OF PRICE AND WAGE STATISTICS

ANDALUSIA [2]

1. *Used*

Years	
1503, 1505, 1507, 1511, 1513, 1515, 1517, 1519, 1530, 1532, 1537, 1539, 1542, 1548-1549.	A. de I., *Contratación*, 39-2-1/8, 40-6-1/2, 32-3-3/22, 32-3-4/23, 32-3-5/24, 39-2-2/9, 39-2-2/9 (2), 32-3-7/26, 40-6-1/3, 39-3-3/1, 32-3-9/28, 36-2-1/9, 30-3-1, 36-2-2/10; *Contadurías*, 3-4-126/3, 2-3-23/24, 2-3-5/6.
1503, 1505, 1507, 1515, 1537, 1539, 1549.	AA, Seville, *Libros de Mayordomazgo.*

[1] All the manuscripts in this section are deposited in the *Sección de Manuscritos* of the Biblioteca Nacional, to the inventories of which the reference numbers correspond.
[2] All of the hospital records listed below are for Sevillan institutions and are deposited in the Archivo del Hospital del Pozo Santo, Seville.

1511, 1517, 1519.   AS, *Contaduría Mayor, Iª Época*, leg. 307.

1544, 1546, 1548–   Hospital de la Sangre, *Libros de Recibos y Gastos*, legs.
1549, 1551, 1554–   453–464.
1555, 1557–1567,
1569, 1571–1573,
1576, 1580, 1582,
1584–1585, 1587–
1589, 1591–1596,
1598–1609, 1611–
1614, 1616–1620,
1622–1650.

1591–1595, 1606–   Hospital del Espíritu Santo, *Cuentas*.
1613, 1618–1620,
1622, 1625–1631,
1635–1637, 1640–
1648.

1598–1639.   Hospital del Amor de Dios, *Cuentas*.

1599–1650.   Hospital del Cardenal, *Cuadernos de Gastos*, legs. 293–
304.

1640–1647.   Hospitalidad de Convalecientes, *Cuentas*, leg. 456.

2. *Not Used*

1500, 1555, 1563,   AS, *Casa Real*, leg. 1; *Contadurías Generales*: *Razón*,
1580–1581, 1600,   legs. 3019, 3020, 3024; *Guerra Antigua*, leg. 100;
1603, 1607, 1619,   *Contaduría Mayor de Cuentas, 2ª Época*, leg. 1324;
1624.   *3ª Época*, legs. 1404, 1381.

1552–1553, 1555,   A. de I., *Contaduría*, 3–1–7/21, 2–3–8/9, 2–3–23/24, 2–
1557, 1559, 1561,   4–73/28, 3–1–9/23, 2–3–12/13, 2–3–17/18, 3–3–
1563, 1565, 1567,   122/26, 3–1–13/27, 2–3–15/16, 3–1–1/1 (1), 2–3–
1569, 1572–1573,   20/21, 2–3–21/22, 2–3–30/31, 3–1–3/3, 3–1–10/33,
1575, 1577, 1579,   2–3–37/38, 2–3–34/35, 3–1–25/39, 3–2–52/10 (1),
1581–1582, 1585,   2–3–40/41, 2–3–41/42, 2–3–44/45, 2–4–47/2, 2–2–
1588–1589, 1591–   72/27, 3–3–112/14, 3–4–131/8, 3–4–133/10; *Contra-*
1599, 1601, 1603–   *tación*, 3902, 30–3–5, 30–3–1, 41–1–1/31, 30–3–6, 36–
1606, 1609, 1611,   2–3/11, 30–3–8, 30–3–7, 36–2–4/12, 30–3–11, 36–2–
1613, 1615, 1617,   5/13, 36–2–8/16, 30–3–9, 35–5–5/28, 30–3–18, 30–3–
1619, 1621, 1626–   19, 41–1–1/12, 30–3–10, 36–2–9/17, 35–5–10/33, 36–
1629, 1637, 1639,   2–10/18, 4316, 36–2–11/19, 40–6–1/2, 36–2–12/20,
1642, 1644–1645,   30–4–41/18, 36–3–13/1, 4317, 35–5–17/40, 41–1–
1647, 1648.   2/13, 35–5–12/35, 35–5–11/34, 30–5–50/2, 30–5–
   56/8, 4318, 4322, 32–5–32, 35–5–14/37, 35–5–16/39,
   35–6–53/16, 35–6–68/31, 33–1–90/23, 30–5–63/15,
   42–6–7/11, 35–6–54/17, 35–6–66/29, 35–6–59/22,
   41–1–3/14, 40–6–2/19, 35–6–63/26, 36–3–15/3, 36–
   3–19/7, 35–6–81/44, 35–6–82/45, 40–6–3/20.

1608–1609, 1611, 1613, 1618–1627, 1632–1635, 1639– 1642, 1644–1647, 1649. Hospital del Cardenal, legs. 297, 299, 301, 302, 303.

1596–1600, 1606– 1609, 1620, 1630– 1642, 1649–1650. AHN, *Clero*, Cádiz, legs. 98, 124, 150, 217, 218, 219, 270.

1561–1566, 1606– 1620. AHN, *Clero*, Córdoba, legs. 38 and 4.

1582–1605, 1621– 1660. AHN, *Clero*, Granada, legs. 196, 81, 82, 84.

1562–1565. AHN, *Osuna*, leg. 2950.

NEW CASTILE

1. *Used*

Years

1500–1521, 1523– 1552, 1555–1559, 1562–1610, 1618, 1620–1623, 1643– 1650. Hospital de Antezana (Alcalá de Henares), *Libros de Gastos*.

1509–1521, 1523– 1524, 1526, 1547, 1551–1566, 1568– 1617, 1620–1638, 1643–1650. AHN, Sección V. *Universidad de Alcalá, Colegios de San Ildefonso, San Lucas y San Nicolás, San Ambrosio, Gramáticos, San Jerónimo, San Pedro y San Pablo, Santiago, San Clemente*, 370 f, 725 f, 743 f–744 f, 746 f–747 f, 769 f–793 f, 795 f–796 f, 816 f, 930 f, 938 f, 1006 f–1007 f, 1017 f, 1023 f–1032 f, 1039 f, 1058 f, 1074 f. Legs. 102, 103, 135–148, 151–154, 381, 423–424.

1511–1562, 1583– 1650. Archivo de la Asociación General de Ganaderos del Reino, Madrid, *Cuentas del Concejo de la Mesta*.

1519–1534, 1537– 1550. AA, Toledo, Hospital de San Pedro, *Libros de Cargo y Data*, 628 and 650.

1540–1543, 1545– 1650. Hospital de Tavera, or San Juan Bautista (Toledo), *Libros de Obras, Despensa, Botillería, Borrador*, and *Gastos Ordinarios y Extraordinarios*.

1621–1645, 1627– 1634, 1629–1650. AHN, *Clero*, Toledo, legs. 268, 693, 144.

2. *Not Used* .

1566–1571. AS, *Obras del Escorial*, leg. 1.

1597–1616. AHN, *Osuna*, 29–49.

1630–1650.   Hospital de Nuestra Señora de la Caridad (Illescas-
              Toledo), *Libros de Cuentas.*

1632–1635.   AS, *Tribunal Mayor de Cuentas*, leg. 1490.

1621–1662.   AHN, *Clero*, Ciudad Real, leg. 21.

1636–1651.   AHN, *Clero*, Cuenca, leg. 55.

1504–1508, 1624–   AHN, *Clero*, Guadalajara, legs. 49 and 43.
1655.

1572–1587, 1617–   AHN, *Clero*, Madrid, legs. 1040, 1036, 715, 660.
1624, 1641–1650.

1590–1602, 1605–   AHN, *Clero*, Toledo, legs. 221, 168, 224, 268, 603, 33,
1610, 1621–1645,   166, 186, 31.
1648–1650.

OLD CASTILE–LEÓN

1. *Used*

Years

1502–1503, 1506,   Hospital de Nuestra Señora Santa María de Esgueva
1510, 1512, 1518–   (Valladolid), *Libros de Cuentas, Gastos de Hijuela*, and
1521, 1523–1524,   *Despensa.*
1527–1528, 1530,
1532–1538, 1541–
1565, 1567–1599,
1601–1614, 1616–
1627, 1629–1640,
1642–1650.

1508–1515, 1517–   AS, *Casa Real* (E.M.), legs. 8–8, 9–1, 9–2, 9–3, 10, 12,
1520, 1537, 1539–   33, 34. *Contaduría Mayor de Cuentas, 3ª y 4ª Épocas,*
1541, 1543, 1584–   leg. 1634.
1595, 1597, 1599–
1601, 1604–1613.

1511, 1513–1519,   AA, Villalón, *Cuentas del Concejo.*
1521–1525, 1527–
1528, 1532–1544.

1518–1530, 1533–   AHN, *Clero*, León, legs. 244–248 (*Cistercienses de*
1567, 1583–1650.   *Nuestra Señora de Sandoval*).

1550–1559, 1561,   Hospital de San Bernabé y San Antolín (Palencia),
1564, 1569, 1574,   *Libros de Gastos* and *Libros de Salarios.*
1576, 1578–1579,
1581, 1587, 1593–
1594, 1597–1599,
1600, 1602–1603,
1606, 1608–1610,
1612–1640, 1642–
1650.

1562, 1564–1568, 1603–1606. AHN, *Clero*, Palencia, legs. 119 and 20.

1638, 1639, 1642–1644. Hospital de la Resurrección (Valladolid), *Libros de Data del Mayordomo*.

2. *Not Used*

1521. AA, Medina de Rioseco, *Mayordomazgo*, 251.

1534–1535, 1539–1549, 1626, 1628, 1631–1632, 1636–1637, 1639, 1644, 1646–1650. Hospital de Dios Padre (Ávila), *Cuentas*.

1536, 1539. Archivo de Santa María (Medina de Rioseco), *Cuadernos de Gastos*.

1562–1565, 1568, 1571–1574, 1593, 1596–1598, 1604, 1623–1625. Archivo de la Catedral de Burgos, *Mayordomía*.

1566–1567. AA, Burgos, *Libros de Hacienda*.

1578, 1630, 1636, 1641–1642, 1644–1646. Hospital de la Misericordia (Ávila), *Cuadernos de Gastos*, legs. 1–8 and 2–28.

1591. AS, *Estado*, leg. 188.

1592–1602, 1604–1608. Convento de Santa Clara (Medina de Rioseco), *Libros de Gastos*.

1595–1596. Hospital de San Juan (Burgos), *Despensa*.

1597–1609. Hospital de Barrientos (Medina del Campo), *Cuadernos de Gastos*.

1625–1627, 1648–1650. Hospital de Santa María Magdalena (Ávila), *Cuentas*.

1634–1638, 1640–1650. Hospital de Santa Escolástica (Ávila), *Cuentas*.

1644–1649. Hospital de Nuestra Señora de la Misericordia (Segovia), *Libros de Cuentas*.

1631, 1637–1640, 1642–1650. AHN, *Clero*, Ávila, legs. 214, 469, 203.

1598, 1602–1650. AHN, *Clero*, Burgos, legs. 473 and 434.

1600–1650.   AHN, *Clero*, León, legs. 177 and 36.

1565–1570, 1608–   AHN, *Clero*, Logroño, legs. 390, 397, 11, 2, 370.
1650.

1520, 1550–1559,   AHN, *Clero*, Palencia, legs. 129, 260, 126, 137, 23.
1621–1624, 1630–
1640, 1645, 1648,
1650.

1552–1600, 1624–   AHN, *Clero*, Salamanca, legs. 197, 170, 186, 229.
1631, 1649.

1620–1628.   AHN, *Clero*, Santander, leg. 27.

1591–1614, 1617–   AHN, *Clero*, Segovia, legs. 534, 281, 282, 36, 280.
1650.

1596–1599, 1602–   AHN, *Clero*, Valladolid, legs. 317 bis, 869, 495, 349, 61,
1604, 1610–1651.   581, 346, 601, 498, 369, 345, 598, 606.

1619–1650.   Hospital de Simón Ruiz (Medina del Campo), *Gastos de
                    Despensa*.

VALENCIA

1. *Used*

Years

1501–1650.   Hospital dels Inocents, *Llibres de Administració, Al-
                    baráns, Contrallibre, Major, Memories, Querns del
                    Hospitaler, Clavería*, and *Rebudes y Dates*.

1502–1506, 1508–   AA, Valencia, *Clavería Censals, Clavería Comuna, Lonja
1512, 1514–1519,   Nova, Obra Nova del Riu, Sotsobrería de Murs y Valls*.
1523–1530, 1532–
1563, 1565–1584,
1591–1597, 1599,
1603–1607, 1610–
1611, 1616–1619,
1623–1650.

1546–1563, 1565–   AR, *Conventos*, libs. 1638, 3596, 4136, 2294, 1824, 2296,
1584, 1596–1650.   2589.

1565–1574, 1585,   Colegio de Santo Tomás, *Libros de Procura*.
1586, 1588–1591,
1594–1599, 1609–
1613, 1621–1625,
1628–1637, 1648–
1650.

2. *Not Used*

1557, 1559–1560, 1565, 1579, 1580–1582, 1585–1586, 1589–1597, 1599, 1625, 1638.	AHN, *Osuna*, legs. 805–806, 808–811.
1579–1608.	AHN, *Clero*, códices 395 and 398.
1585–1591.	AHN, *Clero*, Castellón, leg. 16.
1506, 1517, 1526–1529, 1531, 1537, 1541–1542, 1549, 1554, 1556, 1562, 1571, 1585–1597, 1609–1651.	AR, *Clero*, libs. 493, 955, 1143, 1443, 1683, 1825, 2040, 2064, 2257, 2292, 2312, 2369, 2371–2373, 2375, 2378–2380, 2382, 2502, 2595, 2607, 2757, 3600, 4088, 4149.

AMERICAN TREASURE AND THE PRICE REVOLUTION IN SPAIN, 1501–1650

CHAPTER I

INTRODUCTION

THE sole purpose of the present study, when originally undertaken, was to ascertain the precise quantities of American gold
and silver imported into Europe through Spain from 1503 to 1660
and to examine the effects of the treasure upon Spanish prices,
wages, and economic welfare. During the years required to assemble the raw material, however, other economic questions have
forged to the front, and quantitative data, which, incorporated
in monographs, may provide partial answers, have been sought.
It is obvious that no problem simple enough to admit of definitive
solution solely through statistical compilations, however extensive, could possibly challenge the sustained attention of scholars;
but I believe that the exact measurements rendered possible by
satisfactory monetary, price, and wage statistics can illuminate
many complex social phenomena and enhance the significance of
other ancillary information. No one can foresee all the scientific
ends which the numerical data are likely to serve, and limitations
of space preclude an exhaustive list of obvious possibilities. But a
few of the anticipated by-products may be enumerated.

Particularly favorable appears the prospect of new light upon
the age-old and recondite problem of Spanish economic decadence.
Several venerable explanations of this phenomenon need to pass
through the crucible of quantitative test. The comparison of
special index numbers of commodities produced largely or exclusively by Moriscos with the indices of general prices will doubtless furnish valuable information concerning the economic consequences of the Moorish expulsions. The relative movements
of agricultural and non-agricultural prices should demonstrate
whether industry declined earlier or faster than agriculture or
whether both fell together. Index numbers of fish prices may
help to date the decline of the Spanish fisheries, which were closely
allied with the merchant marine. Special indices of meats and

other animal products will measure the progress of the pastoral industry, while index numbers of fruits and nuts will shed the same light upon horticulture. The separate regional price series may help to determine whether decadence was general or provincial in character, and if the latter, which regions led. The prices of forest products and their derivatives will assist in gauging the course of deforestation. Owing to the paucity and unsatisfactory character of extant vital statistics, the relative movements of wages and prices may supply data concerning depopulation.

Economic events during and immediately after the World War focused attention anew upon the relationship between price behavior and the economic welfare of individuals, classes, and nations; and the course of events from 1920 to 1933 has poignantly demonstrated the utter inadequacy of present economic knowledge for the social control of business oscillations. Until a greater collection of facts from a wider source, both in territory and time, shall have been analyzed by statisticians and economists, scientific knowledge of the business cycle will probably remain fragmentary and obscure. I hope that the price series for Spain may form a small stone in the vast foundation upon which the future theory of the business cycle will rest.

It has long been recognized that the quantity theory of money had its crude beginning in Jean Bodin's observation [1] of the causal connection between American treasure and the Price Revolution.[2] But the last lesson concerning the quantity theory has not been drawn from this phenomenon; nor is the final word likely to be spoken before greater knowledge of the history of banking and of the contemporary influence of credit on prices becomes available. Nevertheless, more exact data than have hitherto been accessible concerning both treasure and prices may afford a partial verification of the quantity theory and also throw new light upon the related question of the connection between

[1] *Vide infra,* pp. 293–295.

[2] *Vide* Henri Hauser, Introduction to Bodin's *Réponse* (Paris, 1932), pp. xliii–xlv, lxxv–lxxvi; M. J. Bonn, *Spaniens Niedergang während der Preisrevolution des 16. Jahrhunderts* (Stuttgart, 1896), pp. 12–13; A. E. Monroe, *Monetary Theory before Adam Smith* (Cambridge, Massachusetts, 1923), pp. 57–58.

prices and the supply of the precious metals, a matter of thought-ful concern to economists throughout the world at present.

The upheaval of European prices during the sixteenth and seventeenth centuries has long attracted the attention of scholars, and elaborate studies have been made of the phenomenon in England, France, and Germany.[1] But nothing worthy of the name of an investigation of Spanish prices has yet been carried out. Contemporary writers were content to make observations concerning the dearness of necessaries — much as men have always complained of the weather and of the high cost of living. But not many authors bothered to state actual prices in an effort to substantiate their contentions; and those who did, adduced very few.[2] The dearth of information concerning Spanish prices in the sixteenth and seventeenth centuries is attested by the eagerness with which writers have accepted the meager data of Diego Clemencín,[3] Manuel Colmeiro,[4] and Konrad Haebler,[5] most of which were derived from secondary sources and price-fixing ordinances.

It is strikingly anomalous that the index number, the modern device for measuring price changes, which was developed by Carli for the purpose of investigating the rise of Italian prices caused by the discovery of the rich American mines and elaborated by Jevons for use in studying the mid-nineteenth-century price fluctuations precipitated by the output of the recently opened Californian and Australian gold fields,[6] has not hitherto

[1] *Vide* J. E. Thorold Rogers, *A History of Agriculture and Prices in England*, vols. iii–vi (Oxford, 1882–1887); Vicomte d'Avenel, *Histoire Économique de la Propriété, des Salaires, des Denrées, et de Tous Prix en Général*, vols. i–vii (Paris, 1894–1926); Georg Wiebe, *Zur Geschichte der Preisrevolution des XVI. und XVII. Jahrhunderts* (Leipzig, 1895); François Simiand, *Recherches Anciennes et Nouvelles sur le Mouvement Général des Prix du XVIe au XIXe Siècle* (Paris, 1932).

[2] *Vide*, for example, Alonso de Carranza, *El Ajustamiento i Proporción de las Monedas de Oro, Plata i Cobre* (Madrid, 1629), p. 180; Sancho de Moncada, *Restauración Política de España* (Madrid, 1746, First ed., 1619), p. 54.

[3] "Elógio de la Réina Católica Doña Isabel," *Memorias de la Academia de Historia*, vi (Madrid, 1821), 550–555.

[4] *Historia de la Economía Política en España* (Madrid, 1863), ii, 424–452.

[5] *Wirtschaftliche Blüte Spaniens im 16. Jahrhundert* (Berlin, 1888), pp. 160–163.

[6] W. C. Mitchell, "The Making and Using of Index Numbers," *Bulletin of United States Bureau of Labor Statistics*, no. 284 (Washington, 1921), p. 7; Irving Fisher, *The Making of Index Numbers* (ed. Boston and New York, 1927), pp. 458–459.

been employed in the study of prices in the country where perhaps as never before or since the influence of an increasing supply of gold and silver upon prices stands in clear relief.

The complete absence of pioneering studies such as Rogers made for England and d'Avenel for France has rendered the collection of material difficult and laborious. Not only has it proved necessary to take every price and wage quotation included in the present series from contemporary manuscripts, but no previous research has facilitated the location of commercial or financial records.[1]

For several reasons it has seemed desirable to maintain regional separation of price series. The possibility of a distortion of data through diversity of weights and measures is materially reduced. Regional price comparisons throw light upon interregional commercial contacts, the evolution of trade, and the diffusion of American treasure from Seville throughout Spain.

In none of the four regions for which index numbers of prices have been constructed do continuous wages or salaries from more than three sources appear. Furthermore, the wage series in every region has been vitiated by the preponderant influence of the salary scales of not more than two institutions, the probable errors of transcription arising from inability to determine the extent of payments in kind, and failure to recognize and properly record fixed gratuities and *ayudas de costa*. Consequently it has seemed best to construct a single index number for Spain by averaging the various regional series. The resultant wage indices are certainly more reliable than any of the regional components taken separately.

Since previous authors have treated Castilian and Valencian money chiefly from the standpoint of numismatics, it has proved necessary to give a more complete economic history of money

---

[1] "La Carestía de la Vida en el Siglo XVI y Medios de Abaratarla," *Revista de Archivos Bibliotecas y Museos*, 3ª Época, XXIV, 36–54, 169–204, 329–354; XXV, 1–18, 199–225, by Don Cristóbal Espejo, whose pen has enriched our knowledge of Spanish economic history through *Las Ferias de Medina del Campo* (in collaboration with Don Julián Paz) and numerous other monographs, is particularly disappointing. The paucity and heterogeneity of data, faulty methods of presentation, and vague references to source material render "La Carestía de la Vida" virtually worthless.

than one usually finds in price studies. Without an extensive investigation of primary sources relating to Castilian and Valencian coinage, it would have been impossible to determine the extent to which monetary debasement affected Spanish prices.

Apart from the Price Revolution and the hegemony of Spain in European politics, Castilian money is worthy of study in the sixteenth century, when the great preponderance of silver in the imports from America revolutionized bimetallic ratios, when Castilian coins enjoyed world-wide prestige, when the Castilian monetary system expanded into the Hispanic colonies of the New World, and when the desire to retain the fabulous imports of treasure dominated monetary policy. In the first half of the seventeenth century Castilian money is not less interesting. The royal impecuniosity inevitably resulting from extravagance and grandiose foreign projects led to inordinate vellon inflation, and a government with imperfect knowledge of monetary theory struggled manfully to attain stability. Out of the conflict between penury and the zeal for reform issued an endless succession of inflationary and deflationary measures that perturbed economic life and played a conspicuous part in the decline of Spain.

PART I

MONEY AND TREASURE

CHAPTER II

IMPORTS OF AMERICAN GOLD AND SILVER[1]

I

THE present chapter deals with imports of gold and silver, not with production in the Indies. The reasons for following this course are two. First, all the American treasure that legally entered Europe during the period under investigation passed through Spain. No other colonizing power found significant mines of gold or silver, and trade with the Spanish colonies was jealously restricted to subjects of the motherland.[2] Second, imports — not production — affected the economic life of Europe.

The amount of treasure drawn by Spain from her American colonies has been a fruitful source of speculation among historians for almost four centuries,[3] and economists have given attention to the matter since the time of Bodin. Notwithstanding the persistence and intensity of interest in the subject, however, most writers have accepted uncritically the often-admitted guesses and rough approximations of contemporary chroniclers and travelers. Scant use has been made of the records [4] of the men who handled the treasure.[5]

---

[1] This chapter covers the period 1503–1660, the dates between the foundation of the House of Trade and the termination of compulsory registration of treasure.

[2] Of course there was interloping, which increased toward the close of the period under investigation; but as late as the beginning of the eighteenth century the anonymous author of *Comercio de Holanda* (p. 95) said that almost all the gold and silver in Europe had been brought to Spain from Mexico and Peru. Manuel Colmeiro estimated that Spain received from 83 to 87 per cent of all the American treasure that reached Europe during the first three centuries after the discovery (*Historia de la Economía Política en España* [Madrid, 1863], II, 434–435). In the eighteenth century the Portuguese found rich gold deposits in Brazil (Adolf Soetbeer, *Edelmetall-Produktion und Werthverhältniss zwischen Gold und Silber* [Gotha, 1879], pp. 83–92).

[3] R. B. Merriman, *Rise of the Spanish Empire*, III (New York, 1925), 636–637.

[4] Now deposited in the Archivo General de Indias (hereafter A. de I.), the repository of official papers pertaining to the Hispanic colonies.

[5] In his admirable study, "American Gold and Silver Production in the First Half of the Sixteenth Century" (*Quarterly Journal of Economics*, XXIX, 433–479), Professor C. H. Haring used the records of the House of Trade in determining the volume of production in the Indies. In this paper and in his *Trade and Navigation*

Among the documents utilized in the present study the registers of caravels and galleons, catalogued as *Registros de Oro, Plata, y Mercaderías para Su Majestad y Particulares*,[1] deserve mention. Unfortunately, none of these papers seems to have been preserved for the first quarter of the sixteenth century, and for most of the ensuing quarter they are incomplete. The registers record numerous shipments, many of which are given by weight in annoyingly odd figures,[2] so that a vast amount of labor is required to add the receipts for a single year.

The *Cuenta y Razón*, a sort of journal of receipts and disbursements, kept by the treasurer of the House of Trade (Casa de la Contratación), contains a fairly complete record of Crown treasure (including shipping point, vessel, captain, weight, fineness, and value) and of the methods of disposing of the gold and silver —

between Spain and the Indies (Cambridge, Massachusetts, 1918) Professor Haring gives the Crown treasure — as shown by the records of the treasurer of the House of Trade — drawn from America, 1503–1559. Don Francisco de Laiglesia (*Estudios Históricos*, II [Madrid, 1918], 227–251) used the same source in calculating the receipts of public treasure through the reign of Charles V. His work contains errors incompatible with the impeccability which he claimed and which one would infer from his inclusion of half-*maravedís*. Apparently Laiglesia considered that debits were made on the books of the treasurer only on account of American gold and silver. Consequently his figures contain such extraneous items as money borrowed from agents of the Fuggers on "exchange," sales of caravels in Spain, sums received for licenses to carry slaves to America, and sales of redundant supplies bought by the House of Trade. The papers of the India House pertaining to imports of public treasure during the last hundred years of the period under investigation, when the influx was greatest, have been little used. For the whole period the facilities of the Archivo General de Indias for determining private receipts — which far outweighed public —, the share of imports contributed by each of the two great producing regions, and the relative importance of gold and silver have remained virtually untouched. It is surprising that the records of the House of Trade concerning gold and silver have not been fully utilized, for in 1629 Alonso de Carranza, in *El Ajustamiento i Proporción de las Monedas* (Madrid, p. 211), pointed out how the quantity of imports might be ascertained; and José de Veitia Linaje's *Norte de la Contratación de las Indias Occidentales*, published in 1672 (Seville), was drawn largely from the correspondence between the House of Trade and the Council of the Indies, the most usable and perhaps most reliable single source of information.

[1] The Archivo de Indias has changed its system of cataloguing documents since the data for this study were collected, but the *legajos* cited may be obtained by presenting the references I am listing.

[2] In a caravel that came from the Indies in 1544 there were 154 separate shipments, of which the first six — 561, 578, 398, 245, 151, and 188 pesos of gold — may be taken as typical. In 1548 the first six of 324 items in the register of a treasure ship were 297, 329, 101, 64, 107, and 303 marks of silver (A. de I., *Indiferente General*, 147-2-12).

such as sale by contract, auction, coinage in the Seville mint, shipment to another mint, or delivery to an agent of the Crown in Seville or some other city. The entries of the journal are posted in *Cargo y Data*, a ledger, found in the same documents. These records proved a valuable source of information from February 14, 1503, when Isabella appointed Sancho de Matienzo treasurer,[1] until the close of the reign of Charles V. Although the accounts, which were intended to establish the responsibility of the treasurer for all sums passing into his stewardship, included extraneous items from the beginning, it was feasible to separate receipts of gold and silver until December 14, 1560, when Philip II ordered the treasurer to receive the *almojarifazgo*, or customs duty, on goods shipped to and from the Indies — to which was added in 1582 the income from the *alcabala*, or sales tax, in Andalusia.[2] About the same time the books commenced to suffer from such defects as faulty summation, entry of receipts more than once, and apparently needless and disorderly transfers of items.[3]

The summaries of receipts of gold and silver, prepared annually by the comptroller of the House of Trade from the registers of treasure ships arriving from the Indies, proved extremely valuable for the period after 1550.[4] Both public and private treasure are listed, together with the name of the vessel, port of shipment, and the like.

Letters from the House of Trade, reporting the annual receipts of gold and silver to the Councils of the Indies and of the Treasury, constitute the most important single source. These reports seem to have been based on the above summaries, but the former

---

[1] A. de I., *Contratación*, 46–4–1/30. The first entry in the records of the treasurer was made on February 25, 1503 (A. de I., *Contratación*, 39–2–1/8). The accounts were well kept until October, 1521, when Sancho de Matienzo died. His work surpassed that of any treasurer or comptroller who followed him.

[2] José de Veitia Linaje, *op. cit.*, lib. 1, pp. 74–75.

[3] At least in the early years, say before 1555, the books of the treasurer were audited by order of the Crown every five or ten years. A summary of the receipts and disbursements was ordinarily made, and a balance struck in favor of or against the treasurer. For example, *vide* A. de I., *Contratación*, 39–2–1/8, 39–2–2/9, 39–3–3/1. The summaries are generally not reliable, but they furnish a rough check on the accuracy of one's work with the journal and ledger.

[4] The first summary I was able to locate is for 1550 (A. de I., *Indiferente General*, 147–2–12).

have been a great deal better preserved than the latter. Unfortunately, the first letters available are for 1558; the earlier ones were probably destroyed by a fire in 1563, which consumed many documents of the House of Trade.[1] Reports were doubtless submitted with more or less regularity from the beginning of the sixteenth century, for on June 15, 1510, a pragmatic was sent to the House of Trade reiterating previous orders that detailed reports on public and private gold coming from the Indies be supplied the Crown.[2]

A "report on reports," covering the period 1583–1613, filed with the papers of the comptroller (contador), proved serviceable in determining the completeness of data and in locating documents. As a rule, no single source listed above has been relied upon without being checked against others.

II

An account of imports would hardly be complete without some consideration of the machinery for transporting and handling bullion in Spain and the Indies.

First, let attention be directed to the House of Trade at Seville,[3] a government bureau instituted for the regulation and development of commerce and travel between Spain and the colonies of the New World.[4] The affairs of the House of Trade, itself under the supervision of the Council of the Indies,[5] were controlled by three judge-officials (jueces oficiales) — the factor, treasurer, and comptroller —, who were in effect chiefs of divisions as well as

[1] José de Veitia Linaje, *op. cit.*, Prólogo, § 18.

[2] *Colección de Documentos Inéditos Relativos al Descubrimiento, Conquista y Organización de las Antiguas Posesiones Españolas de América y Oceanía* (Madrid, 1869), XXXI, 551–554.

[3] The compass of the present study permits only the barest outline of the organization and functions of the India House. For a comprehensive treatment *vide* C. H. Haring, *Trade and Navigation*, or Gervasio de Artíñano, *Historia del Comercio con las Indias* (Barcelona, 1917).

[4] The activities of the House of Trade consisted of the enforcement of decrees affecting the India trade; the assembling, outfitting, provisioning, inspecting, and dispatching of treasure fleets; the control of travel to and from America; the maintenance of postal service with the Indies; the promotion of the science and art of navigation; and the development of pure and applied geography.

[5] R. B. Merriman, *op. cit.*, III, 619.

councilors who helped to formulate policies, and a president,[1] whose principal duties were to coördinate the work of the judge-officials and to represent the India House in external matters.

The Merchant Gild of Seville, established by the Emperor in 1543, was intimately connected with the House in the governance of the India trade.[2] Furthermore, it was often called upon for voluntary or compulsory advances to the Crown, sometimes to finance the convoys of treasure fleets and at other times to meet urgent needs of the government. In fact, the House of Trade and Sevillan Merchant Gild stood in about the same relationship to the Crown as did Sir Thomas Gresham and the Merchant Adventurers to the English government during the reign of Elizabeth.[3]

Only in the case of Huancavélica, the famous Peruvian mercury mine, did the Crown engage in mining. As soon as it had been definitely determined that precious metals could be extracted in the Antilles, royal decrees permitting private individuals to stake claims were promulgated.[4] Upon filing claims, prospectors were bound by oath to bring all bullion to the royal assay offices, where it was assayed,[5] cast in bars or

[1] After 1579. According to Haring (*Trade and Navigation*, p. 46), Philip II created the office of president in October, 1557; but it was permitted to lapse for two decades after the death of the first incumbent, who served little more than a year. Don Gervasio de Artíñano (*op. cit.*, p. 59) says that Charles V named the first president and adduces instructions given the first appointee by the Emperor.

[2] The Merchant Gild relieved the House of Trade of hearing suits between members arising from the India trade and constantly furnished expert counsel concerning financial and commercial matters (for example, *vide* A. de I., *Contratación*, 42-6-12/16).

[3] To be exact, between the years 1551 or 1552 (before the accession of Elizabeth) and 1574.

[4] *Recopilación de Leyes de Indias* (Madrid, 1681) (hereafter *Recopilación de Indias*), lib. IV, tit. XIX, leyes I-XVI. The decrees stated specifically that the rights of Indians to exploit mines were in no way inferior to those of Spaniards and expressly forbade infringement upon the rights of natives. As in many other cases, however, the solicitude for the interests of the Indians expressed in legislation indicates awareness on the part of the home government of a vast gulf between theory and practice.

[5] An ordinance of 1537 required Crown officials personally to supervise the smelting and assaying of bullion (*Recopilación de Indias*, lib. IV, tit. XXII, ley XI) and to keep the offices open for business three hours on every Monday and Thursday morning (*ibid.*, lib. IV, tit. XXII, ley XII). Legislative measures were taken to insure honesty in the analyses. On November 4, 1535, the mixing of base metals with gold, with fraudulent intent, was made punishable by death and the confiscation of the offender's goods (*ibid.*, lib. IV, tit. XXII, ley IV). On July 1, 1646, these penalties

plate,[1] marked, and quinted.[2] Mercury, which became of the utmost importance after the discovery of the amalgamation process for silver,[3] was a Crown monopoly, for which the royal assay offices served as distributing agencies.

Although the law required all bullion to be carried directly to the royal assay offices and expressly forbade Spaniards and Indians to buy, sell, lend, or pawn treasure that had not been assayed and quinted,[4] not all bullion paid the royal quint. The wild and unsettled character of the country, especially in Peru, facilitated evasion of the law. Only well-to-do miners carried their own metals to the assay offices; others generally delivered them at the mine to capitalists, who, through advances of subsistence and equipment for mining, financed their operations. Furthermore, gold and silver dealers made the rounds of the mines, buying unquinted treasure and sending it to the assay offices.[5] These middlemen doubtless furnished a genuine economic service. They could establish regular routes and thereby provide transportation more economically than small producers, each of whom, in order to transport his own metal, would have required facilities used only at infrequent intervals. Moreover, the specialists could protect treasure at much less cost, for this item did not vary proportionately with the volume of gold and

were extended to silver (*ibid.*, lib. IV, tit. XXII, ley v). The decree of July 1, 1646, also directed assayers to halve all pieces of bullion presented for analysis; in case any foreign substance was found, the gold or silver was confiscated and its possessor fined four times its value (*ibid.*, lib. IV, tit. XXII, ley xv). Yet fraudulent and perfunctory assays were not unknown.

[1] Each piece was numbered and stamped with its weight, fineness, and date of assay (Antonio de Ulloa, *Noticias Americanas* [Madrid, 1792], p. 215). Colonial officials were instructed not to send Crown silver in small pieces (José de Veitia Linaje, *op. cit.*, lib. I, p. 274). But neither were they to be too large. In December, 1635 Philip IV ordered the institution of criminal procedure against the smelter (fundidor) making a bar of silver weighing more than 120 marks (*Recopilación de Indias*, lib. IV, tit. XXII, ley IX).

[2] The quint was a severance tax on mining. It was usually, though not always, (as its name suggests) a fifth; under special circumstances, such as infertile or badly situated mines, it was as low as a tenth. In 1552 the fees for assaying, smelting, and marking were fixed at 1½ per cent (*Recopilación de Indias*, lib. IV, tit. XXII, ley XIII).

[3] About the middle of the sixteenth century.

[4] *Recopilación de Indias*, lib. IV, tit. XXIV, ley I.

[5] Archivo General de Simancas (hereafter AS), *Diversos de Castilla*, 45–6; Antonio de Ulloa, *op. cit.*, pp. 215–216.

silver. To transport bullion from the mines to the royal assay offices in Peru, the llama, the only animal able to work in the Andean altitudes or to follow trails through the mountain wilderness that had to be traversed, was used as a pack animal. Certain tribes of Indians gained their livelihood by making bags and cords with which treasure was secured to the llamas' backs.[1]

Treasure bearing the official seal of the assay office could be shipped to other parts of the Indies [2] or to Castile, provided it was listed in the name of its owner [3] in the register kept by the chief notary of mines (escribano mayor de minas) and in the books of a royal official at the port of shipment.[4] Unquinted bullion was contraband throughout the Indies, and its coinage in colonial mints was punishable by death and the loss of the offender's goods; [5] if found on board a vessel, it was confiscated, and the man in charge fined four times its value.[6]

III

From the following American ports gold and silver were sent to Spain: Vera Cruz (sometimes called San Juan de Ulúa) in New Spain,[7] Cartagena in New Granada (Colombia), Amatique and Truxillo in Honduras, and Nombre de Dios and Porto Belo in Panama,[8] where Peruvian treasure, shipped originally from Callao, was placed on the Tierra Firme [9] galleons.

---

[1] Antonio de Ulloa, *op. cit.*, p. 217.

[2] The privilege of intercolonial shipment was restricted after trade between New Spain and the Far East had commenced to drain away, through the port of Acapulco, Peruvian treasure that had been carried thither (*vide Recopilación de Indias*, lib. IX, tit. XLV; Earl J. Hamilton, "Spanish Mercantilism before 1700," in *Facts and Factors in Economic History* [Cambridge, Massachusetts, 1932], p. 224; W. L. Schurz, "Mexico, Peru, and the Manila Galleon," *Hispanic American Historical Review*, I, 395–402).

[3] *Recopilación de Indias*, lib. IX, tit. XLIV, ley X.

[4] *Ibid.*, lib. IV, tit. XXII, ley I.

[5] *Ibid.*, lib. IV, tit. XXIII, ley VI.

[6] *Ibid.*, lib. IX, tit. XXXIII, ley LXIV.

[7] Except as used on p. 43 *infra*, where a special definition is given, "New Spain" means all of Spanish North America west of the Mississippi River and north of Honduras.

[8] Nombre de Dios was the principal port of Panama until about 1594, when it was supplanted by Porto Belo.

[9] "Tierra Firme" means the mainland of South America. Cf. p. 43 *infra*.

For transshipment to the motherland specie was carried from Peru to Panama on the Pacific (Mar del Sur) fleet, which was modeled after the treasure fleets plying between Spain and the Indies. The registers of ships were kept in an identical manner, and the fleet was served by the same classes of officers. These officers were appointed by the Viceroy of Peru, who was also responsible for taking all precautions, such as the provision of adequate artillery and ammunition, making for the safety of public and private treasure.[1] Upon the arrival of the fleet at the Isthmus, it was thoroughly inspected by treasury officials accompanied by an *oidor* named by the president of the *Audiencia* of Panama.[2] The governor of Panama was instructed to supervise the transportation of treasure from the Pacific to the Atlantic port; upon him devolved the selection of guides to lead the caravan over the roads and trails and on the Chagres River. Gold and silver were not moved to Porto Belo until news of the arrival of the treasure fleet had been received, for it was feared that large amounts of specie on the Atlantic might invite attack and that private treasure intended for shipment to Spain might be diverted to other uses, or even make its way to a foreign country.[3]

For a time single vessels, relying upon their own arms for protection, carried private goods and government supplies to the Indies and loaded return cargoes of gold and other products, such as Brazil wood; but early in the 1520's pirates, especially French and Moorish, menaced the ships to such an extent that war vessels, fitted out from the proceeds of the *avería*— a special convoy tax levied on goods carried to and from the Indies—, were used to police the waters around Andalusia, as well as certain ports of the Indies, where the caravels were peculiarly susceptible to attack. Strict regulation of the armaments of vessels engaged in the India trade was instituted later, and each ship was expected to defend itself in case of attack. About the middle of the sixteenth century, however, the bold aggression of pirates and the danger of capture by enemy ships during the perpetual wars of the house of Austria

---

[1] *Recopilación de Indias*, lib. IX, tit. XLIV, leyes V, XV.
[2] *Ibid.*, lib. IX, tit. XLIV, ley XIV.
[3] *Ibid.*, lib. IX, tit. XXXIII, ley IX; lib. IX, tit. XXXIV, ley XXIX.

again caused a change in the methods of protecting treasure ships. Merchant vessels began to sail in fleets convoyed by warships, the expenses of which were borne by the avería. Sporadic sailings of fleets, adequately protected by men-of-war, were maintained until about 1565, when the service was regularized.[1]

At first, single armadas, one sailing in January and the other in April, served all parts of the Indies. The fleet divided in the Antilles, the captain general going to Tierra Firme with part of the vessels and the admiral to New Spain with the others. But this plan was of short duration. A pragmatic issued on October 18, 1564, ordered the fleets to sail separately, the New Spain fleet departing in April and that of Tierra Firme in August.[2] As might be expected, however, the inveterate propensity of the Spaniard to procrastinate defeated the laws regulating the dates of sailing. But there was a limit to the possible delay: the New Spain fleet had to sail before August in order to avoid the hurricanes that sweep the Gulf of Mexico in September.[3]

In view of the popular misconception concerning the amounts of treasure taken by the English, French, and Dutch, one who works with the records is impressed by the paucity rather than the plethora of the specie that fell prey to foreign powers.[4] The dictum of Adam Smith concerning the failure of gold to cover its cost of production is strikingly applicable to the efforts of foreigners to plunder Spanish treasure fleets. The records of the House of Trade abound with accounts of abortive attempts of pirates and foreign powers to capture these vessels; yet few fell into their hands. In only two years were significant portions of a treasure fleet seized by enemies: in 1628 the Dutch took the fleet returning from New Spain, and in 1656 the English prevented most of the specie on the Tierra Firme fleet from reaching the motherland. For the most part, the flotas, teeming with men and bristling with arms, sailed at regular intervals over usual

---

[1] José de Veitia Linaje, *op. cit.*, lib. II, pp. 60–85; *Recopilación de Indias*, lib. IX, tit. XXXIV, ley I.

[2] José de Veitia Linaje, *op. cit.*, lib. II, p. 82.

[3] Anonymous, *Comercio de Holanda* (translated from French into Spanish by Francisco Xavier de Goyeneche in 1717), pp. 100–101.

[4] *Vide* especially A. de I., *Contratación*, 42–6–1/5 to 42–6–13/17.

courses, almost, if not absolutely, without regard to the operations of enemies.[1]

I have made every effort to check the receipts of public and private treasure with the amounts shipped from the Indies. The royal assay offices were required to submit to the Crown annual reports on the sums collected from the quint and fees for smelting, assaying, and marking.[2] Colonial officials also reported to the House of Trade the number, weight, and fineness [3] of each piece of gold and silver sent to the Crown, as well as the number of people and the amount of gold, silver, and merchandise on every ship returning to Spain. The registers of vessels, showing the quantities of public and private treasure carried, were deposited in the House of Trade. To guard against the loss of registers, every vessel leaving an American port was required to carry its own and a copy of that of another ship sailing at the same time.[4] The House of Trade was required to report to the proper colonial officials the amount of Crown treasure received, in order that any discrepancy between it and the quantity dispatched might be ascertained.[5]

From the beginning, smuggling was punished by confiscation, and in 1593 this penalty was supplemented by four years' suspension from office in the case of a captain or minister, and four years' sentence in the galleys for a man of lower rank. In 1634 the severity of the measures was still further enhanced: men of high station became subject to perpetual exile from the Indies and to loss of the privilege of engaging in the India trade, while men of lower status might be sentenced to ten years in the galleys.[6]

[1] This statement needs qualification as regards the closing years of the reign of Philip IV, when the administration became exceedingly lax. Along with other things, the fighting equipment of the galleons deteriorated. In 1656, 1657, and 1658, English men-of-war bottled up the fleets in Spain and delayed or prevented their sailing (A. de I., *Contratación*, 42–6–12/16, 42–6–13/17). It is worthy of note that the disasters of 1628 and 1656 occurred during the reign of the weak Philip IV.

[2] *Recopilación de Indias*, lib. IV, tit. XXII, ley XI.

[3] The fineness was expressed by stating in maravedís the value of a mark of silver or peso of gold (A. de I., *Contratación*, 41–2–5 to 41–2–9).

[4] *Recopilación de Indias*, lib. IX, tit. XXXIII, ley XLIII.

[5] *Ibid.*, lib. IX, tit. I, ley LVII.

[6] José de Veitia Linaje, *op. cit.*, lib. II, p. 196. In theory, gold and silver brought to Spain by soldiers and sailors, including their salaries, were not exempt from regis-

smuggling

Royal officials in the Indies and on the treasure fleets were instructed to take special precaution against smuggling.[1] To encourage the detection of smuggled treasure, the denouncer was promised one-third of all small sums and an adequate reward, to be fixed by the trial judge, in the case of large amounts.[2] The captains general were directed to make every possible effort to ferret out men who embarked as soldiers, sailors, or passengers for the purpose of carrying unregistered treasure.

Officers and seamen were instructed to take special precautions against the removal of gold and silver during the course of the voyage, and fruitful methods of perpetrating this act were called to their attention. For instance, they were cautioned against permitting other vessels to tie on to treasure ships while at sea and against permitting a boat to go to the rescue of a vessel in distress without carrying some man worthy of trust appointed by the captain general.[3]

Efforts to stifle smuggling were redoubled when the fleets approached land. Boats were forbidden to land from the vessels comprising the flota or from galleys that went out to escort it into port. Each sailor in a boat violating this ordinance, even with the permission of the captain general, was subject to a penalty of two hundred lashes and ten years as a galley slave.[4] Fishing boats were forbidden to sail out to meet incoming fleets or to take on board any man who had left a treasure ship.[5] By an ordinance of

tration in the usual manner. In practice, however, since it was virtually impossible to prevent it, the soldiers and sailors were always permitted to bring small amounts of unregistered gold and silver without penalty. But the abuse of this privilege caused it to be circumscribed. An ordinance of May 20, 1646, fixed the amounts which they might bring unregistered at a sum not in excess of their salaries. Passengers were permitted to bring in like manner enough money to defray traveling expenses for themselves and families, provided the funds brought in this way did not exceed the sums they registered (*Recopilación de Indias*, lib. IX, tit. XXXIII, ley LXI).

[1] *Recopilación de Indias*, lib. VIII, tit. XVII, ley I.

[2] *Ibid.* Between 1635 and 1640 the rewards varied from one-sixth to one-third of the treasure denounced. There seems to have been little correlation between the amount of specie and the reward. For instance, in 1637 the man who detected 2,614,481 maravedís was paid one-third, while in 1636 the denouncer of 133,100 maravedís was given one-sixth (A. de I., *Contratación*, 41-1-2/13).

[3] *Recopilación de Indias*, lib. IX, tit. XXXVI, ley XVIII.

[4] *Ibid.*, lib. IX, tit. XXXVI, ley XLIV.

[5] *Ibid.*, lib. IX, tit. XXXVI, leyes XLIV-XLV. It was alleged that fishing boats had made it a practice to meet treasure fleets for the ostensible purpose of

September 25, 1614, the dispatch of messenger boats (barcos de aviso) to ports other than San Lúcar de Barrameda and the firing of salutes were interdicted, since these practices merely served to apprise fishing boats and pirates of the approach of the fleets.[1]

Upon the arrival of a fleet at San Lúcar de Barrameda, the captain general was required to notify the Council of the Indies and the House of Trade, and he was forbidden to permit anyone — passenger, soldier, or sailor — to leave a ship before the fleet had been inspected by an official of the House.[2] The officials were ordered not to allow more than one day to elapse between the receipt of notification and the inspection [3] and to do the work in person, not by proxy.[4] It was intended that this inspection should be thorough, as is attested by the fact that the law ordered the official to require every passenger and seaman to declare under oath whether he had knowledge of anyone's carrying unregistered or unquinted gold, silver, or pearls; taking anything from a vessel during the voyage or after arrival; or registering in his name treasure belonging to another. Then the inspector had to open all chests to ascertain whether they contained contraband or unregistered goods.[5]

The laws against smuggling were not always enforced. In some years — such as 1560, 1593, 1595, and 1597 — when it was suspected that significant amounts of unregistered gold and silver had arrived, pardons were granted to all who confessed and paid the avería.[6] On September 14, 1594, the reason for this procedure was set forth in a letter from the House of Trade to the Council of the Indies. The Council was requested to permit the delivery of unregistered specie, less the avería, to all owners who confessed

showering hospitality upon them, but for the real purpose of receiving a shower of smuggled specie.

[1] *Recopilación de Indias*, lib. IX, tit. XXXVI, ley XLVIII.

[2] *Ibid.*, lib. IX, tit. XXXVI, ley LVII.

[3] *Ibid.*, lib. IX, tit. XXXV, ley LXVI. These inspections were made by one of the judge-officials of the House accompanied by a sheriff, prosecuting attorney, and guards.

[4] *Ibid.*, lib. IX, tit. XXXV, ley LXIV. Upon the arrival of the inspecting officer, all foreign vessels were required to withdraw from the general vicinity of the treasure fleet (*ibid.*, lib. IX, tit. XXXVI, ley LV).

[5] *Ibid.*, lib. IX, tit. XXXV, ley LXIX.

[6] In 1595 one-fourth of the smuggled treasure was confiscated (A. de I., *Contratación*, 42-6-3/7).

before a specified date. Enforcement of the laws against smuggling and rigorous prohibition against the purchase of smuggled gold and silver by silver merchants and silversmiths, it was argued, had occasioned heavy losses in the avería and, what was worse, the export of large amounts of treasure.[1] Realizing that the granting of amnesty encouraged smuggling, Philip III declared on October 10, 1618, that in the future no pardons would be forthcoming.[2] Nevertheless, they were resorted to more than ever in the closing years of the reign of his successor, Philip IV, when receipts of treasure fell off and the proportion of the actual imports registered declined, thus causing the avería to weigh heavily upon the Crown and honest private shippers.[3]

In the beginning, treasure came to Spain in charge of the captains of vessels and later under the control of the captains general of armadas. With the increase in the volume of shipments, it became necessary to have a special officer, the silver master (maestre de plata), to perform this function.[4] The silver master was originally named by the captain general of the armada; but on August 10, 1592, because of past abuses and the opportunities for fraud inherent in the position, the power of appointment was vested in the officials of the House of Trade, with the advice and consent of the prior and consuls of the Merchant Gild.[5]

Silver masters were required to give bond satisfactory to the officials of the House of Trade for 25,000 ducats in silver.[6] Colonial officials were instructed to examine the silver master's bond before delivering treasure to him, and private individuals were expected to take the same precaution.[7]

A letter written to the Council of the Indies by the House of Trade on January 11, 1605, furnishes valuable information concerning the duties and remuneration of the silver master and the type of man selected for the position. Usually captains of in-

[1] A. de I., *Contratación*, 42-6-3/7.

[2] José de Veitia Linaje, *op. cit.*, lib. II, pp. 199-201.

[3] A. de I., *Contratación*, 42-6-12/16.

[4] *Ibid.*, *Contratación*, 36-2-1/9.

[5] José de Veitia Linaje, *op. cit.*, lib. II, pp. 134-135; *Recopilación de Indias*, lib. IX, tit. XXIV, ley I.

[6] *Ibid.*, lib. IX, tit. XXIV, ley III.

[7] José de Veitia Linaje, *op. cit.*, lib. II, pp. 134-135.

*silver
masters*

fantry or ex-admirals were appointed; always the appointee came
from the upper strata of society. For instance, Tomás de Cardona, for years a commanding figure in the India trade, served at
times as a silver master.[1] The remuneration consisted of a fee
amounting to 1 per cent of all registered treasure. In appearance,
the office was a lucrative sinecure; lucrative it was, but no sinecure. The fees collected by the silver master on the flagship
(capitana) of the Tierra Firme armada sometimes amounted to
almost 7,000,000 maravedís. But from this gross income the silver
master had to meet the following expenses involved in handling
treasure: paying a notary and two helpers of irreproachable
probity; providing bags and boxes for packing; loading in the
Indies, as well as unloading and reloading when occasion arose;
transferring, when necessary, to other vessels in San Lúcar de
Barrameda; unloading at Seville; and transporting to the House
of Trade. Furthermore, the silver master ran the risk of theft
during the voyage.[2]

Notwithstanding the care exercised in their selection, silver
masters did not always measure up to the standard of honor requisite for the position. In 1614 Estevan de Arce, silver master of
the *almiranta* of the Tierra Firme armada in the charge of General Lope Díaz de Almendáriz, absconded with a large amount of
treasure on the day announced for the beginning of delivery to
private owners. All the loss fell upon private individuals, presumably because the treasure of the Crown had been delivered
prior to the theft.[3] An ordinance of 1593 — repeated in 1631,
1634, and 1640 — charged the silver masters with complicity in,
or responsibility for, the major part of smuggling and provided
for either offense a penalty of loss of office and four years of exile.[4]

No matter what unusual circumstances arose, the House of
Trade at Seville was the goal of all Indian treasure.[5] When vessels

---

[1] Alonso de Carranza, *op. cit.*, Prefatory note by Tomás de Cardona. Cardona
furnished a factual basis for this monumental treatise, from which a wealth of first-
hand information concerning the India trade can be gathered.

[2] A. de I., *Contratación*, 42–6–4/8.

[3] José de Veitia Linaje, *op. cit.*, lib. II, pp. 135–136.

[4] *Recopilación de Indias*, lib. IX, tit. XXXIII, ley LVII.

[5] The pragmatic of 1529 authorizing sailings to the Indies from divers ports provided a death penalty and the loss of all of his goods for the captain of a ship failing

in distress or in danger of attack were forced to put in at other ports, such as Málaga or Lisbon, the treasure was immediately carried to the House of Trade. No exception occurred until 1659, when the Tierra Firme fleet, fearing contact with British men-of-war, veered to the north and put in at Santander. Apparently the treasure was not shipped to Seville, but was disposed of by an agent of the Council of the Indies.[1] Both civil and ecclesiastical passengers were required to carry their gold and silver to Seville. When the treasure fleets were forced to stop at any port *en route*, passengers were forbidden, under penalty of confiscation of all treasure brought from the Indies, to sell or barter gold, silver, or precious stones, except in case of dire necessity attested by the affidavit of a second party, and then only to the extent of a hundred ducats.[2]

When the treasure arrived at Seville, it was immediately taken to the House of Trade, where it was weighed by an official weigher (balanzario)[3] and placed in chests in the treasure chamber and, occasionally, in the chambers of the Audiencia and Merchant Gild. In normal times the substantial walls, strong doors, and double iron bars over the windows afforded ample protection; but on certain occasions special guards were kept on duty at night.[4] The treasure chamber and chests were provided with triple locks, so that three keys, one of which was carried by each of the three officials of the House, were required to open them.[5]

When gold and silver entered the House of Trade, the duties of

---

to return to Seville (Manuel Colmeiro, *op. cit.*, II, 402; José de Veitia Linaje, *op. cit.*, lib. II, p. 136). That control of the shipment of treasure was the aim of this regulation is shown by the fact that vessels returning from Hispaniola or Porto Rico with cargoes of hides, dyes, and other colonial products were permitted to land and unload at Cádiz, provided any gold, silver, money, or precious stones carried were sent unpacked to Seville and delivered to the officials of the House of Trade (*Recopilación de Indias*, lib. IX, tit. XLII, ley XXVII).

[1] A. de I., *Contratación*, 42–6–13/17.

[2] *Recopilación de Indias*, lib. IX, tit. XXXIII, ley XLVII.

[3] José de Veitia Linaje, *op. cit.*, lib. I, p. 268.

[4] A. de I., *Patronato*, 3–3–15. Treasure that came in the New Spain fleet of 1582 was guarded at night. Twelve watchmen were on duty at a time, and three shifts were used. The men were paid 3 reals each.

[5] A green treasure chest, probably the *arca verde* frequently mentioned in the sixteenth- and seventeenth-century records of the House of Trade, is on display in the Archivo General de Indias at Seville. *Vide supra*, frontispiece.

the silver master did not end. After permission had been received by the House from the Council of the Indies, he had to deliver treasure to private owners, who might be required to prove that the laws governing registration had been obeyed.[1] Barring orders for delay in delivery, or sequestration, this task had to be completed within four months after the arrival of the fleet, and under all circumstances before the silver master could embark on another voyage.[2]

In the early years the officials of the House of Trade undertook to supervise the refinement and coinage, for the most part in the Seville mint, of gold received by the Crown.[3] With this end in view, special equipment for smelting and refining was bought.[4] But not all Crown bullion was coined in the first instance.[5] All told, significant quantities of bullion were delivered to the creditors of the Crown, especially the Fuggers, Shetz, Welsers, Esquetes, Centurións, and Dorias.[6] As was indicated in connection with the sources of this study, the records of the House of Trade do not reveal the disposition made of private treasure in the early years.

The fact that Castilian mints worked only bullion of the fineness requisite for coinage,[7] which necessitated the refinement of treasure by its possessor, together with swelling imports, soon led to the emergence of special machinery, in the form of silver merchants (compradores de oro y plata, literally "gold and silver buyers"), for handling Indian treasure. Since the government was desirous of profiting by the services of a specialized middle-

---

[1] Alonso de Carranza, *op. cit.*, p. 377.

[2] José de Veitia Linaje, *op. cit.*, lib. II, p. 136; *Recopilación de Indias*, lib. IX, tit. XXIV, ley XII.

[3] A. de I., *Contratación*, 41-2-5. Not all bullion was coined at Seville. For instance, early in 1524 gold was sent to be coined in the mint at Burgos (AS, *Contaduría Mayor*: Iª *Época*, 400).

[4] A. de I., *Contratación*, 39-2-1/8. Workmen were paid on a piece-rate basis.

[5] In 1552, 21,000,000 maravedís' worth of bullion brought from Peru was turned over to creditors of Charles V because the officials of the House of Trade thought that the price offered exceeded its mint value (A. de I., *Indiferente General*, 147-2-12).

[6] A. de I., *Contratación*, 39-3-3/1, 41-1-1/12, 41-1-3/4, 42-6-1/5, 42-6-5/9, 42-6-7/11; *Indiferente General*, 147-2-12; AS, *Contadurías Generales: Razón*, 3052.

[7] Juan Surrá y Rull, *Breve Reseña Histórica de la Organización y Régimen de las Casas de Moneda de España* (Madrid, 1869), pp. 1023-1024.

man and of avoiding fraud and collusion, sale at public auction to silver merchants became the normal method of disposing of Crown treasure. As early as 1531, spirited bidding, such as would make for a "fair" price, took place. On August 14 of that year a shipment of bullion sold in the treasure chamber of the House of Trade, where subsequent auctions took place, brought forth twenty-four bids by seven silver merchants.[1] This is a typical case for that period. Though at times the House of Trade was paid for Crown treasure in cash, the typical method was for the stipulated sum to be paid by the mint, usually that of Seville,[2] to which the silver merchant contracted to deliver the bullion.[3]

---

[1] A. de I., *Contratación*, 41-2-5.

[2] The Seville mint was not the only one used. In the late thirties of the sixteenth century the Emperor became so exasperated by what he considered inexcusable delay in coining about 290,000 ducats' worth of bullion sequestered from private treasure brought from Tierra Firme (originally from Peru) that he sent most of it to Barcelona to be coined (AS, *Diversos de Castilla*, 1-27; A. de I., *Contratación*, 39-3-3/1). The famous water-driven mint of Segovia, the pride of Spanish governors and financial administrators, coined a substantial part of the Crown treasure, especially between 1585 and 1590. The following table, showing the amounts of Crown bullion the House was ordered to send to the Segovian mint, may prove instructive (A. de I., *Contratación*, 41-2-6).

Date	Marks of silver	Date	Marks of silver
Nov. 2, 1585	80,000	Dec. 17, 1588	100,000
Dec. 8, 1586	35,000	May 3, 1589	50,000
Dec. 4, 1587	100,000	Feb. 29, 1590	100,000

On December 14, 1606, the House was ordered to send 200,000 ducats' worth of gold and silver to Segovia "to be coined in reals and escudos" (A. de I., *Contratación*, 32-5-34). The *Nuevo Ingenio* at Segovia was patronized by the Crown as late as 1619, when the House of Trade sent the equivalent of 75,050,061 maravedís there to be coined (AS, *Contadurías Generales: Razón*, 271). On November 27, 1620, 400,000 ducats' worth of silver bullion was sent to Madrid, presumably for coinage there (A. de I., *Contratación*, 39-4-16/7). In July, 1639, 50 bars of silver were shipped to the mint at Toledo (A. de I., *Contratación*, 32-5-34).

[3] The following translation of an entry in the accounts of Receipts and Sales (Recibos y Ventas) illustrates the methods employed by the House of Trade in disposing of Crown treasure. "On May 10, 1591, we received from Marcos Rodríguez, captain of the caravel named [break in manuscript], the gold herein described, which was brought — listed on folio 98 of the register — for his Majesty. We offered the said gold for sale at public auction in the treasure chamber in the presence of many merchants of gold and silver and sold it to Luis Hernández, the highest bidder, at 25½ maravedís per carat plus one ducat distributed over the amount offered for sale. The value of the gold is to be delivered to the treasurer of the mint of this city, in gold of the fineness for coining escudos, within 6 days. We protect ourselves and collect by the aforementioned duty of the treasurer to deliver [money], and we hand over the gold weighed by Luis de Castro, assayer of the House of Trade,

Schemes for saving the Crown the profits of silver merchants were not wanting, and occasionally they won favor. In 1563 the Council of the Indies ordered the House of Trade to refine and coin, without the aid of silver merchants, the bullion brought from Tierra Firme in the armada of Pedro Menéndez de Avilés. The House replied, in a letter of June 20, 1563, that it would be far more profitable and expeditious to sell the treasure at auction to the highest bidder among fifteen or sixteen able and experienced silver merchants than to attempt to refine and coin it.[1] The silver merchants, it was argued, were qualified to perform the service, and their wives, children, and servants would help them to do all the work; while the officials of the India House were not competent to handle bullion, and everyone who touched it would have to be paid a salary. On September 15, 1563, the House rendered the further objection that a host of guards would be necessary to prevent embezzlement by the workmen who refined the treasure and that the expense entailed would more than absorb any possible profit. The remonstrance of the House of Trade was successful, for the treasure was sold to silver merchants. In 1609 the Council of the Indies again must have entertained notions of "eliminating the middleman," for in that year the House wrote the Council that it would be far more profitable to sell treasure at auction than to attempt to coin it without the intermediation of silver merchants.[2] In 1621 Crown bullion was actually handled

in the following manner" (A. de I., *Contratación*, 41–2–6). This statement was followed by a description of the gold, setting forth the weight and fineness of each piece. Sales of silver differed from the above only in the requirement that silver of the fineness for coining reals be delivered at the mint. In a few cases the silver merchant was required to "deliver the value of the silver in reals in the treasure chamber of the House" (A. de I., *Contratación*, 41–2–6). In 1581 this practice was fairly common, especially in minor transactions. Contracts calling for payment in another city were not unknown (José de Veitia Linaje, *op. cit.*, lib. I, p. 254).

[1] It is interesting to remark that in answer to a royal letter of July 19, 1551, instructing the House of Trade either to refine and deliver to the mint or to sell enough public treasure to pay a pressing short-term note for 236,000 ducats, on July 31, the officials stated that the bullion was being sold to silver merchants (AS, *Contadurías Generales: Razón*, 3052). On July 14, 1567, the treasurer of the mint at Mexico City argued that the silver merchants of New Spain, far from being parasites, as they had been characterized by the royal attorney (fiscal) of the colony, were a beneficent institution, rendering a genuine economic service (*ibid.*, *Diversos de Castilla*, 45–6).

[2] A. de I., *Contratación*, 42–6–1/5.

by the House of Trade, the factor being in charge of the work. As
the House had anticipated, the experiment proved disastrous.
Veitia Linaje tells us that up to his day (1672) the government
did not again venture upon such a course.[1]

Although the law did not require it, if we may believe Carranza,
long a student and close observer of the India trade, almost all
private treasure was sold to silver merchants;[2] and we know that
in 1620 they bought all the private bullion that was not sequestered.[3] The explanation of this phenomenon probably lies in the
fact that silver merchants developed considerable skill in super-
vising the refining of bullion. In fact, Veitia Linaje was especially
impressed by the circumstance that they advantageously relieved
private owners of this burden.[4]

Before silver masters could deliver private treasure to its original owners or to silver merchants who had bought it, it was necessary for them to obligate the recipient to coin the bullion in one
of the Castilian mints.[5] On December 4, 1620, the Council of the
Treasury (Consejo de Hacienda) ordered the House of Trade to
withhold one-eighth of the private treasure received that year[6]
as punishment for surreptitious exportation of bullion in the past
and to require private owners or purchasing silver merchants to
present to the House, within six months of the date of delivery, a
certificate from the mint of their choice to the effect that the bullion had been delivered for coinage.[7] In 1659 the House of Trade

---

[1] *Op. cit.*, lib. I, p. 91.   [2] *Op. cit.*, p. 189.
[3] A. de I., *Contratación*, 39-4-16/7.
  Owing to the limitations of space and to their secondary importance for the purpose in hand, the ubiquitous sequestrations of private treasure are mentioned only
incidentally. For brief discussions *vide* F. de Laiglesia, *op. cit.*, II, 301–322; C. H.
Haring, *Trade and Navigation*, pp. 169–174.
[4] *Op. cit.*, lib. I, p. 254.
[5] *Recopilación de Indias*, lib. IX, tit. XXIV, ley XIII.
[6] On October 24, 1620, the House received orders not to deliver private treasure
pending further notice (A. de I., *Contratación*, 39-4-16/7).
[7] A. de I., *Contratación*, 39-4-16/7. A report of the president of the House of
Trade on September 2, 1622, showed that 1,277,371,800 maravedís' worth of private
bullion was delivered to the following mints before June 16, 1621 (A. de I., *Contratación*, 39-4-16/7).

Seville	663,735,465 maravedís, or 52 per cent
Segovia	163,881,445 maravedís, or 13 per cent
Toledo	322,613,590 maravedís, or 25 per cent
Madrid	127,141,300 maravedís, or 10 per cent

and Sevillan Merchant Gild agreed that one of the three functions of registration was to provide a means of enforcing coinage within the realm.[1]

As one would expect from the fact that the Seville mint was literally in the shadow of the House of Trade, a significant portion of private treasure was coined there. In the period 1585–1595, 55 per cent and, in 1620, 52 per cent of private bullion was carried to the local mint.[2]

In the beginning not companies but individuals were silver merchants. For the most part, individuals formed banks in their homes and casually engaged in buying treasure, the magnitude of their operations depending on the extent of the funds entrusted to them.[3] But an ordinance of October 11, 1608, providing that only firms composed of two or more partners could buy bullion, wrought a fundamental change in the financial organization of silver merchants and incidentally led to one of the first appearances in Spain of the limited partnership, or *société en commandite*, on a large scale. The contract forming the partnership, which had to state the names of the partners, the name of the active partner, the length of time the partnership was to endure, and so forth, became operative on the approval of the prior and consuls of the Merchant Gild and the officials of the House of Trade. A bond for 40,000 ducats, likewise subject to the approval of the Gild and House, was also required. When copies of a duly approved partnership agreement and bond had been deposited with the comptroller of the House, where anyone who chose might examine them, the concern was privileged to deal in bullion. But additional security was required before a firm was permitted to buy treasure belonging to the Crown or to persons deceased (difuntos).[4]

A more precarious business than that of the silver merchant could hardly be conceived. Paraphrasing John Stuart Mill, one can say that their profits were a function of three variables: first,

---

[1] A. de I., *Contratación*, 42–6–12/16.

[2] These percentages have been calculated from the figures in A. de I., *Contratación*, 39–4–16/7, 42–6–3/7, and the documents — too numerous to mention — used in determining the receipts of private treasure.

[3] José de Veitia Linaje, *op. cit.*, lib. I, p. 252.

[4] *Ibid.*, lib. I, pp. 253–255.

the price paid for treasure; second, the correctness and probity of the assay in the Indies; and, third, the honesty of the workmen who refined the bullion. On July 14, 1567, the treasurer of the mint at Mexico City stated that in New Spain "the profits [of silver merchants] are miserably low, and their risks great." [1] In 1615 the officials of the House of Trade declared that the usual profit on a *castellano* (⅟₅₀ mark) of gold was 3 maravedís, or 0.5 per cent.[2] Veitia Linaje tells us that, when silver merchants had good fortune regarding all three variables, they could clear not more than 4 maravedís (about 0.18 per cent) on a mark of silver and 1 maravedí (about 0.20 per cent) on a castellano of gold.[3] Considering the great risk entailed, the margin of profits was perilously slender; and, as might be expected, there were many failures. On June 20, 1563, the House of Trade wrote the Council of the Indies that there were fifteen or sixteen silver merchants.[4] A few years before 1615, eight companies were in operation; but by July 14, 1615, failures had reduced the number to four.[5] Only three companies—Alonso de Medina y Compañía, Lope de Olloqui y Compañía, and Juan de Olarte y Compañía — bought the private treasure that came from the Indies in 1620.[6]

---

[1] AS, *Diversos de Castilla*, 45–6.

[2] A. de I., *Contratación*, 42–6–6/10.

[3] *Op. cit.*, lib. I, p. 251. Since man has always had a vague feeling that dealing in the precious metals conveys an unrivaled opportunity for profit, the silver merchant doubtless had to bid so much for bullion that only a slender margin of gain was possible in any case. Furthermore, the integrity of the American assays left much to be desired. On several occasions fraud and inexcusable negligence were discovered in the Peruvian analyses. Finally, about the middle of the seventeenth century, the abuses became intolerable, and vigorous measures were employed to eradicate the evil. Some assayers were hanged; others were arrested and sent to Spain, along with their goods, which had been confiscated. One of the assayers "died in the jail of the House of Trade, and another went mad in it." The analysis of bullion in New Spain never gave evidence of fraud, but the integrity of the assay was counterbalanced by flagrant corruption in smelting. In 1621, for example, "it was discovered that the centers and 'souls' of many bars of silver were of copper, more than a fifth of the bars being of this metal, which was placed so that the assayers could not discover it, no matter how large the sample taken to analyze" (*ibid.*, lib. I, pp. 263–264). On account of errors in the American assays, which had been noticed for some time, it became customary after 1603 to sell gold on the basis of analyses made in Castile (*ibid.*, lib. I, p. 250).

[4] A. de I., *Contratación*, 42–6–1/5.

[5] José de Veitia Linaje, *op. cit.*, lib. I, p. 250. Yet in 1615 the silver merchants advanced funds to outfit the treasure fleets (A. de I., *Contratación*, 41–1–1/2).

[6] A. de I., *Contratación*, 39–4–16/7.

Since the government was very solicitous regarding the national stock of specie, silver merchants were obsequiously treated. Their accounts could be examined or their homes searched only with the consent — rarely or never forthcoming — of the president of the House of Trade. Neither could treasure held by a silver merchant be embargoed without the president's permission. Smuggled gold and silver that reached the home of a silver merchant were accorded the full status of registered treasure. On August 27, 1667, a royal commission, formed to seize French goods as a retaliatory measure, was instructed to examine the papers and search the home of everyone suspected of holding French property; but it was enjoined not to molest any silver merchant.[1]

IV

Table 1 shows in pesos [2] the average annual imports of registered treasure for five-year periods — public, private, and total receipts being listed separately. As has been stated, the data for this table came entirely from the records of the men who handled the gold and silver. The figures for private treasure before 1536, for which original records are not available, have been derived from those for public treasure for the same period. From 1536 to 1660 public receipts were 26.2 per cent of the total, and this figure has been used in estimating private treasure for the period 1503–1536. The remainder of the table has been compiled without resort to conjecture or estimate. But the reader should not suppose that the figures listed are absolutely precise for every quinquennium. Aside from the mistakes that exist in my work, an inevitable concomitant of the thousands of calculations required, the original accounts and documents abound in errors. It often proved necessary to accept one of several conflicting statements,

---

[1] José de Veitia Linaje, *op. cit.*, lib. II, pp. 265–266.

[2] In this case *peso* means 450 maravedís' worth of gold or silver. It was equivalent to 42.29 grams of pure silver. "Peso" also had various other meanings, good accounts of which can be found in C. H. Haring, "American Gold and Silver Production," *Quarterly Journal of Economics*, XXIX, 476–479, and W. Lexis, "Beiträge zur Statistik der Edelmetalle," *Jahrbücher für Nationalökonomie und Statistik*, XXXIV, 376–380.

and mistakes of judgment doubtless occurred. Particularly difficult were many decisions as to whether small sums reached the motherland or were expended in the Indies or the Canaries. But not less than 2700 hours were spent upon the collection of the material in the Archive of the Indies, and every effort was made to account for all the treasure that reached Spain and to avoid double counting. I believe that large errors are improbable.

Crown receipts consisted mainly of the royal quint, but also of tribute levied on Indian tribes, sales of papal indulgences, fines and confiscations, profit on token money (before about 1540), and sales of miscellaneous goods. To some extent private treasure consisted of emigrants' remittances and the savings of passengers returning to Spain, but the bulk of it arose from the motherland's favorable balance of trade with the Indies. The colonists, having at their disposal silver mines like Guanajuato and Potosí — the former the richest of all time, the latter throughout the centuries a synonym of great wealth —, found it to their advantage to specialize in mining and to export specie in exchange for importable commodities.[1] The treasure fleets sailed from Spain laden with provisions, wares, and all sorts of merchandise.[2] The return cargo comprised small quantities of colonial produce — such as hides, copper, tobacco, sugar, indigo, and cochineal — and vast sums of silver. The European goods were exchanged for produce and specie in the fairs of Porto Belo,[3] Vera Cruz, and Cartagena.[4] In 1594 gold and silver formed 95.62 per cent of the return cargo, cochineal 2.82 per cent, hides 1.16 per cent, indigo 0.29 per cent,

---

[1] In other words, the colonists had a comparative advantage in mining the precious metals. Consequently, they neglected the production of many commodities to which their resources and aptitudes were suited. Cairnes pointed out that a similar episode occurred in Australia following the gold discoveries in the middle of the nineteenth century ("The Australian Episode," *Essays in Political Economy*, pp. 20–53).

[2] Tomás de Mercado (*Suma de Tratos y Contratos* [Seville, 1571], lib. II, fol. 91) ascribed the rise in prices in the sixteenth century largely to the heavy export of goods to the Indies.

[3] On October 28, 1659, the prior and consuls of the Sevillan Merchant Gild said: "The fair of Porto Belo is the greatest in the world." A few days later the officials of the House of Trade said, "The fair of Porto Belo used to be the greatest in the world" (A. de I., *Contratación*, 42–6–12/16).

[4] A. de I., *Contratación*, 42–6–12/16.

and miscellaneous articles 0.11 per cent. In 1609, 84 per cent consisted of treasure and 16 per cent of other products.[1]

TABLE 1

TOTAL IMPORTS OF TREASURE IN PESOS (450 MARAVEDÍS)
BY FIVE-YEAR PERIODS

Period	Public	Private	Total
1503–1505	97,216.5	273,838.8	371,055.3
1506–1510	213,854.0	602,382.5	816,236.5
1511–1515	313,235.0	882,318.5	1,195,553.5
1516–1520	260,217.5	732,979.0	993,196.5
1521–1525	35,152.5	99,017.5	134,170.0
1526–1530	272,070.5	766,366.5	1,038,437.0
1531–1535	432,360.5	1,217,870.5	1,650,231.0
1536–1540	1,350,885.0	2,587,007.0	3,937,892.0
1541–1545	757,788.5	4,196,216.5	4,954,005.0
1546–1550	1,592,671.5	3,916,039.5	5,508,711.0
1551–1555	3,628,506.5	6,237,024.5	9,865,531.0
1556–1560	1,568,495.5	6,430,503.0	7,998,998.5
1561–1565	1,819,533.0	9,388,002.5	11,207,535.5
1566–1570	3,784,743.0	10,356,472.5	14,141,215.5
1571–1575	3,298,660.5	8,607,948.5	11,906,609.0
1576–1580	6,649,678.5	10,602,262.5	17,251,941.0
1581–1585	7,550,604.0	21,824,008.0	29,374,612.0
1586–1590	8,043,212.5	15,789,418.0	23,832,630.5
1591–1595	10,023,348.5	25,161,514.0	35,184,862.5
1596–1600	10,974,318.0	23,454,182.5	34,428,500.5
1601–1605	6,519,885.5	17,883,442.5	24,403,328.0
1606–1610	8,549,679.0	22,855,528.0	31,405,207.0
1611–1615	7,212,921.5	17,315,199.0	24,528,120.5
1616–1620	4,347,788.0	25,764,672.0	30,112,460.0
1621–1625	4,891,156.0	22,119,522.5	27,010,678.5
1626–1630	4,618,801.0	20,335,725.5	24,954,526.5
1631–1635	4,733,824.5	12,377,029.5	17,110,854.0
1636–1640	4,691,303.0	11,623,299.0	16,314,602.0
1641–1645	4,643,662.0	9,120,140.5	13,763,802.5
1646–1650	1,665,112.5	10,105,434.5	11,770,547.0
1651–1655	2,238,878.0	5,054,889.0	7,293,767.0
1656–1660	606,524.0	2,754,591.5	3,361,115.5
Totals, 1503–1660 ....117,386,086.5		330,434,845.8	447,820,932.3

How important this treasure was, how large it loomed in the lives of the Spanish people, can perhaps best be shown by stating

---

[1] A. de I., *Indiferente General*, 147-2-16. Treasure so far outweighed other colonial products in the eyes of contemporaries, because of both its absolute amount and mercantilist preconceptions, that the fleets plying between Spain and the Indies were spoken of as the "fleets going to the Indies to bring back the gold and silver of his Majesty and private individuals."

that, at the rate prevailing for unskilled labor in Andalusia, the average annual receipts for 1591–1595 would have paid for about twenty-one days' work of all the persons in the country employed for salaries and wages.[1]

Chart 1 presents graphically the data contained in Table 1.

CHART 1

TOTAL IMPORTS OF TREASURE IN PESOS (450 MARAVEDÍS)
BY FIVE-YEAR PERIODS

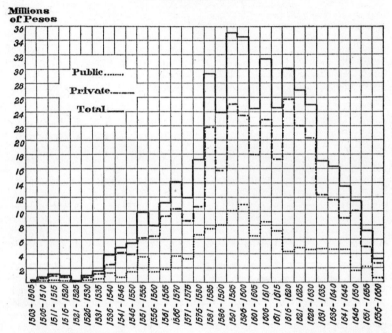

From 1503–1505 to 1591–1595 there was a steady increase in the receipts of treasure.[2] The period 1601–1630 showed a marked

---

[1] There is considerable chance for error in these figures. The data on population have been taken from Tomás González, *Censo de Población de la Corona de Castilla en el Siglo XVI* (Madrid, 1829), the most reliable source known to me; but their accuracy is far below that of a modern census. The percentage of population working for hire has been arbitrarily taken to be that for the United States as shown by the census of 1920. Furthermore, all employees were not unskilled laborers. Wages in Andalusia, the region first flooded with American gold and silver, were higher than in the country as a whole. But all these sources of error do not destroy, though they do impair, the significance of the estimate for the purpose in hand.

[2] The paucity of receipts from 1521 to 1525 may be explained on the ground

decline, and the period 1631–1660 a precipitate drop, in registered gold and silver. Although the scope of the present chapter
does not permit a complete explanation of the dwindling receipts
of specie, the following causes may be named: an increase in interloping; [1] a rise in the expense of mining together with the fixed
prices of the precious metals; [2] a decrease in the fertility of the
mines; [3] an increase in the avería, which in certain years became
confiscatory; [4] decimation of the labor supply by rude work in the

that the colonial officials were reluctant to remit treasure to Castile while she was,
and while they believed her to be, in the throes of domestic turmoil.

It is striking that the largest receipts of precious metals between 1503 and 1660
came in 1591–1595, the quinquennium immediately following the destruction, in
1588, of the so-called Invincible Armada. Obviously the opinion that Spain, unable
to furnish adequate protection to treasure fleets, received a greatly diminished supply of gold and silver from the Indies after this catastrophe has no foundation in
fact.

[1] In 1659 the House of Trade and Sevillan Merchant Gild estimated that a million pesos of Peruvian treasure annually crossed the Andes and made their way to
interlopers in the port of Buenos Aires. On this account the Gild and House recommended that this excellent port be closed (A. de I., Contratación, 42–6–12/16).

[2] That this was a handicap was understood by contemporaries. Vide Alonso de
Carranza, op. cit., pp. 371–375.

[3] This condition seems to have obtained both in New Spain and in the then Peru.
In 1600 Alonso de Oñate, "procurador general de los mineros de la Nueva España,
Nueva Galicia, y Nueva Vizcaya," wrote to the Council of the Indies that formerly
mines produced from 10 to 50 marks of silver per quintal of ore; whereas the mines
then yielding 2 marks per quintal, and with the use of 2 ounces of mercury, were
accounted good (A. de I., Audiencia de Méjico, 60–5–45). Drawing upon Pretensiones de Potosí (Madrid, 1634), by Sebastián Sandoval y Guzmán, Regidor of Lima
and Professor in the University of San Marcós, Antonio de Ulloa contended that in
1545–1571 the mines of Potosí produced a mark of silver per pound of ore, while in
1634 mines yielding 1 mark of silver per 1250 pounds were considered good and
those producing more were thought excellent (op. cit., pp. 255–256). In 1629 Alonso
de Carranza asserted that the decadence of Potosí had become so great that even
the Chinese, fully aware of it, were making and burying huge balls of silver (op. cit.,
pp. 371–375). According to Colmeiro, Potosí commenced to decline in fertility after
1606 (op. cit., II, 427–428). Soetbeer put it about 6 years earlier (op. cit., p. 78).

[4] In 1630, near the beginning of the precipitate decline in registered receipts, the
avería amounted to 31.5 per cent. In 1653 and 1655 it reached 99 per cent, and the
tonnage fee (derecho de tonelada) absorbed the remaining 1 per cent (A. de I.,
Contratación, 5181). In 1656 the avería was 49 per cent (ibid., Contratación, 42–6–
12/16). It should be borne in mind that these figures are not normal; in fact, they
are given in order to show abnormal yearly averías for an abnormal period. From
1620 to 1628 the convoys were financed by the merchants of Seville, who were able
to keep the avería at 6 per cent. In 1629 it rose to 17 per cent. In 1635 and 1636 the
merchants again contracted for the outfitting of the treasure fleets; expenses were
kept low enough for the avería to be 12 per cent. In 1641 and 1642 it was 14 per
cent, but in 1643 it rose to 23.4 per cent (A. de I., Contratación, 30–5–66/18, 42–6–
12/16).

mines; [1] an increase in trade with the Orient; [2] unnecessary delay in the delivery of private treasure; [3] delivery of private bullion in vellon at more than its market value; [4] a revival of the practice of sequestration in the closing years of the reign of Philip IV; [5] and an increase in the wealth and population of the Indies, which caused more treasure to be retained in the colonies.

According to Table 1, the total registered imports of public and private treasure in the entire period 1503–1660 amounted to 447,820,932 pesos.[6] Of course, there was smuggled specie also;

[1] José de Acosta, *Historia Natural y Moral de las Indias* (Barcelona, 1591), pp. 139–140; José del Campillo y Cosío, *Nuevo Sistema de Gobierno Económico para la América* (Madrid, 1789), pp. 2–17; William Robertson, *Works* (Edinburgh, 1829), I, 368.

[2] Immediately after the permanent settlement of the Philippines, the Spanish colonists began to trade with the Orient through the port of Acapulco in New Spain. Realizing that significant quantities of bullion were filtering out of the realm, the government subjected the trade to many vexatious restrictions (*vide Recopilación de Indias*, lib. IX, tit. XLV). As early as 1594, raw silk (presumably Chinese) was carried to Spain by the New Spain fleet; and the accounts for the fleet of 1609 stated specifically that Chinese silk ("seda que biene de China") was brought to the motherland. It is significant that the value of the silk increased from 18,233 ducats in 1594 to 88,687 ducats in 1609 (A. de I., *Indiferente General*, 147-2-16). For the collection of the almojarifazgo the imports into New Spain from the Philippines from May 17, 1603, to May 21, 1604, were valued at 223,486,080 maravedís (A. de I., *Contratación*, 4725). The market value of the goods was doubtless considerably higher. In 1659 the House of Trade and Sevillan Merchant Gild argued that 500,000 pesos' worth of Peruvian treasure annually made its way to China through the port of Acapulco (A. de I., *Contratación*, 42-6-12/16).

[3] In the closing years of the reign of Philip IV registers were sometimes sent to Madrid for examination before delivery was made (A. de I., *Contratación*, 42-6-12/16).

[4] A. de I., *Contratación*, 42-6-9/13.

[5] In 1637, for instance, the Crown sequestered 500,000 ducats' worth of private treasure. It seems that while the royal agent charged with the sequestration of the treasure was awaiting the arrival of the fleets of 1637 the Sevillans threatened to burn his home and injure him corporally (Archivo Histórico Nacional, *Clero*, Madrid, *Nuestra Señora del Paular*, leg. 1037). In 1659 the House of Trade and Sevillan Merchant Gild attributed the decline in registered receipts largely to this flagitious practice (A. de I., *Contratación*, 42-6-12/16).

[6] The estimates of previous writers — summaries of which can be found in Gerónimo de Uztáriz, *Theórica y Práctica de Comercio* (ed. Madrid, 1757), p. 6; A. von Humboldt, *Essai Politique sur le Royaume de la Nouvelle-Espagne* (Paris, 1811), II, 637–642; Manuel Colmeiro, *op. cit.*, II, 431–434; and F. de Laiglesia, *op. cit.*, II, 228–232 — vary from about double to ten times my figures. The glamour of romance surrounding the exploits of the discoverers and conquerors of a new world and the inordinate esteem in which the precious metals were then held doubtless played a part in the overestimation by contemporaries of the imports of gold and silver. But perhaps the largest factor was the wide divergence between the marginal uses of

but, from the nature of the case, no one can say how much. The amount of smuggled treasure has been estimated at from 10 to 50 per cent of the registered, but there is reason to believe that it was rather nearer the former than the latter figure. Smuggling was fraught with danger and expense.[1] Before the accession of Philip IV it was probably significant only when there was grave danger of sequestration or of an extraordinary avería. The trend of Spanish prices, as shown in Part II, indicates that the figures in Table 1 are not seriously vitiated by the fact that there were surreptitious imports of the precious metals.[2]

V

Particularly important is the ratio between gold and silver imports. But unfortunately the available data are neither complete nor satisfactory. The records of the House of Trade deposited in the Archive of the Indies [3] contain separate figures for a large part of the auction sales of gold and silver belonging to the Crown and deceased persons; but these documents exhibit two great defects. First, the Crown receipts, not all of which were sold at auction, comprised only 26.2 per cent of the total; and the treasure imported as legacies was insignificant. Second, a continuous lag in the adjustment of the mint ratio to an ever-increasing market ratio of gold to silver offered a constant inducement to gold miners, in collusion with Crown officials in the Indies, to pay in silver the quint on gold. Furthermore, there was a strong temptation to high colonial officials to collect their salaries in gold rather than silver. Rodrigo de Yllescas wrote Philip II, in 1560, that "accord-

treasure in America and Europe. When the booty derived from the spoliation of Indians arrived and it was learned that gold had been used by the Aztecs for such trivial purposes as the adornment of Indian slippers with 19 bells of gold (A. de I., *Contratación*, 39–2–1/8), it was inevitable that the Spaniards should fancy that the Indians possessed as much gold as they themselves would have required before pushing its marginal use so low.

[1] A. de I., *Contratación*, 42–6–12/16.

[2] The surviving accounts of the Castilian mints have proved disappointing as a means of estimating the extent of smuggling.

[3] Especially the series *Libros de Asientos del Recibo y Venta del Oro y Plata que Venían de Indias* and *Relaciones de los Caudales y Efectos que Venían de Indias en Armadas, Flotas, y Naos Sueltas.*

ing to information from men who have lived in Peru, the quint on gold amounts to more than 150,000 pesos a year," but that the Crown "receives no Peruvian gold because the salaries of the Viceroys, oidores, and officials absorb all of it."[1] A royal order of May 27, 1631, instructing colonial officials to send to Castile gold collected for the quint or any other account complained that in the past heavy losses had fallen upon the public treasury through the exchange of Crown gold for silver.[2] The records of auction sales have been supplemented by the accounts relating to private imports, together with certain reports of colonial officials as to the shipment of specie on the galleons. But the records of private treasure likewise present two weaknesses. First, in less than half the years can the imports of gold and silver be separated, and in nearly all cases there are some doubtful items. The practice of recording treasure in terms of value rather than weight at each link in the long chain from the American assay office to the Castilian mint has rendered difficult the process of separation. Second, since gold was easier to conceal, the percentage that came unregistered doubtless exceeded that of silver. From another source, however, we have data with an opposite bias. The accounts of the treasurers of the mints in Seville, Toledo, Segovia, and Granada — in which almost all the coinage of American bullion occurred — are available for about one-third of the years between 1590[3] and 1650.[4] Since unregistered bullion accepted by a mint was purged of all guilt, the percentage of smuggled treasure coined probably exceeded that of registered specie. That fear of detection of smuggled bullion after its arrival in Castile motivated its disposal is demonstrated by the fact that, in spite of the relative

---

[1] AS, *Estado,* 139.

[2] *Recopilación de Indias,* lib. VIII, tit. VI, ley XIV; lib. VIII, tit. X, ley XX.

[3] Diligent search in all the appropriate national and local archives failed to locate continuous records for any Castilian mint prior to 1590. Discontinuous documents of the Seville mint from 1503 on are available; but it is significant that, on May 27, 1687, the House of Trade wrote the Council of the Indies that it was absolutely impossible to find papers disclosing the amount of seigniorage collected by the Seville mint for any quinquennium before 1590–1594 (A. de I., *Contratación,* 5184).

[4] AS, *Tribunal Mayor de Cuentas,* 913–916, 921; *Contaduría Mayor de Cuentas,* 3ª, 985.

Figures for the mints at Madrid and Valladolid are also available and have been used in this study, but their coinage was insignificant.

ease with which gold might have been transported to distant
mints, the ratio of gold to silver coined in the Seville mint —
about two hundred meters from the House of Trade, where
American treasure was delivered to its owners — was considerably higher than in other mints.[1] Furthermore, unlike gold,
significant quantities of silver coined in the Indies were included
in the imports. By combining the data on coinage with those
for public and private receipts of gold and silver — series characterized by opposing tendencies — and making allowance for
the lack of mint statistics for the years before 1590,[2] I have

TABLE 2

PERCENTAGES OF TOTAL IMPORTS OF GOLD AND SILVER BY WEIGHT

Decades	Silver	Gold	Decades	Silver	Gold
1503–1510	0.00	100.00	1581–1590	98.25	1.75
1511–1520	0.00	100.00	1591–1600	98.50	1.50
1521–1530	3.00	97.00	1601–1610	98.67	1.33
1531–1540	87.50	12.50	1611–1620	98.75	1.25
1541–1550	85.00	15.00	1621–1630	99.10	0.90
1551–1560	85.00	15.00	1631–1640	99.20	0.80
1561–1570	97.00	3.00	1641–1650	99.20	0.80
1571–1580	98.00	2.00			

arrived at the estimates of comparative gold and silver imports
into Castile listed in Table 2. The reader is warned that these
are estimates based on partial information, into the determination of which arbitrary assumptions of correlations have entered,
not exact compilations of complete data.

Chart 2 represents pictorially the data contained in Table 2.

Before the first fruits of the conquest of New Spain reached
Castile, on November 5, 1519,[3] all of the specie imports were in
gold. As mining developed in New Spain the percentage of silver
rose. The effect of the conquest of Peru (1533) was neutralized
by the opening up of New Granada (1537), where the gold output

---

[1] The percentage of gold coined in the Madrid mint was abnormally high; but,
as has been said, the total volume of coinage was extremely small.

[2] Scattering records of the Seville mint for the period 1503–1590 have been
utilized.

[3] A. de I., *Contratación*, 39–2–2/9 (1). By far the greater part of this shipment
consisted of gold. The quantity of silver was too small to be taken into account in
Table 2.

CHART 2

PERCENTAGES OF TOTAL IMPORTS OF GOLD AND SILVER BY WEIGHT

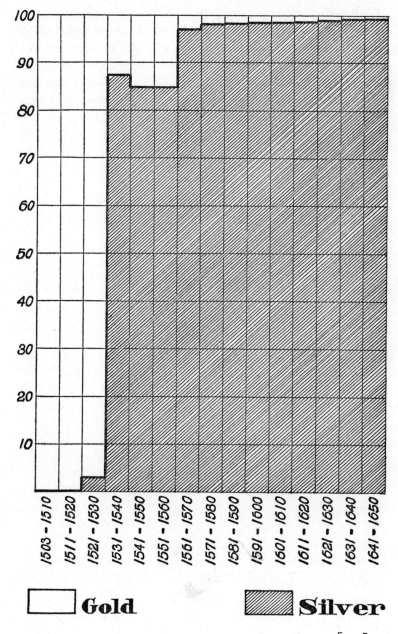

☐ Gold   ▨ Silver

was unusually high. After the discovery of the incomparably fertile silver mines at Potosí, Zacatecas, and Guanajuato and the introduction of the amalgamation process for silver mining, all of which occurred between 1545 and 1558, the mining of gold was eclipsed by that of silver, and the percentage of gold imports declined from that time forward. The proportional decrease in gold imports — and doubtless of production in America as well — continued into the seventeenth century.

VI

To appreciate the influence of the American mines upon Spanish and European bimetallic ratios, we must know the absolute quantities of gold and silver imports as well as the percentage

TABLE 3

Total Decennial Imports of Fine Gold and Silver

(in grams)

Period	Silver	Gold
1503–1510	....	4,965,180
1511–1520	....	9,153,220
1521–1530	148,739	4,889,050
1531–1540	86,193,876	14,466,360
1541–1550	177,573,164	24,957,130
1551–1560	303,121,174	42,620,080
1561–1570	942,858,792	11,530,940
1571–1580	1,118,591,954	9,429,140
1581–1590	2,103,027,689	12,101,650
1591–1600	2,707,626,528	19,451,420
1601–1610	2,213,631,245	11,764,090
1611–1620	2,192,255,993	8,855,940
1621–1630	2,145,339,043	3,889,760
1631–1640	1,396,759,594	1,240,400
1641–1650	1,056,430,966	1,549,390
1651–1660	443,256,546	469,430
Totals 1503–1660	16,886,815,303	181,333,180

distribution. The data in Table 2, together with the Castilian bimetallic ratios and legislation governing the standard fineness of gold and silver coins,[1] have made possible the estimates of decennial imports of fine gold and silver listed in Table 3.

[1] *Vide* Chapters III and IV.

VII

Until about 1515 most of the treasure came from Hispaniola. From 1516 to 1530 Porto Rican exports almost equaled those of Hispaniola, and Cuban exports became about half as great. Before 1531–1535 Tierra Firme and New Spain did not take the predominant positions they were destined to occupy.

CHART 3

PERCENTAGES OF IMPORTS BY PRODUCING REGIONS

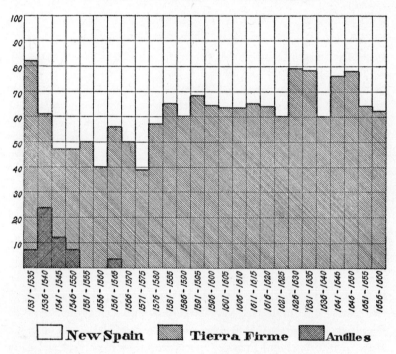

New Spain   Tierra Firme   Antilles

Chart 3 shows the relative amounts of imports drawn from New Spain and Tierra Firme between 1531 and 1660. With the receipts from New Spain I have included those from Honduras; so "Tierra Firme" means South America and "New Spain" North America. It is impossible to distinguish for the whole period the treasure that came from the Antilles, but one can say that it was not of moment after the middle of the sixteenth century. Figures are given in the periods for which I have data.

After 1545, the year that marked the discovery of Potosí, the percentage of receipts coming from Tierra Firme showed a steady increase. From 1581 to 1660, about half the period under investigation, Tierra Firme furnished roughly two-thirds and New Spain one-third of the total Spanish imports.

VIII

Let us examine briefly the effects of American treasure upon the motherland. For a season industry seems to have responded to the rise in prices precipitated by the influx of treasure. The resultant material prosperity, together with the effect of the specie on national psychology, played a part in the passage of Spain through her golden age of literature and art.[1] But ultimately the importation of treasure (the exportation of which was retarded by legal restrictions) in exchange for goods sapped the economic vitality of the country and augmented the Price Revolution, which handicapped export industry. Historians have generally agreed that American gold and silver fanned the flames of Hapsburg imperialism, added to the zeal with which Spanish rulers defended the Catholic faith against Protestant and Mohammedan, furnished sinews of war, and, in short, constituted an important factor in Spain's aggressive foreign policy.[2] Both the absolute amounts of Crown treasure and the stability of the receipts, which made them dependable and reckonable, indicate that this thesis is tenable. Furthermore, private treasure, through sequestration upon arrival, contributed very largely to public revenue. And it should be remembered that, because of the relatively undeveloped state of international finance, specie was then highly prized as a

[1] That Spanish life was directly influenced by American gold and silver is attested by the use Cervantes made of treasure and treasure fleets in *Rinconete y Cortadillo* and *El Celoso Extremeño*, two of his "Novelas Ejemplares," which contain the best descriptions extant of Spanish life and customs.

[2] Professor Merriman, one of the leading recent students of Spanish history, seems to share this opinion (*op. cit.*, III, 45, 255). Though he recognized the general acceptance of this view, Laiglesia (*op. cit.*, II, 230) opposed it as regards the Emperor on grounds that do not seem convincing.

means of supporting military operations in distant countries.[1] So gold and silver from the Indies were a factor in the shedding of the blood of Spain — sacrificed on altars of imperialism and religious fanaticism — on distant European battlefields. Other men, lured by the El Dorados of New Spain and the then Peru, emigrated at their most productive age. American treasure doubtless created the illusion of prosperity and thus fostered extravagance and vagrancy. One cannot escape the conclusion that the gold and silver drawn from the Indies ultimately had baneful effects upon the mother country.

Next let us turn to the effects of Spanish imports of gold and silver upon Hispanic America. One who examines the records of the House of Trade, especially for the early years, cannot fail to be impressed by the enormous part played by American gold in the exploration and development of the New World. The sailors who accompanied Columbus on his first voyage, including the heirs of the men left on Hispaniola, were paid in part with gold brought to Spain between 1513 and 1519.[2] Treasure drawn from the Indies financed the memorable voyage of Magellan, which proved rich in scientific discovery and demonstrated to the lay mind the sphericity of the earth.[3] It paid the salaries of such notable servants of Spain as Amerigo Vespucci and Sebastian Cabot; and it provided the means to purchase and to carry to America the seeds, plants, animals, tools, books, and scientific instruments of the Old World.[4]

[1] Cf. Adam Smith, *Wealth of Nations* (Cannan ed., London, 1904), I, 407–412; F. W. Taussig, *International Trade* (New York, 1927), pp. 274–278. This is one reason why the mercantilists placed great emphasis upon the accumulation of gold and silver.

[2] A. de I., *Contratación*, 39–2–1/8, 39–2–2/9. In the debates over the financing of the first voyage of the Admiral, I have never seen this matter mentioned. It is evident that the sailors themselves made "advances" for a substantial part of the cost of the voyage.

[3] *Ibid.*, *Contratación*, 39–2–2/9.

[4] It is interesting to note that tribute levied upon Indian tribes in New Spain contributed substantially to the construction of the monastery-palace of San Lorenzo del Escorial (AS, *Obras de El Escorial*, leg. 1).

CHAPTER III

GOLD AND SILVER MONEY IN CASTILE

I

THE influx of American gold and silver into Europe, examined in Chapter II, not only lent new impetus to the spice trade and gave rise to the Price Revolution (both of which phenomena were vital factors in the decay of medieval economic institutions and the rise of modern capitalism),[1] but profoundly affected monetary systems. The extension of the Castilian monetary system and mint regime to the Hispanic colonies of the New World, the absolute monopoly of colonial trade, and the legal requirement to coin specie reaching the motherland caused a large part of the American treasure that reached Europe to enter circulation in the form of Castilian coins and endowed the monetary history of Castile with an importance transcending her frontiers.[2] The output of the rich silver mines in New Spain and Peru far surpassed the production of gold, chiefly in New Granada; and the bimetallic ratio, which had remained fairly stable in Western Europe for several centuries, was revolutionized. The present chapter purposes to investigate Castilian gold and silver money — the coinage first affected by the new mines. Vellon [3] coins are included until 1598, when they ceased to be minted with an admixture of silver; but their subsequent history is reserved for Chapter IV.

[1] Earl J. Hamilton, "American Treasure and the Rise of Capitalism, 1500–1700," *Economica*, November, 1929, pp. 338–357.

[2] On December 12, 1577, Juan de Vargas Mexía wrote Philip II from the Spanish Embassy at Paris that "in all this kingdom I see almost no money besides Spanish reals, escudos, and doubloons, not to mention large quantities smelted every day in order to coin other [French] money" (Archives Nationales [Paris], *Négociations France-Espagne*, K 1543, no. 113). According to Paul Raveau (*L'Agriculture et les Classes Paysannes dans le Haut Poitou au XVIᵉ Siècle* [Paris, 1926], p. xii), Spanish reals were "assuredly" used as extensively in Poitou during the sixteenth century as French coins themselves.

[3] Vellon was originally a mixture of silver and copper used for fractional coins. After the restoration of the silver content at the close of the fifteenth century, debasement during the sixteenth century gradually reduced vellon to pure copper.

Castilian gold and silver money, originally based on Roman coins of the time of Julian, passed through recurrent periods of debasement and restoration during the centuries of intermittent warfare to free Castile from the Moslem invader. In the reign of Henry IV (1454–1474), when the struggle was drawing to a close, monetary disorder reached its apogee. Impecuniosity and the importunities of court favorites forced Henry IV to grant possibly as many as 150 mint franchises.[1] Royal supervision, inadequate in the six mints — Burgos, Cuenca, la Coruña, Segovia, Seville, and Toledo — to which coinage had hitherto been confined, now broke down completely. Ordinances governing the weight and fineness of money were boldly disregarded, and the mint concessionaires vied with each other in the coinage of light and base money. Silver was debased; and gold, offering still greater opportunities for profit, was minted with as little as one-third of its legal fineness. Vellon escaped illegal debasement in the new mints, but Henry IV admitted in the Cortes of 1471 that he had sanctioned an issue of pure copper.[2] The circulating media, hitherto consisting largely of foreign and old Castilian coins of widely divergent soundness and state of preservation, were rendered chaotic; and reform became imperative.

In response to general complaint regarding the state of the coinage, probably intensified by economic unrest resulting from the bad harvest of 1470,[3] his Majesty summoned the Cortes and requested certain cities to send monetary experts for consultation by the Cortes and the Council of Castile.[4] On April 10, 1471, in the Cortes of Segovia, Henry IV made a notable attempt at reform. Because of its enlightened character, as well as for its anticipation of the statutory provisions of the great monetary reform of Ferdinand and Isabella of 1497, the pragmatic of Henry IV merits attention.

Particularly important were the provisions of the pragmatic of April 10, 1471, pertaining to the mints. Recognizing that the

---

[1] *Cortes de los Antiguos Reinos de León y Castilla* (hereafter *Cortes*), III, 830; *Actas de las Cortes de Castilla* (hereafter *Actas*), XIII, 358.

[2] *Cortes*, III, 813.

[3] Antonio Vives, *Moneda Castellana* (Madrid, 1901), p. 54.

[4] *Cortes*, III, 813–814.

prevailing monetary disorder was largely attributable to the new mints, Henry IV revoked their licenses and again restricted coinage to the six royal mints. Further coinage in the proscribed mints became tantamount to counterfeiting, punishable by death and the confiscation of goods. Municipal authorities were directed to enforce the pragmatic and, if necessary, to demolish the mint buildings.[1] To frustrate illegal coinage, private individuals were authorized to raze buildings and destroy implements and were guaranteed immunity from prosecution for incidental property damage and personal injury.[2] The mints were organized as private enterprises under the strict surveillance of the government.[3] The treasurers were directed to provide and maintain buildings and complete equipment for coining and were authorized to collect the following fees: 2 *tomines* per mark of gold, 1 real per mark of silver, and 25 maravedís per mark of vellon.[4] The number and the classes of employees were prescribed, and the treasurers were required to pay them on a piece-rate basis according to a stipulated schedule. Besides the treasurer, the officials of a mint consisted of an assayer, an assistant treasurer, a weigher (maestro de balanza), a notary (escribano), guards, and foremen. The weigher and the assayer tested the bullion presented for coinage, as well

---

[1] *Cortes*, III, 831.

[2] *Ibid.*, III, 832.

[3] Castile's early experiment in the private operation of mints under royal supervision has been uncritically praised (*vide*, for example, Juan Surrá y Rull, *Breve Reseña Histórica de la Organización y Régimen de las Casas de Moneda de España* [Madrid, 1869]). It seems, however, that no special benefits were derived from this regime. That satisfactory operation in the sixteenth century was due to able administration by strong monarchs, not to the nature of the system employed, is indicated by the inefficiency and scandals that arose in the seventeenth century (Archivo de Simancas [hereafter AS], *Contadurías Generales: Razón*, 272, 273), when weak monarchs were on the throne. Furthermore, inability to require the coinage of small denominations of silver, a matter of great concern to the Cortes (*vide*, for example, *Cortes*, v, 752), resulted from the fact that the minting of large coins proved more remunerative to the private entrepreneurs. Instead of seeking able entrepreneurs offering the greatest advantages to the public, the Crown delivered the mints to court favorites as sinecures. For instance, in 1596 the Conde de Chinchón was treasurer of the two mints at Segovia (AS, *Tribunal Mayor de Cuentas*, 897), and in 1625 the Duque de Lerma was treasurer in perpetuity of the mints at Burgos and Madrid (*ibid.*, *Contadurías Generales: Razón*, 272). The Valencian mint was also operated privately under strict government regulation (*vide*, for example, Archivo Regional, *Maestre Racional, Tesorería*, legs. 357-358).

[4] *Cortes*, III, 828.

as the money delivered to its owners; and the notary witnessed and certified the weights and assays. The foremen supervised, and the guards watched over the processes of coinage. In addition to the appointment of the treasurer and to intervention in the selection of all officers and employees, the government exercised control by requiring the authorities of cities having mints to name two *regidores* to serve as inspectors for terms of two months. A regidor was not eligible for reappointment before all of his colleagues had served in turn.[1] The pragmatic described the technical operations of coinage and fixed definite responsibility throughout the mint hierarchy. Nepotism was prohibited, and the officers and employees of mints were forbidden to coin bullion privately or in partnership.[2] A death penalty confronted the operative who had unauthorized bullion at his furnace or workbench,[3] failed to return his tools to a guard at the end of the day,[4] withdrew money from a mint through irregular channels,[5] or coined before sunrise or after sunset.[6] Recalling the baneful effects of recent efforts to profit from coinage, Henry IV renounced seigniorage. All fees collected by the mints were retained by the officers and employees.[7]

The pragmatic of April 10, 1471, provided for free and unlimited coinage of gold, silver, and vellon. Following the advice of the experts consulted, Henry IV authorized the coinage of 50 *enriques* from a mark of gold not less than 23¾ carats fine. Mints were ordered to coin one-third the bullion delivered in half-enriques and the remainder in enriques or multiples thereof. The weight of the silver real was reduced from ⅟₆₆ to ⅟₆₇ of a mark, with the fineness remaining 11 dineros 4 grains (93.06 per cent). Fractional coinage was supplied by vellon *blancas* (half-maravedís) and half-blancas, of which 205 and 410 respectively were struck from a mark containing 10 grains of silver (3.47 per cent). The enrique was tariffed at 420 maravedís, the real at 31 mara-

---

[1] *Cortes*, III, 825.
[2] *Ibid.*, III, 822–823. Subsequently the treasurers were forbidden to act as silver merchants (AS, *Contadurías Generales: Razón*, 273).
[3] *Cortes*, III, 821. [4] *Ibid.*, III, 824.
[5] *Ibid.*, III, 826. [6] *Ibid.*, III, 827.
[7] *Ibid.*, III, 821.

vedís, and the blanca at ½ maravedí.[1] The mints were ordered to
deliver coins to their owners by weight rather than by count.[2] A
mark of reals containing more than 67 and a mark of enriques
containing more than 50 might not be released for circulation.
A discrepancy of 4 blancas more or less than standard was permitted.[3] The owners of vellon coins and of gold coins other than
doblas de la banda and florins of Aragon were authorized to smelt
them in the mints for recoinage. For smelting money outside a
mint the death penalty was provided.[4]

In spite of its sagacious provisions the ordinance of April 10,
1471, did not end monetary disorder. As in the case of other
exemplary legislation enacted during his reign, the utter failure
of Henry IV to enforce the pragmatic rendered it nugatory.[5] Even
the death penalty against smelting coins outside the six royal
mints was ineffective. In the Cortes of 1473 the *Procuradores* informed his Majesty that many of his subjects, "blinded by inordinate greed," were smelting reals and blancas in order to
counterfeit reals from the bullion.[6]

II

When Ferdinand and Isabella ascended the throne (1474),
Castilian money was in a deplorable state. Counterfeiters and the
horde of mints chartered by Henry IV had flooded Castile with
defective silver and vellon. Besides the base gold coined by the
"new" mints, considerable foreign gold, short in weight and uneven in fineness, was in circulation. If we take the first tariffs
assigned by the Catholic Kings, we find that gold coins of the following tales expressed in maravedís were in use: 265, 328, 335,
365, 435, 445, 480, 575, and 860. To heighten the confusion, coins
of defective weight were permitted to circulate according to a
schedule of legal deductions, and the tariffs were often changed
in an effort to adjust the legal ratings to economic values.

---

[1] *Cortes*, III, 813–815.   [2] *Ibid.*, III, 821.
[3] *Ibid.*, III, 818.   [4] *Ibid.*, III, 816.
[5] Cf. Andrés Marcos Burriel, *Informe de Toledo sobre Pesos y Medidas* (Madrid,
1758), pp. 26–27.
[6] *Cortes*, III, 879.

The monetary chaos rendered reform inevitable, but during the first twenty-three years of their reign the Catholic Kings were so engrossed successively in rivalry with *La Beltraneja*, the reconquest of Granada, and the persecution and expulsion of infidels that no sweeping monetary reform was attempted. Only minor changes, such as alterations of the tariffs of coins, were effected. But on June 13, 1497, Castilian money was subjected to a thorough renovation.

As in 1471, monetary experts were summoned for consultation. The statutory mint regulations of June 13, 1497, were essentially the same as those of April 10, 1471; but the administrative ability of the Catholic Kings secured adequate enforcement. Important changes were introduced in gold, silver, and vellon money.

Ferdinand and Isabella consulted the experts as to the advisability of continuing the existing gold coinage or supplanting it by a new coin and inquired whether bimetallic ratios were properly adjusted. The experts replied that silver was undervalued at the mint and recommended the adoption of a new gold coin modeled on the Venetian ducat, one of the most prevalent and acceptable gold coins circulating in Castile.[1] Following this advice, the Catholic Kings instituted the *excelente de Granada*, an exact duplication of the Venetian ducat.[2] From a mark of gold 23¾ carats (98.96 per cent) fine 65 excelentes were coined, and their tariff was fixed at 375 maravedís. The weight and fineness of the silver real were not altered; but its tale was increased to 34 maravedís, at which figure it was destined to remain for about three and a half centuries. The changes in gold and silver raised the mint ratio of silver to gold,[3] as had been recommended by monetary

---

[1] Diego Pérez, *Pragmáticas y Leyes* (1549), fols. 85–86. Since the pragmatic specifically states that the Venetian ducat was taken as a model, it is difficult to understand why Antonio Vives (*op. cit.*, p. 22) contended that the Aragonese ducat was copied.

[2] In more than two years devoted exclusively to the collection of Spanish price and wage statistics for the period 1501–1650 I have not seen "excelente de Granada" in a commercial document. As early as 1504 "ducat" was used instead of "excelente de Granada" in official papers (Archivo de Indias [hereafter A. de I.], *Contratación*, 39–2–1/8), and in the pragmatic of November 23, 1566, Philip II mentioned the "ducat" coined by his grandparents (*Recopilación de Leyes de España* [Madrid, 1640] [hereafter *Recopilación*], lib. v, tit. xxi, ley [Declaraciones] xiii). [3] *Vide* Table 4.

experts. Perhaps the greatest alteration occurred in vellon. The fineness was reduced from 10 grains of silver to 7 (2.43 per cent); and 192 blancas were struck from a mark. Realizing that, although the commodity value of vellon — including the fee for coinage — approximated its mint price, depreciation would ensue if the quantity exceeded the requirements for change and petty transactions, the Catholic Kings limited the amount that might be coined to 10,000,000 maravedís. This maximum, far too low, served as a precedent and paved the way for the obnoxious circulation of foreign vellon in the reign of the Emperor. As in 1471, the Crown exacted no seigniorage, all sums collected by the mints being retained as fees for coinage.[1] The circulation of foreign and old Castilian gold, silver, and vellon money was authorized during a provisional period, upon the termination of which they were to be suppressed;[2] but the prohibition did not materialize. The period of grace for gold coins was successively extended,[3] and their tariffs were altered in accordance with every change in the gold coinage until December 23, 1642, when they were finally suppressed. As will be shown presently, foreign vellon continued in circulation for at least seventy years.

Although the pragmatic of Medina del Campo of June 13, 1497, was important and has been the object of extravagant praise by scholars, it did not find immediate favor. On December 20, 1497, the Catholic Kings stated that the recent monetary alterations

---

[1] The following fees were fixed: gold, 1¾ tomines per mark; silver, 1 real per mark; and vellon, 25 maravedís per mark. These fees represented legal maxima. The treasurers of mints were permitted to charge less. At the beginning of the sixteenth century the Seville mint collected the legal tariff (A. de I., *Contratación*, 39-2-1/8, 41-2-5), but subsequently competition led the various mints to resort to price cutting. In fact, the royal mint (Nuevo Ingenio) at Segovia engaged in predatory price competition (AS, *Tribunal Mayor de Cuentas*, 879). In a tying contract of June 30, 1603, the Seville mint bound Manuel Ruiz de Vidacaval, Bernadino de Bidarte y Cía., gold and silver merchants, not to send over 90,000 marks of American silver to other mints in the next three years in consideration of a rebate of 360,000 maravedís on coinage fees. Upon complaint from the Segovian mint against this unfair practice the Crown prohibited such agreements (AS, *Contadurías Generales: Razón*, 271). But the competitive strength of the Seville mint did not prevent the bankruptcy of the treasurer in January, 1626 (*ibid.*, *Contadurías Generales: Razón*, 272).

[2] Diego Pérez, *op. cit.*, fols. 85–86.

[3] Archivo del Ayuntamiento (hereafter AA), Madrid, *Moneda*, 3-413-44; AA, Burgos, *Sección Histórica*, 2485.

introduced to provide Castile with sound money had evoked complaints from numerous cities. The mints and certain municipalities were invited to send delegates to a monetary conference beginning on January 20, 1498,[1] but no important changes resulted.

The administrative ability of the Catholic Kings was never more clearly demonstrated than in the enforcement of monetary and mint ordinances. The precedent of effective and adequate administration of monetary legislation was more powerful than were the beneficent provisions of the pragmatics themselves in establishing the tradition of sound money that obtained in Castile during the sixteenth century.

In 1517 rumors to the effect that the Seville mint was coining gold of defective weight and fineness were widely circulated. Since the treasure of the Indies, then consisting entirely of gold, was passing through the Seville mint, general alarm ensued; and the Crown ordered Dr. Sancho de Matienzo, treasurer of the House of Trade, and a Dr. Calvete to investigate. On February 14, 1517, Drs. Matienzo and Calvete reported that all the gold coins, ten in number, found in the mint had been weighed and assayed in their presence by the best assayer available assisted by two men experienced in weighing and refining gold. Two gold coins minted in 1513, two in 1515, and two in 1516 that had not entered circulation were taken from the coffers of the House of Trade and likewise weighed and assayed. All the coins tested proved perfect in weight and fineness. The report not only exonerated the mint, but praised the ability and integrity of its officers and the skill of its employees.[2]

III

During the reign of Charles V (1516–1556) the Cortes were not always upholders of sound money. The mercantilist expedient of debasement in order to conserve specie was repeatedly proposed to the Emperor during the first half of his reign. In the Cortes of

---

[1] Biblioteca Nacional (hereafter BN), *Sección de Manuscritos*, Ms. 13,111; AA, Burgos, *Sección Histórica*, 2484.

[2] AS, *Diversos de Castilla*, 43–17.

1518,[1] 1520,[2] and 1523 [3] the Procuradores petitioned his Majesty to lower the fineness of gold coins in order to prevent their export. As was probably intended in 1518 and 1520, proportional inflation of the silver real was requested in 1523. The petitions of 1518 and 1520 availed little, but in 1523 Charles V ordered the mints, the Merchant Gild of Burgos, and the merchants and silversmiths of certain other cities to study the proposal for inflation and to send written recommendations by a delegate competent to give further advice to the Council and Cortes. A committee composed of these delegates, representatives of the Council of Castile, and "other experienced officials and silversmiths," appointed by Charles V, recommended a policy of mild inflation. To stop the loss of gold to France, the chief concern of the Cortes, a reduction in the fineness of the ducat (excelente de Granada) from 23¾ to 21½ carats, weight and tariff remaining unchanged, was proposed. Close approximation to the French crown of the sun, a half-carat finer and .0006 mark lighter, could thus be secured. To effect a corresponding debasement of the silver real, a decrease in weight from $\frac{1}{67}$ to $\frac{1}{71}$ of a mark — with fineness and tale remaining constant — was recommended. A reduction of the fineness of the blanca from 7 to 6 grains of silver (2.08 per cent) and an increase in the tariffs of Flemish coins circulating in Castile were also favored. The Crown was requested to order Aragon, Catalonia, Valencia, Naples, and Navarre — members of the Spanish Empire not then using the Castilian monetary system — to adopt the new ducat and to harmonize their silver and vellon coinage with it. Charles V, a champion of sound money, did not accept these recommendations; but either to ascertain public opinion or to delay action he instructed the Procuradores to refer the proposals to their constituencies.[4] In the Cortes of 1528 [5] and 1534 [6] the Procuradores renewed their request that the ducat be debased in

---

[1] Manuel Colmeiro, *Historia de la Economía Política en España* (Madrid, 1863), II, 486.

[2] *Cortes*, IV, 328.

[3] *Quaderno de Cortes de 1523* (1535), Petición 85.

[4] *Cortes*, IV, 388–393.

[5] *Quaderno de Cortes de 1528* (1546), Petición 120; *Cortes*, IV, 505.

[6] *Ibid.*, IV, 609; *Quaderno de Cortes de 1534* (1550), Petición 95.

order to check the flow of gold abroad, but no action was taken until 1537.

In 1537 Charles V provided for the coinage of *escudos* 22 carats (91.67 per cent) fine, weighing ⅟₆₈ of a mark, the weight and fineness of the "best escudos" of France and Italy, and tariffed at 350 maravedís.[1] In Catalonia the escudo had been coined earlier. In 1535 the Emperor, vexed by the delay of the Seville mint in coining the first spoils of the Incan conquest, sent gold to Barcelona to be coined into "imperial escudos," sixty-eight of which were struck from a mark 22 carats fine, thus duplicating the weight and fineness of the "best Italian coronas." The tale was fixed at 350 maravedís. Either these escudos or others circulated at 350 maravedís in Seville before 1537.[2]

The substitution of the escudo for the ducat[3] met with resistance. In 1537 the Cortes, protesting against the debasement of gold, which they had advocated for almost twenty years, contended that in many parts of the kingdom the escudo was accepted reluctantly.[4] A letter from the Crown to the officials of the House of Trade on November 26, 1538, ordered them to send for the purchase of munitions and supplies in Málaga 20,000 ducats in "reals and ducats," not in escudos, because escudos were less acceptable there than other coins.[5] But objections to the escudo were short-lived, and it circulated more than a hundred years without a change in gold content.

In 1518[6] and 1528[7] the Cortes informed his Majesty that there was a dearth of vellon and petitioned him to authorize the coinage of additional supplies, and in 1542 the Procuradores from Granada requested a permit to coin 2,000,000 maravedís in the Granada mint to lessen the handicap to trade and relieve the suffering of alms-receivers due to a lack of fractional coins.[8] In-

---

[1] *Recopilación*, lib. v, tit. xxi, ley (Declaraciones) x.

[2] A. de I., *Contratación*, 39-3-3/1.

[3] The ducat as a unit of account equivalent to 375 maravedís continued in use for at least two centuries. After 1537 it was divorced from all actual coins.

[4] *Quaderno de Cortes de 1537* (1545), Petición 104; *Cortes*, iv, 671-672.

[5] A. de I., *Contratación*, 39-3-3/1.

[6] *Cortes*, iv, 273.

[7] *Ibid.*, iv, 273; *Quaderno de Cortes de 1528*, Petición 161.

[8] *Cortes*, v, 196-197.

formed by the Cortes of 1548 that petty trade was languishing from a scarcity of vellon, Charles V sanctioned an issue and ordered the Council to fix the quantity and apportion it among the mints.[1] But a rise in the price of copper since 1497 had rendered it unprofitable to coin vellon containing 7 grains of silver, and the pragmatic was not in itself effective. In answer to a royal letter of January 22, 1550, instructing him to determine whether the Cuenca mint had coined the 500,000 maravedís allocated to it,[2] the *Corregidor* replied that the vellon had not been coined because of the great loss which the high price of copper would have entailed. On January 27, 1551, the Emperor ordered the Municipality of Cuenca to subsidize the coinage and to effect it without delay. In a letter of February 25, 1551, Charles V directed the Corregidor not to permit other money to be minted before the new vellon entered circulation; to submit a report on the cost of coinage, including the subsidy; and to advise whether the new issue proved adequate.[3] The episode of the Cuenca mint was probably typical, for the Cortes which met in 1551 informed his Majesty that because of the high price of copper no vellon was being coined and that the dearth of fractional money rendered it difficult to find change for a real. The Crown was petitioned to decrease the fineness of vellon, "because the value of the copper will compensate a reduction of silver content," and to authorize an additional issue.[4] The obstruction of coinage by the dearness of copper had undoubtedly produced an acute scarcity of fractional money. Informed by mint officials, municipal authorities, and monetary experts whom he had consulted that vellon 7 grains fine could not be coined without considerable loss and that high intrinsic value was causing it to be exported, on May 23, 1552, Charles V reduced the fineness to 5½ grains.[5] A petition from the Cortes of 1555 [6] to increase the vellon circulation was rejected on the ground that the supply was already adequate.

---

[1] *Quaderno de Cortes de 1548* (1549), Petición 149; *Cortes*, v, 437–438.
[2] AA, Cuenca, caj. 8, leg. 1.
[3] *Ibid.*, Cuenca, caj. 7, leg. 2.   [4] *Cortes*, v, 549–550.
[5] BN, *Raros*, 15,431. The Emperor refused to follow the recommendation of the experts to reduce the fineness to 5 grains.
[6] *Ibid.*, *Raros*, 14,090.

The scarcity of fractional coins facilitated the importation and circulation of foreign vellon — particularly the *tarja*, a vellon coin of Navarre.[1] Far from filling the hiatus in Castilian money to the satisfaction of the public, exotic vellon occasioned no less complaint than had the dearth of fractional coins itself. The Cortes of 1525,[2] 1528,[3] and 1532[4] petitioned the Crown with cumulative importunity to prohibit the importation and circulation of foreign vellon. The petition of 1532 contended that tarjas were circulating at almost one-third more than their commodity value, that they had driven ducats completely out of circulation, and that the unacceptability of foreign vellon was destroying trade. A pragmatic of March 4, 1533, provided for the confiscation of vellon imported or accepted from smugglers. Because of their prevalence, tarjas were permitted to circulate, with their tariff reduced from 10 to 6 maravedís, during a period of ten months, upon the expiration of which they were to be debarred from circulation.[5] This pragmatic was evidently not effective, for the Cortes of 1534[6] and 1537[7] requested his Majesty to prohibit the importation of tarjas, which "had become a regular business," and their circulation at 10 maravedís. In the Cortes of 1537 Charles V prohibited the circulation of tarjas after the end of the year; but the provisional currency of six months — allowed with the naïve expectation that within this period the national stock could and would be "spent" (presumably exported or smelted) — proved utterly ineffective.[8] Once realized, the demonetization of

---

[1] A great deal of ambiguity characterized the use of "tarja" in official documents. It was usually applied to large denominations of the vellon money of Navarre. But occasionally it was used as a generic term to include *placas, ardites,* and the other foreign vellon that entered Castile on the northern and eastern frontiers.

From July, 1505, to August, 1512, the coinage of tarjas greatly exceeded the needs of Navarre (Archivo de la Cámara de Comptos [Pamplona], caj. 167, no. 51).

[2] *Quaderno de Cortes de 1525* (1526), Petición 12; *Cortes,* IV, 410.

[3] *Ibid.,* IV, 458; *Quaderno de Cortes de 1528,* Petición 16.

[4] *Cortes,* IV, 546.

[5] AA, Burgos, *Sección Histórica,* 3732. The Hospital de Antezana in Alcalá de Henares wrote off a loss of only 196 maravedís on the tarjas it held (*Libro de Gastos de 1533*).

[6] *Quaderno de Cortes de 1534,* Petición 94; *Cortes,* IV, 609.

[7] *Ibid.,* IV, 673–674; *Quaderno de Cortes de 1537,* Petición 110.

[8] AA, Madrid, *Moneda,* 3-413-45; *Quaderno de Cortes de 1537,* Petición 110; *Cortes,* IV, 673–674.

the tarja, which the Cortes had repeatedly requested, provoked more clamorous protest than had its circulation. Upon the representation of several municipalities that the holders of tarjas were suffering financial loss and that trade was languishing because of general refusal to accept foreign vellon, on November 6, 1537, the Emperor revoked the demonetization of the tarja; but, to placate the opposition to foreign vellon on the ground that its extrinsic exceeded its intrinsic value, the tariff of the tarja was reduced from 10 to 9 maravedís and that of the half-tarja from 5 maravedís to 4.[1] The ordinance was preconized in cities and villages, and officers of the law were admonished to enforce it.[2] The pragmatic of 1537 apparently satisfied the public and the Cortes, for no serious complaints arose in the next two decades.

The monetary alterations of Charles V were limited to the institution of the gold escudo in 1537, the increase in vellon circulation authorized in 1548, and the reduction of the silver content of vellon in 1552.[3] Near the end of his reign the Emperor probably contemplated a thorough monetary reform, and there is slight evidence that he intended to depart from the tenets of sound money. In 1551 Charles V requested various business men and monetary experts to submit plans for monetary reform and instructed the Viceroy and Captain General of Navarre to investigate with all possible haste and dissimulation the state of the French coinage.[4] The Viceroy was directed to ascertain the causes of the abundance of money in France and of the surreptitious export thither of Castilian coins; to collect and forward to his Majesty samples of all French coins, together with an accurate statement of the tariff of each; to ascertain and report the quantity of each class of money exchanged for Castilian reals and es-

---

[1] It seems that the tarjas were stamped in Castilian mints to indicate legality and reduction in tariff. On June 6, 1538, Charles V recalled the dies supplied the mints ninety days earlier for the "stamping of tarjas of 9 and 4 maravedís" (AA, Madrid, *Moneda*, 3–413–46).

[2] *Ibid.*, Córdoba, *Moneda*, 4 and 5; *ibid.*, Burgos, *Sección Histórica*, 3734; *ibid.*, Madrid, *Moneda*, 3–413–45.

[3] It appears that an issue of vellon in denominations of 2 and 4 maravedís was authorized in the early 1530's, but that the coinage was discontinued by royal order before an appreciable quantity had entered circulation (*Cortes*, IV, 546).

[4] On January 23, 1550, France had inflated her money, but only slightly (Paul Raveau, *op. cit.*, p. ix; *Bulletin de Statistique et Législation Comparée*, XXIII, 9).

cudos in France; and to report upon recent monetary inflation and deflation in France, giving particular attention to the *distribution of gains and losses therefrom*.[1] No immediate monetary alteration resulted from the inquiry instituted in 1551, but it probably influenced legislation in the following reign.

IV

As regards vellon money the reign of Philip II (1556–1598) presents two distinct periods offering curious contrasts. In roughly the first half of his reign the Cortes continuously pressed for more and baser vellon, while in the second half few matters occupied their time more than efforts to limit its quantity and improve the quality.

In 1558 the Cortes petitioned Philip II to authorize a vellon issue of 20,000 ducats, or 7,500,000 maravedís — one-half in blancas and the remainder in *cuartos* (4 maravedís) and half-cuartos—, and to fix the fineness at a figure which would preclude loss on the coinage. The issue of vellon was authorized, but its fineness was not reduced.[2] As had occurred ten years earlier, the high price of copper deterred coinage; and the permissive legislation availed little or nothing. The Cortes of 1559 complained that no vellon was being minted because of the certain loss which the high silver content and dearness of copper would entail and contended that trade was declining and the poor were suffering from a dearth of fractional money. To induce abundant coinage and prevent the export of vellon, the Cortes prayed for a reduction of its fineness from 5½ grains of silver to 3½ (1.22 per cent).[3] Pending the report of a monetary commission, action was deferred until December 14, 1566, when the fineness of blancas was reduced to 4 grains of silver (1.39 per cent) and their weight to 1⁄220 of a mark. By the same pragmatic a new and more transportable type of vellon, known as *vellón rico* and *vellón de la nueva estampa*, was instituted. From a mark containing 62 grains of silver (21.53 per cent) 680 maravedís — one-third in *cuartillos* (8½ maravedís),

---

[1] AS, *Diversos de Castilla*, 48–18.
[2] *Cortes*, v, 752. [3] *Ibid.*, v, 857.

one-third in cuartos (4 maravedís), and the remainder in *ochavos* (2 maravedís) — were struck. The fee for coinage was fixed at 60 maravedís and seigniorage at 34 maravedís. As in the case of the old type of vellon, coinage was not free, but controlled by royal permits.[1] Counterfeiting and hoarding of rich vellon forced Philip II to suspend its coinage before the contemplated quantity had been minted.[2] The absence or infrequent occurrence of *rich vellon* in contemporary financial records suggests that a significant quantity never circulated.

On June 25, 1567 — before the pragmatic of 1566 had borne fruit —, Burgos petitioned the Crown to increase the supply of Castilian vellon.[3] From the lack of further requests for about fifteen years, it may be inferred that the expansion of the ordinary vellon circulation resulting from the ordinance of 1566 met the needs of trade.

The increased mint price of gold in 1537, which in certain districts occasioned momentary reluctance to accept the escudo at par, was soon rendered too low by the preponderance of silver production in the Indies. On April 25, 1548, the Cortes complained that all the gold money of Castile had been exported;[4] the same Cortes protested against the increase in the tariff of the escudo in Aragon and Valencia to 10 maravedís above its tale in Castile and petitioned the Crown to force these kingdoms to conform to the Castilian rating of gold.[5] Most of the plans for monetary reform presented by the experts consulted in 1551 placed great emphasis upon the discrepancy between bimetallic ratios in Castile and other countries, particularly France.[6] In 1560 Rodrigo de Yllescas wrote Philip II that gold commanded a premium of 15 per cent over silver in Peru and that the Crown suffered an annual loss of over 25,000 ducats by permitting the

---

[1] *Recopilación*, lib. v, tit. xxi, ley xiv.

[2] Sebastián González de Castro, *Declaración del Valor de la Plata, Ley y Peso de las Monedas Antiguas de Plata Ligada de Castilla y Aragón* (Madrid, 1658), p. 18; José García Caballero, *Breve Cotejo y Valance de las Pesas y Medidas* (Madrid, 1731), pp. 150-151.

[3] AA, Burgos, *Sección Histórica*, 3740.

[4] *Cortes*, v, 356.

[5] *Ibid.*, v, 438. This petition was repeated in 1551 (*ibid.*, v, 571).

[6] AS, *Diversos de Castilla*, 48-18.

salaries of Peruvian officials to be paid in gold.[1] The Cortes of 1563 complained that the low mint ratio of gold as compared with neighboring states was driving gold coins out of Castile and prayed for immediate remedial legislation.[2] The mint officials and monetary experts consulted by Philip II agreed that the mint ratio in Castile was lower than in neighboring states and provinces and argued that this undervaluation was largely responsible for the export and resultant scarcity of gold. Hence on November 23, 1566, Philip II increased the tariff of the escudo — weight and fineness remaining constant — from 350 to 400 maravedís,[3] a figure at which it was destined to remain more than forty years.

Prejudice against tarjas, which subsided after the reduction in their tariff in 1537, reappeared early in the reign of Philip II. The Cortes of 1563 petitioned his Majesty to debar them from circulation,[4] and in response to a letter from the Corregidor of Burgos stating that tarjas of 9 and 20 maravedís were accepted either reluctantly or not at all a royal order of September 12, 1566, directed local peace officers to force their acceptance.[5] But the attempted compulsion proved utterly futile. On June 25, 1567, Philip inquired of the authorities of Burgos whether many tarjas of 9 and 20 maravedís were held there, whether tarjas were short in weight, and whether compulsory circulation would conduce to the public welfare. Burgos replied that tarjas were abundant, abraded, and generally unacceptable and requested his Majesty to debar them from circulation.[6] A royal order of March 11, 1569, ended efforts to coerce the inhabitants of Burgos into using foreign vellon. Since the supply of Castilian fractional money became adequate about this time, neither public desire nor official effort to restore the legal-tender status of tarjas again arose.

It appears that by the early 1580's the Price Revolution had again rendered the supply of fractional money insufficient for

---

[1] AS, *Estado*, 139. Cf. *Recopilación de Leyes de Indias* (Madrid, 1681), lib. VIII, tit. VI, ley XIV; lib. VIII, tit. X, ley XX.
[2] *Actas*, I, 261, 278–279.
[3] BN, *Varios*, 1–49–32; *Raros*, 14,090; *Recopilación*, lib. V, tit. XXI, ley XIII.
[4] *Actas*, I, 278.
[5] AA, Burgos, *Sección Histórica*, 3738.
[6] *Ibid.*, *Sección Histórica*, 3740.

change and petty transactions. The Cortes of 1583-1585 petitioned Philip II to authorize the issue of additional vellon and to require the coinage of small denominations of silver.[1] Either on his own initiative or in response to this request permits were issued for the coinage of sufficient vellon to provoke immediate protest from the Cortes. Upon a motion by the Procuradores from Burgos on May 23, 1587, the Cortes voted to memorialize the Crown against the great harm and inconvenience resulting from redundant vellon. That commerce was languishing because untransportable vellon represented "almost the only money in circulation in the cities, towns, and villages of Castile" was adduced by the Cortes on September 30, 1587, in support of a petition to his Majesty to restrain the issue of permits to coin vellon, to state in all permits the gross amounts that might be minted, and to be vigilant in limiting coinage to the stipulated figures.[2] In a typical mercantilist protest against licenses for the export of money granted by Philip II as a means of financing foreign military operations, on May 23, 1590, the Cortes complained that in spite of the enormous receipts of gold and silver from the Indies every year, by the middle of the year no money except vellon was to be found.[3] Because of the "inconvenience and injury to trade and the difficulty of collecting royal revenues" resulting from the plethora of "vellon coined and circulating in the kingdom," on May 22, 1591, Philip II ordered the mints to suspend the coinage of vellon and not to resume it without his express license.[4]

The precise date of the resumption of coinage is not clear, but by May 21, 1597, the Cortes were waxing warm over the sale of a royal privilege to coin vellon in the new mint (real ingenio) at Segovia to one Juan Castellón.[5] Immediate efforts by the Cortes to obstruct the issue of vellon proved futile.[6] In fact, only with difficulty could the Procuradores require Philip II to produce a copy of the permit. According to a memorial to the Crown on July 24, 1597 — drawn up by Procuradores who had seen the

---

[1] *Actas*, VII, 795-796.   [2] BN, *Varios*, 1-49-6; *Actas*, IX, 387-390.
[3] *Ibid.*, XI, 366. The Procuradores inconsistently added "and even of this there is little."
[4] AA, Cuenca, leg. 260, fols. 297-298.
[5] *Actas*, XV, 491.   [6] *Ibid.*, XV, 492, 513, 523, 526, 641-642.

license granted Juan Castellón —, 100,000 ducats a year were to be coined. The silver content was reduced to 1 grain (.35 per cent), and the number of maravedís struck from a mark was increased to 144.[1] Although upon several occasions in the reigns of Charles V and Philip II abrasion and the prohibitive cost of extraction had been adduced by the Cortes to demonstrate that the silver content of vellon represented a social loss,[2] the near elimination of silver evoked vehement protests and predictions of dire consequences.[3]

But Philip II, never easily coerced by the Cortes, was overwhelmed by service on the public debt and the enormous expenses of administering a world-wide empire; the need for ready cash which impelled him to violate the policy of limiting vellon circulation to the quantity required for change and petty transactions — expressed in the pragmatic of December 14, 1566 [4] — forced him to reject all proposals to stem the flood of vellon from the new Segovian mint.

Of particular interest to the economist and student of financial history is the effect of the excessive issue upon the parity of vellon. Undoubtedly there was a preference for gold and silver in León as early as June 2, 1576,[5] and about the same time unmistakable prejudice against vellon existed in Galicia.[6] But I have been able to find no evidence that the objection to vellon in any part of the kingdoms of Castile and León became great or general enough to force it below par. The contentions of the anti-vellon memorial adopted by the Cortes on October 19, 1594,[7] that the

---

[1] Actas, XV, 524–525.
[2] Vide, for instance, Cortes, IV, 504–506; Actas, I, 260.
[3] Ibid., XV, 641–642.   [4] Recopilación, lib. V, tit. XXI, ley XIV.
[5] AA, León, Sección Primera, 535.
[6] Ibid., Sección Primera, 539, 541.
[7] Actas, XIII, 351–359. This memorial is noteworthy because it foreshadowed most of the objections advanced during the first half of the seventeenth century, when depreciation was acute and chronic. The leading indictments may be briefly summarized as follows: vellon (1) drove gold and silver out of circulation; (2) stimulated the importation of foreign vellon; (3) forced up prices; (4) occasioned disputes and litigation over the media in which obligations were due; (5) depressed the sums which tax farmers, anticipating collection in vellon, bid for royal revenues; (6) placed an inequitable burden on the poor, who held a relatively large share of vellon; and (7) deprived carriers of merchandise of the opportunity to load return cargoes.

effective premium on silver in terms of vellon — in the form of loss of interest on advances in vellon to be repaid in silver without an agio — was 8 per cent and that the discount in the purchase of goods amounted to 25 per cent, not to mention the higher estimate of 50 per cent inconsistently advanced, are manifestly absurd. There was certainly more ground for depreciation after the permits for excessive coinage had been issued in the late 1590's than at any time during the reign of Philip II. Yet careful examination of the financial records — including daily expense accounts — of charity hospitals in Valladolid, Palencia, Alcalá de Henares, Toledo, and Seville and of the Colegio Mayor de San Ildefonso of the University of Alcalá de Henares has failed to disclose a single instance of an agio on an exchange of vellon for silver or a discount on vellon paid for commodities or services. Furthermore, we know that as late as August 12, 1598, Cosme Ruiz, Lope de Cámara and Company accepted 7000 reals in vellon at par from solvent debtors.[1] The slow emergence and the moderation of the premium on silver in the face of unrestrained coinage and the doubling of the tariff on vellon at the beginning of the reign of Philip III — when, with a weaker administration, the hazard of violating the law against a premium diminished — furnish additional ground for presuming that the preference of the public for gold and silver was not great enough before the death of Philip II to give rise to a discernible discount on vellon in money or commodity markets.

No change occurred in silver money during the reign of Philip II. In 1566, when an unfavorable turn of the war in Flanders coincided with Moorish uprisings in Spain, he rejected the recommendations of experts to debase silver;[2] and near the close of his reign, when necessity might conceivably have driven him to such a course, public opinion was unalterably opposed to tampering with silver.[3]

---

[1] *Vide infra*, p. 91.

[2] AS, *Diversos de Castilla*, 1–31.

[3] For instance, a motion introduced in the Cortes on June 9, 1595, to increase the tale of the real to 40 maravedís was rejected by an overwhelming majority (*Actas*, XIV, 111–115).

V

A pragmatic of November 23, 1609, increased the tariff of the escudo — weight and fineness remaining constant — from 400 to 440 maravedís.[1] That the purpose of this pragmatic was to adjust the mint price of gold to the market price is attested by the fact that severe penalties were fixed for the payment or acceptance of more than 440 maravedís for an escudo, while no sanction was provided against a market tale of less than the legal rating.[2] No other changes in the escudo or real occurred until well into the reign of Philip IV (1621–1665), when ephemeral silver inflation took place. On December 23, 1642, the number of reals struck from a mark of standard fineness was increased from 67 to 83¾,[3] and the tariff of the silver in circulation was raised proportionately. The piece of eight (real de a ocho), for instance, became 10 reals. To maintain the existing bimetallic ratio the tariff of the escudo was increased from 440 to 550 maravedís. Philip IV attempted to rationalize this inflation on the ground that the radical deflation of vellon by the pragmatic published on September 15, 1642, and a heavy export of specie had created a dearth of money.[4]

The pragmatic of December 23, 1642, offers two additional points of interest. First, old Castilian coins, which, continuing in circulation with their tariffs altered proportionately to each change in the escudo, had occasioned considerable confusion and friction in the last hundred years,[5] were debarred from circulation. Second, owners of silver plate were accorded the privilege

---

[1] A. de I., *Contratación*, 42–6–6/10, fol. 190.

[2] *Quaderno de Leyes Añadidas a la Nueva Recopilación* (1610), fol. 67.

[3] The only contemporary copy of the ordinance which I have been able to locate lists the number of reals as 83¼, but this seems to have been a mistake. The purpose was to decrease the weight by one-fourth (Academia de Historia [hereafter AH], *Leyes y Cédulas de Castilla*, 8²–23–5).
4499

[4] *Ibid.*, *Leyes y Cédulas de Castilla*, 8²–23–5.
4499

[5] The auditor of the accounts of the Convento de Nuestra Señora de Sandoval (León) for 1518 wrote by the entry of a *castellano* at 485 maravedís "I do not know what coin a castellano is" (Archivo Histórico Nacional [hereafter AHN], *Clero*, León, 247). As early as 1544 the Cortes complained that even judges were not well informed as to the rating of old gold coins (*Cortes*, v, 315–316).

of coining it into "rich vellon" of the weight and tale authorized by Philip II in 1566 but with the fineness lowered from 62 to 46½ grains of silver in harmony with the reduced weight of the real. The sale of silver except to silversmiths was interdicted, and mints were instructed to facilitate deliveries of plate. The Crown renounced seigniorage and, on March 12, 1643, ordered the mint officers and operatives to forego coinage fees.[1] The reluctance of the holders of plate to part with it in a time of financial instability and monetary disorder defeated this attempt to rehabilitate the vellon coinage.[2]

A 25 per cent debasement of gold and silver was the essence of the nostrum for monetary reform which Tomás de Cardona proposed at the beginning of the reign of Philip III and ably defended for more than a quarter of a century. According to Cardona, the debasement advocated would end or greatly diminish the smuggling of specie on the American treasure fleets; prevent the drain of gold and silver from Spain and the colonies to foreign countries; eliminate frauds in the royal quint, or severance tax on gold and silver mining; aid in restoring the parity of vellon; and revive the languishing mining of the precious metals in the Hispanic colonies of the New World. Coming from a royal servant thoroughly familiar with every phase of mining and transporting the precious metals, these extravagant claims engaged public fancy and ministerial attention. Several monetary commissions were formed to consider the scheme, and on more than one occasion it had a fair prospect of adoption. In 1629 the sound exposition and able defense of Cardona's scheme by Alonso de Carranza,[3] one of the most celebrated jurists of his time, revived and heightened the public interest, and the following writers either praised the project of Cardona or advanced similar plans: Gerónimo de Cevallos (1623),[4] Pedro de Castro

---

[1] AH, *Leyes y Cédulas de Castilla*, 8²-23-5.
4499

[2] After 1640, when the receipts of gold and silver from America dropped to insignificant sums, repeated efforts were made to induce Castilian subjects to disgorge their holdings of plate; but all of them proved ineffectual.

[3] *El Ajustamiento i Proporción de las Monedas de Oro, Plata i Cobre* (Madrid, 1629).

[4] Juan Sempere y Guarinos, *Biblioteca Española Económico-Política*, III (Madrid, 1804), liii–liv.

(1627),[1] and Guillén Barbón y Castañeda (1628).[2] By a law of January 20, 1643, the Crown attempted to retain bullion at its former price in the Indies, as Cardona had recommended.[3] As the Licentiate Francisco Pérez Manrique affirmed in 1650,[4] the nostrum of Cardona undoubtedly influenced and may have determined the inflationary legislation of 1642.

But many economists regarded silver debasement with disfavor, and public opinion solidly opposed such a course. Several of the treatises on money and schemes for monetary reform evoked by inflation during the first half of the seventeenth century held that debasement of gold or vellon was relatively innocuous, but that ruin would follow if silver, "the nerve of commerce," were tampered with. Many writers and reformers who did not share this opinion recognized that public opposition to alteration of the real was a great obstacle to the acceptance of their theories or nostrums. Recognizing the unpopularity of the coinage of light silver, on March 12, 1643, Philip IV restored the real to its former weight and reduced the tariff of the silver coined under the act of December 23, 1642, accordingly.[5] The pragmatic of March 12, 1643, nominally reverted to the old weight of the real until the arrival of the next treasure fleets and then until his Majesty should decree otherwise, but the weight remained ⅟₆₇ of a mark until October 14, 1686.

As early as 1616 the escudo circulated in Madrid at 442 maravedís;[6] by 1630 its market value in Toledo rose to 500 maravedís and by 1631 to 510.[7] As early as 1632 the treasurers of the mints paid the Crown 476 maravedís in lieu of escudos collected as seigniorage.[8] In 1634 and 1635 isolated exchanges at 476 mara-

---

[1] BN, *Raros*, 17,270.
[2] Juan Sempere y Guarinos, *op. cit.*, III, lix–lx.
[3] *Recopilación de Leyes de Indias*, lib. IV, tit. XXIV, ley VI.
[4] AH, Ms. 11–1–6.
[5] *Ibid.*, *Leyes y Cédulas de Castilla*, 8²–23–5.

4499

[6] AHN, *Clero*, Madrid, 1040.
[7] On January 4, February 4, March 11, April 15, and May 24 exchanges were effected at 510 maravedís (*Pensiones que se Pagan al Cardenal Sandoval* [Archbishop of Toledo], an uncatalogued manuscript found in the basement of the Diputación Provincial in Toledo).
[8] AS, *Tribunal Mayor de Cuentas*, 915–916.

vedís were effected in Madrid,[1] but the escudo doubtless reacted from this low figure.[2] Since the increase in the rating of the escudo in 1642 merely offset the concurrent change in silver, gold remained undervalued at the mint; and on January 12, 1643, the legal tariff of the escudo rose to 612 maravedís.[3] When the weight of the real was restored on March 12, 1643, the tale of the escudo was fixed at 510 maravedís.[3] Since the escudo seems to have circulated at exactly 510 maravedís from the second quarter of 1643 through the end year of 1650,[4] the bimetallic ratio of 15.45 to 1 established on March 12, 1643, doubtless coincided with the market ratio.

VI

In 1650 it was discovered that reals of defective fineness, coined in Peru "in the last few years," had entered circulation in Castile.[5] A pragmatic of October 1, 1650, stated that Peruvian reals had

[1] AHN, *Clero*, Madrid, 715, 1037.

[2] It is not safe to lean too heavily upon the assertions of contemporary economists, particularly when the supposed machinations of foreigners are involved; but it is worthy of note that, in 1640, José Pellicer de Ossau believed that the drain of specie to France was taking the form of gold. He argued that Frenchmen gave 25 reals per escudo intended for export (Juan Sempere y Guarinos, *op. cit.*, III, cxlvi-cxlvii). The high valuation of gold at the French mint from 1636 to 1640 naturally served as a magnet for the escudo.

[3] AH, *Leyes y Cédulas de Castilla*, 8²-23-5.
4499

[4] On account of the paucity of gold in circulation, few data concerning the escudo have survived in commercial documents; and the existing figures are rendered obscure by the current practice of allowances for abrasion of the escudo and slightly inexact by the fact that records of no direct exchanges between gold and silver are available. Making an appropriate reduction for the discount on vellon, we find that from April, 1643, to December, 1650, most of the market tariffs of the escudo ranged from 504 to 517 silver maravedís. The mode and the mean are about 510; and that this figure represents the true commercial rating of the escudo, from which there is dispersion because of a lack of absolutely precise information concerning the discount on vellon for the requisite days and localities, admits of little doubt.

[5] The evil may have been of long standing. For on October 9, 1602, his Majesty instructed the treasurers of the mints to have refined all the base Peruvian 4- and 8-real pieces which might be delivered for recoinage in pursuance of the pragmatic of October 1 and to coin the bullion without seigniorage (AS, *Secretaría de Hacienda*, 273).

In 1613 there must have been a significant quantity of counterfeit reals in Madrid. On February 28 the Cartujos de Nuestra Señora del Paular found that 240 of 1080 reals they attempted to spend were false (AHN, *Clero*, Madrid, 1040).

been debarred from circulation in Navarre, Aragon, and Valencia and that, like bullion, they were acceptable in Italy and Flanders only by weight and assay. Government assays had shown variable fineness, "some coins being short almost half their silver." The owners of Peruvian reals were allowed two months in which to carry them to a mint to be refined and recoined or to be cut in half, after which they might either be hoarded or refined and converted into plate. Peruvian reals might also be exchanged for vellon at par or for Castilian or Mexican reals in the ratio of 8 to 5 at royal agencies established for the purpose. The government refined and recoined the reals collected. His Majesty renounced all seigniorage and ordered the treasurers of mints to reduce the fees for coinage as much as possible.[1] The possession of defective Peruvian reals after December 1, 1650, was punishable by confiscation of the money and two years' exile,[2] but an ordinance issued on October 6, 1650, allowed holders of the reals the option of passing them at 75 per cent of their nominal value or carrying them to a mint for recoinage.[3] On March 24, 1651, the period in which Peruvian reals might circulate at the 25 per cent discount was limited to May 15, 1651, after which time they were to have the status of counterfeit money.[4]

Between January 23 and December 5, 1651, 42,810 marks of Peruvian reals refined in the mint at Burgos produced 37,367 marks of the fineness requisite for coining reals.[5] On April 28, 1651, the steward (mayordomo) of the Hospital de la Sangre of Seville charged the Hospital with a loss of 576 reals on 3204 Peruvian reals that had been smelted because "they could not be passed."[6] Debasement, 17.98 per cent, was much greater than in

---

[1] AS, *Tribunal Mayor de Cuentas*, 916. On November 21, 1650, his Majesty contracted with Juan Ortiz and Gerónimo de Fonseca, silversmiths, to smelt the reals in the mint at Granada and convert them into bullion 11 dineros 4 grains fine (the fineness requisite for coining reals). The fees were fixed at 131 maravedís per mark, as had been agreed upon for the mints at Segovia, Madrid, and Burgos (AS, *Contadurías Generales: Razón*, 273).

[2] BN, *Varios*, 1-60-98.

[3] AH, Ms. 11-1-6; BN, *Varios*, 1-60-97. Hospital del Amor de Dios, *Libros de Gastos Extraordinarios*, 70.

[4] AS, *Contadurías Generales: Razón*, 273; BN, *Varios*, 1-60-98; AH, Ms. 11-1-6.

[5] AS, *Tribunal Mayor de Cuentas*, 909.

[6] Hospital de la Sangre, *Libros de Recibos y Gastos*, 464.

the Burgos sample. Discrepancy between the above percentages indicates that the degree of debasement was not uniform, but even the higher figure suggests that the discounts at which Peruvian reals were received by the government and at which they were permitted to circulate were excessive.[1]

Immediate steps were taken to insure the integrity of Peruvian reals; but, owing to the time required for communication, the importation of base coins continued for almost two years. On July 9, 1652, his Majesty instructed the President and officials of the House of Trade to have the Peruvian reals on the galleons that had recently arrived refined in the Seville mint before delivery to their owners.[2] By 1653 reform of the mint at Potosí had restored the quality of the reals reaching Castile, but prejudice against them had not waned. On September 23, 1653, a royal order assured the kingdom that the Peruvian reals imported in that year were not inferior to those coined in Castile, the only difference being in the pattern, and interdicted discrimination against them.[3]

VII

One of the most important consequences of the enormous output of the precious metals in the Hispanic colonies of the New World was the complete upsetting of the fairly stable bimetallic ratio which had obtained in the Occident for several centuries.[4] Since the imports of treasure that legally entered Europe passed through Castile, it was presumably in this kingdom that the first and greatest effect of the influx of specie upon the market ratios between gold and silver was felt.

Soetbeer's erroneous opinion that the percentage of gold production remained stable after 1580 [5] led him into an awkward at-

---

[1] The extent of debasement shown by the assays at Burgos and Seville discredits the extreme statements in a memorial which the Licentiate Francisco Pérez Manrique presented to Philip IV on December 8, 1650. Pérez Manrique averred that, through the issue of base reals, the "thieves, traitors, and enemies of mankind in Peru" had perturbed the commerce of all Europe (AH, Ms. 11-1-6).

[2] AS, *Contadurías Generales: Razón*, 273.

[3] AA, Burgos, *Sección Histórica*, 1125.

[4] Adolf Soetbeer, *Edelmetall-Produktion und Werthverhältniss zwischen Gold und Silber* (1879), pp. 114-120.

[5] *Ibid.*, pp. 55, 60, 63-64, 69-70; Tafeln i and ii.

tempt to explain the phenomenal increase in the mint ratio of gold
to silver in Western Europe in the period 1621–1660 on the side
of demand.[1] Tables 2 and 3 demonstrate conclusively that the
change in the relative supplies of gold and silver influenced greatly
and may have determined the course of European bimetallic
ratios.   silver to gold ?

The rising market ratio of gold to silver, which inevitably resulted from the great preponderance of silver imports, forced frequent alterations in the Castilian mint ratio.[2] Legal bimetallic
ratios from 1497 to 1650[3] are listed in Table 4.

TABLE 4
BIMETALLIC RATIOS

Years	Ratio
1497–1536	10.11 to 1
1537–1565	10.61 to 1
1566–1608	12.12 to 1
1609–1642	13.33 to 1
1643–1650 [4]	15.45 to 1

As Table 4 demonstrates, from 10.11 to 1 in 1497 the legal
bimetallic ratio rose to 15.45 to 1, or by over 50 per cent, in 1643.
The mint ratio remained close to this figure for more than two
centuries.

Availing ourselves of the data in Table 4, we may arrive at a
rough approximation of the values in terms of present money of

[1] *Op. cit.*, pp. 126–127. Cf. Karl Helfferich, *Geld und Banken* (Leipzig, 1910), I, 117–118.

[2] This phenomenon was not confined to Castile. Similar changes occurred in other countries (W. A. Shaw, *The History of Currency* [London, 1896], pp. 69–70; Adolf Soetbeer, *op. cit.*, pp. 120–127).

[3] Owing to imperfect technique, the actual fineness of coins probably did not conform perfectly to legal requirements. *A priori* one might expect to find lax assays in the reign of Philip IV. The Valencian mint uniformly rated the Castilian reals smelted and recoined there during the reign of Philip IV at 11 dineros 2 grains — 2 grains below their legal fineness (Archivo Regional, *Maestre Racional, Tesorería*, leg. 358, cas. 8583, 8586–8589); but the invariability of this rating elicits the suspicion that it rested upon an arbitrary official valuation, not upon the results of actual assays. It is significant that the analyses of the Castilian gold coins of Philip IV by Pierre-Frédéric Bonneville (*Traité des Monnaies d'Or et d'Argent* [Paris, 1806], p. 36) show as little discrepancy between the legal and actual gold contents as do his figures for the contemporary gold money of other countries.

[4] The mint ratio of 14.84 to 1, established on January 12, 1643, and revoked exactly two months later, has been omitted from Table 4 because of its transitory character and doubtful influence upon practice.

Castilian gold and silver coins. The modern equivalents of gold money are easily established by a comparison of fine gold contents; but, owing to frequent shifts in bimetallic ratios, no such simple operation is possible in the case of silver. To overcome this difficulty, the best method seems to be to establish the modern gold equivalent of the real on the basis of the bimetallic ratio obtaining in 1497 and to alter the rating in accordance with each successive change in the mint ratio. Using this method, I have calculated the equivalents listed in Table 5.

TABLE 5

MODERN EQUIVALENTS OF CASTILIAN COINS

Gold

Coin	Years	Value in modern gold pesetas
Excelente de Granada	1497–1536	12.00
Escudo	1537–1650	10.68

Silver

Coin	Years	Value in modern gold pesetas
Real	1497–1536	1.09
Real	1537–1565	1.04
Real	1566–1608	0.91
Real	1609–1642	0.83
Real	1643–1650	0.71

Examination of changes in prices from the sixteenth century to the present, or of money measured in purchasing power, is beyond the scope of the present study. It may be remarked, however, that the imports of American gold and silver into Europe during the sixteenth and the early part of the seventeenth century not only raised prices to approximately the level at which they stood during most of the eighteenth and nineteenth centuries, but raised the mint ratio of gold to silver from approximately 10.00 to 1, a point toward which it had gravitated for several centuries before the discovery of America, to the neighborhood of 15.50 to 1, the approximate center for the oscillations of the next two centuries.

CHAPTER IV

VELLON INFLATION IN CASTILE, 1598–1650

I

IN MONETARY stability (as in literature, art, and empire) Castile passed through her golden age in the sixteenth century, the only century in history that has not witnessed serious departures from parity by one or more forms of Castilian money. But this golden age was followed literally by one of bronze. In the absence of paper money and of modern devices for printing, inflation could not reach the heights attained in several belligerent countries immediately after the Great War; but through copper money and the best known types of mint machinery, installed at Segovia by German engineers, debasement profoundly affected the economic life of Castile. The present chapter purposes to study this phenomenon — with its antecedents, concomitants, and consequences — during the first half-century after its inception.

Aside from the increases in the value of gold and vellon, which called forth the remedial ordinances of 1537, 1552, and 1566, the different forms of Castilian money circulated at par from 1497 to 1598. Both Charles V and Philip II steadfastly refused to debase the coinage, regardless of the chronic bankruptcy of the treasury, when both were waging bitter wars to consolidate and extend world-wide empires and to protect and propagate the Catholic faith. There is evidence that toward the close of his reign Charles V wavered, but he did not yield to the temptation.[1] Philip II opposed unsound money no less tenaciously than he fought the cults of Luther and Mohammed. Exhortation by the Cortes to debase the coinage was of no avail. In 1566, when an unfavorable turn of the war in Flanders coincided with Moorish uprisings in Spain, he rejected the report of a monetary commission recommending debasement that promised an immediate

---

[1] Archivo de Simancas (hereafter AS), *Diversos de Castilla*, 48–18.

yield of about 151,110 ducats and an annual income of some
232,664 ducats.[1] During most of his reign Philip II was particularly resolute with regard to vellon. Believing that it could be
maintained at parity only by limitation of its quantity to that
required for change and petty transactions,[2] he was exceedingly
careful to restrict the supply. But the staggering financial burdens at the close of his reign led Philip II to permit the coinage of
sufficient vellon to threaten its parity.

II

Though Charles V and Philip II maintained sound money,
forces were at work during their reigns that rendered debasement
inevitable as soon as a weak ruler ascended the throne. Goaded
by imperialistic ambition and religious fanaticism, these two
monarchs shed the blood and squandered the wealth of Spain on
battlefields throughout the world. Extravagance of the royal
family and courtiers, intrigues of Philip II, and disturbances in
the Spanish possessions in Italy, Holland, Portugal, Flanders,
Germany, Austria, and Africa helped to multiply the financial
burdens awaiting Philip III (1598–1621). Toward the close of the
reign of Philip II decadence of agriculture, industry, and commerce — attributable in part to the persecution, expulsion, maim-
ing, and killing of thousands of the most productive subjects during the Inquisition, the depletion of man power through military
ventures, the great growth of non-productive religious orders, the
fostering of vagrancy by indiscriminate poor relief, the emigration
of men to America at their most productive age, and the illusion
that American gold and silver would enrich the nation without
work — rendered public revenues, which came largely from the
alcabala and *millones* (sales taxes) and *almojarifazgo* (customs
duties), inadequate for the enormous expenditures.

Upon ascending the throne, Philip III found most of the ordinary and extraordinary revenues for 1599 and 1600 assigned to

---

[1] AS, *Diversos de Castilla*, 1–31.
[2] *Recopilación de Leyes de España* (hereafter *Recopilación*), lib. v, tit. xxi, ley
(Declaraciones) xiv.

money lenders.[1] The outlays occasioned by war, the extravagance of a pleasure-loving court, and the necessity of living with
the pomp and splendor commensurate with Spain's theoretical
position as a world power brought Philip III face to face with a
precariously unbalanced budget; and he sought solvency through
issues of base money.

In 1599 Philip III, maintaining that the silver ingredient of
vellon was useless, authorized the coinage of vellon of pure copper. In *cuartos* and *ochavos* 140 maravedís were struck from a
mark.[2] Since a mark of copper was worth about 34 maravedís,[3]
the fees for coinage were 34 maravedís, and a coined mark was
passed on to the public at 140 maravedís, the Crown realized more
than 100 per cent profit. In 1599 [4] and 1600 [5] the Cortes protested
against the issue of copper vellon, and in 1602 they made futile
efforts to oblige the Crown to desist from its coinage.[6] But a
worse issue was soon to follow. An ordinance of June 13, 1602,
provided for a 50 per cent reduction in the weight of copper vellon,
280 maravedís — in denominations of 1, 2, 4, and 8 — being
coined from a mark.[7] The Crown alleged that this step was taken
to reduce the cost of handling and transporting vellon, but the
use of some of the proceeds to pay officers and soldiers of the gar-
risons of Castile salaries five years in arrears suggests that there
was a different motive.[8] To combat the rising price of copper resulting from the large issues of vellon, his Majesty fixed a maximum price of 24 ducats per quintal, or 45 maravedís a mark, for
copper delivered at the mints.[8] The cost of the copper and the

---

[1] *Actas de las Cortes de Castilla* (hereafter *Actas*), XVIII, 510–511.

[2] Biblioteca Nacional (hereafter BN), *Sección de Manuscritos*, Ms. 3207.

[3] José García Caballero (*Breve Cotejo y Valance de las Pesas y Medidas* [Madrid, 1731], pp. 154–155) and Juan Surrá y Rull (*Breve Reseña*, pp. 39–40) agree on this figure. On November 2, 1600, 20 ducats a quintal, or 37½ maravedís a mark, were paid for copper delivered at the mint in Segovia (AS, *Tribunal Mayor de Cuentas*, 912). In view of the probable rise in the price of copper between 1599 and 1600, 34 maravedís per mark seems a plausible price for 1599.

[4] *Actas*, XVIII, 157, 568–573.

[5] *Ibid.*, XVIII, 596–599.

[6] *Ibid.*, XX, 143–153, 169–178, 421–422; *Quaderno de Leyes Añadidas a la Nueva Recopilación* (hereafter *Quaderno de Leyes*) (Madrid, 1619), Cortes de 1602, fol. 4.

[7] AS, *Contadurías Generales: Razón*, 271; BN, *Sección de Manuscritos*, Ms. 3207.

[8] AS, *Contadurías Generales: Razón*, 271.

profit on coinage.

fees for coinage amounted to 79 maravedís per mark; the profits of the Crown were 201 maravedís, or 254.43 per cent.

An opportunity for further gain was seized by the government. On September 18, 1603, the holders of the pure copper vellon authorized in 1599 were ordered to carry it to mints within thirty days for restamping to double its tale. After the period of grace — later extended by twenty-five days "because it has not been possible in all the provinces to carry the money to the mints in the time allowed" — coins not bearing the special stamp were debarred from circulation. The owners received in restamped vellon the number of maravedís they delivered plus remuneration for transportation. The profits, 100 per cent less the cost of transportation and the fee for restamping, accrued to the Crown and were held in special accounts by the treasurers of the mints for disbursement by royal order. In order to expedite restamping, treasurers of the mints were instructed to mark immediately a sufficient quantity of vellon to pay for the early deliveries, to provide enough men to count the money delivered and its equivalent without delay, and to employ the greatest number of stampers (marcadores) feasible.[1]

These inflationary measures drove vellon, which had circulated at or above parity for more than a century, to a discount and evoked bitter criticism from the kingdom.[2] Like most rulers who have seen disorder follow debasement, Philip III sought the source of evil in the conduct of others. Between July 2 and September 16, 1604, inspectors were sent to the mints to determine the quantities of vellon coined from 1599 to 1602, the quantities minted after 1602, and the quantities restamped after September 18, 1603. If the sums coined had exceeded the permits or if other excesses or frauds had taken place, the inspectors were to incarcerate the responsible mint officials, embargo their goods, and institute criminal proceedings in royal courts.[3] On August 23, 1605, an ordinance instructed the provincial gov-

---

[1] AS, *Contadurías Generales: Razón*, 271.

[2] On December 4, 1603, the Cortes petitioned the Crown to suspend the coinage and, in particular, the restamping of vellon (*Actas*, XXII, 154, 157–160).

[3] AS, *Contadurías Generales: Razón*, 271.

ernments to ascertain and report the quantities of vellon in circulation.[1]

On July 8, 1600, the Cortes proposed, as a condition for the levy of 18,000,000 ducats, that his Majesty agree not to coin vellon in the next twenty years. The Crown refused to make this concession, but promised "to study the proposal carefully." [2] In 1608 the Cortes were more resolute; and Philip III, having already suspended the coinage of vellon, was disposed to renounce its issue. As a condition for the levy of 17,500,000 ducats (2,500,000 a year for seven years), his Majesty promised on November 22, 1608, not to coin additional vellon, with or without a mixture of silver, for any purpose, not even that of redeeming an outstanding issue, within twenty years from the date the imposts should be voted.[3]

Aroused public opinion prevented significant inflation in the decade following 1606,[4] but in 1617 financial necessity led to a resumption of the coinage of vellon. On July 3, 1617, his Majesty petitioned the Cortes for release from the royal promise of 1608 and requested permission to issue 600,000 ducats. The Crown contended that "almost all the rest of the world are opposed to this kingdom and openly or secretly are enemies of its grandeur" [5] and said that the budget for 1617 showed an enormous deficit, receipts being estimated at 5,375,000 ducats and expenditures at 8,234,113.[6] On July 6, 1617, the Cortes granted his Majesty's request; [7] and on July 17 the *Procuradores* agreed that sufficient vellon might be coined to afford a net profit of 600,000 ducats, provided the total issue did not exceed 800,000.[8] The royal

---

[1] *Ibid., Diversos de Castilla*, 48–16. His Majesty assured the holders of vellon that plans were under way to redeem all outstanding vellon in silver, but these plans never materialized.

[2] *Actas*, XIX, 433.   [3] *Ibid.*, XXIV, 637–639.

[4] *Vide*, for example, *Actas*, XVIII, 600–602; XXIII, 227, 288, 487.

[5] *Ibid.*, XXX, 10–12.   [6] *Ibid.*, XXX, 15–26.

[7] *Ibid.*, XXX, 45–48.

[8] *Ibid.*, XXX, 109–119. On January 12, 1618, the Crown requested permission to coin sufficient vellon to yield a profit of a million ducats, "for some good secret purpose." The Cortes consented the following day (*Ibid.*, XXXI, 191–193, 196–201), and on March 21 Philip IV authorized the issue (AS, *Contadurías Generales: Razón*, 271). With the precedent established, the government continued the coinage of vellon as it saw fit (*vide infra*, pp. 79 ff.).

cédula of September 30, 1617, authorizing the issue of vellon maintained that non-enforcement [1] of the law prohibiting the circulation of copper vellon within a radius of twelve leagues of seaports and frontier towns had facilitated the smuggling of enormous quantities of counterfeit vellon into Castile after debasement had rendered the business highly profitable. The cédula, which renewed the prohibition and exhorted judges and officers of the law to enforce it, was preconized in all places where the new issue of vellon was debarred from circulation.[2]

The revival of the coinage of vellon proved sufficiently unpopular to arouse the opposition of the Cortes, and a promise of his Majesty was again relied upon to curb the evil. The concession of 18,000,000 ducats in additional taxes — 2,000,000 a year for nine years — was conditioned on an obligation by the Crown to refrain from minting vellon of any kind for any purpose during the next twenty years and subsequently to coin only vellon containing the mixture of silver required by law.[3] On June 18, 1619, Philip III accepted these conditions [4] and expressly agreed that release from them could not be given by a petition from the Procuradores, but only by the consent of their constituencies.[5]

Owing to the impecuniosity of Philip III, however, the royal contract of 1619 proved less efficacious than had its predecessor of 1608. Long before its arrival all the Crown treasure that came from the Indies in 1619 had been assigned to money lenders on account, Jacome and Agustín Justiniano being the principal

---

[1] There must have been sporadic enforcement. On March 12, 1609, the Procuradores of León, who also represented Asturias, requested the Cortes to petition his Majesty to remove the prohibition against the circulation of copper vellon in Oviedo. The Procuradores averred that a 4-maravedí alms in Oviedo had recently cost the donor more than 500 ducats. Asturias was pictured as a poor province, with its meager income derived chiefly from the sale of fish, vegetables, and cattle in León and Medina de Rioseco. Since it was illegal to carry the cuartos received in payment to Oviedo, they had to be spent, often to the disadvantage of the Asturians, in León or Medina de Rioseco (*Actas*, XXV, 124–125).

[2] AS, *Diversos de Castilla*, 48–17.

[3] Presumably 4 grains of silver per mark, the fineness that obtained from 1566 until near the end of the reign of Philip II, when a reduction to 1 grain was secretly authorized.

[4] The twenty-year period commenced on August 28, 1619, when the 18,000,000 ducats were levied (*Actas*, XXIV, 491–492).

[5] BN, *Sección de Manuscritos*, Ms. 1320; *Quaderno de Leyes*, fols. 113–115.

recipients.[1] Before the close of his reign (March 13, 1621), Philip III, maintaining that a majority of the cities and towns represented in the Cortes had consented to a further issue of vellon,[2] authorized the coinage of 800,000 ducats. The Council of the Treasury was directed to purchase the necessary copper, apportion it among the mints, and negotiate contracts with the treasurers of mints,[3] determining the fees for coinage.[4] At least as early as January 1, 1621, vellon was being coined in the mint at Toledo,[5] and by March 6, 1621, at Madrid.[6]

III

Especially unfavorable was the economic condition of Castile upon the accession of Philip IV (1621–1665). The wholesale emigration of young men, the enormous increase in religious foundations under royal patronage, and the emergence of more vigorous international competition by northern Europe had caused a progressive decadence of Castilian agriculture, industry, and commerce during the preceding reign. The consequent decrease in public revenue and the poor financial administration of Philip III had resulted in an enormous public debt. Most of the sources of revenue had been alienated, and during the reign of Philip IV a large part of what remained was absorbed by the host

---

[1] AS, *Contadurías Generales: Razón*, 271.

[2] On July 15, 1621, the Cortes, protesting against the coinage of vellon, admitted that a majority of the districts had given their consent for the issue — some for 600,000 ducats and others for 800,000 — but complained that some districts had not been consulted and that the legal requirements for the consultation had not been met in any case (*Actas*, XXXVI, 126–128).

[3] From June 13, 1497, to this date the fees for coining vellon had been 34 maravedís a mark. It seems that the contracts fixed the fees at 28 maravedís. From May 11, 1622, to May 20, 1623, the mint at Granada collected 28 maravedís for each mark of vellon coined (AS, *Contadurías Generales: Razón*, 271). On June 7, 1625, the Crown set a maximum of 28 maravedís per mark, 3 of which were really seigniorage collected and held for his Majesty in a special account. A law of 1447 (*Recopilación*, lib. v, tit. XXI, ley XLVI) fixing the fees at 25 maravedís was cited as a precedent (AS, *Contadurías Generales: Razón*, 272).

[4] *Ibid., Contadurías Generales: Razón*, 271. Although this document is not dated, it is in a *legajo* devoted to money and mints during the reign of Philip III, and reference is made to "one of the conditions under which the kingdom lately granted me the favor of 18 millions."

[5] *Ibid., Tribunal Mayor de Cuentas*, 881.

[6] *Ibid., Tribunal Mayor de Cuentas*, 921.

of tax farmers and collectors, estimated by some writers at from 60,000 to 160,000.[1] In 1621 the twelve years' truce with Holland ended, and the Thirty Years' War, disastrous to Spain, had already begun. During a considerable part of the reign of Philip IV the Spanish Empire waged wars in Europe, America, and the East Indies against the combined forces of the leading military and maritime powers. Such an ambitious program entailed heavy outlays. Furthermore, civil disorder arose within the Empire, revolutions occurring in Catalonia, Italy, and Portugal. After 1630 the remittances of gold and silver from the Indies declined precipitately; and before 1650 they had fallen to an insignificant amount.[2]

Circumstances obliged Philip IV to continue the inflationary policy initiated by his predecessor. In two respects his reign witnessed an increase in monetary disorder: first, debasement was more flagrant; and, second, instability was heightened by deflation as well as inflation.

Philip IV continued the coinage of vellon commenced at the close of the reign of Philip III. In the first five years after his accession the output was enormous.[3] But, as has almost always happened in similar cases, the resultant monetary disorder was attributed to malfeasance, particularly by foreigners, rather than to defective monetary policy. On October 14, 1624, a royal pragmatic provided a penalty of death and the confiscation of goods for bringing vellon money into the kingdom — no matter how small the quantity —, going near a boat in which it was brought to the coast, exchanging it for merchandise or silver, transporting or hiding it, or in any way aiding in smuggling it.[4] For counte-

---

[1] *Vide* Manuel Colmeiro, *Historia de la Economía Política en España* (Madrid, 1863), II, 556.

[2] *Vide supra*, Table 3.

[3] From April 22, 1621, to April 6, 1623, 937,373 marks of copper were coined, yielding 264,144,440 vellon maravedís (AS, *Contadurías Generales: Razón*, 271).

[4] By the middle of the reign of Philip III diplomatic representatives commenced to send home rumors of schemes for the shipment of false vellon into Castile. Following the advice of Don Rodrigo de Cordova, relayed to the Duke of Lerma by the Spanish Embassy at Paris, on January 13, 1609, the Council of State decided to have all French and English vessels coming to Spanish ports from Hamburg and Lübeck searched for counterfeit vellon (Archives Nationales [Paris], *Négociations France-Espagne*, K 1426, no. 110). On April 26, 1613, Gonzalo Gómez de Cárdenas

nancing any of these acts an officer was subject to the same penalties. Cognitive acceptance of smuggled vellon in exchange for goods or in payment of debt was punished by perpetual exile and the loss of half of one's goods. The imposition of these penalties was mandatory upon judges.[1] On February 2, 1627, jurisdiction in the trials of vellon smugglers was transferred to the courts of the Inquisition,[2] and on September 13, 1628, the ordinary death penalty was replaced by burning at the stake.[3]

When the premium on silver reached the neighborhood of 50 per cent, in 1626, and vellon prices rose sharply, reform became imperative; but, in characteristic fashion, Philip IV temporized. Utilizing Italian bankers, who had often got the Hapsburgs into and out of financial difficulties, his Majesty sought rehabilitation of the vellon coinage through a gradual and painless process. On March 27, 1627, after several years of deliberation by ministers and advisers, a Banking Company, with extensive trading privileges, was chartered for the purpose of contracting the vellon circulation without loss or injury to anyone. Banks, each controlled by a governor, were to be established in Madrid, Seville, Granada, Cordova, Toledo, Valladolid, Murcia, Segovia, Cuenca, and Salamanca. Control was vested in a board composed of the governors of the banks. The government intervened through the appointment of a comptroller for each bank and a special committee — on which the Board of Governors had representation — which was supposed to exercise general supervision over the policy of the Company.

There was no paid-up capital, but the Crown assigned the Com-

complained to his Majesty from Antwerp that the introduction of counterfeit vellon into Spain from France, England, Denmark, the Hanseatic cities, the United Provinces, and certain parts of Italy, together with the resultant exportation of gold and silver, was impoverishing Spain and yielding profits of 500 per cent to the smugglers. Acting upon an anonymous warning in 1621 that several merchant vessels had sailed from Holland carrying large quantities of Castilian vellon counterfeited in Amsterdam and Rotterdam (*ibid.*, *Négociations France-Espagne*, K 1478, no. 173), on April 22, 1622, Philip IV instructed the authorities in several Spanish coastal regions to keep on the alert for the Dutch ships (*ibid.*, *Négociations France-Espagne*, K 1456, no. 44).

[1] *Recopilación*, lib. ix, tit. xiii, ley x.
[2] Archivo Histórico Nacional (hereafter AHN), *Inquisición*, lib. 271, fols. 536–539.
[3] Archivo del Ayuntamiento (hereafter AA), Madrid, *Moneda*, 2–159–153.

pany 100,000 ducats a year plus the indeterminate revenue derived from a special subsidy (donativo). The Board of Governors — all Italians [1] — was expected to provide only business experience and sagacity.

The Company was expected to contract the vellon circulation in the following manner: private possessors of vellon were given the privilege of exchanging it at any of the banks for the Company's obligation to pay in silver 80 per cent of its normal value plus interest at 5 per cent. Twenty per cent of this vellon was to be perforated to indicate a 75 per cent reduction in tariff. The vellon received by the Company from the following sources also underwent a 75 per cent deflation: (1) 2 per cent of the income from property and property rights,[2] (2) 20 per cent of the revenue from the subsidy, (3) 25 per cent of all fines, (4) 2 per cent of the vellon exchanged for silver (under the supervision of one of the banks) at a premium greater than 10 per cent — the legal maximum under ordinary conditions, (5) all profits from the lottery conducted by the Company, and (6) 25 per cent of the receipts from the sale of domestic exchange.

To enable the Company to pay operating expenses, accumulate a reserve sufficient to acquire silver for the redemption of vellon, and make profits for the Board of Governors and his Majesty, it was authorized to receive deposits at 5 per cent to be lent at 7 per cent, to deal in foreign and domestic exchange, to conduct a lottery, and "to engage in any business whatsoever that seemed likely to prove profitable." A monopoly of mortgage loans (censos) was established in favor of the Company. After all the obligations of the Company, including the restoration of the capital advanced by the Crown, had been met, 66⅔ per cent of the profits were to accrue to his Majesty and the remainder to the Board of Governors. In case losses were incurred, the Crown became liable for a special assessment.[3]

---

[1] The charter of the Company appointed eight of the Governors, namely, Otavio Centurión, Carlos Trata, Vicencio Esquarçasigo, Luis Espinola, Antonio Balui, Lelio Imbrea, Pablo Justiniano, and Juan Gerónimo Espinola (AA, Madrid, *Moneda*, 2–159–153).

[2] The deflated vellon was returned to the owners (*Ibid.*, Madrid, *Moneda*, 2–159–152); so the tax amounted to 1½ per cent.

[3] *Ibid.*, Madrid, *Moneda*, 2–159–149, 2–159–152, 2–159–153; *Actas*, XLV, 431–434.

Since the success of the scheme depended upon the voluntary surrender of vellon by private possessors, it seemed ill conceived and destined to fail; but it is difficult to explain the uniform decline in the discount on vellon in the three Castilian regions during the last three quarters of 1627,[1] except in terms of the actual or anticipated intervention of the Company. From its inception, however, the Company proved highly unpopular;[2] and the gradual decline in the premium on silver did not placate the public dissatisfaction with the monopolistic privileges accorded the execrated Italian bankers. Even while the charter of the Company was effective, the Cortes[3] and ministers did not relax their efforts to devise an efficacious and more palatable remedy. The most drastic and significant deflationary measure since the days of Ferdinand and Isabella was enacted on August 7, 1628,[4] when the tale of copper vellon was reduced by 50 per cent. Evidently feeling that a definitive solution had been reached, his Majesty solemnly pledged himself and his successors never to raise or lower the tariff of copper vellon and "to allow it to circulate always at the value now assigned it."[5] The charter of the Company, due to expire on March 27, 1631, was revoked; and eleven days later the mints were directed to deliver the 337,838 marks of copper bullion held on May 31, 1626, when the coinage of vellon was suppressed, to an agent of the Crown to be forwarded to the Artillery Factory in Seville.[6] Losses sustained by the private holders of vellon were not indemnified; but, to forestall unrest, the government made a gesture in this direction. The cities were instructed to study the feasibility of raising funds locally — by means other than taxes upon necessities — to pay the possessors

---

[1] *Vide infra*, Table 7.

[2] On May 10, 1627, a summary of the complaints in the Cortes, which had begun as early as April 13, 1627 (*Actas*, XLV, 447–448), was presented (*ibid.*, XLV, 460–464).

[3] On April 27, 1628, the Cortes voted to have five hundred masses celebrated for the "enlightenment of their intelligence" in studying the reform of vellon (*Ibid.*, XLVI, 387).

[4] The ordinance was not preconized in Seville until August 11, 1628 (Hospital de la Sangre [hereafter HS], *Libros de Recibos y Gastos*, 461; Hospital del Cardenal, *Cuaderno de Gastos*, 298).

[5] BN, *Varios*, 1–60–77; AS, *Contadurías Generales: Razón*, 277.

[6] *Ibid.*, *Contadurías Generales: Razón*, 272.

of deflated vellon half the losses they suffered, which were estimated at a fourth of the nominal value of the vellon held;[1] but the municipalities did not put his Majesty's plan into practice.[2] Local government authorities were instructed to ascertain and report the quantities of vellon in the possession of tax farmers, tax collectors, and treasurers on August 7, 1628;[3] and the fiscal agents were credited with the loss in tariff through deflation.[4]

On October 21, 1634, the tale of *calderilla* (vellon coined before 1599, which contained a mixture of silver) was doubled. By a decree raising the tariff of calderilla the Crown would have profited only on that in the public treasury; so, as in 1603, a more lucrative procedure was devised. The calderilla in circulation was called to the mints for restamping, its owners and the Crown sharing equally the profits on the transaction.[5]

The royal promise of August 7, 1628, "never to increase the tale of copper vellon" was observed less than eight years. On March 11, 1636, the possessors of copper vellon were ordered to deliver it at the most accessible mint within eighty days for restamping to treble its tariff. The owners of vellon received the number of maravedís they delivered plus the cost of transporting the money to and from the mints, and the profits accrued to his Majesty. On April 8, 1636, the authorities of the municipalities having mints were instructed to provide agencies, supplied with not more than 15,000,000 maravedís of restamped vellon, to collect deliveries not exceeding two hundred reals and carry them to

[1] AA, Madrid, *Moneda*, 3-413-52.

[2] AHN, *Colección de Reales Cédulas*, tomo I.

[3] The government mistakenly provided that vellon should be returned to its owners immediately after registration had taken place (BN, *Varios*, 1-60-77). Consequently, much vellon was counted several times. On August 28, 1628, a futile effort was made to determine the extent of fraudulent registration in Madrid. All water-carriers and others engaged in public transportation were required to declare under oath the quantities of vellon (or of what appeared to be vellon), as determined by weight, transported between August 7 and August 18, 1628; the owner; point of origin; and point of destination (AS, *Contadurías Generales: Razón*, 274). In the registration of vellon held by fiscal agents at the time of subsequent reductions in tale, municipal authorities were required to place the money under a lock with triple keys, only one of which was given to the holder of the vellon, until registration should be completed (AA, Burgos, *Sección Histórica*, 1192; AHN, *Colección de Reales Cédulas*, tomo I; AS, *Contadurías Generales: Razón*, 277).

[4] *Ibid.*, *Contadurías Generales: Relaciones*, 2695.

[5] Juan Surrá y Rull, *op. cit.*, pp. 41-42.

the mints in large quantities. The agents, paid adequate salaries by the municipalities, were not permitted to charge fees for their services.[1] The mints were urged to restamp the vellon with all possible haste; and on July 31, 1636, the officers of the mint at Granada were cited for meritorious conduct in having increased the coiners to 130, in spite of the statute limiting the number to 100.[2]

In 1638 an ambitious program of monetary reform was adopted, 100 per cent contraction of the vellon circulation being the goal. On January 29, 1638, his Majesty provided that the revenue from subsidies granted by cities after January 1, 1629, money received from municipalities for the extinction of useless offices, and one-fourth of the fines in the courts of the kingdom should be smelted in special factories established in the cities represented in the Cortes.[3] The bullion was to be sold for silver at a price determined by the Council of the Treasury, this silver exchanged for vellon at the current premium, and the process repeated.[4] Because of the diversion of vellon collected for smelting to other uses, a practice which his Majesty unwittingly admitted,[5] only infinitesimal quantities of vellon were retired from circulation.[6] On January 1, 1641, the idealistic scheme, never effective in practice and little more popular than its predecessor of 1627,[7] was formally abandoned.[8]

Revolutions in Catalonia and Portugal in 1640, when the financial burdens of the government were already crushing,[9] could be opposed only by resort to bold inflation. On February 11, 1641,

---

[1] On April 10, 1636, Madrid established two posts, one in the house of Gerónimo de Águila and the other in that of Pedro de León, each provided with 50,000 ducats. Each employed two men to transport the vellon collected to the Madrid mint (AS, *Contadurías Generales: Razón*, 273).

[2] *Ibid., Contadurías Generales: Razón*, 273.

[3] The Procuradores were instructed to consult their constituencies concerning other resources that might be utilized (BN, *Varios*, 1–60–77).

[4] AA, Madrid, *Moneda*, 3–413–58; BN, *Varios*, 1–60–77; AS, *Tribunal Mayor de Cuentas*, 887; AA, Seville, *Escribanía de Cabildo*, siglo XVII, tomo 23, nos. 2 and 10.

[5] BN, *Varios*, 1–60–92.

[6] *Vide*, for example, AA, Madrid, *Moneda*, 3–413–57.

[7] *Ibid., Moneda*, 3–413–59.

[8] BN, *Varios*, 1–60–92.

[9] According to Manuel Colmeiro (*op. cit.*, II, 581), in 1639 the Crown was obliged to pay 70 per cent interest on money borrowed in Seville to outfit treasure fleets.

the holders of 4-maravedí pieces restamped in 1603 were ordered
to carry them to the "nearest and most accessible mint" for restamping to double their tale. The owners of calderilla, which
was to be retired from circulation, were instructed to present it
at a mint for redemption in copper vellon. On October 27, 1641,
all 2-maravedí pieces and the 4's coined after 1603 were called to
the mints to be marked and issued with their tale trebled. Thirty
days were allowed to deliver the vellon, and the officers of mints
were exhorted to complete the restamping in the shortest possible
time. As in 1636, the owners received in restamped vellon the
number of maravedís they delivered plus the expense of transportation, and the profits on inflation accrued to the public treasury.[1]

The prodigious increase in vellon prices and the unprecedented
premium on silver following the inflation of 1641 forced the government to deflate. The Cortes, the Council, and the experts who
had been consulted strongly favored this policy; and his Majesty
averred that a majority of his subjects concurred. By a pragmatic adopted on August 31, 1642, and published on September 15, 1642, the tariff on pieces of 12 maravedís and 8 maravedís
was reduced to 2 maravedís, that of 6's and 4's to 1 maravedí, and
that of 1's to a *blanca*, or ½ maravedí. A committee was appointed to study the possibility of partial compensation of private
losses, but no indemnity was ever given.[2] Fiscal agents of the
government were credited with the reduction in the tale of vellon
in their possession, as shown by the sworn inventories of local
authorities.[3] His Majesty solemnly pledged himself and his successors not to raise the tale of vellon nor to coin any more unless
the extrinsic and intrinsic values were equal and the issue were
designed to retire base vellon from circulation.[4]

But the royal promise not to increase the tariff on vellon was
observed less than six months. Contending that the recent deflation had reduced the quantity below the requirements of commerce, on March 12, 1643, Philip IV quadrupled the tale of the

[1] AS, *Contadurías Generales: Razón*, 273, 277; *Tribunal Mayor de Cuentas*, 908;
BN, *Varios*, 1–60–92.
[2] AS, *Contadurías Generales: Razón*, 277.
[3] *Ibid.*, *Contadurías Generales*, 1788.
[4] AHN, *Colección de Reales Cédulas*, tomo I.

1- and 2-maravedí pieces of calderilla. Unlike previous inflationary measures, however, the pragmatic conceded the possessors of vellon — tax farmers excluded — the benefits derived from the increase in tariff. The holders of calderilla blancas were granted immunity from prosecution for smelting coins outside a mint and ordered to convert them into industrial use within four months. Provision was made for the redemption of blancas at the *cabezas de partidos* after the expiration of the period of grace.[1]

The sharp rise in the premiums on silver in 1650 demonstrated that the evils of debasement had not been surmounted, and Philip IV planned to retire all vellon from circulation in 1651. But the execution of this benevolent design was thwarted by the necessity of "reënforcing the armies of Milan and Flanders and of sending armadas to other territories." To finance these operations, it was necessary to choose between additional taxes and inflation. The rise in prices and the increase in the premium on silver, expected to follow inflation, were feared less than the results of further imposts.[2] On November 11, 1651, his Majesty ordered that all pieces of 2 maravedís be carried to the mints within thirty days for restamping to quadruple their tale. The possession of unstamped coins after the expiration of the period of grace was declared illegal, and their expenditure was subjected to a penalty of death and the loss of one's goods.[3] The holders of vellon received in restamped coins the number of maravedís they delivered plus compensation for transportation to and from the mint at the rate of 4 maravedís per *arroba*-league.[4] The increase in the tale of the 2-maravedí pieces would have deprived the kingdom of this useful denomination. To supply this deficiency, the ordinance provided for the coinage of 100,000 ducats [5] of pure

---

[1] AH, *Leyes y Cédulas de Castilla*, 8²–23–5.
 4499

[2] AS, *Contadurías Generales: Razón*, 277.

[3] *Ibid.*, *Tribunal Mayor de Cuentas*, 866.

[4] To avoid frauds in claims for transportation, the owners of vellon were required to secure at the point of origin notarial certificates of the quantity and of the distance to the nearest mint and to present them to the notary of the mint upon delivering the coins (*Ibid.*, *Tribunal Mayor de Cuentas*, 909).

[5] The ducat was a unit of account equivalent to 375 maravedís. After 1537 it was completely divorced from all Castilian coins.

copper 2's having one-fourth the weight of the 2's then being re-stamped.[1]

IV

Although available documents do not make possible the complete elimination of duplications and omissions, permits granted mints for the coinage of vellon, contracts with business men — such as Genoese bankers and the Fuggers — to supply copper, and reports from the treasurers of the mints furnish satisfactory bases for estimates of the quantities of vellon minted after the issues of pure copper commenced. Coinage was limited largely to three periods: 1599–1606, 1617–1619, and 1621–1626. For the

TABLE 6

VELLON DELIVERED FOR RESTAMPING

Year	Number of ducats
1636	1,500,000 [2]
1641	10,500,000 [3]
1651	3,500,000 [4]

period 1599–1606 I estimate that in round numbers about 22,000,000 ducats were issued.[5] This figure includes the increase in tale from restamping in 1603. For the period 1617–1619 the quantity was much smaller. In round numbers about 5,000,000 ducats were coined.[6] From 1621 to 1626 coinage amounted to about 14,000,000 ducats.[7] Thus a total of approximately 41,000,-000 ducats had been issued by the end of 1626, after which date coinage was inconsiderable, further inflation being restricted to increases in tale through restamping.

The strenuous efforts and stern measures of the government to require the delivery of vellon at the mints for restamping to in-

---

[1] AS, *Contadurías Generales: Razón*, 273; *Tribunal Mayor de Cuentas*, 909.

[2] *Ibid.*, *Tribunal Mayor de Cuentas*, 900.

[3] *Ibid.*, *Tribunal Mayor de Cuentas*, 874, 908.

[4] *Ibid.*, *Tribunal Mayor de Cuentas*, 871, 909–911.

[5] *Ibid.*, *Tribunal Mayor de Cuentas*, 878, 884, 912; *Contadurías Generales: Razón*, 271.

[6] *Ibid.*, *Tribunal Mayor de Cuentas*, 879, 912; *Contadurías Generales: Razón*, 271.

[7] *Ibid.*, *Tribunal Mayor de Cuentas*, 878, 881, 912, 921; *Contadurías Generales: Razón*, 271–272.

crease the tariff availed little, and only infinitesimal quantities [1] were surrendered when deflation was attempted. The preceding table lists in round numbers estimates for the quantities of vellon delivered in compliance with the principal inflationary ordinances.

Only in 1641, when the efforts of the government were intensified and patriotism was aroused by revolutions in Portugal and Catalonia and disturbances in Italy, did the government secure for inflation as much as 10 per cent of the vellon in circulation.

V

The large issues of copper money at the beginning of the reign of Philip III doubtless tended to eliminate gold and silver from circulation. In the official report on vellon submitted in compliance with the pragmatic of August 23, 1605,[2] Cordova stated that little silver was current in that province; Madrid and Orense — farther from Seville, the *entrepôt* of American treasure — reported that no gold or silver was circulating and that it was difficult to find a single real.[3] With the suspension of coinage after 1606, silver reappeared; but the resumption of heavy vellon issues in 1617 again drove it out of circulation. In a memorial to the Crown approved on November 8, 1617, the Cortes affirmed that when the American silver reached Spain, "it immediately goes to foreign kingdoms, leaving this one in extreme poverty," and that Castile "serves as a bridge over which the products of our mines pass to foreign hands, at times even to our worst enemies." [4] On November 24, 1623, the Cortes informed his Majesty that "complaints are very great" against the requirements to pay silver for papal bulls "because of the dearth of silver and plethora of vellon"; [5] and on January 31, 1624, the Cortes added that "a great number of individuals fail to gain papal indulgence, and the dead do not enjoy suffrage because there is no silver money to pay for bulls." [6] As early as 1625 Spanish economists commenced to

---

[1] *Vide*, for example, AA, Madrid, *Moneda*, 3-413-57; AS, *Tribunal Mayor de Cuentas*, 892, 924.

[2] AA, Seville, *Escribanía de Cabildo*, siglo XVII, tomo 23, no. 1.

[3] AS, *Diversos de Castilla*, 48-16.

[4] *Actas*, XXXVII, 295-296.

[5] *Ibid.*, XL, 144.   [6] *Ibid.*, XL, 359-360.

complain that despite the treasure of the Indies vellon had driven gold and silver completely out of circulation; [1] and in pragmatics of January 29, 1635,[2] and September 15, 1642,[3] official acceptance was accorded this view. In 1644 the bookkeeper of the Convento de Nuestra Señora de Sandoval (León) wrote in his accounts: "The smallest coin current is a cuarto.[4] Silver reals no longer circulate, and pieces of eight [reales de a ocho] are a fiction of the imagination, rated at about 11 [vellon] reals." [5] The disappearance of silver from the channels of trade was reflected in accounting, silver being displaced by vellon as the standard.[6] Charity hospitals, for instance, recorded in vellon their occasional receipts and disbursements of gold and silver.[7]

The uniform practice of keeping accounts in terms of vellon after Gresham's law [8] commenced to operate makes it difficult to obtain precise data concerning the extent to which vellon supplanted gold and silver, but for the period after 1630 some information is available. Of 122,670 maravedís spent by the Hospital de Antezana (Alcalá de Henares) in 1631, 116,496, or 95 per cent, consisted of vellon.[9] In 1641–1642, 209,139,903, or 99.96 per cent, of the 209,213,903 reals spent by the Spanish Army with headquarters in Ciudad Rodrigo were in vellon.[10] Between January 1, 1643, and September 30, 1650, vellon constituted 90.88 per cent of the expenditures of the *Cámara de Castilla*.[11] The books of Antonio Baez de Guzmán, of the Council of the Treasury, from Au-

---

[1] Manuel Gaitán de Torres, *Reglas para el Govierno destos Reynos* (1625), p. 140. In 1629 similar complaints were registered by Alonso de Carranza (*El Ajustamiento i Proporción de las Monedas de Oro, Plata i Cobre*, p. 208) and Fernando Manojo de la Corte (*Pruévase que Conviene Reformar los Precios de las Cosas*, fol. 4).

[2] BN, *Varios*, 1-60-85.

[3] AHN, *Colección de Reales Cédulas*, tomo I.

[4] A vellon coin worth 4 maravedís, frequently used as an accounting unit after about 1620.

[5] AHN, *Clero*, León, 246.

[6] It is significant that in his accounts for the year 1624 Don Carlos Coloma, the Spanish ambassador in England, reduced all sums expended in English money to Spanish vellon (BN, *Sección de Manuscritos*, Ms. 18,203, no. 4, fols. 12–18).

[7] *Vide*, for example, HS, *Libros de Recibos y Gastos*, 462.

[8] Known many centuries before the time of Sir Thomas Gresham.

[9] Hospital de Antezana, *Libros de Gastos*, 1631.

[10] AS, *Contaduría Mayor de Cuentas*, 2ª, 1293.

[11] Archivo General Central (Alcalá de Henares), *Hacienda*, 353.

gust 1, 1650, to June 25, 1652, show disbursements of 17,693,099 silver maravedís and 214,563,362, or 92.38 per cent, vellon.[1] In the outfitting of a flotilla of thirty-four vessels that sailed from Seville on August 15, 1655, vellon comprised 95.66 per cent of the expenditures.[2] While I can cite no exact statistics, protracted work with the financial records of charity hospitals in Old Castile, New Castile, and Andalusia has given me the impression that vellon represented at least 95 per cent of the money spent in 1640 and probably more than 98 per cent of that spent in 1650.

VI

A statistical study of the extent of vellon depreciation naturally falls into two periods: first, the years 1601–1619, in which accounts were normally kept in terms of silver and discounts on vellon were sporadic; second, the period after 1620, when silver was at a steady and significant premium and vellon constituted the accounting unit and the chief medium of exchange.

Although the large and increasing output of vellon at Segovia during the closing years of the reign of Philip II incited vigorous complaints,[3] there is no evidence that vellon receded from parity before the accession of Philip III. In fact, we know that on August 12, 1598, Cosme Ruiz, Lope de Cámara y Cía., successors of Simón Ruiz, the great banker and merchant prince, accepted from solvent debtors a large payment in vellon at par.[4] Regardless of the unpopular and redundant issues of copper vellon authorized in 1599 and 1602, a premium of 2 per cent on an exchange of vellon for silver in 1602 [5] constitutes the sole exception to the

---

[1] AS, *Contaduría*, 1789.

[2] Archivo de Indias (hereafter A. de I.), *Contratación*, 40-3-6/18.

[3] BN, *Varios*, 1-49-6; *Capítulos Generales de las Cortes, 1592-1598*, Petición 87.

[4] Letter from Fabio Nelli de Espinosa, Valladolid, August 12, 1598, to Cosme Ruiz, Lope de Cámara y Cía., in the enormous mass of uncatalogued papers of Simón and Cosme Ruiz deposited in the Hospital de Simón Ruiz at Medina del Campo. So far as I know the above datum is the first ever published from this priceless collection. Until some scholar utilizes the journals, ledgers, and thousands of letters from factors in the leading commercial and financial centers of Europe, our knowledge concerning the celebrated fairs at Medina del Campo will remain fragmentary, and the history of Castilian banking and commercial practice obscure and incomplete.

[5] BN, *Sección de Manuscritos*, Ms. 8991, fol. 212.

abundant evidence that in 1599–1602 vellon normally circulated at face value. But the doubling of the tariff of the first issue of pure copper on September 18, 1603, broke the force of customary acceptance of vellon at par and overcame governmental resistance to a premium. One of the earliest manifestations of an agio took the form of vellon loans to be repaid in silver without interest. By December 19, 1603, the Crown was acquiring silver by this method in Seville.[1] On December 26, 1603, his Majesty ordered the treasurer of the mint at Granada to exchange 50,000 vellon ducats for silver "with the utmost haste" at a premium not exceeding 2½ per cent. As late as January 4, 1604, however, the Crown hoped to exchange vellon for silver at par in Cuenca; but instructed the treasurer of the mint to pay as much as 2½ per cent agio in case it should prove necessary.[2] Actual premiums for 1604 are available only for Andalusia, where the figures for January to July ranged from 3 to 4 per cent; but isolated exchanges at par also occurred.[3]

The thousands of pertinent documents utilized in the collection of price and wage statistics and intensive additional search have yielded not a single actual premium for 1605–1610. But the attention given by the Cortes to schemes for reforming the vellon coinage [4] and the complaints of contemporary pamphleteers and economists [5] suggest that the discount on vellon did not disappear with the suspension of coinage in 1606. There is reason to believe, however, that the premium on silver was not great. Only six of the twenty provinces that reported between September 24, 1605, and January 18, 1606, on a plan for the contraction of the vellon circulation requested the redemption of vellon in silver, and one (la Coruña) stated specifically that redemption in silver was not desired.[6] In 1609 Juan de Mariana declared that the premium on silver stood at 10 per cent and predicted that it would soon reach

---

[1] AS, *Tribunal Mayor de Cuentas*, 884.
[2] *Ibid.*, *Contadurías Generales: Razón*, 271.
[3] *Ibid.*, *Tribunal Mayor de Cuentas*, 884.
[4] *Vide*, for example, *Actas*, XXIV, 872; XXV, 380, 426–427.
[5] *Vide*, for example, Juan de Mariana, "Tratado sobre la Moneda de Vellon" (1609), *Biblioteca de Autores Españoles*, XXXI, 587.
[6] AS, *Diversos de Castilla*, 48–16.

15, 20, or 30 per cent;[1] but Mariana's strong opposition to the monetary debasement of Philip III obviously led him to exaggerate its consequences. On October 1, 1609, Francisco Vela de Acuña — interested in making a strong case — told the Cortes that the premium on silver in the interior of the kingdom was about 3 or 4 per cent.[2]

The highest actual premium found in any region before 1620 was 5.8 per cent for Andalusia in the first quarter of 1611, and the next highest was 4.05 for Old Castile in the last quarter of 1619. But in only four of twenty exchanges between vellon and silver for which data are available in 1605–1619 did the premium exceed 2½ per cent, and in an equal number of cases the exchanges were effected at par. Moreover, after the heavy coinage in 1617–1618 the premium stood at exactly 2½ per cent in each of the regions in the first and second quarters of 1619.

In the light of the above data, it seems safe to estimate the average annual premium on silver in Castile as 1 per cent in 1603, 2 per cent in 1604–1615, 1 per cent in 1616, 2 per cent in 1617–1618, and 3 per cent in 1619. The data are inadequate for both regional differentiation and greater exactitude than that afforded by round numbers. Since these figures are primarily intended for use in reducing the index numbers of prices and wages to a silver basis, an effort has been made to avoid errors of underestimation. The fact that the purchasers of goods probably made slight concessions when the fear of punishment and the force of custom militated against or reduced agios on open exchanges of vellon for silver is expected to counteract the preponderance of silver purchases by the institutions whose records have yielded price and wage statistics.

Owing to the mountainous character of the territory, the difficulty of transporting vellon, and the concentration of coinage in

---

[1] Juan de Mariana, *op. cit.*, *Bib. Au. Es.*, XXXI, 587. Mariana was not alone in overestimating the depreciation of vellon. Manuel Colmeiro (*op. cit.*, II, 494) stated that at the beginning of the seventeenth century premiums of 10 or 12 per cent were openly collected in Seville and other centers of maritime intercourse. On May 4, 1619, Gabriel Cimbrón told the Cortes that the premium on silver was more than 6 per cent (*Actas*, XXXIII, 211–212); and on August 30, 1623, a Procurador asserted in the Cortes that the premium had reached 19 per cent (*ibid.*, XXXIX, 284).

[2] *Ibid.*, XXV, 433–436.

the Segovian mint, it seems desirable to maintain regional separation of series for 1620–1650, when exact data supersede estimates. Table 7 lists the average quarterly and annual premiums on silver in terms of vellon.[1] All of the data that enter into this table have been taken from contemporary commercial or financial accounts.[2] The average number of premiums per year in each region is probably not less than twenty-four, but it has proved necessary to interpolate the figures for exactly one-third of the quarters in Table 7.

Chart 4 presents graphically the data in Table 7.

As a result of the heavy issue of vellon at the beginning of the reign of Philip IV, the premium on silver rose steadily; but the first figure above 10 per cent in Table 7 is for the last quarter of 1623. Little regional discrepancy occurred before 1625, when New and Old Castile rose sharply and Andalusia only slightly. Andalusian premiums for each of the last six months of this year are available, and the invariable figure of 10 per cent suggests that either the legal maximum controlled practice or that conventional premiums have been erroneously accepted. The agios in all regions increased greatly in 1626,[3] but Andalusia still lagged considerably behind. The cessation of vellon coinage in 1626 and the intervention of the Banking Company caused a slight decrease in the premium in 1627, and the devaluation on August 7, 1628, occasioned a precipitate drop. From an average of about 17 per cent in 1629 the agio rose steadily, with slight divergence

---

[1] For monthly averages in Andalusia in 1622–1660 and the sources from which they have been compiled *vide* Earl J. Hamilton, "Monetary Inflation in Castile, 1598–1660," *Economic History*, II, 202–204. Additional data have entered into the quarterly and annual averages for Andalusia in Table 7.

[2] In general, the sources coincide with those used for prices and wages; but many additional documents in the Archivo de Simancas, the Archivo de Indias, and the Archivo Histórico Nacional, and in various cathedral archives have been utilized. If the manuscripts were not too numerous to cite, it would be otiose to list them. Most of the premiums in Table 7 are by-products of other investigations. The time required to collect them, had they been sought alone, would not have been a great deal shorter than that required to collect prices and wages. Bating the accounts of the Hospital de la Sangre in Seville, I know of no series of records from which satisfactory quarterly premiums can be obtained for a single year without reading thousands of manuscript folios.

[3] A memorial presented the Crown by the Cortes on December 27, 1625, stated that "the premium on silver has almost reached 50 per cent" (*Actas*, XLIII, 305).

among regions, to approximately 45 per cent in 1640. Since only insignificant quantities of vellon reached the mints for the increases in tariff in 1634 and 1636, no noticeable effect appears in Chart 4. The rise in the average premium in 1638–1640 tends to substantiate the conclusion that little contraction of the circulation resulted from the deflationary scheme in force from January 29, 1638, to December 31, 1640.

The radical increase in the tale of vellon in February, 1641, the necessity of using the profits in the purchase of silver for remittance to rebellious Portugal and Catalonia, and the extraordinary drop in silver imports from America, forced the premium from the neighborhood of 50 per cent in 1640 to its peak of 172–200 per cent in the second and third quarters of 1642. The deflation of September 15, 1642, brought the premium down to about 25 per cent, from which point it rose gradually, and with considerable discrepancy among regions, to slightly above 50 per cent in the last quarter of 1650.

The annual premiums in Table 7 serve satisfactorily for the reduction of the index numbers of prices and wages to a silver basis except for 1625–1627 and 1640–1642, when a flight from copper pulled the premium on silver far out of line with the depreciation of vellon in commodity markets. Incomparably more durable and exchangeable than any commodity, pieces of eight furnished the ideal medium for speculation during periods of inordinate vellon inflation. Moreover, the preponderance of finished goods in the index numbers of prices renders the silver reduction for a single year of great vellon depreciation much less reliable than the average for a quinquennium or decade. Time was required for the high prices of producers' goods to make themselves felt in the markets for finished commodities. In 1629, for instance, a low premium on silver coincides with dear prices, at least partially ascribable to the high expenses of production in 1626–1628, when vellon depreciation was great. The inflexibility of wage and salary scales naturally obviated fluctuations comparable with those of the premium on silver in the years of maximum vellon inflation.

TABLE 7

Premiums on Silver in Terms of Vellon. (Per cent).

Year	Andalusia Jan.-Mar.	Apr.-June	July-Sept.	Oct.-Dec.	Yearly average	New Castile Jan.-Mar.	Apr.-June	July-Sept.	Oct.-Dec.	Yearly average	Old Castile-León Jan.-Mar.	Apr.-June	July-Sept.	Oct.-Dec.	Yearly average
1620	4.00	4.00	4.00	4.00	4.00	3.50	4.00	4.25	3.50	3.81	4.50	5.75	6.00	4.00	5.06
1621	4.00	4.00	4.00	4.00	4.00	3.13	6.96	4.75	5.00	4.96	0.00	4.75	3.45	4.50	3.18
1622	6.00	6.00	4.25	5.65	5.48	4.75	5.00	6.33	7.09	5.79	5.00	5.83	5.60	6.23	5.67
1623	8.27	8.90	9.25	12.50	9.73	8.50	8.50	9.00	15.00	10.15	8.50	9.40	9.67	17.70	11.32
1624	11.75	11.60	11.25	11.20	11.45	12.77	12.35	11.90	11.76	12.20	11.80	12.40	13.00	16.00	13.30
1625	16.00	13.00	10.00	10.00	12.25	17.05	17.60	25.00	33.50	23.29	18.16	19.50	28.00	37.55	25.80
1626	25.00	45.00	47.00	46.75	40.94	42.00	50.00	52.50	51.67	49.04	46.00	55.00	60.00	58.00	54.75
1627	46.50	34.90	34.00	33.00	37.10	51.50	40.00	39.00	38.00	42.13	56.50	48.00	46.25	53.00	50.94
1628	29.00	44.50	60.00	12.75	36.56	50.00	47.33	34.50	17.60	37.36	51.50	47.00	31.20	10.00	34.93
1629	12.75	12.75	19.00	22.75	16.81	17.60	17.60	20.00	17.60	18.20	10.00	10.00	21.40	19.00	15.10
1630	21.00	19.00	25.00	19.60	21.15	16.90	16.00	30.00	19.50	20.60	20.50	23.15	19.50	18.00	20.29
1631	18.00	20.00	20.00	19.00	19.25	17.60	20.00	18.32	17.80	18.48	17.60	19.50	18.25	17.75	18.28
1632	18.00	18.00	18.00	20.00	18.50	17.44	17.05	17.73	21.30	18.38	17.60	19.90	18.00	19.00	18.63
1633	21.75	21.90	22.00	26.00	22.91	23.50	24.00	24.30	24.57	24.09	17.60	24.00	24.25	24.50	22.59
1634	29.00	30.00	25.50	25.00	27.38	25.00	28.95	25.00	26.63	26.40	24.65	25.25	24.35	26.50	25.13
1635	27.50	26.00	22.75	25.00	25.31	28.24	27.20	26.25	29.57	27.82	25.00	25.38	25.00	28.80	27.10
1636	26.00	24.00	24.60	26.00	25.15	27.91	26.10	26.85	29.70	27.64	27.40	24.00	23.88	27.00	25.57
1637	28.50	30.00	29.30	29.75	29.39	29.80	28.52	27.93	28.40	28.66	29.00	31.00	30.00	27.43	29.36
1638	30.00	30.50	40.00	42.50	35.75	29.50	31.37	30.00	36.00	31.72	37.80	29.40	35.00	40.00	35.55
1639	28.00	26.50	34.00	39.11	31.90	37.15	25.00	37.53	40.00	34.92	38.00	31.00	40.00	46.20	38.80
1640	46.00	46.00	50.00	50.00	48.00	46.00	43.50	48.00	49.73	46.81	39.75	32.70	39.50	45.00	39.24
1641	46.00	49.50	68.25	87.00	62.69	41.70	45.50	72.25	99.33	64.70	43.40	47.10	79.00	110.00	69.88
1642	104.22	172.00	181.25	25.00	120.62	97.90	174.90	184.30	25.00	120.50	104.00	200.00	195.00	30.00	132.25
1643	25.00	35.83	38.33	32.50	32.92	23.50	20.80	30.70	30.00	26.25	27.00	24.00	26.00	25.94	25.74
1644	30.67	31.83	31.67	35.00	32.29	27.08	26.25	35.00	31.25	29.90	30.40	28.15	27.50	26.25	28.08
1645	38.25	30.00	37.50	37.50	35.81	28.56	32.85	50.70	29.40	35.38	24.60	23.00	31.30	29.30	27.05
1646	36.50	39.33	44.00	44.89	39.48	43.80	43.60	43.40	28.50	39.83	32.85	34.75	37.50	36.00	35.28
1647	41.33	37.08	42.00	37.50	41.04	37.30	37.37	38.07	25.00	34.59	34.75	43.80	40.70	34.25	40.19
1648	41.21	40.78	41.00	41.17	41.21	38.00	40.35	40.50	40.60	39.86	41.50	43.80	43.85	43.80	43.24
1649	42.28	43.50	44.00	43.50	43.32	42.00	42.97	45.00	44.50	43.62	47.00	48.50	50.00	48.90	48.60
1650	44.92	48.00	50.00	57.33	50.06	50.00	51.00	52.50	55.00	52.13	47.00	49.00	50.00	53.50	49.88

CHART 4

PREMIUMS ON SILVER IN TERMS OF VELLON

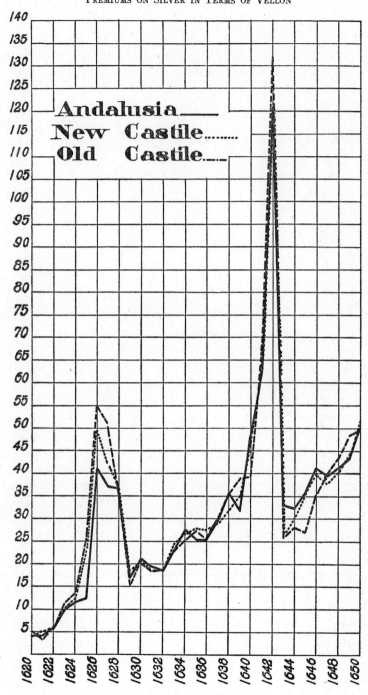

VII

In an epoch of price-fixing, when scholastic philosophy and the Price Revolution evoked ordinances fixing maximum prices for almost all commodities, even for copies of price-fixing ordinances, it was natural that the government should use this device to oppose the premium on silver. Realizing the futility of prohibition, his Majesty shifted to a policy of regulation on March 8, 1625, when a maximum premium of 10 per cent was established. Severe penalties were relied upon to keep the agio within this limit. For the first offense the penalty was confiscation of the silver and vellon exchanged; and for the second, ten years' exile for agents and principals was added.[1] The steadiness of the market premium at about 2½ times the legal figure led, on April 30, 1636, to an incease in the legal rate to 25 per cent until the arrival of the treasure fleets and to 20 per cent thereafter.[2] This ordinance was suspended on November 5, 1636; but on March 20, 1637, it was renewed. The maximum was set at 25 per cent before the arrival of the treasure fleets of 1637 and subsequently at 20 per cent; but agencies enjoying royal franchises were established at Seville, Granada, Toledo, Murcia, and Valladolid and given the privilege of collecting an agio of 28 per cent.[3] The penalty for exceeding the legal premium established in 1625 was supplemented by loss of the offender's goods, offices or royal favors (mercedes), and citizenship. His Majesty's ministers were authorized to proceed in summary fashion against all infractors of this law. On January 21, 1640, the franchises granted royal agencies for the exchange of silver and vellon were revoked; and the 28 per cent maximum premium, formerly reserved for them, was generalized. A specific minister was charged with the supervision of enforcement and was authorized to deal summarily with all offenders.

[1] BN, *Varios*, 1–60–84. The ordinance of March 27, 1627, establishing the Company designed to deflate the vellon coinage exempted from the legal maximum premium all exchanges made under the supervision of one of the banks (AA, Madrid, *Moneda*, 2–159–153); but this measure was repealed on August 7, 1628.

[2] On December 27, 1625, the Cortes, recognizing that the legal maximum premium of 10 per cent was wholly ineffective, had petitioned that it be raised to 25 per cent (*Actas*, XLIII, 305–306).

[3] BN, *Varios*, 1–60–84.

On September 7, 1641, the legal maximum premium was increased to 50 per cent; but for a brief period following the pragmatic of September 15, 1642, absolute prohibition was attempted. Declaring that the intrinsic value of vellon was little below its legal tariff, that the quantity was not redundant, and that the premium on silver was due to malice and greed, on September 18, 1647, Philip IV prohibited agios above 25 per cent on exchanges of vellon for gold or silver and established this figure for reducing to vellon all sums due the royal treasury in silver.[1] But the continuous rise of the premium from about 40 per cent in 1647 to more than 60 per cent in 1651 led to a restoration, on November 11, 1651, of the 50 per cent maximum and to a radical increase in the sanctions. In addition to the loss of goods and citizenship for the first offense, nobles became subject to six years' imprisonment and plebeians to a like term in the galleys; for the second offense the penalty for plebeian or noble was death.[2] Yet violation of this law led the government, on August 14, 1659, to preconize throughout the kingdom that the premium on silver could not legally exceed 50 per cent and that his Majesty intended to enforce the pragmatic of November 11, 1651.[3]

Chart 4 and Table 7 demonstrate that the legal maximum premium, like its counterpart, the legal maximum price, was impotent except within narrow limits. Notwithstanding the adjustments of the legal maximum to the market premium, the latter was usually far above the former. The legal agio seems to have operated only when the freely determined market rate would have approximated the legal figure. For instance, the drop in the Andalusian premium from 16 per cent in the first quarter of 1625 to 13 per cent in the second quarter and 10 per cent in the third quarter may have been influenced by the maximum rate established in March, 1625. But the failure of the premium in other regions to fall to the Andalusian figures in the last three quarters of 1625 and the great rise in the premium in all regions in 1626 demonstrate the impotency of the legal maximum in the face of

---

[1] AA, Burgos, *Sección Histórica*, 1032.
[2] AS, *Tribunal Mayor de Cuentas*, 866.
[3] AA, Burgos, *Sección Histórica*, 1127.

adverse market conditions. The maxima of 50 per cent established on September 7, 1641, and of 25 per cent on September 18, 1647, as well as the prohibition of a premium on September 15, 1642, were utter failures.

VIII

Various factors contributed to the depreciation of vellon in terms of silver. The chief cause was the extraordinary multiplication of the vellon in circulation through excessive coinage and increases in tale. The large issues at the beginning of the reign of Philip III drove vellon to a discount; the heavy coinage in 1621–1626 raised the premium on silver to 45 per cent, and the reduction in tariff in 1628 brought vellon near par. The attempted increases in tale in 1634 and 1636 had little effect because few coins were carried to the mints for restamping. The radical inflation of 1641 was largely responsible for the enormous depreciation of vellon in 1641–1642, and the deflation of 1642 lowered the average premium on silver from 190 to 25 per cent.

Changes in the velocity of circulation were also an important factor in the depreciation of vellon. The frequent consideration of plans for monetary reform by the Cortes [1] and ministers and the numerous inflationary measures in the reign of Philip IV, with little or no compensation to the holders of vellon, occasioned bearish rumors from time to time, which greatly accelerated the expenditure of vellon. On April 18, 1633, public criers announced in Madrid that anyone stating publicly or privately that he knew or had heard that the tale of vellon was going to be changed would receive two hundred lashes and a sentence of ten years in the galleys; [2] and a pragmatic of December 23, 1642, provided severe penalties against rumors of an impending alteration of the vellon tariff.[3] "Because of fear of a reduction in the tale of vellon," on

---

[1] The proceedings of the Cortes were secret, but the discussions of vital economic questions leaked out and affected economic behavior (*vide*, for example, *Actas*, x, 102).

[2] AA, Madrid, *Moneda*, 2–173–11. The same order was preconized in the towns of the province of Madrid before the end of April, 1633 (*ibid.*, *Moneda*, 3–413–56).

[3] AH, *Leyes y Cédulas de Castilla*, 8²–23–5.

February 1, 1638, the Hospital de la Resurrección of Valladolid bought 216 *fanegas* of wheat and 1400 eggs,[1] several times the quantities usually purchased; and on March 4 the Convento de Nuestra Señora del Paular went long on papal bulls "through fear of a drop in vellon." [2] In 1642 the Hospital de Nuestra Señora de la Caridad in Illescas requested the *priostre* to dispose of 994,616 vellon maravedís "so that the expected reduction will not cause a loss." [3] Business men were doubtless at least as well informed concerning proposed changes in vellon as were the hospitals and ecclesiastical establishments, and more active in avoiding the evil consequences. It may be presumed that when vellon deflation was expected, competitive bidding for silver was much more intense than for even the most durable commodities. The rise in the premium on silver after 1642 was partially attributable to the sharp drop in treasure imports from America.

The premium on silver measured public preference for a relatively stable medium and the disutility of counting, handling, storing, and transporting vellon. In the seventeenth century the counting of vellon in large quantities proved impracticable and was supplanted by weighing.[4] The large number of employees required by business men for handling vellon and the space needed to store it were often adduced by the opponents of inflation. The difficulty of transporting vellon alone rendered it a highly unsatisfactory medium of exchange. In August, 1653 the value ratio of vellon to cheese by weight in Seville was 60.70 : 100.00;[5] to hens — assuming that the average weight was 4 pounds — 68.96 : 100.00;[6] and to white wax candles 265.06 : 100.00.[7]

Such irrational explanations of the premium on silver as the smuggling of counterfeit vellon into Castile and the machinations of foreign bankers and money changers, though expounded by a

---

[1] *Cuadernos de Gastos*, 1638.

[2] AHN, *Clero*, Madrid, 715. According to Manuel Colmeiro (*op. cit.*, II, 492), this fear was general in Castile.

[3] *Libros de Recibos y Gastos*, 1642, 1647.

[4] *Vide*, for example, AS, *Contadurías Generales: Razón*, 274; AHN, *Clero*, Madrid, 715, 1037.

[5] A. de I., *Contratación*, 35–6–92/55.

[6] *Ibid.*, *Contratación*, 41–1–3/14.

[7] HS, *Libros de Recibos y Gastos*, 465.

great majority of contemporary economists and accepted by the government, are too preposterous to warrant attention.

IX

A pragmatic interpretation of the development of economic doctrines finds ample support in the progress of economic theory in Castile resulting from monetary inflation in the first six decades of the seventeenth century. Few phenomena in history have given rise to a greater number or diversity of economic treatises or proposals for reform. The incomplete compilation of writers on economics in Manuel Colmeiro's *Biblioteca de Economistas Españoles* includes forty-nine authors who were motivated by or who devoted significant attention to monetary inflation in the seventeenth century.[1] From 1601 to 1650 hardly a year passed in which numerous memorials or nostrums [2] were not presented to one of the royal councils or to the Cortes. Through polemics, memorials, and abstract treatises dealing with debasement of the vellon coinage, economic science flourished in Spain during the seventeenth century, as it did in England at the same time through controversies over the East India trade and in the nineteenth century through disputes over banking and the corn laws.

X

Debased vellon may not have been "the unique and doleful ravage of the Crown and its vassals" [3] nor "more destructive than the wars in Flanders"; but, as contemporaries recognized, it was a powerful deterrent of economic progress. Castile, mistress of the Indies, universally envied because of her monopoly of gold and silver mines, saw the precious metals driven almost com-

---

[1] Among the outstanding authors were Pedro de Cantos y Benitez (*Escrutinio de Maravedises* [1763]) and the following, whose works have already been cited: Alonso de Carranza, Sebastián González de Castro, José García Caballero, and Juan de Mariana.

[2] Almost every shade of opinion concerning monetary reform, from the wisest to the most inane conceivable, was included in these proposals. They had this uniformity, that they were generally advanced with a definite hope of reward.

[3] Francisco Martinez de la Mata, "Memorial," in Juan Sempere y Guarinos, *Biblioteca Española Económico-Política*, III (Madrid, 1804), cclxix.

pletely out of circulation by a cumbrous and unstable monetary
standard. Few matters claimed the attention of the Cortes —
that might well have been devoted to the political problems of the
Empire — more than the formulation of protests against debasement of vellon and the consideration of schemes for its rehabilitation.[1] Vellon inflation prolonged into the seventeenth century
the great Price Revolution generated by the influx of American
gold and silver in the sixteenth. While many beneficial effects
flowed from the constant, and therefore predictable and dependable, rise in prices in the sixteenth century, it was not so with the
sudden inflation and deflation of the seventeenth. The numerous
and wide fluctuations in prices [2] upset calculations, stifled initiative, and impeded the vigorous conduct of business enterprise.
Although in some respects a result of economic decadence, vellon
inflation was one of the most powerful factors in the economic
decline of Castile.

[1] Writing in 1631, Miguel Caja de Leruela (*Restauración de la Abundancia de
España* [ed. Madrid, 1713], pp. 1–2) complained of utter inability to obtain a hearing for his scheme for the economic regeneration of Spain through the restoration of
the ancient privileges of the Mesta, because vellon money had taken first place in
councils, commissions, and conversations with such "arrogance" that what was not
a scheme for the reduction of its tariff fell upon unwilling ears.

[2] The stability of silver prices at this time was of little practical importance, for
business was transacted almost exclusively in terms of vellon.

CHAPTER V

VALENCIAN MONEY

I

As THE two preceding chapters have demonstrated, students of Castilian money in the sixteenth and seventeenth centuries find abundant source material; few significant problems remain without illumination from contemporary documents. To several essential questions pertaining to Valencian money, however, extant original records offer no satisfactory answers. Bating a brief period during the *Germania* revolution, when mints were established at Denia and Segorbe, coinage was limited to the city of Valencia; consequently royal orders to mint officials were fewer and less formal than in Castile, dual circumstances which militated against survival. Since Valencia lacked gold and silver mines, there was no occasion to circulate monetary statutes widely, nor to give them great publicity. The infrequent sessions of the *Corts* diminished the opportunities of the subjects to agitate for monetary reform; and the apparent conviction that Valencia was governed by outsiders slightly interested in the affairs of the kingdom and unlikely to redress grievances averted schemes for monetary reform, which germinated upon every hand in Castile, particularly in the seventeenth century, when vellon inflation was rife. Although undoubtedly a medium of inflation, Valencian vellon did not suffer the precipitate alternations of expansion and contraction which the Castilian underwent in the seventeenth century, and the *Taula*, or Bank, of Valencia [1] largely obviated the creation of special machinery when coins were retired from circulation. The mass of legislation affecting Valencian vellon is

---

[1] Until some economist makes a thorough study of the Taula of Valencia, including the part it played alternately in monetary disorder and stabilization, a definitive treatise on Valencian money will not be possible. In the Archivo del Ayuntamiento, Archivo Regional, Archivo de la Catedral, and other Valencian archives abundant virgin material awaits an investigator. After a partial and incomplete utilization of these records, however, I wonder whether they equal what Professor Abbott Payson Usher has unearthed for his book on the Taula of Barcelona, now nearing completion.

correspondingly insignificant. But the excellent records of the Valencian mint partially compensate for the dearth of monetary statutes, parliamentary proceedings, and excogitations of contemporary economists. Always conserved in the city of their origin, and having escaped the fires from which many long series of Spanish documents have suffered, the accounts of the treasurer of the mint and his reports to the *Maestre Racional*, deposited in the Archivo Regional, furnish remarkably accurate and complete data on the volumes of gold, silver, and vellon coinage.

II

Finding Valencian silver money clipped, sweated, and otherwise defective, Ferdinand (1479–1516) and Isabella demonetized the current coins in 1480 and issued new reals, 72 to the mark 11 dineros (91.67 per cent) fine, tariffed at 18d. A flight from silver by possessors aware of the discrepancy between the nominal and intrinsic values and wary of losses from demonetization generated a sharp rise in prices in the first quarter of 1480; and as early as April 6 the municipal council of Valencia, in an extraordinary session, granted ample powers to a commission appointed to suppress any social uprising that might ensue.[1] If the silver coins expended by the Hospital dels Inocents between May 4 and September 22 constitute random samples, the public misgivings rested on a solid foundation. The Hospital realized only £2 15s. in new reals upon a nominal outlay of £5 5s. 8d. of old silver.[2]

The first gold coin minted in significant quantities by Ferdinand V[3] was the *excelente*, authorized in 1483. From a mark 23⅞ carats fine (99.48 per cent) 33½ excelentes were struck; and denominations of half- and quarter-excelentes were also issued.[4]

---

[1] Archivo del Ayuntamiento (hereafter AA), Valencia, *Manuals de Consells*, A, lib. 41, fol. 316.

[2] Hospital dels Inocents (hereafter H. Inocents), *Administració*, 1480.

[3] Throughout this study the titles of kings are listed as of Castile. Ferdinand the Catholic was Ferdinand II of Valencia. Since Philip I never reigned in Valencia, the titles of the subsequent Philips are one number lower than in Castile.

[4] Archivo Regional (hereafter AR), *Maestre Racional, Tesorería*, leg. 355, ca. 8492; leg. 357, ca. 8558.

It is significant that the title coincided with that of the first gold coin issued in Castile by the Catholic Kings; and, in 1497, when Ferdinand and Isabella, copying the Venetian ducat, adopted the *excelente de Granada*, complete unity of Castilian and Valencian gold money was attained, both the fine gold content and the tariff of the half-excelente and the excelente de Granada being virtually identical.[1]

The records of the Valencian mint indicate that no vellon was coined during the last half of the fifteenth century. The notable increase in population and trade created an acute scarcity of fractional money, and foreign coins inevitably filled the hiatus. Informed that, notwithstanding the constitutional prohibitions against the importation and circulation of foreign vellon, "Aragonese, Catalan, Florentine, and other forbidden coins," certainly worth less than 25 per cent of their nominal value, had recently entered the kingdom of Valencia and begun to circulate, on July 24, 1494, Ferdinand V fixed a penalty of death and the confiscation of goods for the importation of foreign vellon and a fine of 60s. — 500s. in the case of a money changer — for its acceptance.[2] But the dearth of fractional Valencian coins rendered the interdiction of foreign vellon nugatory, and at the close of the fifteenth century his Majesty authorized a domestic issue.[3] A *crida* of February 13, 1500, required the holders of Florentine and Sienese vellon to register it and carried the liberal promise to redeem as much as 40s. per individual, presumably at par.[4] In 1501 11,969 marks of vellon — of which only 300, a truly insignificant portion, were derived from the Florentine and Sienese coins pre-

---

[1] The higher percentage of gold in the half-excelente counterbalanced its relative deficiency in weight. The tariff of the excelente de Granada, 375 maravedís, was equivalent to 21s. 1.8d. in Valencian money, only 1.8d. above the tale of the half-excelente. The common practice of counting the Castilian ducat as 11 reals, or 374 maravedís, made the agreement still closer.

[2] AA, Valencia, *Manuals de Consells*, A, lib. 48, fol. 69.

[3] AR, *Maestre Racional, Tesorería*, leg. 401, ca. 9054, fol. 36; AA, Valencia, *Llibres de Cartes Reals*, h³, lib. 7, fols. 60–61.

In a letter of February 13, 1498, the city of Valencia protested against the supposed intention of the Crown to limit the legal tender of vellon to sums not exceeding 15s. The letter also spoke of the "most urgent need which we have for the new issue of said vellon" (AA, Valencia, *Cartes Misives*, g³, lib. 33).

[4] Biblioteca Universitaria de Valencia (hereafter BUV), *Llibre de Noticies de Valencia*, Ms. 1206.

sented for redemption [1] — containing 1 dinero 20 grains of silver (15.28 per cent) were coined, and from January 10, 1503, to June 12, 1504, 7324 marks were struck. A crida of April 27, 1499, fixed the output per mark at 25s. 8d. for pennies and 26s. 6d. for half-pennies,[2] but the mint records show an average yield of 27s. 7d.[3] From 1504 to 1531 Valencia minted no vellon. Hence the total issued during the reign of Ferdinand amounted to 19,293 marks, which produced about £26,608 6s., roughly equivalent to 9,440,056 Castilian maravedís. In 1497 the Catholic Kings limited the coinage of Castilian vellon to 10,000,000 maravedís; hence the per capita issue in Valencia was more than ten times as great as in Castile.[4] There is not the slightest indication, however, that the Valencian vellon proved redundant. In fact, we know that as late as the autumn of 1502, after about two-thirds of the vellon coined from 1501 to 1531 had entered circulation, crides designed to avert a premium on *menuts* were promulgated and that the Taula de Valencia intervened actively to prevent vellon from circulating above par.[5] The frequent petitions in Cortes for the coinage of vellon and the persistent legislation and complaints against fractional foreign coins, particularly *tarjas*, in the first half of the sixteenth century suggest that vellon was under-issued in Castile. The example of excessive limitation upon vellon coinage imposed by Ferdinand and Isabella in 1497 and the theoretical principles they enunciated concerning its issue — doctrines accepted as dogma and quoted (when convenient) by legislators and monetary theorists for the next two centuries — were partially responsible for the dearth of Castilian vellon in the ensuing fifty years.

---

[1] AR, *Maestre Racional, Tesorería*, leg. 356, ca. 8510. Most of the possessors of the demonetized vellon redeemed only 5 or 10s. worth, and it was widely held (*ibid.*, leg. 356, ca. 8509).

[2] AA, Valencia, *Llibres de Cartes Reals*, h³, lib. 2, fols. 57–60.

[3] AR, *Maestre Racional, Tesorería*, leg. 356, cas. 8509–8511.

[4] If we accept the estimates of the population of Castile in 1594 and of Valencia in 1609 given by Tomás González (*Censo de Población de la Corona de Castilla en el Siglo XVI* [Madrid, 1829], pp. 1–89, 138–142, 390, 393–394) and assume that the same ratio obtained at the beginning of the sixteenth century, the per capita issue of vellon in Valencia was about thirteen times as large as in Castile.

[5] AA, Valencia, *Llibres de Cartes Reals*, h³, lib. 2, fols. 147–149.

III

In the Corts of Monzón in 1510 the Royal Estate (Bras Real) complained that undervaluation at the mint was driving all the silver coins out of circulation and requested his Majesty to authorize an issue sufficient to fill the domestic channels of circulation and to appoint a commission to determine the fineness and tariff, as well as to supervise the coinage of the reals. In principle, Ferdinand V granted the petition and appointed a commission (consisting of the Councilors of Aragon resident in Valencia, the city councilors, the treasurer, and the syndic) to study and report upon the silver question.[1] After conferring with experts and assaying many reals coined by each of the Castilian mints, as well as the mint of Valencia, the committee recommended the issue of 3000 marks 11 dineros fine.[2] To rectify the undervaluation of silver and to enable the Valencian coins to supplant the omnipresent Castilian silver, the committee favored a reduction in the weight of the real from $\frac{1}{72}$ to $\frac{1}{88}$ of a mark.[3] Ferdinand V did not authorize the coinage of silver, however, and the report of the committee remained pigeon-holed until the reign of Charles V (1516–1556).

On May 7, 1520, the Emperor authorized the municipality of Valencia to coin silver; but the permission was not utilized for two years.[4]

Following the example set by Ferdinand V in 1510, the Emperor relied upon a monetary commission to determine the weight

---

[1] *Furs de Valencia*, I, fol. 191.

[2] The ubiquity of permits for the coinage of silver issued by the Crown from 1522 to 1614 suggests that silver was not subject to free coinage.

[3] AR, *Maestre Racional, Tesorería*, leg. 356, ca. 8538; AA, Valencia, *Manuals de Consells*, A, lib. 59, fol. 761.

[4] According to Dr. Felipe Mateu y Llopis (*La Ceca de Valencia y las Acuñaciones Valencianas de los Siglos XIII al XVIII* [Valencia, 1929], pp. 105–106), in 1521 the Viceroy, Diego Hurtado de Mendoza, coined considerable quantities of silver, supplied by the nobility, in mints improvised at Denia and Segorbe. Dr. Mateu intimates that the Viceroy resorted to this expedient because political conditions in Valencia precluded the use of the established mint; yet the Valencian mint coined more gold in 1520–1522 than in any other three consecutive years between 1501 and 1650. It seems that at Denia and Segorbe a mark 11 dineros fine was coined into 72 reals, but precise information is lacking.

and fineness of silver coins; and in accordance with its counsel dated May 21, 1522,[1] a mark 11 dineros fine was coined into 88 reals, tariffed at 18d. Since gold coins remained unchanged, the legal bimetallic ratio became 9.35 to 1 — a rating for silver not only considerably above the Castilian, but higher than obtained in any important European country in the entire sixteenth century.[2]

In 1531 Charles V resumed the coinage of vellon of the weight, fineness, and tariff fixed by Ferdinand V at the close of the fifteenth century. The emissions continued without interruption until 1540,[3] but the moderate quantities were well within the commercial requirements for fractional money.

The gross undervaluation of gold by the market ratio of 9.82 to 1 in 1522 became intolerable after 1537, when Castile raised her ratio to 10.61 to 1. "Having been informed and being cognizant by experience of the great injury and commercial distress" occasioned by the outflow of gold, on October 18, 1539, Charles V granted a petition from the city council of Valencia to prohibit gold exports except to Castile, Aragon, and Catalonia in exchange for necessary food, and then only under a royal or viceregal permit.[4] In response to a petition from the city and kingdom of Valencia to issue gold coins that could not be exported with profit, on August 2, 1544, the Duke of Calabria, Viceroy of Valencia, lowered the fineness of gold to 21⅞ carats and directed mint officials to strike 69.63 *coronas* from a mark.[5] The corona was tariffed at 19s. 8d., but contemporary accounts show that the

---

[1] AA, Valencia, *Manuals de Consells*, A, lib. 59, fol. 261.

[2] Adolf Soetbeer, *Edelmetall-Produktion und Werthverhältniss zwischen Gold und Silber* (Gotha, 1879), pp. 120–127; W. A. Shaw, *The History of Currency* (London, 1896), p. 69.

[3] AR, *Maestre Racional, Tesorería*, leg. 356, cas. 8534, 8536–8540.

[4] *Ibid., Diversorum*, lib. 325, fol. 353. It seems that strenuous efforts were made to enforce the laws prohibiting monetary exports. In the Archivo Regional (*Maestre Racional, Tesorería*, leg. 357, ca. 8549) there is a document of eighty-six folios listing the apprehensions of exporters of money without permits in the brief period from April 26, 1550, to January 9, 1552.

[5] The mint accepted gold 22 carats fine but coined coronas of 21⅞ carats. The remaining ⅛ carat and 1 corona per mark, amounting to 26s. 9d., were absorbed by coinage fees and seigniorage. The mint officials received 13s. 9d. per mark and the Crown 13s. Since 1483 the fees for coinage had been 14s. 6d. and seigniorage 5s. 6d. (AR, *Maestre Racional, Tesorería*, leg. 357, ca. 8558).

usual commercial rating was 20s. from the day the corona entered circulation.[1] The market bimetallic ratio of 10.61 to 1 exactly duplicated the Castilian, and there was heavy coinage of gold from August 4, 1544, to March 11, 1546. In the space of little more than nineteen months 2351.5 marks were minted.

Although divorced from any actual coin after 1544, the ducat continued in use as a money of account equivalent to 21s.

Recognizing that the increase in the mint price of gold in 1544 had diminished its outflow, the city council, treasurer, and syndic of Valencia urged the Crown to curb the disappearance of silver from circulation by issuing reals that could not be smelted or exported at a profit. Following the example of Ferdinand V in 1510, the Crown ordered the royal councilors resident in Valencia and the city officials, with the advice of merchants and monetary experts, to devise means of improving the silver money. The monetary commission recommended a reduction in the weight of reals from ⅟₈₈ to ⅟₉₁ of a mark, with the fineness and tariff unchanged, and the immediate coinage of 5000 marks.[2] The commission also advised that 15,000 marks of vellon 1 dinero 20 grains fine be minted. "To prevent the ruin of the city and kingdom of Valencia by the total cessation of commerce," on July 12, 1547, the Crown ordered the master of the Valencian mint to coin "immediately silver and vellon of the quantity, quality, form, and fineness" recommended by the monetary commission and menaced him with a fine of 1000 florins if he failed to execute the order.[3] Yet no silver issued from the Valencian mint before 1554, and five more years elapsed before 15,000 marks of vellon had been coined.

The market bimetallic ratio of 10.26 to 1 established in 1547 favored silver. Gold was rated considerably lower than in Castile

[1] AR, *Maestre Racional, Tesorería*, leg. 357, ca. 8544. But a commercial tale of 19s. 8d. was by no means unknown (*vide*, for example, AR, *Maestre Racional, Borrador de la Taula*, 508).

[2] The monetary commission recommended and the Viceroy established the collection of 6d. per mark as seigniorage. But this payment did not constitute a net gain for the Crown. The King paid the rent on the mint building and provided tools and implements. Hitherto silver had paid coinage fees, but no seigniorage (AR, *Maestre Racional, Tesorería*, leg. 357, ca. 8575).

[3] AR, *Maestre Racional, Tesorería*, leg. 357, ca. 8550.

or in any important European country. The complaint of the Castilian Cortes of 1548, repeated in 1551,[1] against the change in the mint price of gold in Valencia in 1544 on the ground that gold was attracted to Valencia from Castile appears unwarranted by the ratio of 1544 and absurd after 1547. Yet an inordinately high percentage of coronas in the deposits of the Taula de Valencia in 1546, a percentage unapproached after the decline in the Valencian rating of gold in 1547 took effect,[2] suggests that from 1544 to 1547 there was a drain of Castilian gold to Valencia, probably because of a general misunderstanding of the true bimetallic ratios. But generalization is hazardous for two reasons: first, we lack exact knowledge of the extent of corona deposits in the Taula before 1546; and, second, the undervaluation of gold in 1547 relative to the rest of Europe [3] doubtless tended to drive coronas out of circulation in Valencia.

Notwithstanding the significant reductions in the weight of Valencian silver coins of constant fineness and tale in 1522 and 1547, Castilian reals continued to circulate at 23d. A crida issued by the Duke of Calabria on April 7, 1536, fixing the tariff of the Castilian real at 22d.,[4] had absolutely no effect upon practice.[5]

---

[1] *Quaderno de Cortes de 1548*, Petición 151; *Capítulos y Leyes de las Cortes de 1552* (Valladolid, 1561), Petición 163; *Cortes de los Antiguos Reinos de Castilla y León*, v, 571–572.

[2] The following table lists the percentages of total deposits in the Taula de Valencia (exclusive of the negligible quantities of *albaráns*, which were apparently a species of treasury notes) represented by coronas on several selected days near the fifteenth of the month for eleven years from 1546 to 1563.

Year	Per cent	Year	Per cent
1546	45.65	1557	1.42
1547	7.82	1559	0.00
1550	0.16	1560	0.00
1553	0.15	1561	0.23
1556	0.60	1562	2.55
		1563	0.00

The above percentages have been computed from data found in AR, *Maestre Racional, Tesorería*, legs. 508–509.

[3] For the bimetallic ratios of the leading European countries *vide* W. A. Shaw, *op. cit.*, p. 69 and Adolf Soetbeer, *op. cit.*, pp. 120–127.

[4] AR, *Maestre Racional, Tesorería*, leg. 356, ca. 8538.

[5] There is abundant evidence to support this statement in the accounts of the Hospital dels Inocents and in the financial records of the city of Valencia.

IV

The reign of Philip II (1556–1598) offers little of monetary interest. The real remained constant; and, as Table 9 indicates, not only were there long intervals in which no silver was coined, but the annual average was little higher than in the preceding reign. The activity of the Valencian mint obviously reflected only slightly the great influx of Mexican and Peruvian silver during the reign of Philip II. Gold alterations were limited to an increase in the fineness of the corona from 21⅞ to 22 carats and of its legal tariff from 19s. 8d. to 22s. 6d. in 1591.[1] By 1556 the tale of 21s. had become so well established in commerce that it gained acceptance in the accounts of the mint; in 1561 the market tariff rose to 22s. and in 1571 to 22s. 6d., where it tended to remain until 1614.[2]

During the reign of Philip II the weight, fineness, and tariff of vellon remained constant, and, except in 1577–1581 and 1595–1598, its issue moderate. The rise in prices and wages, however, doubtless rendered the small quantity of vellon grossly inadequate; and it seems that commerce readily absorbed the heavy issues of 1577–1581 and 1595–1598.

In 1576–1577 the Valencian mint temporarily reverted to the coinage of "ducats."[3] But the circumstances that they were 24 carats fine;[4] that the ducats, 118½ marks, were considerably less than the coronas, 263⅝ marks, concurrently minted; and that the coinage ended in 1577, suggest that the ducats, if not intended either for non-commercial purposes or for export, were issued experimentally.

---

[1] AR, *Maestre Racional, Tesorería*, leg. 357, ca. 8575.

[2] According to the accounts of the master of the mint, the seigniorage received by the Crown in 1593–1595 amounted to 17s. 8d. per mark of gold, 9d. for vellon, and 6d. for silver (AR, *Maestre Racional, Tesorería*, leg. 357, ca. 8575). Readers are warned that at no time during the period 1501–1650 was the commercial tariff of the corona invariable. According to my observations, the figure 22s. 6d. represents the most probable mode and median from 1571 to 1614; but after 1600 the frequency of ratings above 22s. 6d. increased notably.

[3] AR, *Maestre Racional, Tesorería*, leg. 357, ca. 8572; leg. 444, ca. 9518.

[4] The mint records do not state the weight of the ducats, but I calculate from the figures given that 67 were struck from a mark.

V

The weight and fineness of the corona remained constant in the first half of the seventeenth century. Bating the quinquennium 1606–1610, when the total of 1940.8 standard marks was reached, only 481 marks of standard gold, a truly insignificant quantity, were coined in the entire reign of Philip III (1598–1621). On the other hand, the output of silver was copious. The number of marks minted during his reign greatly exceeded the total for the preceding century. The mint was especially active in the quinquennia 1601–1605 and 1616–1620.[1]

Continuing the heavy emission of vellon begun by his predecessor, Philip III coined 20,078 marks in 1599–1600. During the ensuing seven years the total dwindled to only 10,733, but in 1608 coinage was resumed on an unprecedented scale. The output of about 501,527 marks in 1608–1613 exceeded the total for 1501–1607 and set the high-water mark for vellon inflation during the period under observation. After the coinage of 6442 marks in the nine months ending on March 6, 1614, the mint was closed to vellon for twenty years.[2]

As the impecuniosity of Philip III determined the course of vellon inflation in Castile during his reign, so the dire financial straits of the Taula were the dominant factor in the concurrent debasement and expansion of silver and vellon in Valencia. Contending that the financial difficulties of the Taula [3] "because of the purchases of wheat and other commodities necessary for the sustenance of the citizens in conjunction with the large total of liabilities on deposits seriously endangered the integrity and credit of the city" and that vellon, "always coined in limited quantities," was insufficient for "daily commerce," in 1607 the city of Valencia petitioned the Crown for permission to coin £400,000

---

[1] In the Corts of 1604 the Three Estates requested his Majesty to send £200,000 worth of gold and silver bullion to the Valencian mint every year. The King replied that he would gladly do so if Valencia furnished him £200,000 a year in pieces of 4 and 8 Castilian reals (*Furs, Capitols, Provisions e Actes de Cort de 1604* [Valencia, 1607], cap. LVIII, fol. 16)!

[2] AR, *Maestre Racional, Tesoreria*, leg. 358, cas. 8579–8580.

[3] *Vide infra*, pp. 133–134.

of vellon, with the fineness reduced from 1 dinero 20 grains to 20 grains (6.94 per cent) and with one-half the resultant seigniorage accruing to the municipality. After considering the advice offered by the Marquis de Caracena, the Valencian Viceroy, and the *Patriarca* Juan de Ribera, Archbishop of Valencia, on December 12, 1607,[1] Philip III reduced the fineness of vellon as requested and conceded the municipality half of the profits; but he restricted the issue in the next six years to £100,000.[2] On March 1, 1608, the coinage of the vellon began, and by June 26 of the following year 82,779 marks had been struck. According to the records of the master of the mint, a mark was coined into 28s. 6d.[3]

It seems that the addition of 82,779 marks to the circulation rendered vellon redundant and embarrassing to its holders.[4] Instead of recognizing its own culpability, however, the government attempted to shift the odium onto counterfeiters — much as do present governments onto speculators. As early as 1559 Valencia prosecuted some thirty-six residents of Moxent, Vallada, Enguera, Arándiga, Játiva, Font de la Figuera, and Balbaid and confiscated their real and personal property on a charge of counterfeiting. But the return of over £100,000 from the confiscated estates, in which the prosecuting witnesses and judges shared, and the disproportionate representation of Moriscos [5] suggest that some of the criminal cases may have rested upon avarice or enmity rather than the falsification of money. In a crida of September 3, 1578, Don Manrique de Lara, the Valencian Viceroy, provided a penalty of four years in the galleys for the possession of "dies or instruments for counterfeiting," unless immediately surrendered to the government, or of counterfeit money in excess of £4 which

---

[1] In AR, *Maestre Racional, Tesorería,* leg. 358, ca. 8578, the date is listed as April 12. I have no way of knowing which date is correct. I am guessing, however, that the more complete document is properly dated.

[2] *Ibid., Maestre Racional, Tesorería,* leg. 402, ca. 9056, fol. 301.

[3] *Ibid, Maestre Racional, Tesorería,* leg. 358, ca. 8579. One cannot be sure that the mint did not attempt to coin 27s. 7d., as formerly.

[4] By August 29, 1608, vellon was sufficiently abundant to cause the city council to permit the sacristy of the Cathedral, hitherto limited to deposits of gold and silver, to accept menuts (AA, Valencia, *Manuals de Consells,* A, lib. 135).

[5] AR, *Maestre Racional, Tesorería,* leg. 357, cas. 8567, 8571.

could not be accounted for satisfactorily.[1] On October 31, 1595,[2] and again on November 6, 1603,[3] the Valencian Viceroy confirmed this crida. But in 1609 the redundancy of vellon evoked more drastic legislation. "Considering the increase in the falsification of money, particularly of vellon, which is filling the kingdom and city with counterfeit coins," on February 27 the Marquis de Caracena, Viceroy of Valencia, increased the penalty for the possession or expenditure of more than £4 of false money, without the ability to prove from whom it was obtained, to six years in the galleys and a fine of £50; for the ownership of implements for counterfeiting to ten years in the galleys and a fine of £50; and for actually counterfeiting to a life sentence in the galleys and a fine of £100. These penalties were mandatory upon judges.[4] To deprive counterfeiters of raw material, on September 12 the Viceroy interdicted the sale of new or used copper and required dealers and artisans to have their utensils sealed by a public authority.[5] Declaring that, in spite of the drastic prohibition, the fabrication and circulation of false money, vellon especially, continued unabated, on November 6 the Marquis de Caracena raised the penalty for illicit possession of vellon to £50 and ten years in the galleys — or the same period of exile in Orán in the case of an army officer — and that for counterfeiting to death and a fine of £100. The statutory punishment remained mandatory.[6] A nostrum to render vellon proof against counterfeiting, advanced by Don Bernardino de Velasco, a native of Palermo, won the attention of the Valencian city council on November 13;[7] but apparently the scheme was never put into practice. On May 8, 1619,[8] and on January 27, 1623,[9] the prohibitions against counter-

---

[1] BUV, *Llibre de Reals Pramàtiques Publicades en la Present Ciutat de Valencia de Doctor Jaume Sánchez del Castellar* (hereafter *Llibre de Reals Pramàtiques*), var. 167, fol. 120.

[2] Institut d'Estudis Catalans, *Follets Bonsoms*, 6602.

[3] BUV, *Llibre de Reals Pramàtiques*, var. 167, fol. 277.

[4] *Ibid., Llibre de Reals Pramàtiques*, var. 167, fol. 307.

[5] *Ibid., Llibre de Reals Pramàtiques*, var. 167, fol. 317.

[6] *Ibid., Llibre de Reals Pramàtiques*, var. 167, fol. 329.

[7] AA, Valencia, *Manuals de Consells*, A, lib. 136.

[8] AR, *Archivo del Real*, lib. 61, cap. 64.

[9] *Ibid., Archivo del Real*, lib. 61, caps. 69–72.

feiting were confirmed, but in routine fashion.[1] The notable correlation of the frequency and the severity of the legislation against counterfeiting with the excessive coinage of vellon from 1578 to 1609 suggests that the evil the government feigned to combat was less real than imaginary.

Launched upon her inflationary program in 1608–1609, Valencia moved in a vicious circle during the next four years. For its own convenience, the government ascribed the superfluity of vellon to counterfeiting; and, on the pretext that the genuine coins were so crudely manufactured as to render them indistinguishable from the false vellon, the Crown decided upon a new issue to retire the outstanding circulation.

Petitioned by the city of Valencia, with the approval of the Viceroy, for permission to coin 400,000 ducats in order to retire the "vast quantity of false vellon which circulates in the city and kingdom," on February 27, 1610, Philip III authorized an issue of £100,000 from bullion 20 grains fine.[2] The proscribed vellon held and subsequently received by the Taula de Valencia was to be recoined, and a municipal bond issue of £100,000 for the purchase of sufficient silver coin and plate to raise the base vellon to standard fineness was sanctioned. A mark was to be coined into 21s. 4d.; but on April 17 the city government reported to the Viceroy upon experiments demonstrating that the new vellon broke and bent so readily that it would be difficult to coin but, paradoxically, easy to counterfeit and requested that the copper alloy and the weight of the penny be increased. On April 20 the Marquis de Caracena lowered the fineness to "12 or 13 grains" and fixed the yield per mark at 17s. 9d.[3] The mint exercised its option of coining vellon 12 grains (4.17 per cent) fine,[4] and neither this

---

[1] It is interesting to note that in 1620 the Inquisition claimed jurisdiction over the case against a servant (familiar) of the Viceroy imprisoned for counterfeiting. In a prolix denial of the competence of the Inquisition to handle the case the Viceroy adduced considerable information on counterfeiting (Archivo Histórico Nacional, *Inquisición*, lib. 271, fols. 43–87, 90).

[2] AR, *Maestre Racional, Tesorería*, leg. 402, ca. 9056, fol. 338; AA, Valencia, *Llibres de Cartes Reals*, h³, lib. 7, fol. 39.

Some documents give February 13 as the date of this issue (*vide*, for example, AA, Valencia, *Manuals de Consells*, A, lib. 136).

[3] AR, *Real Audiencia*, letra S, p̱ 1ª., 1964.

[4] *Ibid.*, *Maestre Racional, Tesorería*, leg. 358, ca. 8579.

percentage nor the number of pence per mark changed during the period under observation.

A series of viceregal and royal decrees issued between March 18 and October 20, 1610,[1] provided for the withdrawal of all outstanding vellon from circulation. On September 22 the Viceroy ordered municipalities to prepare a list of the heads of households, divided into three categories according to wealth; to estimate the quantity of new vellon, not to exceed 15s. per family, required by the community; and to send a syndic to a conference of the municipalities at Valencia on October 5. The cities were instructed to deliver in silver one-half the value of the new vellon they solicited.[2] A crida, preconized in all the cities of the kingdom on October 20, provided that the heads of families should deliver all their vellon to specially constituted authorities the following morning at six o'clock; that the holders of genuine vellon included in the poorest third of the inhabitants should be paid in new money two-thirds of the value, not in excess of £3, which they surrendered, and the other two classes a similar credit in the Taula de Valencia; that foreign or counterfeit vellon and all genuine coins in excess of £3 held by each family should be forfeited, without any compensation except the bullion, "in case it proved to be considerable"; that all the outstanding vellon should be demonetized after October 21 and its possession severely punished; and that the municipalities should forward all the genuine vellon, together with the list of former owners, to the Taula de Valencia.[3]

As a part of the scheme for the withdrawal of the old vellon from circulation, on August 14, 1610, Philip III authorized the coinage of £100,000 of silver, in reals and half-reals, within two years. The fineness and tariff remained constant;[4] but the num-

---

[1] *Vide* Institut d'Estudis Catalans, *Follets Bonsoms*, 6613; BUV, *Llibre de Reals Pramátiques*, var. 167, fols. 371–372, 374, 378; AR, *Real Audiencia*, letra S, p? 1ª., 1964.

[2] Institut d'Estudis Catalans, *Follets Bonsoms*, 6613; BUV, *Llibre de Reals Pramátiques*, var. 167, fol. 371.

[3] *Ibid.*, *Llibre de Reals Pramátiques*, var. 167, fols. 372–376.

[4] This pragmatic and another of August 23, 1614, providing for the coinage of £150,000 of silver, apparently authorized the city of Valencia to debase the bullion sufficiently to add 2d. per real to the seigniorage (AR, *Diversorum*, lib. 383, fol. 66). But if we may rely upon the mint records, the silver coined in pursuance of the

ber of reals per mark rose to 103, which represented an 11.65 per
cent decrease in weight. Probably in order to strengthen the
Taula, Philip III donated to the city of Valencia the seigniorage
on the £100,000 of silver.[1] The coinage of light reals commenced
in March, 1611.[2]

Besides the issues of February 27, 1610,[3] January 9, 1611,[4] and
January 8, 1612,[5] Philip III authorized emissions of £100,000 of
vellon to take the place of the "false coins" retired from circulation and provided that the seigniorage should accrue to the city
of Valencia. The pragmatic of 1612 carried the preposterous
declaration that because of a "dearth of vellon" the issue of
£100,000 "was needed to facilitate petty trade and to provide
change"!

To summarize the events from 1608 to 1614, the heavy coinage
of vellon in 1608–1609, designed to bolster up the Taula, proved
redundant and gave rise to charges of counterfeiting, which led,
in 1610, to the attempted restoration of the coinage. The vellon
issues of 1610–1614 were intended primarily to replace the outstanding circulation. Yet the coinage in 1610–1614, amounting
to £364,911, was 98.26 per cent of the total, £371,362, issued in
the preceding one hundred years, and doubtless greatly in excess
of the quantity actually current, which it was intended to supersede. Furthermore, it is safe to assume that a substantial portion
of the old vellon was not retired from circulation. Diligent search
in Valencian archives has failed to disclose the exact amount collected by the government; but we may infer from the experience
of Castile that the Valencians did not readily seize the opportu-

legislation of 1610 and 1614 was of standard fineness (AR, *Maestre Racional,
Tesorería*, leg. 358, cas. 8579–8580).

[1] AR, *Maestre Racional, Tesorería*, leg. 401, ca. 9056, fol. 345; AA, Valencia,
Llibres de Cartes Reals, h³, lib. 7, fol. 43.

But the municipality agreed to give anyone providing enough silver to coin
£30,000 and depositing half the reals in the Taula three-fourths of the seigniorage
(*ibid., Manuals de Consells*, A, lib. 138).

[2] AR, *Maestre Racional, Tesorería*, leg. 358, ca. 8579.

[3] *Vide supra*, p. 116.

[4] AA, Valencia, *Llibres de Cartes Reals*, h³, lib. 7, fol. 50; AR, *Maestre Racional,
Tesorería*, leg. 401, ca. 9056, fol. 347.

[5] *Ibid., Maestre Racional, Tesorería*, leg. 401, ca. 9056, fol. 359; AA, Valencia,
Llibres de Cartes Reals, h³, lib. 7, fol. 61.

nity to surrender their vellon. The poorest third of the holders probably saw no reason to accept the heavy discount on the old vellon in terms of new coins of undetermined soundness. The remonetization of demonetized coins was a familiar phenomenon in Europe at that time, and it was still more common for proscribed money to continue in circulation. Moreover, the middle and upper classes, especially in the provincial towns, doubtless considered it inconvenient and unsafe, as in this case it turned out to be,[1] to accept deposits in the Taula de Valencia. Hence vellon served as a medium of genuine inflation in the second decade of the seventeenth century.

"Realizing that a great part of the economic welfare of Valencia consisted of having an abundance of gold and silver money" and that the depressed conditions were largely due to the drain of the precious metals to neighboring states, where higher values obtained, on April 18, 1614, Philip III raised the legal tariff of the Castilian real to 24d., its nominal value in Catalonia and Aragon, and of the escudo to 13 Castilian reals. The statute is ambiguous on this point, but its apparent intention was to raise the tale of the Valencian corona to 26s.[2] We know — what is significant — that a difference between the corona and the escudo, the fine gold contents of which were identical, could not have been maintained in practice and that both immediately rose in the market to 26s.[3] The bimetallic ratio of 11.72 to 1 still undervalued gold relatively to Castile and the rest of Europe. The increase in the tale of the Castilian real to 24d., making the Castilian ducat, often counted as 11 reals, equivalent to 22s., caused some doubt as to whether a "ducat" should consist of 22s. in Valencia or 21s. as formerly.[4]

---

[1] On August 2, 1614, Philip III wrote the Viceroy to issue a crida notifying the municipalities that the Taula de Valencia would not and could not pay the sums deposited and authorizing the levy of *sisas* or other special taxes to enable the cities to repay the losses of their inhabitants (Institut d'Estudis Catalans, *Follets Bonsoms*, 6622).

[2] *Ibid.*, *Follets Bonsoms*, 6620.

[3] In a few isolated instances ecclesiastical institutions counted escudos and coronas as little as 20s., even in the 1620's and 1630's (AR, *Conventos*, libs. 2294, 2296).

[4] For instance, there was a good deal of correspondence between the Crown and the Treasurer of Valencia (Maestre Racional) concerning the number of shillings to be received or paid on "ducat obligations" (AR, *Maestre Racional, Tesorería*, leg. 402, ca. 9056, fols. 369–371; leg. 402, ca. 9057, fol. 25; leg. 444, ca. 9520).

But the confusion soon cleared away, and the ducat continued in use as a money of account equivalent to 21s.

VI

The coinage of vellon, suspended in 1614, was resumed in 1634. As in 1607, the difficulties of the Taula were a primary factor in the issue. Informed by the city council of the "calamitous financial case of the Taula and municipality of Valencia and of the desirability of a vellon emission for their economic rehabilitation," on January 25 Philip IV authorized the coinage of £50,000 and renounced the seigniorage in favor of the city of Valencia.[1] The coinage of the £50,000 terminated in 1636; and no further issues occurred until 1645–1647, when a little over £24,000 were minted.[2] In 1634–1636 and 1645–1647 the weight, fineness, and tariff of vellon remained as in 1614.[3] The mint was closed to vellon in 1648–1650; so the total coinage from 1621 to 1650 slightly exceeded £74,000, a sum which could have been absorbed easily had not the heavy issue of 1610–1613 already filled the channels of circulation with fractional coins.

The issue of vellon which began early in 1634 immediately evoked cries of counterfeiting, and crides of September 22 and October 6 provided for the withdrawal of "false coins" from circulation. The Viceroy ordered the holders of suspicious vellon to deliver it for inspection before the end of October. In case the vellon proved to be counterfeit its possessors had the option of selling it to the Taula at 4s. per mark or of having the coins cut in half and returned to them. Anyone due more than £10 was no longer required to accept vellon unless the coins had been inspected and declared genuine by experts at the Taula or at one of the receiving stations.[4]

No changes occurred in the weight or fineness of the corona from 1621 to 1650, and the legal tariff remained at 26s. at least until 1631. The best guess seems to be that this figure obtained

---

[1] AR, *Maestre Racional, Tesorería*, leg. 404, ca. 9063, fol. 14.
[2] *Ibid.*, *Maestre Racional Tesorería*, leg. 358, ca. 8588.
[3] AA, Valencia, *Llibres de Cartes Reals*, h³, lib. 9, fols. 253–257.
[4] BUV, *Pragmáticas del Reino de Valencia*, Ms. 168, no. 7.

through the end year of 1650. Since the coinage of gold ended in 1631, the mint records no longer list the legal or market tale of gold coins; and so few coronas circulated that inadequate tariffs appear in the accounts utilized for price and wage statistics. Furthermore, such quotations as do occur are often entangled with the rates of exchange on foreign centers. The most probable guesses from the incomplete data available seem to be that the commercial rating of the escudo tended to hover in the neighborhood of 26s. until about 1631 and somewhere near 32s. from then until 1650. Instead of being abrupt in 1631, however, the increase in tariff appears to have taken place gradually over several years; but the paucity of data will not permit one to measure precisely the year to year changes.

The gross undervaluation of gold at the mint limited its coinage in 1621–1650 to the trifling total of 252.8 standard marks.

The weight, fineness, and tariff of the real remained unaltered in 1621–1650, but the outstanding monetary phenomenon in Valencia was the remarkable increase in the coinage of silver. In 1627–1629 alone more marks of silver were minted than in the preceding 126 years, and in 1641–1650 the coinage more than doubled that of the entire sixteenth century, which witnessed the greatest proportional increase in the supply of silver the world has ever known. For an explanation of the unprecedented deliveries of silver at the Valencian mint one must turn to Castile, the mistress of Zacatecas and Potosí. As was shown in the preceding chapter, the heavy issues of vellon in the reigns of Philip III and Philip IV virtually drove silver out of circulation. The flight from vellon through the exportation of Castilian silver doubtless reached its apogee in the years of maximum vellon depreciation — namely, 1626–1628 and 1640–1650. If we allow sufficient time — say twelve months — for exported silver to reach the Valencian mint, we find a notable correlation between the quantity coined and its probable displacement in Castile. Smelted Castilian reals furnished by far the greater part of the silver bullion in 1627–1629 and more than 90 per cent in 1641–1650.[1] Besides the high ratio of silver to gold, which tended to

[1] AR, *Maestre Racional, Tesorería*, leg. 358, cas. 8587–8589.

attract silver bullion to the mint, after 1611, when the weight
of the Valencian real was reduced, without a change in fineness or
tale, the tariff of the Castilian real was considerably lower in
terms of the fine silver content than that of the Valencian real.
From 1611 to 1614 the full-weight Castilian reals at 23d. were
undervalued about 15.8 per cent. After deducting 6s. 3d. per
mark for seigniorage and coinage fees and accepting the low assay
of 11 dineros 2 grains, which the Valencian mint invariably assigned Castilian reals, a clear profit of approximately 13.1 per cent
rewarded the conversion of Castilian into Valencian silver. In
1614, when the tariff of the Castilian real rose to 24d., the profit
remained about 9 per cent. In the beginning the quantity of
Castilian reals was sufficient to supply the demand for conversion
at a low premium, but the heavy coinage of the late 1620's reduced the quantity and raised the agio. Only in 1631–1637 and
1645, however, did the premium on Castilian silver obliterate the
profit on its recoinage into Valencian reals.

By crides of July 9, 1650, and March 28, 1651, Valencia attempted to retire the recently coined Peruvian and other defective reals from circulation. The residents of the kingdom were
instructed to deliver any base or counterfeit silver they might
possess at the Valencian mint, where the government would redeem it at the value determined by two experts. If a holder considered the appraisal unfair, he might have the silver smelted or
coined at his expense in the Valencian mint. The government
placed a limit of £1000 per individual upon the indemnity for
defective reals.[1]

The mercantilist attitude toward treasure was not confined to
Castile. Unable to feed herself, Valencia had found it necessary
since the fourteenth century to permit specie exports in return for
victuals; and the issue of licenses by the *baile* upon the syndic's
certificate that food had been imported had become an established
practice. Shortly before 1626, however, the Viceroy attempted to
restrict treasure exports by subjecting the issue of permits to his
own scrutiny. But the Crown granted a petition from the Corts
of 1626 to enjoin the Viceroy not to interfere with the victualing

---

[1] BUV, *Varios*, 249, fol. 468.

of Valencia and to revert to the former method of granting licenses to export money.[1]

In the same Corts a petition from the Three Estates to revoke the requirement of a permit for the domestic shipment of money, "because the guards, having advance notice, have perpetrated many robberies and committed murders to escape detection," was rejected by Philip IV on account of "the injury which would result from fraudulent exports of money." [2]

TABLE 8

BIMETALLIC RATIOS

	Market	Legal
1501–1521	12.00:1	11.43:1
1522–1543	9.82:1	9.35:1
1544–1546	10.61:1	10.43:1
1547–1555	10.26:1	10.09:1
1556–1560	10.77:1	10.09:1
1561–1570	11.29:1	10.09:1
1571–1590	11.54:1	10.09:1
1591–1610	11.48:1	11.48:1
1611–1613	10.14:1	10.14:1
1614–1631	11.72:1	11.72:1
1632–1650	14.42:1	11.72:1 [3]

VII

Table 8 lists the Valencian bimetallic ratios. Since the legal ratio controlled the coinage of gold and silver and the market ratio the tendency for each metal to continue in or disappear from circulation,[4] both ratios are given.

A comparison of Tables 4 and 8 will show that Valencia overvalued gold relatively to Castile until 1522, and — except for 1544–1546 and 1556–1565, when the Valencian market rose above

[1] *Furs, Capitols, Provisions e Actes de Cort de 1626* (Valencia, 1635), cap. x, fol. 10.
[2] *Ibid.*, cap. xx, fol. 12.
[3] Since no gold was coined from 1632 to 1650, it is impossible to state categorically what the legal bimetallic ratio was. The fact that no gold entered the mint indicates that it was undervalued; and because of inability to find evidence of a change, I am assuming that the ratio of 11.72 to 1 remained effective through the end year of 1650.
[4] If the Valencian mint had coined bullion for its owners, as did the Castilian mints, obviously the market bimetallic ratio would have controlled both coinage and circulation. But the Valencian mint, paying money of whatever description happened to be available, bought outright the bullion delivered for coinage.

the Castilian legal rating of gold — silver thereafter. Valencia lagged behind the Castilian and almost every other European monetary system in adjusting the mint price of silver to its declining market value.

VIII

Table 9 lists the marks of standard gold and silver, the marks of pure gold and silver, and the nominal value of the gold, silver, and vellon coined in the Valencian mint from 1501 to 1650. The figures have been compiled from the accounts and reports of the master of the mint deposited in the Archivo Regional and catalogued under *Maestre Racional, Tesoreria.*[1] An effort has been made to secure accuracy to the nearest shilling and tenth of a mark. But aside from the mistakes that have doubtless crept into my work, minor errors abound in the accounts of the mint. Records of underweight and overweight, transcribed at great pains, have been dropped in computing the quantities of gold and silver coins from the number of marks of standard fineness, because experimentation demonstrated that their utilization did not afford substantially greater accuracy. The same is not true of vellon, but in this case excesses of weight largely cancel shortages.[2] If account were taken of all departures from normal weight, the figures for quinquennial vellon coinage would differ slightly from those given below. In computing the monetary yield of gold bullion, the market rather than the legal tariff of the coins has been considered.

In the first half of the sixteenth century almost eight times as much money was coined from gold as from silver, and vellon produced less than 10 per cent of the total. Gold doubled silver in the

---

[1] The number of manuscript folios probably does not exceed 5000; but the collection of the data included in Table 9 proved laborious, largely because of repetition and of a lack of order in the accounts. An accurate record of the time required in the Archive has not been kept, but it was undoubtedly more than 1000 hours. I must admit my error, however, in striving for greater accuracy than the records will permit.

[2] Upon counting sample marks of coins in seven years between 1560 and 1575, the mint officials found extreme variations of 6d. of excess and shortage and only one case of exact weight (*AR, Maestre Racional, Tesoreria,* leg. 357, cas. 8561–8572). These figures may be taken as typical of the entire period 1501–1650.

TABLE 9

Gold, Silver, and Vellon Coinage

A. *Gold*

	Standard marks	Fine marks	Monetary yield £	s.
1501–1505	....	....	....	..
1506–1510	1,214.9	1,208.6	85,468	4
1511–1515	1,294.3	1,287.6	91,054	..
1516–1520	1,176.2	1,170.0	82,745	14
1521–1525	2,452.5	2,439.8	172,533	8
1526–1530	1,584.5	1,576.3	111,469	12
1531–1535	546.7	543.8	38,460	6
1536–1540	207.0	205.9	14,562	10
1541–1545	2,049.5	1,875.0	142,800	16
1546–1550	380.0	346.4	26,461	6
Total, 1501–1550	10,905.6	10,653.4	765,555	16
1551–1555	268.8	245.1	18,717	18
1556–1560	484.4	441.5	35,416	18
1561–1565	329.0	393.8	33,091	4
1566–1570	179.7	163.8	13,765	..
1571–1575	192.1	175.1	15,049	2
1576–1580	711.3	658.9	56,561	10
1581–1585	38.1	34.8	2,984	16
1586–1590	....	....	....	..
1591–1595	1,572.0	1,441.0	123,150	10
1596–1600	35.1	32.2	2,749	14
Total, 1551–1600	3,810.5	3,586.2	301,486	12
1601–1605	164.7	151.0	12,902	12
1606–1610	1,940.8	1,779.0	152,042	6
1611–1615	21.4	19.6	1,739	6
1616–1620	42.1	38.6	3,811	2
1621–1625	9.9	9.1	896	4
1626–1630	211.7	194.0	19,164	2
1631–1635	31.2	28.6	2,824	8
1636–1650	....	....	....	..
Total, 1601–1650	2,421.8	2,219.9	193,380	0
Total, 1501–1650	17,137.9	16,459.5	£1,260,422	8s.

TABLE 9 (*continued*)

B. *Silver*

	Standard marks	Fine marks	Monetary yield £ s.	
1501–1520	....	....	....	..
1521–1525	4,771.0	4,373.4	31,488	12
1526–1530	1,905.0	1,746.3	12,573	..
1531–1535	511.3	468.7	3,374	5
1536–1540	7,167.9	5,670.6	47,308	..
1541–1545	342.0	313.5	2,257	4
1546–1550	....	....	....	..
Total, 1501–1550	14,697.2	12,572.5	97,001	1
1551–1555	640.9	587.5	4,374	4
1556–1560	4,606.6	4,222.7	31,440	..
1561–1570	....	....	....	..
1571–1575	314.1	288.0	2,143	18
1576–1580	751.9	689.3	5,132	..
1581–1590	....	....	....	..
1591–1595	3,259.8	2,988.2	22,248	9
1596–1600	12,456.5	11,418.5	85,015	12
Total, 1551–1600	22,029.8	20,194.2	150,354	3
1601–1605	17,451.0	15,996.8	119,103	2
1606–1610	5,160.0	4,730.0	35,217	..
1611–1615	8,868.0	8,129.0	68,505	6
1616–1620	19,402.0	17,785.2	149,880	9
1621–1625	17,030.0	15,610.8	131,556	15
1626–1630	131,330.0	120,385.8	1,014,524	5
1631–1635	2,428.9	2,226.5	18,763	1
1636–1640	3,825.0	3,506.3	29,548	3
1641–1645	43,882.2	40,225.3	338,989	13
1646–1650	65,433.0	59,980.3	505,469	19
Total, 1601–1650	314,810.1	288,576.0	2,411,557	13
Total, 1501–1650	351,537.1	321,342.7	£2,658,912	17s.

TABLE 9 (*continued*)

C. *Vellon*

	Standard marks	Monetary yield £	s.
1501–1505	19,293.0	26,608	6
1506–1530	....	....	..
1531–1535	10,745.0	14,819	2
1536–1540	14,751.8	20,345	2
1541–1545	....	....	..
1546–1550	11,929.8	16,453	2
Total, 1501–1550	56,719.6	78,225	12
1551–1555	5,844.5	8,060	10
1556–1560	6,219.5	8,577	14
1561–1565	1,912.0	2,637	0
1566–1570	5,258.5	7,252	6
1571–1575	217.0	299	6
1576–1580	31,515.0	43,464	8
1581–1585	22,419.9	30,920	14
1586–1590	....	....	..
1591–1595	14,945.0	20,611	12
1596–1600	47,245.0	65,158	14
Total, 1551–1600	135,576.4	186,982	4
1601–1605	9,464.0	13,052	8
1606–1610	180,031.0	204,895	2
1611–1615	315,184.0	279,725	16
1616–1630	....	....	..
1631–1635	52,812.0	46,870	14
1636–1640	3,545.0	3,146	4
1641–1645	....	....	..
1646–1650	27,062.0	24,017	10
Total, 1601–1650	588,098.0	571,707	14
Total, 1501–1650	780,394.0	£836,915	10s.

next fifty years, but the precipitate decline in the coinage of gold reduced the total to less than 40 per cent of that from 1501 to 1550. The phenomenal increase in the coinage of silver in Castile during the sixteenth century was paralleled in Valencia during the first half of the seventeenth. In spite of the heavy vellon issues Valencian reals constituted 75.9 per cent of the total coinage, while gold continued to decline absolutely and relatively.

IX

Financial accounts were invariably kept, and prices generally quoted in pounds, shillings, and pence. Prices appeared occasionally in terms of ducats and Valencian reals and often in Castilian reals, especially in the sixteenth century; but the totals were always reduced to pounds, shillings, and pence. It seems, however, that the bulk of the monetary circulation in the sixteenth century, at least, consisted of Castilian reals. No Valencian coin occurs with comparable frequency in the accounts of the Hospital dels Inocents. Random samples from the journals of the Taula for eleven years from 1546 to 1563 indicate that the sums deposited in Castilian reals exceeded those in Valencian silver coins in the ratio of almost 7½ to 1.[1] Although exact statistics are not available after 1563, there can be little doubt that Castilian reals furnished the basis for the Price Revolution in the second half of the sixteenth century, when the total output of the Valencian mint was about 30 per cent lower than in 1501–1550.[2] Since Valencian reals served principally as subsidiary coins, the reductions in their weight in 1522 and 1554 had little effect upon the monetary circulation. It is safe to assume that throughout the sixteenth century the penny, in terms of which the price and wage series run, represented ⅟₂₃ of a Castilian real, or approximately 0.1389 gram of pure silver.

The heavy vellon issues at the end of the sixteenth and the beginning of the seventeenth century did not supplant the Castilian real as the chief medium of exchange, and through 1609 the

---

[1] AR, *Maestre Racional, Borrador de la Taula*, legs. 508–509.

[2] Credit expansion by the Taula could not have been responsible, for it was not (except illegally on certain occasions) a bank of discount.

penny continued to represent 0.1389 gram of fine silver. But from 1610 forward, excessive coinage of Valencian vellon and silver forced the Castilian real above par and out of use as the basis for money of account. Before estimating the silver equivalence of the penny after 1609, we must consider the extent of vellon and silver depreciation.

The first documentary evidence of discrimination against vellon appears in legislation. As early as July 8, 1606, a crida prohibited agios on exchanges of gold or silver for vellon; but not until the heavy issue of 1608–1609 had entered circulation did the Viceroy make a strenuous effort to maintain vellon at par. Having "heard that premiums of 15, 20, and even 25 per cent had been paid on exchanges of vellon for gold or silver" and that "£4 of vellon had been exchanged for 20 Castilian reals and even less," on October 15, 1609, the Marquis de Caracena fixed a penalty of £100, the confiscation of the money involved, and three years in the galleys — or of exile in Orán in the case of an army officer — for the principals and intermediaries in sight exchanges of vellon for gold, silver, or drafts on the Taula at a premium.[1] Complaining that silver had virtually ceased to circulate and that the general disinclination to accept vellon was resulting in great hardship to the poor, who had no other means of buying provisions, on November 4, 1609, the Viceroy provided a penalty of £25 and thirty days' imprisonment for the rejection of a tender of genuine Valencian vellon.[2]

In a ban of October 16, 1610, the Patriarca Juan de Ribera, Archbishop of Valencia, added ecclesiastical interdiction to the viceregal prohibition of discounts on vellon and fixed the penalty for principals and intermediaries at *excommunion major late sententiae*, absolution from which he reserved to himself.[3] An apparent lull in the legislative efforts to maintain vellon at par was broken on October 6, 1634, shortly after the revival of coinage, when the Viceroy forbade contracts in terms of Valencian reals

---

[1] BUV, *Llibre de Reals Pramátiques*, var. 167, fol. 325.

[2] *Ibid.*, *Llibre de Reals Pramátiques*, var. 167, fol. 327.

[3] Archivo de la Catedral de Valencia, 40:31. The Cardinal showed little mercy toward the conduct which his own advice, in 1607, to authorize the over-issue of vellon helped to render inevitable.

and fixed a penalty of £25 for refusal to sell goods except in terms of silver.[1]

As in Castile before 1621, it is extremely difficult to find agios on gold or silver in terms of Valencian vellon for the whole period 1610–1650. But sufficient information is available to show that the estimate of the Viceroy on October 15, 1609, that the premium on silver ranged from 15 to 25 per cent, not to mention his figure of 100 per cent for Castilian reals, was absurdly high. On September 20, 1609, the Colegio de San Pablo exchanged £531 14s. of vellon for silver at 0.3 per cent premium;[2] and on April 15, 1610, it seems that the premium was potential rather than actual, for a contract was made for the future payment of £231 10s. 1d. "in silver if the creditor should so desire."[3]

The cost of coining vellon, including fees and seigniorage, was only about 15 per cent below its nominal value. Hence a greater depreciation was possible only in the case of a decline in the monetary requirements after vellon had been issued; and the demand for vellon either fell insignificantly or remained stationary from 1610 to 1650. Furthermore, vellon was never over-issued sufficiently for its depreciation to approach the limit set by cost of production. Although isolated exchanges at off figures undoubtedly occurred, there is no evidence that Valencian silver stood for a considerable period at a premium of more than 2 per cent in terms of Valencian vellon. Except in 1616–1619, 1626, and 1631–1636, when the agio on Valencian reals ranged from 1 to 2 per cent, either Valencian silver and vellon circulated at par or menuts were at a discount of not over 0.5 per cent. The inadequate data available suggest that parity was the usual phenomenon.

Although vellon greatly influenced the money of account after 1609, Valencian reals rather than menuts replaced Castilian silver as the unit in terms of which accounts were kept, and prices quoted. But inasmuch as the Castilian real gradually lost its position as the accounting unit, it seems desirable to utilize the

---

[1] BUV, *Pragmáticas del Reino de Valencia*, Ms. 168, no. 7.

[2] AR, *Conventos*, lib. 4136.

[3] *Ibid., Conventos*, lib. 3600.

agios on Castilian silver in terms of Valencian reals for the reduction of index numbers to a silver basis. Thus we approach reality more closely than if we jumped suddenly from the fine silver content of the Castilian to that of the Valencian real as a basis for our operations.

Satisfactory quotations in private accounts not being available, two principal sources have been drawn upon for the compilation of the data in Table 10; first, the records of the Maestre Racional,[1]

TABLE 10

PREMIUMS ON CASTILIAN SILVER IN TERMS OF VALENCIAN SILVER

Year	Per cent	Year	Per cent
1610	1.00	1631	14.00
1611	1.00	1632	13.50
1612	1.00	1633	11.30
1613	1.00	1634	10.40
1614	2.00	1635	9.60
1615	2.00	1636	10.60
1616	2.00	1637	9.90
1617	2.00	1638	5.95
1618	2.00	1639	8.75
1619	1.60	1640	5.75
1620	2.05	1641	4.60
1621	2.80	1642	6.20
1622	3.00	1643	6.00
1623	3.15	1644	7.05
1624	3.40	1645	9.00
1625	1.30	1646	7.00
1626	1.75	1647	7.30
1627	4.60	1648	5.65
1628	4.70	1649	4.30
1629	6.15	1650	4.25
1630	8.15		

who made frequent purchases of Castilian reals and of foreign exchange in their terms; and, second, the proceedings of the Valencian municipal council,[2] a constant buyer of Castilian reals in the open market to pay for the perennial imports of foodstuffs, particularly wheat, from Sardinia, Sicily, Castile, and Corsica. A few premiums have been taken from the account-books of the Colegio del Patriarca, the Cathedral, the Hospital dels Inocents,

[1] AR, *Maestre Racional*, legs. 38, 42–46.
[2] AA, *Manuals de Consells*, A, libs. 138, 143–148, 151–164.

and the Colegio de Santo Tomás. But in general the best sources of price and wage statistics have proved glaringly deficient for the investigation of monetary depreciation. As in the case of all other phenomena treated quantitatively in the present study, I have found it necessary to take all the data from contemporary manuscripts; and no printed material has rendered assistance in the location of serviceable documents.

Although quarterly averages were calculated from ample data as a preliminary step in the computation of the premiums in

CHART 5

PREMIUMS ON CASTILIAN SILVER IN TERMS OF VALENCIAN SILVER

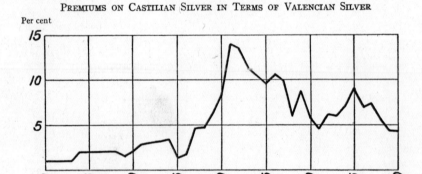

Table 10, it would be otiose to list the seasonal figures. There were few significant and no inordinate rises or slumps in the premiums as between consecutive quarters; and, unlike Castilian vellon, Valencian silver was not subjected to radical inflation and deflation. Hence seasonal data are not required in order to measure the repercussions of monetary legislation.

Chart 5 presents pictorially the data in Table 10.

On account of the interchangeability of Valencian silver and menuts in conjunction with the over-issue of the latter, a premium on Castilian reals averaging about 1 per cent emerged in 1610. After remaining steady at this figure for about four years, in 1614 the agio rose to 2 per cent, where it continued through 1618. With a relapse in 1625–1626, the premium rose from 1.6 per cent in 1619 to 8.15 per cent in 1630. In the period 1631–1637 Valencian silver reached its nadir, represented by premiums on Castilian reals ranging from 9.6 to 14 per cent. Only in these seven years did the agio rise high enough to render it unprofitable to smelt and recoin Castilian reals in the Valencian mint;[1] consequently the coinage of Valencian silver dropped sharply.[2] From 1638 to 1650 the premium fluctuated slightly, never rising above 9 nor falling below 4.25 per cent. As a natural result of the tendency for the exports of Castilian reals to vary directly with the domestic premium on silver in terms of vellon, from 1625 to 1650 there was a remarkably close inverse correlation between the discounts on Castilian vellon and Valencian silver.[3]

The premiums listed in Table 10 have been utilized in the reductions of the Valencian index numbers to a silver basis, and the absence of abrupt changes in the agios renders them much more reliable than the corresponding figures for Castile. Only in the period 1631–1637 is there a reasonable possibility that a lack of confidence in Valencian money forced the premium on Castilian silver out of line with the discount on Valencian reals in terms of commodities and services. And there were no extraordinary declines in the premium which the commodity markets were unable to follow with equal rapidity, as occurred in Castile on two or more occasions.[4]

At least from 1525 on Valencian institutions habitually kept deposits in the Taula de Valencia and made a considerable proportion of their large payments through transfers on its books. For that day, bank deposits played an unusual rôle in the Valencian monetary system. But the Taula was not nominally a bank of discount. Hence if it had been administered in accordance with the law, it could hardly have been an agency for currency expansion or the cause of monetary disorder. On many occasions, however, the Taula made illegal loans to the city of Valencia, as well

---

[1] In 1645 one could have only broken even.
[2] Cf. Table 9.
[3] Cf. Charts 4 and 5.
[4] *Vide supra*, p. 95.

as to its own officers and influential members of the municipal council.

Correspondence between Philip II and the Count of Benavente, Viceroy of Valencia, in 1567, disclosed not only that the city of Valencia was on the verge of using the deposits of the Taula to purchase wheat, but that the municipality had exhausted the Taula's cash for this purpose on many occasions in the past, with the inevitable result that its obligations to depositors could not be fulfilled.[1] But even more sordid disclosures were forthcoming. In a criminal suit against Francisco March, a member of the city council, in 1590, for the illegal withdrawal of £600 from the Taula, in collusion with José Molina, the keeper of the ledger ("qui regia lo llibre major"), testimony was produced to show that the city officials had habitually received illegal personal advances; had failed to audit the accounts quarterly, as required by law; and had permitted other irregularities in the administration of the Taula.[2]

In view of the long-standing mismanagement and abuses of authority, the bankruptcy and reorganization of the Taula in the spring of 1613 excite little wonder.[3] In spite of the precautionary measures adopted at that time, the Taula failed and was reorganized in 1634[4] and again in 1649.[5] The three bankruptcies of the Taula forced its deposits and *albaráns*, a species of treasury notes, much farther below par than Valencian silver or vellon fell at any time during the period under observation. In 1613–1614 the discount on albaráns and deposits in the original Taula reached 16⅔ per cent in terms of Castilian reals, and in 1634 the premium on pieces of eight ranged from 26.5 to 30 per cent. The heavy discount on albaráns and Taula deposits emerged at least two years before the last bankruptcy. In 1647–1648 the premium on

---

[1] AA, Valencia, *Llibres de Cartes Reals*, h³, lib. 5, fol. 164.

[2] AR, *Real Audiencia, Procesos de Madrid*, letra F, no. 166.

[3] Manuel Peris y Fuentes, "La Taula de Valencia," *III Congrés d'Historia de la Corona d'Aragó*, I, 514–515, n. 1.

[4] AA, Valencia, *Llibres de Cartes Reals*, h³, lib. 9, fols. 175–179. The legal arrangements controlling the reorganization, dated March 20, 1634, are strikingly modern in tone.

[5] Manuel Peris y Fuentes, *op. cit., III Congrés d'Historia de la Corona d'Aragó*, I, 515, note.

Castilian silver fluctuated between 30 and 40 per cent, and in 1649 it reached 50 per cent. But neither albaráns nor deposits in the defunct Taula served as money of account; and the perturbation of economic life resulting from their depreciation was not comparable to that which occurred in Castile, for example, when vellon inflation was at its apogee.

PART II

THE PRICE REVOLUTION

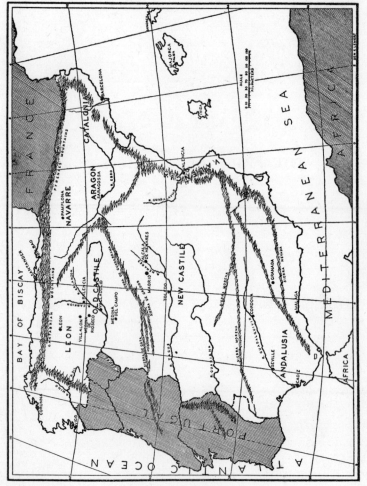

MAP OF SPAIN

CHAPTER VI

SOURCES AND METHODS

I

THE accounts of charity hospitals constitute by far the best single source yet unearthed for Spanish prices and wages in the sixteenth and seventeenth centuries. From the eleventh century forward these benevolent institutions arose in the leading municipalities of Christian Castile and figured among the earliest foundations in each successive city wrested from the Moors during the Reconquest. In the first few centuries of their existence, however, the hospitals either failed to keep or did not preserve records of their expenditures. The oldest significant price records commence with 1413 in Valencia and approximately ninety years later in Castile. But systematic methods of bookkeeping did not evolve until about 1540, before which date the statistics tend to be scant and irregular.

Bating the associations for outdoor charitable relief, which often adopted the title "hospital" without assuming the correlative functions, the hospitals had to feed, house, clothe, and treat their patients and to bury their deceased. The upkeep of edifices entailed by the possession of large blocks of urban real estate required steady purchases of building materials. To heal the curables and regale the doomed, the hospitals bought a rather wide variety of wholesome foods. Since a chapel figured as an indispensable department and rituals were performed faithfully, the commodities employed by the Catholic Church for sacramental purposes usually abound in the hospital accounts. Almost invariably the institutions had their own pharmacies. Purely medicinal articles have generally been omitted, but purchases for the hospital pharmacies have strengthened the quotations for several foods such as sugar, honey, and lard.

Perhaps the greatest advantage of the hospital records lies in their accessibility. Most of the accounts remain deposited in the hospitals, institutions not affected by the ubiquitous *fiestas* which impede research in the public archives. Not only was it possible in all cases except in Valencia (where I was limited to an eight-hour day, Sundays and holidays excluded) to work seven days a week, but no obstacles to a day of eleven to thirteen hours were encountered. Hence one could average considerably more than twice as many hours per month as the various national archives were open and more than three times as many as in the typical municipal or provincial archive. Furthermore, I was permitted everywhere to handle the documents freely; so progress was not obstructed by the slow service unfortunately characteristic of Spanish archives [1] and libraries.

Several difficulties encountered in the utilization of hospital records are worthy of mention. Only at Ávila did I find serviceable catalogues or inventories,[2] and it happened that the accounts themselves were virtually worthless. Unreliability deprived the inventory of the Hospital de la Sangre accounts at Seville [3] of all value, and the catalogue of the Esgueva papers at Valladolid constituted a considerable handicap.[4] Complete freedom to handle the records, coupled with the fact that the accounts were usually bound, rendered the lack of inventories and the disorderly arrangement less formidable than they appear. The strong tendency to record expenditures in several books increased the labor of transcription, and the lack of heat in winter and the deficiency of light all the year often made one wonder whether the game was worth the candle.

The account-books of convents [5] are probably the second best

---

[1] At least from 1927 to 1933 the Archive of Simancas has been an exception.

[2] The inventories cover the records of the following hospitals: Dios Padre, Santa María Magdalena, Misericordia, and Santa Escolástica, all deposited in the Hospital Provincial.

[3] Deposited in the Hospital del Pozo Santo.

[4] The books of account had been catalogued numerically without reference to chronological sequence and shelved accordingly. Had there been no inventory, the records could have been rearranged. The catalogue was not always reliable; for instance, the accounts for several years that did not appear in the inventory were utilized.

I am glad to state, however, that the Esgueva records have recently been transferred to the Archivo del Ayuntamiento and recatalogued.

[5] In this study "convent" is used as a generic term to include both monasteries and convents in a narrow sense.

source of price statistics. Even during the Reconquest and the palmiest days of the Inquisition the plethora of convents and the growth of mortmain evoked strong complaints from the Cortes and aroused the opposition of several enlightened prelates. But from the thousands of convents few accounts sufficiently continuous for adequate price statistics survived the transfers occasioned by the various acts of disentailment and suppression from the reign of Philip V to that of Isabella II. With rare exceptions, the economic records were confiscated and provisionally stored in the *Delegaciones de Hacienda* of the provincial capitals, whither they were transported in carts. It is persistently rumored among archivists that the muleteers were accorded and freely used the privilege of jettison on mountain roads. Thousands of *legajos* were assembled in the Archive of the Real Academia de la Historia and later transferred to form the nucleus of the Archivo Histórico Nacional. After subsequent remissions from the provinces, the central collection now consists of about 13,910 legajos. Hundreds of account-books of convents still remain in several Delegaciones de Hacienda, almost invariably uncatalogued and often poorly sheltered. In the sixty-six years since the vast collection of ecclesiastical records has been deposited in the Archivo Histórico Nacional no catalogue containing more information than the number of legajos from each convent has been prepared. Only the industry and intelligence of Don Miguel Bordonau, of the Sección de Manuscritos of the Biblioteca Nacional and sometime Director of the Archive of Simancas, who, as a member of the National Corps of Archivists, was able to gain direct access to the collection, have made the papers useful for the present study. In three months of arduous labor he examined each of the 13,910 legajos and, with consummate skill, made notes covering the thousand or more containing significant price statistics. With the resultant critical inventory, one can utilize the accounts of convents in the Archivo Histórico Nacional for the present purpose at least as readily as any other economico-historical manuscripts in Spain.

Since the prohibition of meats during Lent did not rigorously bind patients, the accounts of convents often complemented hospital records, especially in fish prices. Inasmuch as the vows of poverty and abstinence from the mundane apparently did not extend to dietaries, the expenditures of convents proved rich in food prices.

Intensive search among the existing manuscripts of the Universities of Salamanca [1] and Valencia [2] disclosed nothing of value for the present study, but the kitchen accounts of the Colegio Mayor de San Ildefonso of the University of Alcalá de Henares [3] proved extremely valuable for the sixteenth century and fair for the first half of the seventeenth. The Colegios de San Pablo and San Lucas y San Nicolás have furnished some material for bridging gaps.

No continuous prices have been found in the records of the royal household. The expense accounts of Juana la Loca in Tordesillas for 1508, 1511, 1513, and 1517–1520 [4] have been utilized to fill lacunae, as have the kitchen expenditures of Philip II, then Crown Prince, in Valladolid for 1539–1541, 1543–1545, and 1547. [5] It is unfortunate that the continuous accounts of the royal household have not been available, for the expenditures of Juana and Philip II covered an extensive list of commodities.

The records of municipalities and cathedrals furnished a few data, but these sources proved disappointing. Since the commodity expenditures of both institutions were limited largely to construction projects and to the articles used in rituals and processions, the number of articles for which quotations are available is intolerably small. [6] Furthermore, few cathedral accounts are

---

[1] Still deposited in the University.

[2] In the Archivo del Ayuntamiento.

[3] In the Archivo Histórico Nacional. There is a good manuscript inventory of the records of the Universities of Alcalá de Henares and Plasencia. The latter contain no significant price statistics.

[4] Archivo de Simancas, *Casa Real* (E.M.), 8–8, 9–1, 9–2, 9–3. Strenuous efforts to locate the remainder of these documents in the Convent of Santa Clara in Tordesillas, where Juana was immured, and in the Royal Palace in Madrid, whither the mother superior and the chaplain reported that the accounts had been transferred, produced negative results.

[5] Archivo de Simancas, *Casa Real* (E.M.), legs. 33–37.

[6] The few surviving accounts of jails are no good. It seems that the public authorities farmed out the feeding of prisoners. The records of orphan asylums are worthless for the same reason; most of these institutions appear to have been agencies for the placement of homeless children in private families at a fixed rate per month.

continuous, and the disbursements of municipalities are often heavily diluted with extraneous items. At best cathedrals and municipalities have furnished material to bridge gaps in other series.

All efforts to locate significant expense accounts of prelates [1] and noble families [2] have failed. And no satisfactory private accounts have been found. The journals of Simón and Cosme Ruiz at Medina del Campo [3] abound in textile and wine prices; but the commodities were purposely diverse, and the descriptions seem inadequate for the compilation of homogeneous price series. Furthermore, the prices extend over less than half a century. No public records concerning the prices of grain or other commodities in particular markets such as were kept in other countries for guidance in fixing legal maximum prices seem to be available. It might be possible to calculate market prices from the *alcabala*, or sales tax; but the obvious incentive to understate the price in order to lessen the heavy *ad valorem* impost rendered alcabala returns unreliable indices of market prices. Furthermore, it is unsafe to assume a constant percentage of undervaluation; for the extent of fraud probably varied inversely with the strength of the administration and directly with the height of the tax.

Records of the outfitting of ships by the House of Trade at Seville furnish prices for many years, but numerous long gaps and the fact that the purchases did not always fall in the same season vitiate the price series. Neither continuous nor wholly satisfactory prices occur in army or navy accounts. Although the records of the Mesta supplied salaries and wages, they proved to be worthless for prices. Since the Mesta neither owned sheep nor traded in wool, even the prices of these commodities fail to appear in its account-books.

The suspicion that embezzlement was not entirely absent in the

[1] In the archives of the bishoprics of Palencia, León, and Barcelona and the archbishopric of Valencia I not only encountered no obstructive tactics, but received cheerful assistance from the archivists.

[2] The archives of the Dukes of Alba and Medinaceli have proved particularly disappointing. The collection of Osuna papers, one of the largest of its kind in existence, in the Archivo Histórico Nacional is of little or no account for price statistics.

[3] In the Hospital de Simón Ruiz.

financial administration of institutions, particularly hospitals, over a century and a half has kept me constantly on guard against the distortion of series through the acceptance of fraudulently dear prices. Consequently the quotations from each institution have been compared with those from as many different sources as possible. In New Castile, for instance, prices from the Hospital de Tavera in Toledo, the best single source, were compared with those paid by the Colegio Mayor de San Ildefonso of the University of Alcalá de Henares, several convents in Toledo, and the Hospital de Antezana in Alcalá de Henares. For the Andalusian series from 1551–1650, taken chiefly from the Hospital de la Sangre in Seville, the accounts of the municipality, cathedral, House of Trade, three other Sevillan hospitals, and of convents in Cádiz, Cordova, and Granada served as controls. In Old Castile-León the quotations from the Convento de Nuestra Señora de Sandoval in Villaverde de Sandoval (León) and the Hospital de Esgueva in Valladolid were compared with prices from the Hospital de San Bernarbé y San Antolín in Palencia, Hospital de Simón Ruiz in Medina del Campo, Hospital de la Resurrección in Valladolid, the municipality of Villalón, and several convents. For the principal series in Valencia, taken from the Hospital dels Inocents, the records of the municipality, the Colegio de Santo Tomás, and of several convents were used as controls. The dearth of fraud uncovered by the critical comparison of records suggests that the frequent audits of most institutional accounts [1] caused dishonest purchasing agents to elect the easier course of overstating quantities rather than prices. The fact that contemporary complaints of shortages in weights and measures greatly outnumbered denunciations of suspiciously dear prices confirms this hypothesis.[2]

---

[1] In many cases the records were inspected thoroughly. For example, the auditor of the account-books of the Hospital de la Sangre for 1573 (*Libros de Recibos y Gastos*, leg. 455) wrote "exorbitantly dear almonds" beside an entry. In 1604 the inspector of the records of the Hospital de Antezana denounced the excessive expenditures for charcoal, firewood, and olive oil (*Gastos Ordinarios de 1604*, 17–18 de Abril), and in 1605 the auditor of the accounts of the Hospital de la Sangre gave vent to his wrath over the squandering of funds intended for charity upon fine Segovian cloth for decorative mule blankets (*Libros de Recibos y Gastos*, leg. 459, 6 de Febrero).

[2] As will be shown in a study now in preparation, corruption was much more frequent in institutional purchases in 1651–1800 than in 1501–1650.

One cannot affirm that absolutely no dishonesty escaped detection, but the number and variety of the controls and the slight discrepancies among the prices of the four regions indicate that the index numbers have not been distorted by the use of fraudulent records.[1]

II

Owing to the vast area, diversity of climate and resources, and mountainous character of peninsular Spain — triple circumstances sufficiently potent to differentiate the speech, customs, dress, and economy of the major regions; the great scarcity of internal waterways; and the fact that Andalusia, specifically Seville, was the goal of all the Mexican and Peruvian silver legally entering Europe, it seemed unusually desirable to maintain strict regional separation of Spanish price series from 1501 to 1650, when land transportation was slow and expensive and interregional trade presumably undeveloped. Hence for the investigation of prices the country has been divided into four large districts, which probably included not less than 67 per cent of the area and population.

As the map on page 138 shows, Andalusia, New Castile Old Castile-León,[2] and Valencia — the regions selected — constituted natural economic units separated by well-defined geographic boundaries. Political impediments also restricted trade between Castile and Valencia. In view of the close commercial contacts between New Castile and Estremadura, the index numbers for the former region doubtless furnish a reliable measure of prices in the latter. If continuous prices in Estremadura had been unearthed,[3] however, either the two regions would have been combined or the Estremenian series would have been used as a control for the New Castilian. Owing to the small area of the Crown of

---

[1] For comments on the efficiency of institutional purchasing *vide infra*, p. 187, n. 2.

[2] For brevity this region is invariably designated "Old Castile" in the charts which follow, and the text almost always refers to Old Castilian-Leonese data as "Old Castilian."

[3] I attempted to find continuous data in Zafra, Badajoz, Mérida, Trujillo, Cáceres, and Guadalupe.

Aragon any one of the three constituent kingdoms would have served as a fair sample of the whole. But the economic importance of Catalonia, including its French appendages, and the relatively central location of the capital would have made a price series for Barcelona, other things equal, the most desirable choice. Both Catalonia and Aragon proper were eliminated, however, by failure to discover satisfactory price statistics in Barcelona or Saragossa.[1] Valencia, the second choice, was selected because of the relative abundance and satisfactory character of the available data. In view of the intimate commercial contacts maintained with Catalonia by both Valencia and Aragon proper, it seems that the Valencian series should be fairly representative of prices in the limited area of the Crown of Aragon. The index numbers for Old Castile-León, the region that included the fairs at Medina del Campo, Medina de Rioseco, and Villalón, probably measured the movements of prices in Galicia, Asturias, Guipúzcoa, Vizcaya, and Navarre with reasonable accuracy. In view of the close agreement among the price indices for regions as widely separated as Andalusia, Valencia, and Old Castile-León, it seems highly improbable that the movements of prices in a single important district of Spain departed significantly from the index numbers for the region with which it traded most actively.

III

After the regions had been selected all the historically important towns [2] were visited, and the manuscripts considered likely to yield price statistics inspected.

[1] Perhaps the best series found in Barcelona was in the accounts of the *Casa d'Infants Orfens*, which begins in the middle of the sixteenth century and continues through 1650. The strong tendency to record expenditures without any indication of prices or quantities renders the series almost worthless. The accounts of the Sea-Consulate contain some salaries and wages, but the years are too scattered to permit the compilation of satisfactory wage statistics. I could locate no useful hospital records, and continuous accounts of particular convents do not seem to be available in the Archivo de la Corona de Aragón. The accounts of the municipality and of the cathedrals (Nuestra Señora del Pilar and la Seo) of Saragossa furnish a fair series for building materials, but I could not locate a good general price or wage series.

[2] In Old Castile-León, for instance, efforts were made to locate material in Burgos, Valladolid, Palencia, Simancas, León, Salamanca, Tordesillas, Medina del Campo, Villalón, Medina de Rioseco, Ávila, Cuellar, and Segovia.

The best accounts from the standpoints of intrinsic worth and the economic significance of the locality supplied the principal series for each region, and the remaining material filled hiatuses and served as controls. The primary records were exploited in the following fashion. The prices of all homogeneous commodities except medicines and other articles not generally consumed were recorded at five- or ten-year intervals, according to the apparent uniformity or variability of the records, and frequency tables constructed. All important commodities occurring in 60 per cent or more of the years, or in a smaller number if past experience and preliminary inspection of the complementary series indicated the probable existence of acceptable data for filling the gaps, were printed alphabetically on four-faced folios 23 by 33½ centimeters. Usually about fifty commodities were printed, and space was left at the bottom of each list to enter approximately twenty-five more. After the quotations for each printed commodity had been completed, sufficient space remained on most lines to record prices for another article; so approximately 125 commodities could be included on each page. Radically short abbreviations of monetary and metrological units economized both time and space. Since penmanship and a knowledge of paleography proved to be a rare combination, prices were dictated to clerks, who repeated each entry aloud, as a safeguard against error.

The calendar year was divided into the following quarters: January–March, April–June, July–September, and October–December. The earliest four purchases [1] in each quarter were recorded; so a total of sixteen quotations per year for each commodity was sought. The quantity, as well as the price, was invariably transcribed. When prices for several materially different grades or quantities of a significant commodity recurred frequently, four quarterly quotations of each were recorded.[2] Cartage was uniformly either included or excluded in transcribing the prices of bulky commodities such as wine, grain, and building

---

[1] Obviously erroneous or abnormal data were omitted.

[2] For instance, four wholesale and four retail quotations of white, brown, and loaf sugar, making a possible total of twenty-four entries per quarter, were recorded when they occurred frequently.

materials. The practice of the contemporary accountants was usually adopted, but in all cases it proved necessary to make adjustments for changes in the accountants' methods of entering local transportation costs.

After practice had demonstrated the undesirability of multiple forms for each year, the secondary series in each region were transcribed on the same folios with the primary data in a different color of ink.

Even prices from the same locality were not crudely averaged with the main series unless substantially similar quantities of identical quality were bought at prices that agreed closely. Otherwise, local series were combined, as were those of different towns, only by means of average correlations. To avoid the distortion of annual averages by missing quarterly quotations, the data were subjected to elaborate statistical treatment. Appendix I describes the methods employed in computing the annual averages included in the regional index numbers of commodity prices.

IV

To economize space in printing and to lessen bias in the index numbers, separate price series for each of the half-centuries included in the present study have been compiled.

Owing to the cardinal importance of wheat and barley, particularly the former, the adoption of a "grain harvest year" from July 1 to June 30 was considered; but this procedure was rejected for the following reasons. Harvests of olive oil and common wine,[1] commodities that rivaled grain in importance, reached the market in the first quarter rather than the third, while rice, oranges, and nuts were a full quarter later than wheat. A difference of several weeks in the seasons would require different datings of the harvest year for Andalusia and Old Castile-León. All commodities considered, it seems that no better harvest year than the calendar

---

[1] The Ordinances of Valladolid approved by Charles V on July 20, 1549, prohibited the sale of unripe wine and declared that it could not ripen before *San Andrés* (November 30) next following the harvest (*Ordenanzas de Valladolid* [Valladolid, 1737], Ordenanza xli). In fact, however, new wine did not reach the market in large quantities before late December or early January.

year itself can be contrived. Bating cases of original records in terms of harvest years, as Thorold Rogers found in England, data for calendar years can be transcribed and elaborated with considerably less difficulty. For the above reasons I have adopted the calendar year.

Regardless of the upward bias in this type of index number, the simple arithmetic mean has been chosen for the index numbers of prices and wages. To lessen, if not to eliminate, the effect of the bias, all the indices have been constructed on the averages for the middle decade as a base. This device was probably effective except in the second quarter of the seventeenth century, when wide dispersion of relatives resulting from unbridled vellon inflation doubtless produced an upward bias not counteracted by a similar tendency in the index numbers for 1601–1625, when inflation was moderate. Aside from its relative ease of construction, the simple arithmetic index number has been recognized as a desirable type for measuring changes in the purchasing power of money,[1] the greatest single desideratum of the present study. Furthermore, historians and other scholars, less familiar than economists and statisticians with the sophisticated averages embodied in the more complex index numbers employed at present, are likely to find the simple arithmetic index number the most comprehensible type. The simple arithmetic is used more frequently than any other index number to measure current social phenomena, and few laymen are familiar with any other kind.[2] I believe, moreover, that it would be absurd and otiose to apply hair-splitting methods to price tables no more accurate than the best that can be constructed for the sixteenth and seventeenth centuries.

With few exceptions, all the homogeneous commodities occurring in thirty-five or more years in each half-century, as well as unusually important articles appearing less frequently, have been

[1] W. C. Mitchell, "The Making and Using of Index Numbers," *Bulletin of the United States Bureau of Labor Statistics*, no. 284 (Washington, 1921), pp. 63, 71, 76–78.

[2] It might be argued on the other hand that only technicians understand the mechanics of even the simplest index numbers; that the average reader is likely to ascribe to statistical tables and charts greater precision than their compilers attempted or pretended to attain; and that therefore the most exact type of index number known should be used.

tabulated and included in the index numbers. Because of the scarcity of data for the first half of the sixteenth century, however, commodities having quotations for over half the years have been utilized. The number of articles was materially reduced by the rejection of all heterogeneous commodities such as mules, horses, cows, old wine, fine cloth, and precious ornaments as well as all goods sold by variable or indefinite weights and measures. Lambs and hens, for instance, have been accepted because the number purchased, usually totaling dozens or hundreds, furnished reliable averages.

A complete list of articles tabulated in one or more regions in at least one of the fifty-year periods, together with the Castilian and Valencian equivalents and the metrological units, appears in Appendix II.

A lack of space limits description of the commodities to the staples, several grades of which might have occurred. No one should suppose, however, that the bewildering variety of products to which we are accustomed at present existed in the sixteenth and seventeenth centuries. For instance, hospitals and even university students generally used an identical grade of olive oil for culinary purposes and sacramental illumination.[1] The prices of some of the leading commodities run in terms of the following grades: hulled white rice, average milling wheat, mattress wool, fresh (but not strictly fresh) eggs, white writing paper, laundry soap, milk cheese, unbleached and unfinished domestic, new wine (either red or white), fresh sardines, and live hens. Chemically prepared raisins (pasas de lejía) appear in the price tables for New Castile and sun-dried (pasas del sol or pasas azules) in the other regions. Mixed meal (tres farines) contained barley, horse beans (habas), and ivy beans (hiedras). It seems that beef and veal were indiscriminate cuts from the fore- or hind-quarters, but adequate descriptions have not been found. Ordinarily mutton was bought by the carcass, kid by the quarter, and salt pork by the side; and the respective pound prices run in terms of the average quality for these purchases. Lamb prices are for live animals

---

[1] Esgueva, *Libro de Cuentas de 1562*; Archivo Histórico Nacional, *Universidades, Colegio de San Ildefonso,* 768 f, 772 f.

averaging about 29 pounds (13.37 kilograms) when dressed. Brown sugar appears in the price tables for Andalusia and Old Castile-León, white sugar for Valencia, and loaf sugar for New Castile.

One of the outstanding defects of the index numbers is the dearth of textile prices. Many varieties of expensive cloth occurred frequently, but inadequate descriptions defeated every effort to assemble satisfactory price series. Realizing the weakness of textiles in most historical price studies, I spared no pains to fill this anticipated hiatus; yet if we classify twine, cotton lamp wicks, naval cables, hempen sandals, and burlap as textiles and count bedticks, shrouds, and four classes of thread, only twelve textiles occur in the consolidated list of commodities in Appendix II. The percentage of metals is still lower—lead, horseshoes, and large nails being the only (and not very satisfactory) representatives of this group. It should be remembered, however, that metals ranked far below textiles in importance at least until the end of the eighteenth century. Roughly two-thirds of the commodities are foods, with both vegetable and animal products well represented. Satisfactory series are also available for the following special groups: building materials, fruits and nuts, poultry, grain, fish, forestry products, and spices.

CHAPTER VII

WEIGHTS AND MEASURES

THE present chapter purposes to trace (solely from the point of view of the historian of prices)[1] the evolution of metrological standards, to describe regional and local departures from official units, and to discuss the weights and measures most commonly employed in commerce. Vast differences between their metrological systems require separate treatment for Castile and Valencia:

I. CASTILE

The most constant uniformity encountered by students of Castilian economic history is heterogeneity, and few economicohistorical phenomena in Castile have exhibited greater or more persistent diversity than has the evolution of weights and measures. The Moorish conquest obliterated the uniformity achieved by the Romans and maintained by the Visigoths, and the incomplete substitution of Christian for Moorish standards during the eight centuries of reconquest accentuated the confusion. In the definitively reconquered territory the diversity was perpetuated and intensified by the large measure of municipal autonomy in the Middle Ages, the climatic and ethnologic differences, the impediments to commerce and communication imposed by mountain ranges, the particularistic proclivities of the Castilians, the predilection of the Moriscos for their customary standards, and the aberrations of taxation. Throughout the modern period heterogeneity, incongruity, and inscrutability have characterized Castilian metrological usage.

---

[1] I disavow any pretension of exhaustive or even satisfactory treatment of Spanish metrology; but the possession of incomparably more original data than anyone has yet employed, together with the conviction that all systematic observations of perplexing phenomena encountered in pioneering price studies should be made available to economists, statisticians, and historians, amply justifies the present chapter.

Initiating a long series of futile projects for unification, on March 7, 1261, Alfonso X declared the *cahiz* of Toledo to be the standard for arid measures, the *moyo* of Valladolid for wine, the 10-pound *arrelde* of Burgos for meat, and the *vara*, or yard, and the *Alfonsí* mark (together with a pound of 16 ounces, an *arroba* of 25 pounds, and a quintal of 100 pounds, its common multiples), "which I send you," for lineal measures and weight respectively. The law provided severe penalties, rising to thirty days' imprisonment upon the third conviction, for sealing or using units not in conformity with the above standards.[1] In the Cortes of Jerez de la Frontera, in 1268, Alfonso X substituted the moyo of Seville for that of Valladolid and reduced the arrelde from 10 to 4 pounds.[2] The *Fuero Real* and the *Siete Partidas* enjoined the use of official weights and measures, but did not alter or even specify the standards.[3]

In the celebrated *Ordenamiento de Alcalá*, promulgated in the Cortes of 1348 in Alcalá de Henares, Alfonso XI declared that "in the kingdoms of our domain there are local weights and measures by which buyers and sellers receive great injury" and attempted to realize his learned grandfather's ambition to reform and unify Castilian metrology. Of the official units only the arrelde remained constant. The Toledo cahiz gave way to its much more frequently used fraction, the *fanega*, and the *cántara* of Toledo supplanted the moyo of Seville. But a true standard for liquids was not established. The cántara applied only to wine, and the law provided that such staples as olive oil and honey should be sold by weight. Standards of weight suffered the most revolutionary alterations. The Alfonsí mark was superseded by the Cologne mark for gold, silver, and vellon, and the Troy mark, with the multiples established in 1261, for all other commodities.

---

[1] Manuel Colmeiro, *Historia de la Economía Política en España* (Madrid, 1863), I, 452–453; Andrés Marcos Burriel (hereafter Burriel), *Informe de Toledo al Consejo de Castilla sobre Igualación de Pesos y Medidas* (Madrid, 1758), pp. 7–9, 391–393. The *Informe* was published as an official report from the city of Toledo, in which the name of Andrés Marcos Burriel does not appear; but it is generally recognized that the learned priest was its author. For brevity and the convenience of readers I have changed the Roman pagination of the first edition to Arabic.

[2] *Cortes de los Antiguos Reinos de Castilla y León* (hereafter *Cortes*), I, 75–76.

[3] Burriel, *op. cit.*, pp. 9–11.

In accordance with Moorish practice, the 10-arroba quintal of olive oil was recognized as standard in Seville and near the frontiers of the Moslem kingdoms of Málaga and Granada. The Castilian yard became the lineal standard. The requirement that cloth be measured along the selvedge on a plane with one inch in each yard doubled back — one of the most constant elements of subsequent metrological statutes [1] — made its first appearance.[2] If we may judge by the petitions of the Cortes, the attempted reform of 1348 failed flatly. In 1367 and again in 1369 the *Procuradores* informed Henry II that some cities, towns, and villages had neglected to adopt the national standards and urged his Majesty to enforce the law of 1348.[3]

Complaining that metrological chaos impeded commerce and detracted from the public welfare, the Cortes of 1435 petitioned John II to unify weights and measures throughout Castile. Accordingly, a sweeping reform was undertaken. The fanega of Ávila superseded that of Toledo. Existing contracts in terms of the Toledo measure remained valid; but the Ávila fanega became the legal standard for future engagements, and notaries were forbidden to certify a contract in terms of a different unit. The law of 1435 failed to mention the arrelde and left the standard for wine unchanged. The yard of Toledo, one-eighth longer than the Castilian, became the legal (but not the actual) standard for lineal measures. For weighing silver the mark of Burgos was adopted, as was that of Toledo for gold; but these marks were of identical magnitude.[4] The pound, arroba, and quintal of Toledo, where the pound consisted of 16 Cologne ounces (or 2 Cologne marks), supplanted the corresponding units based on the pound of 16 Troy ounces for all commodities, except jewels and the pre-

---

[1] *Vide*, for example, Biblioteca Nacional (hereafter BN), *Varios*, 1–49–7; *Cortes,* III, 227–229, 322; IV, 664; V, 441–442; *Actas de las Cortes de Castilla* (hereafter *Actas*), XVI, 651.

[2] *Cortes*, I, 534; Manuel Colmeiro, *op. cit.*, I, 454–455; *Recopilación de Leyes de España* (hereafter *Recopilación*), lib. V, tit. XIII, ley I.

[3] *Cortes*, II, 149, 181–182.

[4] Both cities having adopted the Cologne mark, the only difference was that the usual fractions of the Burgos standard corresponded to those of the silver mark and of the Toledo unit to those of the gold mark (Manuel Colmeiro, *op. cit.*, I, 456; Burriel, *op. cit.*, pp. 21–24; José García Caballero, *Breve Cotejo y Valance de las Pesas y Medidas* [Madrid, 1731], p. 6).

cious metals. Apparently for the first time, elaborate provisions were made for the dissemination of the official weights and measures. Hitherto the central government had relied upon each municipality to procure, without compulsion, the national standards; but the law of 1435 instructed the cities, towns, and villages to send to Ávila for a fanega, to Burgos for the silver mark, and to Toledo for all other standards before the end of May. Municipal authorities were ordered to preconize in markets and public squares that the new units would become effective on June 1, 1435.[1]

Doubtless because of superior provision for its enforcement, the statute of 1435, unlike previous metrological legislation, immediately influenced practice; and with characteristic fickleness, the Cortes hastened to denounce the reform they had instigated. In petition number I the Cortes of 1436 opposed unification of weights and measures on the general principle that national laws should not run counter to local customs. The Procuradores also adduced several specific objections. They argued that the pound of 16 Cologne ounces was approximately 2 ounces lighter than the Troy pound, which it had superseded, but that sellers, fewer in number and better organized than buyers, had not abated their pound prices upon the adoption of the new standard. The Cortes complained that similar solidarity of sellers had enabled them to increase yard prices by one-fourth, whereas the standard had been augmented only one-eighth. They urged the Crown to revert to the units of weight established in 1348, that is, to the Cologne mark for the precious metals and jewels and to the pound of 16 Troy ounces for all other commodities. Advocating a still more backward step, the Procuradores urged his Majesty to legalize the unofficial local measures for cloth, grain, and wine in use before 1435. To justify the legalization of local *de facto* units for grain and wine, they advanced the absurd argument that small measures favored the producing regions, whereas large ones benefited consuming areas.[2] From a belief in 1436 that the statute of

---

[1] *Cortes*, III, 227–229; Burriel, *op. cit.*, pp. 28–30; Manuel Colmeiro, *op. cit.*, I, 455–457.

[2] *Cortes*, III, 255–257.

1435 had produced excessive uniformity and proved injurious because of the sudden suppression of local units, by 1438 the Cortes had veered to the conviction that local custom had rendered the law nugatory, that "in many places the weights and measures that prevailed formerly are used." The Procuradores entreated his Majesty to enforce the law of 1435 and to require that salt and vegetables be measured by the Ávila fanega and honey and olive oil — hitherto sold by weight — by the cántara of Toledo.[1] John II granted this petition; but there is no evidence that olive oil was ever measured by the Toledo wine standard, and the subsequent sale of honey by weight appears constantly in some regions and occasionally in others. In 1462 the Cortes complained that in certain cities, towns, and villages unofficial standards of weight and measure were in general use and requested the Crown to enforce the prohibitory laws. Henry IV acceded; but since the royal authority was then at its nadir, his resolution availed little.[2] In fact, the city of Toledo, which, more than any other municipality, furnished Castile her metrological units, had to issue an ordinance the following year to forestall the introduction of Medina del Campo standards.[3]

Although adequate data are lacking, one naturally infers that — despite judicious legislation — baronial anarchy under Henry IV entailed further regional divergency of weights and measures and that upon the accession of the Catholic Kings chaos was rife. Like other internal improvements, however, metrological reform had to await the settlement of grave dynastic and political problems. Not until 1488, nine years after La Beltraneja had taken the veil and one after the capture of Málaga and the progress of the siege had rendered inevitable the fall of Granada, did Ferdinand and Isabella set themselves seriously to unify weights and measures. In harmony with their centralizing proclivities they began in 1488 to assume the responsibility for the construction, custody, and dissemination of a true standard of weight. On April 12, 1488, the newly created *marcador mayor* (chief of standards) was directed to prepare the marks and their fractions em-

---

[1] *Cortes*, III, 322; Burriel, *op. cit.*, pp. 30–32.
[2] *Cortes*, III, 720; Burriel, *op. cit.*, p. 32.   [3] *Ibid.*, p. 143.

ployed in weighing gold and silver and to carry or send these standards to the mints and the *cabezas de partidos*.[1] To extirpate the discrepancies between ounces and thus to attain absolute unity, on October 13, 1488, the Catholic Kings decreed that the weights of all commodities should conform to the recently distributed standards for the precious metals.[2] In all probability these standards were based upon copies, more or less exact, of the Cologne mark, the official unit for treasure since at least 1348 and for all commodities since 1435.[3] In 1494 the Catholic Kings issued four pragmatics concerning lineal measures, but did not name the standard.[4] On January 7, 1496, they extended the legislation of 1488 to measures; provided for the hierarchical distribution of arid and liquid standards, as units of weight had been diffused in 1488; ordered the cabezas de partidos and ecclesiastical sees to procure immediately the standards for arids from Ávila and for liquids from Toledo; and instructed municipalities to secure copies of these units within thirty days after the preconization of the pragmatic. The statute fixed severe penalties for the manufacture or use of unauthorized measures and forbade notaries to write or certify and judges to enforce contracts in terms of unofficial cántaras or fanegas.[5]

As in the case of monetary reform, the metrological advance of the Catholic Kings sprang largely from superior administration of preëxisting statutes rather than from progressive legislation. While altering no standard, they devised administrative machinery peculiarly amenable to control by the Crown and assiduously enforced the laws.

With the burden of empire and the cares of state constantly upon him, Charles V had little time for such a prosaic matter as

---

[1] Manuel Colmeiro, *op. cit.*, I, 457–458; Burriel, *op. cit.*, pp. 36–38; *Recopilación*, lib. v, tit. xxii, leyes v, vii, ix. The cabeza de partido was the capital of an administrative and judicial subdivision of the province.

[2] *Recopilación*, lib. v, tit. xxii, ley xix; Burriel, *op. cit.*, pp. 40–41.

[3] Burriel (*op. cit.*, pp. 329, 362) maintains that the Alfonsí mark adopted in 1261 was identical with the Cologne mark.

[4] *Ibid.*, p. 41.

[5] *Pramáticas del Reyno, Recopilación de Algunas Bulas* . . . (Alcalá de Henares, 1528), fols. 129–130; *Recopilación*, lib. v, tit. xiii, ley ii; Manuel Colmeiro, *op. cit.*, I, 458–459.

weights and measures. Regardless of the deluge of petitions from the Cortes,[1] he neglected metrological reform; and the same is largely true of his illustrious successor. In 1563 Philip II confirmed the law of 1438 adopting the Ávila fanega for arids and enjoining the sale of honey "and all other things which by similar measures may be sold" by the Toledo wine measure.[2] But the confirmation of the injunction to use the Ávila fanega and the Toledo cántara proved no more effective than the original enactment. The sale of produce by weight continued unabated, and nowhere was the cántara of Toledo used consistently for honey, least of all in Toledo. On June 24, 1568, the Castilian yard, nominally at least, superseded that of Toledo. Philip II ordered the cabezas de partidos to obtain and distribute the Burgos standard in the usual fashion.[3] The complete absence of a decline in textile prices after 1568, with due allowance for the general Price Revolution, and a lack of protests from the Cortes or the public such as usually attended the introduction of a new standard suggest continuation of the previously existing lineal unit. In fact, the text of the pragmatic of 1568 indicates on the part of the framers ignorance of the adoption of the Toledo vara in 1435 and signifies the intention of the Crown to enforce the legal vara, adopted in 1348, rather than to impose a new standard.[4]

Uncritical examination of lib. v, tit. XXIII, ley I of the *Recopilación* has led some writers [5] to assert that Philip II reverted to the Toledo fanega and the Troy mark. The *Recopilación* erroneously lists the pragmatic of June 24, 1568, endorsing uniformity of weights and measures and readopting the Castilian yard as a confirmation of the law of 1348; but it is highly probable that

---

[1] *Vide*, for instance, *Cortes*, IV, 548–549; V, 144, 250–251, 396, 554.

[2] *Recopilación*, lib. v, tit. XIII, ley III.

[3] BN, *Varios*, 1–49–7; Burriel, *op. cit.*, pp. 55, 161–162; *Recopilación*, lib. v, tit. XIII, ley I.

[4] If we accept the testimony of the pragmatic itself, the use of a yard "much shorter than that of *Burgos*" in the fair at Medina del Campo, the center of the cloth trade, and complaints against the diversity of lineal measures precipitated the legislation. The pragmatic does not mention the Toledo vara and refers to failure to accept the standard adopted by Alfonso XI.

[5] For instance, Manuel Colmeiro (*op. cit.*, II, 522) and José García Caballero (*op. cit.*, p. 107). Caballero erroneously states that the Cologne and Troy ounces were of equal magnitude (*op. cit.*, pp. 106–107).

Philip II did not attempt to restore the Toledo fanega or the Troy mark, and certain that, in case he did, the effort availed nothing.

From June 24, 1568, to the adoption of the metric system, in 1849, no changes occurred in Castilian metrological standards. But in 1601 the institution of the national *sisa* — a special tax on wine and olive oil, extended to vinegar in 1602 — introduced duality into liquid measures. Technically the cántara remained unchanged, but dealers were ordered to deliver 7 *azumbres* and to pay the government a sisa equivalent to the value of 1 azumbre per cántara sold to final consumers.[1] Since retail purchasers ordinarily bought wine by the azumbre or *cuartillo* (quarter-azumbre) and olive oil by the pound or *panilla* (quarter-pound), these measures were affected most of all. As formerly, grocers and tavern keepers received the standard cántara of wine, but retained one-eighth the nominal quantity of each sale and paid the corresponding tax to the government. Retailers bought and sold olive oil in identical fashion. Institutions and large households purchased both wine and olive oil by the cántara or arroba and, presumably by paying a higher price — in which case the sisa became a true excise tax —, received the full measures. It was the normal, though not invariable, practice of the hospitals and convents to obtain the cántara of 8 azumbres of wine and the arroba of 25 pounds of olive oil.[2] Naturally there was a long-run tendency for the price to rise by approximately the amount of the tax; so the economic result of the sisa was the same whether the price rose or the measure fell. With the concomitant confusion easily imagined, the sisa uniformly reduced the fractional measures of wine, vinegar, and olive oil by one-eighth and introduced new arrobas and cántaras,[3] the *menores* or *sisadas*, one-

[1] *Actas*, XVIII, 621; XIX, 48, 680–684, 761–767; XX, 129, 689–696. Cities having a local sisa on wine petitioned the Crown for permission to substitute a sisa on some other commodity (*Actas*, XIX, 682).

[2] One cannot be sure that purchases by convents or even hospitals, virtually all of which were ecclesiastical foundations, paid the sisa before 1618. On August 8, 1618, Pope Paul V formally conceded Castile the authority to collect the sisa on wine, olive oil, vinegar, and meat from churches, convents, monasteries, and religious orders. The papal grant was conditioned upon the expenditure of the resultant funds in defense of the Catholic faith (*Actas*, XXXIV, 353–357).

[3] The Convent of Santa Ana in Valladolid recorded more sales than receipts of wine from the harvest of 1643 and ascribed the anomaly to the use of standard

eighth smaller than the *mayores* or *no sisadas*. Fortunately, the accounts of hospitals and convents usually record arroba and cántara prices, and in these entries the old measure survived. Although unqualified generalization is not possible, one may say that in institutional records the simple terms *arroba* and *cántara* refer to the sixteenth-century standards. When the new units are employed, the accounts ordinarily, though not invariably, make the fact clear. At any rate, these have proved sound hypotheses in attacking new series of price records.

Particularly important were the manner and degree of inspection of weights and measures. Through the *almotacenes* or *fieles*, among the oldest and most important functionaries, the municipalities had long exercised effective control over local units. In keeping with the traditions of medieval municipal liberty, the Castilian monarchs vested the administration of the incipient national standards in the *concejos*. In 1261, 1268, and 1348 the Crown had relied upon the municipalities to procure, without compulsion, the official weights and measures and upon local inspectors to require their observance. Noting the obstinate retention of local units, John II ordered the cities to provide themselves with the standards adopted in 1435. But after a season of partial effectiveness the decree was nullified by perfunctory municipal inspection. In 1462 the Cortes denounced the perplexing diversity of weights and measures and requested the King to send two royal representatives throughout the kingdom to require conformity with national standards.[1] By granting their request, Henry IV took the initial step in establishing royal inspection, a *sine qua non* of uniformity. The chaos engendered by baronial and dynastic strife stifled the new institution under Henry the Impotent; but, in characteristic fashion, the Catholic Kings utilized the precedent thus established to centralize control in the Crown.

On April 12, 1488, Ferdinand and Isabella charged Pedro Vegil de Quiñones, the first marcador mayor, with the construction,

---

cántaras for receipts and azumbres and cuartillos sisados for their sales (Archivo Histórico Nacional [hereafter AHN], *Clero*, Valladolid, *Convento de Santa Ana*, leg. 346).

[1] *Cortes*, III, 720.

custody, and dissemination of official weights. Moreover, the marcador became responsible for inspecting the weights and measures of the cabezas de partidos; and a sealer, royally appointed and responsible to the Castilian marcador, in the beginning at least, was placed in each cabeza de partido. Still another medium of royal control was devised. The *corregidor*, one of the most important instruments of the Catholic Kings and the Hapsburgs in the suppression of municipal liberty, also became an effective agent for the generalization of metrological standards. Upon taking office, the corregidor required everyone to present his weights and measures for inspection and, if necessary, adjustment to the official units.[1] At last, reasonably efficient machinery for imposing metrological uniformity emerged; and had the Catholic Queen lived longer, satisfactory unity might have been attained. But her successors, obsessed with diplomacy and external aggrandizement, neglected the standardization she inaugurated.

The intelligence, industry, and probity of Pedro Vegil de Quiñones and Diego de Ayala, the first two marcadores mayores, contrast strikingly with the incompetence, dishonesty, and negligence of their successors. Beginning in 1553, when Juan de Ayala succeeded his father, Diego, the post became a sinecure; and appointments rested on favoritism rather than fitness. Bureaucratic inertia was followed by blackmail, extortion, and vice. Writing in 1572, the celebrated Juan de Arphe y Villafañe [2] complained that the marcadores mayores had ceased to construct and seal standards, that commercial weights and measures were being adjusted to the units supplied the cabezas de partidos by Diego de Ayala, and that most of the weights — presumably too light because of abrasion — had been repaired by the addition of tin.

By 1593 Antonio Muñoz, a silversmith who had temporarily succeeded Juan de Ayala, commenced to send deputies into the provinces to inspect commercial weights and measures. Regardless of the fact that the new practice, when honestly conducted,

---

[1] Complying with a petition of the Cortes in 1534, Charles V ordered the corregidores to allow his subjects a reasonable interval — after preconization of the order — in which to present their weights and measures for inspection (*Cortes*, IV, 599; *Recopilación*, lib. V, tit. XIII, ley IV; lib. III, tit. V, ley XIX).

[2] *Vide* Burriel, *op. cit.*, pp. 366–367.

furnished the surest possible means of unification of standards, if we may judge by a protest from the Cortes on February 12, 1593, the activity of Muñoz proved more unpopular than the lethargy of Ayala.[1] Before the royal signature was affixed to his title as marcador mayor in 1596, Felipe de Benavides began to deputize sealers, who, by officious conduct throughout the kingdom, promptly incurred public disfavor.[2] On February 13, 1597, the Cortes approved a memorial to the Crown charging that instead of inspecting weights and measures, the minions of Benavides were extorting bribes from petty tradesmen for protection from prosecution, collecting exorbitant fees for adjusting and sealing, and punishing violations of the law only in order to share in the fines.[3] On the same date began the ardent and protracted struggle of the Cortes to limit the prerogatives of the marcador mayor to those enjoyed by Juan de Ayala. Insisting that the time-honored institution of local inspection was efficient and adequate, the Procuradores asked Philip II to restrict the marcador mayor to the impotent rôle of supplying standards to the cabezas de partidos from a fixed domicile.[4] To obtain data for the commissioners negotiating with the Crown, on August 8, 1597, the Cortes instructed the Procuradores to consult their respective cities concerning the excesses and outrages committed by the deputies of Felipe de Benavides.[5]

By 1599 Juan Beltrán de Benavides, the most unpopular of all the marcadores mayores, had succeeded his father. In a memorial to the Crown, on February 27, the Cortes denounced his agents as brigands, unjustly punishing bold traders in order to participate in their fines and exacting tribute from the timorous for immunity from prosecution. The Procuradores alleged, moreover, that by enjoining local inspectors from sealing during their visits the agents of Benavides hampered honest metrology, that their blackmail and pillage were shamelessly frequent, and that they collected exorbitant and illegal fees for adjusting and sealing.[6]

[1] *Actas*, XII, 322–323.
[2] *Ibid.*, XV, 122–123, 135–136.
[3] *Ibid.*, XV, 418–419.
[4] *Ibid.*, XV, 417, 420.
[5] *Ibid.*, XV, 533.
[6] *Ibid.*, XVIII, 160–163.

Remonstrance having proved fruitless, the Cortes exploited the impecuniosity inherited by Philip III. In 1600 they conditioned the grant of 18,000,000 ducats upon his Majesty's promise to revert to the functions of the marcador mayor exercised by Juan de Ayala.[1] Dependent upon this subsidy to avert state bankruptcy, Philip III accepted the terms of the Cortes.[2] On January 1, 1601, he limited the authority of the marcador mayor to that of furnishing standards to the cabezas de partidos and revoked the increase in fees conceded the Benavides,[3] and in a pragmatic of February 7, 1602, he formally limited the prerogatives of the marcador to those enjoyed by Juan de Ayala.[4] The ambiguity of this pragmatic, coupled with the aggressiveness of the marcador mayor, the Cortes, and several municipalities, immediately evoked litigation before the Council of Castile.[5] In August, 1607, while a suit before the Council was pending, the Procuradores wrote the cities represented in the Cortes that under the terms of a subsidy to the Crown Benavides could furnish standards to the cabezas de partidos; that he could inspect the standards he issued; that the inspection of commercial weights and measures rested entirely with municipal authorities; that neither Benavides nor his agents should usurp judicial functions; and that in case the marcador or his henchmen should exceed the authority exercised by Juan de Ayala they should be arrested and sent to the capital, where the Cortes would institute criminal proceedings.[6] Few matters elicited more parliamentary discussion in 1607–1609 than did the inspection of weights and measures; and the service of 17,500,000 ducats was granted only upon a royal promise, embodied in a pragmatic of September 4, 1609, to limit the marcador mayor to the function of furnishing standards to the cities represented in the Cortes, which in turn should supply the cabezas de partidos, and to a biennial inspection of the units he issued. He and his agents were specifically forbidden to seal commercial weights and measures or to exercise judicial authority.[7] In the

---

[1] *Actas*, XIX, 169, 176, 410–411, 433, 441.   [2] *Ibid.*, XIX, 433, 451, 694–695.
[3] *Ibid.*, XIX, 711–712.   [4] *Ibid.*, XXXII, 69.
[5] *Ibid.*, XXI, 435; XXII, 345.   [6] *Ibid.*, XXIII, 266–267, 327–328.
[7] *Ibid.*, XIII, 369, 468–469, 576–577; XXIV, 776–777; XXXII, 69; *Recopilación*, lib. v, tit. XXII, ley XXI.

midst of the litigation before the Council of Castile and of the adverse parliamentary criticism, Benavides, far from being cowed into submission, secured a mandamus from the *alcalde*, Fernández Portocarrero, directing every dealer in Madrid to submit his weights and measures to the marcador mayor within twenty days and enjoining the municipal marcador from sealing in the interim. Armed with the mandamus, Benavides haughtily proceeded to inspect commercial units, and for violation of the injunction he imprisoned the local sealer.[1] Victory in the litigation before the Council of Castile and assiduous negotiation with the Crown availed little in the struggle of the Cortes to curb the activity of the marcador mayor; and by 1615, when the Council of the Treasury began to sell the post of municipal sealer at public auction, the last vestige of local control was irreparably impaired.[2] In 1618[3] and again in 1632[4] the Cortes wrested from the Crown, as a condition for a subsidy, a promise — virtually a renewal of that of 1609 — to restrict the powers of the marcador. But by this time the impotence of the Cortes was rivaled only by the weakness of the Crown, and there was nothing to make the agreement less fragile than its predecessors.

In 1614 Philip III installed in the public granary at Seville a measurer of wheat (medidor de trigo), with more than a score of lieutenants, empowered to collect a fee of 4 maravedís per fanega.[5] Apparently this institution was confined to Seville, but it immediately incurred public disfavor. Apprehending a spread of the office to other cities, the Cortes of 1618 and 1632 required the Crown, as a condition for the grant of a subsidy, to agree not to establish municipal grain measurers nor to authorize the collection of fees for this service.[6]

The inveterate adherence of custom-bound and particularistic Castile to local units — together with the prevalence of dishonest, haughty, and incompetent marcadores mayores and deputies —

---

[1] *Actas*, XXIV, 151, 243–244, 250, 522, 528; XXV, 64–65, 210–211.
[2] *Ibid.*, XXVIII, 130–131, 217.
[3] *Ibid.*, XXXII, 69–70.
[4] *Recopilación*, lib. v, tit. XXII, ley XXI.
[5] *Actas*, XXVIII, 131, 247; XXXII, 315.
[6] *Ibid.*, XXXII, 315–316; *Recopilación*, lib. v, tit. XIII, ley VIII.

defeated the efforts to unify weights and measures through centralized control. Some progress toward standardization resulted from the institution of the marcador mayor, but local units did not entirely disappear. In fact, the Bourbons failed to establish a national system. Writing in 1731, José García Caballero,[1] marcador mayor of Castile, said: "Rare is the city, town, or hamlet in which the weights or measures conform to the standards of the kingdom"; and throughout the eighteenth century the Cortes deluged the Crown with petitions to unify weights and measures. In 1801 Charles IV extended the Castilian units to the remainder of Spain, but Manuel Colmeiro wrote in 1863 [2] that in Aragon, Catalonia, and Valencia both the Castilian and the metric systems had successively failed to supplant the ancient standards in retail trade. Even yet petty traders in the most important commercial centers of Spain (Seville, Valencia, Madrid, and Barcelona, for example) have not entirely abandoned the old local or regional units.

Chronic diversity of weights and measures followed Castilians to the New World.[3] On November 12, 1626, Andrés Deza, for twenty-eight years a resident of Peru, memorialized the Crown against the great divergence between the metrological units of adjacent Peruvian municipalities and requested Philip IV to adopt the standards of Seville in the Hispanic colonies.[4]

The persistence of local units in defiance of prohibitory legislation favors not less than it hinders the historian of prices who maintains rigid regional separation of data. Although weights and measures varied widely among different districts, resistance to metrological reform conduced to perdurable uniformity in a given locality,[5] an important desideratum of the price historian, chiefly concerned with protracted homogeneity of data. Not only

---

[1] *Op. cit.*, p. 8.

[2] *Op. cit.*, II, 523.

[3] On September 28, 1512, Ferdinand the Catholic extended the authority of Diego de Ayala, the Castilian marcador mayor, to the Indies (Archivo de Simancas [hereafter AS], *Títulos Rasgados*, 1).

[4] BN, *Raros*, 17,270, fols. 124–127.

[5] Burriel argued that, with the exception of the vara, the weights and measures established by Alfonso X, on March 7, 1261, "had subsisted for 500 years . . . without substantial variation" in Toledo (*op. cit.*, p. 9).

is there sharp separation of regions in the present study, but quotations from a particular city serve as the standard for each commodity. Interpolations from other localities are made only by average correlations. Hence constant discrepancies in local standards, however great, can hardly disturb the uniformity of a series.

Let us consider the evolution, regional variations, and present equivalents of the metrological standards used in Castile from 1501 to 1650. The reader should recall that precise measurements are modern phenomena, both consequences and causes of scientific and industrial progress. In no country did the arts of weighing and measuring prior to 1650 even approach present standards of proficiency. The dearth of manufactures and the dependence of Spain upon foreign engineers [1] indicate relative technological backwardness. Burriel tells us that Castilian marcadores, unable to construct accurate weights, were forced to import units, which, after adjustment, served as standards.[2] The necessity of a formal prohibition near the end of the fifteenth century against the use of wheat grains to weigh coins,[3] the failure of metrological statutes and ordinances to specify whether arid measures should be heaped or stricken, and the persistence of such inaccurate units as "load," "bag," and "basket" attest the crudity of Castilian metrology. There is no reason to believe that successive purchases of nominally equal amounts of, say, wheat on the same day in a given locality necessarily represent identical magnitudes.[4] Every effort has been made to detect and allow for variations in local units,

---

[1] For instance, Philip II relied upon German engineers to build and operate the water-propelled mint at Segovia and employed them extensively in the silver mine at Guadalcanal (AS, *Estado*, 138).

[2] *Op. cit.*, pp. 369–370.

[3] José García Caballero, *op. cit.*, p. 11; *Recopilación*, lib. v, tit. xxii, leyes iii–vi. But medieval Castile was not alone in using wheat grains as a metrological standard. For instance, an act of Henry III (51 Henry III) in 1266 states "that by the consent of the whole realm of England, the measure of our Lord the King was made, viz., an English penny, called a sterling, round and without any clipping, shall weigh 32 wheatcorns in the midst of the ear; and 20 pence do make an ounce, and 12 ounces a pound; and 8 pounds do make a gallon of wine, and 8 gallons of wine do make a bushel, which is the eighth part of a quarter" (H. W. Chisholm, *On the Science of Weighing and Measuring* [London, 1877], p. 55).

[4] Modern examples of crude metrological standards and practices abound in rural North America. Furthermore, in the most advanced urban communities commercial weights and measures are considerably less accurate than those of scientific laboratories, themselves not absolutely precise.

once established. Since alterations of standards caused a similar variation of prices, one may be fairly certain that significant changes have not escaped notice. But the reductions to modern equivalents are much less certain. Since the needs of the present study are met by establishing either the constancy or percentage of change in a unit, no extensive inductive inquiry into modern metrological equivalents is justified. Hence on this point I have relied upon critical utilization of the work of others, and the reader is warned that Spanish metrology has proved singularly unattractive to scholars.

Arid Measures

Of the commodities included in the present index numbers only barley, wheat, rye, bran, chick-peas, filberts, walnuts, ashes, coriander, beans (habas), lentils, mustard, plaster of Paris, lime, acorns, and occasionally chestnuts were exchanged by arid measures. The percentage of the total ranged from 6.41 in New Castile to 14.09 in Old Castile-León and averaged 11.2 in the three regions. Wheat and chick-peas, two of the chief articles of food, enhance the significance of these commodities; but barley and bran were used almost exclusively to feed animals, and rye was seldom grown or sold outside of León and northern Castile. Walnuts and filberts appear almost entirely as a Christmas delicacy. Lime and plaster of Paris were leading building materials, but coriander and mustard ranked as unimportant condiments. The consumption of chestnuts, acorns, and lentils was always small, and habas occurred only in Andalusia. Used directly in laundering as well as in the manufacture of lye, ashes were not trivial.

The following table lists the multiples and fractions of the fanega, the standard for arid measures.

TABLE 11

ARID MEASURES IN CASTILE

12 cucharas	= 1 celemín or almud [1]	12 celemines	= 1 fanega
4 cuartillos	= 1 celemín	4 fanegas	= 1 carga (grain)
4 celemines	= 1 hemina	12 fanegas	= 1 cahiz

[1] The *almud*, a Moorish term, prevailed in Andalusia, the region longest under Moslem domination, and the *celemín* in Old and New Castile and León.

The *cuchara* and the cuartillo were too small, and the cahiz was too large for general use; so the celemín and the fanega governed most purchases. The former occurred more frequently in retail and the latter in wholesale trade. The *hemina* appeared only in León [1] and the neighboring districts of Old Castile. Large quantities of grain were sold by the *carga* — invariably equivalent to 4 fanegas — almost exclusively in León, often in Old and New Castile, and occasionally in Andalusia. This measure should not be confused with the carga of lime or plaster of Paris, which was generally, though not always, equivalent to 1 fanega, nor with the indefinite term *carga*, or load, which represented the capacity of a boat, vehicle, or pack animal.

The estimates of most modern writers for the fanega of Ávila, official for the kingdom of Castile after 1435, range around 55.5 liters,[2] and this figure may be considered roughly correct.

With characteristic inexactitude, Castilian metrological pragmatics fail to mention heaped or stricken measures. In this respect I have only indirect evidence concerning even the official standards. Through diligent search I have unearthed wheat and barley prices in Ávila for ten years in the second quarter of the sixteenth century and eleven in the second quarter of the seventeenth.[3] In the absence of better data these obviously inadequate prices furnish some basis for comparing Ávila measures with those of the regions for which grain quotations are abundant. In accordance with the statute of 1435 Toledo adopted the fanega of Ávila; yet there is satisfactory evidence that in the ensuing three centuries the Ávila fanega slightly exceeded that of Toledo.[4] Municipal ordinances indicate that heaped measures prevailed in Toledo in the second half of the fifteenth century,[5] and fanega prices do not reflect a departure from this custom before 1650.

[1] The hemina was a very common unit in León (*vide*, for example, AHN, *Clero*, León, *Convento de Nuestra Señora de Sandoval*, legs. 244, 246–248).

[2] J. F. Saigey (*Traité de Métrologie Ancienne et Moderne* [Paris, 1834], p. 142) gives the slightly higher figure of 56.3 liters.

[3] Hospital Provincial, Ávila, *Dios Padre*, 1–3, 2–8; *Misericordia*, 2–28; *Santa Escolástica*, 2–7, 3–1, 3–4; *Santa María Magdalena*, 2–18, 2–19.

[4] Besides my comparisons of grain prices I have the testimony of Burriel (*op. cit.*, pp. 334–335) at the middle of the eighteenth century. Manuel Colmeiro agrees that the fanega of Ávila was slightly larger than that of Toledo (*op. cit.*, I, 456).

[5] Burriel, *op. cit.*, pp. 136–139, 141.

That the arid measures of Ávila were also heaped is a reasonable inference. The Ordinances of Valladolid approved by Charles V on July 20, 1549, provided that 50 per cent of the measures of oats and lime should be heaped and the remainder stricken.[1] Although other arids are not mentioned, it is highly probable that the Ordinances merely applied customary methods to oats, a grain rarely exchanged, and lime, a commodity frequently sold by the load. A municipal ordinance forbidding the sealer to approve arid units not equally wide at the base and the mouth and requiring the gratuitous sealing of straightedges[2] confirms the hypothesis of alternation between heaped and stricken measures in Valladolid. Comparisons of prices and the estimates of metrologists indicate that Burgos and Palencia adopted the Ávila fanega and that the arid measures of León were about 20 per cent below the Castilian standards. The great increase in Seville grain quotations during the Price Revolution invalidates price comparisons, but metrological estimates place the Seville fanega at 54.7 liters, or about 1.5 per cent below the Castilian standard. The fanega of Valladolid is estimated at 54.8 liters, and average prices suggest rough equivalence to that of Ávila.[3]

Lineal Measures

The great dearth of satisfactory textile quotations renders lineal measures the least important of all the metrological standards. Lineal units measured only about 1.25 per cent of the total commodities included in the index numbers for the three regions. The following table lists the customary fractions of the vara, or yard.

TABLE 12

LINEAL MEASURES IN CASTILE

12 pulgadas = 1 pie	4 palmos = 1 pie	
16 dedos = 1 pie	3 pies = 1 vara	
	2 codos = 1 vara	

---

[1] *Ordenanzas con que se Rige y Gobierna la República de Valladolid* (ed. Valladolid, 1818), ordenanzas IV, LVI.

[2] *Ordenanzas de Valladolid*, ordenanza XXI.

[3] The slight discrepancy may be due to the fact that 50 per cent of the measures in Valladolid were stricken, but the difference appears too small to substantiate this hypothesis.

Only the vara and the *palmo* occur frequently as textile measures. The *pulgada* and the *dedo* were too small for general commercial use, and sales by the *pie* or *codo* were rare.

Estimates of the equivalence of the Burgos, or Castilian, yard
— the *de jure* standard for the kingdom of Castile after 1568 and
the *de facto* standard in most cities from 1501 to 1650 [1] — range
from .8359 to .8379 meter, and one may consider .84 meter approximately correct. Only León, Toledo, and Valladolid furnish
continuous textile prices, and linen alone provided a homogeneous
series in each locality. Insufficient knowledge of the grade and
width of the cloth excludes metrological comparisons through
average prices; but the linen quotations of Valladolid and León
suggest a common unit, and metrologists agree that both cities
employed the standard of Burgos. That the Toledo yard remained constant from 1501 to 1650 is all that I venture positively
to affirm. The normal rise of linen prices after 1568 indicates
either that, contrary to law, the Castilian yard prevailed prior to
this date or that the unit of Toledo illegally continued afterward.
Burriel cited municipal ordinances to prove that the Castilian
yard, along with the local unit, enjoyed legal status in Toledo
after 1435,[2] when it lost acceptance as a national standard; and
in 1758 he placed the lineal units of Toledo 2 per cent below those
of Madrid, Segovia, and Ávila, where the vara of Burgos had been
adopted.[3] This estimate agrees with those of modern metrologists. Hence it is safe to assume that the attempted substitution
of the ancient yard of Toledo for the Castilian, in 1435, failed even
in Toledo; that in 1568 Philip II merely legalized the firmly established *de facto* unit; and that from 1501 to 1650 Toledo employed
a slightly debased Burgos standard.

Liquid Measures

Measuring only 4.23 per cent of the total commodities in Old
Castile-León, 7.61 per cent in Andalusia, and 10.26 per cent in
New Castile, liquid units rank next to last among metrological
standards. Olive oil, widely used for cooking, seasoning, and

---

[1] *Vide supra*, p. 158.
[2] *Op. cit.*, pp. 90–93.　　　　　　　[3] *Op. cit.*, pp. 164–165.

sacramental purposes, and wine, surpassed only by wheat as a
staple food, raise the significance of the liquid group above its
relative numerical strength. Milk, vinegar, and honey [1] further
exalt liquids; but sweet almond oil, linseed oil, brandy, and ink
— all trivial commodities — lower their position.

Divided into at least three categories, liquid measures offer
peculiar difficulties to the historian of prices. Fortunately, however, the wine measures, the most important liquid units, prove
the least recondite.

The following table lists the multiples and fractions of the
Toledo cántara, the standard for wine, vinegar, ink, and brandy.

TABLE 13

WINE MEASURES IN CASTILE

4 cuartillos	= 1 azumbre
8 azumbres	= 1 cántara or arroba
7 cántaras	= 1 carga
16 cántaras	= 1 moyo

Used frequently at the close of the Middle Ages and occasionally in the early sixteenth century, the moyo gradually fell into
desuetude. The carga seldom occurred outside New Castile, and
the cuartillo served only for small retail sales. Measuring most
institutional purchases, the azumbre and cántara were the only
wine units in terms of which the price series have been compiled.

Metrological estimates of the present equivalence of the Toledo
cántara range from 16 to 16.24 liters.[2] The most ubiquitous and
nearest average figure, 16.13 liters, may be regarded as roughly
correct. As constant complaints from the Cortes indicate,[3] wine
measures in most cities departed from the Castilian standard.
If we may rely upon metrological estimates, the cántara contained approximately 15.65 liters in Seville and Valladolid, 15.75
in Palencia, and 15.85 in León. That these cities adopted the
Toledo unit and subsequently debased it in varying degrees —
possibly on account of local sisas — is a reasonable hypothesis.

---

[1] As will be shown presently, honey was often sold by weight.

[2] Contemporary metrologists agreed that the cántara was equal in volume to
34 pounds of clear water from the Tagus in Toledo.

[3] For example, *Cortes*, IV, 548–549; V, 144, 250–251, 396, 544, 753; *Actas*, XV, 408.

Uncertainty concerning the quality of wine and vinegar, the only two relevant commodities quoted continuously in all regions, and the dependence of both commodities upon local conditions render price comparisons useless as indices of the narrow regional discrepancies in wine measures.

In 1601 the national sisa, applied to vinegar in 1602, introduced a new type of wine measure, the menor or sisada, 12½ per cent less than the former units.[1] The new standard, adopted only for sales to final consumers, affected little the measures in terms of which prices are quoted in the present study. Purchasing wine and vinegar in large quantities, hospitals and convents received the old measures; and sales to middlemen were exempt from the sisa.

To the extent of actual collection, institutions generally preferred to pay an excise tax equal to the sisa rather than to take the reduced measure.

The earliest legislation concerning olive oil prescribed sale by the Castilian arroba. Because of greater convenience, however, a measure based on weight soon evolved; and the liquid arroba, equal in volume to twenty-five pounds, became the standard. Of the articles included in the index numbers, the above unit measured only the three oils — linseed, olive, and sweet almond.

The following table lists the usual fractions of the arroba.

TABLE 14

OIL MEASURES IN CASTILE

4 ounces	=	1 panilla
4 panillas	=	1 libra
25 libras	=	1 arroba

Too small for commercial use, the ounce was only a nominal unit, and sales by the panilla seldom occurred. The *libra* dominated retail trade, as did the arroba wholesale transactions.

Metrological estimates of the modern equivalence of the olive oil standard range from 12.5 to 12.63 liters, and 12.55 is probably not far wrong. The cities of Toledo and Seville conformed to the

---

[1] When he said that the sisa affected only measures smaller than the azumbre, Burriel (*op. cit.*, pp. 344–345) erred. Considerable purchases by the cántara or arroba menor sometimes occurred in Old Castile-León, New Castile, and Andalusia.

Castilian standard; but Burriel complained that great diversity characterized olive oil measures in the province of Toledo,[1] while the arroba menor — a survival of the old Moorish unit of 18 pounds,[2] equivalent to approximately 9.6 liters — and the arroba of Marchena, 15 per cent greater than the *mayor*, or local standard,[3] plagued Seville. The arroba of Palencia was roughly equivalent to 12.25 liters. Price comparisons indicate that the Valladolid arroba roughly equaled and that of León slightly exceeded the Palencian. In each of the three periods León prices of olive oil averaged a little over 10 per cent higher than those of Valladolid and Palencia. Unless it cost considerably more to transport this commodity to León than to Valladolid or Palencia — an unlikely assumption — the León arroba must have exceeded the Castilian standard by more than 5 per cent. The persistent protests of the Cortes against the diversity of olive oil measures [4] appear amply justified.

Bating that of León, all the price series of olive oil have been compiled in terms of the standard arroba — approximately 12.55 liters. As in the case of wine, after 1601 institutions generally purchased by the old unit. The adoption of the sisa chiefly affected the smaller measures, utilized in retail transactions; and these units, employed only as substitutes for the arroba by average correlation, have distorted the price data little, if at all. Sweet almond oil and linseed oil did not pay the sisa.[5]

According to José García Caballero, the wine standard measured milk in Castile; [6] but in Toledo at least there was a special unit. Writing in 1758, Burriel said that in Toledo the azumbre of milk had been equivalent to 5 wine cuartillos since December 5,

---

[1] *Op. cit.*, pp. 356–357.

[2] According to Burriel (*op. cit.*, pp. 82, 84–86, 347–356) the arroba of 18 pounds was official in Toledo until 1438, when the 25-pound standard was adopted.

[3] *Vide*, for example, Pozo Santo, Hospital del Cardenal, *Libros de Gastos*, 301; Hospital de la Sangre, *Libros de Gastos*, 1657.

[4] *Vide*, for example, *Cortes*, III, 322; IV, 548–549; V, 144, 250–251, 396, 554; *Actas*, I, 353.

[5] It is possible, however, that — occasionally at least — the pound measure for olive oil, reduced by 12 ½ per cent, measured linseed and sweet almond oil after 1601. The price series indicate that this practice was not generally adopted, but my information is inadequate.

[6] *Op. cit.*, p. 261.

1458, when a municipal ordinance prescribed this magnitude.[1] Although cántaras varying from 4 to 9 azumbres were not unknown in Madrid,[2] 8 seem to have been the normal number. Saigey, one of the few metrologists to notice Castilian milk measures, estimated the present equivalence of the arroba at 20 liters.[3] If we assume that the cántara contained 8 azumbres, each equivalent to 5 wine cuartillos, Saigey's estimate closely approximates that of Burriel. Aside from the uniformity of milk prices, I have no information concerning the measures of Seville.

The only continuous milk quotations available, the series for Andalusia and New Castile, run in terms of the azumbre. Although unable to furnish a better estimate of the present equivalence than that of Saigey, I can say that in both regions the azumbre remained sufficiently stable to permit the compilation of a trustworthy price series.

Until 1438, when John II provided for the sale of honey by the wine cántara of Toledo,[4] the arroba of 25 pounds by weight was the legal standard. But practice ignored the law of 1438, as it did the restoration of the ponderal arroba to *de jure* status in 1568.[5] In Old Castile-León and New Castile fluid and ponderal arrobas and cántaras, varying from 25 to 50 pounds, appear simultaneously in given localities, often without any description of the unit. The most common types are arrobas or cántaras of 25, 33, 48, and 50 pounds.[6] Hoping that they may be of metrological interest, I am listing honey prices in the series for New Castile and Old Castile-León.[7] Unable to eliminate metrological differences, however, I am excluding the commodity from the index numbers for these regions. In Andalusia honey measures permit the compilation of satisfactory price series. Only the ponderal arroba of

---

[1] *Op. cit.*, pp. 136–137, 342.

[2] AHN, *Clero*, Madrid, *Cartujos de Nuestra Señora del Paular*, leg. 715.

[3] *Op. cit.*, p. 142.

[4] *Cortes*, I, 534; Burriel, *op. cit.*, p. 83; *Recopilación*, lib. v, tit. xiii, ley iii.

[5] *Ibid.*, lib. v, tit. xiii, ley i.

[6] In Olías, a small town in close proximity to and in intimate commercial contact with Toledo, the arroba of honey weighed 50 pounds, whereas that of Toledo normally weighed 25 (H. Tavera, *Botillería*, 1618). The *arroba de hierro*, a common unit in Old Castile, ordinarily weighed 50 pounds.

[7] The honey series for New Castile has been compiled as nearly as possible in terms of the Toledo arroba and for Old Castile-León in terms of the Valladolid cántara.

25 pounds and the fluid arroba of 33 pounds [1] occur frequently, and it is possible to identify each. The price series run in terms of the fluid arroba equal in volume to 33 pounds.

Tale

Although effecting the exchanges of 15.35 per cent of the commodities in the three Castilian regions and taking second rank among metrological standards, tale offers no special problems to the price historian and requires only brief treatment. Hens, eggs, oranges, bricks, and sardines were among the most important articles; and the unit, pair, dozen, hundred, and thousand were the commonest units. Freak methods of counting such as a baker's dozen did not appear in any region.[2] Paper was sold by the ream (resma) and the quire (mano),[3] and garlic by the string (ristra).[4]

Weight

When compared with weight, all measures pale into insignificance. The percentage of commodities weighed ranged from 61.97 in Old Castile-León to 66.3 in Andalusia and averaged 64.73 in the three Castilian regions. Even the important articles are too extensive to name.

The following table lists the leading weights encountered in price studies.

TABLE 15

WEIGHTS IN CASTILE

4 cuartas = 1 ounce	4 pounds = 1 arrelde
16 ounces = 1 pound	25 pounds = 1 arroba
32 ounces = 1 carnicera pound	4 arrobas = 1 quintal [5]

---

[1] Occasionally the liquid arroba contained only 32 pounds (Pozo Santo, Hospital de la Sangre, *Libros de Recibos y Gastos*, leg. 462).

[2] In isolated instances abnormal notation occurred. For instance, on December 4, 1525, the Convento de Nuestra Señora de Sandoval (León) bought 20 dozen dried fish, "which have in each dozen 14 fish from Ireland" (AHN, *Clero*, León, leg. 248). But this idiosyncrasy seems to have been imported with the fish.

[3] In all regions the ream invariably contained 20 quires.

[4] In small wholesale transactions garlic is still sold by the string. Even in Seville petty dealers insist that they find the string a satisfactory standard. According to the accounts of the Convento de Cartujos de Nuestra Señora del Paular, 66 strings of garlic bought in October, 1644 weighed 11 arrobas (AHN, *Clero*, Madrid, leg. 715).

[5] The quintal *macho*, often employed for iron and steel, weighed 150 pounds.

The cuarta and the ounce were limited almost exclusively to spices.[1] More than 80 per cent of the articles weighed and over half of the entire list of commodities were sold by the pound. Weighing bulky goods,[2] the arroba and quintal account for one-sixth of the articles sold by weight. The arrelde, used only for meat, rarely occurred in Andalusia and virtually disappeared in Old and New Castile by 1550.

Regional relationship of average prices, the relative pound-arroba value ratios for given localities, and perfect agreement between the Sevillan *carnicera* and the unqualified pound demonstrate that — despite legislation specifically requiring the unit of 16 ounces for pound sales of meat and fish [3] — the carnicera pound invariably weighed fish, meat, lard, and butter in Seville,[4] but not in New Castile or Old Castile-León. Hence the Andalusian price series for these commodities run in terms of the carnicera pound. Arrobas and quintals, however, consisted, respectively, of 25 and 100 normal pounds. Unlike lard and butter, tallow and cheese were sold by the pound of 16 ounces.

In the celebrated fairs of Medina de Rioseco, Villalón, and Medina del Campo [5] the carga was a common unit for wholesale transactions in fish.[6] Affirming that indefinite weights enabled the seller, possessing exact quantitative information, to deceive the purchaser, the Cortes repeatedly inveighed against and urged the Crown to prohibit fish sales by the carga and lot (a ojo).[7] But the arguments of the Procuradores lacked cogency. It was gen-

---

[1] Occasionally spices were sold by the *adarme* (1/16 ounce) and *pesante* (1/32 ounce); but these weights, although doubtless the principal units in sales to private consumers, usually occur not more than once in twenty-five years of institutional accounts.

[2] In 1527 Charles V ordered merchants to sell wool and other bulky goods by the arroba rather than the pound (Burriel, *op. cit.*, p. 49).

[3] *Recopilación*, lib. v, tit. XIII, leyes I–II; *Cortes*, III, 228.

[4] When the sisa on meat was extended for nine years, in 1618, the government, doubtless thinking of the carnicera pound in Andalusia, provided that the tax of 1 maravedí per pound of 16 ounces should increase proportionately to larger units (*Actas*, XXXII, 280).

[5] *Vide infra*, pp. 203–204.

[6] AHN, *Clero*, León, *Convento de Nuestra Señora de Sandoval*, legs. 244, 248; *Universidad de Alcalá de Henares*, leg. 768; *Clero*, Madrid, *Nuestra Señora del Paular*, leg. 715.

[7] *Vide*, for instance, *Cortes*, V, 146–147, 442, 555, 659; *Actas*, I, 85, 343–344.

erally recognized that the carga contained about 10 arrobas and that at worst the tare did not exceed 2 arrobas.[1] Inexact standards in retail trade would have occasioned the exploitation of consumers; but wholesale purchasers, although at some disadvantage in lot transactions, were not sufficiently at the mercy of sellers to warrant state intervention. In Old Castile-León the *tercio*, a unit varying from 4½ to 5 arrobas,[2] and the *cesto*, or basket, of indeterminate size were also used in fish sales. Fortunately, however, it has proved unnecessary to compile any of the price series for fish in terms of indefinite weights or measures.

The pound of 16 ordinary ounces weighed wax, spices, and other commodities embodying great value in small bulk.

The quotations for several articles included in the index numbers originated in purchases for hospital pharmacies. Not being medicines, however, the commodities were sold by ordinary weights and measures. Hence there is no occasion to consider medicinal standards.

Metrologists agree that the Castilian pound of 16 ounces weighed 460.093 grams and the other units accordingly.[3] Bating tale, weights were probably the least variable of all Castilian metrological standards. No such problems as heaped and stricken measures or cántaras mayores and sisadas arose. The carnicera pound rarely or never perplexes the price historian, for a change between it and the regular unit could hardly escape detection. Furthermore, there was considerably less regional discrepancy in weights than in measures. None of the cities that serve as bases

---

[1] AHN, *Clero*, León, *Nuestra Señora de Sandoval*, leg. 244; *Cortes*, v, 442. A carga contained about 2500 sardines (AHN, *Clero*, León, *Nuestra Señora de Sandoval*, leg. 248).

[2] *Vide*, for example, AHN, *Clero*, León, *Nuestra Señora de Sandoval*, leg. 244; *Clero*, Madrid, *Nuestra Señora del Paular*, leg. 715; *Universidad de Alcalá de Henares*, 768 f.

[3] At the close of the sixteenth century the pound — theoretically at least — was reduced imperceptibly. On February 15, 1599, Philip III instructed the agents of the Licentiate Juan Beltrán de Benavides, marcador mayor, to tolerate weights adjusted to the old standard but to make his inspections according to the reformed unit, which, according to the law of this date, was 1 ½ ounces per quintal (.09375 per cent) lighter (Burriel, *op. cit.*, p. 368). It is highly probable that this alteration of the legal standard never became effective. In fact, one wonders whether the contemporary appliances and technique of weighing could have put this hair-splitting change into practice.

for price series failed to adhere to the Castilian standard.[1] Hence all the prices run in terms of the official Castilian weight.[2]

It is fortunate that weight and tale, standards that approximate the price historian's ideal of absolute invariability, account for more than 80 per cent of the commodities in the three Castilian regions.

II. VALENCIA

Valencian metrology requires much less extensive treatment than has been accorded Castilian standards and usage. Since the city of Valencia, the capital and undisputed metropolis, furnished all the prices included in the index numbers, regional discrepancies may be ignored. The Castilian standards became official for all Spain early in the nineteenth century, whereas the Valencian units not only failed to pass the frontiers, but were encroached upon at home before they lost official status. Furthermore, both primary and source material are much less abundant than for Castile. The infrequency of meetings of the Valencian *Corts* in the sixteenth and seventeenth centuries deprived the subjects of an opportunity to express their opinions concerning metrological reform; and the viceregal decrees have been less faithfully preserved than the Castilian pragmatics. Economic historians have neglected Valencia. In fact, no other comparable area in Spain has elicited so little scientific study.[3]

Aragonese and Catalan influence upon the earliest Christian legislation proved strong enough to eradicate the effect of pro-

[1] Several cities and regions not included in the present investigation used local weights. For instance, the arroba of fish in Bilbao seems to have exceeded the Castilian by something like 12½ per cent (AHN, *Clero*, Madrid, *Nuestra Señora del Paular*, leg. 715). J. F. Saigey (*op. cit.*, pp. 141-143) lists for different Castilian provinces pounds ranging from 434 grams in Murcia to 713 grams in Santander.

[2] Except, of course, the pound prices for fish and meat in Andalusia.

[3] Anomalous as it may seem, the principal reason probably lies in the excessive concentration of Valencia upon economic pursuits, with emphasis upon domestic rather than foreign trade. Far more than in proportion to its relative intrinsic importance, commercial and maritime, but warlike, Catalonia has attracted the attention of economic historians, many of whom in the past (devoid of both training and interest in economics) have cultivated the discipline casually and as an adjunct to political history. One must recognize, however, that the energy and intelligence of native scholars have also directed attention to the economic and political past of Catalonia.

tracted Moorish domination upon Valencian metrology and to introduce a marked Roman element, exemplified by the prevalence of duodecimals.

With great care for his day, James the Conqueror formulated the basic laws governing weights and measures. For wine he established the fluid arroba equal in volume to 30 pounds. The fanega of 8 almudes was adopted for barley, oats, wheat, and other grains. Unlike Castilian monarchs, who failed to specify whether arid units should be heaped or stricken, James I specifically adopted stricken standards. It seems that the grain fanega was a new measure smaller than the current standard, also consisting of 8 stricken almudes, which James I legalized for "salt, chestnuts, filberts, barley, lime, and other similar things," [1] for early in the seventeenth century Valencia engaged in litigation to retain the customary salt measures; and in 1604 the Corts requested the Crown to prohibit the use of grain measures by the salt monopoly.[2] For weights James I adopted the mark of 8 ounces, the pound of 12 ounces, the carnicera pound of 36 ounces, the arroba of 30 pounds, and the quintal of 4 arrobas. He decreed that wool, grapes, cheese, silk, flax, hemp, jute, figs, raisins, flour, and "all other things, large and small," should be weighed by the above standards. It is significant that James I created no special weights for fish or flour and that he failed to mention the arroba of 36 pounds,[3] which proved a source of subsequent confusion.[4]

The sealer of weights and measures was among the most ancient and important officials of the Valencian metropolis, and his prestige and authority remained unabated under the Hapsburgs. The political and economic hegemony of the capital, together with the strong traditions of municipal liberty in the kingdoms of the Crown of Aragon, rendered impossible such a conflict as occurred in Castile between local and royal sealers during the last decade of the sixteenth century and the first two decades of the seventeenth.

---

[1] *Furs, Capitols, Provisions e Actes de Cort* (Valencia), pp. 238, 260.

[2] *Ibid.*, cap. XXXIII, fol. vi.

[3] Probably imported from Aragon, the kingdom that played the leading rôle in the conquest of Valencia and powerfully influenced her institutions.

[4] *Furs, Capitols, Provisions e Actes de Cort*, pp. 238, 260.

Arid Measures

Accounting for 13.56 per cent of the articles included in the index numbers, arid measures rank third among metrological standards. But the importance of the commodities — wheat, chick-peas, beans, bran, lime, plaster of Paris, salt, and ashes — raises the arid group above its relative numerical position.

The following table lists the units most frequently encountered in historical price studies.

TABLE 16

ARID MEASURES IN VALENCIA

4 cuarterones	= 1 almud	2 barchillas	= 1 fanega
4 almudes	= 1 barchilla	6 fanegas	= 1 cahiz

Of the eight arid commodities, institutions usually bought five by the cahiz, one by the *barchilla*, and two by the almud. Although doubtless prevalent in sales to private families, the *cuarterón* was too small to measure institutional purchases.

Metrologists estimate the barchilla at 16.75 liters, the cahiz at 201 liters, and the remaining units accordingly. Presumably these figures are for grain standards, which seem to have differed from salt measures, at least until 1604. Whether bran, plaster of Paris, and lime were sold by this standard — according to the original decree of James I — or by the grain measures I am unable to say; but their prices reflect no significant metrological alteration, and the lack of data concerning a duality of arid units suggests that the salt standard lost acceptance for other commodities before 1501. The exact metrological equivalence of salt measures, as well as their fate after 1604, remains a mystery. But it is probable that they exceeded the grain standard only slightly, perhaps by no more than the difference between heaped and stricken units.

Lineal Measures

Lineal standards measured only one of the fifty-nine commodities (1.69 per cent) entering into the price series, but they also served as units for piece-rate wages. The Valencian yard was an exact reproduction of the Roman vara. Although the modern term *vara* superseded *alna* about 1600, the yard remained invariable and occasioned no metrological problems. Table 17 lists the usual fractions of the yard.

TABLE 17

LINEAL MEASURES IN VALENCIA

12 pulgadas = 1 pie	16 cuartos = 1 palmo
3 pies = 1 vara	4 palmos = 1 vara

Only the yard and palmo occur as textile measures — the former for length and the latter chiefly for width.[1]

According to most metrological estimates, the Valencian yard was equivalent to about 91 centimeters.[2]

Liquid Measures

If one excludes honey and turpentine, obviously sold by weight, liquid standards account for only three articles (5.08 per cent) and rank next to last among metrological units. But the importance of the commodities — vinegar, wine, and olive oil, particularly the latter two — places liquids far above their relative numerical level.

As in Castile, there were dual liquid measures: one standard for wine and another for olive oil.

Table 18 gives the common units for wine and vinegar.

TABLE 18

WINE MEASURES IN VALENCIA

8 cuartillos = 1 azumbre	15 cántaras = 1 carga
4 azumbres = 1 cántara	4 cargas = 1 bota seixentena

---

[1] Cloth was frequently sold by the piece. Contemporary price records indicate that each piece contained 22 yards, and on November 27, 1625, the city council of Valencia required craftsmen and merchants to deliver and accept this quantity as a *piece* (Archivo del Ayuntamiento [hereafter AA], Valencia, *Crides*, xx, lib. 3).

[2] On May 8, 1610, the Hospital dels Inocents of Valencia bought a bolt of French linen containing 236 French alnas and recorded it as 306½ alnas of Valencia (Hospital dels Inocents, *Clavería de 1609–1610*, fol. 187). If we accept the common metric estimates of the French alna, this ratio gives us almost exactly 91 centimeters for the Valencian yard.

Institutions ordinarily bought both wine and vinegar by the cántara. Although common units in small retail transactions, azumbres and cuartillos are seldom found in institutional accounts. The carga also appears infrequently; and the *bota* (pipe), perhaps the most common measure for institutional purchases in the succeeding period, 1651–1800, seldom occurs.

In the Corts de Monzón of 1626 the Three Estates voted the Crown an annual subsidy of £72,000 for fifteen years and decided to raise the requisite revenue through a tax on wine production ranging from 12s. to 20s. per bota *seixentena* (4 cargas), according to the producing region, with a countervailing import duty. In order "to shift a part of the burden onto the consumers," the Corts decided to reduce all wine measures, large or small, by one-sixteenth so that the current botas would hold about 64 cántaras.[1] On November 27, 1627, the Viceroy decreed that the new wine measures should become effective on December 1 and remain in force fifteen years.[2] The quality of ordinary wine was too variable and the quantity too dependent upon good or bad harvests for the price to indicate whether the metrical change of only 6.67 per cent became effective or operated as an excise tax. The fact that the Hospital dels Inocents continued to receive only 60 cántaras per bota suggests that the measures remained constant, but the data are too meager to permit positive generalization.

Metrologists commonly estimate the cántara at 10.77 liters and the other units proportionately.

Table 19 lists the fractions of the arroba for olive oil. Since the measure originated as the more convenient equivalent of a weight, the nomenclature is based on ponderal units.

TABLE 19

OIL MEASURES IN VALENCIA

12 ounces　=　1 pound
30 pounds　=　1 arroba
12 arrobas　=　1 carga

The carga being too large and the ounce too small for general commercial use, only the arroba and the pound occurred frequently.

---

[1] *Furs . . . e Actes de Cort de 1626*, fol. 100.　　[2] AA, Valencia, *Crides*, xx, lib. 3.

The arroba was approximately equivalent to 11.93 liters, and the other units varied accordingly.

Tale

Accounting for 25.42 per cent of the articles, tale ranked second to weight and was far more important than in Castile and León, where the percentage was 15.35. Owing to the complete absence of freak notation, however, no explanation of tale is required.

Of the fifteen commodities in this group, six were sold by the dozen and six by units, while the pair, gross (144), and thousand accounted for one each.

Weight

Fortunately, only 54.24 per cent of the articles were sold by weight. Unlike Castile, where the maximum certainty pertains to this group, Valencia presents her greatest metrological problems in the ponderal standards.

The following table lists the weights most frequently encountered.

TABLE 20

WEIGHTS IN VALENCIA

4 adarmes	= 1 cuarta
4 cuartas	= 1 ounce
12 ounces	= 1 pound
16 ounces	= 1 small fish pound
18 ounces	= 1 large fish pound
36 ounces	= 1 carnicera pound
30 pounds	= 1 arroba prima
36 pounds	= 1 arroba grosa
4 arrobas (primas or grosas)	= 1 quintal (of 120 or 144 pounds)

The ounce and its fractions were limited almost exclusively to spices. The pound of 12 ounces served for all commodities except fish and meat. According to metrologists, the pound of small fishes consisted of 16 ounces. Primary data permitting ounce-pound comparisons are too scant to show the number of ounces in the pound of eels, perch, and perch *de Calp*, the only small fishes in the price series. Until adequate information becomes available, one must accept tentatively the statements of metrolo-

gists; but all that one can affirm positively is that price behavior
does not reflect a change in the number of ounces to the pound
during the period under observation. Extensive comparisons of
pound and arroba prices of codfish and tuna fish in Valencia and
Seville and of pound-arroba relationships in Valencia demonstrate
that the Valencian pound of large fishes contained 18 ounces and
the arroba 36 of these pounds.[1] The pound carnicera of 36 ounces
weighed mutton and salt pork, the only meats in the price tables.

Differing by only 6 pounds and often unidentified, the two
arrobas frequently perplex the price historian. But the unmistakable tendency to use one of the arrobas almost exclusively for
each commodity and to note discrepancies facilitates the compilation of homogeneous series. Hemp, flax, soap, firewood, and
honey were normally sold by the arroba of 36 pounds or the corresponding quintal of 144. When the arroba *prima* was used,
ordinarily the fact stood out. Since pound prices of borage,
pumpkin, and carob beans do not occur and inasmuch as the accounts fail to identify the units, one cannot be certain whether the
price series run in terms of arrobas primas or *grosas*. The most
likely guess is that the arroba of carob beans and of pumpkin
weighed 36 pounds and that of borage 30. The arroba prima undoubtedly weighed rice and sugar. There is abundant evidence
that an unqualified arroba of each weighed 30 pounds; the few
instances of arrobas grosas are almost invariably marked accordingly. The carga of 360 pounds was the most frequent weight for
rice and a common unit for sugar. In the case of sugar the carga
was a net weight of 360 pounds; but, occasionally at least, the
carga of rice was a gross weight including from 5 to 10 pounds of
tare. Apparently turpentine was sold by the arroba prima, but
the data are inadequate for positive generalization. Metrological
tables ordinarily include a special arroba of 32 pounds for flour,
but I have omitted this unit because *tres farines*, a composite
meal, seems to have been exchanged by the arroba of 30 pounds.

The most indefinite weight or measure included in the price

---

[1] But this was not invariably the case. Some convents counted 24 pounds of
18 ounces an arroba of large fishes (*vide*, for example, Archivo Regional [hereafter
AR], Valencia, *Conventos*, lib. 1638).

series for Valencia (or, with the possible exception of garlic, for any other region) is the *sarrie*,[1] or bag, of charcoal. Single purchases rarely exhibit erratic fluctuations, and the number of quotations suffices to render the annual average trustworthy. The average ratio of 23 strictly comparable sarrie and quintal prices indicates that the sarrie weighed about 1.67 quintals of 144 pounds, and several comparisons of a less satisfactory character tend to confirm this figure.

Loads of straw and of sand have been omitted from the price series because of the variability of the units. A load would prove a satisfactory standard only in case many were bought every quarter, or at least every year, a condition not satisfied by straw. Numerous quotations for sand, always by the dozen loads,[2] occur; but the price of this commodity generally depends altogether upon the cost of transportation. A homogeneous price series could be constructed only in the case of both a fixed source and a fixed destination. Although numerous quotations for alfalfa occur in almost every quarter of the 150 years, metrological variation eliminates the commodity. Occurring in terms of *reals* and *sous*, the prices originally represented the quantity exchanged for a fixed sum of money. That this phenomenon subsisted during the period under observation is indicated by the abnormal stability of quotations throughout the Price Revolution.

According to metrological estimates, the pound of 12 ounces contained 355 grams,[3] the arroba prima 10.65 kilograms, and the arroba grosa 12.78 kilograms. From these figures anyone interested may calculate the metrical equivalents of the remaining weights.

---

[1] Sometimes written *cullera*.

[2] The records of the municipality, the Hospital dels Inocents, and the Colegio de Santo Tomás invariably list sand by the *dozen* without any description. Not until the collection of prices for the period 1351–1500 was begun in the Cathedral did it become clear that the term meant a dozen loads.

[3] If we make allowance for the fact that 31 Valencian ounces approximately equaled 32 of Castile and consider the Castilian pound equivalent to 460.093 grams (an assumption that admits of little doubt), the estimate of 355 grams for the Valencian pound is confirmed by numerous statements of equivalence between Valencian and Castilian weights in the records of the purchases of delicacies in Valencia from 1508 to 1513 for consumption by Juana la Loca in Tordesillas (AS, *Casa Real* [E.M.], 9–1, 9–2, 10–1).

CHAPTER VIII

THE PRICE REVOLUTION BEGINS, 1501-1550

MANY historically-minded economists and students of Spanish history have long been interested in the beginning of the Price Revolution in Spain. Most previous authors have attempted to show whether the phenomenon commenced before some specific date, as 1540 or 1550, and to ascertain roughly the extent of the rise in prices before the abdication of Charles V.[1] But the data adduced have consisted largely or exclusively of complaints in the Cortes against the high cost of living, phenomena as old as the Cortes themselves; price-fixing ordinances; and legislation implying a decrease in the purchasing power of money, such as prohibitions against the slaughter of certain young meat animals, which by proper causes might have become dearer, or the agitation for increased compensation by public employees, who may have felt that altered political rather than economic conditions favored their demands. Sufficient statistics to date scientifically the beginning of the Price Revolution have not hitherto been available.

The weakest element in the price statistics for 1501-1550 is the Andalusian series, which has been taken largely from the records of the outfitting and victualing of treasure ships at Seville.[2] In number and character the commodities are fairly adequate, but the paucity of years and the complete absence of prices for all except the last year of the base period vitiate the data. Furthermore, the purchases did not always fall in the same season, and there lurks the danger that the sudden demand for ships' supplies may have forced up prices in the early years of the sixteenth century before the economic life of Seville and its hinterland became

---

[1] Konrad Haebler (*Wirtschaftliche Blüte Spaniens* [Berlin, 1888], pp. 160-163) and Francisco de Laiglesia (*Estudios Históricos*, II [Madrid, 1918], 325-330, 347-351), interested in proving that Charles V did not increase the real burden of taxation, attempted to demonstrate that taxes lagged behind prices.

[2] For a description of the sources *vide* Earl J. Hamilton, "American Treasure and Andalusian Prices, 1503-1660," *Journal of Economic and Business History*, I, 10-17.

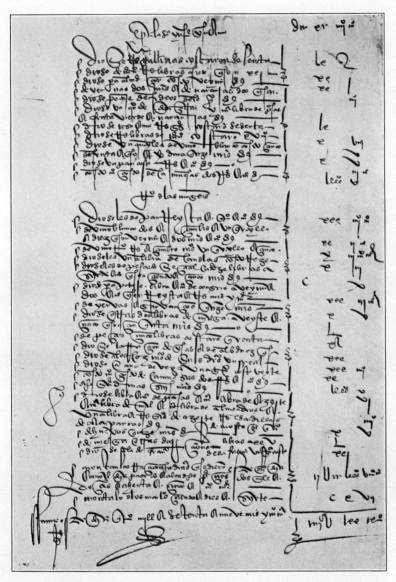

PAGE FROM THE ACCOUNTS OF *JUANA LA LOCA* IN TORDESILLAS
FOR SUNDAY, FEBRUARY 13, 1513

(Archivo de Simancas, *Casa Real* [E. M.], 9–2)

adjusted to the heavy periodic requirements of colonial navigation and commerce. But the few comparable prices in the records of the municipality and the Cathedral of Seville agree closely with those of the House of Trade; and in 1551–1600, when the fleet system was in its heyday and commerce between Spain and the Indies reached its apogee, there is no greater discrepancy between the price series of the House of Trade and those of three Sevillan charity hospitals than may have resulted from the different compositions of the indices. Certainly the index numbers for the House of Trade did not rise more than those of the hospitals, the only noticeable differences being in 1565–1574 and 1581–1589, when the House of Trade indices lagged behind.[1] Hence there is strong reason to believe that the Andalusian index numbers for 1501–1550, though highly unsatisfactory for many purposes, correctly portray the secular trend of prices.[2]

The series for New Castile, furnished by the accounts of the Hospital de Antezana and the Colegio Mayor de San Ildefonso of the University in Alcalá de Henares and the San Pedro and Tavera Hospitals[3] in Toledo, are little better than the Andalusian data; but the weaknesses are reversed. In this case the dearth of commodities counteracts the absence of lacunae in the table of annual prices.[4] Acceptably continuous quotations are

---

[1] Cf. Earl J. Hamilton, op. cit., I, 26, and Table 23, infra. Hospital prices are high in 1562, when figures for the House of Trade are lacking. Only in 1557 and 1597 did the House of Trade index number greatly exceed that of the hospitals.

[2] The charge of incompetent buying by the House of Trade, given wide currency by Alonso de Carranza (Ajustamiento i Proporción de las Monedas [Madrid, 1629], p. 323), had little, if any, basis. In fact, we know that Carranza drew heavily upon data supplied by Tomás de Cardona, who, having represented the Gild Merchant of Seville in negotiations with the Council of the Indies, in 1620, for the contractual victualing and outfitting of the treasure fleets in 1621–1626 (Archivo de Simancas, Contadurías Generales, 3052), was interested in proving that the House of Trade purchased less efficiently than merchants.

The purchasing agents of hospitals were probably less lethargic and incapable than has often been assumed. For instance, on January 22, 1557, the Hospital de Esgueva (Libro de Cuentas de 1557) bought 30 cargas (120 fanegas) of wheat at 44 reals per carga "from Gracián Astete, because he wanted to do the institution a good turn, although wheat was selling at 50 reals a carga." On more than one occasion the representatives of hospitals secured significant price concessions and at the same time obtained from the sellers donations in kind.

[3] The Tavera accounts begin in 1540, but before 1553 they cover little besides building materials.

[4] Vide Appendix III.

limited to twelve articles;[1] and the index numbers for 1535 and
1546 represent the averages of only four relatives, while for four
other years only five commodities are available.

As Appendix III indicates, the series for New Castile is a hybrid
of Alcalá de Henares and Toledo prices, quotations for each commodity from one or the other of the two cities having been selected as the standard for that article. Never crudely combined
with the main series, prices from outside the chosen locality were
interpolated or extrapolated only through average correlations.[2]
Toledo prices represent nine of the twelve commodities and
Alcalá quotations the remainder. But in many cases the Toledo
price was taken as the standard for the sole purpose of preserving
uniformity throughout the three fifty-year periods.

The excellent accounts of the Convento de Nuestra Señora de
Sandoval [3] in Villaverde de Sandoval, about 12½ kilometers from
León, and of the Hospital de Esgueva in Valladolid, supplemented
by the records of the municipality of Villalón and scattering data
from Medina de Rioseco, Tordesillas, and Ávila, have supplied a
price series for Old Castile-León infinitely superior to the statistics for Andalusia and New Castile. The annual prices for the
forty-one varied commodities included in the index numbers [4]
represent the averages of satisfactory quarterly quotations; so
seasonal fluctuations have not vitiated the results. The outstanding defect of the Old Castilian series is the lack of sufficient data
for eight of the first sixteen years and for 1531 to permit the construction of index numbers. The lacunae have doubtless resulted
from a fire in the Convento de Nuestra Señora de Sandoval on
August 5, 1614, which destroyed the abbot's cell, where the invaluable account-books for 1501–1517 and 1531–1532 were
stored.[5]

---

[1] Prices of hens and spring chickens occur frequently; but both commodities were
omitted because the stability of their quotations and other internal evidence indicated that the prices represented arbitrary commutations of feudal dues.

[2] For a description of the statistical methods employed *vide infra*, Appendix I.

[3] Cistercian monks.

[4] Forty-two commodities appear in the table of prices in Appendix III, but
erratic metrological units excluded honey from the index numbers. *Vide supra*,
p. 174.

[5] Archivo Histórico Nacional, *Clero*, León, 246.

TABLE 21

INDEX NUMBERS OF COMMODITY PRICES, 1501–1550
Base = 1521–1530

	Andalusia	New Castile	Old Castile-León	Valencia
1501	...	68.51	...	69.88
1502	...	69.68	73.43	83.32
1503	65.84	68.88	76.84	85.16
1504	...	71.18	...	80.81
1505	70.59	80.04	...	82.63
1506	...	110.63	98.16	86.36
1507	92.36	108.43	...	79.28
1508	...	95.88	90.17	86.72
1509	...	74.54	...	75.50
1510	...	76.21	80.50	79.19
1511	67.72	84.06	80.17	86.32
1512	...	72.86	77.53	84.55
1513	65.43	80.27	78.22	89.29
1514	...	85.26	...	87.70
1515	78.33	87.90	...	85.35
1516	...	80.73	...	88.75
1517	74.29	76.34	77.43	92.38
1518	...	86.23	89.19	91.54
1519	85.16	82.79	84.86	92.77
1520	...	73.99	83.96	91.62
1521	...	87.85	93.38	97.95
1522	...	109.99	96.02	103.01
1523	...	85.74	101.24	103.93
1524	...	95.27	96.94	99.93
1525	...	99.55 ·	99.44	99.56
1526	...	103.83	91.80	96.15
1527	...	96.70	105.16	100.24
1528	...	96.44	102.91	96.72
1529	...	107.90	105.81	97.79
1530	122.45	117.95	106.64	109.81
1531	...	118.37	...	110.21
1532	108.79	103.48	121.48	106.77
1533	...	100.69	98.13	102.30
1534	...	125.18	91.67	102.63
1535	...	85.55	92.11	99.51
1536	...	107.70	100.36	106.77
1537	121.65	102.50	104.39	100.25
1538	...	118.63	104.28	109.48
1539	133.12	110.50	107.91	103.95
1540	...	121.25	100.98	109.36
1541	...	104.54	103.23	101.26
1542	150.41	127.45	105.71	106.81
1543	...	124.91	110.46	107.96
1544	...	119.43	110.47	103.37
1545	...	105.45	107.13	112.06
1546	...	129.48	113.23	122.06
1547	...	127.45	109.08	110.42
1548	162.68	131.19	125.99	117.00
1549	152.20	170.09	128.28	120.78
1550	...	145.23	132.62	125.49

Again we have a hybrid price series, with quotations from León representing twenty-eight commodities and from Valladolid the remaining fourteen.

The statistics for Valencia outrank those for all other regions. As in Old Castile-León, forty-one commodities enter into the index numbers; and, as in New Castile, no lacunae mar the annual data. The continuity and excellence of the accounts of the Hospital dels Inocents [1] and of the municipality, especially the former, and the preponderance of the metropolis in the economic life of the kingdom, which insured the representative character of the series, obviated the necessity of utilizing prices from outside the city of Valencia.

Table 21 lists the index numbers of commodity prices for the four regions.

Chart 6 presents pictorially the data in Table 21.

The decennial averages of the price indices are given in Table 22. Since prices for 1530 alone are available for Andalusia in the third decade, no average can be listed.

TABLE 22

DECENNIAL AVERAGES OF INDEX NUMBERS OF COMMODITY PRICES, 1501–1550

Base = 1521–1530

Decades	Andalusia	New Castile	Old Castile-León	Valencia
1501–1510	76.26	82.40	83.82	80.89
1511–1520	74.19	81.04	81.62	89.03
1521–1530	...	100.12	99.93	100.51
1531–1540	121.19	109.39	102.37	105.12
1541–1550	155.10	128.52	114.62	112.72

The above tables and following chart demonstrate conclusively that the Price Revolution in Spain began at the opening of the sixteenth century. Resulting largely from bad harvests, the peak in 1506–1508, common to all regions, proved ephemeral; but the troughs of 1510 and 1512 remained considerably above 1501

---

[1] Bating a gap of five months in 1512, when a fiscal year beginning on June 1 supplanted the calendar year, the records of extraordinary expenditures run unbroken from 1501 to 1650. But the Querns del Hospitaler, which list "ordinary" or daily recurring expenditures, are unbound, moth-eaten, and replete with missing months and years.

CHART 6

Index Numbers of Commodity Prices, 1501–1550 [1]

Base = 1521–1530

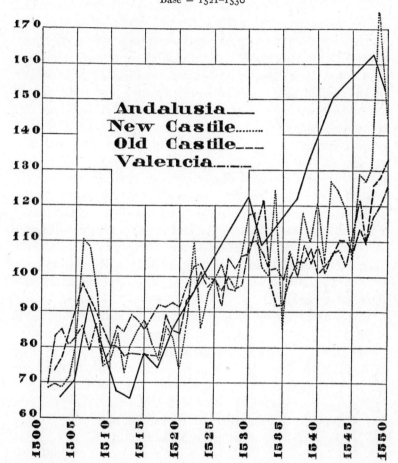

and 1502. Although the trend was unmistakably upward from 1512 to 1518, the Price Revolution made little progress; but during the decade 1521–1530 a general upheaval occurred in all regions, the advance being particularly marked in 1521 owing to the Wars of the Comuneros and Germanías and in 1522 on ac-

---

[1] For brevity, "Old Castile" appears instead of "Old Castile-León" in all charts.

count of bad harvests. On the average, prices in the four regions rose about 51.5 per cent in the first quarter of the century.

Relative price stability characterized the decade 1531–1540, the sharp decline of the first five years,[1] apparently of a cyclical nature, being largely neutralized by the uprise from 1536 to 1540. The average for 1531–1540 in New Castile was about 9.24 per cent and for Old Castile about 2.43 per cent above that of the preceding decade. The data are inadequate for a decennial comparison in Andalusia, and in Valencia the average for 1531–1540 registered an advance of only 4.59 per cent. The upturn of prices in 1536 continued through 1550, the rise being particularly sharp in all regions during the last quinquennium of the period under observation. At the end of the second quarter the index numbers for the four regions averaged about 37.03 per cent higher than at the beginning. In the entire first half of the sixteenth century prices slightly more than doubled. To be specific, if we consider only 1501 and 1550, the advance was about 107.61 per cent. As Chart 6 demonstrates, the rise in prices occurred largely in the first, third, and fifth decades. From 1511 to 1520 the Price Revolution made little or no headway, and the fourth decade witnessed an increase of only 2.5 per cent.

The order of regional emergence of the Price Revolution was in strict accordance with *a priori* expectations. The increase in prices during the first half of the sixteenth century was greatest in Andalusia, where the bulk of the early receipts of American gold and silver first entered circulation. New Castile, the region in the closest commercial contact with Andalusia, experienced the second greatest price upheaval. Valencian and Old Castilian prices rose similarly but lagged considerably behind those of the other two regions. Political barriers to trade between Castile and Valencia apparently counterbalanced the greater geographical separation between Old Castile and the *entrepôt* of American treasure.

Particularly unfortunate have been most generalizations con-

---

[1] The paucity of articles and the abnormally high prices for lard, raisins, and wine forced the Old Castilian index number for 1532 out of line with the other regions; and a high index number for New Castile in 1534 resulted from poor grain and wine harvests.

cerning Spanish prices in the first half of the sixteenth century. Space does not permit consideration of all the uncritical deductions from inadequate data which have made their way into historical and economic literature; but certain errors demand attention. In carefully guarded statements, as one would expect from a scholar conscious of a glaring inadequacy of data, Professor Roger B. Merriman suggested that the general rise in prices did not occur before 1540;[1] but he categorically affirmed that during the reign of the Emperor "the court was constantly moving from place to place, and wherever it went prices rose by leaps and bounds,"[2] and that "the Burgundian court . . . was the chief cause of such rise in prices as occurred during the early part of the [Emperor's] reign."[3] Yet the regional index numbers reflect no definite connection between high price levels and the peregrinations of "Charles's spendthrift Burgundian court."[4] The fact that prices in Old Castile-León, where the court resided most frequently in the first half of the sixteenth century, lagged considerably behind those of Andalusia, where the court almost never went, and New Castile, whither it seldom repaired, renders Professor Merriman's theory untenable.[5] It cannot be argued in

---

[1] *Rise of the Spanish Empire*, III (New York, 1925), 32, n. 1, 124, 199–200.

[2] *Ibid.*, III, 124. Professor Merriman cites J. Bernays ("Zur inneren Entwicklung Castiliens unter Karl V," *Deutsche Zeitschrift für Geschichtswissenschaft*, I, 398–399) to support his theory concerning the rôle of the Burgundian court in the beginning of the Price Revolution. But Bernays' mere ascription of the phenomenal rise in royal expenditures to the extravagant tastes and customs introduced by the Emperor's foreign retainers does not warrant such a course. In fact, Bernays states: "Hence the Burgundian etiquette, not higher prices, caused the increase in the expenditures of the court" (*op. cit.*, p. 398).

[3] *Ibid.*, III, 200.

[4] For the purpose in hand it is instructive to compare the course of prices shown by Chart 6 and Table 21 with the movements of the Emperor in Spain as recorded by the Marquis de Foronda (*Estancias y Viajes del Emperador Carlos V* [Madrid, 1914]). Since Charles V rarely remained in one region a whole year, the unpublished quarterly prices measure the influence of his presence more accurately than do the annual averages. The quarterly data certainly register no revolutions of prices in the cities where the Emperor and his retinue sojourned; at the most they reflect a slight upward influence.

[5] According to Professor Merriman (*op. cit.*, III, 32, n. 1), the Valladolid prices for 1548 listed by Gómara (*Annals of the Emperor Charles V* [R. B. Merriman, Editor, Oxford, 1912], pp. 138–139) were "in a place where everything was exceptionally high on account of the presence of the royal court." Yet the index number for Old Castile-León, based largely on Valladolid prices, stood little above the Valencian and far below the Andalusian and New Castilian indices for that year.

defense of the above thesis that the present index numbers fail to measure accurately changes in the prices of commodities affected by the presence of the court; for Professor Merriman obviously thought in terms of general prices, and no significant discrepancy between the corresponding prices in Appendix III and those paid by the households of Juana la Loca in Tordesillas from 1508 to 1520 and Philip II in Valladolid from 1539 to 1547 is discernible. Furthermore, on *a priori* grounds there is no reason to suppose that an index number composed of the commodities consumed by courtiers would have "risen by leaps and bounds" in medium or large cities when the court arrived. The ratio of the courtiers to the population of a city was small, and the arrival of the court was known in advance and anticipated by the business community.[1]

Konrad Haebler's statement that the prices of necessaries trebled in the first half of the sixteenth century[2] considerably overshot the mark, while the estimates of Maurice Ansiaux[3] and Diego Clemencín[4] that prices trebled by 1555 and 1558 respectively proved little more accurate.

---

[1] The erroneous impression that a local "Price Revolution" occurred wherever the court went doubtless arose from the fact that the protests of the royal attendants had greater survival value than the common run of complaints against the high cost of living.

[2] *Op. cit.*, pp. 35, 160–163.

[3] "Histoire Économique de l'Espagne," *Revue d'Économie Politique*, VII, 548.

[4] "Elógio de la Réina Católica Doña Isabel," *Memorias de la Real Academia de la Historia*, VI (Madrid, 1821), 292, n. 1.

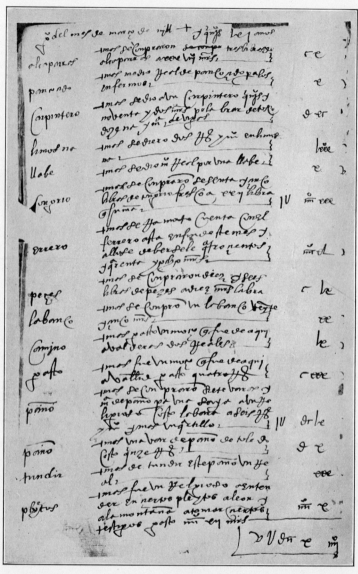

PAGE FROM THE ACCOUNTS OF THE CONVENTO DE NUESTRA
SEÑORA DE SANDOVAL FOR MARCH, 1561
(Archivo Histórico Nacional, *Clero*, León, Leg. 247)

CHAPTER IX

THE PRICE REVOLUTION CULMINATES, 1551-1600

THE second half of the sixteenth century, with the loss of the Holy Roman Crown, the battles of Saint Quentin and Lepanto, protracted insurrection in the Low Countries, the continuation of fanatical religious wars, the annexation of Portugal and her colonial domains in Africa and the East Indies, the destruction of the Invincible Armada, and the pillage of Cádiz, was among the most eventful and critical periods in the political annals of Spain. Yet this epoch was not less pregnant with transcendent economic developments. The crushing public debt inherited by Philip II steadily mounted, and by 1575 weighed so heavily upon the royal treasury that suspension of payments proved the only recourse. As has been shown, the initial steps were taken toward the unbridled vellon inflation which was destined to drive gold and silver out of circulation and force Castile, the mistress of New Spain and Peru, onto a copper standard. According to most historians, the second half of the sixteenth century witnessed the nascent stages of the agricultural, maritime, and industrial decadence which characterized the economic life of Spain under the last three Hapsburgs. The invention of the mercury amalgamation process of silver mining and the discoveries of the Potosí, Guanajuato, and Zacatecas deposits bore full fruit. And the resultant deluge of treasure imports into Spain revolutionized prices, wages, and debtor-creditor relationships.

The strategic position of Spain, the recipient and distributor of American treasure and presumably the fountainhead of the European Price Revolution, renders it not less important to date the culmination, trace the progress, and determine the extent of the Spanish price upheaval than to illuminate its emergence and initial developments. Though by no means adequate for all purposes, the price data available for the second half of the sixteenth century, unlike those for the preceding period, leave few significant questions unanswered.

As in the first half of the sixteenth century, Andalusian prices, derived almost exclusively from the records of the Hospital de la Sangre in Seville, with the accounts of the Cathedral, House of Trade, and Hospital del Espíritu Santo, all of Seville, as controls, are decidedly the weakest regional series. The fifty-six articles included in the index numbers are adequate in quantity; and, except for the ubiquitous paucity of textiles and metals, most important groups of commodities are satisfactorily represented.[1] Samples from the accounts of convents in Cádiz, Cordova, and Granada confirmed the hypothesis that the commercial hegemony of Seville, the monopolist of American trade and navigation, lent a representative character to Sevillan prices. The most salient defect of the Andalusian series is the inadequacy of data for the construction of reliable index numbers for fifteen years, which unfortunately include half the base period 1571–1580 and seven of the decade 1574–1583. The lacunae probably vitiate the secular trend little, if at all; but they greatly impair the value of the data for cyclical measurements and for the investigation of relationships between economic and political events.[2]

In the second half of the sixteenth century New Castilian prices constitute by far the strongest regional series. The excellent accounts of the Hospital de Tavera [3] in Toledo and of the Colegio Mayor de San Ildefonso of the University of Alcalá de Henares furnish continuous quotations for sixty-eight commodities, sixty-seven of which enter into the index numbers, honey being eliminated by an inextricably erratic combination of metrological units. The records of the Hospital de Antezana and of several of the minor colleges of the University of Alcalá de Henares were utilized for comparison and interpolation. As in the preceding half-century, the price series, combining Toledo and Alcalá de

---

[1] Building materials are an exception, quotations for lime, bricks, and nails not being available.

[2] It is interesting to note that in 1576 regular consumption of potatoes by patients in the Hospital de la Sangre commenced (*Libros de Recibos y Gastos*, leg. 455).

[3] The records of ordinary expenditures begin in 1553 and apparently continue for a little over three hundred years without a gap of a single day. It proved necessary, however, to use the bookkeepers' scratch pads for a few years for which the final accounts were missing. Numerous lacunae unfortunately occur in the records of extraordinary disbursements.

Henares quotations, are binary; and again the Toledo prices, embracing all but fifteen of the articles, overwhelmingly predominate. The index numbers include a wide variety of commodities and are marred by no lacunae.

The statistics for Old Castile-León rank second only to those of New Castile. The records of the Convento de Nuestra Señora de Sandoval in Villaverde de Sandoval and the Hospital de Esgueva in Valladolid furnish continuous prices for fifty-six articles; and fifty-four commodities enter into the index numbers, honey being eliminated by variable measures and vinegar by apparently heterogeneous quality. Again we have a binary price series, the quotations for twenty-nine commodities being from León and the remainder from Valladolid. The excellent records of the Hospital de San Bernarbé y San Antolín in Palencia proved invaluable for interpolations, and the accounts of several convents were utilized as controls. Sufficient data are available to permit the construction of index numbers for every year, and most of the important groups of commodities ordinarily found in sixteenth-century documents are satisfactorily represented. The outstanding weakness of the series consists of a hiatus in León prices from 1568 to 1582,[1] making it necessary either to interpolate the base prices for all Leonese commodities from Palencian or Valladolid quotations or to improvise bases by averaging quotations for the two years immediately before and after the gap.

Bating the Andalusian series, the Valencian statistics are the least satisfactory regional data for the second half of the sixteenth century. No gaps occur in the index numbers; but the irregularity and the long lacunae in the *Querns del Hospitaler*, or accounts of ordinary expenditures, of the Hospital dels Inocents, the principal source of the data, reduce the number of commodities for which continuous quotations are available to thirty-five and distort the group representation. Continuous quotations for fruits, nuts, and vegetables are completely lacking,[2] while fish prices are restricted

[1] This gap, like the one from 1501 to 1516, resulted from the fire of August 5, 1614, which destroyed a part of the documents of the Convento de Nuestra Señora de Sandoval stored in the abbot's cell (*vide supra*, p. 188).

[2] It is worthy of note that fruit and vegetable prices for Valencia, "the garden of Spain," are decidedly weaker than in the other regions from the sixteenth century

TABLE 23

Index Numbers of Commodity Prices, 1551–1600
Base = 1571–1580

	Andalusia	New Castile	Old Castile-León	Valencia
1551	68.85	62.96	71.75	74.03
1552	...	71.16	68.52	75.60
1553	...	65.47	68.57	75.91
1554	72.52	63.46	72.47	78.63
1555	72.46	59.85	73.35	78.40
1556	...	61.85	77.27	76.48
1557	76.18	72.15	88.67	81.95
1558	75.50	72.12	98.14	77.93
1559	71.65	72.67	87.14	79.99
1560	72.79	80.42	81.48	81.66
1561	85.86	82.79	87.79	90.87
1562	104.42	85.26	90.87	85.42
1563	88.55	85.86	94.21	90.02
1564	85.83	88.30	95.87	84.67
1565	99.33	88.54	98.17	83.48
1566	89.87	91.63	94.00	85.65
1567	91.18	92.74	94.33	85.37
1568	...	93.73	93.73	90.28
1569	94.77	91.75	85.10	89.10
1570	...	93.52	95.50	88.35
1571	103.41	95.36	96.42	94.94
1572	95.26	96.38	100.26	97.36
1573	95.32	101.57	101.29	98.11
1574	...	97.25	102.17	98.75
1575	...	101.06	107.95	106.84
1576	93.99	97.43	94.39	96.79
1577	...	96.62	93.26	92.12
1578	...	96.79	97.96	102.60
1579	...	113.35	103.06	104.67
1580	103.21	104.15	97.59	106.11
1581	...	102.95	101.33	104.51
1582	111.48	102.33	101.06	111.40
1583	...	107.98	104.26	109.80
1584	112.68	115.65	104.83	108.28
1585	108.75	116.16	108.39	112.10
1586	...	109.45	106.24	106.77
1587	106.58	113.07	109.74	115.80
1588	108.91	104.20	103.82	113.56
1589	112.45	112.71	108.95	118.23
1590	...	118.11	107.32	117.46
1591	113.06	113.50	110.84	113.52
1592	114.75	115.67	117.62	120.42
1593	111.00	111.91	111.59	119.23
1594	113.55	113.50	114.83	115.09
1595	110.94	114.08	112.38	118.91
1596	123.70	113.63	115.65	113.46
1597	...	114.38	126.40	127.23
1598	130.02	126.32	140.76	133.11
1599	133.13	134.00	131.61	140.95
1600	141.15	130.70	136.16	140.91

to codfish. The records of the municipality of Valencia strengthened the quotations for building materials. If virtually all of the
sixteenth-century accounts of the Colegio de Santo Tomás, which
ran unbroken from 1553 to 1931, had not been destroyed in the
anticlerical rioting of May 12, 1931, a few hours after their utilization had commenced, they would have proved valuable complements of the hospital data.[1]

Table 23 lists the regional index numbers of commodity prices.
Chart 7 presents pictorially the data in Table 23.

In the following table decennial averages of the index numbers
are given.

TABLE 24

DECENNIAL AVERAGES OF INDEX NUMBERS OF COMMODITY PRICES, 1551–1600

Base = 1571–1580

Decades	Andalusia	New Castile	Old Castile-León	Valencia
1551–1560	72.85	68.21	78.74	78.06
1561–1570	92.48	89.41	92.96	87.32
1571–1580	98.24	100.00	99.44	99.83
1581–1590	110.14	110.26	105.59	111.79
1591–1600	121.26	118.77	121.78	124.28

After six years of unusually stable prices, the index numbers in
all regions rose sharply from 1556 to 1562, registering an average
advance of about 26.58 per cent in the space of six years. The
trough in New Castilian prices from 1554 to 1556 was apparently
of a cyclical nature, and the peak for Old Castile in 1558 was
largely due to a bad season for fruits, vegetables, and grains,
though fish and meat were also dear. The abnormally high prices
for Andalusia in 1562 are less easily explained. Poor harvests of
grain and olive oil cannot escape responsibility; but the prices of

to the eighteenth. Only in Valencia, a land of orange groves, are orange prices
elusive; but the reason for the deficiency is not far to seek. Most institutions either
had their own gardens and orchards or found no difficulty in obtaining their fruits
and vegetables as alms. Much more than in other regions the payment of alms in
kind was a firmly established practice. For instance, all the silk prices listed in
Appendix IV represent the sales of charitable donations to the Hospital dels Inocents. Prices for hens are missing in 1615–1616 because the Hospital begged the
several hundred required to feed its patients.

[1] Two assistants and I left Santo Tomás within fifteen minutes of the time the
students had to abandon the building before the fury of the mob.

such diverse commodities as firewood, mutton, resin, raisins, and soap were also exorbitant. Furthermore, the index number, which includes only twenty-five commodities, or less than half the total, may fail to measure the general price level with absolute precision.[1]

CHART 7

INDEX NUMBERS OF COMMODITY PRICES, 1551–1600

Base = 1571–1580

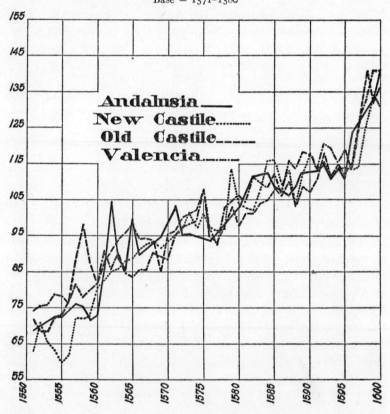

From 1562 to 1569 a second plateau was reached, a considerable advance being registered only in New Castile; but in 1570–1575 there was a sharp upturn in all regions for which adequate data

[1] It is unfortunate that quotations from the House of Trade are not available for 1562.

are available. The gap from 1573 to 1576 destroys the validity of the Andalusian series for the purpose in hand. It is significant, however, that index numbers based on quotations from the House of Trade rose from 90 in 1573 to 101.7 in 1575,[1] thus agreeing closely with the course of prices in the other regions. Even with a straight-line interpolation for the Andalusian lacuna, a method which (in this case) introduces a downward bias, the average increase in prices for the four regions from 1569 to 1575 was about 15 per cent. Using the same method, we find that in the third quarter of the sixteenth century prices rose by 49.5 per cent.

After a sharp cyclical drop in 1576–1577, following the royal bankruptcy of 1575, prices reacted in 1578 and continued to rise in all regions until 1584. The peak for New Castile in 1579 was largely due to an exceptionally poor fruit crop. From 1584 to 1595 the price levels in all regions remained unusually stable, with a slight upward tendency. The abnormally low index numbers for Old Castile largely reflect bountiful harvests of fruits, nuts, and grains. In 1596 the Andalusian index number soared, and the next year Valencian and Old Castilian prices followed. But the upward movement was delayed until 1598 in New Castile. The average advance for the four regions in the brief space of three years was about 16.19 per cent, the most phenomenal general rise of silver prices in the entire period 1501–1650 occurring in this interval. In the last quarter of the century prices rose about 32.31 per cent and in the last half-century about 97.74 per cent. That the advance of prices during the second half of the century so nearly duplicated that of the first half is indeed a remarkable coincidence.

Little would be gained by systematic consideration of the estimates of the general price upheaval in its various stages registered by the *Procuradores* in Cortes and contemporary writers,[2] whose

---

[1] *Vide* Earl J. Hamilton, "American Treasure and Andalusian Prices, 1503–1660," *Journal of Economic and Business History*, I, 26.

[2] For an example of how far from the mark these estimates have carried even a competent historian one may consult the work of Don Antonio Ballesteros (*Historia de España*, IV, pt. II [Barcelona, 1927], 147–148). An examination of the data listed by Professor Ballesteros will show that few of the years pointed out as being sterile and dear were actually so.

knowledge was glaringly defective and whose expressions were colored by the tendency, uniformly characteristic of human nature, to complain against an actual or fancied high cost of living and by a desire to secure fiscal advantages for their constituencies; but it is worthy of note that in a memorial to the Crown dated May 22, 1581, the renowned engineer, Juan Bautista Antoneli, affirmed that "the prices of goods . . . have risen so much that *seigneurs*, gentlemen, commoners, and the clergy cannot live on their incomes."[1] In 1600 Francisco Soranzo, a Venetian envoy, reported that "in all Spain are found a very great scarcity and an inexpressible dearness of all things,"[2] and a memorial to the Crown adopted by the Cortes on November 18, 1600, complained that as consequences of exorbitant prices, nakedness and sickness stalked the land, that the number of beggars, thieves, and prostitutes had increased, that only through hypothecation of property had the rich been able to live, and that the poor were dying of hunger.[3]

The sharp rise in prices which began in 1596 continued until 1601, when the apogee, represented by an index number of 143.55 on a 1571–1580 base, was reached.[4] If we consider only 1501 and 1601, the nadir and zenith respectively, we find that on the average the regional price indices more than quadrupled. To be specific, the average price level was 4.32 times as high in 1601 as in 1501. Since silver prices never fully descended from the peak attained at the close of the sixteenth century, it seems correct to say that by 1600 silver prices in Spain had risen permanently to a level four times as high as that at which they stood in 1501. But the extent of the Price Revolution was not equal in all the regions. Reflecting wide discrepancies among the regional series in the

---

[1] Juan Sempere y Guarinos, *Biblioteca Económico-Política*, I (Madrid, 1801), lxxv.

[2] Cited by Maurice Ansiaux, "Histoire Économique de l'Espagne," *Revue d'Économie Politique*, VII, 1027.

[3] *Actas de las Cortes de Castilla*, XIX, 554–555. The list of prices and wages for 1588 and 1600 included in the memorial, which has occasionally been cited to indicate the course of the Price Revolution (*vide*, for example, Cristóbal Espejo, "Carestía de la Vida en el Siglo XVI," in *Revista de Archivos, Bibliotecas y Museos*, 3ª Época, XXV, 211), greatly exaggerates the extent of the upheaval between these dates.

[4] The only higher silver index number subsequently attained was for 1629, but in all probability this figure was spuriously high (*vide infra*, Chapter XIII).

Silver index numbers for 1501–1650 on 1571–1580 as a base are shown in Chart 20.

first half of the century, prices more than quintupled in Andalusia, more than quadrupled in New Castile, but rose only about 3½-fold in Old Castile and Valencia.

The outstanding phenomenon revealed by the present chapter is the almost incredibly close agreement among the regional index numbers of prices. Chart 7 demonstrates that less disparity appears among the price series from 1580 to 1600 than in the base period 1571–1580, when they are artificially brought together, and that the curves are little farther apart in 1561–1570. Although the index numbers measure relative movements rather than the relationships among absolute prices, the inevitable conclusion is that, despite the mountainous character of the territory and the dependence upon land transportation over poor highways, carried on in the primitive fashion of the day, interregional trade probably covered a wider range of commodities and was more active than anyone has yet supposed, and that the fairs, especially those of Medina del Campo, Medina de Rioseco, and Villalón, served as great central markets and clearing houses, which regulated wholesale prices throughout the realm.

The principle that the wholesale prices in the leading fairs should govern retail prices won recognition in municipal legislation. The ordinances of Valladolid approved by Charles V on July 20, 1549, provided that the municipality should send a delegate to each of the fairs at Medina del Campo to report upon the prevalent wholesale prices of spices and groceries. To fix the maximum retail prices which should obtain until the next fair, the *regidor* and justices of Valladolid added to the Medina del Campo wholesale quotations just compensation for the expenses and labor of the retailer.[1] For failure to obtain, to post in their establishments, and to abide by the maximum retail price list within three days after its preparation had been preconized grocers were subject to a fine of 500 maravedís and twenty days' imprisonment.[2] After having received the report of a representative sent to Valladolid to investigate price control in that city, on

---

[1] In 1549 the municipality of Valladolid informed a representative of the city of León that the retail prices in Valladolid were fixed 10 per cent above wholesale prices in the fairs at Medina del Campo (*Ordenanzas de León* [León, 1669], fol. 202).

[2] *Ordenanzas de Valladolid* (Valladolid, 1737), ordenanza XXVII.

December 9, 1549, León decided to base the maximum retail prices of groceries upon wholesale quotations in the fairs at Medina del Campo, Medina de Rioseco, or Villalón.[1]

But the most striking evidence of the regulatory influence of the fairs upon Spanish prices is furnished by the high percentages of the wholesale purchases of cloth, fish, groceries, medicine, and miscellaneous commodities made in Medina del Campo, Medina de Rioseco, and Villalón by hospitals and convents as far away as Toledo and by the regular liquidations of large financial obligations in the fairs by institutions and business men in Seville and Valencia. That the influence of the fair at Medina del Campo transcended the Spanish frontiers and linked domestic prices with those of the leading commercial emporia of Europe in the second half of the sixteenth century is amply attested by the accounts of Simón and Cosme Ruiz, the great bankers and merchant princes of Medina, and their correspondence from factors scattered throughout the Occident.[2] During the entire sixteenth century the Convento de Nuestra Señora de Sandoval regularly bought the bulk of its spring supplies of clothing and non-perishable provisions in the March fair at Villalón. In 1565, for example, the purchases included rice, saffron, sugar, twine, soap, chick-peas, raisins, lentils, paper, pins, cinnamon, cloves, pepper, alum, incense, dates, figs, five classes of fish, and several kinds of cloth.[3] In the second quarter of the sixteenth century the Convent also procured a large percentage of its fall supplies in the September fair at Medina de Rioseco, but after about 1558 this fair virtually passed out of the picture.

The political hindrances to trade and the strict prohibitions of treasure exports from Castile to Valencia render the perfect agreement of the price movements in Valencia and the three Castilian regions all the more remarkable. For instance, the goods bought in Valencia in March, 1508 for the household of Juana la Loca at Arcos, "two leagues from Burgos," had to pay export duties upon leaving the Mediterranean kingdom;[4] and in February, 1555

---

[1] *Ordenanzas de León*, fol. 202.   [2] *Vide supra*, p. 91, n. 4.
[3] Archivo Histórico Nacional, *Clero*, León, 247.
[4] Archivo de Simancas, *Casa Real* (E.M.), 9–1.

Valencian convents paid export duties on saffron purchased in Aragon.[1] By a royal order of July 20, 1592, Philip II granted the Monasterio de San Lorenzo del Escorial the special privilege of importing annually from Valencia through Requena a hundred arrobas of wax duty-free.[2] In the Valencian *Corts* of 1626 the Three Estates complained to the Crown that when Valencians attempted to return to their homes with surplus funds they had carried into Castile to purchase "wheat and other things," the Castilian customs officials were "obstructive and vexatious." [3]

In view of the research in price history now being conducted in various European countries, it would be otiose and hazardous to attempt at this time an exhaustive or even an accurate comparison of Spanish prices with those of other nations. But it may not be amiss to contrast the revolution of Spanish prices with the upheavals in other important European countries as limned by the data now available. Inasmuch as the conclusions will necessarily be tentative, the index numbers constructed by Georg Wiebe [4] from the statistics supplied by Vicomte d'Avenel, Thorold Rogers, and others [5] appear sufficiently accurate for the present purpose. Unfortunately Wiebe omitted annual index numbers and shifted from quarter-century averages for France to decennial for England, Germany, and Italy. Furthermore, the English decades subsequent to 1561–1570 fail to coincide with those employed in other countries. Since a common unit of time has proved unattainable, twenty-five year averages have been calculated for comparison with French prices; and the decennial averages most nearly synchronous with Wiebe's decades for England have been utilized. All of Wiebe's index numbers are of the simple arithmetic type and have been constructed from prices expressed in terms of a constant weight of fine gold or silver,[6] and

---

[1] Archivo Regional de Valencia, *Conventos*, lib. 1368.

[2] *Quaderno de Leyes Añadidas a la Nueva Recopilación* (Madrid, 1619), fols. 177–178.

[3] *Furs, Capitols, Provisions e Actes de Cort de 1626* (Valencia, 1635), cap. XXXIII, fol 13.

[4] *Geschichte der Preisrevolution des XVI. und XVII. Jahrhunderts* (Leipzig, 1895), pp. 369–379.

[5] *Ibid.*, pp. 325–366.

[6] Only the prices for Münster run in terms of gold.

the Spanish index numbers have been either computed on or reduced to a pure silver basis. Since Wiebe adopted 1451–1500 as a base and the continuous index numbers in the present study have a 1571–1580 base,[1] the first time-unit common to both sets of index numbers has been chosen as a point of reference for all comparisons.

The dating of the Price Revolution in France and Spain seems to have been similar. According to d'Avenel,[2] French prices turned upward during the reign of Louis XII (1498–1515); and the highest average index of commodity prices in any quarter-century from 1501 to 1650 occurred in the last quarter of the sixteenth century, when prices stood about 2.19 times as high as in 1501–1525. Spanish prices also rose from the beginning of the sixteenth century, and the upheaval in Spain was much more violent, each quarter of the century showing a greater advance over the preceding one than occurred in France. The Spanish price level was 2.66 times as high in the last as in the first quarter of the sixteenth century;[3] and instead of declining sharply, as in France, the index for 1601–1625 rose to a point 3.13 times as high as in 1501–1525. If we combine wages, or the price of labor, with commodity prices in the ratio of 1 to 2, thus approximating the combination suggested by Mr. Carl Snyder[4] for an "index of the general price level" as closely as our data will permit, we find that Spanish prices in 1576–1600 exceeded those of 1501–1525 in the ratio of 2.56 to 1 and that the corresponding ratio for France was

---

[1] Owing to his adoption of the late fifteenth-century base, the upward bias of Wiebe's unweighted arithmetic index numbers tends to exaggerate the price upheavals in the various countries which he studied, whereas the selection of a 1571–1580 base, near the end of the Price Revolution in Spain, tends to produce the opposite effect upon my simple arithmetic indices.

[2] *Histoire Économique de la Propriété, des Salaires, des Denrées, et de Tous les Prix en Général*, 1 (Paris, 1894), 15.

A difference in the time-units renders comparison difficult; but it appears that, when reduced to a silver basis, the prices published by M. Paul Raveau in his excellent study, *L'Agriculture et les Classes Paysannes dans le Haut Poitou au XVIe Siècle* (Paris, 1926), pp. i–xxxvi, agree fairly closely with those of d'Avenel reproduced by Wiebe.

[3] All the decennial and quarter-century averages used for comparisons in this chapter include interpolations of lacunae in the regional index numbers, but no interpolations enter into the averages in Table 24.

[4] *Business Cycles and Business Measurements* (New York, 1927), p. 138.

1.92 to 1. The highest average "general price level" attained in
Spain, in 1601–1625, was 3.18 times as high as a hundred years
before, while the peak for France, in 1626–1650, was only 1.93
times as high as in 1501–1525.

The different modes of comparison uniformly indicate that the
revolution of silver prices was considerably more violent in Spain
than in France.[1] The synchronism of the price movements in the
two countries suggests that close commercial contacts were maintained, either directly or through the Spanish possessions in Italy
and the Low Countries, in spite of the bitter political rivalry and
protracted hostilities between the French kings and the house of
Austria.

Although French prices attained their peak in 1576–1600, the
upward movement in other leading European countries continued
into the seventeenth century. The data now available indicate
that English prices commenced to rise at the opening of the
sixteenth century and that the decennial averages increased
rapidly, although irregularly, from 1540–1549 [2] to 1643–1652,
when they reached their zenith.[3] From 1501–1510 to 1593–1602
commodity prices rose in the ratio of 1 to 2.56, and in 1643–1652
the commodity index was 3.48 times that of 1501–1510. The
Spanish price level in 1591–1600 was 3.03 times that of 1501–1510;
and by 1601–1610, when they reached their apogee, prices were
3.4 times as high as a hundred years before. In other words,

---

[1] Owing to persistent monetary debasement, however, the rise of prices in Haut
Poitou during the sixteenth century in terms of current money (*vide* Paul Raveau,
op. cit., pp. xiii–xxxvi), the only prices of practical significance to contemporaries,
was no less revolutionary than in Andalusia. It is easily possible that the average
increase in current French prices exceeded the average in Spain.

[2] The results of Thorold Rogers show a sharp drop in prices in 1541–1550 as compared with the preceding decade, but a preliminary unpublished report from Sir
William Beveridge to the International Scientific Committee on Price History indicates that English prices rose considerably in the decade 1540–1549. With the scant
material at his command, Adam Smith concluded that English prices did not begin
to rise before 1570; that the Price Revolution ran its course by 1636; and that silver
declined in value by two-thirds (*Wealth of Nations* [Cannan ed., London, 1904],
I, 191–192).

[3] The decennial averages in 1673–1682 and 1693–1702 were slightly higher than
in 1643–1652; but the general average for 1653–1702 was lower than in 1563–1652.
The decennial averages available indicate that the Price Revolution ended in 1643–
1652 and that remarkable stability of prices characterized the ensuing fifty years.

commodity prices rose considerably more in Spain than in England during the sixteenth century, and the peak in Spain, reached in the eleventh decade of the Price Revolution, was almost exactly as high as the peak in England, which developed in the fifteenth decade.

If we combine the index numbers of prices and wages in each country in the ratio of 2 to 1 and compare the resultant indices of the "general price level," we find that the upheaval of general prices in Spain was incomparably greater than in England. The general index for England in 1593–1602 was only 2.14 times that of 1501–1510, while from the first to the last decade of the sixteenth century the Spanish index rose 2.94-fold. At the zenith, in 1601–1610, Spanish prices were 3.46 times as high as in 1501–1510, while the peak of English prices, in 1643–1652, exceeded the level of 1501–1510 in the ratio of only 2.94 to 1.

Bating decennial averages for wheat and maize, which continue through the seventeenth century, we have no commodity prices for Italy posterior to 1600; and Wiebe's index numbers for the sixteenth century rest upon extremely inadequate data. One may infer, however, that commodity prices in north Italy approximately doubled in the sixteenth century, and the apparent fall in grain prices in the seventeenth century suggests that the zenith of Italian prices was reached in the neighborhood of 1600.[1] Lacking wage statistics, we cannot consider movements of the "general price level." Unfortunately index numbers for the Low Countries — like Italy, a cradle of modern capitalism — are lacking. According to d'Avenel,[2] the remuneration of Spanish officials in Flanders was increased in 1527 on account of higher living costs. Wiebe's index numbers for Münster, which was doubtless in close commercial contact with the Low Countries, may throw some light upon the movements of Flemish as well as German

---

[1] According to the recent investigation by Amintore Fanfani ("La Rivoluzione dei Prezzi a Milano nel XVI e XVII Secolo," *Giornale degli Economisti* [Luglio, 1932], pp. 465–482), Milanese silver prices were almost exactly twice as high in 1615–1619, the peak for the period 1500–1629, as in 1510–1514. But Signor Fanfani's study includes very few commodities; and the quotations, based on legal maximum schedules, are questionable and discontinuous.

[2] *Op. cit.*, I, 15.

prices. From 1501–1510 to 1551–1560, when the data end, prices in Münster rose in the ratio of 1 to 1.47; and, owing to the deplorable lag of wages behind prices, the "general price level" in 1551–1560 was only 1.37 times that of 1501–1510. In the same period commodity and "general prices" in Spain rose 1.85- and 1.82-fold respectively. The only other German index numbers listed by Wiebe are for Saxony in the sixteenth century. The data for the first three decades are so scanty, however, that the base period 1467–1500 and the fourth decade must be taken as points of reference. The peak of commodity prices in 1591–1599 was 2.39 times the base and 1.5 times as high as in 1531–1540. As has been indicated, Spanish prices rose 3.03-fold from the first to the last decade of the sixteenth century; and the average for 1591–1600 was 2.23 times that of 1531–1540.

I regret that inability to read Polish renders it impossible for me satisfactorily to compare Spanish prices with the statistics for Lemberg published by the eminent Polish scholar, Professor Fr. Bujak.[1] It is hazardous for one unable to understand Polish to use the brief summary and the price tables written in French;[2] but it appears that from 1521 to 1530, when Professor Bujak's decennial averages of unweighted general index numbers in terms of a fixed weight of silver begin, through 1641–1650,[3] the decennial averages of the composite silver indices for Spain[4] are higher than the Polish indices in each decade save the first and last. In most cases the difference is substantial.[5]

Whether the sixteenth-century increase of prices in Spain was the greatest long-term upheaval on a specie basis in modern times is an interesting question. Although current research in price history in other countries may revise the above estimates of the extent of the Price Revolution, it appears extremely unlikely that in the course of the sixteenth and seventeenth centuries the "gen-

---

[1] *Ceny we Lwowie w XVI i XVII Wieku* (Lemberg, 1928).

[2] *Ibid.*, pp. 158–287, 316–322.

[3] *Op. cit.*, p. 283.

[4] For the annual indices *vide infra*, Appendix VIII. For the above comparison I have reduced my indices to a 1521–1525 base, the one selected by Professor Bujak.

[5] It is highly probable, however, that Professor Bujak's index numbers designed to measure the cost of living (*op. cit.*, pp. 283, 320) registered a greater advance than similar indices for Spain would show.

eral price level" rose as much in any other country of the Old World as it did in Spain from 1501 to 1601.[1] With the exception of Mexican silver production, no significant increase in the output of the precious metals occurred in the eighteenth century; so we may focus our attention upon the nineteenth century and the first three decades of the twentieth, in which fertile gold and silver mines were discovered and new processes and improved technique came into general use. Yet the nineteenth- and twentieth-century annals of the leading countries of the Western World afford no example of a hundred-year price upheaval in terms of a fixed-weight monetary standard [2] comparable to that which occurred in Spain during the first century of the Price Revolution. If we examine the period 1820–1920, for example, in order to include the peak of the Great War prices, we find that commodity index numbers in the United States rose considerably less than 100 per cent, or not half as much proportionately as did those of Spain in the sixteenth century.

[1] Although he correctly inferred from the scanty material available that in its early stages the Price Revolution was more violent in Spain than in any other European country, Georg Wiebe (*op. cit.*, p. 162) went far from the mark when he guessed that the total advance of prices was little greater than in France or Germany and perhaps less than in England. Wiebe underestimated the rise in Spanish prices during the sixteenth century largely because he labored under the impression that the fine silver equivalent of the maravedí fell throughout the century (*op. cit.*, pp. 38, 414–415). One must recognize, however, that Wiebe (*op. cit.*, pp. 14, 37–38, 414) was aware of the glaring inadequacy of the monetary and price data at his disposal.

[2] Had not silver been demonetized, the enormous production of this metal in the last sixty years would have raised price levels immensely.

CHAPTER X

PRICES UNDER VELLON INFLATION, 1601–1650

THE emphasis now swings from the impact of ever increasing treasure imports upon prices in terms of the soundest European currency to price behavior under sharply declining receipts of American gold and silver and progressive depreciation of base money. As Chapter IX demonstrates, the Price Revolution in Spain culminated in 1601, when prices in terms of a fixed weight of silver reached their apogee; but the reader should bear in mind that "culminated" refers to the upheaval of prices in the sixteenth and seventeenth centuries which occurred independently of monetary debasement. From the standpoint of contemporaries the course of Castilian silver prices in the first quarter of the seventeenth century was incomparably less important than the movement of vellon prices; and in the second quarter silver prices, which can be obtained in significant quantities only as the derivatives of vellon quotations, exercised no influence upon economic life. Only as means to certain scientific ends, such as international price comparisons and the determination of price behavior under declining treasure imports from the New World, can the compilation of silver prices or the construction of silver index numbers find practical justification.

As Chapter IV sets forth, vellon did not consistently fall below par until 1603, when the doubling of the tariff of the pure copper issues authorized by Philip III in 1599 and 1602, following the heavy coinage of near-copper at the end of the reign of Philip II, drove silver to a premium in the open market. But the next two decades witnessed no further increases in the tale of vellon, and unbridled coinage did not occur before the accession of Philip IV. The vigorous opposition of the government to the slight discount on vellon favored the operation of Gresham's Law; but while the stock of specie was being replenished by heavy annual receipts from the Indies, considerable time was required for vellon to displace the vast quantities of silver that had circulated in Castile at the end of the sixteenth century. In the first two decades of the seventeenth century Castilian silver and vellon remained current, and indiscriminate entries in terms of both appear regularly in contemporary commercial documents. But the inordinate issues of vellon early in the reign of Philip IV greatly accelerated the hitherto gradual displacement of silver as the money of account. In the quinquennium 1621–1625 the premium on pieces of eight reached such heights that even the crude principles of bookkeeping then obtaining could no longer countenance mixed entries of silver and vellon receipts and disbursements, and the virtual disappearance of reals from circulation left a clear field for *cuartos.* It is impossible to date exactly the definitive establishment of vellon as the chief circulating medium and sole accounting unit, but the change took place around 1622–1623 in most of the records I have utilized. It seems safe to say that throughout the second quarter of the seventeenth century prices and wages were uniformly quoted in terms of vellon. And in this period the alternation of sudden inflation and precipitate deflation wreaked havoc upon the economic life of Castile.

As Chapter V demonstrates, not vellon, but Valencian silver, supplanted Castilian reals as the monetary standard and accounting unit in the Mediterranean kingdom; and debasement never approached the extremes registered in Castile.

From the last position in the two preceding periods the Andalusian series — with ninety-two commodities in the index numbers and only one missing year — rises to first place in 1601–1650. The accounts of the Hospital de la Sangre, available every year except 1610, 1615, and 1621, remain the chief source; but the records of the Hospitales del Cardenal and Amor de Dios form valuable additions to the Espíritu Santo papers as sources to fill lacunae, and convent records from Cádiz, Cordova, and Granada supplement the accounts of the Casa de la Contratación as controls. As in the sixteenth-century series, it has proved unnecessary to utilize prices from outside Seville, the Andalusian metropolis and center of the West Indian trade. Bating metals, all important groups of commodities for which satisfactory quo-

tations are ordinarily available in seventeenth-century documents are adequately represented.[1] The fish series is particularly
rich, and the quotations for cotton lamp wicks, twine, and
three grades of thread diminish the characteristic weakness of
textiles.

Owing to deterioration of the Hospital de Antezana and the
University accounts, the number of commodities in the New
Castilian price table falls to fifty-nine; and the Alcalá de Henares
quotations, with only five representatives, almost disappear. The
high quality of the account-books of the Hospital de Tavera is
maintained, however; and the New Castilian index numbers,
chiefly based on Toledo prices, virtually become unitary rather
than binary, as in the two preceding periods. The records of four
convents in Madrid, Toledo, and Guadalajara and of the Hospital de Caridad in Illescas filled lacunae and served as controls.
Aside from the inevitable weakness of the textile and metal quotations, the outstanding defect of the New Castilian series is the
dearth of fish prices, which resulted from the abnormally low consumption by the Hospital de Tavera. That this hiatus was not
altogether due to the inland location of New Castile is attested by
the prevalence of fish purchases in the accounts of Madrid and
Toledo convents.[2]

With no missing years and continuous quotations for sixty-four
commodities, sixty-two of which enter into the index numbers,[3]
the prices for Old Castile-León are highly satisfactory. The Old
Castilian-Leonese series remains binary. Of the sixty-two articles
included in the index numbers, quotations for forty have been
taken from the excellent records of the Convento de Nuestra

[1] It is interesting to note that the Hospital de la Sangre apparently served its
patients tomato salad much earlier than it is generally believed that tomatoes commenced to be used as food. The kitchen accounts for July 20, 1608, record a purchase of 4 pounds of tomatoes at 12 maravedís a pound, and on August 17 two
pounds were bought at 8 maravedís (*Libros de Recibos y Gastos*, leg. 459). The entry
of the tomatoes in the kitchen rather than in the pharmaceutical accounts, the
quantities bought, and the concurrent purchases of cucumbers "for salad" indicate that the tomatoes formed an ingredient of salad.

[2] *Vide*, for example, Archivo Histórico Nacional, *Clero*, Madrid, legs. 660, 715;
Clero, Toledo, legs. 166, 186.

[3] Honey prices have been omitted because of erratic measures, and heterogeneous quality eliminated vinegar.

Señora de Sandoval in Villaverde de Sandoval and the remainder from the accounts of the Esgueva and Resurrección [1] Hospitals in Valladolid. The Archive of the Hospital de San Bernarbé y San Antolín in Palencia supplied by far the best data relegated to the position of filling gaps in the series for any region or period. The remarkable kitchen accounts of the Hospitales de Barrientos and Simón Ruiz in Medina del Campo, along with fragmentary material from the records of five hospitals in Ávila and Segovia and several convents in widely scattered localities, have been utilized as controls. The outstanding defect of the Old Castilian series is the lack of quotations for lime, bricks, and plaster of Paris, the three leading building materials. The exceptional strength of the grain series deserves special mention.

The *Querns del Hospitaler*, or records of daily recurring expenditures, of the Hospital dels Inocents having been better preserved, the Valencian series — with no missing years and fifty-two articles in the index numbers — is incomparably better than in the preceding period. With the exception of metals, most important groups of commodities usually found in historical price studies are satisfactorily represented. One of the most notable features of the Valencian series is the relative abundance of textile quotations. Twine, hempen sandals, bedticks, shrouds, and unbleached domestic give coarse textiles a representation of almost 10 per cent of the commodities. As in the sixteenth century, the account-books of the Hospital dels Inocents were the principal source, and the records of the Ayuntamiento and the Colegio de Santo Tomás continued to supply data to fill gaps. The papers of various convents, deposited in the Archivo Regional, afforded much more adequate controls than were available for the sixteenth century. Again it has proved unnecessary to utilize data from outside the city of Valencia, and the preponderant commercial position of the metropolis assures the representative character of the series.

Table 25 lists the index numbers of commodity prices for the Castilian regions in terms of silver for 1601–1602 and of vellon

---

[1] Stored in the Hospital Provincial. The Esgueva papers are deposited in the Archivo del Ayuntamiento.

TABLE 25

Index Numbers of Commodity Prices, 1601–1650

Base = 1621–1630

	Andalusia	New Castile	Old Castile-León	Valencia
1601	93.91	84.05	94.31	107.31
1602	88.23	79.63	93.43	104.48
1603	93.68	79.03	91.75	105.20
1604	99.23	81.12	94.33	100.77
1605	98.22	86.69	96.76	98.76
1606	91.42	86.61	95.09	94.79
1607	91.28	84.81	91.87	88.94
1608	90.29	84.41	91.20	92.70
1609	89.29	80.96	80.13	90.88
1610	87.83	82.27	83.54	96.87
1611	80.67	79.95	83.06	94.11
1612	82.46	78.22	79.95	96.33
1613	83.66	82.92	79.50	93.35
1614	83.75	88.29	85.97	94.66
1615	81.43	84.17	83.84	94.60
1616	84.05	88.56	88.36	95.97
1617	84.63	89.98	86.89	99.02
1618	88.57	88.38	82.84	99.79
1619	82.79	80.62	84.94	98.50
1620	88.57	86.24	85.27	94.94
1621	...	82.69	85.86	96.14
1622	90.08	89.48	83.21	95.22
1623	87.64	87.51	87.49	100.61
1624	88.78	93.24	95.52	96.52
1625	96.38	93.68	92.15	93.72
1626	113.39	107.74	102.13	99.01
1627	113.04	113.76	116.03	101.40
1628	110.61	109.17	117.12	100.47
1629	99.88	112.99	117.06	108.12
1630	99.79	109.69	106.64	106.78
1631	96.17	105.23	110.13	107.11
1632	100.60	111.43	108.10	111.31
1633	99.84	104.71	102.92	112.90
1634	96.10	107.39	99.84	109.54
1635	98.42	100.52	98.23	110.92
1636	105.24	105.34	94.21	118.20
1637	118.30	109.11	100.40	118.61
1638	107.29	112.82	116.01	109.53
1639	104.92	108.23	105.43	106.38
1640	104.76	106.05	103.25	111.82
1641	110.40	114.70	110.04	113.67
1642	131.58	122.95	123.72	108.97
1643	114.14	112.39	114.50	111.67
1644	115.61	111.88	105.37	118.85
1645	113.68	113.28	103.42	111.69
1646	123.62	113.17	112.59	106.72
1647	125.69	109.18	109.25	115.69
1648	126.44	119.05	120.51	114.60
1649	136.00	120.44	124.96	111.22
1650	157.53	122.78	124.58	114.10

thereafter. The Valencian indices run in terms of Castilian silver in 1601–1609 and of Valencian silver in 1610–1650.[1]

Chart 8 presents graphically the data in Table 25.

CHART 8

INDEX NUMBERS OF COMMODITY PRICES, 1601–1650

Base = 1621–1630

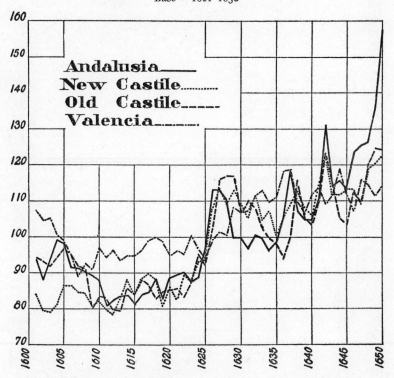

The averages of the silver index numbers for the four regions on 1571–1580 as a base appear in Chart 20. The appropriate premiums listed in Tables 7 and 10 and the data in Appendix II will enable anyone interested in silver prices to convert the regional indices in Table 25 into terms of a fixed weight of silver.

[1] *Vide infra*, Appendix II.

In Table 26 the decennial averages of the index numbers in Table 25 are given.

TABLE 26

DECENNIAL AVERAGES OF THE INDEX NUMBERS OF COMMODITY PRICES, 1601–1650

Base = 1621–1630

Decades	Andalusia	New Castile	Old Castile-León	Valencia
1601–1610	92.34	82.96	91.24	98.07
1611–1620	84.06	84.73	84.06	96.13
1621–1630	99.95	100.00	100.32	99.80
1631–1640	103.16	107.08	103.85	111.63
1641–1650	125.47	115.98	114.89	112.72

Beginning at the highest average for the four regions reached by silver prices in the entire period 1501–1650, the index numbers uniformly displayed a downward tendency until 1610. The decline of the Valencian price level from 1603 to 1607 [1] and of the Andalusian from 1606 to 1610 was apparently cyclical in character, while the fall of more than ten points in the Old Castilian index number in 1609 largely reflected abnormally low prices for spring fruits, fish, and animal products. The protracted recession was interrupted only by a significant cyclical upturn in Andalusia in 1603–1604 and in the two Castiles in 1604–1605 and a slight rise in all regions except Andalusia in 1610. From 1601 to 1610 the average price level in the four regions fell almost 7.5 per cent.

Remarkable stability of prices characterized the period 1611–1620. As Chart 8 demonstrates, a rise and fall in the indices for all regions accompanied a complete revolution of the business cycle. But the extreme fluctuations, ranging from 6.44 points in Valencia to 11.76 in New Castile, were confined within narrow limits. The trend was slightly but unmistakably upward, the average of the four regional index numbers for 1620 being 1.44 per cent higher than in 1610.

The heavy coinage of vellon in the quinquennium 1621–1625 upset the price stability of the preceding decade, which had resulted largely from the quasi-equilibrium between the coinage of silver and vellon and the disappearance of reals from circulation through hoarding and exportation. Under the stimulus of vellon

---

[1] The prices of animal products fell sharply.

inflation prices rose sharply in the three Castilian regions from 1621 to 1625; only in Valencia, a region relatively free from currency expansion, was there a net decline in the price level. The rise from 1621 to 1625 almost exactly neutralized the fall from 1601 to 1610, the average of the regional index numbers in 1625 being about 0.3 per cent lower than in 1601. The acceleration of the velocity of circulation of vellon resulting from the fear of a drastic reduction in tariff precipitated in 1626–1627 one of the most violent price upheavals registered in the annals of Castile. The average indices for the three Castilian regions rose 13.68 points in 1626 and 6.53 in 1627, making a total of 20.21 points in the two years. The advance continued until August 7, 1628, when a 50 per cent reduction in the tale of vellon called a sudden halt and brought prices sharply downward. Relatively low prices at the end of the third quarter and throughout the fourth were largely offset by the inordinate prices before August 7; so the index numbers for Andalusia and the two Castiles in 1628 receded only slightly from the peaks in 1627. The drastic deflation produced its full effect upon Andalusian prices in 1629, when the index number fell 10.73 points; but the corresponding decline did not occur in Old and New Castile until 1630. The uprise of Valencian prices from 1626 to 1629 reflected the concomitant silver inflation. Since the Valencian real was not deflated, however, the relapse of Castilian prices in 1629–1630 had no counterpart in the Mediterranean kingdom. On the average the indices for the four regions rose about 20 per cent from 1621 to 1630.

Fluctuating between 96.2 and 100.6, Andalusian prices remained steady in the quinquennium 1631–1635; but the indices for the two Castiles, largely reflecting good grain harvests and low prices of poultry and animal products, fell precipitately.[1] In spite of the general downward tendency in 1632–1633, the enormous output of Valencian reals in 1626–1630 and the monetary disorder resulting from the impending failure of the *Taula* forced Valencian prices upward. After a slight reaction in 1634, when the Taula was reorganized, and stationary prices in 1635, the Valencian index number, stimulated by the vellon issues of 1634–

---

[1] Fruit and fish prices also fell sharply in Old Castile.

1636, rose 7.28 points in 1636. Valencian prices advanced negligibly in 1637, but a cyclical reaction in 1638 and excellent crops in 1639 reduced the index number 12.23 points, 5.44 of which were regained in 1640. In 1636–1638, unlike other occasions when bearish rumors concerning vellon spread abroad, efforts to avoid losses from a reduction in tariff generally took the form of long purchases of commodities rather than of pieces of eight. The downward trend of the Old Castilian index numbers after 1631 continued until 1636, but prices rose violently in 1637–1638, registering an advance of 21.8 points. The upheaval of Andalusian prices occurred in 1636–1637, when the index numbers rose 19.88 points, but bountiful crops in 1638 neutralized the rapid circulation of vellon and lowered the price level. The rise of New Castilian prices spread over 1636–1638 and was less violent than in Andalusia and Old Castile. Reflecting abundant harvests and the decreased velocity of circulation of vellon after the anticipated deflation had proved to be mild, the price levels of the three Castilian regions fell sharply in 1639 and slightly in 1640. The average index for the three regions was 0.82 per cent higher in 1640 than in 1631.

Owing to the inordinate increase in the tariff of vellon to finance military operations against rebellions in Catalonia, Italy, and Portugal, prices in the three Castilian regions surged strongly upward in 1641–1642, the advance in the Andalusian series being 26.82 points, in the New Castilian 16.90, and in the Old Castilian 20.47. Had not drastic vellon deflation by the pragmatic published on September 15 reduced prices materially in the last quarter, the index numbers for Andalusia and the two Castiles in 1642 would have risen considerably higher. As in 1626–1627, speculation in pieces of eight in an effort to avoid a loss from vellon depreciation or deflation outstripped long purchases of even the most durable commodities. Consequently prices, which measured the depreciation of vellon in terms of commodities, rose incomparably less than the premium on silver. The price decline in Andalusia and the two Castiles in 1643 resulting from the deflation of vellon almost exactly counteracted the rise in 1642; but only in Old Castile, where the fall continued in 1644–1645, did prices return to the 1640 level. After remaining fairly steady in 1641–1643, the Valencian index number, reflecting high quotations for wine, vinegar, hemp, animal products, and fish, rose considerably in 1644; but the gain was lost in 1645, and the decline, apparently cyclical in character, continued in 1646. High prices for agricultural products and their derivatives were largely responsible for the sharp upturn of Valencian prices in 1647. Following moderate declines in 1648–1649, the Valencian index rose slightly in 1650. The quinquennium 1646–1650 witnessed the fourth great price upheaval of the first half of the seventeenth century in Andalusia and the two Castiles. The upward surge of the Old and New Castilian indices can be ascribed to the concomitant depreciation of vellon as indicated by the mounting premium on silver.[1] But the violent upswing of Andalusian prices in 1649–1650 must be attributed largely to the terrible pestilence which ravaged Andalusia in 1648–1650.[2] The rise in 1649 occurred in spite of good crops in 1648, but the disastrous harvest of 1649 was an important factor in the extraordinary advance of 21.53 points in 1650. The 1650 index for Andalusia also reflected the exceptionally dear prices of fish, spice, and other imported commodities, which probably resulted from the impediments to navigation and commerce imposed by municipal authorities in their efforts to avoid further infections during the epidemic.

The average price level in the four regions was approximately 38.7 per cent higher in 1650 than in 1625. Hence the net advance under the stimulus of vellon inflation in Castile and silver inflation in Valencia in the second quarter of the seventeenth century was not far behind the most violent upheaval of silver prices in any quarter-century of the Price Revolution. Owing to the horizontal trend in 1601–1625, however, the uprise in the entire first half of the seventeenth century was less than half as great as that which occurred in each half of the sixteenth. Since it was generally recognized, however, that unsound currency was chiefly

---

[1] *Vide* Table 7 and Chart 4.

[2] Archivo del Ayuntamiento, Seville, *Escribanía de Cabildo*, siglo XVII, tomo 23, no. 81; Antonio Ballesteros, *Historia de España*, IV, 2ª parte (Barcelona, 1927), p. 149; Albert Girard, "Le Chiffre de la Population de l'Espagne," *Revue d'Histoire Moderne*, Janvier-Février, 1929, p. 10.

responsible for the rise in prices, the complaints against the high
cost of living emanating from economists and the Cortes were
decidedly more general and bitter than in the sixteenth century,
when a plausible explanation of the Price Revolution compatible with the prevailing mercantilist philosophy could hardly be
devised.

The remarkably close agreement among the regional price
movements observed in the sixteenth century, especially in 1551–
1600, continued in the first half of the seventeenth, the divergence
among the three Castilian series, except for a few years, such as
1636 and 1650, being slight. The discrepancy between the Castilian and the Valencian indices arose from the differences in
monetary inflation in the two kingdoms. The divergence from
1610 to 1623, the only protracted period of significant disagree-
ment, was chiefly due to the heavy coinage of *menuts* in 1608–
1613. Price analysis of the commodities produced predominantly
by Moriscos suggests that their expulsion in 1609–1613 exercised
little or no influence upon the course of Valencian prices.

The striking harmony among the various regional price movements demonstrates conclusively that, in spite of the decline of
the fairs, the probable economic decadence of Spain, and the
necessity of employing a cumbersome medium of circulation,
commerce among distant regions remained extremely active. Particularly notable was the failure of the preponderant coinage and
restamping of vellon in the Segovian mints to raise prices in the
two Castiles earlier or more violently than in Andalusia.

CHAPTER XI

GROUP PRICE MOVEMENTS

HITHERTO the movements of the general price level have been stressed and the prices of particular commodities and cognate groups considered only when they explained discrepancies among or aberrant changes in the regional index numbers. But alterations of the prices of many groups of commodities transcend their importance as elements of the changes in the general price level registered by unweighted index numbers. It is obviously desirable to study the price behavior of the leading groups of commodities under the successive impacts of steadily increasing imports of the precious metals, the diminishing receipts of American treasure, the transition to a copper standard in Castile and a debased silver standard in Valencia, and the recurrent vellon inflation and deflation. Perfect stability of prices resulting from the mutual cancellations of divergent changes would have inflicted serious hardships upon certain groups of producers and bestowed corresponding windfalls on others; but when the average price level rose or fell sharply, the producers of commodities whose prices moved contrarily, especially when the deviations reflected alterations of demand, found their economic positions revolutionized. The economic consequences of uneven price movements varied with the percentage of the population required to produce the aberrant commodities and the percentage of the average man's money income expended upon their purchase. Obviously a change in the price of wine affected larger numbers of producers and was of greater import to consumers than a proportional alteration in the price of incense. Dear wheat meant hunger to a considerable portion of the population, while cheap wheat, not resulting from correspondingly bountiful harvests or counterbalanced by commensurate declines in general prices, spelled penury for thousands of peasant families. The divergent price trends of different commodities and groups may cast faint light upon the nature and the causes of Spanish economic decadence.

Since the sources are identical with those employed for general prices, little criticism is required; ordinarily the group index numbers have been constructed only when continuous quotations for three or more articles were available, and the indices have generally been omitted for the years affording only two relatives. In all cases unweighted arithmetic index numbers have been constructed for each of the three half-centuries on the middle decade as a base. To render possible the presentation of the price movements of each group of commodities in a single chart, the bases for 1501–1550 and 1601–1650 have been shifted to 1571–1580, thus providing continuous index numbers; and to facilitate rough comparisons of group and general price movements, the averages of the four regional index numbers on 1571–1580 as a base have been included in each of the group charts.[1]

I   FORESTRY

Adequate data for the construction of index numbers of the prices of forest products have been found for only two regions: Andalusia and Valencia. From 1512 to 1650 the Valencian series includes charcoal, ashes, and firewood; and for 1551–1650 turpentine prices are also available. Quotations for forest products in Andalusia are lacking in the first half of the sixteenth century; but, with prices for ashes, charcoal, firewood, pitch, and resin, the series for 1551–1650 is extraordinarily rich.

Chart 9 portrays the index numbers for the forestry group.

As the following chart demonstrates, the prices of forest products in Valencia moved counter to general prices from the second to the sixth decade of the sixteenth century, the index number for 1557 being 23.81 points lower than in 1512 and the average for 1551–

[1] Obviously it would be desirable to compare graphically the group and the general commodity index numbers for each region, but a prohibitive number of charts would be required. The reader is warned that comparisons of group and general prices for particular regions repeatedly occur in this chapter, although the movements of the latter are not shown in the charts. Arranged according to the priority and the extent of the rise in general prices, the different regions ranked as follows: Andalusia, New Castile, Old Castile, Valencia — with only a slight difference between the last two (*vide* Charts 6–8). The curve of composite general prices in Charts 9–16 rose less than the Andalusian and New Castilian general commodity indices, more than the Old Castilian and Valencian.

1560, 13.41 points below that of 1512–1520. A sharp reaction
began in 1560, and by 1570 the indices had regained the loss sustained in the preceding fifty years. Unfortunately, the lacunae in
the Andalusian index numbers render it difficult to ascertain the
trend from 1551–1570, but it appears that prices fell. In the last
three decades of the sixteenth century the forestry indices in both

CHART 9

INDEX NUMBERS OF THE PRICES OF FOREST PRODUCTS

Base = 1571–1580

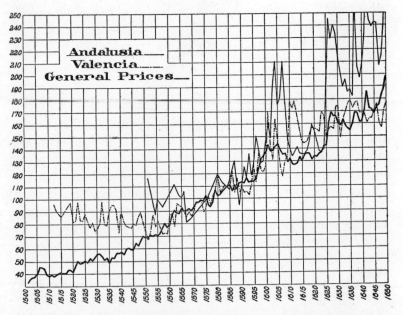

Andalusia and Valencia agreed closely with those of general commodity prices, but in the first half of the seventeenth century
the prices of forest products in both regions forged considerably
ahead of the corresponding commodity indices. From 1601 to
1650 rarely were the forestry indices as low as the commodity
indices in either Andalusia or Valencia. The discrepancies between the prices of forest products and those of general commodities were particularly great in Andalusia in the years marked
by violent monetary disorder.

The decline in the index numbers of forest products in Valencia from 1512 to 1557 reflected a precipitate drop in the price of ashes. Since the quotations for firewood and charcoal advanced in harmony with the general commodity indices, it appears that a decrease in the demand for ashes, probably resulting from the substitution of soap for laundry purposes, depressed their price.[1] The pronounced upswings of the forestry index numbers for Andalusia in the years of phenomenal vellon depreciation — particularly 1625–1626, 1637, and 1641–1642 — doubtless resulted from the suitability of the extraordinarily durable commodities for speculative purchases. The tendency for the index numbers of forest products to rise faster than the commodity indices in Andalusia and New Castile in the first half of the seventeenth century suggests scarcity symptomatic of deforestation. But the evidence is too slight to support a positive generalization. Technological changes or currency expansion, to name only two possibilities, may have increased the demand for forest products. It is unfortunate that indices are not available for Old and New Castile, the regions ravaged most by the migrations and pasturage of the Mesta sheep herds.

II

Although scattering quotations are available for ducks, capons, turkeys, and roosters [2] for every region in almost every fifty-year period, the index numbers of poultry prices include only eggs, hens, and spring chickens. Owing to the complete lack of satisfactory data, indices could not be constructed for Andalusia and New Castile in 1501–1550; [3] but adequate material is available

---

[1] Apparently the substitution of soap continued through the middle of the seventeenth century, for the price of ashes rose little either during the Price Revolution or in periods of marked vellon depreciation.

[2] The Hospital de Esgueva bought one rooster per year for over a hundred years. Since there are no means of knowing whether the rooster was average, the article has been excluded from the price tables and the index numbers.

[3] As has been stated (*vide supra*, p. 188, n. 1), quotations for hens and spring chickens are available for New Castile; but both commodities have been rejected because the invariability of the prices and other internal evidence suggested that the "purchases" represented commutations of feudal dues. Occasional prices for eggs and hens in Andalusia have been taken from the records of the House of Trade, but gaps and the lack of seasonal uniformity in the purchases eliminated both commodities.

for eggs, hens, and spring chickens in Old Castile for 1502–1650, in Valencia for 1512–1650, in New Castile for 1554–1650, and in Andalusia for 1580–1650. When two or three relatives could be averaged, the index numbers were computed; but years having only one relative were omitted.

Chart 10 presents the index numbers of poultry prices.

CHART 10

INDEX NUMBERS OF POULTRY PRICES

Base = 1571–1580

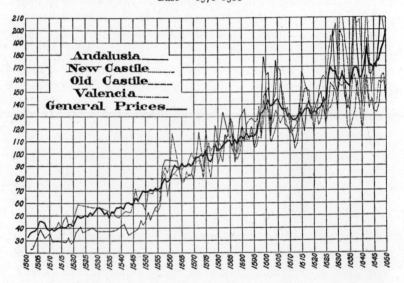

In the first half of the sixteenth century poultry prices in Old Castile lagged considerably behind the general commodity indices, but the sharp rise in the former from 1551 to 1557 brought the two into line. The poultry indices tended to rise faster than the commodity indices in Valencia from 1512 to 1561; but, except for the peak in the last year, the discrepancy was slight. The remarkably close agreement of the trends of poultry and general prices in the second half of the sixteenth century and the first half of the seventeenth indicates that monetary causes were responsible for the advance of the poultry indices, that the conditions of demand and supply remained stable.

Chart 10 discloses sharp cyclical movements of poultry prices, but does not reveal a constant period. The prices of eggs also exhibited marked seasonal fluctuations. The averages for the first and last quarters in Old Castile, Valencia, and Andalusia [1] were approximately equal, while the second- and third-quarter prices averaged about 18 and 6 per cent respectively less than those of the first and fourth quarters. Although numerous discordant short-run movements of the regional poultry indices are shown by Chart 10, the coincidence of peaks and troughs, especially as between contiguous regions, suggests either that commerce was active [2] or that identical natural causes were operative.

III

Favored by aridity, a mild climate, and mountainous topography, the pastoral industry was a basic element of Spanish economy, and the consumption of raw and fabricated animal products was correspondingly high.[3] Fortunately, the data are sufficiently abundant and varied to gauge satisfactorily the prices of animal products in Valencia in 1512–1550 and 1601–1650, New Castile in 1524–1650, and Andalusia and Old Castile throughout the period under investigation. The following commodities have been included in the animal group: beef, butter, tallow candles, cheese, kid feet, lamb feet, kid, lambs, lard, milk, mutton, fresh pork, salt pork, rabbits (conejos),[4] sheepskins, tallow, veal, and wool.

---

[1] New Castile has been omitted because, with only five breaks in the quarterly data for a hundred years, it was not worth while to compute the percentage of seasonal variation as a preliminary step in the calculation of annual prices.

[2] Data concerning interregional purchases are lacking in institutional accounts, but most of the hospitals bought hens over an unusually wide area. For instance, the Hospital dels Inocents of Valencia frequently purchased in such distant towns as Orihuela, Elche, and Castellón de la Plana — localities that probably traded in hens with other regions. Furthermore, the hens purchased by institutions in their immediate localities may have originated in another region and been transported thither by traders.

[3] Inasmuch as Spaniards preferred wine and olive oil, the consumption of milk and butter was exceptionally low.

[4] The inclusion of rabbits, which may well have been game rather than domesticated animals, is a doubtful procedure. But if the classification is erroneous, relatively little harm has been done; for the article occurs only in the Andalusian series for 1551–1600 and 1601–1650, when quotations for ten and thirteen indubitable commodities respectively are available.

Anyone desiring to ascertain the commodities included in the various regional index numbers in the different fifty-year periods may consult either Appendix II or the price tables in Appendices III–V.

The only satisfactory data being for mattress wool in Andalusia and Old Castile in the first half of the seventeenth century,

CHART 11

INDEX NUMBERS OF THE PRICES OF ANIMAL PRODUCTS

Base = 1571–1580

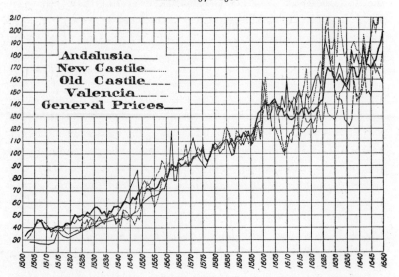

the dearth of wool prices deserves special mention. Diligent efforts to unearth continuous quotations for the leading grades of this great Spanish staple have yielded negative results, but the presence of mutton, lambs, lamb feet, and sheepskins attenuates the defect.[1]

Chart 11 presents graphically the index numbers of the prices of animal products.

The prices of animal products moved in striking harmony with those of general commodities in the first half of the sixteenth cen-

---

[1] One must bear in mind, however, that all of these commodities were joint products of wool and that, as such, to use a Marshallian term, their "supply [not market] prices" tended to be inversely influenced by variations of wool prices.

tury. But from the late 1540's to about 1560 the indices for animal products rose inordinately in the three regions for which data
are available, the advance being particularly great in the two
Castiles. It is significant that the years of the greatest relative
upswing of the animal indices synchronize remarkably with a
precipitate decline in the size of the *transhumante* sheep flocks
and with the years in which Dr. Julius Klein placed "the begin-
nings of Mesta decadence."[1] The close agreement of the price
trends of animal products and general commodities from about
1560 to 1650 in all regions for which data are available indicates
that monetary factors determined the course of prices for the
animal group. The cyclical price movements, which would probably be disclosed by the products of each separate species, are lost
in the averages of goat, sheep, cow, and swine derivatives.

IV

The plethora of Catholic fast days and the difficulty of wresting
sustenance from inhospitable soil having conduced to a high consumption of fish,[2] prices abound in sixteenth- and seventeenth-
century accounts. But owing to the exemption of many patients
in hospitals from the religious inhibitions against the eating of
meat on fast days, the frequent shifts from one class of fish to another, and the often inadequate descriptions of the multiple forms
in which several leading fishes were purchased,[3] sufficient data
for the construction of reliable index numbers of fish prices on
1571–1580 as a base are limited to New Castile in 1551–1592,[4]
Andalusia in 1551–1650, and Old Castile in 1517–1650.

Five kinds of fish enter into the Valencian commodity indices
in the first half of the sixteenth century and four in the first half

---

[1] *The Mesta* (Cambridge, Massachusetts, 1920), pp. 27–28.

[2] *Vide infra*, p. 276.

[3] For example, fresh, dried, salted, and pickled conger eels were purchased by
every institution whose accounts have been utilized.

[4] The dearth of fish prices after 1592 and the weakness of the series from 1551
to 1592 have resulted from the abnormally low consumption by the Hospital de
Tavera rather than from the difficulty of transporting fish into the interior, as the
copious quotations in the accounts of Madrid and Toledo convents for the second
quarter of the seventeenth century attest. Unfortunately, no continuous convent
records for 1601–1650 have been unearthed.

of the seventeenth; but, with common quotations for only tuna fish in the first and second fifty-year periods and codfish in the second and third, the bases cannot be shifted to 1571–1580 so as to provide continuous indices.

Since the fishes included in the regional index numbers can easily be ascertained by consulting Appendices III–V, it is need-

CHART 12

INDEX NUMBERS OF FISH PRICES

Base = 1571–1580

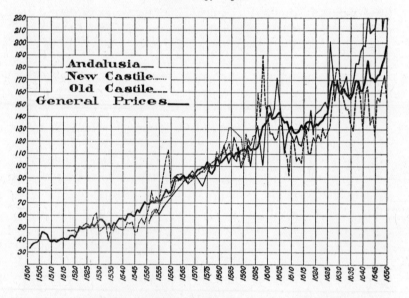

less to list them here. But the wealth of the Andalusian series, with continuous prices for nine varieties in 1551–1600 and fifteen in 1601–1650, deserves special mention.

Chart 12 pictures the index numbers of fish prices.

The price trends of fish and of general commodities in the two Castiles were harmonious at all times for which data are available. Only in 1635–1650, when fish prices rose considerably more than general prices, was there a notable divergence in Andalusia. The hostilities with France after 1635 and with Portugal after 1640 possibly reduced the supply of fish in the Seville market. Fish prices in Valencia rose considerably more than general prices in the first quarter of the sixteenth century. The two indices moved consonantly from 1526 to 1550 and from 1601 to 1625; but in 1632 the Valencian fish index on a 1621–1630 base soared 34.52 points and remained considerably above the general commodity index until 1645, when the fish series ended. Since the three celebrated Old Castilian fairs at Medina del Campo, Medina de Rioseco, and Villalón served as clearing houses for a large part of the fish brought into the Cantabrian and Galician [1] ports, as well as for that consumed in the two Castiles, the fish indices for Old Castile probably gauge New Castilian prices satisfactorily. The fairly close agreement of the Old and the New Castilian fish indices from 1551 to 1591, in spite of the inadequacy of the latter,[2] tends to confirm *a priori* expectations.

Since speculative long purchases of such perishable commodities obviously did not afford an avenue of escape from the reduction in tariff or depreciation of vellon, Andalusian and Old Castilian fish prices remained relatively stable in 1625–1627, 1637–1638, and 1641–1642 — years marked by a mad flight from Castilian vellon.

V

Because of the inveterate predilection of the Spaniard for highly seasoned food, which the liberal consumption of meat and fish and the easy communication with the Levant doubtless fomented, spice prices are plentiful in sixteenth- and seventeenth-century account-books. But the irregularity of the purchases, which limited the articles in the Valencian series to saffron in 1501–1650 and pepper in 1501–1550 and 1601–1650, prevented the construction of index numbers for this region; and continuous data for Andalusia and New Castile in the first half of the sixteenth century are completely lacking. Containing only cinnamon and

---

[1] Petition XLVII of the Cortes of 1558 incorrectly alleged that "all the fish consumed in Castile" came from Galicia (*Cortes de los Antiguos Reinos de León y Castilla* [hereafter *Cortes*], v, 758. *Vide* also *ibid.*, v, 470–471; *Actas de las Cortes de Castilla* [hereafter *Actas*], I, 295).

[2] Of the three fishes in the New Castilian indices only sardines were included in the Old Castilian series.

pepper, the New Castilian series for 1601–1650 is markedly weak; and in 1551–1600 cloves are missing. From 1518 to 1650 in Old Castile and from 1580 to 1650 in Andalusia [1] satisfactory prices are available for cinnamon, cloves, pepper, and saffron.[2]

Chart 13 presents the index numbers of spice prices.

CHART 13

INDEX NUMBERS OF SPICE PRICES

Base = 1571–1580

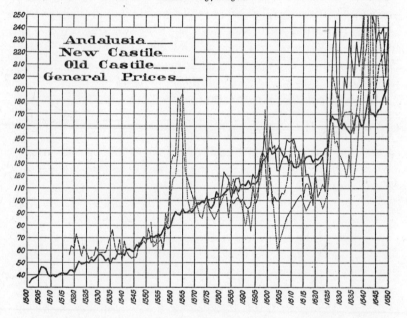

Despite the rise of general commodity prices, the spice indices for Old Castile moved horizontally until about 1546. The ensuing decade witnessed little divergence between the spice and the general commodity indices, but from 1558 to 1563 in Old Castile and 1558 to 1565 in New Castile the level of spice prices almost

---

[1] The Andalusian quotations commence in 1551, but on account of gaps it has seemed undesirable to construct index numbers before 1580 (*vide* Appendix IV).

[2] Mustard, cumin-seed, lavender spike, and other commodities that might be classified as spices are included in the commodity indices for certain regions and periods (*vide* Appendices III–V), but it has seemed best to limit the components of the spice index numbers to the four staples: cinnamon, cloves, pepper, and saffron.

trebled. The precipitate decline of spice prices in 1564–1570 in Old Castile and 1566–1567 in New Castile obliterated the discrepancy between the spice and the general commodity indices; but, after having moved harmoniously with general prices for some fifteen years, from about 1584 to 1625 in Old Castile and 1587 to 1636 in New Castile, the spice indices lagged considerably behind. From 1580 through 1625 the trends of the Andalusian spice and commodity prices agreed fairly closely; but, bating brief intervals such as 1631 and 1649–1650, the spice indices stood considerably above those of general commodities throughout the second quarter of the seventeenth century.

The general upheaval of spice prices in 1558–1565 reflected dear quotations of the three imported articles: cinnamon, cloves, and pepper. Only in 1561–1562 were the prices of saffron, a domestic product, abnormally high. There is reason to believe that dear spice prices in 1558–1565 were not confined to Spain,[1] and it seems that a plausible explanation of the phenomenon must be sought outside of Spanish economics and politics.[2] Whether speculation in spices on the Antwerp exchange, which, as R. Ehrenberg has pointed out,[3] was extremely active and characterized by many of the modern devices for artificially raising and depressing prices, may not have been largely responsible is an interesting question.

The lag of the spice indices in roughly the last fifteen years of the sixteenth century and the first quarter of the seventeenth largely reflected the low quotations for cinnamon. The horizontal trend of the index numbers of New Castilian spices, of which cinnamon formed one-third in 1551–1600 and one-half in 1601–1650, is pronounced. Inasmuch as the customs barriers between the two countries subsisted and since political union went little beyond allegiance to a common sovereign, the rough synchronization of low spice prices and the Spanish domination of Portugal

---

[1] *Vide,* for instance, Georg Wiebe, *Geschichte der Preisrevolution des XVI. und XVII. Jahrhunderts* (Leipzig, 1895), pp. 376, 379, 383.

[2] It would be interesting to know whether the extremely dear spice prices of the immediately preceding years partially motivated the voyage of Legazpi to the Philippines in 1564, the initial step in the colonization of the Islands.

[3] *Das Zeitalter der Fugger* (Jena, 1896), II, 14 ff.

are worthy of remark. It seems that in some inscrutable fashion the solidarity of dynastic interests effectively smoothed the path between Spain and the great Lisbon market. The new route for the spice trade opened by Philippine commerce, largely conducted through the Manila galleons [1] and the New Spain treasure fleets, affords an additional, or possibly an alternative, explanation of the forty years of low prices; for spices tended to be cheap when the trade was active, and the upswing of the indices in the last quarter of the seventeenth century synchronized with the decline of commerce between Castile and New Spain.

VI

The construction projects of institutions and municipalities and the maintenance of buildings, walls, and streets required heavy purchases of building materials; but, owing to the intermittent nature of the operations in Andalusia and Old Castile, continuous quotations for a sufficient number of articles to permit the calculation of index numbers are lacking.[2] The Valencian indices for building materials include bricks, lime, and plaster of Paris in each of the three half-centuries. In New Castile data for lime, nails, and plaster of Paris extend from 1504 through 1650; and the indices for 1601–1650 also include pitch and roof-tiles (tejas). In all regions occasional quotations for lumber occur, but the lack of continuity and inadequate descriptions preclude their utilization.

Chart 14 presents pictorially the index numbers for building materials.

Although the prices of building materials rose from the beginning of the sixteenth century, the indices lagged behind those of general commodities in New Castile and Valencia until about 1545. Bating the period 1553–1569, when the indices for building materials averaged 7.75 points higher than those of commodities,

---

[1] Plying between Acapulco and Manila.

[2] Tolerable indices for Old Castile in 1501–1550, when prices for lime, nails, and plaster of Paris are available, and for Andalusia in 1601–1650, with quotations for lime, bricks, and plaster of Paris, could have been constructed; but the scarcity of data for 1571–1580 would have precluded accurate shifting of the bases.

and 1604–1607, when commodity prices lagged behind, remarkable uniformity characterized the courses of the two sets of indices in Valencia during the last half of the sixteenth century and the first half of the seventeenth. From 1545 to 1582 the price trends of building materials and general commodities in New Castile also

CHART 14

INDEX NUMBERS OF THE PRICES OF BUILDING MATERIALS

Base = 1571–1580

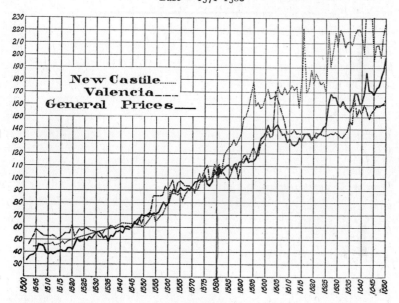

agreed; but from 1583 to 1595 building materials — largely reflecting exorbitant prices for bricks and plaster of Paris, particularly the latter — gained 55 points on general commodities in New Castile,[1] and on the average something like half the gain was retained through the end year of 1650.

Particularly significant is the fact that the depopulation at the

[1] It is significant that the price of plaster of Paris did not rise abnormally in other regions. Since the commodity was too bulky for distant commerce, regional discrepancies might easily have occurred; but the possibility that the data may have been vitiated by a variation in the quality of the plaster of Paris in the New Castilian series must be recognized.

close of the sixteenth century and in the first half of the seventeenth failed to counteract the upward impulse to the prices of building materials imparted by monetary phenomena.

VII

For two reasons fruits and nuts have been combined in a single group. First, with the exception of cantaloupes and green and ripe grapes, the twenty-five articles occurring in one or more regions in one or more of the fifty-year periods were arboreal; and, second, desserts and seasonal delicacies largely accounted for the consumption of most of the commodities.

The plethora of fruits and nuts in Valencia and the firmly intrenched custom of alms in kind [1] limited the continuous price series to almonds in 1501–1550, quinces in 1601–1650, and raisins in the entire period under investigation. No data are available for New Castile in the first half of the sixteenth century, and the Andalusian quotations for almonds and raisins are inadequate for the construction of index numbers. Hence Chart 15 exhibits fruit-nut prices for Old Castile alone prior to 1550. On account of long and frequent gaps in 1551–1579 the Andalusian indices begin in 1580, after which date they are excellent, as are the data for the two Castiles in 1551–1650.

Ranging from six in Old Castile in 1501–1550 and Andalusia in 1551–1600 to eighteen in New Castile in 1551–1600, the commodities included in the various regional indices in the different periods are too extensive to enumerate. By reference to the price tables in Appendices III–V one may learn the components of the fruit-nut indices for the different regions and periods.

Until about 1580 the trends of the fruit-nut prices agreed fairly closely with those of general commodities; but subsequently, the first decade of the seventeenth century excepted, the three regional fruit-nut indices lagged considerably behind the respective commodity indices, the divergence being particularly great in Andalusia.

More than to any other single cause the relative inertia of fruit-nut prices after 1580, particularly in 1610–1650, was prob-

[1] *Vide supra*, p. 197, n. 2.

ably due to the sluggish adjustment of production to depopulation, a phenomenon which naturally resulted from the extreme longevity of most fruit and nut trees. Fresh fruits composed almost two-thirds of the present group, and virtually all of the components were both perishable and, not being articles of gen-

CHART 15

INDEX NUMBERS OF THE PRICES OF FRUITS AND NUTS

Base = 1571–1580

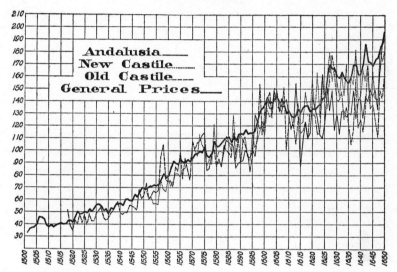

eral consumption, incapable of finding a ready wholesale market. Hence flights from the currency rarely or never assumed the guise of speculative purchases of these commodities, and relative stability characterized the index numbers in the years of unbridled vellon depreciation.

VIII

For two reasons grain prices deserve extensive treatment. First, grains, particularly wheat, constituted the most important element in the consumption of a vast majority of the population and absorbed a high percentage of the average man's money income. Second, the efforts of the central governments to control prices, through comprehensive price-fixing legislation in Castile and import subsidies in Valencia, were largely focused upon wheat.

Lacking price statistics for public grain markets such as are available for France in the *mercuriales*, data of the type compiled by local authorities in England as bases for the assizes of bread and ale, and continuous records of sales by feudal estates such as Thorold Rogers and Sir William Beveridge have unearthed in England, I have been forced to collect the Spanish grain series almost exclusively from the account-books of municipalities, cathedrals, convents, and hospitals — sources that leave much to be desired. The possession of grain-producing estates by hospitals and convents, which not infrequently produced the approximate amounts required for the annual consumption of the institutions, thus obviating both purchases and sales, tended to render the quotations discontinuous. Because of the inveterate lack of precision in accounting methods, belated liquidations of grain purchases — unfortunate consequences of the apathetical financial administration of most institutions — were occasionally recorded as cash transactions as of the dates of settlement and often listed in such a fashion that it proved impossible to ascertain the exact date of purchase. Therefore it has been difficult to determine the precise extent of seasonal variation and to make the corresponding adjustments in the annual averages for breaks in the quarterly data.

Although lentils and chick-peas might have been classified as grains, it has seemed best to limit the components of the series to the four cereals: barley, rice, rye, and wheat. In fact, there are strong reasons to question the presence of rice, which was planted in the spring, cultivated exclusively in irrigated fields, confined to a few small producing areas along or near the Mediterranean coast, and harvested much later than the other three grains, and which, for all of these reasons, was affected by peculiar weather conditions. The almost incredible paucity of quotations in the four regions indicates that oats were rarely grown,[1] while the cul-

---

[1] In the fourteenth and fifteenth centuries oats were an important element in the maintenance of the horses belonging to the royal household of Navarre (*vide*, for example, Archivo de la Cámara de Comptos, tomos 130 and 484).

tivation and consumption of rye seem to have been largely confined to Old Castile-León,[1] the only region for which continuous quotations are available. Hence the exclusion of rye from the Old Castilian series would have conduced to uniformity and facilitated comparisons among the regional grain indices. The substitution of barley grits for barley in Valencia was an extremely dubious expedient. Powerfully affected by custom, as were the prices of most inexpensive commodities bought and consumed in extremely small quantities, the quotations of barley grits tended to remain inflexible in the face of violent short-run fluctuations in the cost of the raw material. Hence the commodity is a tolerable substitute for barley only if one's principal purpose be to gauge the secular trend.

Data for only rice and two grades of naval biscuit, which might conceivably have been employed as wheat substitutes, being accessible in the first half of the sixteenth century, index numbers for Andalusia have not been constructed; and in 1555–1600 there are several long hiatuses in the indices, which, like the highly satisfactory ones for 1601–1650, include barley, rice, and wheat. The New Castilian index numbers comprise barley and wheat prices in the three fifty-year periods and also rice in the second half of the sixteenth century. In all periods quotations for barley grits, rice, and wheat constitute the Valencian series, and the Old Castilian index numbers for the three half-centuries include barley, rice, rye, and wheat.

The Andalusian grain series represent Seville quotations, supplied by the account-books of various hospitals [2] (particularly the Hospital de la Sangre), the Cathedral, and the House of Trade.[3] Toledo prices, derived from purchases and sales by the San Pedro and Tavera Hospitals and supplemented by Alcalá de Henares quotations, furnished by the records of the University

---

[1] Although the quotations are preponderantly from León, in the remainder of this chapter the Old Castilian-Leonese grain series will often be designated "Old Castilian."

[2] *Vide supra*, pp. xxx–xxxi.

[3] The hospitals bought grain when harvests were poor and sold in years of abundance. In the accounts of the Hospital de la Sangre purchases predominated. The Cathedral ordinarily sold grain, and the House of Trade invariably purchased.

and the Hospital de Antezana, form the New Castilian series.
The Valencian grain prices are based on purchases in the kingdom
of Valencia by the municipality and the Hospital dels Inocents.

The relative strength of the grain series for Old Castile-León
deserves special mention. With strikingly adequate seasonal [1]
quotations for barley, rye, wheat, and rice, the accounts of the
Convento de Nuestra Señora de Sandoval afford incomparably
more complete prices for 1501–1650 than are available in any
other Spanish source yet unearthed. Furthermore, the Sandoval
quotations derive a certain measure of uniformity not generally
shared by other Spanish series from the fact that the prices of
barley, rye, and wheat always represent large sales from the surplus produced by the Convent's estates in the fertile valley of the
Esla, while rice quotations were for wholesale purchases. But the
value of the León grain prices is impaired by the long gap from
1569 to 1584, resulting from a hiatus in the accounts of Nuestra
Señora de Sandoval, and by the fact that the measures, 20 per
cent smaller than the official Ávila standards, brought the prices
which would have prevailed in an unregulated market close
enough to the *tasas* for the latter to influence the market quotations for barley, rye, and wheat in most years of normal harvest.[2]
The Cathedral at Burgos, the Hospital de Esgueva, and the Hospital de San Bernabé y San Antolín supplied material for interpolations. The fragmentary grain quotations in the accounts of the
Dios Padre and Escolástica Hospitals in Ávila and of many convents served as controls.[3]

Chart 16 presents the index numbers of grain prices. On account of the transcendent importance of this group, the indices
are listed in tabular form in Appendix VI.

Until about 1570 there was little divergence in any region between the trends of the grain and the general commodity indices,

---

[1] In 1518–1615 and 1625–1629 grain sales were entered on a monthly or quarterly basis; but in 1616–1624 and 1630–1650 the accounts, including the grain quotations, were divided into periods of four months.

[2] *Vide infra*, p. 259.
The unusual stability of the Old Castilian wheat, rye, and barley prices in Appendices III–V was chiefly due to the peculiar operation of the legal maximum
tariffs in León.

[3] *Vide supra*, pp. 165–166.

and through the end year of 1650 the substantial agreement per-
sisted in Old Castile and Valencia. But in roughly the last half of
the period under investigation grain prices rose considerably more
than those of general commodities in Andalusia and New Castile.

CHART 16

INDEX NUMBERS OF GRAIN PRICES

Base = 1571–1580

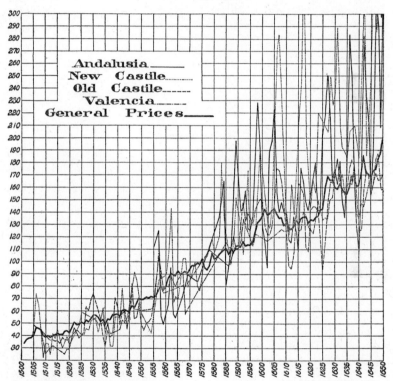

With no statistics for the output of grain and competing agricultural products and only flimsy demographical data, a satisfactory explanation of the discrepant trends of the regional grain
indices appears unattainable. But certain observations may not
be amiss. The advance of the Andalusian grain indices after about
1570 was largely due to the notable increase in the population of

that region, particularly in Seville, Cádiz, and Cordova, collectively considered.[1] The advance of the New Castilian indices in the first half of the seventeenth century in spite of a decline in population was probably due, in part at least, to the increased demand from Andalusia and to the heavy planting of vineyards on wheat land [2] in response to the inordinate rise of New Castilian wine prices in the first half of the sixteenth century.[3] Depopulation [4] and the tasa afford a plausible explanation of the lag of Old Castilian grain prices behind those of other regions, and the constant imports into Valencia from Corsica, Sicily, and Sardinia — territory affected less than that of Valencia by the imports of American treasure [5] — seem to account for the comparatively stable trend of the Valencian grain prices.

The causes of the relative infrequence and the moderation of the peaks and valleys in the Old Castilian and the Valencian grain indices are not far to seek. The presence of a greater number of articles in the Old Castilian series than in those of any other region softened the effects of good and bad harvests, and the superior efficacy of the tasa in León,[6] the district that furnished the bulk of the grain quotations, seems to have depressed prices disproportionately in the years of poor harvests. The inclusion of barley grits, whose prices were powerfully influenced by custom, and the fact that grain was drawn from an area wide enough to preclude the concurrence of bountiful and scant harvests [7] tended to prevent extreme fluctuations in the Valencian index numbers. Furthermore, the never-failing surpluses of certain grains for export — rice from Valencia and barley, rye, and wheat from León — served as buffers against famine prices in both regions.

---

[1] Tomás González, *Censo de Población de la Corona de Castilla en el Siglo XVI* (Madrid, 1829), pp. 83–85.

[2] Cf. Konrad Haebler, *Die Wirtschaftliche Blüte Spaniens* (Berlin, 1888), p. 40; *Actas*, XV, 759; XVIII, 483; Jean Bodin, *Response au Paradoxe de Malestroit* (Henri Hauser, ed., Paris, 1932), p. 36.

[3] *Vide* Appendix III. The abnormally slight advance of the New Castilian wine prices after 1580 suggests that production increased, but one must allow for the effect of depopulation.

[4] Tomás González, *op. cit.*, pp. 1, 7, 20, 22, 25, 28, 40, 43, 48, 56–57, 61.

[5] Owing to favorable monetary statutes in both kingdoms, a significant drain of treasure from Castile into Valencia occurred in the first half of the seventeenth century (*vide supra*, pp. 117–118, 121–122).

[6] *Vide infra*, p. 259.   [7] *Vide infra*, pp. 257–258, n. 4.

IX

Although the limitations of space will not permit comprehensive treatment, the legal maximum prices of grain deserve consideration. They precipitated in the Cortes acrimonious discussions of (1) the state of agriculture, (2) the economic functions of the state, and (3) the efficacy and consequences of price-fixing legislation; stimulated economic speculation; and, through heated polemics among economists and political theorists, played an important rôle in the development of Spanish economic literature. Incredible as it may seem, scholars have attempted to deduce from the maximum grain tariffs the terminal dates and the magnitude of the Price Revolution in Spain;[1] and the resultant pseudo-scientific generalizations have gained wide acceptance.

Legal maximum prices had been fixed for wheat and other commodities, mostly necessities, in the Caliphate of Cordova and by various Christian monarchs in medieval Castile;[2] but weightier affairs absorbed the energies of the Catholic Kings during most of their reign and delayed the promulgation of price-fixing statutes until the close of the dear year of 1502.

Destined to serve as models for subsequent legislation, the enactments of the Catholic Kings deserve special attention. Declaring that an investigation precipitated by exorbitant prices had disclosed that the last harvest throughout the kingdoms of Castile and León had been bountiful and that the supply was ample, but that peasants had been forced to market their crops in order to pay pressing debts, with the result that the entire national stock — not held by landowners under no pressure to sell — had passed into the hands of regraters, in a *cédula* issued at Alcalá de Henares on December 23, 1502, Ferdinand and Isabella affirmed that the constantly increasing wheat prices were obliging the poor to alienate their property in order to maintain their families and fixed the maximum cash or credit price at 110 maravedís per fanega for wheat, 60 maravedís for barley, and 70 maravedís

---

[1] For example, *vide* Moritz Julius Bonn, *Spaniens Niedergang* (Stuttgart, 1896), pp. 25–30.

[2] Cristóbal Espejo, "Carestía de la Vida en el Siglo XVI," *Revista de Archivos, Bibliotecas, y Museos* (hereafter RABM), 3ª Época, XXV, 215; *Actas*, XXI, 339–340.

for rye, values regarded as fair to both buyers and sellers. Contrary to the prevailing Castilian legislative practice, the validity of the cédula was limited to the definite period of ten years. Galicia and the Cantabrian region ten leagues inward from the sea, territories invariably dependent upon grain imports, were exempted from the statute. The penalties for requesting or accepting more than the tasa, or legal maximum tariff, were confiscation of the grain and a fine of five hundred maravedís per fanega, to be distributed equally among the judge, the accuser, and the royal *cámara*.[1] Furthermore, in localities "where grain was needed either for local consumption or for transportation to some other part of Castile or León" the *corregidor* or the *alcalde*, two *regidores*, and two good men (buenas personas) selected by the municipal council were enjoined to force the possessors of surplus grain to cede it at prices not above the legal maxima. For refusal to surrender condemned grain, a fine of 300 maravedís per fanega was provided. With prophetic vision, the Catholic Kings endeavored to forestall the breakdown of the statute through apathetical administrative procedure and the deeply ingrained opposition of local officials to grain removals. For neglecting to heed a request to condemn grain or for "excusing" sales already enjoined, municipal officials became liable to a fine of 20,000 maravedís; and for obstructing withdrawals for domestic shipment, judges and feudal lords were fined 50,000 maravedís.[2]

Informed that the price regulations were being evaded by sellers of flour, who maintained that the wheat tasa applied only to the raw product, on March 4, 1503, Ferdinand and Isabella limited flour prices to the maximum for wheat plus the cost of milling.[3] But the sale of bread at market prices and either the acceptance of gifts such as gold, silver, and silks or the compulsory purchase of "rye, oats,[4] iron, olive oil, wine, salt pork, or other goods" with unregulated prices along with the wheat largely nullified the tasa.

---

[1] This was a well-nigh universal method of distributing fines in Castile.

[2] Archivo de Simancas, *Registro del Sello*, Diciembre de 1502; *Pramáticas del Reyno: Recopilación de Algunas Bulas* . . . (Alcalá de Henares, 1528), fols. 164–165.

[3] *Ibid.*, fol. 165.

[4] The enforcement of the rye tasa was obviously a matter of secondary importance to the Catholic Kings. It is interesting to note that the pragmatic of December 23, 1502, also regulated the price of oats.

A royal order of April 20, 1503,[1] forbade ulterior considerations and joint sales of wheat and other commodities and provided that the price of bread should not exceed the maximum tariff of wheat plus the cost of milling and bread-making, including a reasonable profit on these operations. At the same time Ferdinand and Isabella repeated the provisions of earlier legislation rendering all grain, even that in the hands of the farmers of royal and ecclesiastical rents, subject to condemnation at tasa prices; complained against the indifferent enforcement of the price-fixing statutes; and threatened to send royal inspectors throughout the land to proceed against the persons and property of delinquent judges.[2] Inveterate neglect by municipal authorities to locate and condemn surplus grain elicited the royal order of May 2, 1503, providing for the confiscation of all grain not registered with municipal authorities within three days after the preconization of the statute. The fixation of the bread tasa at two maravedís per pound and the stipulation that the price of flour should not exceed the cost of wheat by more than twenty maravedís per fanega circumscribed the legal allowances for the expenses of milling and baking.[3]

The grain tasas expired on December 23, 1512; and, so far as I have been able to ascertain, remained in abeyance almost twenty-seven years. The reasons for this long lapse are obscure; but the patent demonstration of the inefficacy of the statutory regulations in 1504–1507 [4] — years of markedly poor harvests —, the moderation of prices for at least three years before and eight after the expiration of the statute, and the unsettled conditions during the interregnum in Castile were probably contributory factors.

The sharp advance of grain prices resulting from the poor harvest of 1539 was the proximate cause of the revival of legal control. In a royal order of October 10,[5] 1539, strongly reminiscent of the cédulas of 1502 and 1503, Charles V attributed the dearness of grain to regrating, complained that unregulated prices would force poor families to sell their property (haciendas) in order to

---

[1] Published at Alcalá de Henares on April 21.
[2] *Pramáticas del Reyno: Recopilación de Algunas Bulas* . . . fols. 165–166.
[3] *Ibid.*, fols. 166–167.
[4] *Vide* Appendix III.   [5] Published on October 11.

subsist, required holders of grain to declare it before municipal authorities within thirty days following the preconization of the statute, forbade gifts and joint sales, provided for the condemnation of grain needed for consumption in any part of León or Castile, and threatened judges with dire punishment for any delinquency that might be detected by royal inspectors. Galicia and the Cantabrian region ten leagues inward from the sea were again exempted from the price control, and the flour tasa was not altered. Unlike those of 1502, the maximum prices were evidently intended for points of origin rather than of consumption,[1] for sales at the legal figure plus the cost of transportation, including a reasonable profit (honesta ganancia), were allowed. For the province (reino) of Toledo Charles V fixed the maximum price of wheat at 170 maravedís a fanega, of barley at 85 maravedís, and of rye at 114 maravedís, while the following higher scale was established for the remainder of Castile and León: wheat 240 maravedís,[2] barley 120 maravedís, and rye 160 maravedís. Neither the royal order nor the comparative levels of prior and subsequent regional grain prices reveal any justification for the lower scale of prices for Toledo.[3] The penalties for violating or neglecting to enforce the various provisions of the royal order remained as established by the Catholic Kings in 1502–1503. The statute became effective on November 11, 1539, and was to "remain valid in the ensuing year and thereafter during his Majesty's pleasure."[4] The frequent sales at the tasa found in the accounts

[1] Informed that the addition of transportation costs to the maximum price of wheat in Cuenca — a city never supplied by local production — was inflicting great hardship upon the poor, on February 29, 1504, the Catholic Kings forbade wheat sales in Cuenca at more than 110 maravedís per fanega (Archivo del Ayuntamiento [hereafter AA], Cuenca, caj. 11, leg. 39).

[2] In practice the legal price was often considered 7 reals, or 238 maravedís (for example, *vide* Archivo Histórico Nacional [hereafter AHN], *Clero*, León, leg. 246).

[3] Cf. the levels of grain prices in Appendices III–V.

On August 30, 1623, a *Procurador* stated in the Cortes that the greater demand for wheat and smaller supply in Toledo caused prices to be higher than in Old Castile, that in Toledo wheat was worth 12 reals a fanega "one year with another," and that in "some" (implicitly "most") years the price was 4 reals in Old Castile (*Actas*, XXXIX, 250).

[4] I am indebted to García Rico y Cía. for having placed a printed copy of the price-fixing legislation of October 10, 1539, at my disposal. The place and date of publication are lacking, but the paper and the type suggest that it was contempo-

of the Convento de Nuestra Señora de Sandoval indicate that the tariffs fixed in 1539 remained in force almost twenty years.[1]

The policy of price regulation was the object of considerable deliberation in high political circles in 1546 and 1551–1552,[2] but the matter did not progress beyond the discussional stage until the dear prices of 1557 stimulated positive action. On March 9, 1558, Philip II raised the tasas to the following scale: wheat 310 maravedís a fanega, barley 140 maravedís, and rye 200 maravedís. The spread between the cost of wheat and the price of flour was increased to 30 maravedís per fanega. To attract imports, "the said grain which comes from outside these kingdoms [Castile and León] by sea" was exempted from the price control. The tasas were valid throughout Castile and León, except in Galicia and the Cantabrian region, where the freedom of the grain market subsisted. The statute became effective on April 20, 1558, and remained in force until it was superseded in 1571.[3] Since the provisions for enforcement, prohibitions, penalties, and the like remained as in 1539, they need not be repeated.[4] On April 16, 1558, Philip II limited the allowance for the expenses of interurban transportation to 6 maravedís per fanega-league for wheat and rye and 5 maravedís for barley. To guard against fraud, transporters were ordered to obtain a notarial certificate of quantity at the point of origin and to present it to a judicial authority at the destination.[5] An oath professing innocence of fraud was also required of sellers who exceeded the maximum prices on account of transportation costs.

The tasas of 1558 elicited spirited debate in the Cortes on April 21, 1563, being opposed on the ground that they "benefited only merchants and officials" and that "since there is no [central]

---

raneously printed. I have failed to locate the pragmatic in any public library or archive, but Don Cristóbal Espejo (*vide op. cit.*, RABM, 3ª Época, XXIV, 45, n. 1) has a printed copy in his private library.

[1] AHN, *Clero*, León, legs. 246–247.

[2] Cristóbal Espejo, *op. cit.*, RABM, 3ª Época, XXIV, 169 ff.

[3] The barley schedule was altered in 1566.

[4] AA, Valladolid, *Actas*, 1554–1560; Biblioteca Nacional (hereafter BN), *Raros*, 15,431; *Recopilación de Leyes de España* (hereafter *Recopilación*), lib. v, tit. xxv, ley 1. The unabridged body of the pragmatic is available in the *Recopilación*.

[5] BN, *Raros*, 15,431; *Recopilación*, lib. v, tit. xxv, ley 11.

price control of other goods, let there be none for grain." But the motion for reform was defeated by a majority of three votes.[1]

Informed that the low maximum price and the high cost of production had diminished the cultivation of barley, Philip II issued a pragmatic, on August 29, 1566, increasing the tasa to 187 maravedís per fanega. In order to encourage sowing in the fall of 1566, judges were instructed to compel the holders of barley to sell to farmers at 140 maravedís a fanega, "in accordance with the preceding pragmatic." [2]

To the Cortes convoked on December 1, 1566, several Procuradores bore instructions to agitate for increases in the maximum tariffs on the ground that greatly augmented expenses of production in conjunction with the low tasas had depressed grain cultivation sufficiently to render the kingdom dependent upon imports or even to threaten famine in sterile years. On March 19, 1567, a committee was appointed to study price-fixing legislation,[3] and Petition XIX of the Cortes of 1566–1567 urged his Majesty either "to annul the maximum prices and to institute special schedules for the different provinces or to issue an order requiring that as much land as formerly be sown [to grain]." Philip II referred the proposal for forced cultivation to the Council of Castile, but refused to alter the system of price control.[4] On March 2, 1570, the Cortes adopted a motion to request the Crown to raise the tasa of rye to 7 reals a fanega and of wheat to 11 reals,[5] and Petition XIII of the same Cortes advocated either increases of the wheat and rye schedules to the above figures in order to offset the high expenses of production and thus arrest the progressive diminution of the grain supply or a royal proclamation commanding farmers to sow as much land as formerly, "as was requested in the last Cortes." [6] Although Philip II noncommittally replied that the Petition would be referred to the Council, on October 8, 1571, he raised the maximum price of wheat to 11 reals, or 374 maravedís, per fanega. The legal tariffs of barley and rye, the spread of 30 maravedís per fanega between the cost of wheat and

[1] *Actas*, I, 85–86.
[2] BN, *Raros*, 14,090.
[3] *Actas*, II, 219.
[4] *Ibid.*, II, 431.
[5] *Ibid.*, III, 34.
[6] *Ibid.*, III, 365–366.

the price of flour, and the exemption of Galicia and the Cantabrian region were not altered;[1] but in almost every other respect the legislation broke new ground.

The most salient aspects of the pragmatic of 1571 were the divers provisions designed to preclude the evasions and infractions which, as the pragmatic expressly recognized, had largely nullified the previous price-fixing statutes. To the existing penalties for selling above the tasas two years' exile from the infractor's place of residence and the town where the crime occurred was added for the first offense; for the second conviction all penalties were doubled; and for the third offense half the infractor's goods were confiscated, and he was exiled from the kingdom for two years. Intermediaries, overlooked in previous legislation, became liable to the same penalties. The buyer who denounced purchases at illegal tariffs within thirty days could recover his entire outlay, or, after the lapse of this period, the excess over the maximum price. Judges were directed to suppress false claims for transportation, which, according to the pragmatic, had proved a prolific medium for evading the price regulations. That "judges had dissimulated and countenanced infractions of regulatory legislation, thus legitimizing violation and satisfying the infractor's conscience," was recognized and roundly condemned; and Philip II appealed to his subjects to observe the pragmatics through conscientious and patriotic motives. Alleging that the negligence and connivance of judges were patent factors in the defeat of the price control, the Crown warned the judiciary that executors of the periodic inspections (residencias) would bear specific instructions to inquire into the enforcement of the grain tasas and that "in due time" special inquisitors would be dispatched. The pragmatic of September 14, 1568, prohibiting non-bakers to make or sell bread either directly or in partnership with bakers was confirmed; the penalties were increased to those against exceeding the maximum prices; and bakers who, having received wheat on a profit-sharing basis, turned state's evidence within twenty days

---

[1] A royal order of May 11, 1595, authorized specie exports in return for wheat, barley, or rye brought into the ports of Biscay. On several subsequent occasions of scarcity, down to February 7, 1630, this royal order was preconized (AA, Bilbao, caj. 2, leg. 1, no. 23).

were promised immunity from prosecution and the grain as a reward. Judges were enjoined to "take great care that local markets be well provided with bread" and were authorized to condemn,[1] "when necessary," wheat or flour in excess of household requirements and turn it over to bakers to make bread "to be sold at just and moderate prices . . . so that there may be neither want nor price disorder, as there have been heretofore." Royal patents exempting certain municipalities from the price control because of the invariable dependence upon grain from other provinces were suspended during forty days, the period allotted the local governments in which to present the patents to the Council of Castile for revocation or confirmation.[2]

The representatives of Burgos in the Cortes of 1576 were instructed to favor the following reforms in the grain price control: (1) that public granaries should be permitted to sell at cost "even when the cost exceeded the maximum price"; (2) that sales by public granaries should be exempted from the alcabala, or sales tax; and (3) that after a lapse of two or three months one should be immune from prosecution for violation of the price-fixing statutes.[3] The Procuradores from Burgos were also instructed to call the attention of the Cortes to the fact that many poor peasants were failing to sow grain because of inability to borrow money to buy seed and to argue that municipal seed-loans in kind would insure abundant harvests.[4] On August 8, 1576, Juan Vázquez, a royal secretary, wrote the Corregidor of Burgos that the amendments [5] to the price-fixing legislation advocated in his letter of July 20 "would be good for Burgos but possibly injurious in many other places";[6] and the proposals from Burgos were rejected by the Cortes.

---

[1] The text of the pragmatic, which, because of accessibility in the *Recopilación* (lib. v, tit. xxv, ley IV), need not be reproduced here, does not specify the compensation; but presumably market prices, up to the statutory maximum as a limit, were contemplated.

[2] BN, *Varios*, 1–49–29 and 31; *Raros*, 19,985; *Recopilación*, lib. v, tit. xxv, ley IV.

[3] In Petition LXXXI the Cortes of 1579–1582 proposed the enactment of a statute of limitations with a period of four months, but Philip II flatly rejected the petition (*Actas*, VI, 870).

[4] *Ibid.*, V Adicional, 132–133.

[5] Presumably those advanced by the Procuradores from Burgos.

[6] *Actas*, V Adicional, 139.

Petition LXXI of the Cortes of 1579–1582 maintained that the low tasa of rye, overlooked when the recent increases in the grain tariffs were decreed, was causing much land unsuitable for barley and wheat to lie idle and requested Philip II to raise the rye tasa from 200 to 250 maravedís per fanega.[1] The Crown referred the Petition to the Council of Castile, where its consideration may have influenced the legislation of 1582.

A pragmatic issued at Lisbon on September 24, 1582,[2] raised the maximum price of wheat to 14 reals (476 maravedís) per fanega, of barley to 6 reals (204 maravedís), and of rye to 8 reals (272 maravedís), and drastically increased the penalties against exceeding these limits. Sellers at illegal rates became liable to the confiscation of a fourth of their goods and to six years' exile from their place of residence for the first offense; to the loss of half their goods and ten years' exile from the kingdom for the second offense; and to the confiscation of all their goods and perpetual banishment from the realm for the third offense. The efforts to end fraudulent claims for transportation and judicial laxity and corruption were notably intensified. Henceforth the notarial certificate had to specify the point of origin, the quantity of grain, and the names of the owner and the transporter and to be countersigned by either the corregidor or the mayor of the town. One who exacted a transportation allowance without having complied with the above formalities exposed himself to the penalties against illegal grain prices. Judges of first instance were forbidden "to moderate or suspend the statutory penalties" and to reverse their own sentences, "as they ordinarily do with artifice and dissimulation"; and the privilege of bail for the accused was circumscribed. Conviction upon the testimony of three witnesses was authorized, and the penalties against lethargic and fraudulent conduct throughout the entire judicial hierarchy became more drastic. The pragmatic declared "that in many places zealous efforts have been made to violate the said [price-fixing] laws and pragmatics by mixing barley, oats, rye, and other grains with wheat; [by adulterating it] with straw, dirt, and garbage; and by

---

[1] *Actas*, VI, 863.

[2] The *Recopilación* gives September 22 as the date.

wetting it to cause it to swell." Judges were instructed to enjoin the cleaning of adulterated wheat; to require sellers to restore the ill-gained portion of the purchase price; and rigorously to punish all cases of intentional adulteration.[1]

On March 11, 1582, the allowance for interurban transportation was increased to 10 maravedís per fanega-league for rye and wheat and to 8 maravedís for barley;[2] and, owing to the frequent disputes that had arisen over the ambiguity of the term "league," on January 8, 1587, Philip II ruled that the law contemplated the common, or vulgar, rather than the legal variety.[3]

On January 15, 1590, farmers were authorized to convert the wheat from their own harvests in excess of household requirements into bread and to market it at prices determined by public authorities at the points of sale,[4] but this trifling privilege was revoked on January 10, 1591.[5]

Possibly because the public causally linked the measure with the dear prices of the following year, the elevation of the tasas in 1582 proved highly unpopular. Several Procuradores in the Cortes of 1583–1585 had instructions from their constituencies to protest against the recent increases in the grain schedules. On August 3, 1585, the Cortes voted to request the Crown to revert to the maximum prices adopted in 1571,[6] and Petition XXXVI ineffectually laid the demand before Philip II.[7] On November 4, 1587, the Cortes resolved to consider the proposal of the representatives from Jaén to abolish the tasas; but the measure was defeated on December 11, 1587,[8] and on January 25, 1588, a motion by the Procuradores from Cordova to adopt the policy of adjusting the maximum prices to each harvest met a similar fate.[9]

---

[1] BN, *Raros*, 7673; *Recopilación*, lib. v, tit. xxv, ley v.

[2] *Ibid.*, lib. v, tit. xxv, ley vi.

[3] *Ibid.*, lib. v, tit. xxv, ley viii.

[4] BN, *Sección de Manuscritos*, Ms. 13,125, fols. 58–59; *Raros*, 7673; *Recopilación*, lib. v, tit. xxv, ley ix.

The Cortes of 1579–1582 had petitioned Philip II to enact similar legislation (*Actas*, VI, 861–862).

[5] *Recopilación*, lib. v, tit. xxv, leyes vii and x.

[6] *Actas*, VII, 756–759. It is interesting to note that five of the twenty-five Procuradores present on August 3, 1585, favored abolition of the price control.

[7] *Ibid.*, VII, 816–817.

[8] *Ibid.*, IX, 201, 205, 209, 254–256.   [9] *Ibid.*, IX, 317–318.

Four months later Cristóbal de Figueroa, a Procurador from Salamanca, advocated complete freedom of the grain market, but the proposition was killed without protracted debate.[1] On September 18, 1593, Alonso de Fonseca, from Toro, introduced a bill for the removal or annual fixation of the tasas; but the Cortes refused to consider it.[2] A motion either to increase the maximum tariffs or to suspend them for a few years, which the representatives of Segovia presented to the Cortes on August 18, 1597, was also denied consideration.[3]

On September 6, 1593, the Council of Castile submitted to the Cortes a project to increase the maximum price of barley beginning with the 1594 harvest; but the Procuradores disapproved the proposal on the ground that the enhanced tariff would stimulate the cultivation of barley at the expense of wheat.[4] In August, 1597 the Procuradores from Burgos and Segovia favored an increase in the barley tasa,[5] but their plan fell on deaf ears. It was upon the initiative of the Council of Castile, whose most telling argument seems to have been that the low barley schedule had reduced cultivation to a purely subsistence basis, that on July 21, 1598, Philip II raised the maximum price to 7 reals per fanega beginning with the 1599 harvest.[6]

By 1593 the appointment of special judges to inquire into violations of the price regulations, an expedient to which the Crown had threatened to resort in practically every major price-fixing statute of the preceding ninety years, had become a reality. On June 10, 1593, Rodrigo Sánchez Doria, a Procurador from Seville, lodged a complaint before the Cortes;[7] and two days later the Procuradores formally petitioned Philip II to withdraw the commissions.[8] The eruption of loud and bitter complaints in the autumn of 1599[9] indicates that the royal justices were still at large; but in response to a memorial approved by the Cortes on

---

[1] *Actas*, x, 97, 103, 105.
[2] *Ibid.*, XIII, 37–42.
[3] *Ibid.*, xv, 534, 539–543, 546.
[4] *Ibid.*, XIII, 14, 16–22, 35–36.
[5] *Ibid.*, xv, 534, 540–541.
[6] BN, *Varios*, 1-1-37; *Raros*, 22,472; *Recopilación*, lib. v, tit. xxv, ley xi.
[7] *Actas*, XII, 504.
[8] *Ibid.*, XII, 505.
[9] *Ibid.*, XVIII, 378–381, 401, 407.

November 4, 1599,[1] the Crown agreed to recall them.[2] The lack of subsequent protests suggests that Philip III fulfilled his promise and that the execrated institution was not revived.

From the late summer of the extremely dear year of 1598 until the early summer of 1600 the regulation of grain prices was a favorite topic of discussion in the Cortes,[3] with the opponents of moderation or abolition in the ascendancy. Through requests for advice the Council of Castile initiated several of the debates. Although defeated in 1598 and desultorily discussed, without decisive action, in 1599–1600, the Council's proposal to exempt grain sold by the producer seemed to gain support as the deliberations progressed. After eleven months of intermittent discussion of the tasas, on June 13, 1603, the Cortes — largely motivated by a desire to alleviate agricultural distress — petitioned Philip III to permit peasants to sell the surplus from their harvests at market prices.[4] The retention of the price-fixing statutes, as a bulwark against the cupidity of regraters, was advocated; but the Procuradores rightly believed that the proverbially weak bargaining power of peasants guaranteed the public against exorbitant prices in an unregulated market.

On September 2, 1605,[5] Philip III raised the legal maximum prices of barley and wheat to 9 and 18 reals per fanega respec-

---

[1] *Actas*, XVIII, 408–409.   [2] *Ibid.*, XVIII, 436.

[3] *Vide Actas*, XV, 654–656, 658–667, 688, 748–765; XVIII, 128, 417–418, 421, 459, 471–489, 491–495, 497–499, 501, 512, 617–622; XIX, 371, 376; Cristóbal Espejo, *op. cit.*, RABM, 3ª Época, XXV, 8–13.

[4] *Actas*, XX, 377–378, 380, 409, 476, 492, 542, 548, 565, 611, 613; XXI, 90, 170, 174–189, 198, 202–204, 287, 289–290, 318–348, 352–353, 356–360, 362–366, 400–402, 431–432.

[5] Previous writers have accepted the erroneous date, October 15, 1600, listed by the *Recopilación* (lib. V, tit. XXV, ley XII). For example, *vide* Moritz Julius Bonn, *op. cit.*, pp. 27–28; Cristóbal Espejo, *op. cit.*, RABM, 3ª Época, XXV, 1–2, 221; Francisco Cárdenas, *Historia de la Propiedad Territorial en España* (Madrid, 1873), II, 320; Diego Clemencín, "Elógio de la Réina Católica," *Memorias de la Real Academia de la Historia*, VI (Madrid, 1821), 292, n. 1. Yet there can be no doubt concerning the correct date. A memorial presented to the Cortes on May 5, 1603, placed the maximum price of wheat at 14 reals per fanega (*Actas*, XXI, 318), the tariff adopted in 1582, as did a Procurador from Murcia four days later (*ibid.*, XXI, 354–355). The accounts of the Convento de Nuestra Señora de Sandoval (AHN, *Clero*, León, leg. 244), which list tasa prices for every quarter-year from 1600 to 1605, mention the "new maximum prices" of 18 reals per fanega for wheat and 9 reals for barley for the first time in the third quarter of 1605. Had the pragmatic been issued in 1600, it could not have failed to provoke discussion in the Cortes of 1602–1603.

tively,[1] the highest points they were destined to reach during the period under investigation. If one may accept the parliamentary debates as evidence, the enhanced tariffs proved highly unpopular. On April 28, 1607, a request from the Duke of Lerma, the favorite of Philip III, to consider the price-fixing legislation for grain was laid before the Cortes, and the Procuradores decided to write their cities for instructions.[2] In the unusually animated parliamentary discussions which ensued during the summer and fall of 1607 and the spring and summer of 1608, the support of the recent pragmatic was virtually nil, and the denunciation of regrating particularly vitriolic.[3] When a vote was finally taken, in October, 1608, the Cortes favored a reduction of the maximum price of barley to 7 reals per fanega and of wheat to 14 reals and the exemption of sales by producers.[4]

After 1608 depopulation and the depreciation of the vellon coinage largely crowded the control of grain prices out of the parliamentary deliberations. On July 1, 1609, the Cortes voted not to press the Crown for a reply to the memorial submitted on October 21, 1608;[5] in June of the following year a Procurador from Seville ineffectually advocated regulation of agricultural wages in order to mitigate the losses of entrepreneurs and thus to avert the diminution of the grain supply;[6] and in 1612 isolated complaints were registered against imports.[7]

Freedom to sell grain from their own harvests at unregulated prices was finally conceded to farmers on May 18, 1619;[8] but because "experience has shown the evils which result from the said law . . . designed to stimulate cultivation and thereby lower prices," on September 11, 1628, producers were again subjected to the tasas established in 1605.[9] In 1629[10] and 1632 the Cortes

---

[1] *Quaderno de Leyes Añadidas a la Nueva Recopilación* (Madrid, 1610), fol. 69.
[2] *Actas*, XXIII, 48–49.
[3] *Ibid.*, XXIII, 4, 21–25, 48–49, 174–177, 193, 195, 370, 393, 531, 588; XXIV, 126, 299, 320, 326–327, 329, 331, 386, 390, 394, 398, 403, 407–411, 417–419, 422–423, 473–475, 545–546, 553–556, 560–565.
[4] *Ibid.*, XXIV, 560–568.   [5] *Ibid.*, XXV, 293.
[6] *Ibid.*, XXV, 772–773.   [7] *Ibid.*, XXVII, 265, 307.
[8] *Recopilación*, lib. IV, tit. XXI, ley XXVIII.
[9] *Autos Acordados* (Madrid, 1772), lib. V, tit. XXV, auto III.
[10] *Actas*, XLVII, 252–254, 428–429.

conditioned grants of subsidies upon the restoration of the liberty of peasants to sell grain at market prices; accordingly a pragmatic of July 27, 1632, repealed the legislation of September 11, 1628, and revalidated that of May 18, 1619.[1] During the period under investigation the price of grain sold by its producers was not again subjected to public control. But through the end year of 1650 the tasas adopted in 1605 [2] and confirmed in 1631 remained applicable to grain not produced by the seller.

It is interesting to note that the policy of encouraging grain imports manifested in the parliamentary discussions and legislation of roughly the first eight or nine decades of the period under investigation was finally superseded by interdiction. On March 26 and April 12, 1612, the representatives of Jaén and Cordova unsuccessfully laid before the Cortes a proposal to forbid imports into Andalusia except in sterile years upon the unanimous request of Granada, Seville, Cordova, Murcia, and Jaén.[3] Arguing that domestic agriculture needed protection, that foreign wheat menaced public health, and that grain imports occasioned specie exports, the Cortes of 1626 conditioned the grant of a subsidy upon the prohibition of barley, rye, and wheat imports.[4] A pragmatic of February 7, 1626, fulfilled the royal engagement,[5] with the reservation that in years of such scarcity "that certain provinces cannot provide themselves from other provinces at moderate prices" the Crown should permit shipments of foreign grain into the stricken area.[6]

Throughout the period under investigation there was a ban on grain exports, but the domestic trade of Castile and León was theoretically free. In practice, however, local authorities often impeded outward domestic shipments; and, although the Cortes strenuously objected, royal permits for exports were granted from time to time.

---

[1] *Recopilación*, lib. v, tit. xxv, ley xiii.

[2] The rye tasa (8 reals a fanega) established in 1582 remained in force through 1650.

[3] *Actas*, xxvii, 265, 307.

[4] *Ibid.*, xliv, 73–74.

[5] Galicia, the Cantabrian region, and Murcia were excepted.

[6] *Actas*, xliv, 243–246.

It seems that in almost all cities and important towns of Castile and León there were public granaries, but accessible knowledge of their administration is too meager to support generalization concerning their influence upon prices.

Whereas Castile relied upon statutory limits to insure reasonable grain prices, the kingdom of Valencia attempted to reach the same end in an unregulated market through governmental intervention to guarantee an abundant supply. The chronic dependence of Valencia upon imports, a phenomenon which largely resulted from her comparative advantage in the production of rice and fruit, led to medieval legislation permitting treasure exports in return for foreign grain; [1] and the regulation remained in force throughout the period under investigation.

Few matters absorbed more attention in the infrequent sixteenth-century sessions of the Valencian *Corts* than the efforts to maintain the medieval *foral* privilege of importing grain from Sicily upon the payment of nominal export duties.[2] The Corts also endeavored to procure, while the Castilian Cortes opposed, the issue of royal licenses for grain exports from Castile into Valencia.[3] But the principal governmental activity designed to insure an abundance of grain and to control the price consisted of the subsidies and loans to importers through the *Taula de Valencia*, usually for one year, with gratuitous interest for six months. The two methods of attracting foreign grain were alternately pursued until about 1540, after which date loans were almost invariably granted.[4]

---

[1] Earl J. Hamilton, "Spanish Mercantilism before 1700," in *Facts and Factors in Economic History* (Cambridge, Massachusetts, 1932), p. 221.

[2] *Fori Valentie Extravaganti*, ii, fols. 71–72; *Furs . . . e Actes de Cort de 1537* (Valencia, 1545), fols. viii–ix; *Furs . . . e Actes de Cort de 1585* (Valencia, 1588), cap. iv, fols. iv–v.

[3] For example, *vide Furs . . . e Actes de Cort de 1547* (Valencia, 1555), cap. vi, fol. ii; *Actas*, vii, 213–216, 218.

[4] The above data have been taken from *Claveria Comuna, Claveria de Censals,* and *Manuals de Consells* of the Archivo del Ayuntamiento of Valencia and the various series of documents of the Hospital dels Inocents (*vide supra*, pp. xxxiv–xxxv) utilized as sources of price and wage statistics. An enormous quantity of extremely important virgin manuscripts in the Valencian Municipal Archive awaits the future historian of the Spanish grain trade.

The loan and subsidy contracts state whence the grain was to be imported. Sardinia and Sicily were the predominant granaries; but Andalusia, Castile, Cata-

Because of the heavy superstructure of generalizations respecting the course of Spanish prices resting upon the grain tasas, it may be profitable to consider their relation to market prices. Although economic historians have subsequently gone astray, there is abundant evidence that contemporaries were fully, indeed painfully, aware of the glaring ineffectiveness of the regulations. As has been indicated, many of the price-fixing statutes, with enumerations of evasive "artifices and subterfuges," stern measures against judicial delinquency, and progressively severe penalties for infractions, bore eloquent testimony of their own inefficacy. The parliamentary proceedings abound with asseverations that the tasas were flagrantly disregarded, especially by lay and ecclesiastical magnates. In 1569 the administration of the Hospital de la Sangre of Seville, evidently feeling obligated to apologize for the sale of two lots of wheat at the legal maximum price, explained that the grain was worm-eaten.[1]

If we consider the fact that the arid measures of León were about 20 per cent smaller than the official Castilian standard and neglect (for the time being) the allowance for transportation and the exemptions of farmers' sales, we find that roughly two-thirds of the annual wheat and barley prices of Andalusia and New Castile exceeded the tasas, that a little less than half of the Leonese wheat prices and about three-fourths of the barley and rye quotations surpassed the legal limits, and that only about 4 per cent of the annual averages in the three Castilian regions precisely equaled the legal maximum schedules.

The above statistics obviously fail to gauge accurately the extent of the observance of the price regulations. As has been indicated, after 1539 the statutes authorized the addition of interurban transportation costs to the tasas, and in 1619–1628 and 1632–1650 grain sold by the producer fell without the price control. Exercising the authority inherent in the Crown to suspend

lonia, Corsica, Málaga, Murcia, Naples, Paris, Ronda, Rumania, and Turkey were drawn upon from time to time. In the fiscal year 1602–1603, which may be considered typical, wheat was transported to the Hospital dels Inocents (*Memorias*, 1602–1603, fols. 55–64) from more than a hundred towns and cities in the kingdom of Valencia.

[1] *Libros de Recibos y Gastos*, leg. 455.

or repeal legislation by decree, Philip II temporarily lifted the regulations in particular localities on occasions of great scarcity.[1] On the other hand, one cannot be certain that the modicum of exchanges nominally concluded at tasa prices were not influenced by ulterior considerations.

But the manifold sources of distortion do not render the above statistics valueless as indices of the observance of the price-fixing statutes. Approximately half of the quotations entering into the annual averages for Andalusia and New Castile represent the sales of grain received as rent by institutions. These sales were never exempt from the statutory schedules, and they almost invariably took place before expenses of interurban transportation had been incurred. Most of the grain purchased by institutions in Seville and Toledo was probably produced in their respective localities, and there is strong reason to doubt that farmers often sold as large lots as the institutions ordinarily bought. Hence there is ample foundation for the belief that in Andalusia and New Castile the tasas were illicitly exceeded in more than half the transactions. In accordance with *a priori* expectations, the statutory limits exerted a strong pull on prices which would have been slightly higher than the tasas in an unregulated market, for a low reward was insufficient to motivate violation of the law. Since the small arid measures tended to bring the normal market prices within the magnetic field of the regulatory schedules, a high percentage of Leonese grain sales nominally occurred at the maximum tariffs. In terms of the official Castilian standard these prices were illegal, but it would be incorrect to argue that the statutory limits did not bear a fairly constant ratio to and tend to moderate the market prices of grain in León.

Perhaps it is superfluous to conclude that maximum tariffs consistently disregarded in two of the three Castilian regions [2] did

---

[1] For example, *vide* AA, Cuenca, caj. 7, leg. 31; BN, *Varios*, 1–49–38.

[2] Whether allowances for transportation, the temporary suspensions of the price control, and the exemption of peasant sales may have rendered legal a higher percentage of the prices in Appendices III–V than I have presumed is irrelevant to the question under consideration. The authors who have relied upon the legal maximum schedules to indicate the course of Spanish prices have not — and, in fact, could not have — allowed mathematically for these elements of elasticity.

not accurately represent the course of grain prices in the entire
country; and, as Chart 16 reveals, there was a marked divergence
between the short- and long-term movements of the grain indices
and those of general commodities.[1]

X

The articles in Appendices III–V have been divided into agricultural and non-agricultural groups on the basis of origin. The
products of agriculture marketed in a raw state have been classified as agricultural, while the goods of non-agricultural prove-

CHART 17

INDEX NUMBERS OF AGRICULTURAL AND NON–AGRICULTURAL PRICES

Base = 1571–1580

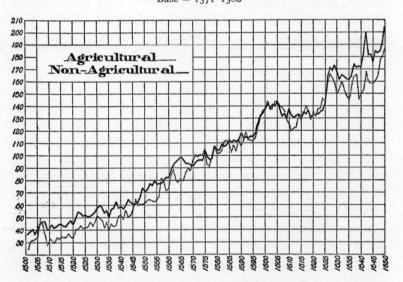

nance and those manufactured from agricultural raw materials,
whether on farms or in industrial establishments, have fallen into
the non-agricultural category. For instance, olives and grapes
have been considered agricultural; olive oil and wine, non-agri-

---

[1] If the present book succeeds in dispelling the widely disseminated and obsti-
nately held view that the legal grain tariffs listed in the *Recopilación* render research
in the history of Spanish prices supererogatory, I shall feel that it has not been
written in vain.

cultural. The present taxonomic method is open to the objection that it fails to bring into clear relief the effects of harvests upon agricultural prices and that the contemporaneous fabrication of many products as an adjunct to farming distorts the agricultural and non-agricultural dichotomy. It seems, however, that the charts of grain and fruit-nut prices supply ample data concerning the results of good and bad seasons and that no alternative method of classification would divide all the commodities into the two groups more logically or satisfactorily. Obviously it would be desirable to examine the regional movements of agricultural and non-agricultural prices; but on account of the limitations of space the four sectional indices for each group have been combined and presented in Chart 17.

Throughout the first three quarters of the sixteenth century agricultural prices rose considerably faster than the non-agricultural; from 1575 to 1625 the two groups of index numbers moved harmoniously; but in the second quarter of the seventeenth century the non-agricultural indices forged ahead.

The relatively rapid upswing of agricultural prices in the first half of the period under consideration suggests a comparative decline of agricultural production,[1] but the fact that imports — whose prices reflected the influx of American treasure less than did domestic goods — comprised a higher percentage of the commodities tended to moderate the advance of the non-agricultural index numbers. In the second quarter of the seventeenth century the conditions were reversed. Apparently agricultural production decreased less than the non-agricultural, but the relatively high representation of imports, which felt the full impact of vellon depreciation, accentuated the rise of non-agricultural prices.

---

[1] Chart 17 obviously casts doubts upon the thesis of Konrad Haebler (*op. cit.*, pp. 34–35) that Spanish agriculture was in its heyday from 1550 to 1560 and tends to support Manuel Colmeiro's (*Historia de la Economía Política en España* [Madrid, 1863], II, 80–81) conclusion that agricultural decadence began as early as the second quarter of the sixteenth century.

CHAPTER XII

WAGES: MONEY AND REAL

SINCE the sources of the wage statistics largely coincide with those consulted for prices, extensive criticism may be omitted. As in the collection of all other quantitative data included in the present study, I have found it necessary to utilize manuscripts altogether; and no printed material has furnished a clew to their location. The relative superiority of hospital account-books as a source of wage statistics is even greater than in the case of prices. In addition to the physicians, surgeons, barber-bleeders, and attendants needed to supply medical attention and the priests, chaplains, sacristans, and nuns required to console the suffering, perform rituals and administer sacraments for the community, render extreme unction to the moribund, and celebrate masses for the patients and decedents, the hospitals employed legal counsel, superintendents, accountants, notaries, and divers classes of domestic servants. The maintenance of the hospital buildings and residential dwellings held as investments necessitated the frequent employment of the various grades of labor in the building trades; but unfortunately the repairs seldom extended throughout a half-century, and homogeneous substitutes were usually unobtainable. Furthermore, the hospitals occasionally exploited vineyards or wheat land by wage labor; but this was never an enduring policy, and consequently wages for agricultural workers are available for only one region in a single half-century. Not only furnishing no continuous series, but supplying few data to bridge gaps and to serve as controls, the account-books of convents are virtually worthless for the present purpose. I have located no serviceable private payrolls; and, except in one case, it has not seemed desirable to make use of the readily obtainable salaries of municipal and national employees.

Although sporadic wages and salaries were taken from the records of the House of Trade and the municipality and Cathedral of Seville, the quotations for Andalusia in 1501–1550 were so discontinuous that a satisfactory series could not be compiled.[1] The data proved useful only as a control for the extrapolation of Andalusian wages in the first half of the sixteenth century. But in 1551–1600 the accounts of the Hospital de la Sangre supplied continuous monthly salaries for 25 grades of labor, of which 8 were professional, 8 skilled, and 9 unskilled.[2] Sufficient quotations were found for every year to permit the computation of index numbers; and 1552–1553, with 6 relatives each, represent the only weak links in the chain. The series for the first half of the seventeenth century is incomparably more satisfactory than that for the preceding period. From the accounts of the Espíritu Santo, Amor de Dios, and de la Sangre Hospitals, all Sevillan institutions, monthly or annual salaries for 39 kinds of labor and daily wages for 5 classes have been obtained; and, when compared with the series for 1551–1600, the percentage of both professional and skilled labor declined, the professions having 11 representatives and the trades 13. No lacunae mar the indices; for no year were there less than 30 relatives; and in all except five cases the annual averages were over 90 per cent complete.[3]

[1] Subsequent research has not significantly enlarged the material in my "Wages and Subsistence on Spanish Treasure Ships," *Journal of Political Economy*, XXXVII, 430–450.

[2] The following principles have governed the tripartite classification of workers:

A. *Professional.* Individuals engaged in work requiring considerable formal education, usually the degree of *bachiller* or its equivalent, and those occupying administrative posts. Lawyers, notaries, physicians, priests, and hospital superintendents, for instance, fall into this category.

B. *Trades or skilled workers.* Individuals engaged in work requiring a moderate amount of education or a long apprenticeship and those occupying minor administrative positions. Masons, carpenters, bookkeepers, overseers, and foremen are examples.

C. *Unskilled laborers.* Individuals whose occupations required little or no education or supervisory capacity. Specialized knowledge, as in the case of cooks, was sometimes necessary; but the type and the degree of skill included in this category were either acquired quickly or absorbed from one's environment without special effort. Helpers in the building trades, hospital orderlies, doorkeepers, and the like have been considered varieties of unskilled laborers.

[3] It is interesting to note that in 1563 the Hospital de la Sangre (*Libros de Recibos y Gastos*, leg. 454) paid 50 ducats for a female slave, Ana la Esclava, who was assigned the duties of chief cook. One ducat per month, the salary formerly paid, was credited toward the amortization of her purchase price. As soon as the Hospital recouped its outlay, Ana was manumitted.

For two principal reasons the salaries of the Mesta officials and employees have been placed in the New Castilian series. First, of the regions included in the present study, New Castile maintained the closest commercial contact with Estremadura, a stronghold of the Mesta; and the most central region was perhaps the logical place for a series that could not be definitely located. Furthermore, most of the ambulatory employees traversed New Castile on the biennial migrations.[1] Second, without the Mesta salaries the New Castilian series would have been largely dominated by the wage policy of the Hospital de Antezana in Alcalá de Henares, a small hospital in a small city. For 1501–1550 the account-books of the Mesta, which unfortunately do not begin until 1510, and the records of the Hospital de Antezana supply salaries or wages for only 13 classes of labor: 6 professional, 6 skilled, and 1 unskilled. Although there are no gaps, the index numbers for 1501–1509 and 1513–1514, being averages of from 3 to 6 relatives, are clearly dubious. For the second half of the sixteenth century the above sources and the records of the Hospital de Tavera in Toledo, which contributed satisfactory quotations for unskilled labor in the building trades and for master and journeymen carpenters and masons, furnished continuous wages or salaries for 9 professional, 11 skilled, and 2 unskilled grades of labor, giving the index numbers 22 components. Aside from the abnormally high representation of the professions and trades, the gap in the Mesta payrolls from 1563 to 1582, twenty years that include the base period, constitutes the outstanding defect of the series. Neither in the second half of the sixteenth century nor in the first half of the seventeenth, for which identical sources were employed, was there a hiatus in the index numbers; and remarkable completeness of the annual averages characterized the latter period. The series for 1601–1650 included 12 professions, 5 trades, and 5 varieties of unskilled labor.

Although continuous quotations could be drawn from only one source, the account-books of the Hospital de Esgueva in Valladolid, Old Castilian wages in the first half of the sixteenth century

---

[1] *Vide* Julius Klein, *The Mesta* (Cambridge, Massachusetts, 1920), map facing p. 19.

take second rank among the regional groups. Monthly or annual salaries for only 10 categories of workers are available; but the records of the exploitation of 3 vineyards supplied daily wages for 9 classes of agricultural laborers, and the maintenance of buildings necessitated the frequent employment of journeymen carpenters and master roof-tilers (trastejadores). Consequently 21 classes of workers entered into the index numbers. With 3 professions, 9 trades, and 9 kinds of unskilled labor represented, the group distribution was highly satisfactory. Although the payrolls of the Hospital de San Bernabé y San Antolín in Palencia supplement the Esgueva papers, the statistics for 1551–1600 are inferior to those of the preceding period. Since the Hospital de Esgueva abandoned the exploitation of vineyards, wages for agricultural workers were not accessible.[1] The components of the index fell to 20; and the group distribution, with 6 professions, 4 trades, and 10 varieties of unskilled labor, deteriorated. For 1601-1650 the Esgueva and San Bernabé y San Antolín records supplied salaries for 7 professions, 5 trades, and 10 classes of unskilled workers, making a total of 22. From 1551 to 1650 neither hiatuses nor weak years vitiated the Old Castilian index numbers; but owing to a lack of data, an index could not be made for 1501. In 1504 and 1513–1517 there were only 7 relatives, while in 1529 the number fell to 6.

Since political rather than economic considerations largely determined the wages and salaries of all forms of public employees, they have generally been omitted. When there was also the possibility, as in the case of military and naval personnel, that the labor was either involuntary or was patriotically motivated, the data were invariably rejected as unreliable. But owing to the continuous and varied programs of public works (including the maintenance of the wall, streets, and towers, and the construction and upkeep of irrigation canals), the operation of the Taula, and the diversified activities resulting from the paternalism of the municipality, an exception has been made of the payrolls of the city of Valencia. The wages and salaries derived from the municipal records are not free from the objection that non-economic

---

[1] Unless one classifies an urban grain-sifter as an agricultural laborer.

considerations influenced their magnitudes, but the economic rather than political or administrative nature of much of the work probably minimizes the distortion. The accounts of the municipality of Valencia and of the Hospital dels Inocents, the sole records of continuous wages yet unearthed, yield by far the best regional series for each of the three half-centuries. The index numbers are complete from 1501 to 1650, and satisfactory quotations for at least 49 categories of labor are present in each of the fifty-year periods. The index numbers for the first half of the sixteenth century include 14 professions, 22 trades, and 13 classes of unskilled labor, making a total of 49 components. In 1501, when 8 relatives are averaged, the index is dubious; but 1503 and 1507 are the only other years having quotations for less than 39 kinds of workers. In 1551–1600 wages or salaries for 17 professions, 16 trades, and 17 varieties of unskilled labor, or a total of 50, are available; and for no year are the data less than 90 per cent complete. The series for the first half of the seventeenth century includes 20 professions, 17 trades, and 19 classes of unskilled workers, totaling 56; and in every year except 1612 and 1615, with 41 and 52 relatives respectively, at least 95 per cent of the data are present.

Aside from the invariable lack of adequate controls, evident from the above discussion of the sources, the compilation of the wage series involved numerous difficulties not encountered in the collection and elaboration of price statistics. Many professional servants of institutions — attorneys, notaries, and surgeons, for example — were employed on a part-time basis, and descriptions of their duties appeared at infrequent intervals. Since the trend of salaries from 1501 to 1650 was upward, it was not always easy to detect a spurious increase in remuneration resulting from enhanced part-time duties. Furthermore, the full-time employee was not infrequently assigned additional tasks, especially during the temporary vacancy of a similar position, with a correlative increase in pay;[1] and the accountants seldom took the trouble to

---

[1] The ingrained tendency of salaried workers to seek additional part-time employment, which must impress every observant visitor in Spain to-day, was firmly established in the sixteenth century.

clarify the phenomenon. Evolutions in the nature of occupations and changes in the title of the same employment would have distorted uncritically compiled wage series extending over a half-century. The "salaries" of institutional employees frequently included extraneous items. There is at least one case in which the apothecary of a hospital suddenly became a contractor of pharmaceutical supplies; and the payrolls for several ensuing years carried his total annual receipts as a labor income. Although the shepherds of more than one hospital had to provide pasturage, their compensation was recorded year after year without any indication of the irregularity; and the same holds for the contractor who "put out" the laundry of the Convento de Santa Clara in Medina de Rioseco. Occasionally the wives, and still less often the children, of hospital employees assisted them; and, when wages were rising, it was seldom easy to identify the specious salary increases which accompanied the transition from an individual to a family basis. The payrolls, especially in the first half of the sixteenth century, often omitted the occupations of the workers; in almost all cases, however, internal evidence enables one to surmount this obstacle.

In addition to his monetary reward virtually every worker included in the regional index numbers received goods and services ranging from a half-azumbre of wine and 16–24 ounces of bread daily in the case of unskilled laborers to free house rent, 24 fanegas of wheat and 12 of barley annually, and free admissions to bullfights for the upper stratum of professional employees. The hospitals generally supplied lodging for the single and a house for the married employee and paid in kind sufficient bread, meat, and wine for the consumption of the worker, which theoretically varied directly with his economic and social category; but there was a progressive tendency for monetary payments to supersede the food and drink. At first the commutations corresponded closely to the true prices of the meat, bread, and wine; but the adjustment of the nominal to the actual market prices became more infrequent with the passage of time. Particularly in the last quarter of the sixteenth century and the second quarter of the seventeenth, the commutations tended to lag behind the composite prices of

the food and drink, which entailed a corresponding loss in real
wages. Unfortunately, it proved impossible to ascertain the exact
monetary equivalents of the total annual payments in kind. One
could have included the dietaries in about one-third of the cases;
but, since there is no means of knowing the value of the house
rent or lodging nor of the miscellaneous goods and services, the
wage tables could not have been made to represent the total compensation of workers. Furthermore, the data concerning food and
drink are so fragmentary in many cases that interpolation would
be dubious, and at times information is completely lacking. Hence
the annual averages have been compiled and the index numbers
computed purely on the basis of monetary remuneration, that is,
without taking into account payments in kind. Success seems to
have attended the constant efforts to prevent the payments in
lieu of dietaries from creeping into the wage statistics, but there
is a possibility that at times the commutations of the grain originally paid a few professional employees may have been trans-
scribed as money wages. The magnitude and frequency of gratuities in money and kind designed to offset the mounting cost of
living apparently increased until the vellon inflation of the seventeenth century upset the finances of hospitals — institutions
largely dependent upon charitable donations, mortgage loans,
government obligations, and quasi-fixed urban rentals. Only
when the gratuities had attained sufficient certainty and regularity to motivate labor were they considered wages; and their
unavoidable exclusion during the process of evolution tended to
accentuate the slight upward bias imparted to the index numbers
by the occasional inclusion of the grain allowances. It seems,
however, that the error resulting from the combination of these
factors was not large.

That the regional statistics depict with tolerable accuracy the
movements of the wages and salaries paid by the institutions
whose accounts have been consulted admits of little doubt, but
there are ample reasons to question their validity for general
wages in the regions they represent. On *a priori* grounds one
would expect the lack of controls and the preponderance of the
wage scales of two or three institutions — which inevitably re-

flected their labor policies and financial circumstances — to impair the reliability of the regional data. That the salary schedules of particular hospitals should fall and remain for a considerable period out of line with the trend of wages was a natural phenomenon; for an unusually high percentage of hospital employment was professional in character, and even a large part of the domestic labor was specialized. Since the institutions were not operated for profit, there was doubtless little competition for the specialized labor; and the employees, being below the average in responsiveness to economic stimuli and lacking initiative,[1] were probably less aggressive than the generality of salaried workers in bargaining with their employers and seeking more remunerative posts elsewhere. The labor policy and the fortunes of the Mesta doubtless affected the compensation of its employees, and political factors probably influenced the wages paid by the municipality of Valencia.

The disparities among the regional index numbers tend to confirm the above hypotheses casting doubt upon the validity of each of the four series. It is true that the revolution of wages was greater in Andalusia and New Castile than in Valencia and Old Castile, as theoretical considerations would lead one to expect; but the lack of harmony among the regional wage movements over long and short periods must be ascribed to the non-representative character of the data. Satisfactory information concerning contemporary migrations of workers is lacking, but there is certainly greater reason to believe that a lower price differential was required to move labor from one region to another than was necessary in the case of bulky commodities. That economic prospectiveness induced migration in sixteenth-century Spain is attested by the rapid growth of Seville and Cádiz.[2] Yet the regional price movements of all important groups of commodities agree more closely than do those of the wage indices.

The statistical methods described in connection with prices have generally been followed.[3] For each quarter I have trans-

---

[1] A cause and a consequence of the habitual performance of routine labor.
[2] Tomás González, *Censo de Población de la Corona de Castilla en el Siglo XVI* (Madrid, 1829), pp. 83–84.
[3] *Vide* Chapter VI and Appendix I.

scribed the first four wages for every grade of labor paid on a daily basis and, when quarterly data were lacking, adjusted for seasonal variations in computing annual averages. Discontinuous wage series from different localities have been combined only through average correlations, but the wages and salaries of homogeneous classes of labor from different establishments in the same town and from different localities of the same region when extending over entire half-centuries have been crudely averaged. Wood-cutters, linen weavers, and linen measurers were the only piece-rate workers whose wages could be utilized. Fortunately the width of the linen — a datum almost invariably excluded from the entries of textiles in contemporary accounts — was always expressed, and the units of wood were usually definite. Separate series for each of the half-centuries from 1501 to 1650 have been compiled, unweighted arithmetic index numbers constructed on the middle decade of each period as a base, and the bases for 1501–1550 and 1601–1650 shifted to 1571–1580 in order to provide continuous index numbers for 1501–1650.

As has been indicated, the indices for each region are vitiated by the preponderance of the wage scales of two or three institutions. But if we average the regional index numbers to form a national series, for each of the fifty-year periods there are 8 or more sources and wages covering from about 50 to almost 100 grades of labor, including the earnings of hundreds of workers.[1] Hence there is little reason to question the representative character of the national indices which have been constructed by averaging the index numbers for the four regions. The greatest defect of the composite series consists of the abnormally high percentage of professional labor included. The fact that hospital records supplied approximately 70 per cent of the data is a much weaker objection; for the institutions were sufficiently numerous and scattered for most of the aberrations of their labor supply and demand to cancel one another.[2] The close agreement of the

---

[1] The annual averages for several grades of domestic labor included as many as 15 workers in single regions, and the number of completely unspecialized and unskilled day laborers was occasionally higher.

[2] In the only case of a major influence affecting all hospitals alike, the wage indices moved counter to *a priori* expectations. Dependent upon fixed-yield invest-

TABLE 27

COMPOSITE INDEX NUMBERS OF MONEY WAGES, 1501–1650

Base = 1571–1580

Year	Index number	Year	Index number	Year	Index number
1501	37.51	1551	69.59	1601	144.82
1502	42.07	1552	70.35	1602	150.15
1503	44.42	1553	72.18	1603	157.61
1504	42.56	1554	77.80	1604	159.23
1505	44.09	1555	78.41	1605	161.81
1506	43.36	1556	79.22	1606	163.09
1507	46.27	1557	80.27	1607	162.23
1508	46.01	1558	82.34	1608	165.18
1509	46.04	1559	86.46	1609	165.68
1510	49.55	1560	87.59	1610	166.73
1511	48.06	1561	88.58	1611	167.01
1512	48.10	1562	88.29	1612	163.19
1513	49.45	1563	90.52	1613	164.94
1514	49.40	1564	90.55	1614	164.43
1515	48.80	1565	93.55	1615	165.06
1516	48.91	1566	89.59	1616	164.44
1517	49.77	1567	93.97	1617	163.81
1518	51.44	1568	97.80	1618	167.65
1519	51.79	1569	97.52	1619	166.77
1520	52.81	1570	99.06	1620	163.89
1521	52.34	1571	97.12	1621	163.54
1522	52.94	1572	97.34	1622	165.78
1523	53.67	1573	96.49	1623	165.42
1524	53.85	1574	98.40	1624	162.84
1525	53.85	1575	97.67	1625	162.86
1526	52.65	1576	98.97	1626	164.03
1527	54.32	1577	100.13	1627	165.74
1528	54.59	1578	100.73	1628	170.72
1529	53.57	1579	105.41	1629	173.54
1530	51.87	1580	105.71	1630	175.81
1531	53.86	1581	108.56	1631	176.25
1532	54.66	1582	107.76	1632	176.72
1533	54.57	1583	108.61	1633	177.24
1534	55.12	1584	113.10	1634	177.97
1535	55.82	1585	113.82	1635	177.43
1536	56.36	1586	113.03	1636	179.21
1537	57.57	1587	114.80	1637	179.64
1538	56.95	1588	120.14	1638	179.44
1539	58.70	1589	121.36	1639	179.19
1540	59.54	1590	120.64	1640	180.55
1541	58.11	1591	121.41	1641	181.22
1542	59.42	1592	121.95	1642	182.48
1543	59.46	1593	121.45	1643	174.49
1544	60.96	1594	121.63	1644	175.92
1545	62.54	1595	121.26	1645	178.31
1546	63.69	1596	121.09	1646	177.58
1547	62.19	1597	122.51	1647	180.42
1548	63.36	1598	123.30	1648	179.84
1549	66.12	1599	123.32	1649	183.39
1550	67.40	1600	125.31	1650	185.17

averages of regional wages and prices supports the theoretical ascription of reliability to the former.

Because of the limitations of space and the erratic nature of the regional data, it is not worth while to publish the complete annual averages of wages; but, inasmuch as absolute wage levels sometimes interest economists and historians, composite tables containing fifteen grades of labor selected from the different regional series are listed in Appendix VII.

Table 27 lists the composite index numbers of money wages.[1]

In Table 28 decennial averages of the composite indices are given.

TABLE 28

DECENNIAL AVERAGES OF THE INDEX NUMBERS OF MONEY WAGES

Base = 1571–1580

Years	Wages	Years	Wages
1501–1510	44.19	1581–1590	114.18
1511–1520	49.85	1591–1600	122.32
1521–1530	53.37	1601–1610	159.65
1531–1540	56.32	1611–1620	165.12
1541–1550	62.33	1621–1630	167.03
1551–1560	78.42	1631–1640	178.36
1561–1570	92.94	1641–1650	179.88
1571–1580	99.80		

ments for most of their income, hospitals found it difficult to adjust expenditures to receipts in the second quarter of the seventeenth century. Endowments tended to keep pace with the rise in prices during the sixteenth century, but there was no such tendency in the seventeenth. From about 1625 to 1645 most of the hospital records consulted showed a steady excess of disbursements over receipts, with a corresponding encroachment upon capital. In the late 1640's the expenditures were reduced; and, to the discredit of the trustees, the economies took the form of a decrease in the number of patients admitted to the institutions. As early as August 11, 1599, a Sevillan municipal councilor had complained that the salaries of the officials and employees, particularly the former, largely absorbed the incomes of the four Sevillan hospitals, — Amor de Dios, Espíritu Santo, Sangre, and Cardenal, — thus defeating the purposes of the founders and benefactors (Hospital del Cardenal, *Cuaderno de Gastos*, leg. 366). Particularly noteworthy is the fact that most charity hospitals maintained or raised salaries and wages in 1626–1650, regardless of the budgetary difficulties which rising prices and virtually stationary incomes entailed.

[1] Data for Andalusia in 1501–1550 have been extrapolated in the following fashion. The average of the 10 ratios of the quinquennial averages of the Andalusian indices to the sum of the corresponding quinquennial averages of the New Castilian, Old Castilian, and Valencian indices for 1551–1600 is 29.4 per cent. Multiplication of the yearly sums of the indices for the other three regions for 1501–1550 by 0.294 gave tentative indices for Andalusia. Relatives for carpenters' wages in Seville, which appeared to be typical of general wages, averaged about 78.2 per cent of the tentative indices, and the final indices for Andalusia were arrived at by multiplying the tentative figures by 0.782.

Chart 18 presents graphically the annual index numbers of wages contained in Table 27. To facilitate comparison, composite index numbers of prices, representing the averages of the regional data, with straight-line interpolation for missing years in Andalusia and Old Castile, are also given.

CHART 18

COMPOSITE INDEX NUMBERS OF WAGES AND PRICES, 1501–1650

Base = 1571–1580

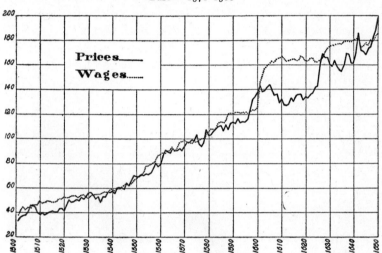

The above tables and chart indicate that the upward movement of money wages made itself felt at the opening of our period and continued, with strikingly few plateaus and recessions, through the first decade of the seventeenth century. After declining slightly from 1611 to 1625, the curve rose from 1626 to 1642 under the stimulus of vellon depreciation. The deflation of September 15, 1642, reduced wages in 1643; but they reacted in 1644 and, with slight drops in 1646 and 1648, continued to advance through the end year of 1650, when the phenomenal increase in Andalusian daily wages resulting from the pestilence of 1648–1650 made itself felt.[1] The increase registered by each decennial average over its

---

[1] *Vide supra*, p. 220.

predecessor attests the constancy of the rise in the wage indices. If we consider only the first and last years, wages rose about 79.7 per cent in 1501–1550, and the average for 1541–1550 stood about 41 per cent above that of 1501–1510. In 1600 the index was 85.9 per cent greater than in 1550, and the average for 1591–1600 was 96.25 per cent above that for 1541–1550. Largely reflecting the sharp upswing in 1601–1610, the wage index for 1650 exceeded that of 1600 by 47.77 per cent, and the average for 1641–1650 was 47.06 per cent higher than in 1591–1600.

Experimental comparison of special index numbers for skilled and unskilled labor with the general wage indices shown in Table 27 and Chart 18 has demonstrated that, regardless of the abnormal representation of the professions, the composite index numbers roughly limn the trend of wages for craftsmen and unskilled laborers; but the oscillations of daily wages greatly exceeded those of the combined wage and salary indices. For instance, wages responded more suddenly and violently than salaries to the epidemics at the close of the sixteenth century and at the middle of the seventeenth. The Old Castilian series for agricultural labor in 1501–1550 rose considerably more than did the general wage indices.[1] Agricultural wages are lacking for the other three regions in the first half of the sixteenth century and for all Spain in 1551–1650.

The complete lack of data concerning the fluctuations of employment renders impossible an exact determination of the effect of the Price Revolution of the sixteenth century and the inflationary rise of prices in the second quarter of the seventeenth upon total labor incomes. Since Spain was predominantly an agricultural country with little or no industry beyond the handicraft stage, the volume of employment probably varied within narrow limits, rising slightly in periods of prosperity and declining insignificantly during depressions. Hence perfect index numbers of wages would gauge the money incomes of the men who worked for hire with tolerable certainty and in conjunction with index

---

[1] Agricultural wages rose significantly in 1501–1520, fell in 1521–1530, and soared in 1531–1550.

numbers of the cost of living would crudely measure changes in real wages.

Only index numbers weighted according to the expenditures of the average family accurately measure changes in the cost of living. But accessible information concerning private budgets during the period under observation is limited to partial and discontinuous data for the royal household in the first half of the sixteenth century and to a few testaments and isolated expense accounts of prelates, grandees, and merchant princes. Such material obviously fails to indicate the relative importance of different items in the disbursements of the average working-class family. In all probability exact information will never be unearthed, but diverse institutional and public records avert total darkness. Itemized daily rations for sailors and soldiers on the treasure fleets and for the complements of naval vessels on duty in the Mediterranean have been obtained from documents in the Archives of the Indies [1] and Simancas.[2] The kitchen accounts of the Colegio Mayor de San Ildefonso of the University of Alcalá de Henares for the second half of the sixteenth century [3] disclose the proportional expenditures upon different articles of food. The account-books of the Hospital de Esgueva occasionally summarize the annual purchases of a few important commodities, and the yearly balance sheets of the Hospital dels Inocents group the disbursements in a manner strikingly similar to that adopted in Chapter XI. But the information derived from each of these sources is an unreliable indicator of the relative importance of the various commodities and services upon which wages were spent. The primitive knowledge of conserving foods, the necessity of protracted storage, and the difficulty and danger of cooking at sea in stormy weather differentiated the dietaries of seamen from those of landmen of similar economic category. Designed to heal and regale patients, the food bought by hospitals was presumably more wholesome and expensive than that consumed by working-

---

[1] *Vide* Earl J. Hamilton, *op. cit.*, pp. 433–437.

[2] *Vide*, for example, *Guerra Antigua*, leg. 100; *Estado*, legs. 486, 1327.

[3] Archivo Histórico Nacional, *Universidades*, 725 f, 743 f–744 f, 746 f–747 f, 769 f–793 f, 795 f–796 f, 816 f, 930 f, 938 f, 1006 f–1007 f, 1017 f, 1023 f–1032 f, 1039 f, 1058 f, 1074 f.

class families. Drawn largely from the upper social and economic strata, university students doubtless demanded better fare than the typical craftsman or salaried employee could afford.

Making what appear to be appropriate adjustments for the unrepresentative character of the available data, I estimate that the average head of a family dependent upon explicit labor income distributed his expenditures, exclusive of house rent, as follows: olive oil 2 per cent, beans (aluvias and habas) and chick-peas 5 per cent, poultry 3½ per cent, textiles 4½ per cent, fish 5 per cent, fuel 5 per cent, wine 10 per cent, meats 15 per cent, wheat 20 per cent, and miscellaneous 30 per cent.[1] The reader should not forget that judgment has necessarily entered into the compilation of these percentages to a great extent and that the possible error is large. Perhaps the most doubtful estimates are for wine, probably abnormally low,[2] and meats, possibly too high. The estimates are intended as averages for the country as a whole, to which the data for separate regions do not closely conform. For instance, olive oil was a more important article in Andalusia and Valencia than in the two Castiles; whereas the reverse was true of lard. The consumption of rice was incomparably greater in Valencia, the great producing center, than in the rest of Spain.

Two of the most serious defects of the unweighted commodity index numbers as indicators of the cost of living are the complete lack of information concerning house rent and the dearth of prices for clothing, particularly textiles. But the fabrication by the worker and his family of a significant portion of the cloth required for home use, together with the presence of a few raw materials and partly finished products in the commodity series, attenuates the weakness of the textile quotations. On the other hand, the validity of Engel's law for Spain in the sixteenth and seventeenth centuries, the fact that even skilled laborers were not far above the Ricardian minimum of subsistence, and the vast preponder-

---

[1] Cf. Francisco Bernís, *El Problema de las Subsistencias* (Salamanca, 1911), cited by Wesley C. Mitchell, "The Making and Using of Index Numbers," *Bulletin of the United States Bureau of Labor Statistics*, no. 284 (Washington, 1921), p. 334.

[2] *Vide* Earl J. Hamilton, *op. cit.*, p. 440.

ance of foods in the price statistics lend special strength to the simple index numbers for the present purpose.

Index numbers weighted in accordance with the estimated expenditures of the working class would show greater year-to-year fluctuations than do the simple indices, but comparisons of averages for the two types of index numbers in 1501–1505 and 1546–1550 suggest that the secular trends in the first half of the sixteenth century would differ little. The exceptional rise in wine and wheat prices, especially the former, was largely offset by the opposite tendency of the quotations for olive oil, fuel, meats, and fish. But the quinquennial averages for 1551–1555 and 1596–1600 indicate that the unweighted index numbers for the second half of the sixteenth century underestimate the total advance in the cost of living by possibly 10 per cent. The sluggish increase of fuel, meat, and fruit-nut prices did not counterbalance the sharp advances of the curves for fish, wheat, and poultry. By the same method of comparison, one finds that the unweighted index numbers tend to overestimate the total rise in the cost of living in the first half of the seventeenth century by something like 2 per cent.

As has been pointed out, the wage indices probably gauge the trend of the money earnings of the average urban worker with fair precision. Hence the proportional movements of the index numbers of money wages and commodity prices roughly measure the course of real earnings and the economic welfare of laborers and salaried employees in 1501–1550 and 1601–1650. Owing to the inaccurate delineation of the cost of living by the unweighted commodity indices in the second half of the sixteenth century, the index numbers of real wages are extremely crude; but they will doubtless prove valuable until they shall have been superseded by more reliable information.[1]

Table 29 presents the index numbers of real wages obtained by dividing the indices of money wages in Table 27 by the composite index numbers of commodity prices.

---

[1] In a book on *American Treasure and the Rise of Capitalism*, which I plan to publish soon after the material on prices and wages for the European countries represented on the International Scientific Committee on Price History becomes available, I hope to present more accurate data on both money and real wages in Spain in the sixteenth and seventeenth centuries.

TABLE 29

Composite Index Numbers of Real Wages

Base = 1571–1580

Year	Index number	Year	Index number	Year	Index number
1501	112.78	1551	100.27	1601	100.88
1502	115.55	1552	98.64	1602	108.68
1503	118.96	1553	102.76	1603	112.80
1504	111.56	1554	108.40	1604	111.94
1505	108.62	1555	110.41	1605	112.10
1506	92.47	1556	109.60	1606	116.80
1507	99.68	1557	100.66	1607	119.60
1508	102.75	1558	101.75	1608	121.35
1509	117.06	1559	111.05	1609	127.83
1510	127.84	1560	110.75	1610	125.49
1511	120.80	1561	102.02	1611	130.56
1512	126.85	1562	96.50	1612	127.96
1513	125.48	1563	100.96	1613	128.09
1514	122.04	1564	102.12	1614	122.85
1515	118.56	1565	101.27	1615	126.57
1516	120.62	1566	99.22	1616	121.45
1517	123.87	1567	103.37	1617	119.81
1518	118.36	1568	105.80	1618	122.90
1519	119.77	1569	108.14	1619	127.08
1520	125.56	1570	105.56	1620	121.61
1521	112.61	1571	99.58	1621	122.11
1522	104.81	1572	100.02	1622	121.85
1523	109.89	1573	97.40	1623	120.16
1524	109.36	1574	100.11	1624	114.64
1525	106.87	1575	94.18	1625	113.82
1526	105.66	1576	103.47	1626	101.15
1527	102.26	1577	106.52	1627	97.82
1528	106.62	1578	102.95	1628	102.44
1529	100.15	1579	97.81	1629	104.22
1530	91.35	1580	102.86	1630	109.31
1531	94.39	1581	104.43	1631	110.89
1532	99.40	1582	101.12	1632	107.79
1533	106.25	1583	100.09	1633	111.11
1534	102.43	1584	102.48	1634	113.47
1535	114.03	1585	102.22	1635	114.60
1536	104.49	1586	106.01	1636	111.63
1537	108.19	1587	103.14	1637	105.83
1538	99.82	1588	111.63	1638	105.86
1539	104.06	1589	107.31	1639	110.81
1540	102.30	1590	105.85	1640	111.59
1541	103.73	1591	107.70	1641	106.13
1542	98.23	1592	104.12	1642	98.07
1543	97.24	1593	107.07	1643	101.30
1544	101.45	1594	106.47	1644	102.45
1645	105.14	1595	106.29	1645	105.91
1546	98.36	1596	103.84	1646	102.07
1547	99.28	1597	99.00	1647	103.10
1548	95.54	1598	93.02	1648	98.20
1549	93.61	1599	91.40	1649	97.53
1550	97.61	1600	91.31	1650	93.30

Chart 19 presents graphically the data in Table 29.

Table 30 shows the decennial averages of the index numbers of real wages.

TABLE 30

DECENNIAL AVERAGES OF THE COMPOSITE INDEX NUMBERS OF REAL WAGES

Base = 1571-1580

Decade	Average index	Decade	Average index
1501–1510	110.73	1581–1590	104.43
1511–1520	122.19	1591–1600	101.02
1521–1530	104.96	1601–1610	115.75
1531–1540	103.54	1611–1620	124.89
1541–1550	99.02	1621–1630	110.75
1551–1560	105.43	1631–1640	110.36
1561–1570	102.50	1641–1650	100.81
1571–1580	100.49		

CHART 19

COMPOSITE INDEX NUMBERS OF REAL WAGES

Base = 1571-1580

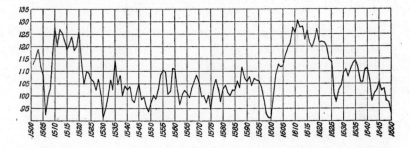

On account of the extremely dear commodity prices resulting from poor harvests, real wages fell precipitately in 1504–1506 and remained low in 1507–1508. The significant decline in the cost of living and simultaneous increase in money wages carried real earnings sharply upward in 1509–1510; and the gain was maintained in 1511–1520, when the decennial average was about 10 per cent greater than in 1501–1510 and more than 15 per cent above the highest average for any subsequent decade of the sixteenth century. The enormous drop in real wages in 1521–1522 resulting largely from the abrupt rise in commodity prices during and immediately after the revolt of the *Comuneros* continued, with interruptions in 1523 and 1528, until 1530, when the index was about 27 per cent less than in 1520. The rapid fall of living costs and synchronous increase in money wages in 1532–1535 carried real waegs approximately 14 per cent above the 1571–1580 level and some 3 per cent higher than the average for 1501–1510. From 1536 to 1549 the purchasing power of labor time steadily declined, the nadir in 1549 being about 18 per cent lower than in 1535 and roughly 20 per cent under the average for 1501–1520. The upswing of money wages in 1551–1560 notably ameliorated the economic circumstances of workers, but the rapid advance of living costs in 1561–1562 absorbed most of the gain. Under the impetus of rising money wages and stable commodity prices real earnings soared nearly 9 points in 1566–1569, but the slight decline of wage rates and simultaneous increase of living costs in 1570–1575 calamitously depressed real earnings. From 1575 to 1588 the economic position of workers improved by almost 19 per cent. Wage earners lost ground moderately in 1588–1595, disastrously in 1597–1598, and slightly in 1599–1600, when real incomes fell to the lowest point for the period under observation. If we allow for the fact that the unweighted commodity indices apparently underestimate the advance in the cost of living by something like 10 per cent, the decline of real wages at the end of the sixteenth century exceeds that shown in Chart 19. Interpolating the 10 per cent discrepancy between weighted and unweighted index numbers evenly at the rate of 2 per cent per decade, at best a crude procedure, one finds that real earnings fell steadily from 1551–1560 to 1591–1600, the decrease being about 12 per cent. With few interruptions, the trend was downward from 1520 to 1600. The financial status of the average urban worker was approximately one-fourth less favorable in the last than in the first quinquennium of the sixteenth century. From the high-water mark in 1511–1515 to the low-water mark in 1596–1600 the purchasing power of labor time declined almost 30 per cent.

 Thus we find that the great streams of treasure from the Indies, which, according to the prevailing mercantilist philosophy, were expected to enrich Spain after the fashion of King Midas, spelled unremitting economic retrogression for wage earners, one of the largest and most necessitous social classes. It seems, however, that Spanish workers fared infinitely better during the Price Revolution than did those of England, France, Germany, and Poland.[1]

Reflecting the abrupt increase of money wages resulting from the decimation of the population by the pestilence which ravaged Spain at the close of the sixteenth century [2] and the natural reaction to the rapid forward movement of commodity prices in 1596–1601, real wages rose by leaps and bounds in 1603–1604 and considerably in 1606–1611. In the brief space of eleven years the deleterious effects of the Price Revolution in the preceding eight decades were nullified. Although the slight advance of commodity prices in conjunction with stationary money wages in 1614–1620 absorbed a part of the previous gain, the highest decennial average of real earnings in the period under investigation was registered in 1611–1620. The sluggish response of money wages and rapid adjustment of living costs to the depreciation of Castilian vellon money in 1622–1627 caused real wages to drop more than 20 per cent. The continuation of the rise in money wages while commodity prices were falling in 1628–1635 raised real earnings about 17 points, but the greatly augmented living costs in 1636–1637 largely precipitated by the mad flight from vellon money obliterated about half the gain. The violent decline of Castilian prices in 1639, which followed the restoration of confidence in the vellon coinage, forced real wages upward almost 5 points, and there was a slight further increase in 1640; but the gravest monetary disorder in Castile since the days of Henry IV occasioned a sharp rise in the cost of living in 1641–1642, which inflicted upon workers a loss of more than 12 per cent. The drastic reduction in the tariff of Castilian vellon by the decree of August 31, 1642, reduced both prices and money wages in 1643; but

---

[1] D. Knoop and G. P. Jones, "Mason's Wages in Medieval England," *Economic History*, II, 484–492; Georg Wiebe, *Geschichte der Preisrevolution des XVI. und XVII. Jahrhunderts* (Leipzig, 1895), pp. 369–379; Earl J. Hamilton, "American Treasure and the Rise of Capitalism," *Economica*, November, 1929, pp. 350–353; Fr. Bujak, *Ceny we Lwowie w XVI i XVII Wieku* (Lemberg, 1928), p. 283.

[2] *Vide infra*, p. 306.

thereafter the greater fall in the former rendered the condition of workers more favorable, and real wages continued upward until 1645, when they stood nearly 8 per cent above the 1642 level. Under the impetus of vellon inflation money earnings and the cost of living soared in the last quinquennium of our period, but the preponderant advance of living costs steadily depressed real wages. Consequently the index for the end year of 1650 was approximately 10 per cent less than in 1645 and considerably under that for 1627, the next lowest point in the first part of the seventeenth century. The average for 1641–1650 was not far above the "adjusted" figures for the last three decades of the sixteenth century.

The calamitous depreciation of the inflated Castilian vellon and debased Valencian silver coinage in 1623–1650 impaired the economic welfare of workers no less catastrophically than had the influx of American gold and silver in the last eight decades of the sixteenth century. Real wages rallied after the three deflationary reforms, but the apex of each successive recovery fell short of the preceding peak; and recurrent increases in the tariff of the Castilian vellon money, never long delayed, swept away the advances in real earnings and forced workers almost down to the low level of subsistence experienced in the darkest days of the Price Revolution.

CHAPTER XIII

WHY PRICES ROSE

ACCORDING to Adam Smith,[1] "the discovery of the abundant mines of America, seems to have been the sole cause of this diminution [between 1570 and 1640] in the value of silver in proportion to that of corn. It is accounted for accordingly in the same manner by every body; and there never has been any dispute either about the fact, or about the cause of it." Yet, for reasons which will be shown presently,[2] a vast majority of the multitudinous contemporary explanations of the Price Revolution in Spain, the mistress of Zacatecas and Potosí, failed to mention "the abundant mines of America."

There are two principal sources of contemporary speculation concerning the causes of the Price Revolution: first, the parliamentary petitions and the legislation designed to reduce the cost of living and, second, treatises on economics, politics, and moral philosophy. Exhaustive discussion of the efforts of statesmen and theorists to account for the price upheaval which they experienced is beyond the scope of the present study, but certain views implicit in statutes and parliamentary proceedings and explicit in the works of scientists and the nostrums of reformers will be briefly considered.

Inasmuch as the dearness of particular commodities attracted attention before the advance of the general price level had been perceived, the earliest explanations concentrated upon the forces governing the values of specific goods. All four sessions of the Castilian Cortes in 1520–1528 complained of the high cost of grain and meat;[3] and the animosity toward foreigners engendered

---

[1] *Wealth of Nations* (Cannan ed., London, 1904), I, 191.

[2] *Vide infra*, pp. 294–295.

[3] *Cortes de los Antiguos Reinos de León y Castilla* (hereafter *Cortes*), IV, 333–334, 385, 415–416, 466; Maurice Ansiaux, "Histoire Économique de la Prospérité et de la Décadence de l'Espagne au XVIe et au XVIIe Siècles," *Revue d'Économie Politique*, VII, 547; Manuel Colmeiro, *Historia de la Economía Política en España* (Madrid, 1863), II, 323.

In an ordinance of August 9, 1504, Ferdinand and Isabella had ascribed the dear

by the recent Flemish domination probably influenced the ascription of the phenomenon to exportation, rendered possible by royal licenses and non-enforcement of the prohibitive legislation enacted at least as early as the reign of Henry II.[1] To end the "immoderate prices" exacted by the regraters who bought growing wheat, barley, oats, and rye and to protect peasants against exploitation, on August 5, 1524, Charles V interdicted purchases of unharvested grain.[2] Attributing the scarcity and the high prices of beef to the heavy consumption of veal, on August 27, 1525, Charles V forbade the butchering of calves in the country as well as in towns.[3] The Cortes of 1528 maintained that exports of hides had occasioned "very excessive shoe prices" [4] and advocated prohibition of the slaughter of lambs and calves [5] for two and four years respectively and a ban on narrow-mesh nets for ten years as means of alleviating the dearth and lowering the cost of beef, mutton, and fresh-water fish.[6] In 1532 the Procuradores complained that the Genoese, having bought all the soap in the kingdom and taken a leading position in its manufacture, had forced prices to exorbitant levels.[7] Petition CXI of the Cortes of 1537 attributed the advance in the value of horses to the spirited demand by professional and business men,[8] while Petition CXIII affirmed that "meat prices have risen and are rising every year"

current price of wheat in Andalusia to exportation (*Documentos de Asunto Económico Correspondientes al Reinado de los Reyes Católicos* [1475–1516], Eduardo Ibarra and Students, eds. [Madrid, 1917]). The Cortes of 1518 complained that the exports of meat had created acute scarcity, but made no specific reference to high prices (*Cortes*, IV, 283); and in 1532 the *Procuradores* affirmed that exports had caused exorbitant grain quotations (*Cortes*, IV, 548).

[1] Alfonso Díaz de Montalvo, *Copilación de Leyes* (Burgos, 1488), lib. VI, tit. IX, ley XXVI.

[2] Archivo del Ayuntamiento (hereafter AA), Salamanca, *Reales Cédulas*, leg. 2, no. 50.

[3] Biblioteca Nacional (hereafter BN), *Varios*, 1–1–1; *Recopilación de Leyes de España* (hereafter *Recopilación*), lib. VII, tit. VIII, ley XII.

[4] *Cortes*, IV, 479.

[5] The statutory interdiction of the slaughter of calves in 1525 apparently remained valid throughout the sixteenth century, but the kitchen accounts which have been consulted for price statistics demonstrate conclusively that from its inception the prohibition was frequently violated. Hence the subsequent parliamentary petitions against the butchering of calves were not anomalous.

[6] *Cortes*, IV, 497.

[7] *Ibid.*, IV, 569; Maurice Ansiaux, *op. cit.*, VII, 540.

[8] *Cortes*, IV, 674.

and recommended that the slaughter of lambs and calves be prohibited.[1] The Cortes of 1548 declared that regrating in cloth and
silks at the fairs of Medina del Campo and Villalón "had increased a great deal"[2] and ascribed the dearness and the acute
scarcity of fish to exports from Galicia, the region which, it was
argued, supplied Castile.[3] The royal proclamation of March 20,
1551, instructing municipalities to reconvert common pastures
reduced to arable in the preceding decade was issued in response
to a complaint from the Cortes of 1548 that meat prices had
doubled, thus forcing the poor to substitute cheaper and less
wholesome food.[4] To combat the rising cost of cloth a statute
of April 22, 1552, interdicted regrating in wool;[5] and on the
following day the sale of livestock which had been acquired in
an identical condition was forbidden.[6]

By the middle of the reign of Charles V the forward movement
of the general price level[7] had been observed; and, although time
had mitigated the extreme antipathy to foreigners, much of the
blame was laid at their door. The Cortes of 1537 attributed the
phenomenon to the diffusion of the dear prices resulting from excessive pasture rents;[8] but Petition CXXIV of the Cortes of 1548
informed the Emperor that "in the last few years the heavy purchases of wool, silk, iron, steel, other merchandise, and provisions
by foreigners" had forced prices so high that natives could no
longer subsist on their incomes nor trade on their capital.[9] Ascrib-
ing the insufferable dearness of commodities to the brisk American
demand, the Cortes of 1548 petitioned the Emperor to encourage
the establishment of colonial industries for the fabrication of the

---

[1] *Cortes*, IV, 675.

[2] *Ibid.*, V, 445–446.

[3] *Ibid.*, V, 470–471. The petition concerning fish exports from Galicia was repeated in 1551 (*ibid.*, V, 555).

[4] BN, *Raros*, 15,431.

[5] AA, León, *Sección Primera*, 425.

[6] BN, *Raros*, 14,090.

[7] In 1523 the Procuradores had successfully petitioned the Crown to permit two
oidores to adjudicate and three to review civil suits involving greater sums of money,
but neither the parliamentary petition nor the royal order it elicited stated or im-
plied that a change in the price level motivated this judicial reform (*Cortes*, IV, 375).

[8] *Cortes*, IV, 476.

[9] *Ibid.*, V, 425.

bountiful supplies of wool, hides, silk, and other raw materials; to strive to render the colonies self-sufficing in manufactures; and to ban exports of merchandise from Spain.[1] In 1551 the Procuradores maintained that "the principal cause of the rising prices of bread and other food is that [resident] aliens speculate in all kinds of provisions."[2] The pragmatic of May 25, 1552, restricting regrating and forbidding the exportation of many commodities was specifically designed to abate the high cost of living.[3]

Since the legislation and the parliamentary proceedings of the second half of the sixteenth and the first quarter of the seventeenth century evinced no greater penetration of the causes of the Price Revolution than had been shown during the reign of Charles V, a detailed examination is unnecessary. The efforts of the Cortes and the Crown to avert dear prices of animal products and their derivatives were overshadowed only by the protracted attempt to control grain prices.[4] Numerous statutes and parliamentary petitions attributed the high cost of meat, leather, shoes, wool, and cloth to the copious slaughter of calves and lambs;[5] to exports of live stock;[6] to engrossing and regrating in live animals, especially when combined with forestalling or with credit sales;[7] and to the machinations of brokers in fairs and markets.[8] The Cortes of 1583–1585 ascribed the dearness of sugar to the inordinate purchases for export by the Genoese[9] and other foreigners, and in 1615 the Procuradores argued that the high prices of thread and linen were due to speculation in flax.[10] The legislation and

[margin handwritten note: perused cursed]

---

[1] *Cortes*, V, 472–474.

This truly remarkable petition ran counter to the dominant theory and practice of Spanish mercantilism (cf. Earl J. Hamilton, "Spanish Mercantilism before 1700," *Facts and Factors in Economic History* [Cambridge, Massachusetts, 1932], pp. 214–239).

[2] *Cortes*, V, 554. Charles V was too deeply obligated to foreign bankers and money lenders to heed the parliamentary petitions to exclude aliens from domestic trade.

[3] BN, *Raros*, 15,431.

[4] *Vide supra*, pp. 243–257.

[5] *Vide*, for example, *Actas de las Cortes de Castilla* (hereafter *Actas*), IV, 441–442; VI, 863–864; XVI, 540; *Furs, Capitols, Provisions e Actes de Cort de 1604* (Valencia, 1607), cap. XLV, fol. 17; BN, *Varios*, 1–59–5, 1–59–6; *Raros*, 22,472; *Recopilación* (ed. 1775), lib. VII, tit. VIII, leyes XIV, XVII–XX.

[6] For instance, *vide Actas*, III, 433; V, 568–569.

[7] BN, *Raros*, 15,431; *Actas*, XXII, 437, 444; XXVII, 370.

[8] BN, *Raros*, 15,431.   [9] *Actas*, VII, 832.   [10] *Ibid.*, XXVIII, 540.

parliamentary petitions pertaining to grain prices demonstrate conclusively that the maximum tariffs were designed largely to foil the cupidity of engrossers, regraters, and large landowners and that public authorities considered exports a secondary cause of dearness.[1]

That the government was fully aware of the advance of the general price level cannot be doubted; [2] yet searching analyses of the phenomenon by the public officials who faced the problem of providing remedies, if actually made, do not seem to have survived. In 1563 the Cortes attributed the high cost of living to unrestrained commodity speculation by alien capitalists and the native business men who imitated their nefarious methods.[3] The Valencian *crides* of 1578, 1595, 1604, and 1619,[4] designed to lower the general price level, prohibited forestalling,[5] regrating, restraint of trade, and engrossing and restricted wholesale trade, credit transactions, and the exportation of provisions. Near the close of the reign of Philip II the Castilian Cortes ascribed the sharp advance of commodity prices to the debasement and the copious issue of vellon money; [6] and during the reign of Philip III, when vellon inflation was a favorite topic of debate, no other cause of the high cost of living elicited more than passing mention in the Cortes.

Although the trite complaints that regrating, engrossing, exporting, and speculating by alien business men were responsible for the prevalent dearness occasionally cropped out in the parliamentary proceedings of the second quarter of the seventeenth century,[7] the glaring depreciation of vellon forced the Procuradores to recognize that the monetary factor surpassed all other causes of the contemporaneous price upheaval. The clauses of the inflationary pragmatics threatening to frustrate and punish any attempt of avaricious merchants to raise prices attested the aware-

---

[1] *Vide supra*, pp. 243–257.

[2] *Vide*, for instance, *Actas*, III, 370, 372; IV, 432, 455; V, 576–577; XXII, 446.

[3] *Ibid.*, I, 346.

[4] Institut d'Estudis Catalans, *Follets Bonsoms*, 6591, 6602, 6624, 7119.

[5] Cf. *Furs, Capitols, Provisions e Actes de Cort de 1585* (Valencia, 1588), cap. CVI, fol. 17.

[6] *Vide supra*, p. 63, n. 7.

[7] *Vide*, for example, *Actas*, XLV, 478–479.

ness of the Crown of a direct correlation between the quantity of money and the height of prices. After preambles imputing the abnormal price level to the evil conduct of business men and to the importation of foreign vellon, the recurrent deflationary pragmatics often placed the blame squarely upon the previous increases in the tariff of vellon — where it belonged.

Throughout the period under observation the Castilian municipalities fixed maximum tariffs for most necessities; prohibited regrating, forestalling, and engrossing;[1] and acted positively to guarantee the regularity and the adequacy of the food supply. To control prices, the city of Valencia relied upon legal regulations[2] less and on abundance of supply more than did the Castilian municipalities. The Valencian metropolis not only subsidized imports of wheat and of all kinds of meat;[3] but, capitalizing its political preponderance, wrested from the Crown, with the approval of the *Corts*, authority to send agents throughout the kingdom armed with plenary powers to buy provisions at the average prices prevailing in the local markets on the date of their commissions and to requisition work animals at fair rentals for the transportation of the victuals.[4] The notable increase in the cost of living apparently failed to intensify municipal price-fixing, but the inflationary upheaval of commodity prices in 1626–1627 led the Castilian government, which had hitherto confined its regulatory activity largely to the grain tariffs, to fix legal maximum prices and wages for an extensive list of commodities and services. The pragmatic, issued on September 13, 1627,[5] and amended on February 26, 1628,[6] provided severe penalties for infraction of the price and wage regulations and embodied ingenuous measures to

---

[1] *Vide*, for example, AA, Burgos, *Libros de Hacienda*, 1567; *Ordenanzas de Valladolid* (sanctioned by Charles V on July 20, 1549), ordenanzas IV, V, X, XIII, XXXIV, XLI, XLV; *Cortes*, V, 119–120, 242.

[2] *Vide*, for example, AA, Valencia, *Crides*, XX, lib. 3.

[3] Chiefly through loans by the *Taula de Valencia* for periods of one year, with free interest for six months (*vide* AA, Valencia, *Clavería Comuna*, J, 97, 123, 127, 131, and 137 and the series *Manuals de Consells*).

[4] *Furs, Capitols, Provisions e Actes de Cort de 1604* (Valencia, 1607), cap. LXVIII, fol. 17.

[5] BN, *Varios*, 1-60-72; *Sección de Manuscritos*, Ms. 13,120, fols. 152–175, 267–272; *Actas*, XLV, 470, 478–479; XLVI, 4–5.

[6] BN, *Varios*, 1-51-44.

forestall evasion; nevertheless the statute proved no more effective than had the grain tariffs. It is interesting to note that, although the Crown had placed upon the printed copies of the price-fixing proclamation of September 13, 1627, a legal maximum price of 62½ maravedís, on October 10, 1627, the Hospital de Tavera of Toledo was forced to pay 85 maravedís, 36 per cent more than the legal maximum.[1] Regardless of its signal failure to control prices the statute of 1627 proved unpopular; and, on March 5, 1629, Philip IV agreed, as one of the conditions prescribed by the Cortes for the concession of a subsidy, to repeal "the legal regulations of prices in general."[2]

Neither the municipal ordinances nor the royal proclamations establishing maximum tariffs give evidence of deep insight into the causes of the protracted upheaval of prices. The most remarkable characteristic of the attempts of the Cortes, the Royal Ministers, the Crown, and the municipal authorities to account for the high cost of living which they strove to abate is the apparent failure to mention the "abundant mines of America." Prolonged search of contemporaneous public records has disclosed no references, nor even allusions, to the influx of American treasure as a contributory cause of the Price Revolution.[3]

Before the close of the Emperor's reign Spanish economists were cognizant of the rise in prices,[4] but during the sixteenth century their explanations were little, if any, stronger than those formulated by contemporary statesmen. Cristóbal de Villalón (1542),[5] Luís de Alcalá (1546),[6] and Francisco García (1583),[7] learned authors whose treatises constantly verged upon commod-

---

[1] Hospital de Tavera, *Libros de Despensa*, 1627. The Cortes of 1592–1594 complained that primers (cartillas para enseñar a leer niños), the legal maximum price of which was 4 maravedís, were being sold at from 12 to 16 maravedís (*Actas*, XVI, 674).

[2] *Ibid.*, XLVII, 253.

[3] Of course, it has been impossible to examine all the pertinent documents in Spanish archives. A lifetime would not suffice. Abundant evidence that more than one contemporaneous public official appreciated the influence of American treasure may be unearthed some day.

[4] *Vide* Diego de Covarrubias y Leiva, *Veterum Collatio Numismatum* (ed. Salamanca, 1556), fol. 39.

[5] *Provechoso Tratado de Cambios y Contrataciones* (Valladolid).

[6] *Tratado de Préstamos* (Toledo).

[7] *Tratado Utilísimo . . . de Todos los Contratos* (Valencia).

ity price levels, did not attempt to account for the advance in living costs which they had experienced.

According to Luís Saravia de la Calle, value depends upon the quantitative relationship between goods and sellers on the one hand and of buyers and money on the other; but "the principal determinants of whether an article is cheap or dear are the quantity of money and the number of buyers."[1] Nevertheless Saravia de la Calle declared that "if one penetrates to the roots of the high prices of goods in the realm, all or the greater part is traceable to usury," which forced merchants to raise prices in order to recoup their expenses;[2] and as contributory causes he listed only regrating and forestalling.[3] Tomás de Mercado (1569) expounded a theory of value strikingly similar to that of Saravia de la Calle;[4] but, like his predecessor, largely threw it aside while attempting to explain the increase of commodity prices. Although Mercado recognized the theoretical importance of the quantity of money as a price determinant, attributed the inordinate living costs in the Indies to the plethora of specie,[5] and resided in Seville, the *entrepôt* of American treasure, he apparently failed to mention the heavy output of the Mexican and Peruvian mines as a cause of the Price Revolution in Spain.[6] Mercado ascribed the upheaval of prices to the brisk American demand for the goods produced in and those reëxported from the motherland,[7] to the increase in credit sales resulting from the periodical nature of the Indian trade,[8] and to the prevalence of regrating.[9]

In 1587 Alonso de Morgado[10] declared that the "armadas and flotas depart for the Indies so heavily laden with merchandise that Sevillan prices are forced to fantastic heights."[11] A memorial addressed to the Crown by Fernando del Pulgar in 1595 argued

---

[1] *Instrucción de Mercaderes* (Medina del Campo, 1544), fol. 27.
[2] *Op. cit.*, fol. 99.
[3] *Ibid.*, fol. 70.
[4] *Suma de Tratos y Contratos* (ed. Seville, 1571), lib. II, fols. 39, 93.
Francisco García (*op. cit.*, I, 233) also enunciated a substantially identical theory of value.
[5] *Op. cit.*, lib. II, fol. 15.   [6] Cf. p. 295, n. 2, *infra*.
[7] *Op. cit.*, lib. II, fols. 15, 90.   [8] *Ibid.*, lib. II, fols. 73–74, 90.
[9] *Ibid.*, lib. III, fol. 124.   [10] *Historia de Sevilla* (Seville, 1587), fol. 55.
[11] This is a free translation.

that the legal maximum grain tariffs discouraged cultivation, thereby raising market prices, and that grain quotations determined the cost of food, upon which all other prices depended.[1] In a similar fashion Lope de Deza (1618) attributed the high cost of living to the decline of agriculture,[2] and Miguel Caxa de Leruela (1631) attempted to trace the Price Revolution almost exclusively to the advance in the quotations of animal products — which he regarded as pivotal — resulting from the derogation of royal favors to the Mesta.[3]

In the second quarter of the seventeenth century most writers, like the Procuradores in Cortes, ascribed the advance of commodity prices largely to the debasement and the overvaluation of the vellon coinage;[4] but ruinous taxation,[5] depopulation,[6] market manipulation,[7] high labor costs,[8] vagrancy,[9] luxury,[10] the enclosure

---

[1] BN, *Varios*, 1-49-38.

[2] *Govierno Polytico de la Agricultura* (Madrid), fols. 21-65.

[3] *Restauración de la Abundancia de España* (Naples), fol. 3.

[4] For example, *vide* Sebastián González de Castro, *Declaración del Valor de la Plata, Ley, y Peso de las Monedas Antiguas de Plata Ligada de Castilla y Aragón* (Madrid, 1658), pp. 10-18; Alonso de Carranza, *El Ajustamiento i Proporción de las Monedas . . .* (Madrid, 1629), p. 201; Fernando Manojo de la Corte, *Pruévase que Conviene Reformar los Precios de las Cosas* (?, 1629), fols. 4-6; BN, *Varios*, 1-124-44 and 1-158-59.

This view had been expressed by Juan de Mariana in 1609 ("Discurso sobre la Moneda de Vellón," *Biblioteca de Autores Españoles*, XXXI [Madrid, 1854], 586). But Sancho de Moncada (*Restauración Política de España* [Madrid, 1619], discurso III, fol. 24) had declared that the increase in the tariff of vellon by Philip III, in 1603 (*vide supra*, p. 76), did not raise prices.

In view of his familiarity with the development of Spanish economic thought, it is difficult to understand why Manuel Colmeiro (*op. cit.*, II, 452) fell into the error of claiming originality for his observation that monetary debasement forced prices upward.

[5] Manuel Gaitán de Torres, *Reglas para el Buen Govierno destos Reynos y de los de las Indias* (Jerez de la Frontera, 1625), p. 148; Guillén Barbón y Castañeda, *Provechosos Advitrios al Consumo del Vellón* (Madrid, 1628), fol. 9; Alonso de Carranza, *op. cit.*, pp. 341-343; Pedro Fernández Navarrete, *Conservación de Monarquías y Discursos Políticos* (Madrid, 1626), p. 124.

[6] Guillén Barbón y Castañeda, *op. cit.*, fol. 10. The author voiced the following strange and untenable view of the order of causation: "The dearness of all commodities, which we experience, results from that of provisions [mantenimientos], and this results from depopulation. . . ."

[7] Pedro Fernández Navarrete, *op. cit.*, p. 143; Fernando Manojo de la Corte, *op. cit.*, fol. 3.

[8] Pedro Fernández Navarrete, *op. cit.*, pp. 80, 143.

[9] *Ibid.*, p. 69.

[10] Guillén Barbón y Castañeda, *op. cit.*, fols. 26-27.

of common pastures and forests,[1] and the machinations of alien business men, particularly the Genoese,[2] were often enumerated as contributory causes.

While attempting to account for the Price Revolution, Spanish writers did not entirely overlook the American mines, as public officials seem to have done; but of all the causes mentioned by contemporaries the influx of specie was recognized the latest and discussed the least. In the nature of the case, priority in observing the connection between American treasure and Spanish prices cannot be settled. At least as early as 1558 Francisco López de Gómara voiced the opinion that "the great quantity of silver and gold which has come to us from the Indies" was responsible for the alteration of commodity prices.[3] But instead of taking the trouble to elaborate his thesis and to offer evidence in support of it, Gómara dismissed the matter in a single sentence. It is altogether possible that a casual remark of similar tenor was recorded prior to 1558. That Gómara's observation substantially influenced scientific thought is more than doubtful. The *Annals* remained inedited until 1912, and it seems that very few manuscript copies were made, "possibly only the original (which was very likely lost) and the two seventeenth-century copies in the Biblioteca Nacional at Madrid and in the British Museum in London."[4] Professor Merriman did not find evidence that more than four authors had utilized the manuscripts of the *Annals*, and one may safely assume that few cases escaped his thorough search. Of the four works, only one, Prudencio Sandoval's *Historia de la Vida y Hechos del Emperador Carlos V* (1604–1606), appeared before 1650.[5] Unmistakably following Gómara, without acknowledgment as usual, Sandoval mentioned Indian treasure as a theoretical determinant of prices, but seemed to ascribe the advance during the preceding fifty-four years to luxury and ostentation, particularly in dress and houses, and to the flagrant idleness of

---

[1] Guillén Barbón y Castañeda, *op. cit.*, fols. 9–10.

[2] Sancho de Moncada, *op. cit.*, discurso 1, fol. 9; Guillén Barbón y Castañeda, *op. cit.*, fol. 10.

[3] Roger B. Merriman (editor), Gómara's *Annals of the Emperor Charles V* (Oxford, 1912), pp. lii–liii, 2, 162.

[4] *Ibid.*, p. xxxix.　　　　　　　　　[5] *Ibid.*, pp. xxxix–xl.

women.[1] There is not a shred of evidence that the seventeenth-century Spanish economists who recognized the influence of American gold and silver upon prices took the idea from Gómara, either directly or through Sandoval.

So far as I know, Jean Bodin, in his *Response au Paradoxe de Malestroit Touchant l'Encherissement de Toutes Choses*, published in 1568,[2] was the first to demonstrate by careful analysis that the American mines were the principal cause of the Price Revolution,[3] to amplify this view, and to refute rival explanations. The data collected by Professor Merriman[4] suggest that Bodin could not possibly have known of Gómara's ascription of the Price Revolution to American treasure, and the great scholar's express claim to priority[5] indicates that his work was wholly original.[6] So far as I have been able to determine, the earliest unequivocal printed explanation of the Price Revolution in terms of the influx of American treasure by any Spanish economist appeared in 1600. Martín González de Cellorigo,[7] the author, frequently cited Bodin's *Six Livres de la République*, in which the French savant

---

[1] *Op. cit.* (ed. Pamplona, 1614), II, 660–661.

[2] For an excellent edition of this scarce tract, with a scholarly introduction and illuminating notes, *vide* Henri Hauser (editor), *La Response de Jean Bodin a M. de Malestroit* (Paris, 1932). All subsequent references are to this edition.

A good English version of the *Réponse* is available in A. E. Monroe (editor), *Early Economic Thought* (Cambridge, Massachusetts, 1924), pp. 123–141.

[3] Especially pp. 9–10.

Learned authors have credited Noël du Fail with having first mentioned the influence of American treasure upon European prices (*vide*, for example, A. E. Monroe, *Monetary Theory before Adam Smith* [Cambridge, Massachusetts, 1923], p. 56, and the authors cited in Professor Hauser's Introduction to *La Response de Jean Bodin*, p. lxix, n. 1). But I have examined all the editions, including the modern reprints, of the works of Noël du Fail in the Bibliothèque Nationale, and find that he did not mention the connection between American treasure and European prices prior to 1585 (*Les Contes et Discours d'Eutrapel* [Rennes], fol. 125); and then, as Professor Hauser has remarked (Introduction to Bodin's *Réponse*, p. lxix), not only the idea, but the phraseology was taken from Bodin.

[4] *Op. cit.*, pp. xxxix–xl, liii.

[5] *Op. cit.*, p. 9.

[6] An incontrovertible demonstration that he departed from some other author's simple observation of a causal connection between the American mines and the level of European prices would detract little from Bodin's right to fame, which fundamentally rests upon the orderly and cogent presentation of his thesis and its influence upon scientific thought.

[7] *Memoriales de la Política Necessaria y Util Restauración á la República de España* (Valladolid, 1600), fol. 22.

epitomized his *Réponse*.[1] Writing in 1619, Sancho de Moncada, credited by Konrad Haebler [2] with having been "the first to make the discovery," stated that American specie had called forth the Price Revolution.[3] Sancho de Moncada often referred to the work of Bodin. The prestige enjoyed by Moncada, Professor of Theology in the University of Toledo, among the Spanish economists and moral philosophers of the seventeenth and eighteenth centuries conduced to the acceptance of his explanation of the rise in prices. Although Pedro Fernández Navarrete [4] and Diego Saavedra Fajardo,[5] the only remaining Spanish economists known to me,[6] who, in books published before 1650, ascribed the Price Revolution to the influx of American gold and silver, cited neither Bodin nor Moncada, they were doubtless conversant with the work of the latter. It is interesting to note that none of the Spanish writers who accounted for the advance of prices in terms of the American mines explained the mechanism through which the increase in the quantity of money operated. Bating González de Cellorigo and Fernández Navarrete, the writers dismissed the matter in one or two sentences; and it seems that all the Spanish authors prior to 1650 devoted less than a thousand words to the influence of American treasure upon prices, while entire chapters and even books were written upon several imagined causes of the high cost of living.

The reason for the comparative neglect of American gold and silver by the economists and statesmen who attempted to explain the Price Revolution is not far to seek. Recognition of the fact that rising prices may stimulate industry and commerce is a distinctly recent achievement; but contemporary consumers grasped the significance of dear commodities, and producers understood

---

[1] Bk. VI, ch. II.

[2] *Wirtschaftliche Blüte Spaniens* (Berlin, 1888), p. 160.

[3] *Op. cit.*, discurso III, fol. 22.

[4] *Op. cit.*, p. 143.

[5] *Idea de un Príncipe Político Cristiano* (Monaco, 1640), pp. 383–384, 386.

[6] It is needless to say that I have read only a small part of the numerous books on economics written by Spaniards in 1501–1650, not to mention the myriads of tracts and pamphlets. A thorough exploration of the sources, which could not be accomplished without an enormous outlay of time, would doubtless enlarge and substantially modify my conclusions.

the handicap to export industry imposed by high price levels relatively to those of other countries. Only with difficulty could mercantilists ascribe the advance of prices, which caused "evils" of such magnitude, to the accumulation of specie, the *summum bonum* in most of their eyes.[1] At least in some instances it seems that the brevity of the discussions may have been due to a laudable desire to avoid expatiation upon the obvious;[2] and, being pragmatists, the Spanish mercantilists devoted their attention to causes for which remedies compatible with their philosophy seemed attainable.[3]

Although excellent studies have enriched our knowledge of many phases of Spanish economic history,[4] only scanty data concerning the activity of agriculture, industry, and commerce in the sixteenth century are accessible. Monographs involving decades of research in national and local archives will have to be written before our knowledge of the volumes of commercial and financial transactions can pass beyond the nebulous stage. But in the absence of more satisfactory information certain theoretical determinants of long-run changes in the supply of commodities may be examined with profit.

During the first half of the sixteenth century the Cortes inveighed against the increase in mortmain and urged the spiritual and temporal authorities to forbid the acquisition of rural estates by ecclesiastical institutions, lest all the land in the kingdom should pass into their hands.[5] The extension of primogeniture

---

[1] Martín González de Cellorigo was a notable exception. Students of the history of monetary theory may peruse fols. 21–22 of his *Memoriales* with profit.

[2] Many passages in Tomás de Mercado's *Suma de Tratos y Contratos* strongly suggest that he was aware of the influence of American treasure upon prices and that he neglected to say so because he thought everyone else knew as much.

[3] As has been pointed out, the Cortes of 1548 recommended the stimulation of American industry in order to alleviate the insufferable dearness at home precipitated by the colonial trade; but one suspects either that the Procuradores expected to obtain the American treasure anyway — through taxation, emigrants' remittances, and the like — or that the petition to the Crown was ill considered (*vide supra*, pp. 285–286).

[4] For example, *vide* Ignacio Asso, *Historia de la Economía Política de Aragón* (Saragossa, 1798); Julius Klein, *The Mesta* (Cambridge, Massachusetts, 1920); Konrad Haebler, *op. cit.*; Albert Girard, *Le Commerce Français à Seville et Cadix au Temps des Habsbourg* (Bordeaux, 1932).

[5] *Cortes*, IV, 255, 276, 379, 413–414, 465, 556, 584, 588, 668.

(mayorazgos) to commoners by the Laws of Toro, in 1505,[1] also promoted the increase in the number and size of the latifundia. It has ordinarily been assumed that the growth of mortmain diminished agricultural efficiency, but there are adequate grounds for believing that the relative incompetence and lethargy of the managers of ecclesiastical estates have been exaggerated. That priests and monks were far above the average landowner in culture is beyond question, and the fact that statesmen and economists feared aggressive bargaining by ecclesiastical sellers of grain indicates that the Church was not devoid of interest in economic administration. The deleterious effect of the extension of primogeniture developed so slowly that it was probably of little consequence in the sixteenth century. The economists often complained of the economic loss which the excess of religious holidays entailed;[2] but I have seen no evidence that the number of *fiestas* significantly increased during the Price Revolution, and contemporaneous payrolls demonstrate conclusively that the rank and file of workers observed a much lower percentage of the holidays than is generally believed. The growth of the secular and regular clergy and the increase in the number of nuns unquestionably diminished national productive power.[3] Largely owing to the enervating climate of most of the Peninsula and to the glorification of war during the eight centuries of the Reconquest, Spaniards of the upper social strata were averse to physical toil, while vagrancy and vagabondage were common vices among the lower classes.[4] But there is scant reason to believe that indolence and idleness augmented significantly in the sixteenth century. To the maximum grain tariffs many economists have imputed responsibility for a diminution of cultivation and a consequent rise in prices,[5]

[1] Maurice Ansiaux, *op. cit.*, VII, 532; *Recopilación*, lib. v, tit. VII, leyes I–VII.

[2] For instance, *vide* Pedro Fernández Navarrete, *op. cit.*, pp. 79–83.

[3] It is significant that Pedro Fernández Navarrete (*op. cit.*, pp. 285–294), who occupied high ecclesiastical posts at the time he was writing, decried the increase in the number of nuns, monks, and priests. Cf. *Actas*, XX, 186; XXII, 435; XXVI, 280; XXVII, 372.

[4] *Vide* Juan Sempere y Guarinos, *Biblioteca Española Económico-Política* (Madrid, 1801–1821), I, chs. I–XXII; Manuel Colmeiro, *op. cit.*, II, 17–42. Cf. the view of Jean Bodin, *op. cit.*, pp. 14–16.

[5] Fernando del Pulgar, *Discurso*; Pedro Fernández Navarrete, *op. cit.*, p. 276; Jacinto Alcazar Arriaza, *Medios Políticos para el Remedio . . . de España* (Madrid,

but it is difficult to reconcile this view with the flagrant violation of the price-fixing ordinances.[1]

The increase in taxation, which Manuel Colmeiro rated at parity with the influx of American treasure as a cause of the advance of prices,[2] does not appear to have been a major factor. Perhaps no salient aspect of the past economic life of Spain is so completely shrouded in ignorance as is the history of taxation. Since the Crown contracted (encabezaba) with many cities for fixed annual payments in lieu of the *alcabala*, or general sales tax, the principal instrument of royal taxation was not uniform throughout Castile; and apparently no investigator has disclosed the total excise and sales taxes paid the central government, not to mention the municipal levies, on staple goods in any given locality. Data concerning the extent of collection of the taxes legally due are lacking, and the accessible information regarding social exemptions is inadequate. It is well known that the royal revenues rose during the reigns of Charles V and Philip II, but most of the increase seems to have been derived from the enhanced yields of *ad valorem* taxes as the Price Revolution progressed. If we make allowances for the repercussions of the taxation of one commodity upon the demand for other commodities and for the probable failure to collect a substantial portion of royal and local taxes, all the available evidence suggests that the increases in the alcabala and the *sisa*, the introduction of the *cientos* and *millones*, and all other additions to the burden of taxation could hardly have been responsible for more than 5 per cent of the rise in the unweighted index numbers of general commodity

---

1646), fol. 26; Maurice Ansiaux, *op. cit.*, VII, 1030; Francisco Martínez Mata, *Memoriales*, reprinted in Conde de Campomanes, *Apéndice a la Educación Popular* (Madrid, 1777), IV, 64; Konrad Haebler, *op. cit.*, p. 39. Cf. *Actas*, XIII, 37–40; XVIII, 483.

But the maximum grain tariffs had defenders (*vide* Tomás de Mercado, *op. cit.*, lib. II, fols. 34–43; lib. III, fols. 113–153; Fernando Manojo de la Corte, *op. cit.*, fols. 1–18; *Actas*, V, 595–596; XIX, 555–557).

[1] *Vide supra*, pp. 258–260, 288–289.

Several contemporaries inconsistently argued that sales above the legal maximum price were notoriously common, but that the rigid limitation of prices by the maximum tariffs in sterile years depressed cultivation (for example, *vide* Fernando del Pulgar, *op. cit.*; Sancho de Moncado, *op. cit.*, discurso VII, fols. 1–2).

[2] *Op. cit.*, II, 233. Cf. *Actas*, XIV, 56; XIX, 555–556; XLIV, 412; XLV, 145; Jacinto Alcazar Arriaza, *op. cit.*, fols. 15, 26.

prices in Andalusia and the two Castiles. Since the perpetuation of the traditional Aragonese liberties enabled Valencia to shirk her share of the imperial expenses, the increase of taxation under the Hapsburgs exerted even less upward pressure upon commodity prices in the Mediterranean kingdom than in Castile.

Although one must allow for a wide margin of error in Spanish demographical statistics, which largely rest upon the infrequent contemporaneous enumerations of taxpayers and of adult males for fiscal and military purposes,[1] there can be little doubt that the population of every city of Andalusia and the two Castiles from which the principal series of prices and wages in the present study have been drawn was substantially greater in 1594 than in 1530;[2] and, with the possible exception of Valladolid, the same holds for the territory within each city's sphere of economic influence.[3] In fact, it seems that the population of the kingdom of Castile, and probably of Spain, rose considerably during the reigns of Charles V and Philip II.[4] A vast majority of the large cities, where the censuses were presumably taken with the least inaccuracy, registered

[1] Deposited in the Archivo de Simancas and published by Tomás González, *Censo de Población de la Corona de Castilla en el Siglo XVI* (Madrid, 1829).

[2] One must not forget that the censuses published by González were largely intended as bases for the allocation of taxes and that the social exemptions from the levies were greater in 1530 and 1646 than in 1594 (Tomás González, *op. cit.*, "Advertencia Preliminar" and p. 99).

[3] *Ibid.*, pp. 20, 22, 25, 28, 43, 48, 69–73, 83–84.

[4] Cf. Ignacio Asso, *op. cit.*, pp. 307–308, 331–332, 337–340; Konrad Haebler, *op. cit.*, pp. 144–159; Tomás González, *op. cit.*, pp. 126–157, 160–170, 312, 390–391, 393–394.

Largely through comparisons of the estimate of Castilian population by Alonso de Quintanilla, Contador Mayor, in 1482 with the subsequent censuses published by González, M. Albert Girard ("Le Chiffre de la Population de l'Espagne dans les Temps Modernes," *Revue d'Histoire Moderne*, Novembre–Décembre, 1928, pp. 425–426, 430; Janvier–Février, 1929, pp. 3–5) and Manuel Colmeiro (*op. cit.*, I, 238–239; II, 11–13) concluded that the population of Spain was lower at the end than at the beginning of the sixteenth century; but the wide divergence among contemporaneous demographical guesses (cf. *ibid.*, I, 248–250; II, 7–8; Konrad Haebler, *op. cit.*, pp. 152–153) attests their unreliability. As Haebler (*ibid.*, p. 146) observed, the low governmental estimate of the number of taxpayers in 1495, a figure which no reasonable allowance for the effects of the Jewish expulsion of 1492 can reconcile with the "census" of 1482, and the steady increase in population shown by the enumerations of 1530, 1541, and 1594 create a strong presumption of overestimation by Quintanilla. Inasmuch as Quintanilla estimated the population while advancing a nostrum for enhancing the military strength of Castile (*vide* Tomás González, *op. cit.*, pp. 94–95), he may have been predisposed to exaggeration.

many more inhabitants in 1594 than in 1530. There is strong reason to believe that the loss of population through emigration to the Indies was altogether negligible.[1] Many Spanish soldiers were sacrificed to imperial ambition and religious fanaticism on foreign battlefields; but, inasmuch as no enemy force passed beyond the periphery of the Peninsula, the civilian population was almost entirely spared the heavy direct and indirect losses which invasion entails. Epidemics of a minor character occurred at short intervals throughout the sixteenth century, but not until 1599 was the population decimated by an infectious disease.

The phenomenal growth of Segovia, Toledo, and other industrial centers suggests that the production of manufactured goods flourished, under the stimulus of rising prices and lagging wages, until near the end of the sixteenth century.

As Chart 6 indicates, commodity prices rose in all regions from the beginning of the sixteenth century, but at first the upheaval was greatest in Andalusia, the center of the West Indian trade; and the advance in New Castile, the region having the closest commercial contact with Andalusia, ranked second. The order of emergence of the Price Revolution suggests that some of the initial causes were connected with the American commerce. That the gold imports from the Antilles significantly influenced Andalusian and New Castilian prices even in the first two decades of the sixteenth century is beyond question. The notable increase in the use of credit, which the growth of banking and the periodical nature of the American trade entailed, and the demand for provisions for the ships plying between Spain and the Indies and for the colonists, who, engrossed in the search for treasure, neglected the production of food,[2] also

---

[1] Assuming that the summary figures of Luis Rubio y Moreno (*Pasageros a Indias, 1492–1592* [Madrid, 1917], p. 41) are roughly accurate, we find that only about 8000 Spaniards legally emigrated to America during the first century after the discovery and that the clergy constituted about 17½ per cent of the total.

[2] The heavy exports to America in the first half of the sixteenth century appear to have been largely responsible for the phenomenal upswing of wine prices. The price of olive oil rose sharply in Andalusia, but the average advance in the four regions did not exceed that of the general commodity index numbers. The prohibition of the planting of grape vines and olive trees in Peru, a typical example of mercantilist legislation, apparently affected colonial production less than did the great length of time required to bring vineyards and olive groves to fruitage, the

tended to raise the index numbers of prices in Andalusia and New Castile.[1]

The location of the political capital at Valladolid, the migrations of the Mesta, and the preëminence of the fairs at Medina del Campo, Medina de Rioseco, and Villalón as mercantile exchanges and financial clearing houses facilitated the flow of American treasure into Old Castile. The growth of time transactions in Seville probably enhanced the use of credit in the Old Castilian fairs, and the colonial demand for merchandise was immediately felt in wholesale trade, largely centralized in the three celebrated fairs. But the advance of prices in Valencia, a region economically separated from Castile by customs barriers and prohibitions against specie exports, and in England, France, Germany, and northern Italy[2] early in the sixteenth century indicates that forces not generated by the discovery of America, such as the expansion of mercantile and financial credit which accompanied the rise of modern capitalism and the increased output of German silver mines in the last quarter of the fifteenth century,[3] helped to impart the initial impetus to the Price Revolution in Spain.

Chart 20 brings together the average silver index numbers for the four regions[4] and the total quinquennial imports of American gold and silver.

ineptitude of indigenous labor for the industries, and the engrossment of the early Spanish emigrants in the quest for treasure.

The moderation of the advance of wine prices in the second half of the sixteenth century suggests that in the natural course of time production developed in the colonies, including Peru. Admitting, in 1595, that the early interdiction of vines in Peru had failed, Philip II legalized the clandestine planting and levied an excise tax of 2 per cent of the annual production (*Recopilación de Leyes de Indias* [Madrid, 1681], lib. IV, tit. XVII, ley XVIII). But the evidence is not conclusive. The sharp rise of wheat prices in the second half of the sixteenth century may have been wholly or partially due to a conversion of wheat land into vineyards (cf. *Actas*, XV, 759; XVIII, 483) or to the rapid growth of the urban population.

[1] Cf. Gervasio de Artíñano, *Historia del Comercio con las Indias* (Barcelona, 1917), pp. 138–140; José Arias y Miranda, *Examen Crítico-Histórico del Influjo que Tuvo en el Comercio Industria y Población de España su Dominación en América* (Madrid, 1854), p. 62.

[2] Georg Wiebe, *Geschichte der Preisrevolution des XVI. und XVII. Jahrhunderts* (Leipzig, 1895), pp. 369–370, 372–380.

[3] Adolf Soetbeer, *Edelmetall-Produktion* (Gotha, 1879), pp. 14–18; Georg Wiebe, *op. cit.*, pp. 190 ff.

[4] Listed in tabular form in Appendix VIII.

The extremely close correlation between the increase in the volume of treasure imports and the advance of commodity prices throughout the sixteenth century, particularly from 1535 on, demonstrates beyond question that the "abundant mines of America" were the principal cause of the Price Revolution in Spain. Only at the beginning of the sixteenth century, when, as has been

CHART 20

TOTAL QUINQUENNIAL TREASURE IMPORTS AND COMPOSITE INDEX NUMBERS
OF COMMODITY PRICES

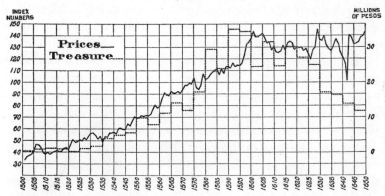

shown, colonial demand, credit expansion, and the increased output of German silver made themselves felt, and at the end of the century, when a devastating epidemic and an overissue of vellon coinage took place, did other factors play important rôles in the price upheaval. The reader should bear in mind that a graphic verification of that crude form of the quantity theory of money which takes no account of the velocity of circulation is not the purpose of Chart 20.[1] In fact, the increase in the world stock of the precious metals during the sixteenth century was probably more than twice — possibly as much as four times — as great as

---

[1] For Chart 20 to achieve this end, it would be necessary to show that the stock of money in 1500 was insignificant and either that the volume of monetary work remained roughly constant, that the proportional use of credit changed little, and that the outflow of specie was approximately equivalent to the inflow or that opposite changes in these factors tended to cancel each other.

the advance of prices in Seville, the recipient and distributor of the legal imports of American gold and silver into Europe.[1]

Instead of seeking ancillary causes of the Price Revolution, as virtually all writers [2] have done, one must account for the failure of the upheaval to keep pace with the increase in the stock of the precious metals. Hoarded specie and bullion not converted to monetary use obviously had no effect upon prices. The ornamental utilization of gold and silver by the church doubtless neutralized a considerable portion of the imports; and after the discovery of the Cape route the flow of gold and silver to the East, a necropolis of European treasure even in Roman days, was incomparably greater than ever before. The seventeenth-century pamphleteers who in tract after tract denounced the English East India Company for draining away the country's treasure were not mistaken as to the facts.[3] Some European goods were carried to the East, but the sales of Western merchandise never matched the avid purchases of oriental spices and luxuries; and the liquidation of the unfavorable trade balance required copious exports of treasure. Because of the inveterate penchant for hoarding, the protracted inflow of specie did not raise oriental prices sufficiently to induce a counter movement.[4] Once in the East, American treasure affected European prices little more than if it had remained in undiscovered mines on Andean peaks. Statistics are lacking, but it seems probable that the Spanish nobility and the

---

[1] I gratefully acknowledge the benefits of Professor François Simiand's illuminating criticism (*Recherches Anciennes et Nouvelles sur le Mouvement Général des Prix du XVIe au XIXe Siècle* [Paris, 1932], pp. 403–420, 457–478, 492, 546) of my previous work on the imports of American gold and silver and Andalusian prices ("American Treasure and Andalusian Prices, 1503–1660," *Journal of Economic and Business History*, I, 1–35, and "Imports of American Gold and Silver into Spain, 1503–1660," *Quarterly Journal of Economics*, XLIII, 436–472). The criticism of the former article by Professor Lucien Febvre ("Le Problème Historique des Prix," *Annales d'Histoire Économique et Sociale*, II, 68–80) has also proved extremely helpful.

[2] Including the present one ("American Treasure and Andalusian Prices, 1503–1660," *Journal of Economic and Business History*, I, 33–34).

[3] It is significant that bitter complaints against the English East India Company commenced about 1640, thus synchronizing with the precipitate decline in the imports of American gold and silver into Europe (*vide supra*, Table 1, p. 34). The vitriolic attacks of pamphleteers evoked notable apologies for the Company.

[4] Earl J. Hamilton, "American Treasure and the Rise of Capitalism," *Economica*, November, 1929, p. 347.

upper stratum of the *bourgeoisie* substantially added to their holdings of plate during the sixteenth century. Although no exact
figures can be adduced, one may safely presume that all of these
outlets for specie did not prevent unprecedented additions to the
monetary stock. But the enhanced production and exchange of
goods which accompanied the growth of population, the substitution of monetary payments for produce rents which the decline
of feudalism entailed, the diminution of mercantile and financial
credit which resulted from the decadence of the Old Castilian
fairs, the shift from wages wholly or partially in kind to monetary
remuneration for services, and the decrease of barter [1] tended to
counteract the rapid augmentation of gold and silver money.

Almost without exception, the economists of the first half of the
seventeenth century complained loudly of agricultural and industrial retrogression; and the tenor of the parliamentary proceedings
corroborated the jeremiads of theorists. One must not forget,
however, that the lamentations of economists have not always
reflected genuine decadence,[2] nor that the views of Spanish authors and statesmen (who were indoctrinated with the prevailing
mercantilist identification of wealth and specie) on general economic conditions were colored by their conviction that the displacement of gold and silver money by the debased vellon coinage
constituted a calamity of the first magnitude and furnished proof
positive of national ruin. Furthermore, there has been a striking
tendency to confuse the loss of Spain's political hegemony with
economic stagnation — interrelated but not necessarily identical
phenomena; and strong biases, all pulling in the same direction,
have vitiated the generalizations of many students of modern
Spanish economic history. The Germans have tended to magnify
the extent of the economic collapse during the seventeenth century in order to glorify the Emperor through contrast, the French
in order to exalt the new economic policy of the first Bourbons,

---

[1] It is easy to overestimate the extent of the decline of barter and of payments in
kind. Navarrese and Valencian account-books of the fourteenth and fifteenth centuries demonstrate that the predominance of money economy and the price system
antedated the dawn of modern times.

[2] For instance, British mercantilists were notoriously pessimistic in many periods
of rapid economic advance.

and the liberals of all countries in order to place absolutism, the
Inquisition, the persecution of minorities, and the Moorish expulsions in a worse light. But no reasonable allowance for overestimation by contemporary and subsequent writers can invali-
date the theoretical presumption that agriculture, industry, and
commerce declined during the first part of the seventeenth century. Furthermore, all the inductive data at our disposal point
to economic decadence. From a leading position in the last quarter of the sixteenth century the Spanish merchant marine lost
ground absolutely and relatively under Philip III and dwindled
to insignificance during the reign of Philip IV.[1] The marked loss
of inhabitants by industrial cities from 1594 to 1646 [2] probably
reflected the deterioration of manufactures, and the drop in the
tonnage of the American fleets registered the decrease of commercial and industrial competitive power. The Castilian fairs and
the Mesta declined sharply, and there is no conclusive evidence
that the gains of sedentary grazing and regular commerce com-
pensated for the losses.

So far as I have been able to determine, the Valencian price
statistics for 1601–1650, in Appendix V, utterly fail to disclose the
dire economic consequences universally attributed to the Moorish
expulsion of 1609. The price stability of most of the commodities
formerly produced by Moriscos in the decade following their expulsion suggests that this despicable act of religious intolerance
can hardly rank as a major cause of Spanish economic decadence.
The Moriscos stood out as producers of wine, and the Koran deterred them from consuming alcoholic beverages; [3] yet the trend
of wine prices in 1610–1620 failed to reflect a notable decrease in
supply with no countervailing drop in demand. The downward
trend of rice quotations (against the current of general prices) in
the decade following the expulsion indicates that the loss of

[1] A. P. Usher, "Spanish Ships and Shipping in the Sixteenth and Seventeenth
Centuries," *Facts and Factors in Economic History*, pp. 202–213; Archivo General
de Indias, *Contratación*, 42–6–5/9 to 42–6–13/17.

[2] Tomás González, *op. cit.*, pp. 57, 61, 66, 70–71; Konrad Haebler, *op. cit.*,
p. 157; Manuel Colmeiro, *op. cit.*, II, 15; Albert Girard, *op. cit.*, Novembre–Décembre, 1928, pp. 426–427, 432.

[3] The nominal Christianity of the Moriscos is immaterial.

Morisco labor from the Valencian rice fields, which largely supplied Spain, did not stifle cultivation.

After 1610 the comparatively stable trend of the composite silver index numbers, which have been derived from the indices in terms of the original monetary units by utilizing the premiums on Castilian silver in terms of Castilian vellon and Valencian silver respectively, was chiefly due to rough cancellation of the diminution in the supply of goods by the reduced imports of specie and the heavy outflow resulting (1) from the displacement of gold and silver by vellon and (2) from the differential between Spanish prices and those prevailing in neighboring countries. The notable drop of silver prices in 1638–1642 was a specious result of the abnormal premiums on silver precipitated by the wild flight from Castilian vellon.

In view of the close correlation between the timing of vellon appreciation and depreciation in terms of silver and the movements of commodity prices in Andalusia and the two Castiles disclosed by Charts 4 and 8 there can be little doubt that vellon inflation and deflation, including speculative anticipations of actual or expected changes in the tariffs, largely shaped the fluctuations of commodity prices in these regions during the second quarter of the seventeenth century. The decadence of agriculture, industry, and commerce, the remarkable decrease of population, and the progressive inflation of the vellon coinage were the primary causes of the upward trend of prices. The forward movement of the index numbers of commodity prices for Valencia was chiefly determined by the heavy coinage of Valencian silver from the Castilian reals driven into the Mediterranean kingdom by vellon depreciation. The overissue of Valencian vellon and a decline in the production and exchange of goods were important contributory factors.

Throughout the sixteenth century the movements of commodity prices tended to govern those of money wages, but the lag of the latter entailed a substantial loss of real income by wage earners.[1] The rise of prices not only engendered aggressive demands from workers, but increased the value product of marginal labor,

[1] *Vide* Chart 19.

thus enhancing the ability and diminishing the reluctance of employers to raise monetary rewards. There is abundant evidence that in bargaining for salary increases public and institutional employees stressed the rise of living costs and that the argument proved effective.

The sharp upswing of the remuneration of virtually every grade of labor in all regions from 1601 to 1605 was principally due to the epidemic of 1599–1600, which swept away a considerable portion of the Spanish population, particularly in Andalusia and New Castile.[1] The Moorish expulsion of 1609 apparently affected neither wages in general nor the remuneration of any particular class of workers. The rise of wages in 1626–1630 was presumably a consequence of the inflationary advance of prices in 1626–1627. Wages dropped with prices in 1643 and followed them upward in 1646–1650. The significant upturn of composite wages and prices in 1649–1650 largely reflected the sharp advance in Andalusia precipitated by the severe epidemic of 1648–1650.[2]

---

[1] The epidemic apparently broke out in the summer of 1599 and, after having remained dormant in the winter, reappeared in the spring of 1600 (AA, Seville, *Escribanía de Cabildo*, siglo XVI, tomo 7, fols. 38–587; AHN, *Clero*, Segovia, leg. 534; *Clero*, León, leg. 244; R. Bona, *Essai sur le Problème Mercantiliste en Espagne au XVIIᵉ Siècle* [Paris, 1911], p. 30; Antonio Marcos Orellana, *Valencia Antigua y Moderna*, I [ed. Valencia, 1921], 173; Sancho de Moncado, *op. cit.*, discurso II, fol. 18; Antonio Ballesteros, *Historia de España*, IV, 2ª Parte [Barcelona, 1927], 148). There is a bare possibility that the severe winter of 1599, which was particularly hard on lambs (BN, *Varios*, 1–59–5; *Furs, Capitols, Provisions e Actes de Cort de 1604*, cap. XLV, fol. 17), may have lowered resistance to the epidemic in 1600. In 1600 the city of Seville was forced to improvise hospitals and to provide extraordinary medical service to care for the afflicted (AA, Seville, *Escribanía de Cabildo*, siglo XVI, tomo 7, fols. 417, 419, 474; siglo XVII, tomo 23, no. 73), and by the early summer the Cofradía de la Caridad had exhausted its reserve for charity funerals (*ibid.*, siglo XVI, tomo 7, fol. 412). The mortality rate of the patients admitted to the Hospital Real in Granada from August 6 to 20, 1600, was extremely high (*ibid.*, siglo XVI, tomo 7, fols. 524–525).

[2] *Vide supra*, p. 220.

APPENDICES

APPENDIX I

METHOD OF DERIVING ANNUAL PRICES FROM CRUDE QUARTERLY DATA

THE methods of computing the annual prices from quarterly averages were not always identical.

In Seville, the prices from the 3 complementary sources were experimentally compared with those of the main series. In 42 cases of concurrent prices distributed among 17 commodities, quotations from the Hospital del Espíritu Santo were greater than those from the Hospital de la Sangre, the principal source, 14 times, identical 13 times, and less 15 times; and in 46 cases, including 16 commodities, prices from the Hospital del Amor de Dios were above those of the Hospital de la Sangre 23 times, below 14 times, and equal 9 times. Quotations from the Hospital del Cardenal, in 42 cases including 25 commodities, were greater than those from the main source 20 times, less 18 times, and equal 4 times. Unless inspection indicated a difference in quality, individual commodities were not subjected to a further correlation test.

The computation of annual prices for cooking apples in New Castile, of which two slightly different grades, *manzanas* and *peros*, were listed, illustrates the combination of data from 2 localities in the same region, the reduction of quotations to a common metrological unit, the substitution of a similar commodity, and the interpolation for missing quarters.

A check list of the prices of manzanas and peros by the pound and the arroba from Toledo and Alcalá de Henares showed that in 1551–1600 the number of prices missing from the first to the fourth quarter were respectively 1, 3, 8, and 1 and in the third period [1] 15, 14, 21, and 5. It also showed that the Toledo pound price for manzanas occurred most frequently. Hence it was selected as the unit for the annual averages.

The second period [2] had 34 full years — that is, years in which quotations for all the quarters occurred — in a common unit, while the third had only 7. The prices from the first and last 2 complete years of each decade in 1551–1600 were listed and the quarters added separately. The same procedure was used for the 7 full years in the ensuing period. In the second period the sums from the first to the fourth quarter were 2277, 2637, 1461, and 1594 respectively, and in the third 1213, 1460, 803, and 860. Since the third quarter occurred least frequently and the sums demonstrated that it could not be taken as equivalent to any other, it was dropped. The prices for the 3 remaining quarters were ranked as first, second, and third lowest. In the first 20 cases the fourth quarter ranked lowest 13 times and tied for lowest 4 times; the first quarter ranked second 10 times and tied for that place 4 times; the second quarter ranked highest 16 times and tied for highest once.

[1] 1601–1650.   [2] 1551–1600.

In the second period all 7 cases ranked as follows: the fourth quarter lowest, the first next to lowest, and the second highest. Since no 2 quarterly sums agreed closely enough for one to be considered equivalent to the other, only the 2 quarters appearing most often — the first and fourth — were employed in calculating the yearly average. The use of 3 quarters would have involved more interpolation.

In 2 years having lacunae in both the first and the fourth quarters substitutes were taken from the second. According to the quarterly sums, the ratio of the first- to the fourth-quarter prices was 1.428 to 1 in the second period and 1.410 to 1 in the third, while the ratio of second- to fourth-quarter prices was 1.654 to 1 in the second period and 1.698 to 1 in the third. Using the combined sums for the second and third periods, we find that the first-quarter price was 1.422 times and the second-quarter price 1.669 times the fourth. Hence fourth-quarter prices multiplied by 1.422 were interpolated for gaps in the first quarter, and first-quarter prices divided by 1.422 filled hiatuses in the fourth quarter. In the 2 years having breaks in both of these quarters, the second-quarter price was divided by 1.669 to obtain the fourth, and the first was deduced from this. The arithmetic averages of the real and interpolated prices for the first and the fourth quarters were used as the yearly averages.

In the second period no substitutes other than the first quarter for the fourth and *vice versa* needed to be used; but in the third period it was necessary to employ Toledo manzana prices by the arroba and both Toledo and Alcalá pero prices by the pound, with preference in the order listed. Toledo arroba and pound prices appeared concurrently in 19 quarters. The 19 ratios of arroba to pound prices averaged 23.73 to 1. Hence arroba prices divided by 23.73 were interpolated for pound prices. Only 8 ratios between manzana and pero prices for Toledo were available. No quotient exceeded unity, and they averaged 0.885. Hence it seemed safe to assume that peros were dearer than manzanas; and, when used as a substitute, their price was multiplied by 0.885. None of the 7 ratios of Toledo manzana prices to Alcalá pero prices fell as low as 1, and their average was 1.192 to 1. Hence the Alcalá pero prices used as substitutes were multiplied by this figure. Had the ratios in either case been distributed about equally above and below unity, the substitute would have been considered equivalent to the basic unit.

In 1501–1550 the quintal prices of salt pork and codfish for Andalusia were divided by 50 to obtain *libra carnicera* prices, and quintal quotations for tallow candles and rice were divided by 100 to get pound prices;[1] but in all other cases concurrent prices in terms of heterogeneous weights and measures were shifted from one unit to another only through average correlation.

---

[1] In Andalusia during this period the annual prices of codfish, rice, salt pork, and tallow candles, all bought in large quantities, were first tabulated with the quintal as the metrological unit. Then the annual figures were reduced to pound or libra carnicera units to conform to those of the following periods.

APPENDIX II

COMMODITIES, MONETARY UNITS, AND METROLOGICAL UNITS

TABLE A lists the commodities included in the tables of prices in Appendices III–V and their equivalents in the language in which they occurred. For the articles appearing only in Valencia the Castilian equivalents are not given, and *vice versa*.

TABLE A

	English	Castilian	Valencian
1	Acorns	Bellotas	
2	Almond oil, sweet	Aceite de almendras dulces	
3	Almonds	Almendras	
4	Alum	Alumbre	
5	Anise	Anís	
6	Apples, cooking	Manzanas or Peros	
7	Apples, pippin	Camuesas	
8	Ashes	Cenizas	Çendra
9	Barley	Cebada	
10	Beans, horse	Habas	
11	Beans, kidney		Fesols
12	Bedticks		Márfegues
13	Beef	Carne de vaca	
14	Borage		Bovina
15	Bran	Salvado	Segó
16	Brandy	Aguardiente	
17	Bricks	Ladrillos	Rajoles
18	Brooms	Escobas	Graneres
19	Burlap	Estopa	
20	Butter	Mantequilla	
21	Cables, naval	Jarcia	
22	Candles, tallow	Velas de sebo	
23	Candles, wax	Velas de cera	
24	Cantaloupe	Melón	
25	Capers	Alcaparras	
26	Carob beans		Garrofes
27	Carrots	Zanahorias	
28	Chambers	Orinales	
29	Charcoal	Carbón	Carbó
30	Cheese	Queso	Formatge
31	Cherries	Guindas	
32	Chestnuts	Castañas	
33	Chickens, spring	Pollos	Pollastres
34	Chick-peas	Garbanzos	Çigrons
35	Chicory	Achicoria	
36	Cinnamon	Canela	
37	Cloves	Clavos	
38	Codfish, dried	Bacalao	Abadejo
39	Conger eel	Congrio	
40	Coriander	Culantro	

TABLE A — Continued

	English	Castilian	Valencian
41	Cotton	Algodón	
42	Cuminseed	Cominos	
43	Cuttlefish	Jibia	
44	Dace	Albures	
45	Dates	Dátiles	
46	Dogfish	Cazón or Mielgas	
47	Dogfish, spotted	Tollo	
48	Eels	Anguilas	Anguiles
49	Eggs	Huevos	Hous
50	Feet, kid	Manos de cabrito	
51	Feet, lamb	Manos de carnero	
52	Figs	Higos	
53	Filberts	Avellanas	
54	Firewood	Leña	Llenya
55	Fish, Calp		Peix de Calp
56	Fish, dried	Pescado cecial	
57	Fish, fresh	Pescado fresco	Peix
58	Flax		Lli
59	Flounders	Acedías	
60	Garlic	Ajos	
61	Grapes	Uvas	
62	Grapes, unripe	Agraz	
63	Grits, barley		Farro
64	Grits, wheat		Sémola
65	Hake	Merluza or Pescada	Lluç
66	Hares	Conejos	
67	Hemp	Estopa	Estopa
68	Hens	Gallinas	Gallines
69	Honey	Miel	Mel
70	Horseshoes	Herraduras	Ferraures
71	Ice	Nieve	
72	Incense	Incienso	
73	Ink	Tinta	
74	Kid	Cabrito	Cabrit
75	Lambs	Carneros	
76	Lard	Manteca	Sagí
77	Lavender spike	Alhucema	
78	Lead	Plomo	
79	Lemons	Limones	
80	Lentils	Lentejas	
81	Lime	Cal	Cals
82	Linen	Lienzo	Llenç
83	Linseed oil	Aceite de linaza	
84	Marmalade, quince	Carne de membrillo	
85	Meal, mixed		Tres farines
86	Milk	Leche	
87	Mustard	Mostaza	
88	Mutton	Carnero	Moltó
89	Nails, large	Trabaderos	
90	Olive oil	Aceite	Oli

TABLE A — Continued

	English	Castilian	Valencian
91	Olives	Aceitunas	
92	Orange blossoms	Azahar	
93	Oranges	Naranjas	
94	Oysters, large	Ostiones	
95	Paper, writing	Papel de escribir	
96	Peaches	Melocotones	
97	Pears	Peras	
98	Pepper	Pimienta	
99	Perch	Peces	
100	Pine nuts	Piñones	
101	Pins, common	Alfileres	
102	Pipes, wine	Pipas	
103	Pitch	Pez	
104	Plaster of Paris	Yeso	Algeps
105	Plums	Ciruelas	
106	Pork, fresh	Tocino fresco	
107	Pork, salt	Tocino salado	Cansalá
108	Potatoes	Patatas	
109	Powder	Pólvora	
110	Prunes	Ciruelas pasas	
111	Pumpkin, candied	Calabazate	Carabasat
112	Quail	Perdiz	
113	Quinces	Membrillos	Codonys
114	Raisins	Pasas	Panses
115	Resin	Resina	
116	Rice	Arroz	Arroç
117	Rye	Centeno	
118	Saffron	Azafrán	Çafrá
119	Salmon	Salmón	
120	Salt		Sal
121	Sandals, hempen		Espardenyes
122	Sardines	Sardinas	Sardines
123	Saucers		Platerets
124	Sea bream	Besugo	
125	Sea eel, Mediterranean	Corvina	
126	Shad	Sábalo	
127	Sheepskins	Pellejos de carnero	
128	Ship biscuit, brown	Bizcocho, ordinario	
129	Ship biscuit, white	Bizcocho, blanco	
130	Shoes		Sabates
131	Shrouds		Mortalles
132	Silk, raw		Seda
133	Sloes	Endrinas	
134	Soap	Jabón	Sabó
135	Sole	Lenguados	
136	Starch	Almidón	
137	Sugar	Azúcar	Sucre
138	Sweetmeats	Confites	
139	Tallow	Sebo	
140	Thread, basting	Hilo de bastar	

TABLE A — Continued

	English	Castilian	Valencian
141	Thread, homespun	Hilo casero	
142	Thread, sewing	Hilo de juntar	
143	Thread, white	Hilo blanco	
144	Tiles, roof	Tejas	
145	Trout	Truchas	
146	Tuna fish	Atún	Tonyina
147	Turnips	Nabos	
148	Turpentine		Trementina
149	Twine	Bramante or Cordel	Cordell
150	Veal	Ternera	
151	Vermicelli		Fideus
152	Vinegar	Vinagre	Vinagre
153	Walnuts	Nueces	
154	Wax, white	Cera blanca	
155	Wax, yellow	Cera amarilla	Çera groga
156	Wheat	Trigo	Forment or Blat
157	Wine	Vino	Vi
158	Wool	Lana	

The abbreviations and symbols used for metrological units in Table B are as follows:

Almud	al		Libra	lb
Arroba	@		Libra carnicera	lb c
Azumbre	az		10 libras	x lb
Barchilla	bs		Mano	qu
Cahiz	ca		Mil	m
Cántaro	k		Onza	oz
Carga	g		Papel	p
Celemín	c		Par	pr
Cien	n		Quintal	q
Docena	d		Resma	r
10 docenas	10 d		Ristra	ri
Fanega	f		Sarrie	bag
Grosa	gr		Vara	v

Table B lists the commodities, indicates the region and period in which each occurred, and gives the metrological unit in terms of which annual prices are expressed in Appendices III–V. The period 1501–1550 is represented by 1, 1551–1600 by 2, and 1601–1650 by 3.

TABLE B

Commodity	Andalusia		New Castile		Old Castile-León		Valencia	
	Unit	Periods	Unit	Periods	Unit	Periods	Unit	Periods
1 Acorns	al	3						
2 Almond oil, sweet	lb	2 3	lb	3				
3 Almonds	@	1 2 3	@	2 3	lb	1 2 3	x lb	1
4 Alum	lb	2 3						
5 Anise	lb	3						
6 Apples, cooking	@	2 3	x lb	2 3	x lb	2 3		
7 Apples, pippin	x lb	2 3	x lb	2 3	x lb	2 3		
8 Ashes	f	2 3					bs	1 2 3
9 Barley	f	2 3	f	1 2 3	f	1 2 3		
10 Beans, horse	f	1 3						
11 Beans, kidney							al	1
12 Bedticks							one	2 3
13 Beef	lb c	1 2 3	lb	1 2	lb	1 2 3		
14 Borage							@	3
15 Bran			c	2 3			ca	3
16 Brandy			az	3				
17 Bricks	m	3	m	2 3			m	1 2 3
18 Brooms			d	2 3			d	3
19 Burlap					v	1		
20 Butter	lb c	2 3	lb	3				
21 Cables, naval	q	1						
22 Candles, tallow	lb	1 2 3	lb	2 3	lb	1 2 3		
23 Candles, wax	lb	1						
24 Cantaloupe			x lb	3				
25 Capers			lb	2				
26 Carob beans							@	1 2 3
27 Carrots			x lb	2				
28 Chambers			d	2				
29 Charcoal	@	2 3	@	2 3	@	2 3	bag	1 2 3
30 Cheese	@	1 2 3	lb	1 2	lb	1 2 3	x lb	1 3
31 Cherries			x lb	2 3	x lb	2 3		
32 Chestnuts	al	2 3	lb	2 3	f	1 2 3		
33 Chickens, spring	one	2 3	one	2 3	one	1 2 3	one	1 2 3
34 Chick-peas	f	1 2 3			f	1 2 3	al	1
35 Chicory			@	3				
36 Cinnamon	lb	2 3	lb	2 3	lb	1 2 3		
37 Cloves	lb	2 3			oz	1 2 3		
38 Codfish, dried	lb c	1 3					lb	2 3
39 Conger eel					lb	1 2 3		
40 Coriander	al	3						
41 Cotton	lb	3	lb	2 3				
42 Cuminseed	lb	3						
43 Cuttlefish	lb c	3						
44 Dace	lb c	2 3						
45 Dates			lb	2 3				
46 Dogfish	lb c	2 3			@	3		
47 Dogfish, spotted	lb c	2 3						

TABLE B — Continued

Commodity	Andalusia		New Castile		Old Castile–León		Valencia	
	Unit	Periods	Unit	Periods	Unit	Periods	Unit	Periods
48 Eels	lb c	3					lb	3
49 Eggs	d	2 3	d	2 3	d	1 2 3	d	1 2 3
50 Feet, kid					d	2		
51 Feet, lamb			d	2 3				
52 Figs					@	1		
53 Filberts	al	3			f	2 3		
54 Firewood	g	2 3	q	3			q	1 2 3
55 Fish, Calp							x lb	1
56 Fish, dried			lb	2 3	lb	3		
57 Fish, fresh					lb	1 2	x lb	1
58 Flax							lb	1 2 3
59 Flounders	lb c	2 3						
60 Garlic	ri	1 2 3						
61 Grapes	x lb	3	x lb	2				
62 Grapes, unripe			x lb	2 3				
63 Grits, barley							x lb	1 2 3
64 Grits, wheat							x lb	1 2 3
65 Hake	lb c	2 3					d	1
66 Hares	one	2 3						
67 Hemp	lb	3	lb	2 3			x lb	1 3
68 Hens	one	2 3	one	2 3	one	1 2 3	one	1 2 3
69 Honey	@	2 3	@	2 3	k	1 2 3	q	1 2 3
70 Horseshoes	pr	3			pr	3	pr	3
71 Ice	lb	3						
72 Incense			lb	2 3	lb	1 2 3		
73 Ink			az	2 3				
74 Kid	one	2 3	lb	2	lb	1 2 3	one	1
75 Lambs					one	1 2 3		
76 Lard	lb c	2 3	lb	2 3	lb	1 2 3	lb	1 2 3
77 Lavender spike	lb	3						
78 Lead	q	1						
79 Lemons			d	2 3				
80 Lentils	f	3	lb	2	c	3		
81 Lime	ca	3	f	1 2 3	g	1	ca	1 2 3
82 Linen			v	1	v	1 2 3	alna	2 3
83 Linseed oil	lb	3						
84 Marmalade, quince					lb	3		
85 Meal, mixed							@	3
86 Milk	az	2 3	az	2 3				
87 Mustard	al	3			lb	3		
88 Mutton	lb c	2 3	lb	1 2 3	lb	1 2 3	lb c	1 2 3
89 Nails, large			lb	1 2 3	lb	1 2 3		
90 Olive oil	@	1 2 3	@	1 2 3	@	1 2 3	@	1 2 3
91 Olives			lb	2	lb	1 3		
92 Orange blossoms	lb	2 3						
93 Oranges			d	2 3	n	1 2 3		
94 Oysters, large	d	3						

TABLE B — Continued

	Commodity	Andalusia		New Castile		Old Castile–León		Valencia	
		Unit	Periods	Unit	Periods	Unit	Periods	Unit	Periods
95	Paper, writing			qu	2 3	r	2 3		
96	Peaches			x lb	2 3				
97	Pears			x lb	2 3	x lb	2 3		
98	Pepper	lb	2 3	oz	2 3	lb	1 2 3	oz	1 3
99	Perch			lb	2	lb	1 2 3		
100	Pine nuts	lb	3						
101	Pins, common					p	3		
102	Pipes, wine	one	1						
103	Pitch	lb	2 3	lb	3				
104	Plaster of Paris	g	2 3	f	1 2 3	f	1 2	ca	1 2 3
105	Plums	x lb	3	x lb	2 3	x lb	2 3		
106	Pork, fresh	lb c	2 3						
107	Pork, salt	lb c	1 3	lb	2 3	lb	2 3	lb c	3
108	Potatoes	@	3						
109	Powder	q	1						
110	Prunes	lb	3	lb	2				
111	Pumpkin, candied ...			lb	2 3	lb	2 3	@	3
112	Quail	one	2 3	one	2	one	3		
113	Quinces			d	2			d	3
114	Raisins	q	1 2 3	@	2 3	@	1 2 3	@	1 2 3
115	Resin	lb	2 3						
116	Rice	lb	1 2 3	lb	2	@	1 2 3	g	1 2 3
117	Rye					f	1 2 3		
118	Saffron	lb	2 3	oz	2	oz	1 2 3	lb	1 2 3
119	Salmon					lb	2 3		
120	Salt							ca	1 3
121	Sandals, hempen							d	2 3
122	Sardines	lb c	2 3	lb	2	n	1 2 3	10 d	1 3
123	Saucers							gr	1 2 3
124	Sea bream	lb c	2 3			lb	3		
125	Sea eel, Mediterranean	lb c	2 3						
126	Shad	lb c	3						
127	Sheepskins	one	1 3			one	3		
128	Ship biscuit, brown .	q	1						
129	Ship biscuit, white ..	q	1						
130	Shoes							pr	2 3
131	Shrouds							one	1 3
132	Silk, raw							lb	2 3
133	Sloes			x lb	2 3	x lb	2 3		
134	Soap	@	2 3			@	1 2 3	@	1 2 3
135	Sole	lb c	2 3						
136	Starch	lb	3	lb	2 3	lb	2		
137	Sugar	@	1 2 3	@	2 3	@	1 2 3	lb	1 2 3
138	Sweetmeats					lb	3		
139	Tallow	q	1	lb	2				
140	Thread, basting	lb	3						
141	Thread, homespun ..	lb	3						

TABLE B — CONTINUED

Commodity	ANDALUSIA		NEW CASTILE		OLD CASTILE–LEÓN		VALENCIA	
	Unit	Periods	Unit	Periods	Unit	Periods	Unit	Periods
142 Thread, sewing	lb	3						
143 Thread, white			lb	3				
144 Tiles, roof			m	3				
145 Trout					lb	1 2 3		
146 Tuna fish	lb c	3					lb	1 2 3
147 Turnips	@	3	x lb	2				
148 Turpentine							lb	2 3
149 Twine	lb	3	lb	2 3	lb	2 3	lb	3
150 Veal	lb c	2 3						
151 Vermicelli							lb	3
152 Vinegar	@	1 2 3	@	2 3	k	2 3	k	1 2 3
153 Walnuts	n	2 3			f	2		
154 Wax, white	lb	2 3	lb	2 3	lb	2 3		
155 Wax, yellow	lb	2 3	lb	1 2 3	lb	1 2 3	lb	1 2 3
156 Wheat	f	2 3	f	1 2 3	f	1 2 3	ca	1 2 3
157 Wine	@	1 2 3	@	1 2 3	k	1 2 3	k	1 2 3
158 Wool	@	3			@	3		

Keys for reducing the metrological units to the metric system may be found on pages 168–178 and 180–185 *supra*.

In Appendices III–V and VII the prices and wages for Andalusia, New Castile, and Old Castile are expressed in *maravedís* and those for Valencia in *diners*. From 1501 to 1602 the maravedí represented 0.094 gram of pure silver. The premiums on silver in terms of vellon (*vide supra*, p. 95 and Table 7) will enable anyone who may care to do so to reduce to silver maravedís the quotations for Andalusia, New Castile, and Old Castile in 1603–1650, which are expressed in vellon maravedís. From 1501 to 1609 the diner was equivalent to 0.1389 gram of pure silver. The premiums in Table 10 may be utilized in reducing Valencian price and wage statistics for 1610–1650 to terms of silver diners.

APPENDIX III

PRICES, 1501–1550 [1]

A. ANDALUSIA (IN MARAVEDÍS)

	1503	1505	1507	1511	1513	1515	1517	1519	1530	1532	1537	1539	1542	1548	1549
1 Almonds	203.5	...	...	340.0	223.0	...	238.0	395.5	400.0	...	306.0	442.0	612.0	...	680.0
2 Beans, horse	104.0	125.0	125.0	...	85.0	100.0	136.0	129.0	263.5	166.0	272.0	246.5	306.0	218.0	306.0
3 Beef	...	6.0	7.0	...	7.0	...	7.0	...	9.5	13.0	...	11.0	15.0	...	15.0
4 Cables, naval	600.0	780.0	1000.0	...	800.0	1075.0	...	710.0	1350.0	820.0	1425.0	1100.0	1250.0	...	...
5 Candles, tallow	8.0	8.0	...	10.0	8.0	12.0	...	10.0	11.0	15.0	15.0	13.6	12.0	...	14.5
6 Candles, wax	34.0	36.0	44.0	...	...	40.0	...	52.0	44.0	40.0	...	50.0	...	...	68.0
7 Cheese	160.0	165.0	...	125.0	140.0	...	165.0	...	250.0	225.0	225.0	238.0	272.0	375.0	255.0
8 Chick-peas	104.0	...	350.0	163.0	...	136.0	153.0	150.5	230.0	161.5	263.5	340.0	375.0	383.0	306.0
9 Codfish, dried	...	6.8	...	...	4.5	2.7	2.3	...	7.6	7.3	9.1	6.7	...	12.1	10.6
10 Garlic	9.0	12.0	...	...	7.0	12.5	13.0	8.5	34.0	8.5	17.0	15.0	20.0	10.0	10.0
11 Lead	...	...	450.0	600.0	500.0	550.0	485.0	640.0	562.5	750.0	680.0	680.0	...	700.0	680.0
12 Olive oil	90.0	80.0	110.0	...	85.0	100.0	153.0	112.0	170.0	204.0	134.0	238.0	153.0	255.0	238.0
13 Pipes, wine	290.0	300.0	375.0	...	306.0	...	...	...	408.0	408.0	408.0	375.0	493.0	...	...
14 Pork, salt	12.0	...	9.0	8.0	7.0	...	14.6	18.0	...	23.0	22.5	22.0	34.0	55.0	31.7
15 Powder	2500.0	...	2000.0	2000.0	2000.0	2800.0	1866.0	2000.0	3375.0	2300.0	3750.0	3750.0	3750.0	...	4500.0
16 Raisins	...	...	...	250.0	...	...	408.0	...	500.0	375.0	612.0	850.0	884.0	...	867.0
17 Rice	...	...	...	5.5	5.5	...	...	...	6.0	...	...	8.2	7.5	8.5	8.0
18 Sheepskins	...	...	34.0	...	40.0	36.0	...	25.0	55.0	60.0	...	72.0	...	...	...
19 Ship biscuit, brown	...	365.0	500.0	170.0	195.0	170.0	250.0	250.0	569.0	544.0	306.0	527.0	612.0	671.5	340.0
20 Ship biscuit, white	388.0	388.0	1079.0	211.5	324.5	...	370.5	441.0	959.5	882.0	...	816.0	...	935.0	850.0
21 Sugar	310.0	...	...	265.0	...	...	400.0	784.0	750.0	...	561.0	782.0	...	...	937.5
22 Tallow	790.0	750.0	750.0	800.0	800.0	1000.0	1000.0	...	1000.0	1100.0	1250.0	1200.0	1632.0	1700.0	1394.0
23 Vinegar	23.0	12.0	20.0	16.0	24.0	17.0	17.0	...	45.0	45.0	41.0	86.5	34.0	54.0	64.0
24 Wine	40.0	32.0	51.0	...	20.0	...	55.0	68.0	85.0	60.0	102.0	70.0	97.5	97.0	151.0

[1] Appendix II lists the metrological units in terms of which prices are recorded and furnishes keys for the reduction of metrological units to the metric system and price quotations to a fixed weight of fine silver.

B. NEW CASTILE (IN MARAVEDÍS)

		1501	1502	1503	1504	1505	1506	1507	1508	1509	1510	1511	1512
1	Barley	3.0	...	...	66.2	66.2	140.6	113.6	77.2	40.8	65.7	68.4	44.1
2	Beef	...	3.0	3.0	3.0	...	...	...	...	...	...	...	...
3	Cheese	...	...	...	...	...	...	...	...	...	...	...	...
4	Lime	...	...	...	19.8	19.8	...	...	...	21.3	21.3	21.3	22.2
5	Linen	...	19.6	...	...	...	...	22.6	18.0	...	24.3	...	23.5
6	Mutton	...	...	5.2	...	5.5	...	...	...	...	...	...	...
7	Nails, large	9.0	...	...	9.0	9.0	...	...	...	10.0	10.0	10.0	10.0
8	Olive oil	155.0	155.0	...	...	...	250.0	310.0	328.0	203.5	196.3	220.0	217.0
9	Plaster of Paris	28.9	28.9	28.9	28.9	28.9	28.9	28.9	...	28.9	28.9	28.9	28.9
10	Wax, yellow	37.2	36.9	35.6	34.4	57.1	51.1	56.7	52.4	43.0	37.4	37.8	38.2
11	Wheat	87.9	128.0	104.7	131.6	179.4	247.6	244.0	165.4	71.8	104.5	100.5	83.7
12	Wine	42.0	...	...	32.5	30.0	40.0	52.0	57.0	55.0	...	72.0	...

		1513	1514	1515	1516	1517	1518	1519	1520	1521	1522	1523	1524
1	Barley	80.0	68.4	72.2	67.6	57.4	73.9	75.0	60.9	40.8	...	65.6	94.9
2	Beef	...	...	...	...	...	...	...	4.1	4.1	4.1	4.3	4.3
3	Cheese	...	...	...	...	...	...	12.5	...	...	...	...	18.0
4	Lime	21.3	21.3	21.8	22.2	21.3	24.4	26.1	...	15.4	...	...	...
5	Linen	...	...	22.4	26.0	18.5	20.4	22.0	22.0	22.0	22.0	...	...
6	Mutton	...	...	...	...	7.5	...	6.6	6.6	6.6	7.5	7.1	6.9
7	Nails, large	10.0	10.8	10.7	10.9	10.5	10.2	10.0	...	...	17.0	...	...
8	Olive oil	187.5	263.0	268.0	255.0	204.0	272.0	...	...	...	...	...	...
9	Plaster of Paris	26.6	...	26.6	28.3	27.6	28.3	28.3	...	34.7	...	...	...
10	Wax, yellow	42.3	43.8	43.0	47.2	43.8	47.2	55.0	48.0	51.8	60.0	...	62.0
11	Wheat	134.0	133.2	179.4	129.5	92.7	...	130.0	108.5	164.0	240.3	187.0	153.0
12	Wine	...	...	56.0	25.0	...	42.0	40.5	28.0	60.8	80.0	37.5	37.0

	1525	1526	1527	1528	1529	1530	1531	1532	1533	1534	1535	1536	1537
1 Barley	...	115.8	...	...	...	...	71.7	82.7	...	102.6	66.2	93.8	56.3
2 Beef	4.5	4.3	6.0	4.7	5.3	4.9	4.3	4.5	...	...	...	...	...
3 Cheese	...	12.0	...	19.0	20.0	17.0	17.0	17.0	17.0	...	...	...	...
4 Lime	...	...	...	21.8	...	...	...	40.0	...	...	...	34.0	31.3
5 Linen	29.6	30.0	29.6	36.0	38.0	38.0	34.0	36.0	32.0	32.5	...	38.0	39.0
6 Mutton	8.5	8.3	7.2	9.0	8.5	7.5	7.6	8.6	7.4	...	...	...	...
7 Nails, large	...	16.5	...	12.0	...	...	...	...	...	...	...	...	...
8 Olive oil	...	...	...	221.0	...	...	263.5	...	272.0	255.0	238.0	...	...
9 Plaster of Paris	...	...	28.9	...	...	36.2	...	...	33.2	...	...	...	...
10 Wax, yellow	53.3	48.1	52.0	48.0	51.5	45.0	56.6	...	49.8	45.5	42.1	45.5	46.4
11 Wheat	187.0	184.0	190.2	144.5	200.5	297.5	238.0	135.5	139.2	244.0	162.7	175.5	113.6
12 Wine	53.6	61.5	39.2	51.8	50.1	91.7	132.4	49.2	68.7	112.0	...	...	88.0

	1538	1539	1540	1541	1542	1543	1544	1545	1546	1547	1548	1549	1550
1 Barley	56.3	93.8	...	93.8	150.0	99.1	75.0	...	...	143.0	97.6	...	115.8
2 Beef	...	4.8	5.0	4.7	5.6	6.0	...	...	...	...	6.8	7.5	7.9
3 Cheese	17.0	...	22.0	14.0	24.0	17.5	14.0	14.5	...	17.3	18.5	19.3	21.2
4 Lime	34.0	...	...	26.8	30.0	28.5	...	29.0	24.9	27.0	...	26.0	26.5
5 Linen	36.0	37.7	38.0	39.0	39.0	38.0	41.0	39.0	36.5	36.0	...	33.5	39.0
6 Mutton	...	8.3	8.0	7.8	9.2	8.5	9.0	...	...	9.5	9.6	9.6	11.0
7 Nails, large	12.0	...	...	13.0	13.0	...	...	...	...	16.0	...	15.0	15.0
8 Olive oil	...	...	...	178.0	304.6	359.0	...	...	...	326.3	272.0	348.1	348.1
9 Plaster of Paris	31.9	33.0	...	43.4	...	44.7	...	...	...	34.0	...	...	34.0
10 Wax, yellow	...	48.0	48.0	46.4	43.8	162.7	49.8	43.0	...	48.5	41.2	50.2	42.0
11 Wheat	113.6	212.3	...	203.3	255.0	136.0	244.0	144.5	376.1	373.0	425.5	304.0	181.8
12 Wine	160.0	72.0	96.0	72.0	91.5	...	105.5	89.0	64.4	77.2	79.8	297.5	223.9

C. OLD CASTILE–LEÓN (IN MARAVEDÍS)

		1501	1502	1503	1504	1505	1506	1507	1508	1509
1	Almonds	...	...	22.4	...	...	25.2	...	...	...
2	Barley	...	...	...	...	...	...	...	68.1	...
3	Beef	...	2.0	...	...	...	...	...	2.3	...
4	Burlap	...	...	...	...	...	...	...	...	...
5	Candles, tallow	...	11.0	11.4	...	...	13.3	...	12.3	...
6	Cheese	...	7.0	6.8	...	...	9.0	...	10.0	...
7	Chestnuts	...	...	...	...	...	...	...	...	...
8	Chickens, spring	...	10.4	10.8	...	...	20.0	...	11.0	...
9	Chick-peas	...	254.7	...	...	...	438.9	...	...	...
10	Cinnamon	...	335.4	...	...	...	...	...	...	...
11	Cloves	...	17.3	...	...	...	...	...	29.0	...
12	Conger eel	...	...	...	...	...	...	...	...	...
13	Eggs	...	8.3	8.8	...	...	13.9	...	17.0	...
14	Figs	...	...	...	...	...	...	...	...	...
15	Fish, fresh	...	6.9	8.1	...	...	8.1	...	9.1	...
16	Hens	...	21.1	20.1	...	...	32.7	...	26.8	...
17	Honey	...	280.3	371.0	...	...	296.8	...	544.0	...
18	Incense	...	...	...	...	...	...	...	...	...
19	Kid	...	...	...	...	...	...	...	...	...
20	Lambs	...	142.9	143.1	...	...	190.9	...	...	...
21	Lard	...	...	...	...	...	18.8	...	23.5	...
22	Lime	...	19.9	18.4	...	...	...	...	...	...
23	Linen	...	13.7	13.7	...	...	14.1	...	...	...
24	Mutton	...	4.8	4.5	...	...	5.7	...	5.0	...
25	Nails, large	...	7.0	6.5	...	...	...	...	...	...
26	Olive oil	...	240.9	253.7	...	...	351.1	...	356.3	...
27	Olives	...	32.6	23.4	...	...	...	...	...	...
28	Oranges	...	...	...	...	...	...	...	...	...
29	Pepper	...	...	...	...	...	...	...	...	...
30	Perch	...	...	...	...	...	...	...	...	...
31	Plaster of Paris	...	...	...	...	...	...	...	...	...
32	Raisins	...	190.8	190.0	...	...	175.0	...	...	...
33	Rice	...	163.3	183.8	...	...	...	...	200.7	...
34	Rye	...	...	...	...	...	...	...	...	...
35	Saffron	...	31.0	29.0	...	...	...	...	...	...
36	Sardines	...	...	...	...	...	...	...	...	...
37	Soap	...	320.0	310.0	...	...	...	...	357.5	...
38	Sugar	...	458.0	460.0	...	...	470.0	...	...	...
39	Trout	...	...	...	...	...	...	...	...	...
40	Wax, yellow	...	43.2	42.4	...	...	59.2	...	...	...
41	Wheat	...	...	...	...	...	271.4	...	160.1	...
42	Wine	...	...	84.0	...	...	32.0	...	72.0	...

C. OLD CASTILE–LEÓN (IN MARAVEDÍS) — CONTINUED

		1510	1511	1512	1513	1514	1515	1516	1517	1518
1	Almonds	...	...	...	...	...	...	...	...	18.6
2	Barley	48.6	36.7	42.1	58.6	...	...	...	...	55.3
3	Beef	...	2.5	...	2.7	...	...	...	2.7	2.7
4	Burlap	...	11.0	...	...	...	...	...	...	...
5	Candles, tallow	16.6	15.0	13.0	12.8	...	...	...	12.0	14.2
6	Cheese	9.5	10.0	6.5	10.0	...	...	...	10.0	11.8
7	Chestnuts	...	...	...	...	...	...	...	...	...
8	Chickens, spring	20.0	11.0	13.3	11.0	...	...	...	10.5	13.4
9	Chick-peas	276.4	...	...	...	...	...	...	...	362.3
10	Cinnamon	268.3	...	503.1	...	...	...	...	...	368.4
11	Cloves	17.3	22.0	...	...	...	...	...	...	35.0
12	Conger eel	...	14.5	...	...	...	...	...	12.7	11.8
13	Eggs	10.8	12.9	9.8	13.4	...	...	...	12.4	11.5
14	Figs	...	...	...	...	...	...	...	...	...
15	Fish, fresh	8.6	12.0	8.1	...	...	...	...	...	8.1
16	Hens	29.1	26.8	28.1	26.8	...	...	...	27.9	32.1
17	Honey	474.1	420.5	387.5	...	...	...	...	280.3	500.0
18	Incense	87.8	...	...	...	...	...	...	...	90.0
19	Kid	...	...	...	...	...	...	...	...	...
20	Lambs	...	...	...	...	...	...	...	...	177.7
21	Lard	...	15.8	...	14.1	...	...	...	...	14.0
22	Lime	...	...	...	...	...	...	...	...	...
23	Linen	14.4	...	13.7	...	...	...	...	...	18.3
24	Mutton	5.7	5.7	6.5	5.7	...	...	...	6.0	6.3
25	Nails, large	...	...	9.5	...	...	...	...	...	9.5
26	Olive oil	295.2	190.6	230.5	...	...	...	...	...	295.2
27	Olives	...	...	...	...	...	...	...	...	27.2
28	Oranges	...	...	...	...	...	...	...	...	68.0
29	Pepper	...	...	...	...	...	...	...	...	115.0
30	Perch	...	...	...	...	...	...	...	...	...
31	Plaster of Paris	19.2	...	16.0	...	...	...	...	...	20.0
32	Raisins	173.7	...	136.0	...	...	...	...	...	192.3
33	Rice	...	150.5	...	150.5	...	...	...	133.8	...
34	Rye	...	...	...	...	...	...	...	...	42.5
35	Saffron	45.0	...	...	...	...	...	...	...	34.0
36	Sardines	40.6	...	59.1	...	...	...	...	67.6	83.2
37	Soap	340.0	450.0	...	375.0	...	...	...	357.5	317.8
38	Sugar	498.7	...	730.0	...	...	...	...	...	750.0
39	Trout	...	...	...	15.4	...	...	...	18.2	17.6
40	Wax, yellow	43.7	...	45.9	...	...	...	...	...	58.1
41	Wheat	61.3	89.4	68.5	93.9	...	...	...	87.6	68.0
42	Wine	84.8	...	51.1	...	...	...	...	34.0	52.0

C. OLD CASTILE–LEÓN (IN MARAVEDÍS) — Continued

		1519	1520	1521	1522	1523	1524	1525	1526
1	Almonds	17.8	16.7	15.0	19.0	20.2	19.0	19.0	17.9
2	Barley	51.9	51.0	55.3	72.7	68.7	66.4	73.7	74.4
3	Beef	3.2	2.7	...	...	3.0	3.5	4.2	3.6
4	Burlap	12.0	15.0	13.5	...	17.0	18.0	17.0	19.0
5	Candles, tallow	13.4	13.2	14.0	13.1	15.0	14.5	14.0	16.0
6	Cheese	11.2	11.5	12.5	12.3	13.5	12.4	...	...
7	Chestnuts	136.0	141.2	170.0	119.0	198.3	144.5	180.0	110.5
8	Chickens, spring	11.6	12.5	18.0	10.0	17.2	17.0	12.8	10.8
9	Chick-peas	190.3	173.4	161.7	...	544.0	520.2	...	238.0
10	Cinnamon	417.5	417.5	420.0	392.9	273.8	343.8	307.0	307.0
11	Cloves	34.0	34.0	42.5	32.0	21.0	33.4	25.0	25.0
12	Conger eel	11.5	13.0	12.5	12.0	10.3	14.0	16.8	12.5
13	Eggs	11.5	11.7	13.5	...	16.6	13.5	...	...
14	Figs	...	68.0	150.0	102.0	100.0	...	147.5	92.0
15	Fish, fresh	11.0	10.9	10.6	10.5	8.9	10.0	11.0	9.0
16	Hens	24.5	26.5	29.3	...	37.4	32.5	...	...
17	Honey	395.8	420.5	765.9	574.4	659.6	574.4	608.2	461.8
18	Incense	62.5	82.5	92.3	85.0	150.0	136.0	130.0	117.8
19	Kid	11.4	...	10.8	12.1	12.2	...	13.7	13.9
20	Lambs	164.7	193.4	161.5	147.4	163.7	146.0	178.8	181.4
21	Lard	...	...	...	...	21.4	17.0	14.5	...
22	Lime	20.0	24.0	24.0	...	...	26.0	28.0	28.0
23	Linen	17.4	19.7	20.0	28.3	22.0	24.0	19.9	24.0
24	Mutton	6.3	6.8	7.3	...	7.5	7.2	...	...
25	Nails, large	10.0	7.0	9.6	16.3	11.0	10.0	...	...
26	Olive oil	280.0	315.0	336.6	376.8	260.3	296.3	258.5	295.1
27	Olives	16.5	14.7	20.0	25.0	19.5	24.0	28.2	27.0
28	Oranges	50.0	51.0	...	34.0	59.0	25.5	51.5	...
29	Pepper	120.0	128.0	145.0	142.0	127.0	134.0	136.0	136.0
30	Perch	...	...	...	4.0	...	...	3.7	...
31	Plaster of Paris	15.8	15.5	15.0	...	25.0	28.7	...	...
32	Raisins	150.0	130.0	175.7	174.9	234.8	189.0	152.7	145.7
33	Rice	185.0	180.0	256.3	325.0	250.0	224.0	225.8	223.0
34	Rye	48.2	50.5	66.1	80.6	78.4	76.5	76.5	85.0
35	Saffron	50.3	42.7	59.5	51.2	61.5	56.0	60.0	40.0
36	Sardines	66.2	80.4	57.1	75.5	94.5	83.2	...	97.0
37	Soap	367.4	317.8	335.6	321.8	385.3	371.4	315.0	321.8
38	Sugar	799.0	895.0	1089.4	796.4	712.5	611.1	657.9	761.8
39	Trout	17.1	12.1	15.7	17.0	20.3	18.6	17.2	18.1
40	Wax, yellow	61.3	57.2	54.5	50.9	...	64.0	...	50.9
41	Wheat	74.6	78.3	107.3	122.8	117.5	92.1	102.5	120.6
42	Wine	88.0	69.3	66.5	69.6	84.0	49.6	135.9	54.8

C. OLD CASTILE–LEÓN (IN MARAVEDÍS) — Continued

		1527	1528	1529	1530	1531	1532	1533	1534
1	Almonds	18.5	19.4	16.2	20.5	...	...	21.4	...
2	Barley	112.7	102.2	121.8	143.8	...	...	100.0	67.7
3	Beef	3.7	4.0	3.6	4.0	...	...	4.3	4.0
4	Burlap	...	19.0	17.3	18.5	...	...	14.0	17.5
5	Candles, tallow	15.0	15.2	12.5	13.0	...	...	16.4	11.4
6	Cheese	...	...	17.0	10.0	...	...	9.4	5.0
7	Chestnuts	...	158.0	176.5	211.8	...	...	...	136.0
8	Chickens, spring	20.3	16.4	...	14.0	...	...	13.0	17.0
9	Chick-peas	255.0	295.6	375.0	628.6	...	...	...	272.0
10	Cinnamon	...	307.0	340.0	384.0	...	...	300.8	...
11	Cloves	28.0	25.0	43.4	35.5	...	...	25.0	...
12	Conger eel	15.0	14.0	12.5	11.2	...	...	17.0	...
13	Eggs	...	17.6	...	17.8	...	...	...	...
14	Figs	126.0	106.5	119.0	160.0	...	...	119.0	119.0
15	Fish, fresh	10.0	12.9	10.0	11.0	...	...	10.5	8.8
16	Hens	29.9	35.5	27.2	32.8	...	...	...	32.0
17	Honey	1148.8	810.9	589.1	527.7	...	700.8	...	...
18	Incense	109.0	102.0	136.0	125.0	...	...	90.0	...
19	Kid	12.2	13.7	12.9	14.5	...	...	12.6	11.9
20	Lambs	206.0	170.0	180.4	135.9	...	...	179.7	187.3
21	Lard	...	16.5	17.0	...	...	29.0	13.5	17.0
22	Lime	28.0	26.8	31.0	34.0	...	...	30.0	25.9
23	Linen	26.4	29.8	22.0	23.0	...	...	19.9	22.0
24	Mutton	7.3	6.9	6.0	7.5	...	7.3	...	7.5
25	Nails, large	...	10.9	11.0	10.9	...	...	10.0	10.5
26	Olive oil	370.3	367.8	355.8	411.7	...	342.6	313.8	331.5
27	Olives	19.4	19.8	20.0	18.5	...	...	16.4	18.6
28	Oranges	85.0	42.4	...	52.9	...	...	56.1	53.8
29	Pepper	...	130.0	125.0	128.0	...	...	170.0	...
30	Perch	4.5	4.3	6.0	4.0	...	...	4.0	3.5
31	Plaster of Paris	18.0	27.3	21.4	16.0	...	...	29.3	24.0
32	Raisins	158.0	200.0	...	186.7	...	218.8	200.0	208.3
33	Rice	276.0	225.0	250.0	272.0	...	...	235.0	...
34	Rye	147.1	144.5	155.8	157.3	...	...	116.2	86.1
35	Saffron	...	50.0	42.6	30.0	...	...	46.0	...
36	Sardines	63.2	105.3	92.6	57.2	...	...	32.8	48.3
37	Soap	335.6	341.9	329.8	383.3	...	...	330.1	...
38	Sugar	850.0	689.1	...	...	...	715.2	588.6	...
39	Trout	21.9	22.3	27.6	18.2	...	...	24.7	...
40	Wax, yellow	57.0	50.9	50.9	57.0	...	...	49.2	48.0
41	Wheat	186.6	195.9	238.9	244.4	...	...	159.4	116.6
42	Wine	75.0	56.8	60.9	72.0	...	102.2	80.9	83.8

C. OLD CASTILE-LEÓN (IN MARAVEDÍS) — Continued

		1535	1536	1537	1538	1539	1540	1541	1542
1	Almonds	15.5	19.0	19.1	20.5	17.0	20.3	19.0	20.0
2	Barley	62.3	87.1	71.7	69.1	121.0	97.5	59.8	90.4
3	Beef	4.1	4.6	...	3.9	3.5	4.0	4.4	4.0
4	Burlap	18.9	14.0	17.9	15.8	14.9	15.3	18.2	19.7
5	Candles, tallow	16.0	16.2	17.5	16.3	12.0	13.6	13.0	19.5
6	Cheese	7.9	12.0	8.0	...	8.0	14.0	8.0	15.0
7	Chestnuts	170.0	170.0	170.0	181.3	...	...	204.0	246.0
8	Chickens, spring	14.0	14.5	...	14.5	...	...	19.5	...
9	Chick-peas	284.0	375.0	513.8	425.0	544.0	459.0	237.9	357.0
10	Cinnamon	...	372.1	294.7	288.6	488.7	...	480.0	400.0
11	Cloves	...	46.0	22.0	24.5	36.4	31.0	39.6	25.0
12	Conger eel	12.6	...	14.9	12.5	15.8	12.3	16.3	17.0
13	Eggs	...	15.3	16.2	15.6	16.4	20.1	17.6	14.3
14	Figs	112.0	136.0	136.0	...	153.0	170.0	102.0	119.0
15	Fish, fresh	12.0	6.8	11.0	13.0	8.5	9.0	10.4	11.0
16	Hens	...	34.0	...	39.0	28.9	36.0	36.3	36.0
17	Honey	723.6	601.9	816.0	728.5	833.5	625.1	529.3	612.0
18	Incense	...	74.0	55.0	68.0	55.5	60.0	62.0	68.0
19	Kid	14.2	13.2	...	14.1	14.2	9.1	13.9	...
20	Lambs	182.9	195.4	227.9	163.8	176.3	178.6	175.9	196.6
21	Lard	15.7	15.5	17.0	17.0	17.0	17.0	16.8	16.9
22	Lime	...	37.4	...	39.7	32.0	32.0	30.0	...
23	Linen	20.2	23.5	23.7	24.8	22.2	18.0	26.0	24.1
24	Mutton	7.8	9.0	8.9	8.0	5.5	8.0	8.0	...
25	Nails, large	...	...	11.4	12.9	11.0	10.6	11.0	11.0
26	Olive oil	310.3	310.0	361.8	337.9	393.0	408.4	388.3	374.0
27	Olives	20.0	25.0	22.0	20.0	21.0	21.0	24.0	24.0
28	Oranges	59.5	45.5	72.5	89.5	107.3	61.2	68.2	50.2
29	Pepper	...	127.6	125.0	138.9	123.3	113.4	136.0	140.0
30	Perch	3.0	6.0	5.8	4.5	4.0	4.7	3.8	4.8
31	Plaster of Paris	22.0	...	24.0	26.7	...	...	24.8	25.5
32	Raisins	200.0	250.0	225.0	227.0	239.3	173.5	172.8	191.4
33	Rice	...	245.0	224.0	200.0	237.5	275.0	262.5	262.5
34	Rye	60.3	81.0	67.6	88.7	181.8	138.7	120.5	135.3
35	Saffron	...	80.0	80.0	55.0	53.4	34.0	42.0	44.0
36	Sardines	...	48.5	47.7	40.7	57.7	61.7	53.4	63.0
37	Soap	357.5	301.7	291.6	301.7	376.3	382.1	348.6	321.8
38	Sugar	745.0	625.0	809.2	1042.0	976.5	969.5	1025.7	927.5
39	Trout	...	19.2	17.3	19.8	19.3	18.6	18.0	18.6
40	Wax, yellow	46.6	46.7	54.3	49.7	43.2	46.1	53.0	43.2
41	Wheat	77.9	118.7	101.8	122.1	236.4	217.4	143.3	186.2
42	Wine	49.2	38.0	154.5	117.8	88.0	32.2	98.0	80.0

C. OLD CASTILE–LEÓN (IN MARAVEDÍS) — CONTINUED

		1543	1544	1545	1546	1547	1548	1549	1550
1	Almonds	20.0	22.0	22.0	28.0	21.0	20.0	22.1	20.0
2	Barley	95.8	74.1	106.2	136.0	90.9	111.4	128.0	85.4
3	Beef	4.6	4.4	3.9	4.2	4.8	5.3	5.0	6.0
4	Burlap	19.2	17.0	18.2	13.8	19.8	23.0	21.5	...
5	Candles, tallow	17.0	15.5	13.7	14.1	16.3	26.2	20.0	23.6
6	Cheese	17.5	7.8	11.0	13.0	9.7	17.0	15.0	19.0
7	Chestnuts	164.0	204.0	195.5	187.0	...	...	261.7	263.0
8	Chickens, spring	13.9	...	12.0	15.0	17.3	17.0	25.0	17.9
9	Chick-peas	...	408.0	442.0	...	...	403.0	...	...
10	Cinnamon	300.8	294.7	374.0	358.0	350.0	294.7	270.1	270.1
11	Cloves	24.0	24.0	23.0	26.6	24.5	24.0	23.0	22.0
12	Conger eel	14.1	16.0	13.4	14.4	15.3	17.0	17.0	17.0
13	Eggs	15.6	...	...	20.2	19.7	24.6	15.1	20.9
14	Figs	136.0	136.0	148.8	136.0	136.0	...	119.0	153.0
15	Fish, fresh	11.0	11.0	10.0	9.3	11.0	13.2	11.5	10.5
16	Hens	29.2	29.5	24.7	28.1	25.7	34.8	27.0	37.0
17	Honey	884.0	890.5	667.9	765.0	722.5	688.5	935.0	799.7
18	Incense	...	85.0	133.0	120.0	92.0	120.0	102.0	85.0
19	Kid	9.1	19.8	12.0	14.8	15.1	17.5	21.3	21.3
20	Lambs	188.1	190.2	206.4	198.8	196.3	197.9	182.0	219.2
21	Lard	21.3	19.0	17.3	16.8	21.2	28.1	34.0	33.2
22	Lime	34.0	47.0	38.3	42.5	34.0	51.0	52.0	...
23	Linen	26.5	25.0	27.0	25.8	28.1	29.7	34.0	35.2
24	Mutton	...	7.5	...	8.5	7.8	10.3	9.0	11.6
25	Nails, large	11.0	12.0	13.0	12.0	...	15.0	16.8	17.7
26	Olive oil	442.0	388.8	403.8	425.3	443.6	442.0	535.5	510.0
27	Olives	25.0	26.0	28.0	26.6	30.0	51.0	37.5	30.0
28	Oranges	51.0	67.1	48.2	64.7	55.0	83.0	102.0	102.0
29	Pepper	136.0	...	136.0	136.0	136.0	140.0	129.5	136.0
30	Perch	4.9	4.5	4.0	3.3	6.0	5.5	5.2	6.7
31	Plaster of Paris	20.0	28.0	31.3	25.5	22.2	22.0	26.5	35.5
32	Raisins	248.7	275.5	287.5	181.0	197.0	204.0	136.0	219.6
33	Rice	300.0	287.4	287.4	325.0	290.5	291.7	340.0	282.5
34	Rye	133.9	87.8	126.8	181.3	103.0	90.7	128.3	89.3
35	Saffron	51.0	51.0	39.0	34.0	79.8	81.3	99.3	91.0
36	Sardines	53.8	51.3	41.3	49.8	43.0	39.2	33.2	35.0
37	Soap	352.0	375.0	347.3	337.6	379.2	362.5	478.7	459.1
38	Sugar	1053.3	1160.0	960.9	901.1	850.0	1250.0	968.0	764.5
39	Trout	22.8	25.2	20.0	21.7	21.2	23.2	20.4	26.3
40	Wax, yellow	42.6	45.7	46.6	45.0	45.0	48.0	51.0	51.0
41	Wheat	173.8	115.3	176.1	290.1	163.8	153.0	187.0	138.9
42	Wine	168.4	134.0	89.6	133.5	81.8	88.0	119.8	210.5

D. VALENCIA (IN DINERS)

		1501	1502	1503	1504	1505	1506	1507	1508
1	Almonds	...	...	...	...	...	...	...	...
2	Ashes	...	...	...	...	8.0	...	...	18.0
3	Beans, kidney	...	...	...	14.8	14.4	14.0	...	13.7
4	Bricks	320.0	283.0	254.7	324.5	391.3	...	288.0	283.0
5	Carob beans	...	...	...	...	...	...	...	...
6	Charcoal	...	...	...	...	...	...	...	...
7	Cheese	...	...	...	45.0	40.6	43.9	40.0	40.8
8	Chickens, spring	...	...	...	...	10.0	...	...	...
9	Chick-peas	...	...	10.0	11.7	10.5	21.0	...	14.8
10	Eggs	...	...	...	9.7	8.0	8.4	8.0	9.3
11	Firewood	14.8	14.0	13.1	13.4	13.8	13.6	13.5	13.8
12	Fish, Calp	...	...	...	...	60.0	55.0	60.0	60.0
13	Fish, fresh	...	...	...	40.0	39.9	42.2	40.0	36.7
14	Flax	6.2	6.5	6.7	7.1	7.7	7.7	8.1	8.3
15	Grits, barley	...	...	...	...	40.0	40.0	...	35.0
16	Grits, wheat	...	...	...	...	...	...	...	...
17	Hake	...	...	...	120.0	120.0	124.5	91.5	94.0
18	Hemp	...	...	...	...	...	...	...	...
19	Hens	...	...	...	...	26.2	24.3	...	22.6
20	Honey	...	...	...	...	488.3	472.5	...	...
21	Kid	...	...	...	...	52.0	63.5	...	...
22	Lard	...	8.0	...	9.0	8.0	...	...	...
23	Lime	...	36.0	54.0	54.0	58.0	53.0	...	51.0
24	Mutton	...	...	13.0	...	13.0	13.0	13.0	13.0
25	Olive oil	77.8	101.3	130.7	124.6	118.6	127.0	143.3	162.9
26	Pepper	...	...	...	6.0	5.0	5.3	...	...
27	Plaster of Paris	...	42.2	40.7	40.7	40.7	42.0	36.0	46.6
28	Raisins	...	...	...	...	34.9	43.9	...	30.1
29	Rice	...	...	...	521.2	633.3	591.4	526.6	592.8
30	Saffron	...	...	...	...	417.7	544.0	...	...
31	Salt	...	...	...	...	96.0	...	96.0	96.0
32	Sardines	...	...	...	26.9	26.9	...	...	...
33	Saucers	...	...	...	...	...	...	...	72.0
34	Shrouds	11.0	...	...	...	...	...	...	...
35	Soap	...	...	...	77.6	88.3	93.1	93.1	105.1
36	Sugar	...	...	...	...	13.0	13.0	12.0	...
37	Tuna fish	...	...	...	5.0	5.2	5.0	...	3.9
38	Vinegar	6.0	...	8.5	9.0	...	8.0	6.7	...
39	Wax, yellow	...	...	...	...	...	...	...	20.0
40	Wheat	319.3	523.0	713.6	508.0	561.5	524.0	497.0	537.8
41	Wine	15.1	18.2	24.0	13.8	13.3	14.5	15.3	13.9

D. VALENCIA (IN DINERS) — Continued

		1509	1510	1511	1512	1513	1514	1515
1	Almonds	...	...	...	50.0	45.0	45.4	45.0
2	Ashes	12.0	...	...	22.0	20.1	...	21.0
3	Beans, kidney	...	...	...	10.0	16.2	10.7	12.2
4	Bricks	294.4	...	306.3	306.5	301.8	300.0	300.0
5	Carob beans	...	...	...	10.0	13.0	15.3	...
6	Charcoal	...	...	...	131.3	124.4	115.8	100.7
7	Cheese	40.0	...	...	33.3	38.3	34.7	37.5
8	Chickens, spring	...	...	...	12.1	12.7	14.2	11.3
9	Chick-peas	12.1	...	...	10.5	15.8	18.0	14.5
10	Eggs	...	...	...	7.5	7.9	8.1	7.9
11	Firewood	15.5	15.0	17.0	16.3	15.9	16.3	16.4
12	Fish, Calp	...	...	...	65.0	63.2	75.0	73.4
13	Fish, fresh	...	...	...	40.4	51.0	57.2	51.9
14	Flax	7.7	7.9	8.1	8.6	8.2	7.4	7.2
15	Grits, barley	...	...	...	30.0	30.0	30.0	30.0
16	Grits, wheat	...	...	...	30.0	30.0	30.0	30.0
17	Hake	96.0	...	...	153.0	159.0	108.0	138.0
18	Hemp	...	...	...	48.3	...	...	...
19	Hens	...	...	...	22.4	23.1	25.3	24.7
20	Honey	...	...	...	462.0	618.0	452.3	447.0
21	Kid	...	...	...	71.1	78.7	105.9	...
22	Lard	...	...	...	...	10.6	6.8	9.5
23	Lime	57.0	48.6	57.2	63.3	59.9	56.1	54.6
24	Mutton	13.0	...	13.0	13.0	13.0	13.0	...
25	Olive oil	111.0	112.3	98.4	99.2	111.3	129.3	105.8
26	Pepper	...	...	...	4.5	4.2	4.2	4.9
27	Plaster of Paris	...	40.7	39.0	36.0	36.0	36.5	39.0
28	Raisins	...	...	...	27.8	33.0	28.0	26.4
29	Rice	...	...	...	540.1	540.1	480.7	490.2
30	Saffron	...	...	...	544.0	318.0	360.0	336.0
31	Salt	...	...	...	96.0	96.0	96.7	96.0
32	Sardines	57.7	...	...	40.4	...	48.1	39.2
33	Saucers	...	...	...	68.0	60.0	60.0	60.0
34	Shrouds	...	...	...	15.0	...	12.0	12.0
35	Soap	...	...	...	79.2	95.7	118.2	93.1
36	Sugar	...	...	...	13.0	15.0	16.0	18.0
37	Tuna fish	...	...	...	6.0	5.7	5.8	4.5
38	Vinegar	4.0	9.0	...	7.5	15.0	...	...
39	Wax, yellow	17.0	...	...	19.0	...	20.3	24.0
40	Wheat	415.0	380.8	364.3	345.3	370.5	387.7	378.8
41	Wine	17.0	16.4	16.9	13.8	12.0	11.5	12.7

D. VALENCIA (IN DINERS) — CONTINUED

		1516	1517	1518	1519	1520	1521	1522
1	Almonds	50.0	57.5	60.0	54.4	...	...	50.0
2	Ashes	...	21.5	22.5	19.5	16.8	17.8	25.0
3	Beans, kidney	13.8	13.8	13.8	...	...	...	...
4	Bricks	300.0	300.0	...	300.0	435.3	300.0	300.0
5	Carob beans	19.0	13.3	...	...	...	...	12.0
6	Charcoal	119.3	154.7	118.0	138.8	105.0	106.7	109.6
7	Cheese	60.0	40.0	40.8	40.0	...	...	...
8	Chickens, spring	14.1	17.9	9.3	10.4	13.9	16.1	12.0
9	Chick-peas	14.0	14.0	14.1	14.5	...	17.3	...
10	Eggs	8.8	8.2	9.0	8.1	8.9	11.4	13.2
11	Firewood	15.2	...	...	18.8	16.8	16.5	18.8
12	Fish, Calp	70.0	70.0	70.0	70.0	...	...	70.0
13	Fish, fresh	50.0	56.3	45.0	60.0	...	...	60.0
14	Flax	7.6	7.7	8.2	8.7	7.9	8.6	8.6
15	Grits, barley	20.0	29.2	30.0	30.0	...	...	30.0
16	Grits, wheat	...	29.4	30.0	30.0	...	...	30.0
17	Hake	153.0	150.0	168.0	156.0	...	180.0	138.0
18	Hemp	...	...	...	30.0	30.0	...	50.0
19	Hens	25.1	24.2	27.8	24.9	27.4	27.0	41.6
20	Honey	470.3	436.5	649.5	456.0	452.7	501.0	554.0
21	Kid	...	104.0	72.0	72.0	...	...	96.0
22	Lard	8.0	8.0	9.0	8.0	...	...	7.0
23	Lime	59.3	66.0	61.5	65.3	61.7	57.0	65.1
24	Mutton	13.0	13.0	13.0	13.0	...	...	13.0
25	Olive oil	111.4	109.2	125.0	138.5	131.8	134.8	184.9
26	Pepper	6.5	5.1	5.8	6.0	...	...	6.0
27	Plaster of Paris	39.0	40.0	...	41.0	39.3	39.0	40.0
28	Raisins	30.0	42.4	50.8	...	...	40.2	47.2
29	Rice	567.1	623.8	523.9	490.2	...	...	...
30	Saffron	299.0	272.0	372.0	291.4	...	...	...
31	Salt	...	96.0	96.0	96.0	96.0	...	...
32	Sardines	80.8	50.0	38.5	...	...	...	...
33	Saucers	...	64.0	60.0	66.0	...	...	...
34	Shrouds	12.0	...	12.5	12.0	13.5	13.3	12.5
35	Soap	...	102.0	108.0	108.6	...	144.8	147.4
36	Sugar	14.0	16.0	19.7	29.0	20.0	9.8	11.0
37	Tuna fish	4.0	5.4	4.0	4.0	...	...	4.0
38	Vinegar	4.0	9.0	...	...	...	...	...
39	Wax, yellow	26.0	26.0	26.0	24.0	...	...	26.5
40	Wheat	433.5	387.1	390.9	400.0	410.2	765.8	1101.0
41	Wine	15.3	17.3	13.6	16.3	11.8	19.3	18.1

D. VALENCIA (IN DINERS) — Continued

		1523	1524	1525	1526	1527	1528	1529
1	Almonds	77.5	55.0	...	50.0	50.0	50.0	...
2	Ashes	18.0	18.2	18.9	17.6	14.3	14.3	13.4
3	Beans, kidney	...	18.0	17.0	14.0	18.0	18.0	20.8
4	Bricks	339.6	344.7	349.8	360.0	356.0	349.8	...
5	Carob beans	13.0	...	11.0	10.5	13.8	11.3	10.5
6	Charcoal	99.8	96.6	103.9	110.1	97.7	114.1	98.0
7	Cheese	45.0	42.5	66.3	51.3	55.6	40.0	...
8	Chickens, spring	...	...	...	...	...	15.1	...
9	Chick-peas	24.0	21.9	14.2	15.0	18.0	...	...
10	Eggs	11.5	10.4	10.4	11.0	11.0	10.9	11.2
11	Firewood	17.5	17.8	19.2	16.0	17.9	17.8	17.0
12	Fish, Calp	...	...	70.0	61.3	65.0	60.0	63.3
13	Fish, fresh	48.8	55.0	53.1	46.0	52.0	46.3	43.3
14	Flax	8.7	10.0	9.2	9.5	9.0	9.0	8.1
15	Grits, barley	35.0	30.0	30.0	30.8	30.0	30.0	30.0
16	Grits, wheat	35.0	30.0	30.0	26.7	27.5	30.0	30.0
17	Hake	213.8	163.5	153.0	134.5	150.0	157.0	150.0
18	Hemp	100.0	...	...	...	...	57.5	...
19	Hens	28.8	34.1	27.0	27.8	35.0	35.7	27.2
20	Honey	569.3	501.3	495.0	574.0	475.0	474.0	639.8
21	Kid	...	66.0	78.0	84.0	99.0	90.0	99.4
22	Lard	7.3	...	...	10.0	10.3	8.0	9.0
23	Lime	59.5	64.5	62.0	65.3	61.5	61.0	55.0
24	Mutton	15.7	15.9	15.7	16.3	16.0	16.0	16.0
25	Olive oil	110.8	122.6	118.1	137.4	128.6	124.4	139.9
26	Pepper	8.0	7.3	6.0	7.0	...	6.4	...
27	Plaster of Paris	46.6	40.0	42.0	42.0	42.0	41.3	43.0
28	Raisins	48.9	46.4	49.2	43.1	55.4	39.5	59.3
29	Rice	558.1	598.5	591.0	582.8	727.3	737.5	761.6
30	Saffron	582.9	466.3	402.0	...	480.0	...	...
31	Salt	...	101.5	95.3	96.0	96.0	96.0	96.0
32	Sardines	...	...	120.0	...	76.9	49.0	48.5
33	Saucers	72.0	73.5	70.5	66.0	...	67.0	...
34	Shrouds	13.0	...	13.0	13.0	12.0	13.0	13.3
35	Soap	108.6	120.0	93.1	124.1	108.0	121.0	99.2
36	Sugar	17.0	24.5	21.0	19.0	19.8	...	...
37	Tuna fish	5.0	5.1	4.3	4.0	4.0	4.1	4.0
38	Vinegar	...	...	...	16.0	18.0	...	...
39	Wax, yellow	24.7	29.0	...	28.1	27.3	24.8	24.0
40	Wheat	576.5	570.9	466.5	474.8	562.5	512.4	789.0
41	Wine	12.8	10.7	17.8	17.5	16.9	22.3	15.3

D. VALENCIA (IN DINERS) — Continued

		1530	1531	1532	1533	1534	1535	1536
1	Almonds	...	75.0	...	...	...	...	60.0
2	Ashes	13.6	14.5	14.8	14.9	14.7	16.0	16.0
3	Beans, kidney	...	25.7	19.4	...	15.5	13.0	17.0
4	Bricks	360.0	330.0	316.3	333.3	360.0	339.6	396.2
5	Carob beans	15.0	...	...	...	...	...	...
6	Charcoal	112.5	127.7	167.5	109.9	107.6	125.2	139.9
7	Cheese	43.3	41.7	50.8	...	57.2	69.1	64.2
8	Chickens, spring	...	14.0	...	...	...	...	...
9	Chick-peas	...	27.0	18.8	...	18.5	20.0	14.0
10	Eggs	12.8	11.5	11.3	10.5	11.2	10.7	11.9
11	Firewood	15.7	15.1	19.4	17.0	16.8	20.2	20.8
12	Fish, Calp	70.0	66.7	70.0	...	67.5	71.3	70.8
13	Fish, fresh	55.0	51.3	49.2	...	50.8	51.3	51.7
14	Flax	7.6	8.5	8.9	8.5	8.1	8.5	8.4
15	Grits, barley	...	40.0	40.0	...	37.5	32.5	39.4
16	Grits, wheat	40.0	40.0	40.0	...	31.1	35.0	39.4
17	Hake	...	169.8	154.5	...	...	160.8	190.5
18	Hemp	...	60.0	75.0	...	...	...	75.6
19	Hens	28.7	36.0	31.2	28.1	28.7	30.0	30.3
20	Honey	766.5	601.0	708.0	560.0	545.8	470.7	546.6
21	Kid	...	...	...	...	114.0	95.9	...
22	Lard	9.0	10.0	8.9	...	8.0	8.0	10.0
23	Lime	56.0	53.0	57.2	61.4	64.0	66.0	66.0
24	Mutton	16.0	16.0	16.0	15.0	15.2	15.0	16.0
25	Olive oil	227.5	198.8	156.0	169.2	155.2	109.0	109.1
26	Pepper	...	8.0	6.5	...	6.0	6.0	6.0
27	Plaster of Paris	40.3	39.5	36.0	39.0	39.8	42.0	42.0
28	Raisins	63.5	57.1	78.4	76.2	54.5	53.6	67.3
29	Rice	831.8	794.0	607.6	...	737.3	675.9	657.6
30	Saffron	...	...	240.0	...	...	...	...
31	Salt	...	...	96.0	...	...	89.1	...
32	Sardines	...	63.1	51.9	...	36.0	46.7	53.8
33	Saucers	...	66.0	60.0	...	72.0	72.0	72.0
34	Shrouds	12.0	12.0	...	...	...	...	...
35	Soap	139.6	133.9	120.0	138.8	156.0	102.5	106.7
36	Sugar	...	17.0	...	...	...	...	...
37	Tuna fish	5.0	5.0	4.8	...	4.0	4.0	4.0
38	Vinegar	30.0	28.0	28.0	...	...	24.0	30.0
39	Wax, yellow	...	...	...	20.0	...	22.5	...
40	Wheat	796.0	640.6	567.5	629.3	595.6	531.5	554.3
41	Wine	14.9	24.0	27.4	20.2	28.6	20.8	20.0

D. VALENCIA (IN DINERS) — Continued

		1537	1538	1539	1540	1541	1542	1543
1	Almonds	...	...	...	...	...	80.0	...
2	Ashes	16.8	18.0	13.4	14.5	16.9	13.0	12.2
3	Beans, kidney	...	...	...	...	...	14.8	14.1
4	Bricks	417.6	369.7	401.3	406.1	397.5	384.1	378.1
5	Carob beans	...	...	...	...	...	...	...
6	Charcoal	142.3	135.1	88.0	145.8	108.5	114.7	...
7	Cheese	...	...	...	...	...	66.7	...
8	Chickens, spring	12.5	12.7	13.4	...	14.3	12.9	...
9	Chick-peas	...	...	...	...	...	18.0	15.0
10	Eggs	10.8	10.3	10.0	11.9	10.7	12.0	13.4
11	Firewood	19.4	17.3	17.6	17.8	16.6	17.2	18.5
12	Fish, Calp	70.0	...	...	...	60.0	68.8	75.0
13	Fish, fresh	40.0	...	...	...	45.0	51.9	42.5
14	Flax	8.7	9.9	8.9	8.5	10.4	9.3	9.2
15	Grits, barley	35.0	...	...	...	35.0	40.0	40.0
16	Grits, wheat	35.0	...	...	...	33.3	40.0	37.7
17	Hake	180.0	175.0	174.0	...	...	206.5	216.0
18	Hemp	40.0	...	...	61.7	50.0	60.0	...
19	Hens	32.7	29.1	27.8	28.4	29.9	31.8	33.5
20	Honey	537.5	693.5	729.4	678.8	582.7	630.0	644.0
21	Kid	104.0	96.0	96.0	142.0	...	...	...
22	Lard	12.0	12.0	8.0	...	...	10.0	10.0
23	Lime	58.8	61.6	58.2	60.0	64.1	60.0	62.0
24	Mutton	16.0	16.0	16.0	16.0	16.0	16.0	16.0
25	Olive oil	108.4	145.3	163.8	135.8	149.1	136.8	156.1
26	Pepper	...	...	...	...	...	...	...
27	Plaster of Paris	41.0	40.7	41.0	40.7	41.0	40.0	40.0
28	Raisins	57.5	96.9	70.8	59.0	58.7	45.7	60.9
29	Rice	554.0	621.8	...	...	615.6	683.3	...
30	Saffron	...	463.3	...	...	324.0	...	...
31	Salt	...	...	...	...	96.0	96.0	...
32	Sardines	...	...	...	...	...	...	70.2
33	Saucers	72.0	...	...	...	60.0	60.0	...
34	Shrouds	14.5	15.5	...	...	...	15.0	15.0
35	Soap	106.7	124.3	131.9	115.6	...	126.0	144.0
36	Sugar	12.0	18.0	23.0	...	...	...	15.2
37	Tuna fish	4.1	...	...	...	5.6	3.8	4.0
38	Vinegar	...	...	10.0	...	...	23.0	...
39	Wax, yellow	22.0	...	24.8	...	...	...	46.0
40	Wheat	445.5	482.8	606.0	837.0	534.0	692.8	559.3
41	Wine	19.5	21.4	27.1	17.7	23.1	24.2	18.9

D. VALENCIA (IN DINERS) — Continued

		1544	1545	1546	1547	1548	1549	1550
1	Almonds	...	70.0	90.0	...	...	...	90.0
2	Ashes	10.8	10.1	10.5	10.5	10.7	11.5	11.6
3	Beans, kidney	18.3	19.8	22.0	...	13.9	...	19.3
4	Bricks	399.6	432.5	447.2	...	480.0	452.8	451.4
5	Carob beans	...	...	...	14.6	10.0	22.2	27.0
6	Charcoal	114.3	131.7	134.5	158.5	171.0	131.2	...
7	Cheese	52.2	47.5	50.0	50.0	70.0	60.7	70.0
8	Chickens, spring	14.5	20.1	26.2	16.0	...	16.3	11.5
9	Chick-peas	20.5	21.6	25.4	22.0	22.0	19.5	20.0
10	Eggs	10.5	11.4	12.7	12.5	12.1	13.1	12.3
11	Firewood	18.4	19.0	16.5	17.0	17.5	17.3	18.4
12	Fish, Calp	65.0	71.7	70.0	70.0	72.5	...	70.0
13	Fish, fresh	48.8	56.7	60.0	55.0	60.0	55.4	58.9
14	Flax	9.2	9.1	9.2	9.2	8.6	9.8	12.2
15	Grits, barley	40.0	40.0	50.0	50.0	...	...	50.0
16	Grits, wheat	40.0	42.5	50.0	50.0	...	...	50.0
17	Hake	192.1	180.0	223.6	192.0	246.0	216.0	231.0
18	Hemp	65.0	60.0	70.0	55.0	75.0	...	...
19	Hens	31.4	27.6	33.0	36.9	32.4	31.2	36.7
20	Honey	720.0	478.0	579.0	474.0	756.0	838.0	809.5
21	Kid	...	124.0	...	...	...	92.3	...
22	Lard	10.7	11.3	11.0	8.0	9.0	8.7	15.0
23	Lime	58.0	60.0	62.0	69.0	61.5	66.0	69.0
24	Mutton	17.0	17.5	17.0	17.0	17.5	18.7	18.8
25	Olive oil	127.5	158.1	182.0	158.9	163.1	186.9	204.8
26	Pepper	...	6.5	7.3	7.7	7.6	7.3	7.8
27	Plaster of Paris	40.0	40.0	...	...	46.6	36.4	46.6
28	Raisins	57.5	77.5	73.1	57.9	74.9	107.0	55.9
29	Rice	677.9	843.9	1012.7	738.7	831.8	752.3	731.3
30	Saffron	312.0	...	340.1	...	773.0	768.0	768.0
31	Salt	108.9	...	156.0	...	96.0	132.0	96.0
32	Sardines	52.9	58.7	54.8	46.2	52.5	34.6	43.8
33	Saucers	60.0	60.0	...	66.0	...	...	72.0
34	Shrouds	18.0	18.0	18.0	18.0	...	19.0	18.0
35	Soap	113.0	113.0	134.0	144.0	150.0	162.0	163.1
36	Sugar	...	...	...	...	27.0	...	...
37	Tuna fish	4.6	3.0	3.0	3.0	4.8	4.0	3.9
38	Vinegar	...	...	...	24.0	...	12.0	26.0
39	Wax, yellow	...	36.0	22.0	...	...	32.3	33.0
40	Wheat	522.0	690.0	1020.0	770.3	672.0	776.5	734.5
41	Wine	15.7	25.6	28.2	17.6	23.6	33.7	25.4

APPENDIX IV

PRICES, 1551–1600 [1]

A. ANDALUSIA (IN MARAVEDÍS)

		1551	1554	1555	1557	1558	1559	1560
1	Almond oil, sweet	...	...	...	89.0	102.0	102.0	...
2	Almonds	586.5	637.5	671.5	677.9	640.3	545.4	544.0
3	Alum	17.0	25.0	...	...	...	...	...
4	Apples, cooking	139.8	150.5	86.0	102.1	...	...	...
5	Apples, pippin	120.0	140.0	99.2	...	...	...	...
6	Ashes	144.0	120.0	...	132.0	156.0	...	...
7	Barley	...	...	272.0	255.0	138.0	121.3	152.0
8	Beef	15.1	15.5	12.2	15.5	...	...	...
9	Butter	...	51.0	43.0	53.0	68.0	...	...
10	Candles, tallow	24.0	29.3	25.3	21.6	23.6	24.0	24.0
11	Charcoal	47.5	33.9	34.2	38.5	33.5	37.7	34.3
12	Cheese	408.0	362.7	399.0	391.5	311.0	375.0	...
13	Chestnuts	49.9	49.9	24.9	44.0	...	...	...
14	Chickens, spring	34.2	32.5	33.4	50.3	39.8	33.0	24.8
15	Chick-peas	187.0	583.8	...	661.7	...	...	...
16	Cinnamon	...	414.4	...	...	541.9	...	...
17	Cloves	...	...	...	...	...	...	...
18	Dace	22.8	...	28.3	18.9	...	...	...
19	Dogfish	10.8	...	12.5	20.9	...	...	...
20	Dogfish, spotted	...	17.0	17.0	17.0	...	...	...
21	Eggs	...	...	...	46.9	...	...	...
22	Firewood	136.0	99.3	85.0	76.5	...	80.0	76.5
23	Flounders	22.0	...	...	...	...	...	...
24	Garlic	15.0	9.0	...	...	...	...	...
25	Hake	17.0	15.5	16.8	...	...	...	...
26	Hares	29.5	36.0	37.3	42.0	...	...	...
27	Hens	64.0	67.8	63.2	112.5	121.0	77.1	66.3
28	Honey	530.4	546.0	468.0	559.0	623.2	520.0	663.0
29	Kid	117.1	117.9	108.0	107.4	...	...	...
30	Lard	29.1	26.2	29.4	...	...	...	...
31	Milk	8.0	10.0	...	...	...	...	...
32	Mutton	26.1	29.7	25.0	25.1	25.1	26.7	22.0
33	Olive oil	221.0	214.5	234.9	204.5	236.0	212.5	238.0
34	Orange blossoms	6.7	10.6	6.7	6.0	...	5.8	...
35	Pepper	...	...	152.8	...	...	...	...
36	Pitch	8.0	5.5	12.0	13.5	...	...	...
37	Plaster of Paris	179.3	160.0	152.0	184.0	...	...	...
38	Pork, fresh	20.7	17.7	26.0	22.0	...	...	...
39	Quail	37.1	35.0	40.0	48.2	...	...	...
40	Raisins	918.0	838.2	500.0	495.8	650.3	612.0	442.0
41	Resin	...	...	12.0	10.0	...	...	...
42	Rice	10.0	16.4	16.3	26.3	...	...	...
43	Saffron	...	...	...	...	...	...	...
44	Sardines	20.9	22.5	15.6	20.9	...	...	...
45	Sea bream	...	19.2	...	...	...	...	...
46	Sea eel, Mediterranean .	...	28.0	24.1	22.0	...	...	...
47	Soap	181.6	194.2	194.2	194.8	194.2	201.9	211.7
48	Sole	...	...	...	...	...	...	...
49	Sugar	875.5	1131.0	998.3	680.0	816.0	880.9	1180.0
50	Veal	20.3	25.5	25.5	25.0	...	...	...
51	Vinegar	79.3	97.0	141.5	68.0	...	...	...
52	Walnuts	20.0	17.0	22.5	17.0	...	...	...
53	Wax, white	76.0	80.0	80.0	80.0	86.9	88.7	85.0
54	Wax, yellow	69.0	80.0	74.0	60.0	77.0	77.7	74.0
55	Wheat	...	188.0	578.0	561.0	210.5	187.0	...
56	Wine	...	171.0	121.2	68.0	93.5	119.0	...

[1] Appendix II lists the metrological units in terms of which prices are recorded and furnishes keys for the reduction of metrological units to the metric system and price quotations to a fixed weight of silver.

A. ANDALUSIA (IN MARAVEDÍS) — Continued

		1561	1562	1563	1564	1565	1566	1567
1	Almond oil, sweet	106.3	102.0	104.0	102.0	102.0	102.0	101.2
2	Almonds	563.8	561.0	714.0	816.0	793.0	513.1	800.4
3	Alum	...	17.0	17.0	...	...	...	22.0
4	Apples, cooking	...	...	...	...	119.0	...	...
5	Apples, pippin	...	...	...	...	...	...	...
6	Ashes	...	...	...	204.7	201.0	147.6	135.4
7	Barley	136.0	153.0	114.8	136.0	140.0	...	163.5
8	Beef	...	...	...	...	...	...	...
9	Butter	102.0	51.0	...	68.0	68.0	...	72.3
10	Candles, tallow	26.5	25.9	21.6	21.2	33.3	34.0	27.0
11	Charcoal	37.0	37.6	42.8	40.1	40.0	41.8	39.5
12	Cheese	...	510.0	442.0	425.0	544.0	...	...
13	Chestnuts	...	...	...	...	...	...	...
14	Chickens, spring	35.2	50.0	44.4	35.3	40.4	38.8	39.9
15	Chick-peas	...	884.0	306.0	...	...	...	...
16	Cinnamon	...	...	1490.1	...	1625.6	...	541.9
17	Cloves	...	...	...	...	...	...	...
18	Dace	...	...	...	...	...	...	...
19	Dogfish	...	...	...	...	...	...	...
20	Dogfish, spotted	...	...	...	...	...	...	...
21	Eggs	...	45.4	...	...	...	...	...
22	Firewood	81.3	110.5	...	...	68.0	...	42.0
23	Flounders	...	...	...	...	...	...	...
24	Garlic	30.0	...	...	...	...	...	...
25	Hake	...	...	...	...	...	...	...
26	Hares	...	...	...	...	...	...	...
27	Hens	80.6	106.4	98.6	79.7	86.8	84.6	84.7
28	Honey	1254.6	1088.0	751.4	557.0	557.6	...	582.2
29	Kid	133.3	...	...	...	...	...	...
30	Lard	...	119.0	...	38.0	...	...	...
31	Milk	...	...	...	...	...	...	...
32	Mutton	25.1	42.4	32.2	30.5	32.3	34.5	43.9
33	Olive oil	273.2	419.1	286.2	348.5	289.0	359.2	377.0
34	Orange blossoms	...	...	...	...	...	...	...
35	Pepper	...	...	...	...	...	...	...
36	Pitch	...	12.0	12.0	13.0	13.3	17.5	11.0
37	Plaster of Paris	...	...	...	...	...	...	...
38	Pork, fresh	26.1	...	...	...	...	...	...
39	Quail	...	...	...	...	...	...	...
40	Raisins	640.3	658.8	714.0	680.0	750.0	672.0	964.8
41	Resin	...	12.0	...	13.0	11.0	15.0	11.0
42	Rice	...	...	11.3	...	...	...	...
43	Saffron	...	...	...	...	...	...	...
44	Sardines	...	...	...	...	...	...	...
45	Sea bream	...	...	...	...	...	...	...
46	Sea eel, Mediterranean .	...	...	...	...	...	...	...
47	Soap	245.7	389.1	294.7	299.8	299.4	300.0	307.0
48	Sole	...	...	...	...	...	...	...
49	Sugar	1248.0	...	1326.0	1326.0	1326.0	1202.3	1275.0
50	Veal	34.0	...	...	...	...	...	...
51	Vinegar	...	...	68.0	148.7	114.8	...	64.0
52	Walnuts	...	...	...	...	...	...	...
53	Wax, white	86.3	82.5	79.3	81.3	85.0	97.5	102.0
54	Wax, yellow	76.0	80.4	76.7	73.3	82.4	87.5	102.0
55	Wheat	306.0	561.0	...	204.0	...	255.0	310.0
56	Wine	102.0	150.8	116.8	120.4	133.4	156.3	207.5

A. ANDALUSIA (IN MARAVEDÍS) — Continued

		1569	1571	1572	1573	1576	1580	1582
1	Almond oil, sweet	110.5	...	119.0	...	110.0	99.0	125.4
2	Almonds	765.0	1109.7	...	918.0	1122.0	714.0	937.8
3	Alum	...	...	...	25.5	22.0	...	21.0
4	Apples, cooking	...	...	...	236.8	170.0	216.8	136.0
5	Apples, pippin	340.0	...	...	595.0	157.5	110.7	200.0
6	Ashes	162.5	143.9	133.6	158.6	156.2	189.2	168.4
7	Barley	187.0	...	...	136.0	...	...	...
8	Beef	...	...	...	24.4	22.5	23.6	25.4
9	Butter	68.0	76.0	...	85.0	31.0	113.5	80.8
10	Candles, tallow	34.0	51.0	...	28.0	35.7	32.0	31.0
11	Charcoal	42.0	36.0	46.0	46.0	50.0	72.0	59.8
12	Cheese	...	476.0	...	510.0	476.0	680.0	459.0
13	Chestnuts	...	...	...	66.0	66.0	107.7	90.5
14	Chickens, spring	42.9	63.1	57.7	42.3	55.7	52.2	67.2
15	Chick-peas	...	...	...	476.0	750.0	629.0	...
16	Cinnamon	541.9	...	...	446.2	451.0	510.0	544.0
17	Cloves	482.8	...	...	...	482.8	680.0	544.0
18	Dace	56.6	...	...	45.5	41.7	48.8	46.6
19	Dogfish	...	...	...	11.5	26.8	25.0	44.3
20	Dogfish, spotted	17.0	...	...	19.5	19.5	20.0	19.8
21	Eggs	44.3	...	...	38.5	38.4	42.5	68.8
22	Firewood	...	...	...				
23	Flounders	...	...	...	40.5	46.3	46.5	46.0
24	Garlic	...	...	...	26.0	21.3	51.0	...
25	Hake	25.6	...	...	27.5	27.3	34.0	32.0
26	Hares	...	...	...	34.0	55.3	56.6	63.1
27	Hens	106.2	121.0	131.0	102.5	99.9	147.1	158.9
28	Honey	735.5	836.4	975.0	...	834.7	663.0	707.2
29	Kid	...	...	...	189.2	173.0	202.0	194.6
30	Lard	68.0	...	...	40.0	42.5	51.0	51.0
31	Milk	14.0	...	...	26.0	...	...	...
32	Mutton	...	...	...	38.1	32.9	36.7	36.4
33	Olive oil	263.5	...	272.0	277.4	...	272.0	382.5
34	Orange blossoms	...	...	...	8.1	9.3	14.0	10.0
35	Pepper	195.3	...	...	140.1	140.1	187.0	187.0
36	Pitch	10.0	...	...	...	15.4	20.0	18.7
37	Plaster of Paris	...	...	...	248.0	...	304.4	408.0
38	Pork, fresh	...	...	...	28.1	27.9	32.6	36.3
39	Quail	...	...	...	53.0	56.7	28.0	61.8
40	Raisins	956.5	714.0	544.0	...	476.0	450.5	501.5
41	Resin	10.0	...	...	...	12.0	10.0	11.8
42	Rice	16.7	...	...	19.5	17.0	24.1	20.3
43	Saffron	1040.0	1222.0	...	1381.9	1268.8	476.0	2244.0
44	Sardines	...	...	...	18.0	21.6	28.6	34.0
45	Sea bream	...	...	...	53.0	45.7	62.0	46.5
46	Sea eel, Mediterranean	...	...	...	22.0	57.5	33.0	71.3
47	Soap	295.3	304.0	283.9	289.0	347.3	347.4	431.5
48	Sole	93.5	...	...	104.7	119.0	85.0	102.0
49	Sugar	1227.2	1355.8	1371.0	1521.3	1526.8	1326.0	1454.4
50	Veal	...	...	...	36.7	38.8	42.5	43.8
51	Vinegar	91.0	83.0	...	119.0	83.8	...	114.5
52	Walnuts	...	...	...	34.0	25.7	35.5	33.0
53	Wax, white	102.0	110.0	113.5	109.5	114.5	113.4	117.5
54	Wax, yellow	102.0	85.0	110.0	85.0	106.3	93.5	106.0
55	Wheat	...	...	238.0	...	...	...	816.0
56	Wine	125.7	272.0	178.5	...	136.0	149.0	150.5

A. ANDALUSIA (IN MARAVEDÍS) — Continued

		1584	1585	1587	1588	1589	1591	1592
1	Almond oil, sweet	136.0	136.0	115.3	114.1	116.9	121.1	121.9
2	Almonds	1156.0	1173.0	1075.3	...	765.0	850.0	1156.0
3	Alum	21.0	24.0	30.0	...	26.0	24.0	24.0
4	Apples, cooking	203.0	198.3	178.5	119.0	204.0	178.5	161.5
5	Apples, pippin	160.0	130.0	160.0	120.0	110.0	120.0	120.0
6	Ashes	179.5	187.0	207.8	207.2	190.6	181.7	140.6
7	Barley	408.0	170.0	204.0	396.4	510.0	238.0	251.6
8	Beef	24.9	26.6	25.9	23.2	22.2	28.9	28.5
9	Butter	76.5	76.0	87.0	87.2	75.9	108.0	102.0
10	Candles, tallow	35.8	29.4	28.2	27.6	35.3	28.6	28.0
11	Charcoal	68.0	68.0	52.0	60.0	46.0	56.0	56.0
12	Cheese	484.5	442.0	425.0	476.0	685.1	544.0	493.0
13	Chestnuts	115.0	64.0	85.0	106.0	102.0	68.0	78.5
14	Chickens, spring	55.4	63.2	50.2	53.8	65.8	62.7	55.8
15	Chick-peas	697.0	578.0	561.0	748.0	1003.0	969.0	918.0
16	Cinnamon	517.5	509.0	561.0	527.0	374.0	476.0	493.0
17	Cloves	476.0	374.0	442.3	510.0	476.0	476.0	476.0
18	Dace	40.4	50.7	50.2	51.3	46.8	52.8	60.4
19	Dogfish	37.9	20.9	22.0	35.0	26.0	39.4	40.3
20	Dogfish, spotted	23.5	23.0	24.0	24.0	24.0	25.3	24.5
21	Eggs	63.1	69.6	49.1	61.3	71.3	69.0	64.5
22	Firewood	59.5	...	...	...	65.5	74.7	50.5
23	Flounders	42.6	48.2	62.5	51.0	52.0	52.9	49.8
24	Garlic	20.0	34.0	22.0	26.0	44.5	48.0	26.0
25	Hake	32.0	32.0	32.7	32.5	32.5	32.0	33.8
26	Hares	51.0	59.4	60.0	55.7	68.0	63.1	37.1
27	Hens	140.9	147.1	102.7	115.1	138.0	179.3	128.6
28	Honey	729.3	707.2	443.3	...	748.0	530.4	527.3
29	Kid	210.1	194.7	190.6	192.2	185.8	193.8	185.0
30	Lard	59.5	63.0	46.8	48.8	55.0	42.5	58.7
31	Milk	24.0	25.0	16.0	21.2	21.3	22.3	24.0
32	Mutton	45.4	41.7	36.7	35.2	39.7	40.5	36.2
33	Olive oil	382.5	314.8	...	352.8	386.0	252.2	294.3
34	Orange blossoms	10.0	13.0	12.5	6.0	7.0	7.0	32.0
35	Pepper	204.0	238.0	272.0	255.0	272.0	238.0	243.7
36	Pitch	12.5	13.5	16.4	14.0	8.4	14.0	18.0
37	Plaster of Paris	278.4	306.0	289.0	293.2	316.3	310.7	297.3
38	Pork, fresh	40.7	40.1	28.9	29.0	35.7	38.9	37.3
39	Quail	72.3	65.2	68.3	66.0	74.3	64.0	68.0
40	Raisins	725.5	1020.0	892.7	637.5	530.0	813.5	926.5
41	Resin	12.5	13.3	20.3	12.2	10.5	20.7	20.8
42	Rice	17.2	17.1	24.5	20.8	21.5	27.6	36.0
43	Saffron	1972.0	1224.0	...	1564.0	1462.0	1479.0	1385.5
44	Sardines	28.2	30.0	34.0	26.6	31.4	24.5	26.6
45	Sea bream	57.5	33.0	34.0	48.5	43.5	36.0	43.0
46	Sea eel, Mediterranean	22.0	83.8	34.5	68.0	30.5	49.0	48.8
47	Soap	425.0	389.0	381.4	396.7	407.8	385.3	359.1
48	Sole	...	102.0	...	110.5	68.0	93.5	102.0
49	Sugar	1476.5	1416.3	1508.8	1331.9	1597.1	1604.9	1698.5
50	Veal	41.6	44.8	45.2	39.7	37.9	44.2	44.5
51	Vinegar	93.5	102.0	153.0	...	108.0	136.0	104.0
52	Walnuts	34.0	37.0	...	28.4	31.2	34.0	33.3
53	Wax, white	124.0	116.6	119.0	116.1	119.0	117.7	114.0
54	Wax, yellow	113.0	106.0	119.0	118.2	119.0	112.5	102.0
55	Wheat	1003.0	331.5	467.5	735.3	1119.9	799.0	601.0
56	Wine	242.3	200.0	136.0	221.0	...	136.0	178.6

A. ANDALUSIA (IN MARAVEDÍS) — Continued

		1593	1594	1595	1596	1598	1599	1600
1	Almond oil, sweet	130.2	130.3	110.3	130.6	204.0	164.3	146.6
2	Almonds	850.0	702.0	1088.0	1434.1	1402.5	1275.0	1224.0
3	Alum	24.0	24.0	...	34.0	42.0	...	24.0
4	Apples, cooking	170.0	178.5	199.8	233.8	212.5	284.8	204.0
5	Apples, pippin	107.5	100.0	135.0	157.5	130.0	170.0	200.0
6	Ashes	183.3	152.0	136.0	136.0	148.8	144.5	...
7	Barley	341.0	204.0	284.8	340.0	612.0	459.0	269.5
8	Beef	30.2	28.9	27.9	29.4	28.8	33.0	37.3
9	Butter	88.0	83.5	106.3	110.0	136.0	119.0	131.8
10	Candles, tallow	30.3	39.7	32.6	31.3	34.0	34.0	57.8
11	Charcoal	56.0	52.0	60.0	72.0	64.0	64.0	76.5
12	Cheese	544.0	476.0	408.0	527.0	663.0	884.0	714.0
13	Chestnuts	102.0	73.7	80.5	119.0	102.0	...	102.0
14	Chickens, spring	57.0	52.2	46.8	50.4	65.2	89.3	76.4
15	Chick-peas	833.0	663.0	442.0	544.0	901.0	960.5	714.0
16	Cinnamon	493.0	476.0	487.3	527.0	510.0	510.0	490.2
17	Cloves	578.0	815.0	612.0	558.9	521.3	476.0	464.7
18	Dace	46.4	50.5	52.5	54.7	44.2	40.0	46.4
19	Dogfish	27.5	34.0	37.0	45.5	26.0	27.5	45.4
20	Dogfish, spotted	26.0	26.0	26.0	...	28.0	31.5	31.4
21	Eggs	66.8	67.5	58.5	65.4	73.6	94.5	85.5
22	Firewood	86.0	60.0	60.0	110.0	76.0	73.3	76.5
23	Flounders	47.5	54.3	56.3	64.7	45.6	55.3	68.0
24	Garlic	30.0	51.0	34.0	40.0	40.0	43.3	52.0
25	Hake	34.0	34.4	34.0	38.3	36.0	42.9	51.0
26	Hares	...	...	59.4	57.5	...	70.5	76.5
27	Hens	113.8	136.9	129.7	129.0	169.3	206.3	205.6
28	Honey	508.3	748.0	696.2	884.0	596.7	884.0	1254.6
29	Kid	139.5	177.5	180.4	196.8	220.7	246.5	306.0
30	Lard	60.5	72.0	44.0	50.0	40.2	37.0	81.8
31	Milk	21.7	22.7	24.5	25.0	28.0	23.3	32.2
32	Mutton	46.0	41.3	37.9	42.6	43.1	38.0	57.5
33	Olive oil	340.0	290.3	...	369.8	493.0	399.5	386.4
34	Orange blossoms	6.0	...	11.0	11.5	14.0	8.0	16.5
35	Pepper	246.5	250.3	260.7	255.0	289.0	408.0	306.0
36	Pitch	16.3	19.6	16.0	20.7	20.0	20.0	21.3
37	Plaster of Paris	304.7	309.0	306.0	...	369.8	...	351.9
38	Pork, fresh	44.2	41.3	33.4	38.5	39.9	39.3	55.9
39	Quail	60.0	85.0	58.3	72.0	68.0	49.4	85.0
40	Raisins	912.3	624.0	635.0	679.0	1012.7	765.0	918.0
41	Resin	22.4	18.7	25.5	23.0	18.4	20.0	18.0
42	Rice	24.2	30.3	28.8	26.0	32.8	30.1	28.8
43	Saffron	1195.7	1195.7	1365.7	1513.0	2314.8	2312.0	1972.0
44	Sardines	26.0	28.0	34.0	34.9	28.0	38.4	38.3
45	Sea bream	34.5	39.0	49.1	53.0	41.5	54.0	59.0
46	Sea eel, Mediterranean	48.8	64.0	69.8	72.3	34.0	55.0	76.5
47	Soap	383.3	398.8	350.3	408.0	408.0	408.0	429.1
48	Sole	78.0	89.3	110.0	117.0	79.9	106.5	152.0
49	Sugar	1318.0	1493.9	1623.5	1292.0	1484.0	2270.8	2384.3
50	Veal	43.1	51.7	40.3	42.4	52.8	51.0	54.3
51	Vinegar	85.0	75.0	...	90.6	119.0	85.0	107.3
52	Walnuts	27.2	32.0	32.3	60.0	34.0	39.1	41.0
53	Wax, white	114.0	117.5	117.9	134.5	131.8	136.0	136.0
54	Wax, yellow	85.0	106.5	112.8	122.5	119.0	119.9	127.5
55	Wheat	879.0	604.5	430.0	529.0	1041.3	986.0	476.0
56	Wine	255.0	223.1	102.0	96.3	181.3	191.3	85.0

B. NEW CASTILE (IN MARAVEDÍS)

		1551	1552	1553	1554	1555	1556	1557	1558	1559	1560	1561	1562
1	Almonds	469.2	619.5	476.0	483.0	572.3	504.0	596.4	596.3		409.3	420.0	509.3
2	Apples, cooking		51.1	64.6	70.0	52.5	50.7	75.0	70.0	60.0	92.5	66.3	87.5
3	Apples, pippin	71.3	67.5	120.0	65.0	81.5	87.1	130.0	80.0	147.5	142.5	115.6	132.8
4	Barley		111.5	85.0	76.9			119.0	183.0		154.7	207.7	190.0
5	Beef	9.5	7.8	10.0		8.2	7.3	8.7	7.2	9.2		11.0	11.0
6	Bran			7.0				6.3			9.6	13.4	12.2
7	Bricks			1374.0				1360.0	1360.0	1360.0	1493.0	1870.0	1600.0
8	Brooms	40.7	68.6	78.0	81.3	76.5	42.7		36.0	36.0	63.1	56.0	56.0
9	Candles, tallow		19.0		24.0		14.6	45.0		25.0	26.0	27.0	24.0
10	Capers	10.5	10.0		11.3	10.3	12.6				16.3	16.0	13.8
11	Carrots		10.0	10.0								10.0	
12	Chambers						85.0	102.0			162.0	136.0	140.4
13	Charcoal	28.8		29.4	35.3	34.3		27.6	28.6		31.0	36.1	33.1
14	Cheese	19.3	20.0	21.0	22.0	14.2	22.7				26.0	28.7	27.3
15	Cherries	73.8		47.5	65.0	60.0	57.5	69.2	50.0	65.0	72.8	72.5	65.0
16	Chestnuts	9.0		10.0		8.5	8.0	10.4	12.1	10.4	11.0	12.0	12.5
17	Chickens, spring	23.9			24.2	24.0	24.6	36.7	36.0	30.4	33.1	38.3	39.9
18	Cinnamon		344.7	269.1		225.4	251.9	322.1	397.7	361.9	351.3	620.4	607.1
19	Cotton			136.0							134.5	134.5	
20	Dates	35.5				48.0	40.0	52.0			30.0	33.0	57.0
21	Eggs	21.5	24.0	25.0	24.6	24.0	28.8	35.7	37.8	30.6	37.5	36.0	35.5
22	Feet, lamb			18.0	17.9	16.5	18.0	20.0	25.1	25.5	25.1	24.0	25.9
23	Fish, dried	13.7	16.0	17.7	16.0	17.0	20.3				17.0	18.5	19.0
24	Grapes	40.0		32.5	40.0	52.5	32.5	45.0	35.0	40.0	40.0	55.0	30.0
25	Grapes, unripe	32.4		35.0	21.3	20.0	22.5	40.0	22.5	30.0	45.0	30.0	40.0
26	Hemp						20.0	20.8				24.0	
27	Hens		76.8	72.7	55.7	53.3	57.1	83.7	89.9	62.3	78.8	84.9	85.4
28	Honey			395.0	374.0			366.0	350.6		420.8	581.5	586.5
29	Incense			98.0					136.0		137.0	144.0	131.9
30	Ink			68.0	80.0	15.8	48.0	24.0	38.7	45.3	48.5	40.0	72.5
31	Kid	16.6	16.4	19.2	16.7	15.8	15.5	17.1	19.0	18.1	21.5	22.7	22.8
32	Lard	22.7	24.0	23.9	15.0	10.0	22.7	22.7	24.0	24.0	34.0	33.5	29.9
33	Lemons	18.3	18.3	25.2	16.8	13.3	15.0	18.9	24.0	12.5	17.0	26.0	33.6

		1551	1552	1553	1554	1555	1556	1557	1558	1559	1560	1561	1562
34	Lentils	11.3	10.0	9.8	10.0	9.9	8.3	...	...	...	12.5	12.7	14.3
35	Lime	...	...	31.0	34.0	33.0	36.0	36.0	36.0	38.0	36.7	38.0	38.0
36	Milk	16.4	36.6	23.5	17.3	16.5	16.0	14.6	20.0	16.0	24.0	27.3	22.0
37	Mutton	12.8	11.9	15.1	14.5	12.1	13.7	13.4	17.0	14.6	15.3	17.0	17.8
38	Nails, large	...	...	17.0	19.3	17.0	...	15.5	17.0	20.0	20.0	20.7	22.3
39	Olive oil	387.5	421.3	337.1	359.0	282.9	399.8	302.1	342.3	...	367.6	512.5	679.0
40	Olives	25.8	...	21.0	...	...	41.0	32.0	...	...	...	47.5	...
41	Oranges	...	...	...	13.5	13.0	11.7	18.0	13.8	20.6	13.8	18.9	24.7
42	Paper, writing	14.7	17.0	17.0	20.0	12.0	16.2	19.8	22.4	18.2	17.5	17.5	17.6
43	Peaches	66.4	...	60.9	...	62.5	52.5	82.5	68.8	...	...	66.4	80.0
44	Pears	...	...	78.8	66.3	60.6	80.0	...	...	100.0	77.5	61.3	80.0
45	Pepper	9.8	12.0	8.0	...	...	12.0	8.0	...	...	...	13.5	15.9
46	Perch	14.3	16.8	21.5	17.3	17.5	18.9	37.3	31.3	35.2	23.0	23.1	30.1
47	Plaster of Paris	...	...	...	34.1	30.2	34.0	30.0	37.5	...	35.0	44.4	43.3
48	Plums	40.7	20.0	20.0	20.0	22.5	24.5	...	...	20.0	60.0	32.5	20.0
49	Pork, salt	...	...	16.0	11.0	12.7	13.8	...	...	...	25.0	21.1	20.3
50	Prunes	...	...	14.8	15.0	...	...	22.0	27.9	20.5	14.3	19.3	15.0
51	Pumpkin, candied	...	...	52.0	48.6	47.4	48.0	55.2	50.9	51.0	60.6	77.8	83.1
52	Quail	...	45.6	...	...	...	60.0	46.6	...	...	...	...	51.0
53	Quinces	...	19.0	12.0	12.0	14.4	15.0	27.0	11.3	12.5	24.0	19.5	14.0
54	Raisins	10.0	...	184.7	196.2	190.8	207.3	213.3	212.1	...	197.9	181.2	233.5
55	Rice	...	10.0	10.0	10.0	11.8	12.4	15.7	15.7	12.3	13.0	13.2	14.1
56	Saffron	...	73.7	61.0	...	52.7	53.0	54.3	65.2	66.9	74.4	101.8	93.5
57	Sardines	14.3	16.7	13.0	16.0	17.3	19.3	...	...	...	21.8	22.0	23.5
58	Sloes	...	...	20.0	30.0	20.0	20.0	60.0	60.0	40.0	70.0	32.5	37.5
59	Starch	...	...	...	...	...	...	24.0	...	25.0	22.9	24.0	23.5
60	Sugar	1151.4	1272.7	1346.7	1373.6	1373.6	1373.6	1433.0	1290.0	...	1616.0	1700.0	1802.0
61	Tallow	...	21.3	...	...	...	12.0	20.0	...	21.8	21.3	22.5	21.9
62	Turnips	20.0	...	20.0	15.0	15.0	20.0	...	...	...	25.0	25.0	25.0
63	Twine	55.1	40.0	32.0	32.0	32.0	32.0	29.5	29.0	37.3	43.3	43.5	42.0
64	Vinegar	...	102.0	53.8	129.0	62.7	39.5	63.0	58.6	85.8	43.0	49.3	56.8
65	Wax, white	83.1	...	...	...	76.0	...	70.0	75.0	95.0	80.0	...	91.0
66	Wax, yellow	...	74.6	...	...	...	73.2	68.0	80.8	79.8	...	...	68.4
67	Wheat	...	...	...	149.3	...	208.1	382.0	...	...	333.5	339.0	289.6
68	Wine	66.4	94.9	91.5	96.1	120.0	107.6	70.0	99.7	130.8	132.6	126.3	163.5

B.   NEW CASTILE (IN MARAVEDÍS) — CONTINUED

		1563	1564	1565	1566	1567	1568	1569	1570	1571	1572	1573	1574
1	Almonds	641.8	628.9	714.0	556.5	459.0	571.0	578.0	714.0	977.5	791.6	697.0	797.1
2	Apples, cooking	90.0	110.0	110.0	100.0	113.8	85.2	115.0	120.0	110.0	102.5	142.5	120.0
3	Apples, pippin	136.7	145.3	95.0	145.0	155.0	150.3	162.5	155.0	150.0	155.0	171.4	168.1
4	Barley	119.7	134.7	137.3	144.6	180.0	182.8	138.2	...	...	184.7	147.2	140.0
5	Beef	11.3	11.0	11.2	11.8	11.6	...	12.0	11.0	11.5	12.3	12.7	13.1
6	Bran	8.8	10.0	9.4	11.4	12.9	...	...	12.0	11.5	10.7	10.7	12.0
7	Bricks	1700.0	1700.0	1700.0	1360.0	1544.6	1700.0	1360.0	...	1360.0	1745.3	1732.0	1564.0
8	Brooms	40.4	55.5	58.2	70.1	60.8	64.0	52.9	60.8	64.1	70.5	64.5	84.8
9	Candles, tallow	...	...	24.0	24.0	24.0	23.0	25.7	29.5	29.5	25.1	22.8	22.9
10	Capers	31.4	36.3	32.8	32.0	36.0	42.0	44.9	34.0	24.0	33.0	33.5	29.0
11	Carrots	15.0	10.0	10.0	10.0	20.0	10.0	20.0	20.0	20.0	16.3	33.5	15.0
12	Chambers	132.0	...	...	...	156.0	144.0	...	...	96.0	120.0	120.0	120.0
13	Charcoal	42.8	30.0	38.6	36.6	35.5	38.0	39.8	36.3	33.2	34.0	44.7	34.4
14	Cheese	22.0	27.1	32.0	29.0	40.0	28.0	25.5	30.0	33.9	35.4	33.0	33.5
15	Cherries	66.3	60.0	60.0	82.5	65.0	100.0	83.8	102.5	88.8	96.3	112.5	62.5
16	Chestnuts	12.0	12.0	12.0	12.0	...	11.1	11.1	15.0	14.0	14.0	15.5	12.0
17	Chickens, spring	38.3	41.8	40.4	42.9	43.6	42.9	46.5	49.7	38.1	38.7	36.9	41.9
18	Cinnamon	877.5	1410.4	1422.4	1150.6	612.0	385.3	408.0	443.0	408.0	402.3	374.0	374.0
19	Cotton	...	161.4	148.0	188.3	186.3	168.1	161.4	148.0	119.0	171.5	211.2	148.0
20	Dates	52.0	...	...	...	40.0	64.0	51.5	58.0	55.0	48.0	77.9	51.0
21	Eggs	36.4	36.0	35.3	36.4	37.8	40.3	40.0	37.5	46.5	47.6	41.0	37.0
22	Feet, lamb	29.6	29.6	27.8	29.0	31.5	31.8	27.0	36.0	36.0	39.0	48.0	39.8
23	Fish, dried	20.0	17.0	19.7	19.9	22.7	21.0	21.0	20.6	20.0	21.0	21.0	21.8
24	Grapes	40.0	40.0	40.0	60.0	40.0	...	75.0	60.0	50.0	40.0	40.0	160.0
25	Grapes, unripe	47.5	40.0	40.0	30.0	30.0	40.0	40.0	40.0	30.0	35.0	60.0	40.0
26	Hemp	...	...	...	44.3	52.6	...	26.0	16.5	...	...	31.0	19.0
27	Hens	96.3	91.4	94.8	93.7	88.1	102.3	108.6	94.3	93.3	94.2	96.7	82.5
28	Honey	544.0	...	500.0	563.7	597.2	627.5	493.0	629.0	697.9	646.0	680.0	807.5
29	Incense	...	126.4	120.2	153.3	...	212.5	198.8	170.0	167.9	151.9	160.5	167.2
30	Ink	54.0	68.0	68.0	136.0	136.0	68.0	102.0	102.0	79.3	152.0	131.8	...
31	Kid	23.4	22.5	23.3	23.4	22.3	22.9	24.7	24.0	23.3	23.8	25.1	24.9
32	Lard	23.8	27.0	22.0	23.0	28.6	...	25.7	22.0	31.5	28.0	30.4	26.0
33	Lemons	19.0	12.0	27.0	18.9	30.0	29.3	14.0	28.4	35.1	27.3	36.5	21.5

		1563	1564	1565	1566	1567	1568	1569	1570	1571	1572	1573	1574
34	Lentils	12.3	11.9	10.8	11.0	16.8	15.0	15.3	12.0	13.4	12.0	13.7	13.2
35	Lime	38.0	41.0	41.0	41.0	41.0	41.0	58.2	60.0	52.0	60.1	68.0	68.0
36	Milk	25.0	21.0	29.2	27.8	22.3	26.6	22.0	24.0	24.0	23.0	23.0	27.0
37	Mutton	16.8	16.4	17.6	18.0	18.0	19.0	18.1	18.0	18.0	18.9	21.3	20.8
38	Nails, large	20.0	20.0	21.0	22.0	21.7	23.0	22.0	22.0	22.8	21.3	24.3	22.0
39	Olive oil	467.9	420.2	394.5	420.0	534.4	441.0	382.8	391.0	487.2	482.1	437.7	407.5
40	Olives	43.7	58.0	53.0	51.0	...	60.0	55.2	45.0	51.0	51.0	51.0	44.0
41	Oranges	20.5	21.5	20.0	24.5	18.8	21.2	17.0	26.3	26.5	33.5	24.0	24.0
42	Paper, writing	17.9	17.8	17.5	19.7	21.0	19.5	18.7	17.0	17.4	19.1	17.5	17.5
43	Peaches	90.0	75.0	80.0	100.0	101.0	...	220.0	155.0	199.3	110.0	137.5	180.0
44	Pears	92.5	117.5	93.8	115.0	81.3	...	91.3	130.0	100.0	122.5	142.5	135.0
45	Pepper	19.8	21.5	23.9	16.0	12.5	16.0	16.0	18.0	14.0	10.0	10.0	13.8
46	Perch	31.9	34.0	34.0	32.4	26.5	34.0	34.0	31.6	33.0	33.9	34.8	35.5
47	Plaster of Paris	44.6	40.9	42.1	38.3	42.0	41.8	42.9	38.8	38.9	43.3	45.6	40.1
48	Plums	40.0	20.0	30.6	40.0	27.5	20.0	20.0	70.0	32.6	45.0	55.0	40.0
49	Pork, salt	21.0	21.2	20.5	18.7	16.5	27.0	24.2	19.0	21.5	22.5	23.3	21.3
50	Prunes	16.5	25.8	16.9	19.5	24.0	20.8	22.0	20.0	21.6	23.6	24.4	25.4
51	Pumpkin, candied	85.0	84.0	81.3	82.0	84.4	83.7	76.0	80.5	89.8	89.5	85.0	85.0
52	Quail	28.5	59.5	...	55.3	51.5	53.5	51.0	53.0	51.0	53.1	50.3	51.0
53	Quinces	...	33.0	...	15.9	60.0	...	...	27.0	57.0	36.0	42.0	47.3
54	Raisins	255.3	253.1	229.5	295.5	205.4	238.0	240.3	246.5	264.2	282.9	340.0	268.8
55	Rice	14.6	14.0	14.5	14.0	13.4	15.0	15.8	13.3	17.8	18.4	15.8	14.0
56	Saffron	64.3	63.2	57.0	58.2	65.5	65.0	62.6	69.8	80.7	87.7	89.4	91.2
57	Sardines	21.2	24.8	22.7	20.7	20.6	20.0	22.0	22.0	23.0	24.0	23.3	21.8
58	Sloes	47.5	37.5	40.0	60.0	50.0	...	45.0	62.5	47.5	60.0	80.0	51.0
59	Starch	...	24.0	...	26.7	24.9	38.3	26.0	21.0	28.4	27.8	23.8	24.0
60	Sugar	1745.3	1668.8	1649.0	1583.5	1595.9	1567.5	1761.5	1807.7	2091.0	2158.0	2091.0	1785.0
61	Tallow	20.0	20.0	20.0	20.4	20.0	20.0	20.0	20.0	20.0	20.0	20.0	20.0
62	Turnips	30.0	23.2	24.4	30.0	30.0	30.0	25.7	23.6	25.0	37.5	27.5	28.8
63	Twine	41.5	40.0	40.0	40.7	42.3	46.0	46.7	45.0	43.9	41.5	44.2	44.0
64	Vinegar	66.8	73.3	96.7	91.1	71.7	62.4	68.0	56.2	59.0	80.2	77.8	104.1
65	Wax, white	80.0	73.5	76.0	80.0	...	92.0	100.0	96.9	106.2	110.0	110.0	114.5
66	Wax, yellow	68.4	74.4	80.8	86.5	83.6	89.0	...	100.0	115.0	...	113.6	113.6
67	Wheat	240.8	244.3	219.8	324.0	378.5	373.5	293.0	393.8	459.0	346.7	285.4	267.8
68	Wine	132.4	183.0	167.7	136.5	130.6	126.9	132.7	154.3	127.2	119.9	164.0	188.8

B. NEW CASTILE (IN MARAVEDÍS) — CONTINUED

		1575	1576	1577	1578	1579	1580	1581	1582	1583	1584	1585	1586	1587
1	Almonds	930.3	936.0	619.3	824.5	701.3	877.5	799.5	840.0	924.0	833.0	833.0	867.0	1122.0
2	Apples, cooking	110.0	97.5	90.0	100.0	117.5	100.0	100.0	107.5	110.0	132.5	127.5	127.5	140.0
3	Apples, pippin	125.0	142.5	117.5	113.8	131.3	126.7	133.8	118.8	120.0	160.0	136.7	177.5	162.5
4	Barley	153.0	187.0	187.0	187.0	211.0	166.5	187.0	206.0	404.1	238.0	192.4	...	184.0
5	Beef	14.0	...	12.4	12.5	12.0	14.0	...	...	...	14.4	17.0	18.0	18.0
6	Bran	12.0	12.1	12.3	15.2	11.8	12.0	...	...	...	21.4	12.7	11.0	...
7	Bricks	1588.5	1663.2	2205.1	1700.0	1707.5	1700.0	...	1700.0	2255.4	2414.0	2414.0	2397.0	2622.0
8	Brooms	80.0	71.1	72.0	50.4	50.3	53.9	64.0	72.0	67.5	124.0	127.5	96.8	98.0
9	Candles, tallow	28.0	29.6	27.1	30.5	31.0	26.0	32.4	32.0	32.0	30.9	33.2	33.0	35.5
10	Capers	32.2	34.0	34.0	34.0	34.0	...	20.0	31.3	34.0	45.2	40.0	...	...
11	Carrots	...	20.0	...	20.0	...	20.0	20.0	20.0	...	...	20.0	20.0	20.0
12	Chambers	120.0	138.0	120.0	120.0	120.0	120.0	120.0	120.0	120.0	120.0	144.0	144.0	136.0
13	Charcoal	33.2	39.5	32.4	38.5	40.4	38.9	...	41.5	48.0	44.0	44.3	44.6	41.9
14	Cheese	32.5	...	32.5	34.0	40.0	32.0	...	32.0	32.0	38.0	31.0	40.0	...
15	Cherries	92.5	77.5	92.5	77.5	97.5	100.0	92.5	100.0	100.0	110.0	95.0	100.0	142.5
16	Chestnuts	13.8	...	13.0	14.0	18.0	14.0	14.0	16.0	12.0	14.0	18.0	14.0	...
17	Chickens, spring	52.3	49.4	50.0	38.9	55.4	44.5	44.6	44.7	49.2	47.3	56.8	51.7	46.8
18	Cinnamon	391.0	...	408.0	378.0	606.0	678.7	...	314.5	352.8	404.9	416.0	442.0	444.8
19	Cotton	170.0	...	170.0	170.0	232.0	204.0	228.0	188.3	224.0	215.2	255.6	255.0	...
20	Dates	66.0	65.2	51.0	...	66.0	85.0	122.0	55.3	60.0	48.0	64.0	51.0	...
21	Eggs	41.6	44.1	43.3	50.9	57.4	52.0	43.1	42.0	54.4	57.4	59.0	53.8	42.6
22	Feet, lamb	42.0	34.5	30.0	32.0	32.0	36.0	36.4	36.0	46.5	45.0	52.0	48.0	48.0
23	Fish, dried	22.0	24.4	22.0	23.0	27.9	26.1	26.1	28.0	26.6	28.0	28.9	26.6	...
24	Grapes	80.0	52.5	...	50.0	77.5	60.0	...	...	...	85.0	...	60.0	...
25	Grapes, unripe	40.0	35.0	40.0	30.0	40.0	30.0	28.8	37.5	40.0	40.0	55.0	40.0	45.0
26	Hemp	...	32.0	28.0	29.0	40.0	35.5	34.0	...	38.0	36.0	44.0	42.5	33.6
27	Hens	101.6	112.9	85.4	100.9	117.9	106.2	102.1	87.4	116.3	109.1	136.3	139.5	115.8
28	Honey	572.4	...	...	548.3	603.5	...	...	...	...	425.0	425.0	510.0	595.0
29	Incense	167.1	181.0	120.0	98.0	102.0	...	120.0	102.0	102.0	111.3	92.5	110.5	102.0
30	Ink	119.0	119.0	...	...	...	...	...	120.0	120.0	...	125.3	...	128.0
31	Kid	23.1	22.8	22.3	23.2	22.4	22.4	22.5	21.4	24.0	27.1	26.0	24.3	23.5
32	Lard	34.0	25.7	34.0	30.0	38.6	34.0	34.0	34.0	34.0	42.0	42.0	22.9	22.0
33	Lemons	24.0	24.0	33.0	34.9	34.5	26.0	31.8	36.0	36.0	36.0	33.0	44.5	25.3

		1575	1576	1577	1578	1579	1580	1581	1582	1583	1584	1585	1586	1587
34	Lentils	10.2	14.0	12.5	13.2	15.3	15.2	13.2	15.3	10.0	12.0	14.7	12.0	
35	Lime	65.0	60.0	41.7	61.5	78.0	73.8	71.3	64.1	67.9	70.5	71.0	75.3	75.1
36	Milk	32.9	23.0	25.3	24.0	20.0	29.0	28.7	45.8	32.1	34.9	32.8	31.5	29.9
37	Mutton	22.0	19.8	17.5	18.0	18.6	19.1	19.0	17.8	18.8	26.8	21.6	21.4	19.5
38	Nails, large	22.0		23.8	25.0	24.0	22.0	25.0	24.0		27.0	30.0	26.8	28.5
39	Olive oil	491.8	538.9	606.3	516.5	634.3	504.3	565.8	429.1	444.1	481.3	684.7	487.0	405.3
40	Olives	44.0		44.0	49.0	49.5	48.5	45.7	51.0	64.0	60.0	76.0	60.0	44.0
41	Oranges	23.8	32.3	27.8	24.0	50.3	24.0	39.0	26.2	31.5	33.8	28.9	35.0	28.8
42	Paper, writing	20.4	19.8	20.8	19.5	22.0	26.0	20.8	20.0	22.0	18.5	24.0	19.0	18.5
43	Peaches	120.0	101.0	170.0	130.0	120.0	105.0	100.0	80.0	151.4	240.0	88.6	126.2	
44	Pears	111.3	100.0	92.5	82.5	120.0	101.3	112.5	117.5	111.7	140.0	115.0	100.0	167.5
45	Pepper	14.0	15.0	13.1	12.5	13.0	18.0	16.0		14.0	17.5	15.5	19.0	
46	Perch	34.1	34.0	34.0	33.8	35.5	34.1	34.0	35.9	43.4	49.0	50.5	51.0	36.8
47	Plaster of Paris	44.5	44.3		41.6	51.3	49.4	50.3	47.7	51.0	51.6	50.6	57.5	56.4
48	Plums	40.0	27.5	50.0	40.8	70.0	36.7	50.0	30.0	40.0	43.3	56.0	35.4	120.0
49	Pork, salt	25.0	24.0	22.1	28.8	31.8	25.9	27.0	25.5	22.9	30.5	34.7	28.1	27.5
50	Prunes	30.2	26.0		23.8	42.5	26.7	20.0	23.5	24.5	31.5		30.0	28.0
51	Pumpkin, candied	83.5	82.8	82.2	87.5	102.4	108.4	108.4	102.5	102.0	80.0	80.0	80.0	80.0
52	Quail	51.0	46.8	53.3	50.0	58.5		57.5	68.0	62.3	51.0	64.0	62.5	54.7
53	Quinces	40.5	14.5	20.7	12.0	72.0	23.0	11.5	55.3	27.0	22.5	18.0	16.0	21.2
54	Raisins	310.5	264.9	274.8	308.3	410.8		296.8		221.1	331.5	333.8	262.2	278.0
55	Rice	17.3	16.0	16.0	19.5	25.3	23.7	21.3	21.3	22.0	22.6	24.1	20.5	17.9
56	Saffron	90.7	129.7		68.0			90.9		132.0	114.8	110.5	102.0	85.7
57	Sardines	24.5	25.5	24.8	25.5	27.5	27.0				32.0	30.0		22.0
58	Sloes	90.0	40.0	60.0	60.0	60.0	50.0	60.0	50.0	30.0	70.0	50.0	40.0	110.0
59	Starch	19.1	19.9	26.1	32.8	34.7	36.7			50.0	34.0	40.2	21.0	
60	Sugar	1858.7	2074.0	1992.8	2365.8	2458.0	2174.9	2351.9	2025.1	1976.2	1617.1	1632.0	2198.7	1983.3
61	Tallow	21.6	20.0	18.6	26.6	20.9	20.9	19.0	17.0	18.2	22.0	20.0	22.0	19.7
62	Turnips	30.0	32.5	35.0	28.4	33.8	30.0	25.0			42.0	40.0	40.0	30.0
63	Twine	42.3	42.2	42.2	45.8	49.0	50.6	47.3	44.0	45.5	42.5	46.3	52.0	51.6
64	Vinegar	136.3	93.4	88.5	97.5	107.4	86.0	86.0	83.3		80.0	80.0	79.5	85.0
65	Wax, white	119.0	117.5	119.0		136.0	108.3	108.4	107.0	110.7	108.7	114.0	114.5	119.0
66	Wax, yellow		106.3	112.0	97.6	112.8	119.0	106.4	107.0	110.0		107.0	117.5	119.0
67	Wheat	340.0	375.9	374.0	422.0	430.7	442.0		459.0	471.0	476.0	492.7	306.0	331.3
68	Wine	168.2	168.4	172.8	183.2	152.0	226.8	124.1	190.3	137.4	188.2	176.5	179.5	314.3

B. NEW CASTILE (IN MARAVEDÍS) — CONTINUED

		1588	1589	1590	1591	1592	1593	1594	1595	1596	1597	1598	1599	1600
1	Almonds	736.7	969.0	845.8	940.7	1048.3	1037.0	840.0	845.5	807.5	1147.5	1215.5	1224.0	1079.5
2	Apples, cooking	133.4	90.0	117.5	150.0	127.5	114.0	114.0	112.5	120.0	122.5	128.4	169.6	133.8
3	Apples, pippin	80.0	138.5	154.5	170.0	180.9	143.9	135.0	140.0	150.0	170.0	160.0	165.0	155.0
4	Barley	204.0	238.0	...	204.0	132.8	225.3	223.2	204.0	191.3	208.3	272.0	242.3	280.5
5	Beef	14.5	...	...	12.0	15.5	...	...	...	...	...	...	...	...
6	Bran	10.3	...	...	14.0	16.0	18.3	20.3	13.4	14.0	15.3	18.8	19.5	16.2
7	Bricks	2414.0	2686.0	2435.6	2380.0	2822.0	...	...	2709.8	2460.2	2425.3	...	2460.2	2986.1
8	Brooms	97.5	93.9	106.5	101.9	90.6	128.0	120.3	120.0	106.8	81.6	104.0	60.0	...
9	Candles, tallow	31.0	32.0	31.0	28.0	28.0	32.5	26.5	26.8	28.0	28.0	28.0	28.5	31.4
10	Capers	...	34.0	25.4	20.3	...	60.0	...	47.5	...	...	...	...	27.1
11	Carrots	20.0	30.0	27.5	25.0	33.3	40.0	20.0	...	30.0	...	35.0	37.5	30.0
12	Chambers	136.0	134.5	136.0	140.0	136.0	102.0	136.0	136.0	130.3	110.0	120.0	144.0	126.0
13	Charcoal	43.5	44.1	50.6	34.9	32.6	26.8	29.9	26.5	41.0	39.9	37.4	39.3	43.0
14	Cheese	...	41.0	48.0	...	34.3	...	28.0	...	40.0	34.0	...	...	40.0
15	Cherries	67.5	112.5	102.5	92.5	100.0	55.3	90.0	97.5	92.5	92.5	132.5	122.5	115.4
16	Chestnuts	...	15.0	...	21.9	20.5	19.7	...	14.0	14.0	17.5	...	20.8	23.3
17	Chickens, spring	50.3	49.5	50.6	47.2	45.2	45.6	50.8	43.4	45.0	48.2	47.5	53.2	57.4
18	Cinnamon	408.0	374.0	408.0	340.0	461.5	340.0	408.0	404.0	391.0	391.0	323.0	597.2	335.8
19	Cotton	238.0	186.0	204.0	188.3	161.4	...	238.0	204.0	196.0	214.0	221.9	240.0	215.2
20	Dates	68.0	84.0	68.3	50.5	52.1	45.5	48.0	55.5	50.3	52.0	55.0	65.3	...
21	Eggs	41.7	48.0	58.9	55.9	52.1	58.9	59.0	47.6	49.1	55.5	54.0	60.5	75.0
22	Feet, lamb	48.0	48.0	...	49.0	47.3	48.0	49.0	48.0	48.0	50.0	66.0	51.7	64.0
23	Fish, dried	28.0	26.7	22.6	21.0	30.0	...	30.0	...	...	30.0	32.8	32.0	32.0
24	Grapes	57.5	80.0	70.0	30.0	...	30.0	50.0	...	...	...	60.0	...	40.0
25	Grapes, unripe	40.0	40.0	37.0	45.0	45.0	30.0	36.0	40.0	37.5	35.0	65.0	40.0	45.0
26	Hemp	34.0	33.3	33.7	34.0	38.0	34.0	40.0	35.2	41.0	42.3	44.5	42.0	45.9
27	Hens	98.7	106.5	127.6	125.1	123.1	110.8	120.4	112.3	110.0	111.6	112.2	128.5	168.4
28	Honey	629.0	635.3	629.0	578.0	527.0	561.0	...	714.0	850.0	663.0	725.5	603.5	748.0
29	Incense	102.1	153.6	161.5	238.5	199.5	136.0	130.3	124.7	134.7	133.3	136.0	149.0	138.7
30	Ink	136.0	136.0	136.0	133.3	136.0	136.0	136.0	136.0	136.0	136.0	137.0	136.0	136.0
31	Kid	23.3	25.2	23.5	24.3	28.2	24.9	24.5	24.3	26.3	25.2	25.8	23.7	32.2
32	Lard	20.0	28.4	34.0	30.1	41.1	32.9	23.6	...	49.7	28.0	34.3	...	50.1
33	Lemons	27.0	28.5	47.6	44.0	31.5	20.3	37.5	30.0	39.2	36.0	34.0	35.0	34.5

		1588	1589	1590	1591	1592	1593	1594	1595	1596	1597	1598	1599	1600
34	Lentils	…	…	…	…	…	14.7	…	…	12.4	…	…	…	…
35	Lime	73.0	74.2	70.9	76.5	76.5	76.2	76.5	74.4	76.2	82.3	85.0	85.0	85.0
36	Milk	27.0	38.0	30.5	38.8	31.6	34.0	31.2	31.0	30.6	32.0	34.0	30.0	41.6
37	Mutton	20.9	21.9	21.4	21.3	21.0	23.5	22.0	18.9	21.8	20.5	19.0	21.5	27.5
38	Nails, large	28.0	27.8	33.5	30.0	24.8	28.0	…	…	…	…	32.0	30.0	…
39	Olive oil	428.0	568.7	617.0	427.7	467.4	599.1	784.1	483.4	464.6	482.3	612.2	595.7	619.9
40	Olives	42.0	55.8	58.0	46.0	60.0	51.0	47.0	64.0	52.5	54.0	60.0	41.0	34.5
41	Oranges	24.0	28.8	44.3	32.8	21.0	22.5	32.5	41.5	26.0	30.5	36.0	24.9	35.0
42	Paper, writing	21.0	22.0	26.6	21.5	26.0	25.0	25.0	21.7	23.0	22.7	24.2	25.7	20.0
43	Peaches	120.0	101.0	120.0	110.7	100.0	151.4	66.4	160.0	200.0	130.0	…	252.4	171.6
44	Pears	112.5	110.0	135.0	129.8	100.0	105.0	111.3	130.0	130.0	130.0	115.0	150.0	125.0
45	Pepper	16.1	15.0	…	12.7	14.8	12.3	18.0	17.5	16.0	16.0	20.0	31.7	22.7
46	Perch	46.5	49.7	33.5	56.3	31.0	60.0	56.3	…	…	51.0	51.0	51.3	…
47	Plaster of Paris	56.4	56.0	61.5	90.0	90.5	101.2	101.2	115.7	93.1	93.7	86.8	99.4	30.0
48	Plums	40.8	60.0	48.9	40.0	60.0	62.5	40.0	80.0	50.0	60.0	50.0	40.0	30.0
49	Pork, salt	24.0	24.0	30.0	28.4	33.5	27.4	38.2	36.0	36.0	32.0	40.0	32.5	35.5
50	Prunes	32.5	32.0	36.3	40.0	…	25.3	23.5	22.0	28.0	…	40.0	40.0	30.0
51	Pumpkin, candied	80.0	80.0	80.0	80.5	81.0	80.0	80.0	82.8	85.0	84.3	90.4	104.4	113.6
52	Quail	42.0	…	68.0	70.8	60.0	68.8	64.0	65.0	64.0	60.2	…	63.8	101.8
53	Quinces	23.6	24.0	24.0	18.7	44.0	…	17.0	29.1	22.5	13.5	24.0	22.0	21.8
54	Raisins	263.4	306.0	456.9	381.8	393.8	305.1	402.5	295.5	331.5	364.8	266.3	510.0	484.5
55	Rice	18.0	18.3	17.7	61.7	27.7	…	26.0	…	21.0	23.2	26.9	26.9	31.4
56	Saffron	85.0	94.0	…	…	60.6	52.0	51.0	…	…	128.0	161.0	136.0	157.0
57	Sardines	…	27.0	30.0	30.5	23.0	40.0	37.5	90.0	45.0	…	36.0	…	60.0
58	Sloes	57.5	80.0	60.0	48.8	60.0	32.0	44.7	28.3	28.1	50.0	60.0	70.0	62.5
59	Starch	24.0	26.2	30.8	34.2	85.0	55.0	63.4	42.5	62.4	53.5	41.1	55.2	42.5
60	Sugar	1942.3	1870.0	1980.5	1908.3	1867.0	1768.0	2060.4	1802.5	1810.5	1853.9	2011.7	2181.7	2800.8
61	Tallow	22.8	29.0	…	20.0	18.6	…	17.8	17.5	24.0	20.5	23.5	18.5	27.2
62	Turnips	…	30.0	32.5	…	35.0	…	…	40.0	36.3	37.5	40.0	40.0	40.0
63	Twine	61.5	46.7	48.0	51.8	55.5	54.0	54.0	54.3	58.7	64.0	65.0	63.3	84.4
64	Vinegar	130.5	85.0	167.5	146.6	85.0	55.0	63.4	42.5	62.4	53.5	63.9	72.0	153.0
65	Wax, white	127.5	131.8	110.2	140.6	140.8	127.5	144.9	144.4	161.9	161.5	162.0	170.0	141.7
66	Wax, yellow	111.5	119.0	110.5	103.0	110.3	110.8	119.0	129.0	143.4	137.3	142.8	130.5	…
67	Wheat	406.2	620.3	600.0	525.6	504.8	515.3	820.5	408.0	442.0	486.3	578.0	908.0	684.4
68	Wine	222.7	184.2	257.0	174.9	235.8	154.0	163.5	108.7	204.1	129.6	251.4	353.2	102.9

C. OLD CASTILE–LEÓN (IN MARAVEDÍS)

		1551	1552	1553	1554	1555	1556	1557	1558	1559
1	Almonds	48.0	25.0	51.0	25.0	28.9	31.4	39.0	30.0	30.0
2	Apples, cooking	65.6	97.6	59.3	92.9	84.9	79.5	105.7	104.6	...
3	Apples, pippin	90.2	71.1	45.5	69.4	76.4	95.3	104.4	164.3	...
4	Barley	80.6	87.3	87.0	91.1	132.3	148.3	154.5	146.3	121.1
5	Beef	6.0	6.8	6.4	6.4	5.5	5.0	6.5	8.0	8.0
6	Candles, tallow	21.4	20.4	26.0	26.0	18.4	23.0	22.0	23.0	21.3
7	Charcoal	56.0	38.4	54.8	51.8	58.0	53.4	69.2	70.0	55.6
8	Cheese	19.0	...	23.8	...	21.1	...	...	...	...
9	Cherries	...	...	63.5	27.1	51.2	89.6	75.0	88.8	...
10	Chestnuts	255.0	272.0	238.0	280.0	340.0	...	408.0	340.0	238.0
11	Chickens, spring	21.0	18.0	20.0	21.3	20.7	22.5	37.2	43.3	...
12	Chick-peas	...	...	408.0	380.6	357.5	425.0	...	782.0	761.1
13	Cinnamon	469.5	257.9	257.9	257.9	408.0	375.0	340.0	612.0	461.0
14	Cloves	22.0	22.0	25.0	23.0	24.0	19.0	18.0	29.6	30.2
15	Conger eel	17.8	24.6	19.8	28.0	14.0	24.6	26.0	32.4	32.4
16	Eggs	20.5	18.9	23.1	24.8	27.4	29.5	34.8	34.1	31.1
17	Feet, kid	17.0	...	...	...	17.0	20.7	17.0	17.0	...
18	Filberts	246.5	221.0	...	238.0	221.0	272.0	408.0	...	374.0
19	Fish, fresh	12.0	16.0	...	...	17.0	12.0	17.0	18.0	...
20	Hens	50.1	44.7	45.3	51.9	50.7	57.1	85.6	89.5	...
21	Honey	680.0	901.0	1312.5	714.0	782.0	867.0	911.1	...	952.0
22	Incense	106.5	85.0	72.0	60.0	...	76.5	82.5	117.5	161.5
23	Kid	21.0	19.7	21.3	22.2	22.0	21.4	23.8	24.2	...
24	Lambs	284.1	259.0	287.6	238.0	294.8	324.4	305.4	409.1	379.7
25	Lard	34.0	28.1	24.7	31.5	27.5	29.0	34.0	33.0	31.5
26	Linen	41.6	44.5	46.8	46.6	44.5	39.3	34.0	39.5	47.0
27	Mutton	11.4	10.5	11.9	12.0	11.8	12.0	12.7	14.7	...
28	Nails, large	17.1	17.0	16.3	17.0	15.4	16.0	16.3	15.4	16.3
29	Olive oil	546.1	495.1	436.4	529.8	416.5	557.3	442.0	482.0	461.5
30	Oranges	66.9	67.2	55.2	97.0	48.7	73.7	109.6	109.6	...
31	Paper, writing	283.5	283.5	283.5	306.0	300.0	425.0	476.0	453.3	371.0
32	Pears	72.5	40.0	50.0	70.1	80.0	69.0	101.3	76.9	...
33	Pepper	160.0	141.8	160.0	155.0	165.0	150.0	147.5	136.0	155.0
34	Perch	8.7	5.8	6.3	6.8	9.2	11.3	12.0	13.0	...
35	Plaster of Paris	32.5	...	33.0	40.0	40.0	40.0	38.0	...	42.8
36	Plums	80.0	60.0	54.4	...	...	50.0	80.0	102.5	...
37	Pork, salt	16.7	...	10.8	...	...	...	...	...	...
38	Pumpkin, candied	50.8	50.4	52.4	60.6	...	60.0	64.0	71.9	59.4
39	Raisins	170.0	222.5	246.5	272.0	188.8	119.0	264.3	296.3	337.5
40	Rice	272.0	275.0	312.5	300.0	289.0	325.0	488.8	362.0	375.0
41	Rye	59.5	93.5	90.8	112.7	144.6	177.6	221.0	202.9	145.0
42	Saffron	68.0	74.0	66.0	64.7	60.0	68.0	42.5	70.0	61.0
43	Salmon	26.0	32.0	28.0	28.0	...	...	25.0	...	34.0
44	Sardines	58.5	66.9	66.1	73.4	75.8	89.4	105.9	90.7	110.5
45	Sloes	80.0	...	...	65.0	...	40.0	80.0	125.0	...
46	Soap	508.9	442.0	464.9	524.2	480.4	462.7	456.8	488.6	383.3
47	Starch	15.0	16.8	...	20.2	...	24.0	24.0	29.1	16.3
48	Sugar	1075.0	1125.0	1088.0	1394.0	1125.0	1173.0	1052.0	1343.5	1105.0
49	Trout	30.0	41.5	35.0	26.8	28.2	31.8	46.8	52.9	...
50	Twine	30.5	...	...	...	...	44.0	48.0	48.8	42.8
51	Vinegar	81.8	102.0	81.3	119.0	...	...	...	26.0	...
52	Walnuts	...	208.3	...	272.0	337.1	357.0	...	...	...
53	Wax, white	63.0	120.0	112.0	110.0	...	136.0	136.0	...	...
54	Wax, yellow	51.0	80.0	76.0	76.5	78.0	78.0	74.0	94.4	83.3
55	Wheat	130.2	134.8	129.9	130.5	203.0	241.5	340.7	303.9	247.0
56	Wine	211.4	198.7	128.0	141.0	149.7	85.8	92.9	147.9	157.0

C. OLD CASTILE–LEÓN (IN MARAVEDÍS) — Continued

		1560	1561	1562	1563	1564	1565	1566	1567	1568
1	Almonds	24.0	30.0	23.9	30.0	32.0	40.0	37.2	61.5	...
2	Apples, cooking	...	...	...	...	80.0	141.6	...	...	...
3	Apples, pippin	...	...	...	120.0	148.5	131.7	89.7	117.2	...
4	Barley	132.4	135.9	133.2	135.2	136.7	137.3	147.0	138.0	83.7
5	Beef	7.0	7.3	7.5	8.0	...	7.5	7.5	8.5	...
6	Candles, tallow	24.6	24.0	21.5	20.8	...	30.0	28.8	26.0	29.3
7	Charcoal	47.6	47.5	45.4	48.3	51.0	46.0	...	41.5	36.0
8	Cheese	16.9	23.2	17.0	16.7	18.0	26.4	23.8	28.5	...
9	Cherries	...	32.8	35.0	...	78.8	128.0	51.2	153.6	...
10	Chestnuts	272.0	272.0	272.0	357.0	357.0	306.0	...	242.4	...
11	Chickens, spring	33.0	28.6	32.0	46.1	44.2	26.8	28.9	30.4	...
12	Chick-peas	306.0	375.0	816.0	448.1	476.0	612.0	...	612.0	868.0
13	Cinnamon	544.0	669.3	697.0	918.0	1252.5	1960.0	1096.5	730.6	...
14	Cloves	...	60.0	60.0	51.1	83.8	40.4	55.3	51.0	...
15	Conger eel	24.6	22.0	24.0	22.9	27.8	24.0	22.9	17.0	...
16	Eggs	...	...	...	37.3	28.6	35.1	...	...	...
17	Feet, kid	...	...	...	17.0	17.0	17.0	...	...	...
18	Filberts	327.3	348.5	340.0	340.0	391.0	425.0	375.0	391.5	...
19	Fish, fresh	17.0	17.0	16.0	16.0	18.5	17.0	17.0	17.0	...
20	Hens	77.0	102.0	74.5	72.9	80.8	74.0	...	68.0	...
21	Honey	1085.0	1263.7	1379.4	972.9	...	...	1216.4	1244.6	...
22	Incense	160.0	150.0	150.0	127.5	122.0	102.0	187.0	255.0	...
23	Kid	...	29.0	27.4	25.0	25.0	25.7	24.4	...	...
24	Lambs	289.0	307.1	328.7	378.5	308.2	337.9	387.8	320.4	463.0
25	Lard	29.0	29.5	35.3	35.5	34.0	...	34.0	34.0	...
26	Linen	48.6	49.9	47.4	46.8	58.3	49.2	58.0	53.8	31.8
27	Mutton	...	...	...	15.2	15.2	14.7	...	16.5	17.0
28	Nails, large	18.0	15.0	15.5	15.7	17.0	15.4	16.3	17.0	17.8
29	Olive oil	480.3	659.3	855.7	888.3	595.0	582.3	578.0	689.5	650.9
30	Oranges	89.6	100.8	101.3	101.6	101.3	98.2	48.2	62.7	...
31	Paper, writing	300.0	298.3	328.7	374.0	310.5	306.0	419.3	425.0	367.2
32	Pears	88.6	...	66.2	112.5	112.5	100.0	105.8	...	...
33	Pepper	238.0	204.0	209.7	238.0	272.0	221.0	272.0	221.0	...
34	Perch	...	9.2	10.0	11.0	...	...	10.0	10.0	...
35	Plaster of Paris	...	...	30.0	...	49.5	40.0	...	26.0	...
36	Plums	...	...	50.0	...	37.5	60.0	60.0	...	...
37	Pork, salt	...	...	...	...	...	...	...	18.7	23.0
38	Pumpkin, candied	61.8	61.9	59.2	69.8	73.3	69.6	69.6	62.7	...
39	Raisins	275.0	273.5	299.3	303.2	282.4	286.1	286.1	243.1	330.8
40	Rice	348.5	334.3	399.5	380.0	387.0	374.0	387.5	408.0	...
41	Rye	174.7	161.5	200.0	197.8	170.0	182.8	191.5	195.5	...
42	Saffron	...	93.5	119.0	78.0	85.3	58.5	68.0	82.3	...
43	Salmon	24.0	23.0	32.0	34.0	23.0	...	32.0	34.0	...
44	Sardines	101.0	133.9	109.3	110.5	119.7	108.8	92.6	...	...
45	Sloes	...	...	...	...	38.8	65.0	...	...	...
46	Soap	377.3	526.9	804.3	707.0	812.5	511.4	563.4	680.0	700.0
47	Starch	15.2	16.0	16.0	18.9	24.0	18.9	...	...	...
48	Sugar	1598.0	1459.7	1624.0	1525.0	1375.9	1538.3	1484.7	1380.7	...
49	Trout	32.9	44.7	42.7	40.3	36.3	41.8	44.7	38.3	...
50	Twine	43.2	42.0	42.0	54.0	45.7	30.5	...	43.1	57.5
51	Vinegar	47.2	...	37.0	67.1	55.2	53.0	...	59.9	59.5
52	Walnuts	297.6	446.3	340.0	297.6	306.0	...	437.5	328.2	...
53	Wax, white	...	110.0	...	...	...	...	...	127.5	119.0
54	Wax, yellow	73.0	76.5	...	80.9	72.0	88.8	83.5	90.0	85.0
55	Wheat	247.0	259.9	277.0	239.1	210.4	278.4	279.4	297.5	192.7
56	Wine	141.0	159.1	152.0	123.8	127.6	149.3	...	96.0	160.0

C. OLD CASTILE–LEÓN (IN MARAVEDÍS) — Continued

#	Item	1569	1570	1571	1572	1573	1574	1575	1576
1	Almonds	39.8	49.1	56.9	52.8	52.8	...	85.4	...
2	Apples, cooking	118.6	135.2	160.1	92.5	...	...	151.4	...
3	Apples, pippin	108.0	136.0	174.9	122.1	151.3	156.9	160.2	123.3
4	Barley	79.3	...	162.6	162.6	162.6	162.6	162.6	162.6
5	Beef	7.7	7.7	7.4	7.7	8.4	...	...	...
6	Candles, tallow	...	22.8	...	...	...	...	26.0	...
7	Charcoal	41.3	39.4	44.8	41.6	31.5	...	...	...
8	Cheese	23.9	23.9	29.4	...	29.4	...	29.4	...
9	Cherries	74.4	117.5	95.0	62.5	91.3	78.8	82.5	130.0
10	Chestnuts	230.7	364.2	...	306.6	...	...	254.9	...
11	Chickens, spring	35.6	35.8	42.7	38.4	41.5	35.0	48.0	48.5
12	Chick-peas	606.9	520.2	693.6	476.9	...	...	552.7	...
13	Cinnamon	402.5	558.4	...	...	...	...	...	...
14	Cloves	...	29.4	...	...	...	...	...	...
15	Conger eel	...	...	...	...	...	...	...	...
16	Eggs	34.1	29.5	37.8	39.3	32.1	30.8	37.6	41.9
17	Feet, kid	17.3	17.0	17.0	17.0	17.0	17.0	17.0	17.0
18	Filberts	293.0	431.8	...	...	...	...	...	...
19	Fish, fresh	...	...	16.9	18.6	...	...	...	...
20	Hens	76.8	73.0	85.4	92.5	89.8	74.5	86.0	98.3
21	Honey	765.0	1292.0	1428.0	...	...	...	...	...
22	Incense	158.5	...	186.5	186.5	186.5	...	223.8	...
23	Kid	26.0	25.7	26.3	26.7	27.7	28.0	27.0	27.3
24	Lambs	...	...	...	...	...	...	584.0	...
25	Lard	...	30.2	34.0	33.6	...	...	...	...
26	Linen	83.4	53.2	60.3	...	...	...	...	...
27	Mutton	13.1	13.3	15.2	17.5	18.9	16.6	15.5	14.8
28	Nails, large	...	...	...	...	...	...	19.0	...
29	Olive oil	505.5	559.0	681.2	790.0	679.6	...	661.1	...
30	Oranges	98.8	112.0	96.0	129.9	96.7	128.9	117.3	84.3
31	Paper, writing	380.5	363.4	329.1	380.5	380.5	...	371.0	...
32	Pears	68.2	136.3	73.8	147.5	117.5	92.5	96.3	75.0
33	Pepper	...	...	...	...	...	...	...	...
34	Perch	...	...	...	...	...	...	...	...
35	Plaster of Paris	42.0	34.0	33.7	38.0	...	...	39.3	...
36	Plums	40.0	72.5	60.0	100.0	100.0	97.5	110.0	40.0
37	Pork, salt	22.0	22.0	21.6	22.0	23.6	...	21.6	...
38	Pumpkin, candied	63.9	64.0	64.0	64.9	62.4	...	85.0	...
39	Raisins	332.3	344.1	381.2	336.0	340.5	330.8	369.8	...
40	Rice	...	...	...	...	...	...	...	...
41	Rye	...	...	...	...	...	...	...	...
42	Saffron	67.3	72.8	81.2	91.0	107.7	...	101.8	...
43	Salmon	...	...	...	...	...	...	...	...
44	Sardines	...	...	...	...	...	...	...	...
45	Sloes	40.0	85.0	60.0	100.0	82.5	100.0	100.0	30.0
46	Soap	493.0	552.1	578.0	612.0	641.5	...	612.0	...
47	Starch	20.3	19.9	20.6	24.0	25.0	...	31.1	...
48	Sugar	1465.9	1190.0	1453.5	1377.0	1541.3	...	...	...
49	Trout	...	...	...	...	...	...	...	...
50	Twine	58.0	58.0	43.0	47.0	47.0	...	55.3	...
51	Vinegar	46.8	50.0	34.0	34.0	37.0	...	85.5	...
52	Walnuts	288.9	364.8	...	...	...	...	456.0	...
53	Wax, white	...	153.0	143.4	136.0	144.5	...	132.0	...
54	Wax, yellow	83.0	111.5	96.5	103.5	121.3	...	102.0	...
55	Wheat	...	...	311.7	311.7	311.7	311.7	308.9	311.7
56	Wine	112.0	128.0	124.7	176.0	112.0	...	202.7	...

C. OLD CASTILE–LEÓN (IN MARAVEDÍS) — CONTINUED

		1577	1578	1579	1580	1581	1582	1583	1584
1	Almonds	...	...	...	...	50.4	51.9	50.2	60.0
2	Apples, cooking	...	98.5	81.8	...	115.3	131.0	103.3	96.7
3	Apples, pippin	78.5	...	86.5	109.3	162.5	123.2	127.2	118.3
4	Barley	...	...	...	...	...	...	181.3	182.9
5	Beef	7.4	7.4	7.9	8.4	8.9	8.4	8.0	10.0
6	Candles, tallow	...	...	...	...	26.9	29.3	26.0	26.0
7	Charcoal	...	...	...	...	42.5	42.0	47.8	54.2
8	Cheese	26.9	26.9	...	24.5	24.5	19.6	31.9	22.5
9	Cherries	76.8	...	69.8	50.7	41.1	58.8	77.5	57.5
10	Chestnuts	279.2	364.2	364.2	333.9	333.9	...	476.0	374.0
11	Chickens, spring	39.8	...	46.7	46.3	...	43.5	45.5	47.0
12	Chick-peas	...	...	...	...	737.0	802.0	680.0	561.0
13	Cinnamon	268.3	...	...	...	...	...	442.0	510.0
14	Cloves	...	...	...	...	...	...	26.0	33.7
15	Conger eel	...	...	...	...	36.7	32.2	24.2	28.0
16	Eggs	42.0	...	39.9	42.3	...	39.0	47.2	42.9
17	Feet, kid	17.0	...	17.0	17.0	...	17.0	17.5	18.7
18	Filberts	354.7	462.7	462.7	424.1	424.1	...	476.0	462.7
19	Fish, fresh	...	...	...	...	18.9	20.1	22.0	24.8
20	Hens	96.3	...	107.9	103.9	...	100.6	108.4	101.1
21	Honey	...	...	...	...	1292.0	1360.0	918.0	1099.3
22	Incense	186.5	186.3	184.3	149.2	145.7	...	119.0	127.5
23	Kid	26.7	...	28.0	29.8	...	26.0	30.3	30.7
24	Lambs	...	...	...	...	...	...	297.6	318.8
25	Lard	...	...	...	...	40.3	40.3	40.0	39.7
26	Linen	...	...	...	74.6	...	74.6	74.6	63.0
27	Mutton	13.7	...	16.7	17.1	18.0	15.8	15.3	17.0
28	Nails, large	...	17.0	17.5	...	18.0	18.0	20.0	17.9
29	Olive oil	...	...	...	756.9	647.4	620.8	518.6	650.5
30	Oranges	114.1	...	121.3	112.0	...	71.3	113.3	74.2
31	Paper, writing	359.6	333.0	329.1	342.5	342.5	340.6	340.0	340.0
32	Pears	63.8	...	91.3	98.2	...	85.0	90.0	100.0
33	Pepper	...	...	...	...	...	...	238.0	238.0
34	Perch	...	...	...	...	...	...	12.0	13.4
35	Plaster of Paris	34.0	...	47.8	...	34.0	40.0	...	...
36	Plums	62.5	...	85.0	47.5	...	55.0	60.0	90.0
37	Pork, salt	19.6	25.0	27.0	26.0	25.5	24.4	26.4	25.0
38	Pumpkin, candied	77.0	68.0	...	...	85.0	85.0	66.0	76.0
39	Raisins	350.3	238.0	505.9	...	310.3	475.0	425.0	473.5
40	Rice	...	...	...	...	...	...	544.0	637.5
41	Rye	...	...	...	...	...	...	200.0	204.2
42	Saffron	85.3	...	88.0	82.0	82.3	90.5	131.0	120.0
43	Salmon	...	...	...	...	...	...	...	36.0
44	Sardines	...	...	...	...	...	...	132.7	114.8
45	Sloes	70.0	...	75.0	45.0	...	42.5	77.5	90.0
46	Soap	688.5	803.3	870.0	654.5	680.0	884.0	595.0	510.0
47	Starch	...	...	...	...	...	33.0	30.3	28.0
48	Sugar	1632.0	1200.0	...	...	1326.0	1496.0	1581.0	1938.0
49	Trout	...	...	...	...	...	...	62.2	67.0
50	Twine	45.7	53.0	58.2	65.3	54.0	52.5	51.5	51.0
51	Vinegar	70.9	...	76.5	73.8	91.4	61.5	49.7	...
52	Walnuts	364.8	456.0	456.0	418.0	418.0	...	555.3	391.0
53	Wax, white	...	...	136.0	136.0	144.5	136.0	148.0	136.0
54	Wax, yellow	...	106.0	102.0	108.0	108.0	108.0	98.0	100.5
55	Wheat	308.9	280.8	...	...	...	...	337.2	314.8
56	Wine	192.0	160.0	128.0	160.0	162.7	136.0	145.4	155.0

C. OLD CASTILE–LEÓN (IN MARAVEDÍS) — Continued

		1585	1586	1587	1588	1589	1590	1591	1592
1	Almonds	62.0	56.0	60.0	55.3	51.0	55.3	51.0	59.0
2	Apples, cooking	117.1	101.7	128.3	142.6	107.9	102.8	108.6	87.4
3	Apples, pippin	123.3	104.6	144.7	132.7	106.6	109.8	117.3	146.5
4	Barley	196.9	171.6	177.2	204.0	189.8	184.2	198.3	203.7
5	Beef	11.8	11.2	8.5	8.5	9.6	9.0	8.0	9.3
6	Candles, tallow	32.6	34.0	33.6	28.0	...	29.6	...	26.0
7	Charcoal	50.8	44.9	44.5	37.2	46.0	50.5	50.4	51.0
8	Cheese	29.2	25.8	22.3	22.0	36.6	23.9	24.2	26.6
9	Cherries	80.0	68.8	116.3	53.8	101.3	103.8	88.1	72.5
10	Chestnuts	408.0	362.0	323.0	291.4	340.0	340.0	442.0	323.0
11	Chickens, spring	46.4	42.5	41.8	39.1	42.5	47.0	46.0	53.3
12	Chick-peas	750.0	680.0	612.0	578.0	592.6	650.3	1190.0	1156.0
13	Cinnamon	408.0	340.0	408.0	408.0	408.0	390.0	351.3	361.3
14	Cloves	35.0	35.0	32.3	...	32.3	40.4	35.9	30.1
15	Conger eel	26.0	33.0	30.0	28.0	30.7	27.9	30.0	29.3
16	Eggs	44.3	40.5	41.9	39.0	39.8	46.3	48.4	55.0
17	Feet, kid	20.0	20.0	20.0	20.8	20.7	20.0	21.3	24.0
18	Filberts	408.0	374.0	408.0	544.0	...	340.0	510.0	620.5
19	Fish, fresh	18.0	22.0	22.0	20.1	21.3	18.0	17.5	22.5
20	Hens	98.4	98.8	86.2	87.1	92.2	101.0	91.7	98.3
21	Honey	1190.0	1088.0	1564.0	1496.0	1496.0	1904.0	1360.0	1243.0
22	Incense	139.3	119.0	90.7	166.7	204.0	221.0	170.0	374.0
23	Kid	32.0	33.2	31.4	30.0	31.0	32.0	31.2	29.0
24	Lambs	426.3	453.0	476.0	393.4	429.3	407.5	354.9	413.6
25	Lard	36.7	41.7	36.1	31.3	36.0	38.4	40.0	35.0
26	Linen	71.8	71.8	65.7	75.1	66.8	76.6	54.9	66.8
27	Mutton	18.8	18.8	16.5	16.0	17.4	17.6	16.0	17.0
28	Nails, large	21.0	19.5	18.0	19.3	18.0	18.0	21.3	20.0
29	Olive oil	782.0	680.0	607.8	622.1	731.0	782.0	654.5	715.9
30	Oranges	93.3	92.8	96.6	101.2	73.1	73.1	82.2	90.3
31	Paper, writing	344.3	340.0	345.7	348.5	453.3	595.0	544.0	583.7
32	Pears	85.0	77.9	115.0	121.3	116.3	59.2	97.5	87.5
33	Pepper	204.0	255.0	272.0	263.5	249.3	233.8	225.3	244.4
34	Perch	13.9	16.0	13.5	17.0	8.0	14.2	14.5	17.4
35	Plaster of Paris	...	40.0	...	...	34.0	34.0	...	59.5
36	Plums	60.0	80.0	100.0	40.0	127.5	40.0	77.5	55.0
37	Pork, salt	32.8	25.0	27.0	24.0	23.0	28.0	28.5	30.0
38	Pumpkin, candied	75.7	72.3	68.0	67.0	69.3	66.0	68.5	68.0
39	Raisins	501.5	402.3	375.0	390.4	459.0	646.0	590.8	493.0
40	Rice	667.3	595.0	566.7	531.3	544.0	624.8	654.5	855.7
41	Rye	231.3	235.2	251.2	272.0	235.9	208.3	272.0	272.0
42	Saffron	115.0	95.5	96.0	97.0	95.8	96.0	96.0	96.0
43	Salmon	34.0	40.0	...	34.0	...	34.0	34.0	35.0
44	Sardines	112.9	134.1	157.5	107.9	113.7	127.4	135.4	125.2
45	Sloes	65.0	80.0	125.0	50.0	120.0	40.0	77.5	95.0
46	Soap	808.3	750.0	740.8	562.5	750.0	850.0	612.0	542.4
47	Starch	28.0	23.2	24.0	17.0	31.0	22.5	28.0	34.0
48	Sugar	1409.9	1266.5	1326.0	1371.3	1377.0	1355.8	1371.3	1428.0
49	Trout	54.0	52.5	44.3	46.4	44.3	45.8	41.8	62.2
50	Twine	51.0	50.6	52.9	56.0	52.5	50.7	60.8	70.5
51	Vinegar	64.0	50.3	67.8	136.0	136.0	119.0	136.0	81.2
52	Walnuts	391.0	436.3	456.0	476.5	396.6	340.0	555.3	510.0
53	Wax, white	161.5	153.0	153.0	153.0	153.0	153.0	153.0	153.0
54	Wax, yellow	124.0	127.5	120.0	110.5	113.0	104.0	106.0	106.0
55	Wheat	272.4	304.3	287.2	343.5	293.9	289.0	376.6	476.0
56	Wine	201.0	230.0	391.0	383.1	317.9	432.0	232.0	209.7

C. OLD CASTILE–LEÓN (IN MARAVEDÍS) — CONTINUED

		1593	1594	1595	1596	1597	1598	1599	1600
1	Almonds	60.0	64.1	68.0	64.0	60.0	80.5	68.0	70.9
2	Apples, cooking	124.2	132.3	91.0	109.6	127.5	151.7	...	...
3	Apples, pippin	125.2	130.8	113.3	123.3	140.8	159.2	169.3	...
4	Barley	204.0	204.0	203.3	204.0	204.0	204.0	221.0	238.0
5	Beef	8.0	8.5	6.8	9.0	12.0	9.0	10.0	12.0
6	Candles, tallow	30.5	33.0	28.0	28.0	27.4	...	28.7	35.3
7	Charcoal	44.0	42.5	52.0	53.5	38.9	42.8	42.5	...
8	Cheese	29.7	29.4	28.2	20.5	26.6	32.4	23.6	27.7
9	Cherries	53.8	43.8	50.0	76.8	51.2	150.0	80.0	...
10	Chestnuts	510.0	374.0	340.0	340.0	569.5	612.0	291.4	340.0
11	Chickens, spring	54.0	56.0	54.0	51.6	59.8	44.3	65.5	...
12	Chick-peas	748.0	952.0	921.2	646.0	884.0	606.9	1496.0	850.0
13	Cinnamon	340.0	425.0	357.0	464.7	...	521.3	374.0	340.0
14	Cloves	36.8	53.8	38.1	32.3	56.5	44.9	37.7	28.3
15	Conger eel	26.0	30.9	30.0	33.9	37.0	40.0	35.0	33.0
16	Eggs	51.0	51.4	46.5	51.0	52.9	51.0	65.6	...
17	Feet, kid	24.0	24.0	21.3	22.7	24.0	24.0	24.0	...
18	Filberts	442.0	340.0	447.2	...	612.0	...	655.4	...
19	Fish, fresh	24.0	18.0	20.1	18.0	24.8	29.3	24.0	25.3
20	Hens	114.8	113.6	121.3	114.1	116.8	100.0	107.4	144.5
21	Honey	1496.0	1496.0	1360.0	1496.0	1360.0	1572.5	1723.2	1669.7
22	Incense	221.0	272.0	215.3	204.0	204.0	204.0	238.0	221.0
23	Kid	34.0	32.5	32.0	34.0	32.8	33.3	32.5	...
24	Lambs	446.1	406.5	387.9	398.1	450.5	451.6	398.0	476.0
25	Lard	42.5	40.9	35.3	39.5	45.3	46.8	34.0	56.9
26	Linen	64.0	61.8	77.6	73.0	87.4	87.1	77.0	99.9
27	Mutton	18.9	16.7	16.3	16.3	17.0	16.7	17.2	...
28	Nails, large	20.0	20.0	20.0	20.0	...	21.0	20.0	...
29	Olive oil	786.3	807.5	636.0	694.3	684.3	833.0	892.3	857.9
30	Oranges	102.7	124.7	152.0	106.7	136.0	109.6	148.0	...
31	Paper, writing	470.3	501.5	476.0	487.3	510.0	515.8	493.0	467.5
32	Pears	81.3	107.5	102.5	122.5	75.0	165.0	78.8	...
33	Pepper	225.3	240.8	247.9	246.5	235.9	265.6	398.6	289.0
34	Perch	...	...	12.8	...	11.2	...	...	12.0
35	Plaster of Paris	...	42.0	44.0	68.0	...	...	...	...
36	Plums	42.5	40.0	66.7	40.0	60.0	175.0	60.0	...
37	Pork, salt	26.0	33.6	29.0	28.7	33.0	31.0	28.3	...
38	Pumpkin, candied	68.0	71.3	74.7	68.0	83.5	84.7	88.0	118.3
39	Raisins	416.5	518.5	437.8	512.0	535.5	570.3	525.4	590.4
40	Rice	612.0	680.0	646.0	510.0	748.0	841.5	850.0	841.5
41	Rye	272.0	272.0	272.0	272.0	272.0	272.0	272.0	272.0
42	Saffron	94.5	87.5	82.0	97.5	132.0	184.5	160.5	109.8
43	Salmon	33.0	36.0	38.0	64.1	43.0	77.0	51.0	...
44	Sardines	163.0	203.3	200.0	284.2	263.5	312.7	272.0	227.4
45	Sloes	52.5	40.0	75.0	40.0	...	...	50.0	...
46	Soap	748.0	675.2	689.5	680.0	663.0	595.8	748.0	764.5
47	Starch	33.2	33.7	24.0	24.0	24.0	39.7	59.5	51.0
48	Sugar	1462.0	1474.7	1453.3	1538.5	1575.3	1751.0	2040.0	1918.4
49	Trout	49.3	53.6	57.6	57.5	46.9	55.5	40.9	65.7
50	Twine	62.3	56.1	53.4	65.5	70.8	65.0	68.0	76.2
51	Vinegar	39.0	55.5	50.5	42.5	62.3	62.0	104.1	113.1
52	Walnuts	408.0	396.6	440.8	371.9	493.0	535.6	646.0	555.3
53	Wax, white	153.0	153.0	153.0	165.0	160.0	158.0	178.0	...
54	Wax, yellow	112.0	113.0	119.0	137.5	148.0	136.0	148.0	140.2
55	Wheat	431.1	476.0	450.5	476.0	476.0	476.0	476.0	411.9
56	Wine	260.7	225.4	264.0	192.3	357.0	420.8	258.3	280.4

D. VALENCIA (IN DINERS)

		1551	1552	1553	1554	1555	1556	1557	1558	1559	1560	1561	1562
1	Ashes	12.8	12.0	12.1	12.1	11.3	9.5	8.5	8.7	10.3	14.0	9.0	9.6
2	Bedticks	...	141.0	150.0	150.0	177.0	...	...	...	204.0	...	150.0	150.0
3	Bricks	455.2	452.8	509.4	566.0	566.0	452.8	471.7	556.5	650.9	596.2	679.2	603.8
4	Carob beans	...	27.0	30.0	...	24.0	25.5	21.9	25.6	20.5	24.0	31.0	...
5	Charcoal	101.0	159.4	...	123.7	163.3	164.8	170.5	167.8	174.4	173.8	205.6	154.0
6	Chickens, spring	18.6	...	15.1	17.5	18.6	20.0	24.1	26.1	23.0	30.8	47.2	...
7	Codfish, dried	...	...	...	...	9.8	11.0	11.0	6.8	...	...	7.0	3.5
8	Eggs	13.6	14.2	13.9	15.5	15.0	15.0	17.1	17.3	17.4	17.0	19.3	17.4
9	Firewood	19.6	19.6	22.8	24.2	24.5	15.0	16.7	17.3	17.5	19.0	23.2	20.2
10	Flax	11.0	10.4	10.8	11.2	10.5	10.9	10.6	...	...	11.0	11.0	12.3
11	Grits, barley	50.0	...	...	50.0	50.0	...	80.0	60.0	60.0	...	...	...
12	Grits, wheat	50.0	...	...	50.0	50.0	...	80.0	60.0	60.0	...	...	...
13	Hens	40.2	45.5	46.5	44.4	41.5	36.1	44.1	50.3	49.3	43.3	46.7	45.2
14	Honey	974.0	1271.8	956.0	999.7	924.5	612.0	689.4	679.0	743.3	1053.0	1238.7	969.3
15	Lard	16.6	14.0	15.0	10.0	10.0	10.0	11.3	13.3	13.3	13.5	12.0	...
16	Lime	66.0	54.0	70.5	72.0	84.0	...	86.0	74.0	80.0	81.3	78.5	81.0
17	Linen	...	...	...	34.8	28.5	...	33.8	36.0	21.0	...	34.0	23.0
18	Mutton	21.5	24.0	25.0	26.0	26.0	25.0	24.8	27.1	28.0	30.9	33.0	32.0
19	Olive oil	234.0	148.0	179.1	155.6	211.7	240.7	196.5	185.1	155.9	183.7	235.8	314.0
20	Plaster of Paris	53.5	59.4	53.5	71.3	63.8	47.5	71.3	72.0	72.0	72.0	72.0	90.0
21	Raisins	67.7	102.8	82.6	76.5	...	...	77.5	80.3	72.9	53.7	47.6	79.4
22	Rice	743.5	877.6	1057.5	908.3	976.7	1163.3	1849.4	1061.7	989.8	813.8	...	...
23	Saffron	580.0	456.0	531.6	576.0	...	480.0	554.5	554.5	576.0	...	945.0	...
24	Sandals, hempen	129.0	138.0	144.0	150.0	161.3	162.0	146.3	144.0	156.0	168.0	165.5	168.0
25	Saucers	96.0	...	...	...	60.0	...	60.0	...	...	...	...	102.0
26	Shoes	84.0	84.0	...	88.2	83.1	88.2	78.0	100.8	...	98.7	95.4	...
27	Silk, raw	352.0	414.0	...	348.0	340.0	350.0	348.0	354.0	480.0	...	547.5	...
28	Soap	186.2	171.1	168.0	163.7	164.5	162.0	164.0	161.0	145.0	164.0	195.0	279.0
29	Sugar	...	...	24.3	29.2	21.1	...	14.6	18.6	...	29.2	...	...
30	Tuna fish	4.0	7.8	7.6	3.6	3.5	4.4	4.5	4.9	5.0	5.7	5.4	...
31	Turpentine	3.1	3.8	...	4.5	4.9	...	...	...	4.1	6.0	...	...
32	Vinegar	36.0	17.0	18.0	40.0	37.5	...	...	12.3	36.0	...	...	...
33	Wax, yellow	32.0	49.0	...	45.0	36.0	...	...	...	36.6	46.0	49.2	...
34	Wheat	780.0	864.5	783.8	636.3	729.0	756.0	1333.3	1027.5	910.9	845.6	875.5	1016.3
35	Wine	22.5	29.4	33.5	39.0	30.1	24.6	23.8	22.7	28.9	30.3	17.1	27.2

	1563	1564	1565	1566	1567	1568	1569	1570	1571	1572	1573	1574
1 Ashes	18.3	7.8	8.8	9.0	9.0	9.2	9.2	10.2	11.9	12.2	12.2	12.2
2 Bedticks	204.0	197.0	198.0	192.0			240.0			168.0		180.0
3 Bricks	566.0	640.0	716.6	679.2	636.8		622.6	594.3	600.0	566.0		420.0
4 Carob beans			33.0	24.0	28.0	38.8	25.0	38.3	36.0			34.1
5 Charcoal	148.0				202.1	196.5	194.8	190.0		198.5	213.0	198.0
6 Chickens, spring		24.7	19.7	19.0	23.0	17.0	20.9	29.3	28.1	35.2	27.7	21.2
7 Codfish, dried	4.2		6.0	7.0	8.0	8.5	5.1			4.8	6.3	
8 Eggs	17.6	18.0	16.5	17.6	18.4	20.3	18.4	20.6	22.2	22.7	20.9	21.0
9 Firewood	20.1	24.6	22.7	21.8	23.4	24.1	24.0	23.6	23.8	24.8	23.9	23.7
10 Flax	13.0	13.0	12.0	11.8	11.8	12.0	17.0	13.6	14.0	17.0	14.0	15.9
11 Grits, barley					60.0	60.0						
12 Grits, wheat					60.0	60.0						
13 Hens	45.4	47.2	45.2	45.8	47.8	50.3	47.0	45.3	49.2	64.1	60.3	52.0
14 Honey	927.0	928.0	980.6	1281.8	1032.3	1176.8	1052.5	1219.0	1151.8	1041.0	1146.5	1797.5
15 Lard	12.0	12.0			12.0	17.5	17.5	12.0	25.0			28.8
16 Lime	79.5	91.0	84.0	84.0	84.0	88.0	86.0	87.0	84.7	85.5	95.3	
17 Linen	44.0		30.0	29.5	44.7	39.0	42.0	23.1		50.0		
18 Mutton	29.8	28.5	30.0	32.0	33.0	34.1	33.9	34.0	33.4	33.0	33.7	37.0
19 Olive oil	338.1	223.8	224.6	267.0	313.5	201.5	228.4	271.3	344.5	276.5	304.5	219.2
20 Plaster of Paris	71.3	72.0	72.0	72.0	72.0	72.0	72.0	67.8	73.5	71.3	72.0	71.3
21 Raisins	91.5	85.0	83.1	74.4	66.1	75.8		87.1		80.2	91.8	90.1
22 Rice				1611.8	1121.0	1168.8	1268.0	1290.0	1536.0	1366.0	1421.5	1282.8
23 Saffron	168.0	168.0	384.0		485.2	462.1	456.0	484.0				
24 Sandals, hempen			162.0	156.0	156.0	156.0	168.0	168.0	169.5	180.0	189.0	186.0
25 Saucers	90.0		78.0		84.0		74.0	78.0	72.0	96.0		92.0
26 Shoes	90.0					92.0	90.0		90.0	91.0		
27 Silk, raw	390.0	414.0	192.0	420.0	384.0	480.0	534.0		224.0		480.0	540.0
28 Soap	282.0	229.5		207.1	231.0	187.5	177.0	186.0		243.0	240.0	213.7
29 Sugar					33.2	39.0	64.5				46.0	52.0
30 Tuna fish				7.0	6.0	6.3						
31 Turpentine						7.0	6.0					5.5
32 Vinegar			9.0		14.4	36.0			8.0		18.0	30.0
33 Wax, yellow			36.0	36.0	43.0	40.0	39.0	48.0	52.0	48.0	52.0	52.0
34 Wheat	951.5	853.5	770.9	1032.8	1047.0	950.3	968.6	1116.0	1471.5	1366.5	1090.9	1173.0
35 Wine	35.0	30.8	30.3	29.6	24.9	31.1	32.0	37.1	23.5	23.4	40.1	46.5

D. VALENCIA (IN DINERS) — CONTINUED

		1575	1576	1577	1578	1579	1580	1581	1582	1583	1584	1585	1586	1587
1	Ashes	12.6	15.5	16.3	16.3	16.2	16.5	14.9	...	...	...	13.7	14.1	15.3
2	Bedticks	...	...	...	...	...	...	...	150.0	...	...	...	...	222.0
3	Bricks	720.0	650.9	641.5	795.4	622.6	705.0	720.0	...	...	...	540.0	674.7	787.5
4	Carob beans	30.6	42.6	...	54.8	38.0	...	28.0	38.7	...	34.0	46.2	27.9	27.0
5	Charcoal	184.0	196.6	173.7	...	...	295.5	197.2	203.1	217.1	216.2	197.6	228.3	194.5
6	Chickens, spring	45.6	21.0	18.2	26.7	26.0	16.7	...	32.4	...	34.1	31.9	28.9	24.5
7	Codfish, dried	...	...	...	5.0	...	5.1	...	...	4.9	...	...	7.2	8.0
8	Eggs	21.0	21.0	21.3	23.8	24.9	24.1	21.6	22.7	23.6	24.0	24.7	27.5	23.0
9	Firewood	21.9	22.5	18.3	19.8	22.7	23.7	25.8	30.2	24.9	25.5	29.1	27.7	25.2
10	Flax	14.2	16.1	15.0	15.0	17.5	16.8	17.7	18.0	21.0	19.3	15.8	16.5	18.5
11	Grits, barley	...	...	...	60.0	...	70.0	...	...	...	...	...	70.0	70.0
12	Grits, wheat	...	...	...	...	...	70.0	...	...	...	...	...	70.0	70.0
13	Hens	54.0	52.6	41.9	54.8	63.6	54.7	59.4	55.1	61.7	61.3	64.3	64.7	61.6
14	Honey	1389.3	1027.0	1178.0	1592.0	1422.7	1553.0	1302.0	1684.0	990.1	1040.1	1251.6	1079.8	1374.8
15	Lard	...	21.5	16.0	27.3	...	24.0	27.7	29.0	...	...	...	20.0	22.0
16	Lime	96.0	120.0	88.3	...	96.0	94.2	102.0	...	96.0	90.9	96.0	96.0	96.4
17	Linen	...	...	28.0	...	...	54.5	...	...	...	51.0	...	...	66.5
18	Mutton	39.8	37.9	32.1	27.3	28.5	31.3	33.0	33.0	34.3	33.0	36.0	36.0	36.0
19	Olive oil	234.5	250.1	361.3	304.5	358.6	367.0	330.3	278.6	303.6	233.9	259.1	198.8	236.1
20	Plaster of Paris	81.0	80.0	78.0	78.0	83.2	83.2	84.0	84.0	...	83.2	84.9	80.0	82.0
21	Raisins	111.9	99.5	102.9	83.8	95.1	98.7	79.5	150.6	114.3	...	177.8	...	109.8
22	Rice	1545.5	1392.7	1422.5	1649.7	1638.0	693.2	...	1793.0	1929.0	...	1589.0	1259.0	1672.5
23	Saffron	...	360.0	...	...	...	...	...	...	...	644.0	644.0	754.4	771.7
24	Sandals, hempen	174.0	180.0	180.0	180.0	180.0	180.0	204.0	200.0	213.5	204.0	204.0	216.0	216.0
25	Saucers	...	84.0	...	...	...	...	168.0	168.0	...	...	192.0	168.0	177.8
26	Shoes	92.0	92.0	90.0	...	...	87.3	90.0	92.0	93.0	...	91.0	...	96.0
27	Silk, raw	...	552.0	...	...	...	588.0	345.0	564.0	...	660.0	...	...	834.0
28	Soap	204.0	234.0	270.0	257.7	270.0	276.0	276.0	266.0	252.0	224.5	226.0	216.0	216.0
29	Sugar	...	...	49.7	...	...	7.0	...	...	...	...	...	...	...
30	Tuna fish	...	...	...	8.0	8.0	9.0	...	...	...	...	...	8.0	9.0
31	Turpentine	...	8.0	7.5	8.0	8.0	...	...	...	9.0	...	...	12.0	8.0
32	Vinegar	46.5	17.5	12.0	12.0	46.0	48.0	51.3	19.0	23.0	...	23.5	18.0	36.0
33	Wax, yellow	52.0	49.0	48.0	48.0	46.0	48.0	...	60.0	52.0	...	...	53.4	52.0
34	Wheat	1179.0	1507.1	1429.3	1773.8	1729.0	1579.9	1363.3	1715.1	1974.3	2154.5	1538.0	1359.8	...
35	Wine	40.6	29.7	26.8	30.0	27.8	23.9	29.5	37.3	36.3	35.8	33.0	30.0	33.3

		1588	1589	1590	1591	1592	1593	1594	1595	1596	1597	1598	1599	1600
1	Ashes	16.8	14.7	13.6	14.5	12.1	12.1	16.9	20.3	17.4	16.6	16.2	16.9	16.2
2	Bedticks	218.0	191.7	184.0	184.0	142.5	...	...	...	184.0	155.3	...	195.5	...
3	Bricks	828.3	600.0	780.0	840.0	873.3	786.9	933.8	940.0	879.3	819.8	958.1	900.0	940.0
4	Carob beans	...	55.7	21.5	42.5	42.3	28.5	53.0	45.0	51.0	45.0	53.0	48.0	33.0
5	Charcoal	208.9	193.6	196.5	204.7	218.3	223.3	208.7	209.2	199.5	206.4	198.3	212.0	209.5
6	Chickens, spring	24.5	28.9	30.5	28.2	...	23.9	29.5	24.2	21.4	40.6	27.0	37.7	32.8
7	Codfish, dried	8.0	7.7	10.0	...	8.5	8.5	...	...	7.0	7.0	8.1	...	...
8	Eggs	22.8	25.8	28.2	26.4	26.6	29.0	28.9	26.6	27.7	27.6	26.4	30.0	31.0
9	Firewood	32.7	31.4	30.5	30.5	29.0	26.0	30.9	29.0	28.5	28.7	32.4	32.8	37.5
10	Flax	17.7	14.0	16.0	19.9	20.5	21.5	19.5	22.5	15.0	19.0	17.5	22.0	24.3
11	Grits, barley	70.0	70.0	70.0	70.0	72.0	80.0	80.0	80.0	80.0	80.0	...	...	...
12	Grits, wheat	70.0	70.0	70.0	70.0	74.4	80.0	80.0	80.0	80.0	80.0	...	...	...
13	Hens	61.1	62.3	70.3	60.8	...	62.5	68.7	72.9	75.7	76.1	72.7	85.8	76.6
14	Honey	1546.3	1787.8	1724.1	1185.7	1275.5	1223.4	1410.3	1144.5	1598.5	1552.9	1419.1	1656.0	1930.0
15	Lard	28.0	27.0	22.7	23.5	33.0	44.2	31.3	23.3	...	...	22.2	30.0	27.0
16	Lime	96.0	96.0	96.0	96.0	96.0	96.0	92.8	102.0	96.0	96.0	96.0	100.7	105.0
17	Linen	46.2	...	65.0	54.2	69.0	56.0	52.0	54.8	54.0	...	54.0	...	...
18	Mutton	37.0	37.0	36.4	36.0	34.0	35.0	35.0	33.0	32.0	34.4	36.0	36.0	41.1
19	Olive oil	256.8	326.0	337.0	316.1	353.3	394.0	284.1	304.5	287.3	339.1	387.1	463.3	455.1
20	Plaster of Paris	82.0	81.0	87.3	95.5	92.0	91.8	91.0	95.0	95.5	97.7	101.5	108.3	108.0
21	Raisins	105.8	179.9	98.5	103.4	127.7	105.3	71.3	117.5	105.0	109.9	142.1	166.6	137.6
22	Rice	1589.3	1617.0	1639.5	1917.8	2435.5	...	1846.4	...	1605.2	2078.1	2448.3	2305.0	2039.3
23	Saffron	685.0	690.0	901.1	659.0	657.3	673.3	714.7	643.3	826.8	935.0	1079.3	1279.1	1344.0
24	Sandals, hempen	216.0	216.0	213.0	210.0	...	258.0	180.0	189.0	189.8	212.8	217.3	215.3	210.0
25	Saucers	207.0	207.0	172.5	179.5	182.9	184.0	184.0	184.0	...	184.0	184.0	182.0	173.7
26	Shoes	102.0	98.0	92.0	96.0	93.4	...	92.0	92.0	92.0	101.3	105.3	96.7	96.3
27	Silk, raw	663.0	...	498.0	...	612.0	648.0	460.0	780.0	887.0	822.0	1171.8	1020.0	989.0
28	Soap	223.0	313.5	303.0	239.7	258.1	283.0	254.1	270.0	280.9	328.1	329.3	359.5	353.0
29	Sugar	51.2	48.0	52.0	48.0	49.3	47.5	47.5	33.0	47.5	43.2	46.4	51.3	57.7
30	Tuna fish	8.0	9.7	10.0	10.0	10.0	...	...	9.6	10.0	...	...	...	...
31	Turpentine	12.0	6.5	...	6.3	7.8	12.0	6.8	...	8.0	16.0	10.4	8.9	...
32	Vinegar	58.0	23.0	27.0	30.0	42.0	48.0	...	54.0	12.0	...	28.5	...	...
33	Wax, yellow	54.0	54.0	54.0	48.0	42.0	...	57.0	...	63.0	76.0	70.0	66.0	78.0
34	Wheat	1523.3	1620.0	1594.0	1621.5	1822.3	1957.5	1983.1	...	1486.0	1488.7	1800.0	1895.0	1684.1
35	Wine	42.8	46.8	44.8	41.0	47.7	53.7	29.5	42.5	34.7	39.0	53.5	74.2	67.6

APPENDIX V

PRICES, 1601–1650[1]

A. ANDALUSIA (IN MARAVEDÍS)

		1601	1602	1603	1604	1605	1606	1607	1608
1	Acorns	51.0	42.0	...	51.0	64.5	55.5	85.0	60.0
2	Almond oil, sweet	144.5	129.6	156.2	170.0	147.3	133.0	123.9	119.0
3	Almonds	1326.0	952.0	1470.5	1428.0	1434.1	1190.0	1122.0	1287.7
4	Alum	35.7	26.0	35.8	...	...	34.0	38.3	24.5
5	Anise	76.3	68.0	69.1	51.0	50.7	63.2	70.7	...
6	Apples, cooking	304.0	255.0	314.5	340.0	332.3	259.3	255.0	272.0
7	Apples, pippin	200.0	200.0	200.0	225.0	190.0	225.0	130.0	...
8	Ashes	170.0	...	324.0	408.0	260.7	208.3	215.7	222.3
9	Barley	204.0	...	487.0	454.8	535.5	340.6	321.8	356.6
10	Beans, horse	558.0	409.2	632.4	748.0	948.6	816.0	850.0	476.0
11	Beef	36.5	29.7	29.6	34.3	30.5	28.3	31.7	29.3
12	Bricks	3740.0	...	...	2040.0	...	...	4125.0	3740.0
13	Butter	159.0	136.0	132.0	96.3	124.7	128.0	119.0	120.5
14	Candles, tallow	46.1	30.8	28.3	32.8	51.6	37.2	28.4	28.0
15	Charcoal	86.0	73.0	79.9	81.6	65.8	70.0	85.4	80.4
16	Cheese	646.0	612.0	595.0	680.0	...	425.0	544.0	967.2
17	Chestnuts	94.0	85.0	119.0	119.0	106.3	102.0	119.0	119.0
18	Chickens, spring	85.0	57.7	76.6	84.4	81.3	77.3	58.9	61.8
19	Chick-peas	544.0	578.0	1292.0	1326.0	1724.4	1700.0	1450.0	918.0
20	Cinnamon	437.8	349.9	361.3	308.1	306.4	331.5	379.7	369.8
21	Cloves	391.0	385.3	384.6	333.2	534.5	630.9	778.2	773.8
22	Codfish, dried	...	...	...	...	...	24.0	21.0	...
23	Coriander	160.4	107.0	118.4	110.5	107.7	122.0	123.3	155.2
24	Cotton	272.0	187.0	...	187.0	187.0	204.0	...	318.8
25	Cuminseed	42.0	93.0	148.8	56.7	59.5	56.5	63.8	68.0
26	Cuttlefish	30.0	31.0	46.0	53.3	45.2	46.0	25.0	38.0
27	Dace	...	68.0	69.2	68.0	65.4	47.9	60.4	57.1
28	Dogfish	38.4	34.4	37.0	57.5	48.7	32.7	37.9	38.0
29	Dogfish, spotted	32.2	28.0	28.0	30.7	28.0	27.1	24.0	27.7
30	Eels	88.4	...	71.9	71.0	72.3	68.0	...	68.0
31	Eggs	87.0	62.3	74.8	97.6	81.9	84.4	75.9	63.0
32	Filberts	136.0	136.0	182.0	187.0	72.3	153.0	142.9	128.0
33	Firewood	76.0	74.0	72.0	70.0	72.0	69.5	68.0	76.5
34	Flounders	68.0	80.7	81.2	85.6	87.2	71.9	63.5	60.8
35	Garlic	45.0	...	20.0	28.0	68.5	49.0	18.0	34.0
36	Grapes	97.5	102.5	66.7	65.0	125.0	65.0	72.5	70.0
37	Hake	55.5	52.5	56.6	66.0	45.9	41.2	26.5	30.0
38	Hares	81.0	64.0	80.8	70.5	74.4	70.0	85.0	68.0
39	Hemp	44.3	45.1	43.3	56.2	54.0	52.8	53.3	42.1
40	Hens	192.3	129.7	155.2	203.6	188.8	198.7	184.5	150.9
41	Honey	837.0	795.6	748.0	816.0	715.0	833.0	952.0	850.0
42	Horseshoes	...	30.0	30.0	30.0	30.0	32.0	34.0	28.0
43	Ice	24.0	...	32.0	34.0	32.0	32.0	24.0	24.0
44	Kid	272.0	250.5	255.3	257.3	240.1	259.4	230.5	242.3
45	Lard	70.5	50.0	58.3	54.6	...	66.7	66.2	72.4
46	Lavender spike	38.0	...	55.7	46.5	32.4	32.2	34.2	22.7

[1] Appendix II lists the metrological units in terms of which prices are recorded and furnishes keys for the reduction of metrological units to the metric system and price quotations to a fixed weight of fine silver.

A. ANDALUSIA (IN MARAVEDÍS) — Continued

	1601	1602	1603	1604	1605	1606	1607	1608
47 Lentils	...	...	...	2033.2	1988.9	2433.9	2255.6	1497.3
48 Lime	875.5	831.1	476.0	680.0	680.0	612.0	705.5	850.0
49 Linseed oil	68.0	...	76.0	60.0	...	68.0	82.0	68.0
50 Milk	25.4	32.0	32.0	45.3	33.3	28.7	32.7	34.0
51 Mustard	136.0	148.0	153.0	238.0	344.3	198.6	219.2	221.0
52 Mutton	59.2	50.8	41.3	53.2	42.1	35.3	34.5	35.3
53 Olive oil	411.2	391.0	525.6	471.3	399.5	346.4	289.0	357.0
54 Orange blossoms	10.0	26.0	15.0	13.0	8.0	7.6	7.0	14.1
55 Oysters, large	16.0	20.0	21.4	20.0	16.0	11.5	15.5	17.0
56 Pepper	340.0	309.6	251.8	232.7	241.2	294.7	272.0	274.8
57 Pine nuts	55.3	66.0	58.0	65.0	60.3	60.6	56.7	49.5
58 Pitch	20.3	19.7	18.4	20.5	24.0	34.0	18.5	19.5
59 Plaster of Paris	412.0	402.6	408.0	423.1	552.0	408.0	408.0	466.2
60 Plums	110.0	125.0	50.0	106.6	57.5	133.2	120.0	107.5
61 Pork, fresh	53.8	35.5	35.8	45.8	48.3	45.5	47.8	51.0
62 Pork, salt	...	...	68.0	60.0	...	69.2	85.0	105.3
63 Potatoes	306.0	272.0	...	306.0	306.0	238.0	384.2	255.0
64 Prunes	26.0	36.0	33.0	44.5	60.0	34.5	30.0	32.0
65 Quail	88.0	68.0	85.0	78.3	68.0	89.3	74.9	63.6
66 Raisins	994.5	743.0	969.0	1292.0	680.0	671.5	696.0	1156.0
67 Resin	18.0	24.4	19.7	17.0	19.0	22.4	68.0	28.0
68 Rice	34.4	26.0	24.9	24.8	24.8	24.0	24.0	23.8
69 Saffron	2167.5	2057.0	2470.7	2091.0	1701.3	1377.0	1225.3	1926.7
70 Sardines	39.2	24.0	31.4	27.5	28.0	22.0	19.8	19.7
71 Sea bream	63.8	64.0	70.5	76.3	62.5	72.0	48.1	58.3
72 Sea eel, Mediterranean	85.0	70.3	62.5	93.5	63.8	34.1	49.3	52.5
73 Shad	68.0	76.0	84.3	102.0	85.0	102.0	70.0	85.0
74 Sheepskins	...	...	144.0	...	136.0	127.5	119.0	...
75 Soap	522.5	646.0	612.0	499.7	490.1	492.0	528.3	522.8
76 Sole	114.8	117.0	130.3	131.8	167.9	157.3	136.0	119.0
77 Starch	25.6	28.0	35.5	48.8	55.8	46.0	38.5	29.0
78 Sugar	2267.1	2584.0	1799.1	1490.3	1659.2	1700.0	1549.8	1635.4
79 Thread, basting	85.0	88.3	79.3	68.0	85.0	87.1	85.0	86.8
80 Thread, homespun	476.0	...	...	...	254.0	442.0	419.3	413.7
81 Thread, sewing	164.3	184.2	144.5	...	170.0	170.0	174.3	164.3
82 Tuna fish	...	...	21.8	50.1	41.1	36.0	13.7	...
83 Turnips	152.0	153.0	150.5	190.8	143.1	144.0	256.0	158.7
84 Twine	...	68.0	...	60.0	...	76.5	...	...
85 Veal	72.0	39.3	35.2	68.0	44.3	52.0	46.3	48.0
86 Vinegar	110.0	102.0	136.0	85.0	119.0	136.0	131.5	111.5
87 Walnuts	48.8	39.0	50.5	43.0	45.9	29.0	60.0	48.0
88 Wax, white	140.3	144.5	136.0	136.0	136.0	143.8	143.0	153.1
89 Wax, yellow	130.7	137.4	136.0	136.0	127.5	125.4	138.8	155.3
90 Wheat	274.1	204.0	941.0	1119.3	1301.5	790.5	631.8	680.0
91 Wine	131.0	252.8	221.0	274.8	175.8	257.8	213.3	279.0
92 Wool	408.0	...	442.0	646.0	646.0	544.0	589.0	684.0

A. ANDALUSIA (IN MARAVEDÍS) — Continued

		1609	1610	1611	1612	1613	1614	1615	1616
1	Acorns	59.5	...	...	...	28.0	51.0	...	44.0
2	Almond oil, sweet	130.3	170.0	143.3	119.0	119.0	113.3	...	113.6
3	Almonds	1568.3	1502.3	901.0	651.7	782.0	935.0	552.3	...
4	Alum	28.0	...	27.0	27.0	22.0	22.0	...	28.0
5	Anise	102.0	...	53.0	59.6	51.0	...	34.0	68.0
6	Apples, cooking	323.0	...	323.0	306.0	357.0	323.0	258.0	306.0
7	Apples, pippin	160.0	...	230.0	180.0	246.7	220.0	...	186.7
8	Ashes	148.8	...	136.0	138.8	153.0	153.0	...	153.0
9	Barley	414.0	272.0	316.2	295.4	306.1	238.0	238.0	478.2
10	Beans, horse	731.0	...	632.4	544.0	...	578.0	...	...
11	Beef	30.8	...	30.1	28.6	29.2	36.4	40.0	33.1
12	Bricks	3400.0	3400.0	3400.0	3400.0	3000.0	3230.0	3400.0	...
13	Butter	150.1	...	127.5	153.0	124.0	144.0	...	170.0
14	Candles, tallow	28.0	...	34.0	34.0	34.0	29.7	35.0	34.0
15	Charcoal	78.9	80.5	67.0	60.0	68.0	64.0	...	66.0
16	Cheese	719.4	...	665.0	967.2	...	374.0	...	806.0
17	Chestnuts	102.0	...	90.6	102.0	102.0	102.0	83.7	93.5
18	Chickens, spring	55.8	80.0	43.5	39.9	55.8	73.4	...	62.9
19	Chick-peas	824.5	552.5	544.0	655.8	663.0	...	...	1207.0
20	Cinnamon	335.8	...	283.2	289.0	284.8	260.7	382.5	340.0
21	Cloves	725.3	...	710.0	612.0	714.0	493.0	710.0	612.0
22	Codfish, dried	16.0	...	20.0	21.7	20.0	21.8	...	23.8
23	Coriander	118.1	...	111.3	107.5	102.0	106.5	140.0	107.7
24	Cotton	237.8	...	272.0	221.0	204.0	170.0	...	178.5
25	Cuminseed	57.0	...	51.0	50.9	51.0	43.7	...	45.0
26	Cuttlefish	34.5	...	33.5	39.0	34.0	34.0	...	38.0
27	Dace	61.3	...	42.3	57.9	48.5	57.3	...	62.5
28	Dogfish	41.0	...	34.5	42.0	35.0	35.8	...	38.3
29	Dogfish, spotted	29.8	...	29.0	30.0	28.3	30.3	...	32.0
30	Eels	122.2	...	68.0	60.0	51.0	51.0	...	88.4
31	Eggs	70.0	...	65.3	64.5	66.0	74.0	61.8	62.9
32	Filberts	142.5	...	136.0	136.0	136.0	128.0	119.0	119.0
33	Firewood	73.3	...	65.5	58.0	58.0	57.0	...	60.0
34	Flounders	70.8	...	53.6	51.1	53.5	54.2	42.7	60.3
35	Garlic	34.7	...	29.1	62.1	41.1	22.0	...	30.0
36	Grapes	100.0	...	...	80.0	160.0	40.0	...	35.7
37	Hake	34.0	...	45.0	31.1	31.5	33.0	...	35.0
38	Hares	85.0	...	60.0	68.0	51.0	68.0	66.0	68.0
39	Hemp	44.7	...	43.7	49.8	51.0	42.8	45.0	50.0
40	Hens	142.4	140.0	156.8	141.9	134.7	159.2	166.5	130.2
41	Honey	919.7	705.5	578.0	629.0	574.6	646.0	...	787.7
42	Horseshoes	34.0	...	34.0	...	34.0	34.0	...	34.0
43	Ice	24.0	...	16.0	16.0	...	...	...	24.0
44	Kid	233.5	...	238.0	218.5	212.0	272.0	244.0	204.5
45	Lard	58.5	68.0	64.0	51.7	51.3	54.0	56.0	54.0
46	Lavender spike	48.0	...	28.0	23.8	26.5	26.0	...	20.0

A. ANDALUSIA (IN MARAVEDÍS) — Continued

	1609	1610	1611	1612	1613	1614	1615	1616
47 Lentils	...	...	1996.4	1539.8	1331.0	2250.9	...	1983.7
48 Lime	612.0	700.0	663.0	510.0	646.0	680.0	680.0	...
49 Linseed oil	73.7	...	68.0	68.0	...	...	...	42.0
50 Milk	30.7	...	31.3	34.7	30.0	34.0	...	27.7
51 Mustard	238.0	...	...	...	226.7	168.4	...	527.0
52 Mutton	47.0	45.1	45.7	43.6	50.4	55.0	59.2	49.8
53 Olive oil	384.0	380.0	430.7	293.3	408.0	357.0	438.9	314.5
54 Orange blossoms	9.5	...	8.0	8.0	6.0	14.0	...	18.0
55 Oysters, large	16.7	...	25.0	16.5	18.0	18.0	...	24.5
56 Pepper	272.0	...	249.3	...	...	254.9	203.8	237.8
57 Pine nuts	55.3	...	51.3	50.8	50.3	51.2	...	49.5
58 Pitch	18.0	...	17.0	21.0	20.0	19.0	17.3	18.0
59 Plaster of Paris	399.5	340.0	340.0	367.0	366.8	355.5	374.0	306.0
60 Plums	60.0	...	110.0	106.6	...	114.5	...	82.5
61 Pork, fresh	43.8	...	38.0	43.2	39.6	55.2	46.5	46.2
62 Pork, salt	...	76.5	68.0	58.0	51.0	66.0	66.0	62.0
63 Potatoes	317.0	...	272.0	255.0	272.0	280.0	238.0	272.0
64 Prunes	34.0	...	28.0	30.7	...	34.0	...	34.0
65 Quail	72.1	...	79.6	71.1	68.9	63.6	90.1	68.0
66 Raisins	1022.4	...	952.0	1124.4	1122.0	782.0	...	629.0
67 Resin	17.0	...	17.0	22.0	20.0	18.5	18.5	17.0
68 Rice	18.1	...	20.0	20.0	20.0	22.8	...	20.0
69 Saffron	2175.2	3077.0	2839.0	2737.0	2550.0	2145.0	2210.0	1178.7
70 Sardines	29.3	...	26.0	32.0	40.0	31.1	...	31.4
71 Sea bream	45.3	...	52.5	43.5	55.0	45.3	...	52.5
72 Sea eel, Mediterranean.	46.5	...	48.3	68.0	45.3	55.1	...	62.0
73 Shad	55.8	...	64.0	51.0	59.8	61.8	...	70.0
74 Sheepskins	153.0	...	136.0	174.3	170.0	...	...	144.5
75 Soap	490.9	...	504.3	476.0	476.0	544.0	510.0	487.3
76 Sole	113.3	...	89.3	136.0	106.5	80.8	...	93.5
77 Starch	33.2	...	28.0	28.2	30.7	33.3	30.0	29.3
78 Sugar	1720.8	1388.6	1445.0	1574.6	1700.0	1536.7	1391.3	1056.1
79 Thread, basting	81.2	...	68.0	68.0	68.0	68.0	...	72.0
80 Thread, homespun	396.7	...	408.0	408.0	408.0	408.0	408.0	408.0
81 Thread, sewing	153.9	...	143.1	131.8	136.0	136.0	...	145.5
82 Tuna fish	34.8	...	26.2	32.0	28.0	30.0	...	33.0
83 Turnips	178.5	...	136.0	136.0	68.0	170.0	...	64.0
84 Twine	60.0	...	60.0	...	60.0	60.0	...	62.7
85 Veal	46.4	...	51.5	48.0	46.8	51.4	...	46.0
86 Vinegar	85.0	90.7	119.0	110.8	195.6	226.7	...	140.0
87 Walnuts	44.7	...	34.0	34.0	30.6	36.0	...	28.9
88 Wax, white	144.4	...	144.0	144.5	144.0	143.8	140.0	144.0
89 Wax, yellow	142.9	136.0	132.4	119.0	139.5	134.6	105.0	137.0
90 Wheat	590.8	705.5	437.8	452.6	719.7	616.3	496.2	905.3
91 Wine	241.2	148.8	195.0	255.0	255.0	314.5	247.0	175.7
92 Wool	680.0	646.0	685.7	884.0	850.0	1160.6	884.0	1178.0

A. ANDALUSIA (IN MARAVEDÍS) — Continued

		1617	1618	1619	1620	1621	1622	1623	1624
1	Acorns	...	29.6	...	41.4	...	29.6	33.4	33.4
2	Almond oil, sweet	120.0	122.1	119.0	130.2	...	136.0	132.0	128.8
3	Almonds	1113.5	1054.0	1081.8	1125.0	...	1292.0	850.0	1325.5
4	Alum	24.0	...	26.7	28.0	...	22.0	...	28.0
5	Anise	82.1	65.0	54.4	50.3	...	50.7	45.8	85.0
6	Apples, cooking	357.0	259.3	340.0	263.5	...	323.0	266.3	314.5
7	Apples, pippin	200.0	186.7	150.0	110.0	...	200.0	180.3	137.9
8	Ashes	146.6	158.3	160.5	153.0	...	152.0	159.9	161.5
9	Barley	307.5	295.4	270.0	364.5	...	472.6	337.0	279.3
10	Beans, horse	646.0	632.4	408.0	1106.7	...	836.0	612.0	561.0
11	Beef	33.8	36.0	36.8	36.7	...	36.5	41.0	46.0
12	Bricks	3000.0	2720.0	2992.0	2856.0	...	2720.0	3060.0	2720.0
13	Butter	127.0	127.0	127.5	110.5	...	136.0	170.0	140.3
14	Candles, tallow	...	...	33.3	...	...	36.0	45.8	34.0
15	Charcoal	68.0	74.0	76.0	76.0	...	64.0	60.0	62.0
16	Cheese	510.0	612.0	612.0	814.1	...	1110.3	725.4	685.1
17	Chestnuts	112.8	88.0	110.0	119.0	...	74.2	119.0	102.0
18	Chickens, spring	76.4	68.8	63.8	65.8	...	78.3	77.5	68.9
19	Chick peas	884.0	1125.8	844.8	510.0	...	845.6	1500.0	1323.4
20	Cinnamon	246.5	216.8	201.9	206.1	...	184.9	191.5	212.5
21	Cloves	566.7	586.5	510.0	578.0	...	680.0	680.0	544.0
22	Codfish, dried	24.0	21.7	23.8	23.4	...	27.0	31.5	32.0
23	Coriander	96.3	97.8	102.0	102.0	...	125.7	175.6	153.0
24	Cotton	204.0	187.0	...	238.0	...	187.0	170.0	153.0
25	Cuminseed	76.7	76.5	51.0	51.0	...	40.8	42.0	37.3
26	Cuttlefish	40.0	38.0	33.0	36.5	...	43.0	34.7	32.0
27	Dace	60.5	57.7	59.5	63.7	...	74.4	68.8	72.3
28	Dogfish	41.0	44.0	45.5	52.5	...	59.0	50.5	57.4
29	Dogfish, spotted	31.5	34.5	32.0	35.8	...	32.0	34.0	36.0
30	Eels	68.0	80.0	55.5	...	...	72.3	76.5	...
31	Eggs	66.7	71.7	61.8	75.2	...	74.1	77.3	69.7
32	Filberts	...	...	134.0	...	...	118.0	120.0	136.0
33	Firewood	60.0	79.0	77.5	64.0	...	66.0	60.0	60.0
34	Flounders	59.6	75.2	67.6	70.4	...	59.3	64.0	60.2
35	Garlic	...	42.5	28.0	27.5	...	47.3	39.0	34.3
36	Grapes	38.8	...	50.0	160.0	...	70.0	40.0	...
37	Hake	38.7	50.0	44.7	41.8	...	36.0	48.3	44.3
38	Hares	51.0	...	76.0	68.0	...	...	72.0	68.0
39	Hemp	46.6	45.4	41.3	42.0	...	36.2	55.5	57.3
40	Hens	159.0	183.6	184.3	152.5	...	169.0	175.8	169.5
41	Honey	892.5	751.4	722.5	501.5	...	612.0	612.0	...
42	Horseshoes	34.0	34.0	34.0	34.0	...	34.0	34.0	34.0
43	Ice	...	20.0	16.0	...	...	16.0	20.0	20.0
44	Kid	225.0	212.5	232.0	234.0	...	232.1	340.0	249.3
45	Lard	65.3	73.5	54.0	53.3	...	93.5	59.0	63.0
46	Lavender spike	52.0	53.3	34.0	29.0	...	22.0	25.0	26.0

A. ANDALUSIA (IN MARAVEDÍS) — Continued

		1617	1618	1619	1620	1621	1622	1623	1624
47	Lentils	1991.6	1927.0	1414.1	930.8	...	1830.1	2091.0	1173.0
48	Lime	652.5	623.3	637.5	646.0	...	484.5	606.7	578.0
49	Linseed oil	102.0	85.0	68.0	60.0	...	85.0	68.0	...
50	Milk	32.7	34.7	34.0	35.8	...	41.3	37.3	34.7
51	Mustard	119.0	168.0	187.0	202.7	...	206.7	209.3	...
52	Mutton	37.5	44.6	55.1	44.0	...	55.9	63.4	55.4
53	Olive oil	...	535.5	412.0	399.5	...	481.2	389.7	625.5
54	Orange blossoms	6.0	8.3	...	9.0	...	...	8.0	...
55	Oysters, large	24.0	12.0	15.0	24.0	...	19.0	12.0	30.7
56	Pepper	272.0	276.3	204.0	257.8	...	266.6	272.0	238.0
57	Pine nuts	54.0	50.3	51.0	53.5	...	49.9	48.1	46.3
58	Pitch	19.0	16.5	21.3	23.0	...	18.0	19.4	19.3
59	Plaster of Paris	397.2	384.4	357.2	379.3	...	386.4	355.5	385.2
60	Plums	106.6	68.7	95.0	105.0	...	70.0	97.5	...
61	Pork, fresh	48.8	50.7	45.4	48.4	...	49.0	53.8	64.5
62	Pork, salt	56.0	68.0	57.0	51.0	...	61.0	51.0	...
63	Potatoes	276.3	259.0	272.0	259.0	...	272.0	187.0	340.0
64	Prunes	30.0	...	30.7	31.5	...	68.5	32.0	28.0
65	Quail	60.0	68.0	76.0	68.0	...	81.1	...	85.0
66	Raisins	1003.0	867.0	884.0	952.0	...	1020.0	901.0	680.0
67	Resin	19.0	16.5	22.0	23.0	...	17.7	18.7	19.0
68	Rice	20.0	22.1	21.3	21.9	...	24.0	23.6	30.5
69	Saffron	...	1258.0	1224.0	2295.0	...	2346.0	2550.0	...
70	Sardines	27.9	43.3	22.9	28.8	...	44.0	22.5	20.0
71	Sea bream	57.5	67.3	74.5	76.5	...	68.0	69.0	64.0
72	Sea eel, Mediterranean.	51.0	85.0	51.5	76.5	...	56.0	66.0	68.0
73	Shad	63.8	79.3	75.8	74.5	...	93.5	80.5	119.0
74	Sheepskins	...	122.0	152.6	191.0	...	178.5	164.3	...
75	Soap	544.0	566.7	552.5	490.9	...	532.7	546.2	707.7
76	Sole	89.3	95.5	74.3	80.8	...	102.0	107.2	94.0
77	Starch	48.0	42.5	28.0	...	...	36.0	39.4	37.0
78	Sugar	1428.0	1394.0	1377.0	1346.4	...	1292.0	1258.0	1428.0
79	Thread, basting	76.0	81.8	99.2	88.7	...	68.0	70.0	76.0
80	Thread, homespun	408.0	407.5	408.0	416.5	...	...	382.5	380.4
81	Thread, sewing	138.0	144.5	180.6	167.2	...	144.5	141.7	136.0
82	Tuna fish	32.0	39.0	32.0	36.0	...	32.0	40.0	46.6
83	Turnips	67.7	201.3	153.0	275.0	...	300.0	178.5	140.3
84	Twine	64.0	68.0	74.0	64.5	...	...	62.0	68.0
85	Veal	48.5	51.0	61.0	51.0	...	46.0	...	68.0
86	Vinegar	...	178.5	87.0	102.0	...	124.6	...	165.8
87	Walnuts	33.2	34.0	30.6	28.1	...	26.4	39.1	35.7
88	Wax, white	144.0	144.0	144.0	142.0	...	136.0	136.0	140.3
89	Wax, yellow	136.0	136.5	136.0	136.0	...	136.0	136.0	136.0
90	Wheat	1125.0	843.6	833.0	777.8	...	871.3	633.3	578.0
91	Wine	221.0	201.2	306.0	198.3	...	221.0	237.8	240.2
92	Wool	646.0	1195.9	970.0	1143.3	...	816.0	...	884.0

A. ANDALUSIA (IN MARAVEDÍS) — Continued

		1625	1626	1627	1628	1629	1630	1631	1632
1	Acorns	40.0	48.0	36.2	36.2	36.0	36.0	32.0	35.5
2	Almond oil, sweet	128.0	158.7	187.0	204.0	178.5	161.5	154.4	148.8
3	Almonds	994.5	1294.2	1994.7	1700.0	...	1399.2	850.0	1343.0
4	Alum	24.0	46.8	34.0	36.0	32.0	39.0	48.1	44.0
5	Anise	99.8	85.6	102.0	90.8	65.8	50.0	56.3	56.6
6	Apples, cooking	300.3	284.0	306.0	306.0	325.0	306.0	323.0	412.5
7	Apples, pippin	...	...	120.0	141.7	180.2	...	159.6	225.3
8	Ashes	153.0	153.0	186.7	172.8	193.6	175.7	204.0	170.0
9	Barley	408.0	520.6	629.0	484.5	306.0	312.0	350.6	348.5
10	Beans, horse	750.0	770.7	558.0	884.0	...	613.8	408.0	680.0
11	Beef	49.7	56.3	57.2	55.2	41.3	41.3	40.2	40.3
12	Bricks	3230.0	3516.7	...	...	3400.0	...	3332.0	4420.0
13	Butter	...	153.0	136.0	153.0	272.0	170.0	204.0	168.0
14	Candles, tallow	...	52.0	54.0	...	...	...	...	37.5
15	Charcoal	78.5	74.3	...	102.0	90.0	106.0	80.0	98.0
16	Cheese	941.0	1094.1	986.0	952.0	816.0	1047.8	714.0	767.7
17	Chestnuts	102.0	151.5	115.5	111.3	110.5	111.3	102.0	68.0
18	Chickens, spring	71.8	81.9	92.6	112.7	86.4	85.0	78.3	87.6
19	Chick-peas	1190.0	1125.0	1224.0	1020.0	672.5	1006.0	833.0	833.0
20	Cinnamon	306.0	306.0	555.3	561.0	476.0	408.0	348.5	507.2
21	Cloves	...	965.6	1931.2	2896.8	1576.2	1448.4	1448.4	2051.9
22	Codfish, dried	32.3	37.2	41.5	30.0	41.8	39.4	40.0	39.0
23	Coriander	136.0	96.0	96.0	111.8	153.0	136.0	136.0	122.5
24	Cotton	310.5	323.0	340.0	289.0	238.0	209.3	...	170.0
25	Cuminseed	100.0	113.7	87.7	80.5	65.3	56.7	50.0	42.5
26	Cuttlefish	31.0	61.3	46.0	46.0	46.5	47.0	46.7	...
27	Dace	74.9	92.8	98.0	80.8	90.7	66.5	85.9	71.9
28	Dogfish	55.0	64.4	64.4	42.3	56.0	55.7	54.9	62.0
29	Dogfish, spotted	50.0	60.5	56.0	48.3	52.0	44.0	44.0	48.0
30	Eels	68.7	112.7	79.2	...	84.0	70.0	68.0	132.6
31	Eggs	62.3	90.0	89.3	91.5	72.0	70.5	...	79.8
32	Filberts	204.0	221.0	...	178.8	195.0	170.0	...	...
33	Firewood	78.5	86.5	106.0	102.0	116.2	93.5	92.0	100.0
34	Flounders	71.2	72.0	75.0	78.0	59.9	56.2	66.6	58.8
35	Garlic	30.0	19.0	42.5	36.8	29.0	18.0	20.0	26.0
36	Grapes	52.5	45.0	40.0	40.0	25.0	57.5	46.7	40.0
37	Hake	48.0	...	68.0	44.0	...	...	...	...
38	Hares	85.0	...	102.0	85.0	94.0	102.0	...	85.0
39	Hemp	64.0	79.3	66.5	47.5	43.7	43.9	...	38.7
40	Hens	149.0	188.1	209.1	242.5	183.3	173.6	185.2	206.6
41	Honey	833.0	782.0	986.0	952.0	731.0	1088.0	918.0	906.1
42	Horseshoes	34.0	40.0	44.0	51.0	...	56.0	52.0	46.1
43	Ice	...	20.0	24.0	24.0	24.0	20.0	24.0	24.0
44	Kid	289.0	306.0	314.5	306.0	289.0	242.0	306.0	309.3
45	Lard	62.1	71.9	58.9	57.4	...	53.0	64.5	69.0
46	Lavender spike	26.0	32.0	68.0	37.0	35.3	28.7	28.0	26.0

A. ANDALUSIA (IN MARAVEDÍS) — CONTINUED

		1625	1626	1627	1628	1629	1630	1631	1632
47	Lentils	1500.0	1497.3	1497.3	1768.0	1652.1	1608.7	1665.0	1598.0
48	Lime	603.5	773.5	816.0	...	...	884.0	748.0	782.0
49	Linseed oil	68.0	119.0	...	119.0	...	...	68.0	...
50	Milk	38.0	42.0	40.7	34.0	34.7	39.3	39.3	42.3
51	Mustard	...	...	283.6	340.0	...	...	...	272.0
52	Mutton	56.7	44.3	59.9	43.4	34.1	32.1	45.6	32.1
53	Olive oil	345.0	540.5	456.0	786.0	552.5	629.0	578.0	716.0
54	Orange blossoms	8.0	8.0	23.0	16.0	8.0	16.0	9.0	19.0
55	Oysters, large	20.0	40.0	24.0	...	24.0	27.5	18.5	20.8
56	Pepper	204.0	305.3	246.0	272.0	...	308.0	...	271.9
57	Pine nuts	58.3	80.5	...	85.0	70.7	55.0	59.0	57.0
58	Pitch	...	30.0	40.0	34.0	32.7	34.0	31.3	24.0
59	Plaster of Paris	374.3	396.8	419.3	424.8	469.2	464.5	403.5	400.8
60	Plums	115.0	120.0	91.6	240.0	75.0	80.1	67.5	186.5
61	Pork, fresh	53.8	72.9	50.5	51.0	52.3	53.0	62.8	65.3
62	Pork, salt	68.0	85.0	...	82.0	68.0	68.0	60.0	110.5
63	Potatoes	340.0	255.0	264.0	208.0	276.3	272.0	280.0	184.0
64	Prunes	24.0	68.0	50.0	48.0	34.0	49.5	51.0	34.0
65	Quail	76.0	78.9	102.0	85.0	85.0	85.0	69.4	88.0
66	Raisins	1054.0	1122.0	1292.0	986.0	612.0	952.0	680.0	680.0
67	Resin	48.0	102.0	40.0	62.3	...	34.0	31.3	26.0
68	Rice	45.0	36.1	37.0	33.1	30.1	40.0	30.5	40.0
69	Saffron	1802.0	2805.0	2669.0	2278.0	1785.0	1875.0	1666.0	1598.0
70	Sardines	27.5	41.8	35.5	38.5	39.3	30.8	37.8	33.0
71	Sea bream	66.3	65.6	75.5	58.5	67.1	74.3	67.3	66.6
72	Sea eel, Mediterranean	68.0	87.1	68.0	70.0	83.0	83.0	102.0	85.0
73	Shad	82.0	127.5	102.0	68.0	94.5	96.3	79.5	74.8
74	Sheepskins	178.5	...	...	...	...	...	136.0	144.5
75	Soap	561.0	544.0	600.0	612.0	680.0	595.0	680.0	612.0
76	Sole	92.3	161.5	102.0	85.0	102.0	95.5	85.0	94.7
77	Starch	29.7	24.0	37.0	42.3	39.0	40.0	32.0	37.3
78	Sugar	1641.3	2074.0	2618.0	1803.0	1921.7	1921.7	1604.9	1952.1
79	Thread, basting	96.5	106.3	102.0	90.7	76.5	85.0	83.3	76.5
80	Thread, homespun	413.3	450.5	476.0	419.3	459.0	442.0	458.0	446.3
81	Thread, sewing	164.7	198.3	181.3	181.3	170.0	155.7	163.0	153.0
82	Tuna fish	38.2	40.0	41.3	41.0	44.0	42.0	43.5	44.0
83	Turnips	136.0	144.5	170.0	108.0	90.7	166.5	184.3	150.0
84	Twine	74.0	90.0	89.5	85.0	102.0	72.0	68.0	72.3
85	Veal	64.0	86.9	87.3	100.7	60.3	68.0	68.0	65.0
86	Vinegar	145.0	170.0	136.0	144.0	...	136.0	92.0	102.0
87	Walnuts	33.2	39.1	34.0	43.4	34.0	40.8	30.6	36.6
88	Wax, white	153.8	238.0	221.0	221.0	221.0	221.0	204.0	187.0
89	Wax, yellow	136.0	210.4	204.0	223.9	196.9	206.8	190.7	153.0
90	Wheat	782.0	994.5	1185.8	1122.0	875.5	718.3	714.0	731.0
91	Wine	314.5	357.0	176.0	188.0	217.2	150.0	284.8	136.0
92	Wool	1385.8	1122.0	1020.0	...	714.0	816.0	1011.8	1212.6

A. ANDALUSIA (IN MARAVEDÍS) — Continued

		1633	1634	1635	1636	1637	1638	1639	1640	1641
1	Acorns	42.8	35.5	30.0	39.8	40.0	35.5	43.8	40.0	...
2	Almond oil, sweet	153.0	153.0	153.0	153.0	153.0	153.0	154.1	153.0	152.0
3	Almonds	1566.0	1479.0	1700.0	1428.0	1326.0	1258.0	1037.0	1360.0	943.5
4	Alum	34.5	34.0	34.0	42.5	38.3	36.0	35.0	38.0	63.8
5	Anise	75.5	68.0	64.0	64.7	72.3	99.2	68.0	51.0	110.0
6	Apples, cooking	327.0	374.0	323.0	433.5	400.0	294.7	357.0	343.0	340.8
7	Apples, pippin	150.0	144.8	200.0	200.0	255.3	200.0	180.0	160.0	180.3
8	Ashes	170.0	159.5	170.0	168.6	170.0	170.0	170.0	170.0	175.7
9	Barley	374.0	351.3	425.0	480.3	484.5	367.0	240.1	170.0	340.0
10	Beans, horse	612.0	612.0	646.4	1054.0	1156.0	750.0	510.0	521.3	632.4
11	Beef	39.9	34.7	31.0	31.2	41.0	45.5	46.0	42.9	44.7
12	Bricks	3000.0	2771.0	2822.0	2958.0	...	...	3060.0	3077.0	3162.0
13	Butter	170.0	170.0	151.5	...	187.0	204.0	136.0	102.0	...
14	Candles, tallow	42.0	41.7	44.5	48.0	44.0	44.9	48.0	40.0	60.0
15	Charcoal	83.5	94.0	87.5	94.0	107.4	100.0	90.0	93.5	88.0
16	Cheese	850.0	848.0	748.0	850.0	1122.0	918.0	...	850.0	1020.0
17	Chestnuts	111.3	111.3	102.0	119.0	102.0	119.0	123.5	110.5	114.5
18	Chickens, spring	81.1	68.5	77.4	106.3	123.1	85.3	93.7	74.4	83.9
19	Chick-peas	850.0	765.0	765.0	1889.0	1360.0	850.0	493.0	510.0	578.0
20	Cinnamon	620.5	752.0	555.3	485.2	564.8	577.3	580.9	566.7	1130.5
21	Cloves	1408.6	1388.1	1247.2	1271.6	1040.9	1086.3	964.2	1058.6	1088.0
22	Codfish, dried	39.0	38.3	36.6	40.0	45.6	45.0	48.0	45.2	46.7
23	Coriander	136.0	96.0	163.2	127.5	96.0	103.4	93.5	136.0	116.0
24	Cotton	170.0	178.5	255.0	246.5	238.0	215.3	195.5	199.8	204.0
25	Cuminseed	...	48.0	109.8	136.0	102.0	93.5	85.0	65.7	68.0
26	Cuttlefish	57.0	42.5	52.0	58.7	54.0	64.0	60.0	62.0	70.0
27	Dace	66.2	56.4	66.0	68.0	74.4	68.3	81.7	79.9	81.0
28	Dogfish	45.9	49.8	55.3	55.5	65.5	64.5	72.0	80.5	68.5
29	Dogfish, spotted	47.5	46.0	47.2	53.3	52.0	...	52.0	56.0	...
30	Eels	...	...	...	76.0	136.0	76.0	...	85.0	92.0
31	Eggs	68.0	69.0	78.1	100.0	125.1	99.1	76.8	67.8	71.7
32	Filberts	175.0	134.0	136.0	144.0	195.5	187.0	204.0	204.0	221.0
33	Firewood	113.5	103.5	106.3	93.5	119.0	89.3	92.5	87.8	88.0
34	Flounders	68.8	58.9	60.9	62.3	71.8	73.5	79.1	85.5	87.0
35	Garlic	34.0	24.0	18.0	34.0	68.0	51.0	42.5	24.0	32.0
36	Grapes	42.5	40.0	50.0	40.0	50.0	40.0	66.7	52.5	53.3
37	Hake	102.0	69.9	68.3	58.0	...	77.0	78.0	80.0	...
38	Hares	87.3	85.0	101.0	70.0	82.8	85.0	89.3	84.8	102.0
39	Hemp	42.7	44.0	52.5	64.0	72.1	74.0	66.0	56.6	62.7
40	Hens	173.7	167.5	164.1	193.8	267.3	241.7	196.7	159.4	171.6
41	Honey	850.0	884.0	680.0	663.0	680.0	600.7	637.5	782.0	612.0
42	Horseshoes	47.0	44.0	48.0	48.0	48.0	48.0	48.0	48.0	49.5
43	Ice	24.0	28.0	24.0	24.0	26.0	...	24.0	24.0	28.0
44	Kid	246.5	246.5	289.3	255.0	289.0	226.0	300.0	280.5	272.0
45	Lard	69.0	53.9	40.0	55.0	77.0	62.0	...	83.3	58.0
46	Lavender spike	27.0	25.0	24.0	28.7	31.6	34.3	33.7	34.0	38.3

A. ANDALUSIA (IN MARAVEDÍS) — Continued

	1633	1634	1635	1636	1637	1638	1639	1640	1641
47 Lentils	1360.0	1695.2	1564.0	2078.9	2250.0	3672.0	1088.0	1613.9	2278.0
48 Lime	1043.9	819.8	777.8	799.5	...	750.0	612.0	748.0	714.0
49 Linseed oil	119.0	...	...	...	136.0	119.0	...	...	...
50 Milk	43.3	44.0	45.3	42.7	46.0	45.3	48.0	42.7	45.3
51 Mustard	338.7	272.0	...	272.0	250.8	...	...	288.0	283.3
52 Mutton	32.1	34.3	39.6	45.3	61.8	57.5	49.0	46.2	44.3
53 Olive oil	617.0	476.0	578.0	484.5	519.9	501.5	357.0	548.1	493.0
54 Orange blossoms	8.0	...	9.0	13.0	14.0	...	...	12.0	14.0
55 Oysters, large	21.0	28.0	24.0	24.0	28.0	24.0	24.0	26.0	20.0
56 Pepper	238.0	204.0	310.0	255.0	433.1	340.0	408.0	694.2	613.0
57 Pine nuts	54.0	52.5	51.5	51.0	51.0	58.3	52.0	67.0	67.3
58 Pitch	28.0	24.0	25.3	24.0	37.5	34.0	31.3	...	46.8
59 Plaster of Paris	374.0	374.0	379.7	374.0	419.2	374.0	458.8	423.0	425.0
60 Plums	115.0	67.5	106.7	105.9	97.5	...	125.0	198.4	70.0
61 Pork, fresh	67.2	51.4	45.0	49.3	68.3	60.0	73.8	64.3	54.0
62 Pork, salt	...	69.5	56.0	54.0	88.0	68.0	85.0	81.5	71.0
63 Potatoes	298.0	...	238.0	323.0	...	220.0	263.5	...	...
64 Prunes	68.0	67.0	69.5	...	85.0	24.0	32.5	48.0	34.0
65 Quail	85.0	85.0	85.0	90.1	102.0	106.0	102.0	102.0	102.0
66 Raisins	782.0	680.0	714.0	748.0	748.0	671.5	1105.0	680.0	714.0
67 Resin	28.0	24.0	24.0	24.0	68.0	34.0	31.3	...	46.8
68 Rice	30.0	24.0	24.0	55.0	37.6	31.0	29.3	28.4	33.5
69 Saffron	1836.0	3451.0	3054.3	3264.0	3094.0	2686.0	3320.7	2588.0	2669.0
70 Sardines	34.3	34.8	36.0	34.0	35.3	40.8	39.3	41.3	58.5
71 Sea bream	72.3	64.5	68.5	65.0	78.0	71.5	75.0	74.5	80.3
72 Sea eel, Mediterranean	67.0	66.5	60.0	70.0	68.0	81.0	93.5	75.5	84.0
73 Shad	83.0	74.5	68.0	102.0	102.0	84.8	85.0	101.5	102.0
74 Sheepskins	172.7	...	170.0	170.0	...	153.0	153.0	174.3	161.3
75 Soap	646.0	595.0	561.0	646.0	732.5	595.0	595.0	680.0	699.1
76 Sole	99.9	85.0	76.3	110.0	102.0	...	...	155.9	...
77 Starch	34.4	32.0	37.5	52.0	64.9	47.0	...	29.3	31.0
78 Sugar	1604.9	1873.5	2184.9	2141.9	2412.9	2032.8	2613.1	1937.6	2138.7
79 Thread, basting	76.0	79.0	68.0	68.0	68.0	69.3	70.7	68.0	68.0
80 Thread, homespun	442.0	442.0	442.0	442.0	442.0	453.3	486.6	476.0	430.7
81 Thread, sewing	153.0	158.7	153.0	153.0	164.3	171.2	170.0	170.0	170.0
82 Tuna fish	43.0	40.0	44.0	44.5	44.0	45.5	45.3	43.7	44.0
83 Turnips	96.3	180.0	323.0	102.0	300.0	176.0	153.0	147.5	113.3
84 Twine	...	68.0	60.0	59.0	66.7	68.0	68.0	63.8	69.0
85 Veal	...	62.0	52.0	49.5	62.2	74.5	58.0	60.0	52.3
86 Vinegar	94.0	85.0	110.0	148.0	144.0	127.6	119.5	136.0	178.5
87 Walnuts	32.3	51.0	34.0	35.7	51.9	53.5	49.3	37.4	44.2
88 Wax, white	187.0	193.5	187.0	185.9	186.5	196.5	193.0	192.7	199.5
89 Wax, yellow	184.4	170.0	144.0	168.8	144.5	173.6	170.0	171.1	178.5
90 Wheat	497.3	518.5	884.0	1473.3	1428.0	782.0	505.8	386.8	637.5
91 Wine	170.0	323.0	190.0	204.0	195.0	217.0	213.0	157.3	323.0
92 Wool	1020.0	918.0	1074.0	831.5	831.5	900.8	1160.6	1281.9	850.0

A. ANDALUSIA (IN MARAVEDÍS) — Continued

		1642	1643	1644	1645	1646	1647	1648	1649	1650
1	Acorns	32.0	40.0	...	...	...	...	...	76.9	80.0
2	Almond oil, sweet	211.8	225.8	217.8	254.0	259.3	269.2	238.0	263.1	272.0
3	Almonds	876.3	1394.0	1868.6	1436.5	1836.0	1224.0	...	3009.0	1810.5
4	Alum	68.0	89.3	51.0	46.8	68.0	44.7	38.3	42.5	42.0
5	Anise	68.0	67.0	144.5	68.0	133.0	69.5	65.9	72.5	102.0
6	Apples, cooking	400.0	376.5	335.8	323.0	318.8	376.3	340.0	442.0	476.0
7	Apples, pippin .	200.0	240.0	180.0	...	180.0	195.0	185.0	...	280.0
8	Ashes	170.0	171.5	170.0	187.0	170.0	170.0	170.0	170.0	340.0
9	Barley	646.0	484.0	524.9	264.6	414.8	779.2	805.9	596.9	929.3
10	Beans, horse ..	544.0	818.4	986.0	816.0	918.0	1224.0	1106.7	1122.0	884.0
11	Beef	50.0	43.8	42.0	46.5	46.4	50.8	59.7	78.8	68.7
12	Bricks	5522.0	3060.0	3230.0	3252.7	3447.5	...	4080.0	...	...
13	Butter	...	161.5	102.0	141.0	...	...	96.0	136.0	...
14	Candles, tallow	54.0	...	...	44.0	64.0	...	56.0	71.3	61.0
15	Charcoal	124.4	93.5	85.5	93.7	96.5	85.0	110.0	129.5	104.8
16	Cheese	884.0	1125.0	1020.0	1360.0	1122.0	1125.0	1500.0	850.0	...
17	Chestnuts	110.5	119.0	139.1	155.3	162.3	140.6	149.9	126.7	68.0
18	Chickens, spring	106.9	92.5	92.7	102.0	98.4	101.0	123.2	186.0	123.2
19	Chick-peas	...	782.0	902.0	680.0	1345.8	1632.0	2483.5	1326.0	1683.0
20	Cinnamon	1235.3	901.0	991.0	981.8	929.3	753.7	722.5	566.7	850.0
21	Cloves	1327.7	965.6	933.7	986.0	1207.0	1277.3	1904.0	1314.7	1428.0
22	Codfish, dried .	48.0	50.0	42.5	46.5	45.0	48.3	40.1	40.7	43.2
23	Coriander	130.4	85.0	149.6	136.0	119.0	136.0	259.8	238.0	136.0
24	Cotton	269.8	238.0	212.0	204.0	209.7	249.3	192.7	204.0	238.0
25	Cuminseed	59.3	40.5	68.0	76.3	76.5	70.8	57.0	50.3	102.0
26	Cuttlefish	68.0	68.0	68.0	76.0	68.0	74.2	70.0	73.0	77.3
27	Dace	104.2	87.0	77.4	90.3	108.3	96.3	65.5	104.9	105.8
28	Dogfish	84.0	78.0	78.7	88.8	78.7	90.8	84.0	83.2	81.6
29	Dogfish, spotted	...	68.0	...	...	80.0	60.0	60.0	60.0	...
30	Eels	109.9	67.5	...	...	110.0	...	102.0	105.5	120.0
31	Eggs	98.9	77.7	79.0	74.5	83.5	112.4	115.3	137.0	120.4
32	Filberts	238.0	...	170.0	136.0	204.0	192.0	204.0	391.0	...
33	Firewood	119.2	98.4	91.7	93.3	85.0	84.2	85.0	134.0	116.2
34	Flounders	103.0	82.7	85.4	90.0	109.0	112.0	105.5	119.7	137.1
35	Garlic	68.0	...	...	28.0	47.0	61.5	52.0	94.0	58.1
36	Grapes	50.0	56.3	60.0	70.0	60.0	40.0	51.3	60.0	60.0
37	Hake	...	...	...	...	...	...	...	...	...
38	Hares	85.0	84.5	90.7	85.0	102.0	110.5	102.0	97.8	164.3
39	Hemp	68.8	58.8	56.0	56.0	54.9	64.0	62.0	60.0	85.0
40	Hens	213.5	194.5	188.0	203.0	184.8	181.3	260.3	336.3	260.7
41	Honey	799.0	544.0	646.0	637.5	841.5	952.0	1003.0	1266.5	952.0
42	Horseshoes	62.0	...	56.0	56.0	56.0	...	56.0	68.0	62.7
43	Ice	24.0	28.0	27.0	26.0	26.0	28.0	28.0	28.0	28.0
44	Kid	297.5	295.4	279.9	272.0	334.3	310.3	234.4	362.7	459.0
45	Lard	58.0	66.2	87.0	103.7	96.0	84.0	85.0	94.0	88.0
46	Lavender spike	35.0	36.7	40.0	42.0	42.0	45.0	30.0	35.0	44.7

A. ANDALUSIA (IN MARAVEDÍS) — Continued

	1642	1643	1644	1645	1646	1647	1648	1649	1650
47 Lentils	3060.0	1500.0	1254.7	1700.0	2145.0	2397.0	2601.0	2414.0	2040.0
48 Lime	1173.0	1020.0	833.0	772.7	750.0	750.0	918.0	1020.0	...
49 Linseed oil	187.0	...	...	...	...	102.0	112.0	85.0	...
50 Milk	45.3	40.0	43.0	42.7	40.7	41.3	42.7	40.0	53.3
51 Mustard	229.5	170.0	271.8	260.7	263.5	187.0	238.0	280.0	442.0
52 Mutton	59.0	47.0	50.9	55.6	70.3	70.7	71.2	98.1	92.9
53 Olive oil	841.5	511.2	408.0	464.7	457.0	408.0	539.8	457.5	459.0
54 Orange blossoms	14.0	17.0	14.0	16.0	12.0	14.7	21.0	...	28.0
55 Oysters, large	29.0	23.0	23.0	23.0	28.0	34.0	16.0	24.0	48.0
56 Pepper	538.0	578.0	433.1	328.7	...	316.6	238.0	245.6	297.5
57 Pine nuts	65.2	68.0	62.3	60.0	60.0	68.0	124.7	56.0	102.0
58 Pitch	48.9	51.0	48.8	48.2	51.0	...	36.8	34.0	42.5
59 Plaster of Paris	612.0	476.0	340.0	464.0	385.3	510.0	546.0	612.0	1088.0
60 Plums	183.2	142.5	62.9	77.5	76.4	73.4	90.0	...	166.7
61 Pork, fresh	55.0	62.5	65.8	75.5	80.0	72.5	81.3	86.8	78.5
62 Pork, salt	94.0	68.0	85.0	97.5	95.5	85.0	102.0	102.0	110.0
63 Potatoes	238.0	...	...	...	...	...	...	...	...
64 Prunes	66.5	24.0	89.3	80.0	76.5	...	54.0	48.0	...
65 Quail	119.0	...	119.0	119.0	119.0	90.1	97.6	85.6	181.3
66 Raisins	544.0	717.0	850.0	680.0	884.0	884.0	1088.0	782.0	1394.0
67 Resin	50.0	47.5	53.8	48.2	51.0	51.0	35.7	34.0	...
68 Rice	42.4	50.8	47.5	39.0	29.5	34.3	38.2	30.5	62.7
69 Saffron	2289.3	1634.5	1445.5	1361.0	1500.0	2881.0	2935.1	2720.0	2720.0
70 Sardines	60.5	47.5	48.5	52.0	48.0	76.5	56.5	54.3	105.5
71 Sea bream	97.8	95.0	96.0	102.5	119.0	116.9	103.5	105.0	119.5
72 Sea eel, Mediterranean	102.0	92.5	102.0	102.0	110.7	106.6	108.3	112.0	122.0
73 Shad	102.0	110.5	136.0	93.5	107.7	114.8	102.5	113.5	127.8
74 Sheepskins	153.0	187.5	...	189.8	189.1	158.7	187.0	204.0	...
75 Soap	1145.7	...	590.7	552.7	637.5	550.5	620.5	510.0	680.0
76 Sole	153.0	...	...	...	153.0	...	136.0	102.0	238.0
77 Starch	40.0	...	43.8	40.7	39.5	...	...	...	...
78 Sugar	3024.4	2295.5	2201.5	2389.7	2660.5	2620.0	2690.1	3076.6	3077.3
79 Thread, basting	90.7	72.0	68.0	68.0	68.0	68.0	68.0	141.7	229.5
80 Thread, homespun	351.3	335.8	450.5	442.0	459.0	...	272.0	...	748.0
81 Thread, sewing	204.0	170.0	170.0	170.0	170.0	170.0	170.0	255.0	357.0
82 Tuna fish	...	62.7	...	38.2	65.4	68.0	...	66.9	...
83 Turnips	195.0	225.0	136.0	137.5	153.0	145.0	204.0	160.0	187.0
84 Twine	82.2	...	...	68.0	76.5	...	68.0	...	161.5
85 Veal	68.0	54.0	52.0	60.0	68.0	68.0	69.5	99.8	102.0
86 Vinegar	178.5	...	153.0	141.5	204.0	262.0	195.5	170.0	...
87 Walnuts	44.2	44.2	44.2	44.2	37.4	40.1	51.0	44.2	...
88 Wax, white	278.4	195.5	187.0	188.5	199.8	205.4	206.1	265.6	256.4
89 Wax, yellow	242.3	166.5	166.8	161.5	183.8	192.3	183.2	216.8	238.0
90 Wheat	1445.0	881.9	671.5	629.0	952.0	1865.8	1317.5	840.6	1020.0
91 Wine	442.0	153.0	306.0	314.5	408.0	272.0	345.7	272.0	220.8
92 Wool	1582.5	1037.0	1224.0	1212.6	918.0	1394.0	...	1351.5	1224.0

B. NEW CASTILE (IN MARAVEDÍS)

		1601	1602	1603	1604	1605	1606	1607	1608
1	Almond oil, sweet	167.5	174.8	181.3	183.8	170.0	170.0	153.0	158.7
2	Almonds	986.0	799.0	1139.0	986.0	1088.0	935.0	986.0	1007.3
3	Apples, cooking	166.3	136.3	146.7	136.3	133.8	125.0	133.8	130.0
4	Apples, pippin	179.7	199.9	189.9	200.0	201.4	189.9	220.0	145.0
5	Barley	...	238.0	238.0	253.8	...	374.0	461.0	...
6	Bran	17.8	17.0	17.0	17.1	26.0	17.8	21.8	22.8
7	Brandy	65.3	119.0	106.3	76.7	81.0	60.0	115.0	56.0
8	Bricks	3030.0	...	2635.0	2720.0	2720.0	...	2968.1	3060.0
9	Brooms	101.6	96.0	96.0	111.0	114.0	...	72.0	92.3
10	Butter	123.3	102.0	73.9	84.0	80.0	80.7	68.0	76.5
11	Candles, tallow	38.0	32.0	42.5	30.0	40.0	38.5	35.0	36.0
12	Cantaloupe ..	50.0	40.0	...	80.0	50.0	...	...	...
13	Charcoal	32.5	37.2	42.2	42.5	42.0	42.6	44.0	43.3
14	Cherries	102.5	115.0	110.0	105.0	97.5	115.0	112.5	102.5
15	Chestnuts	21.9	14.0	...	23.0	25.8	...	...	...
16	Chickens, spring	46.8	44.3	49.1	45.2	54.6	61.4	51.8	57.8
17	Chicory	34.0	38.0	38.0	...	34.0	38.0	42.5	42.5
18	Cinnamon ...	288.6	255.0	...	180.4	270.6	289.0	...	246.5
19	Cotton	187.0	185.6	176.8	192.0	254.0	204.0	220.0	306.0
20	Dates	60.0	62.7	72.5	68.0	81.0	85.0	60.0	85.0
21	Eggs	61.0	49.5	52.1	63.0	62.6	81.5	72.8	63.4
22	Feet, lamb ...	69.0	61.5	59.0	69.0	66.0	72.0	72.0	72.0
23	Firewood	83.1	62.7	67.0	83.6	86.2	83.6	62.7	91.4
24	Fish, dried ...	...	...	...	28.0	...	...	...	...
25	Grapes, unripe	55.0	53.3	57.5	60.0	65.0	70.0	50.0	80.0
26	Hemp	59.8	45.0	32.4	50.2	51.7	58.6	48.5	46.0
27	Hens	148.8	117.5	115.9	116.6	127.5	150.9	169.6	142.5
28	Honey	1020.0	787.7	705.5	539.8	623.3	731.0	787.0	714.0
29	Incense	131.0	134.3	133.3	140.0	168.0	169.0	131.8	148.8
30	Ink	136.0	147.3	136.0	136.0	136.0	136.0	136.0	136.0
31	Lard	55.5	39.3	28.6	34.0	...	34.0	...	38.0
32	Lemons	36.0	48.0	78.0	66.0	72.0	36.0	52.0	54.0
33	Lime	85.2	86.7	83.9	66.8	90.0	...	102.3	98.0
34	Milk	32.0	...	40.0	44.0	40.0	40.0	40.0	36.0
35	Mutton	33.0	26.5	25.3	28.1	26.0	20.5	21.0	22.5
36	Nails, large ..	...	37.7	37.9	37.5	37.9	...	34.0	37.9
37	Olive oil	638.5	587.8	635.2	567.5	556.9	504.0	562.2	605.9
38	Oranges	44.0	39.0	35.5	30.7	54.0	45.0	39.5	38.4
39	Paper, writing	28.0	...	24.7	26.3	28.0	26.0	25.0	24.5
40	Peaches	...	...	...	...	...	...	...	...
41	Pears	142.5	131.3	140.0	135.0	177.5	162.5	135.0	160.0
42	Pepper	24.5	22.3	16.7	10.7	...	...	21.4	16.1
43	Pitch	...	17.5	18.0	24.0	22.0	16.0	15.0	16.0
44	Plaster of Paris	102.7	85.0	89.8	82.9	89.3	104.7	93.5	97.1
45	Plums	60.0	60.0	33.8	60.0	40.0	50.0	60.0	60.0
46	Pork, salt	40.0	38.0	24.0	29.0	29.0	30.0	...	...
47	Pumpkin, candied	124.6	133.0	123.5	120.1	119.0	119.0	113.7	110.3
48	Raisins	425.0	482.8	419.7	387.5	425.0	544.0	374.0	372.7
49	Sloes	60.0	55.0	40.0	60.0	40.0	47.5	60.0	80.0
50	Starch	39.3	30.3	29.0	30.5	43.7	58.5	55.5	45.0
51	Sugar	2874.0	2992.0	3094.0	2643.5	2554.3	2493.0	2061.5	2065.0
52	Thread, white	382.5	467.5	416.5	340.0	340.0	344.8	272.0	300.1
53	Tiles, roof	4560.5	...	...	3910.0	4080.0	4430.2	4284.0	4284.0
54	Twine	70.3	64.0	64.0	64.3	64.0	68.0	64.0	61.7
55	Vinegar	62.0	73.9	58.3	80.7	91.1	84.4	64.7	56.7
56	Wax, white ..	170.0	159.5	182.0	168.5	168.0	176.8	200.0	204.0
57	Wax, yellow ..	155.8	144.5	150.0	144.0	136.0	153.0	151.0	161.5
58	Wheat	382.5	474.4	438.0	539.8	...	1204.2	1123.1	828.8
59	Wine	162.4	105.6	...	164.6	173.8	197.1	186.4	184.3

B. NEW CASTILE (IN MARAVEDÍS) — CONTINUED

		1609	1610	1611	1612	1613	1614	1615	1616
1	Almond oil, sweet	178.7	221.0	178.5	170.0	157.5	169.3	178.5	165.8
2	Almonds	1467.7	1700.0	1101.2	892.7	929.9	1106.0	1011.3	947.8
3	Apples, cooking	152.5	126.7	128.8	130.0	110.7	150.0	177.5	145.3
4	Apples, pippin	...	157.5	217.5	120.0	180.5	184.0	146.5	162.5
5	Barley	307.4	267.8	238.0	327.3	223.9	289.0	310.6	433.5
6	Bran	18.8	18.6	17.5	18.0	18.5	19.8	19.5	21.8
7	Brandy	97.8	97.8	80.0	...	65.0	136.0	75.3	...
8	Bricks	3230.0	...	2992.0	2958.0	2890.0	...	3133.4	...
9	Brooms	104.0	120.0	114.0	72.0	156.0	122.0	66.0	...
10	Butter	68.0	68.0	75.0	68.0	85.0	85.0	...	102.0
11	Candles, tallow	36.0	37.6	40.2	40.0	41.0	38.0	34.7	32.0
12	Cantaloupe ..	...	43.3	...	...	57.5	60.0	35.0	...
13	Charcoal	39.0	44.0	38.9	43.7	42.6	43.1	44.6	42.8
14	Cherries	82.5	105.0	110.0	85.0	78.8	107.5	68.8	120.0
15	Chestnuts	...	...	...	...	...	...	18.5	23.0
16	Chickens, spring	54.2	52.6	49.2	...	55.8	52.1	95.7	77.4
17	Chicory	46.0	40.1	42.5	34.0	34.0	34.0	34.0	68.0
18	Cinnamon ...	...	...	255.0	238.0	246.5	255.0	246.5	263.5
19	Cotton	...	...	238.0	...	170.0	221.0	181.3	238.0
20	Dates	85.0	68.0	53.0	51.0	55.5	76.5	42.5	68.0
21	Eggs	60.0	60.8	50.0	52.5	54.4	57.4	64.5	69.8
22	Feet, lamb ...	66.0	72.0	72.0	72.0	72.0	72.0	66.0	72.0
23	Firewood	88.8	101.9	88.8	...	109.7	77.3	81.3	76.0
24	Fish, dried ...	30.2	...	...	...	...	...	30.0	33.1
25	Grapes, unripe	44.2	70.0	59.3	45.0	60.0	75.0	47.5	40.0
26	Hemp	42.0	39.3	36.7	...	50.8	50.5	53.0	49.5
27	Hens	140.2	134.0	131.3	121.3	131.8	151.0	146.9	151.2
28	Honey	680.8	654.5	433.5	442.3	680.0	663.0	637.5	561.0
29	Incense	160.5	162.0	149.3	136.0	132.0	121.8	144.5	144.5
30	Ink	136.0	136.0	136.0	136.0	136.0	136.0	136.0	136.0
31	Lard	34.3	31.5	33.6	28.6	...	34.0	38.6	37.2
32	Lemons	36.0	48.0	39.0	68.6	...	40.0	51.5	72.0
33	Lime	98.0	106.0	102.0	67.0	99.3	93.5	102.0	...
34	Milk	40.0	40.0	40.0	39.0	40.0	40.0	40.0	40.0
35	Mutton	23.5	24.5	27.0	28.5	24.5	27.5	25.6	23.5
36	Nails, large ..	37.2	...	38.0	38.2	36.0	...	35.0	45.2
37	Olive oil	534.1	670.0	519.8	503.8	488.8	606.4	560.5	645.7
38	Oranges	33.0	...	42.0	31.5	39.0	36.0	38.5	39.5
39	Paper, writing	20.0	...	22.8	...	22.8	38.0	24.0	...
40	Peaches	259.4	...	...	181.6	...	168.6	194.6	142.7
41	Pears	112.5	167.5	110.0	125.0	110.0	160.0	120.0	120.0
42	Pepper	...	...	...	...	21.4	...	22.1	17.0
43	Pitch	11.7	17.0	16.7	...	18.3	16.7	...	24.0
44	Plaster of Paris	92.2	...	97.1	89.5	92.3	86.4	98.0	116.7
45	Plums	50.0	40.0	55.0	40.0	60.0	40.0	40.0	40.0
46	Pork, salt	...	...	...	...	28.0	30.0	41.5	38.5
47	Pumpkin, candied	110.1	110.0	110.0	110.0	110.0	110.3	110.5	108.4
48	Raisins	391.0	298.6	354.2	531.3	444.2	505.8	459.0	310.3
49	Sloes	50.0	50.0	80.0	55.0	60.0	45.0	60.0	45.0
50	Starch	42.6	44.7	28.3	29.0	34.3	34.2	44.7	46.3
51	Sugar	2414.0	2493.3	2337.5	2260.9	2087.5	1904.0	2048.5	2479.2
52	Thread, white .	...	340.0	340.0	...	314.5	323.0	331.5	340.0
53	Tiles, roof	4284.0	...	4250.0	4760.0	4420.0	4420.0	4420.0	5212.0
54	Twine	68.0	...	60.7	58.5	58.3	60.0	62.0	68.0
55	Vinegar	51.0	85.0	76.5	...	164.3	259.1	204.0	106.3
56	Wax, white ..	187.0	187.0	160.5	177.3	194.5	194.5	178.0	182.5
57	Wax, yellow ..	157.3	149.5	153.5	145.9	153.0	148.5	140.0	140.5
58	Wheat	718.3	482.4	392.4	513.1	542.9	652.6	894.1	864.1
59	Wine	176.1	130.3	208.6	247.6	270.2	370.7	207.4	227.4

B. NEW CASTILE (IN MARAVEDÍS) — Continued

		1617	1618	1619	1620	1621	1622	1623	1624
1	Almond oil, sweet	136.0	198.3	204.0	229.5	210.4	186.0	184.9	181.3
2	Almonds	1096.7	1082.7	1159.6	1666.0	1328.6	1113.9	1117.9	1132.4
3	Apples, cooking	169.5	160.0	142.8	132.0	137.9	158.5	156.6	142.0
4	Apples, pippin	206.5	164.9	138.0	189.9	179.7	220.0	192.3	180.0
5	Barley	473.2	476.0	...	268.8	323.0	306.0	451.6	...
6	Bran	24.0	21.3	17.6	16.9	16.8	19.1	21.1	21.3
7	Brandy	...	110.5	59.0	85.0	78.0	112.3	112.3	101.0
8	Bricks	3060.0	3060.0	...	3060.0	2890.0	...	2890.0	2890.0
9	Brooms	102.0	144.0	...	...	128.0	136.0	96.0	111.0
10	Butter	...	...	76.0	76.5	76.5	102.0	102.0	110.5
11	Candles, tallow	39.5	36.5	34.0	34.0	34.0	34.4	40.0	39.0
12	Cantaloupe ..	60.0	42.5	47.5	40.0	...	60.0	...	60.0
13	Charcoal	34.0	47.4	59.5	60.0	54.8	65.2	61.1	63.0
14	Cherries	105.0	95.0	110.0	117.5	95.0	143.4	110.0	142.5
15	Chestnuts	...	...	...	...	15.2	...	18.0	20.0
16	Chickens, spring	65.0	68.4	51.0	72.8	52.1	69.4	77.7	78.5
17	Chicory	...	42.5	42.5	42.5	34.0	...	34.0	...
18	Cinnamon ...	...	238.0	238.0	...	...	238.0	272.0	238.0
19	Cotton	187.0	202.1	202.1	204.0	204.0	204.0	176.8	240.0
20	Dates	64.0	68.0	...	...	68.0	60.0	48.0	...
21	Eggs	64.5	65.6	60.0	57.8	63.0	68.3	63.8	71.9
22	Feet, lamb ...	72.0	72.0	72.0	72.0	72.0	72.0	72.0	...
23	Firewood	84.0	112.0	100.0	96.0	80.0	88.0	88.0	82.7
24	Fish, dried ...	31.5	29.3	31.5	...	32.0	32.0	34.0	34.9
25	Grapes, unripe	40.0	60.0	40.0	...	40.0	60.0	...	65.0
26	Hemp	...	48.0	39.0	41.0	43.3	52.2	51.0	64.0
27	Hens	167.9	157.0	136.6	125.6	136.1	142.1	167.3	156.7
28	Honey	612.0	476.0	374.0	654.5	357.0	527.0	...	...
29	Incense	136.2	108.5	73.7	98.0	127.3	111.7	110.0	162.7
30	Ink	136.0	136.0	136.0	136.0	136.0	136.0	136.0	128.0
31	Lard	42.9	64.0	31.5	34.0	...	45.8	64.0	67.0
32	Lemons	91.5	...	48.0	51.5	68.6	64.4	72.0	...
33	Lime	86.4	89.3	102.0	112.7	...	110.5	110.5	112.5
34	Milk	40.0	44.0	40.0	...	40.0	...	40.0	42.7
35	Mutton	24.6	27.3	25.0	28.1	22.7	29.5	36.0	32.6
36	Nails, large ..	...	34.0	36.0	...	...	34.0	34.0	34.0
37	Olive oil	871.8	830.2	559.9	491.6	502.8	633.2	763.2	777.1
38	Oranges	48.0	34.0	39.0	33.0	40.0	...	57.6	48.0
39	Paper, writing	24.0	24.0	24.0	...	24.0	24.0	24.0	24.0
40	Peaches	157.0	119.0	272.4	181.6	...	160.0	155.6	...
41	Pears	120.0	120.0	130.0	145.0	...	200.0	122.5	170.0
42	Pepper	21.4	21.4	...	21.4	22.7	21.4	17.0	21.4
43	Pitch	...	...	...	...	...	20.0	16.0	20.0
44	Plaster of Paris	...	91.4	112.7	89.4	102.0	99.8	108.4	92.9
45	Plums	80.0	55.0	45.0	120.0	60.0	80.0	40.0	90.0
46	Pork, salt	...	...	...	36.0	37.8	39.5	37.5	45.0
47	Pumpkin, candied	102.0	102.0	102.0	102.0	102.0	102.0	102.2	94.1
48	Raisins	395.3	561.0	453.3	484.5	374.0	467.5	400.2	422.8
49	Sloes	80.0	80.0	65.0	120.0	80.0	110.0	40.0	105.0
50	Starch	46.0	38.3	36.7	35.0	34.0	34.0	35.7	40.0
51	Sugar	2261.0	2130.7	2048.5	2051.3	2125.0	1824.7	2720.0	1780.2
52	Thread, white	328.7	306.0	289.0	289.0	272.0	249.3	314.5	272.0
53	Tiles, roof	4420.0	4420.0	...	4420.0	4873.2	...	4420.0	4420.0
54	Twine	68.0	76.0	68.0	65.7	62.0	62.0	68.0	72.0
55	Vinegar	76.5	60.0	72.3	85.0	73.0	83.9	85.7	85.7
56	Wax, white ..	187.0	187.0	187.0	187.0	187.0	187.0	...	...
57	Wax, yellow ..	144.5	153.0	153.0	145.0	153.0	153.0	...	182.0
58	Wheat	872.3	512.0	539.8	496.5	554.6	510.0	680.0	727.3
59	Wine	248.6	309.6	258.5	241.6	251.0	265.5	265.8	205.5

B. NEW CASTILE (IN MARAVEDÍS) — Continued

		1625	1626	1627	1628	1629	1630	1631	1632
1	Almond oil, sweet	187.0	187.0	317.3	...	348.5	328.7	323.0	340.0
2	Almonds	884.0	1471.8	1848.2	2038.2	1769.1	1596.2	1338.0	1338.0
3	Apples, cooking	218.0	175.0	180.0	180.0	144.8	193.8	136.3	193.8
4	Apples, pippin	239.1	205.0	210.0	210.0	205.0	200.0	175.0	190.0
5	Barley	...	...	348.5	408.0	408.9	306.0	442.0	357.0
6	Bran	23.5	25.0	26.7	28.0	28.0	28.0	28.0	25.5
7	Brandy	187.3	172.0	153.0	204.0	108.3	169.0	119.0	144.5
8	Bricks	...	3570.0	3060.0	...	3400.0	3230.0	4845.0	3400.0
9	Brooms	123.7	118.0	159.4	102.7	90.0	162.6	84.0	120.0
10	Butter	148.8	178.0	...	...	170.0	144.5	...	180.0
11	Candles, tallow	37.8	39.6	40.0	36.0	40.3	40.0	40.0	40.0
12	Cantaloupe ..	...	40.0	40.0	40.0	60.0	40.0	40.0	45.0
13	Charcoal	56.7	80.9	77.1	77.0	80.2	74.0	71.4	66.0
14	Cherries	150.0	135.0	240.0	190.0	165.0	172.5	140.0	155.0
15	Chestnuts	...	24.4	24.0	16.0	24.0	21.0	20.7	16.1
16	Chickens, spring	83.6	95.8	93.6	76.5	92.1	85.0	105.7	85.2
17	Chicory	42.5	...	51.0	...	42.5	42.5	...	42.5
18	Cinnamon ...	292.5	345.0	578.0	476.0	487.3	442.0	340.0	510.0
19	Cotton	202.1	...	...	...	300.3	...	214.7	170.0
20	Dates	68.0	68.0	64.3	...	68.0	68.0	60.0	80.0
21	Eggs	62.3	75.0	84.5	101.3	94.5	73.0	93.8	102.5
22	Feet, lamb ...	48.0	72.0	77.3	69.0	84.0	96.0	72.0	84.0
23	Firewood	96.0	135.9	...	120.0	120.0	120.0	96.0	...
24	Fish, dried ...	34.0	37.9	40.0	39.9	54.3	49.3	53.0	54.4
25	Grapes, unripe	40.0	...	66.7	60.0	60.0	40.0	40.0	40.0
26	Hemp	68.0	85.0	90.3	87.9	79.2	84.0	84.7	63.7
27	Hens	159.9	166.9	191.1	189.7	202.2	179.7	199.4	234.3
28	Honey	850.0	735.3	884.0	906.7	...	...	612.0	561.0
29	Incense	174.3	148.0	136.0	...	382.5	340.0	254.0	306.0
30	Ink	127.0	148.0	148.0	142.0	140.3	137.0	136.0	136.0
31	Lard	54.0	68.7	56.0	70.0	41.5	68.0	54.3	68.0
32	Lemons	32.0	...	96.0	120.0	66.0	57.0	96.0	48.0
33	Lime	108.4	136.0	119.0	...	136.0	136.0	136.0	136.0
34	Milk	48.0	44.0	58.0	48.4	44.0	48.0	48.0	58.0
35	Mutton	33.6	37.3	41.5	34.7	38.6	36.2	35.8	37.2
36	Nails, large ..	...	...	...	34.0	...	...	40.0	40.0
37	Olive oil	626.2	825.6	772.5	911.6	868.8	893.8	821.0	782.7
38	Oranges	69.1	70.0	48.0	36.0	54.0	65.5	54.0	52.5
39	Paper, writing	31.3	35.0	40.0	34.0	34.0	38.7	48.0	58.0
40	Peaches	190.0	259.4	255.0	153.3	221.4	160.0	250.0	280.0
41	Pears	135.0	160.0	220.0	182.5	200.0	175.0	120.0	182.5
42	Pepper	20.1	...	24.0	23.8	24.0	20.0	...	20.0
43	Pitch	20.0	27.3	...	...	28.0	...	20.0	30.0
44	Plaster of Paris	89.5	115.5	119.0	...	129.6	123.2	120.0	100.0
45	Plums	65.0	60.0	...	42.5	75.0	80.0	40.0	80.0
46	Pork, salt	36.0	52.0	56.0	48.0	42.0	40.0	44.0	64.2
47	Pumpkin, candied	119.0	141.9	143.5	146.9	136.0	137.1	136.0	123.4
48	Raisins	350.4	450.5	425.8	498.7	420.8	442.0	408.0	421.5
49	Sloes	70.0	80.0	...	45.0	80.0	80.0	...	120.0
50	Starch	35.8	37.1	38.7	45.7	44.3	52.3	52 7	45.9
51	Sugar	2366.7	2824.9	3895.0	2776.5	3032.5	2873.0	3111.0	2886.1
52	Thread, white	288.0	408.0	408.0	...	416.9	340.0	311.4	340.0
53	Tiles, roof	...	5440.0	4216.0	...	4760.0	4760.0	4845.0	4802.5
54	Twine	85.0	90.5	...	94.0	99.0	93.0	66.3	...
55	Vinegar	136.0	132.2	...	123.3	119.0	102.0	102.0	102.0
56	Wax, white ..	195.5	291.7	289.0	314.5	272.0	259.3	204.0	238.0
57	Wax, yellow ..	178.0	189.0	272.0	243.7	238.0	238.0	204.0	214.6
58	Wheat	509.4	...	780.4	976.0	811.8	1088.0	1200.9	802.2
59	Wine	331.5	261.7	246.6	304.5	300.8	207.8	206.8	261.9

B. NEW CASTILE (IN MARAVEDÍS) — Continued

		1633	1634	1635	1636	1637	1638	1639	1640	1641
1	Almond oil, sweet	331.5	318.8	314.5	289.0	277.7	280.5	263.5	272.0	271.5
2	Almonds	1282.3	1020.0	1496.0	1332.4	1360.3	1070.4	1087.1	...	...
3	Apples, cooking	128.6	290.7	187.4	375.2	170.3	393.7	214.4	171.5	214.4
4	Apples, pippin .	160.0	201.3	185.0	190.0	200.0	215.0	192.5	182.5	165.0
5	Barley	296.1	374.0	374.0	391.0	...	348.5	...	408.0	489.6
6	Bran	25.3	24.7	24.0	24.0	24.0	24.0	24.0	24.0	26.3
7	Brandy	136.0	136.0	136.0	136.0	136.0	163.3	184.0	150.0	152.0
8	Bricks	3400.0	3056.3	3400.0	3400.0	3400.0	3060.0	2983.4	3384.2	3060.0
9	Brooms	...	120.0	103.5	96.0	125.0	108.0	...	...	156.0
10	Butter	113.3	170.0	204.0	...	...	181.4	125.0	...	114.0
11	Candles, tallow	45.5	41.5	41.0	43.3	38.0	38.0	38.0	38.0	37.0
12	Cantaloupe ...	60.0	60.0	40.0	40.0	40.0	45.0	...	65.0	70.0
13	Charcoal	66.6	70.4	66.2	64.5	71.1	67.3	69.4	63.0	68.0
14	Cherries	130.0	153.8	117.5	145.0	130.0	153.4	145.0	135.0	142.5
15	Chestnuts	20.7	26.5	16.0	19.5	21.8	24.0	17.2	17.2	19.5
16	Chickens, spring	102.2	89.6	64.0	75.1	89.5	92.0	99.8	89.9	94.2
17	Chicory	42.5	42.5	42.5	...	42.5	...	34.0	34.0	51.0
18	Cinnamon	544.0	603.8	510.0	476.0	612.0	546.3	652.7	690.1	1107.0
19	Cotton	306.0	323.0	306.0	306.0	303.1	277.9	252.6	239.0	...
20	Dates	68.0	68.0	...	...	85.0	...	...	...	68.0
21	Eggs	74.0	75.3	76.5	80.3	108.8	94.5	89.8	75.0	80.3
22	Feet, lamb	72.0	73.5	72.0	72.0	72.0	72.0	72.0	72.0	72.0
23	Firewood	68.0	80.0	80.0	80.0	80.0	72.0	80.0	...	...
24	Fish, dried	40.4	40.0	43.0	54.0	61.9	61.3	59.2	54.0	58.5
25	Grapes, unripe .	40.0	40.0	57.6	30.2	...	40.0	58.1	54.6	60.0
26	Hemp	68.0	66.5	68.0	70.0	68.0	68.0	68.0	68.0	68.0
27	Hens	182.8	166.3	154.1	153.3	195.8	203.4	206.9	162.3	163.8
28	Honey	...	...	631.2	...	586.5	442.0	566.7	748.0	552.5
29	Incense	277.7	238.0	280.5	289.0	289.0	221.0	221.0	212.5	129.5
30	Ink	136.0	135.5	136.0	136.0	136.0	136.0	136.0	136.0	136.0
31	Lard	63.0	40.0	41.0	56.0	55.0	40.0	44.5	64.0	42.9
32	Lemons	61.5	73.6	54.0	84.0	45.3	81.0	66.0	72.0	62.0
33	Lime	136.0	166.4	136.0	136.0	147.8	153.0	144.5	136.0	...
34	Milk	57.0	48.3	54.4	47.1	68.0	58.0	48.0	...	58.0
35	Mutton	35.3	30.7	26.5	23.2	32.0	36.8	38.8	27.2	33.0
36	Nails, large ...	40.0	...	40.0	40.0	40.0	47.1	45.2	45.2	42.5
37	Olive oil	861.2	825.6	746.3	707.1	755.5	686.9	728.0	702.9	929.3
38	Oranges	54.0	48.0	52.5	48.0	50.5	53.5	54.5	38.0	48.0
39	Paper, writing .	57.0	47.5	56.0	56.8	54.5	51.0	54.7	50.0	32.0
40	Peaches	190.0	280.0	160.0	207.5	290.0	...	...	234.0	207.5
41	Pears	162.5	160.0	140.0	150.0	160.0	175.0	130.9	145.0	165.0
42	Pepper	20.8	26.8	20.0	20.0	26.0	26.8	31.0	46.5	48.0
43	Pitch	24.0	24.0	26.0	27.0	24.0	...	...	20.0	20.0
44	Plaster of Paris .	101.0	110.0	109.5	94.3	127.8	129.1	128.9	129.6	123.2
45	Plums	53.3	75.0	45.0	60.0	60.0	86.7	40.0	50.0	80.0
46	Pork, salt	56.4	44.0	40.0	40.0	42.8	49.4	58.8	57.0	52.9
47	Pumpkin, candied	128.0	125.3	129.3	135.0	136.0	127.8	132.0	153.0	...
48	Raisins	450.5	458.7	365.5	442.0	487.4	493.0	461.8	272.0	461.1
49	Sloes	75.0	80.0	40.0	80.0	60.0	120.0	40.0	75.0	93.3
50	Starch	49.0	40.7	42.8	50.8	45.8	47.0	45.0	40.0	48.0
51	Sugar	2698.8	2754.0	3105.3	3187.5	3273.8	3420.9	3691.1	3141.6	3060.0
52	Thread, white .	282.0	384.0	284.0	...	391.0	398.0	397.0	343.3	398.0
53	Tiles, roof	4760.0	4762.5	4760.0	4760.0	4760.0	4420.0	5100.0	...	4420.0
54	Twine	...	...	...	...	...	...	88.0	...	102.0
55	Vinegar	98.0	97.0	106.9	97.1	97.1	95.3	120.0	90.0	163.2
56	Wax, white ...	221.0	221.0	212.5	204.0	214.6	204.0	...	229.5	238.0
57	Wax, yellow ...	204.0	174.3	180.5	195.5	195.5	174.3	...	204.0	221.0
58	Wheat	792.5	...	579.9	695.8	729.1	814.7	630.7	504.3	885.4
59	Wine	276.3	237.7	313.1	302.8	221.2	337.6	291.7	246.5	292.8

B. NEW CASTILE (IN MARAVEDÍS) — Continued

		1642	1643	1644	1645	1646	1647	1648	1649	1650
1	Almond oil, sweet	323.0	272.0	238.0	323.0	306.0	272.0	283.3	323.0	311.7
2	Almonds	...	1427.2	1338.0	1338.0	1516.4	1577.7	1700.0	1394.0	1856.5
3	Apples, cooking	...	96.9	173.2	214.4	150.1	171.5	242.2	180.9	174.8
4	Apples, pippin .	240.0	185.0	166.7	168.5	134.8	179.9	200.0	200.0	220.0
5	Barley	680.0	306.0	476.3	544.0	781.4	424.0	722.0	578.0	1128.7
6	Bran	28.5	24.0	25.5	27.5	28.0	28.0	28.0	32.0	32.0
7	Brandy	168.0	168.0	215.0	...	...	226.7	...	...	...
8	Bricks	2550.0	...	3840.9	2853.4	...	3740.0	3740.0	3185.1	...
9	Brooms	106.0	114.0	122.0	144.0	84.0	96.0	...	123.0	128.0
10	Butter	136.0	...	...	110.0	120.0	136.0	150.3	168.0	136.0
11	Candles, tallow	42.0	40.0	40.0	45.3	48.0	46.7	...	...	40.0
12	Cantaloupe ...	60.0	110.0	52.5	80.0	40.0	30.0	40.0	42.5	60.0
13	Charcoal	86.7	65.3	59.2	62.6	63.2	70.2	71.3	73.3	67.4
14	Cherries	170.0	155.0	147.5	165.0	120.0	150.5	150.0	135.0	155.0
15	Chestnuts	14.9	16.1	...	21.0	20.7	18.4	...	19.5	...
16	Chickens, spring	119.0	84.7	63.8	80.5	80.2	83.0	102.0	85.0	91.4
17	Chicory	60.0	...	57.5	...	...	51.0	38.0	...	43.0
18	Cinnamon	930.2	862.6	1121.4	977.6	977.6	...	970.4	714.0	...
19	Cotton	378.9	265.2	304.0	...	265.2	347.3	...	322.0	...
20	Dates	50.0	85.0	...	68.0	85.5	...	...	85.0	...
21	Eggs	89.6	78.8	67.9	80.3	78.8	87.8	94.8	91.8	87.0
22	Feet, lamb	74.0	72.0	72.0	80.3	88.0	78.0	76.0	96.0	96.0
23	Firewood	...	...	112.0	...	80.0	88.0	84.0	...	80.0
24	Fish, dried	63.6	53.7	51.0	57.7	54.8	47.3	54.3	58.6	52.5
25	Grapes, unripe .	60.0	80.0	60.0	57.5	60.0	40.0	55.0	68.0	59.3
26	Hemp	72.0	68.0	68.0	68.0	72.7	72.0	82.7	79.8	79.3
27	Hens	211.5	173.5	157.1	162.3	161.9	197.9	220.5	215.1	190.3
28	Honey	629.0	...	...	...	...	...	459.0	...	...
29	Incense	263.0	215.5	220.3	212.3	204.0	187.0	206.7	229.2	237.8
30	Ink	136.0	136.0	...	136.0	...	109.3	136.0	136.0	136.0
31	Lard	42.9	35.8	45.8	48.0	...	64.0	...	85.0	64.0
32	Lemons	55.2	48.0	48.0	96.0	60.7	68.6	144.0	96.0	120.0
33	Lime ..·......	219.8	187.7	175.1	111.2	...	100.4	117.4	123.6	...
34	Milk	68.0	46.0	53.0	54.2	48.0	48.0	51.0	48.0	44.0
35	Mutton	41.0	39.5	40.5	43.5	43.8	41.5	41.4	49.5	44.9
36	Nails, large ...	53.7	45.2	45.2	...	44.0	42.0	...	45.2	44.0
37	Olive oil	1247.4	612.0	643.1	662.2	836.7	594.0	764.6	824.0	760.2
38	Oranges	51.5	44.5	39.5	43.0	42.5	37.0	60.0	48.0	60.0
39	Paper, writing .	53.2	40.0	38.0	45.6	59.0	47.5	56.5	56.0	53.0
40	Peaches	...	...	138.2	260.0	160.0	259.4	240.0	442.0	213.3
41	Pears	130.0	160.0	130.0	160.0	140.0	160.0	180.0	162.5	156.3
42	Pepper	...	48.0	36.0	...	28.0	22.7	...	21.4	...
43	Pitch	23.8	24.0	...	20.0	20.0	20.0	20.0	22.0	22.0
44	Plaster of Paris .	129.6	129.6	129.6	129.6	112.3	134.9	109.3	136.0	132.0
45	Plums	70.0	80.0	45.0	45.0	45.0	60.0	80.0	60.0	80.0
46	Pork, salt	52.3	48.2	48.0	52.8	61.0	48.0	65.0	62.7	64.0
47	Pumpkin, candied	93.0	128.0	119.0	136.0	...	140.0	166.1	187.0	206.8
48	Raisins	566.3	402.5	431.4	425.0	612.0	386.8	333.6	493.0	442.0
49	Sloes	80.0	100.0	80.0	60.0	50.0	60.0	105.0	60.0	110.0
50	Starch	36.0	48.0	41.0	48.0	45.0	42.9	39.9	39.0	38.7
51	Sugar	...	3272.3	3074.6	3090.5	3393.4	3910.0	4043.0	4454.0	5119.7
52	Thread, white .	425.0	391.0	374.0	374.0	442.0	385.3	340.0	331.5	285.9
53	Tiles, roof	5316.2	5100.0	5131.6	5316.2	...	5100.0	5100.0	5100.0	...
54	Twine	...	...	...	84.0	104.8	85.0	...	105.3	104.9
55	Vinegar	150.7	88.0	224.4	228.6	171.4	213.9	85.7	107.7	98.1
56	Wax, white ...	...	221.0	221.0	215.0	244.6	255.0	252.2	272.0	272.0
57	Wax, yellow ...	234.0	212.5	204.0	187.0	187.0	238.0	204.0	163.5	255.0
58	Wheat	965.2	725.3	629.0	782.0	816.0	1210.5	969.0	985.5	1142.2
59	Wine	390.9	302.7	398.5	301.7	316.1	264.1	184.3	260.9	305.3

C. OLD CASTILE-LEÓN (IN MARAVEDÍS)

		1601	1602	1603	1604	1605	1606	1607	1608	1609	1610	1611	1612
1	Almonds	67.8	64.0	68.0	68.0	59.5	68.0	68.0	68.0	63.9	72.3	68.0	68.0
2	Apples, cooking	167.7	148.1	159.2	150.7	173.3	172.6	146.4	119.4	150.0	86.7	188.0	119.2
3	Apples, pippin	190.6	172.5	175.8	205.0	186.7	188.3	175.6	166.7	181.7	126.4	193.3	159.6
4	Barley	235.9	215.0	205.1	209.7	272.4	301.8	303.2	282.8	234.8	173.0	161.5	170.1
5	Beef	13.3	11.0	14.0	12.0	16.0	13.2	10.8	10.0	8.5	9.5	10.3	10.0
6	Candles, tallow	40.0	36.3	33.2	34.0	39.9	39.0	32.0	26.2	26.0	26.0	34.0	33.5
7	Charcoal	...	59.3	72.3	97.5	88.5	...	60.0	55.5	74.3	47.5	43.5	43.0
8	Cheese	31.5	34.6	39.7	37.0	34.8	37.3	30.7	35.2	28.5	25.0	25.8	25.0
9	Cherries	82.5	63.8	65.0	65.0	80.0	66.0	120.0	105.0	35.0	75.0	60.0	80.0
10	Chestnuts	493.0	385.2	442.0	493.0	408.0	374.0	612.0	544.0	272.0	323.0	408.0	408.0
11	Chickens, spring	70.7	50.9	62.0	57.0	75.0	71.0	47.3	52.3	53.0	41.9	51.0	42.5
12	Chick-peas	799.0	712.4	748.0	816.0	1122.0	...	937.4	1020.0	1088.0	689.7	921.2	1037.0
13	Cinnamon	374.0	208.7	289.0	170.0	267.8	289.0	272.0	289.0	384.3	442.0	284.0	238.0
14	Cloves	30.1	17.0	22.9	26.9	37.7	43.9	59.2	65.9	68.0	65.9	...	65.9
15	Conger eel	42.4	41.8	43.0	30.9	34.6	46.0	29.0	34.0	20.5	34.1	30.6	32.0
16	Dogfish	822.6	1129.0	1028.2	790.5	850.0	850.0	850.0	952.0	822.6	1360.0	952.0	1088.0
17	Eggs	55.1	46.5	49.5	55.5	60.0	62.6	54.8	57.8	55.1	54.0	49.5	41.6
18	Filberts	624.8	510.0	714.0	632.3	612.0	408.0	663.0	551.2	722.5	476.0	476.0	493.0
19	Fish, dried	816.0	671.5	603.5	637.5	680.0	816.0	...	518.5	404.8	603.5	629.0	523.6
20	Hens	138.6	126.8	134.5	158.5	162.8	157.8	140.4	120.9	134.6	122.9	95.0	95.6
21	Honey	2102.5	2040.0	2448.0	1904.0	1904.0	1904.0	1904.0	1822.1	1768.0	1822.1	1261.5	1156.0
22	Horseshoes	...	34.0	...	...	32.4	31.4	32.0	...	28.6	28.0	31.0	30.0
23	Incense	136.0	136.0	187.0	175.5	170.0	155.8	195.5	221.0	249.3	204.0	238.0	225.3
24	Kid	39.0	35.0	36.0	37.5	37.3	38.3	34.7	35.2	34.5	34.5	34.0	35.0
25	Lambs	638.9	419.3	430.3	506.8	546.1	471.8	395.8	386.2	393.6	397.4	412.3	482.6
26	Lard	61.8	45.0	51.0	45.5	34.0	48.2	34.0	37.0	36.8	34.6	35.7	38.3
27	Lentils	...	...	51.0	51.0	51.0	102.0	85.0	68.0	...	56.0	44.0	51.0
28	Linen	110.5	98.4	102.5	106.3	92.8	93.5	102.0	71.0	74.2	73.1	80.5	85.0
29	Marmalade, quince	106.3	119.0	113.2	99.8	99.9	102.0	...	107.3	104.4	93.5	104.3	102.0
30	Mustard	195.1	195.1	146.3	165.0	195.1	...	172.2	146.3	119.0	122.0	122.0	97.6
31	Mutton	24.3	22.3	22.7	24.3	25.3	21.0	19.3	20.7	18.7	21.7	23.0	24.7
32	Nails, large	...	...	26.0	...	30.0	26.0	19.0	31.0	23.0	24.0	28.0	25.3

		1601	1602	1603	1604	1605	1606	1607	1608	1609	1610	1611	1612
33	Olive oil	890.4	918.0	960.5	950.3	807.5	833.0	790.5	849.5	818.8	893.2	808.9	707.6
34	Olives	85.0	109.9	80.8	85.0	76.5	85.0	85.0	85.0	77.8	68.0	85.0	68.0
35	Oranges	139.8	170.7	120.9	107.1	91.3	77.6	107.1	80.3	84.0	107.1	89.3	107.1
36	Paper, writing	459.0	...	459.0	481.7	490.2	476.0	470.3	419.3	436.3	382.5	374.0	374.0
37	Pears	140.0	156.3	157.5	142.5	147.5	136.3	116.3	172.5	67.5	132.5	105.0	90.0
38	Pepper	323.0	272.0	238.0	293.3	221.0	272.0	272.0	272.0	272.0	272.0	260.7	212.5
39	Perch	12.0	...	...	17.0	24.0	17.0	15.9	12.0	13.0	15.4	16.4	12.0
40	Pins, common	85.0	85.0	59.5	...	68.0	...	...	...	85.0	68.0	68.0	68.0
41	Plums	80.0	95.0	40.0	115.0	75.0	100.0	40.0	115.0	30.0	90.0	55.0	70.0
42	Pork, salt	37.9	33.9	32.2	32.4	30.7	34.0	37.0	29.0	29.0	32.0	33.7	27.8
43	Pumpkin, candied	94.0	111.4	118.3	111.4	111.4	111.4	110.5	131.7	...	104.0	121.3	113.0
44	Quail	58.0	...	56.5	45.0	51.0	50.4	...	51.0	34.0	35.0	34.0	42.0
45	Raisins	515.7	569.5	500.0	649.2	684.3	620.5	527.0	428.3	450.5	393.6	542.8	620.5
46	Rice	748.0	612.0	816.0	861.3	731.0	1009.1	918.0	850.0	782.0	727.5	674.8	544.0
47	Rye	258.5	251.3	221.4	244.4	272.0	272.6	272.0	272.0	257.8	201.0	187.9	179.4
48	Saffron	161.8	152.0	154.5	152.1	136.0	115.0	96.5	115.5	147.3	207.0	203.8	219.5
49	Salmon	51.0	53.8	42.5	45.0	44.0	36.0	38.6	38.0	42.0	44.8	43.3	30.9
50	Sardines	...	...	...	...	...	173.8	...	130.3	120.9	131.3	156.7	136.0
51	Sea bream	36.7	31.5	25.0	41.5	40.0	33.5	31.5	33.0	18.4	31.9	30.0	27.0
52	Sheepskins	48.8	61.8	63.5	73.6	67.9	62.3	59.4	31.5	29.4	41.4	45.2	40.5
53	Sloes	80.0	110.0	40.0	106.7	75.0	95.0	40.0	160.0	20.0	120.0	40.0	72.5
54	Soap	806.2	918.0	848.6	867.0	806.2	773.5	748.0	785.0	748.0	782.0	748.0	680.0
55	Sugar	2439.6	2567.0	2286.5	2040.0	1955.0	1921.0	1958.8	2074.0	1997.5	1904.0	1956.3	1819.0
56	Sweetmeats	114.0	120.6	115.0	103.9	102.1	102.0	102.0	101.8	103.8	102.0	104.8	102.0
57	Trout	52.3	52.3	66.4	52.1	44.1	51.0	44.3	37.7	34.8	35.5	41.5	36.5
58	Twine	73.1	74.6	72.1	73.0	76.8	79.2	74.0	72.0	72.0	76.0	82.0	80.5
59	Vinegar	127.5	178.5	210.0	204.0	90.7	144.0	68.2	60.0	51.0	51.0	37.0	88.0
60	Wax, white	184.0	182.0	176.5	170.0	170.0	170.0	170.0	170.0	170.0	174.0	178.5	170.0
61	Wax, yellow	140.0	140.0	144.5	142.3	140.0	140.0	144.0	144.5	144.5	144.5	144.5	144.5
62	Wheat	297.4	330.0	300.1	320.4	428.8	578.0	604.9	563.0	472.5	429.9	210.9	241.6
63	Wine	274.5	423.7	569.5	280.0	426.3	365.5	488.0	348.5	292.0	296.0	278.0	229.5
64	Wool	263.5	386.8	476.0	476.0	...	476.0	...	272.0	208.3	180.8	357.0	357.0

C. OLD CASTILE-LEON (IN MARAVEDÍS) — CONTINUED

		1613	1614	1615	1616	1617	1618	1619	1620	1621	1622	1623	1624
1	Almonds	63.8	60.0	47.0	48.7	60.0	64.0	68.0	68.0	61.0	64.5	68.0	57.3
2	Apples, cooking	119.8	128.8	…	94.2	169.5	127.1	133.3	147.5	…	135.0	143.7	154.3
3	Apples, pippin	131.7	153.8	…	133.3	199.5	135.0	133.3	153.3	162.2	173.3	133.3	143.3
4	Barley	176.2	205.1	276.8	286.2	230.9	201.3	174.6	265.6	273.4	285.5	286.2	199.8
5	Beef	10.0	10.2	8.8	10.0	12.5	12.6	12.6	13.3	10.9	12.5	13.5	15.3
6	Candles, tallow	31.4	34.9	33.0	28.0	30.1	34.4	33.0	34.0	36.0	38.0	38.0	40.0
7	Charcoal	48.0	47.8	…	53.4	34.0	46.0	40.0	47.3	60.7	45.0	44.0	42.7
8	Cheese	28.1	40.8	20.4	31.5	…	25.5	25.9	29.5	26.1	22.2	31.4	36.0
9	Cherries	40.0	95.0	73.4	100.0	40.0	76.3	80.0	82.5	66.0	81.3	60.0	112.5
10	Chestnuts	408.0	330.7	340.0	471.9	527.0	310.3	510.0	442.0	471.9	416.4	530.9	374.0
11	Chickens, spring	47.3	53.3	46.2	58.8	69.9	62.0	76.0	46.8	48.5	43.5	47.0	64.0
12	Chick-peas	1020.0	952.0	1509.9	1658.2	823.7	563.6	632.1	455.2	…	901.0	1836.0	1018.8
13	Cinnamon	272.0	272.0	272.0	272.0	285.1	258.5	208.7	204.0	178.0	…	187.0	272.0
14	Cloves	…	…	42.0	…	…	54.0	…	82.5	…	…	56.5	61.9
15	Conger eel	34.0	24.0	30.0	38.5	33.5	39.6	26.0	39.0	42.5	35.5	51.0	38.6
16	Dogfish	612.0	816.0	1156.0	877.4	…	877.4	932.3	795.2	1054.0	1014.5	822.6	1041.9
17	Eggs	47.6	57.8	66.2	63.0	50.8	55.5	47.6	54.0	63.8	56.5	57.3	58.1
18	Filberts	486.4	544.0	768.0	578.0	…	578.0	612.0	689.0	551.2	578.0	578.0	689.0
19	Fish, dried	743.0	578.0	739.5	884.0	561.0	617.2	952.0	697.7	1088.0	875.5	788.4	767.9
20	Hens	84.0	98.9	…	142.5	148.8	117.0	101.0	93.5	117.3	112.8	116.3	125.1
21	Honey	1224.0	1156.0	1148.8	1086.7	1326.0	1261.5	1088.0	1088.0	1088.0	1682.0	1682.0	1541.8
22	Horseshoes	…	29.5	26.0	…	28.0	28.0	…	…	…	…	29.4	25.0
23	Incense	229.5	204.0	228.0	289.0	149.2	…	204.0	170.0	153.0	204.0	158.7	…
24	Kid	34.0	38.0	37.0	36.0	31.0	34.0	36.0	32.0	…	31.8	36.0	45.7
25	Lambs	404.8	500.5	413.6	…	…	348.8	…	452.7	442.0	374.0	592.1	637.5
26	Lard	36.3	41.3	34.0	46.2	46.3	39.2	35.6	34.5	39.4	40.2	42.5	50.8
27	Lentils	42.5	44.5	76.5	68.0	85.0	…	50.0	51.0	…	62.3	80.5	102.0
28	Linen	73.7	88.3	94.0	…	94.0	110.5	85.0	88.0	68.0	…	89.7	94.7
29	Marmalade, quince	…	102.0	…	102.0	85.0	87.3	85.0	85.0	85.0	85.0	76.5	79.3
30	Mustard	97.6	93.5	68.0	97.6	…	146.3	170.7	146.3	146.3	…	102.0	146.3
31	Mutton	22.9	23.3	…	21.7	26.0	22.7	20.5	20.5	22.2	25.5	28.2	27.7
32	Nails, large	…	24.0	…	…	24.0	24.0	22.0	22.0	25.0	…	24.0	24.0

		1613	1614	1615	1616	1617	1618	1619	1620	1621	1622	1623	1624
33	Olive oil	716.2	790.5	837.3	969.0	1042.7	991.7	785.2	761.3	760.4	852.6	936.8	1039.8
34	Olives	...	38.9	64.8	...	85.0	85.0	85.0	77.8	...	50.7	85.0	85.0
35	Oranges	104.2	120.6	119.2	113.2	80.6	106.1	93.2	87.7	91.0	69.1	98.7	103.6
36	Paper, writing	382.5	391.0	391.0	391.0	386.8	416.5	382.5	408.0	391.0	442.0	442.0	442.0
37	Pears	78.8	120.0	...	100.0	...	75.0	110.0	130.0	125.0	103.8	80.0	160.0
38	Pepper	236.1	238.0	272.0	272.0	272.0	272.0	272.0	272.0	152.0	272.0	272.0	204.0
39	Perch	12.8	12.5	11.5	16.0	12.0	12.0	16.0	13.0	12.0	12.0	...	...
40	Pins, common	68.0	68.0	68.0	60.0	85.0	...	76.0	85.0	100.0	...	68.0	85.0
41	Plums	50.0	110.0	53.0	65.0	...	40.0	110.0	80.0	100.0	...	40.0	160.0
42	Pork, salt	28.0	31.0	...	33.5	39.8	39.8	32.0	34.0	32.2	31.5	31.7	40.0
43	Pumpkin, candied	98.0	96.0	...	93.3	96.0	...	96.0	...	80.0	...	83.5	97.5
44	Quail	51.0	38.3	42.5	36.2	49.0	62.5	...	42.5	47.0	38.3	46.0	46.7
45	Raisins	765.0	667.3	...	493.0	437.4	546.7	503.0	442.0	442.0	450.0	544.0	612.0
46	Rice	634.1	667.3	850.0	748.0	1190.0	722.4	751.9	738.6	751.9	718.7	612.0	789.5
47	Rye	216.7	267.8	272.0	269.2	249.2	192.7	186.7	262.1	272.0	272.0	272.0	216.0
48	Saffron	201.0	175.0	...	102.0	96.0	92.0	100.0	148.5	172.8	188.7	172.0	136.0
49	Salmon	43.3	37.1	...	43.5	40.8	38.0	48.3	47.9	46.2	43.3	46.8	40.2
50	Sardines	128.4	137.1	178.5	182.7	132.4	114.0	111.2	146.3	127.5	135.8	182.9	160.1
51	Sea bream	30.6	28.0	28.0	34.0	27.1	31.9	30.0	30.0	28.0	...	...	...
52	Sheepskins	67.8	71.4	55.3	51.6	47.8	60.8	61.5	51.5	44.4	43.7	63.8	60.8
53	Sloes	20.0	70.0	...	50.0	...	40.0	80.0	80.0	80.0	45.0	45.0	150.0
54	Soap	612.0	731.0	867.8	717.1	1060.8	918.0	748.0	629.0	678.9	666.2	857.1	848.6
55	Sugar	1688.7	1581.0	1710.0	1765.2	1496.0	1598.0	1700.0	1615.0	1564.0	1530.0	1343.0	1487.0
56	Sweetmeats	102.0	99.0	102.7	106.4	101.1	102.0	102.0	103.4	102.0	102.0	93.7	93.5
57	Trout	35.9	41.4	39.3	43.6	49.8	43.8	55.3	47.5	46.2	39.9	41.3	44.3
58	Twine	79.0	79.7	...	80.8	80.0	64.7	72.0	69.3	83.0	76.0	83.3	78.3
59	Vinegar	210.6	172.3	...	68.0	187.0	184.2	187.0	34.0	93.5	80.8	113.7	129.2
60	Wax, white	170.0	187.3	187.0	170.0	187.0	...	187.0	...	187.0	168.0	170.0	170.0
61	Wax, yellow	144.5	134.8	133.2	144.5	129.5	...	...	...	138.0	149.4	136.0	140.0
62	Wheat	300.3	466.4	565.7	571.6	400.9	282.6	279.8	401.6	403.8	399.2	395.3	299.7
63	Wine	328.5	338.5	167.0	166.0	153.0	316.0	287.6	289.0	256.3	192.0	250.0	296.3
64	Wool	510.0	525.6	327.3	331.5	...	391.5	399.5	612.0	323.0	342.2	456.9	450.5

C. OLD CASTILE-LEÓN (IN MARAVEDÍS) — Continued

		1625	1626	1627	1628	1629	1630	1631	1632	1633	1634	1635	1636	1637
1	Almonds	58.0	67.2	66.3	....	123.9	....	68.0	....	102.0	81.1	129.8	....	68.0
2	Apples, cooking	226.7	191.7	191.7	....	....	167.7	208.1	191.7	167.7	191.7	....	143.7	104.0
3	Apples, pippin	226.7	145.0	173.3	....	138.0	204.8	173.3	166.7	156.3	173.0	191.7	141.8	143.0
4	Barley	146.3	189.1	282.6	291.8	276.3	275.5	301.8	270.6	289.7	276.3	294.0	290.4	298.9
5	Beef	14.3	18.3	18.0	19.7	16.8	12.0	12.0	13.3	14.0	13.0	11.0	12.0	12.0
6	Candles, tallow	36.9	54.0	68.0	....	....	44.0	47.7	42.6	36.0	38.9	39.1	36.0	43.4
7	Charcoal	41.4	55.8	48.0	....	46.0	51.0	59.5	50.0	40.0	45.0	....	....	44.2
8	Cheese	35.2	30.5	47.5	36.0	35.0	43.5	40.3	35.7	37.0	25.9	26.1	23.9	27.3
9	Cherries	85.0	80.0	120.0	175.0	80.0	87.5	70.0	80.0	60.0	112.5	77.5	92.5	115.0
10	Chestnuts	459.0	589.9	484.5	....	569.5	476.0	544.0	390.0	442.0	399.0	374.0	544.0	612.0
11	Chickens, spring	49.4	60.0	69.0	83.1	54.0	48.0	101.0	76.0	68.0	42.0	53.3	50.0	51.0
12	Chick-peas	1088.0	884.0	1054.0	816.0	647.0	687.9	1617.4	1315.5	1020.0	....	816.0	544.0	....
13	Cinnamon	408.0	374.0	550.1	544.0	544.0	544.0	540.3	464.0	629.0	680.0	544.0	....	....
14	Cloves	51.0	96.3	187.0	....	136.0	119.0	....	170.0	....	44.0	136.0	129.2	....
15	Conger eel	38.0	47.3	42.3	41.9	57.0	58.9	49.4	49.1	41.5	....	....	....	51.8
16	Dogfish	1151.6	1122.0	1632.0	....	....	1496.0	1530.0	1122.0	....	1122.0	1190.0	1156.0	156.0
17	Eggs	57.0	54.0	58.1	63.6	64.4	53.3	79.1	69.4	54.0	46.5	48.0	53.3	52.5
18	Filberts	578.0	826.8	551.2	544.0	....	689.0	1020.0	782.0	510.0	680.0	442.0	486.4	648.5
19	Fish, dried	850.0	867.0	901.0	1020.0	1122.0	1130.5	1190.0	1122.0	1058.3	1105.0	1088.0	1224.0	1530.0
20	Hens	124.6	127.0	147.0	....	147.7	140.0	144.0	206.7	153.4	137.0	98.5	116.9	134.1
21	Honey	1360.0	1682.0	1723.2	1914.7	1914.7	1471.7	1148.8	1238.9	1441.7	1148.8	1531.8	1335.8	1126.3
22	Horseshoes	28.0	29.5	33.2	28.8	33.3	33.5	33.7	33.7	33.0	32.0	33.0	32.0	33.0
23	Incense	....	492.0	....	....	476.0	476.0	411.1	204.0	408.0	212.0	....	340.0	272.0
24	Kid	45.0	....	44.0	39.6	51.8	....	25.9	....	24.1	....	31.8	35.0	....
25	Lambs	584.0	1007.3	884.0	884.0	872.7	632.6	....	760.8	704.8	737.3	568.8	498.7	....
26	Lard	45.9	55.3	59.0	51.0	59.5	38.2	45.3	46.2	30.0	30.0	41.0	48.0	46.5
27	Lentils	68.0	68.0	68.0	68.0	90.7	68.0	119.0	68.0	136.0	119.0	68.0	....	....
28	Linen	102.0	114.0	102.0	93.5	129.5	93.2	....	102.0	102.3	102.0	89.3	110.0	159.1
29	Marmalade, quince	102.0	102.0	102.0	150.6	131.2	....	153.0	....	119.0	127.5	139.0	136.0	136.0
30	Mustard	146.3	136.0	136.0	170.0	92.0	68.0	....	158.0	126.0	102.0	272.0	....	....
31	Mutton	26.2	27.8	32.7	30.0	30.0	26.7	22.7	25.3	28.7	22.7	22.0	20.7	21.3
32	Nails, large	27.0	29.0	38.1	....	32.0	30.7	29.3	27.5	29.2	32.0	23.0	30.0	26.7

		1625	1626	1627	1628	1629	1630	1631	1632	1633	1634	1635	1636	1637
33	Olive oil	903.5	1151.8	1109.3	1099.2	1232.5	1258.0	1099.3	1025.7	996.8	986.0	909.5	846.5	876.5
34	Olives	...	97.2	97.2	129.6	85.0	102.0	102.0	102.0	102.0	63.4	85.0	...	51.0
35	Oranges	96.2	134.3	134.3	179.0	150.2	117.3	155.7	120.1	90.2	69.9	90.2	90.2	103.6
36	Paper, writing	589.3	680.0	544.0	527.0	740.4	646.0	753.9	884.0	527.0	748.0	748.0	838.7	977.5
37	Pears	130.0	112.5	152.5	...	...	120.0	92.5	125.0	92.5	120.0	66.7	87.5	80.0
38	Pepper	294.7	306.0	340.0	340.0	328.7	306.0	204.0	255.0	...	160.0	170.0	161.5	204.0
39	Perch	12.0	10.0	...	18.0	...	17.0	14.5	14.0	14.1	16.4	12.0	...	...
40	Pins, common	102.0	...	136.0	136.0	...	68.0	52.0	110.5	102.0	...	102.0	102.0	136.0
41	Plums	90.0	40.0	160.0	70.0	120.0	80.0	65.0	105.0	80.0	85.0	75.0	40.0	60.0
42	Pork, salt	40.5	37.5	40.0	...	44.0	40.8	45.5	46.5	52.0	44.0	37.0	31.0	34.0
43	Pumpkin, candied	83.5	136.0	144.0	...	152.0	140.0	118.7	142.7	136.0	136.0	125.3	144.0	144.0
44	Quail	37.2	46.8	59.5	53.3	51.0	46.8	51.0	45.5	51.3	51.0	45.9	51.0	54.0
45	Raisins	483.1	556.7	560.7	578.9	477.1	442.0	344.3	297.5	357.0	331.5	278.0	238.0	306.0
46	Rice	782.0	915.6	850.0	928.8	995.2	1108.0	1156.6	867.3	952.0	751.0	850.0	850.0	973.1
47	Rye	150.2	195.5	259.3	272.0	272.0	272.0	272.0	272.0	272.0	272.0	272.0	272.0	272.0
48	Saffron	147.6	204.0	153.0	...	159.5	101.8	...	136.0	...	...	207.5	204.0	183.2
49	Salmon	40.2	38.6	78.8	85.0	...	94.0	77.3	61.8	49.5	51.0	52.5	53.3	52.5
50	Sardines	181.4	156.6	135.0	153.0	182.7	132.1	133.8	163.8	149.0	130.7	124.4	74.8	...
51	Sea bream	34.0	51.0	34.0	51.0	59.7	50.5	51.0	51.0	66.0	55.0	42.5	...	...
52	Sheepskins	45.1	138.8	162.1	46.6	64.9	57.4	...	29.8	44.5	29.9	55.0	44.4	36.9
53	Sloes	40.0	45.0	...	...	120.0	80.0	65.0	130.0	77.5	102.5	55.0	40.0	55.0
54	Soap	848.6	933.5	927.1	1549.7	1272.9	1031.0	1018.3	1018.3	975.9	975.9	891.0	897.4	933.5
55	Sugar	1974.9	2321.1	1812.5	...	2659.4	2755.0	2646.3	2764.0	2720.0	2550.0	3196.0	3125.0	2974.0
56	Sweetmeats	107.0	115.0	145.0	170.0	153.0	150.3	155.8	137.7	136.2	140.3	141.7	153.0	136.0
57	Trout	44.4	45.0	59.0	64.0	66.4	...	42.2	49.8	35.5	44.6	43.2	39.0	41.5
58	Twine	94.8	93.5	102.5	127.5	129.0	94.0	92.8	80.0	100.0	96.0	92.0	92.0	...
59	Vinegar	221.0	186.0	143.3	187.0	170.0	102.0	76.5	51.0	51.0	110.5	51.0	48.0	98.0
60	Wax, white	204.0	272.0	272.0	...	306.0	238.0	240.8	246.5	195.0	204.0	202.5	205.3	206.1
61	Wax, yellow	170.0	...	238.0	...	235.9	204.0	185.9	182.8	170.0	169.0	163.6	186.3	184.6
62	Wheat	214.3	259.5	398.4	511.1	490.9	556.0	599.3	578.0	574.5	501.7	508.9	535.5	462.3
63	Wine	226.0	181.0	216.0	310.6	192.0	256.0	160.0	...	176.0	256.0	236.6	150.0	266.0
64	Wool	629.0	884.0	578.0	731.0	629.0	...	323.0	351.0	...	348.5	408.0	374.0	391.0

C. OLD CASTILE-LEÓN (IN MARAVEDÍS) — CONTINUED

		1638	1639	1640	1641	1642	1643	1644	1645	1646	1647	1648	1649	1650
1	Almonds	68.0	76.5	59.5	64.9	93.5	73.0	93.5	90.8	64.9	…	…	97.3	97.8
2	Apples, cooking	125.7	…	206.7	…	185.0	176.7	208.3	167.7	…	155.5	200.5	213.0	268.5
3	Apples, pippin	185.5	160.0	178.5	204.0	254.0	265.6	290.4	169.2	192.0	297.5	272.0	267.8	289.0
4	Barley	374.0	255.0	…	…	…	…	…	251.2	281.4	…	…	…	…
5	Beef	13.5	14.0	14.0	14.0	15.3	12.7	12.8	…	16.0	16.0	14.0	14.0	16.5
6	Candles, tallow	40.2	45.6	45.6	34.2	52.0	54.3	34.7	40.0	39.1	48.0	51.0	46.8	45.1
7	Charcoal	46.0	50.0	43.0	…	36.0	31.0	…	40.4	36.0	…	40.4	…	38.0
8	Cheese	…	23.2	20.9	31.5	37.0	34.5	37.1	85.0	33.0	24.5	30.1	32.8	32.8
9	Cherries	143.0	67.5	55.0	91.7	70.0	120.0	57.5	85.0	55.0	62.4	80.0	87.5	80.0
10	Chestnuts	476.0	365.5	476.0	408.0	589.9	444.2	748.0	510.0	499.7	425.0	646.0	612.0	807.5
11	Chickens, spring	76.0	60.0	50.0	58.2	85.0	64.0	68.0	54.5	54.0	54.0	68.0	76.0	64.0
12	Chick-peas	970.4	1293.9	…	751.8	…	970.4	970.4	1460.0	1536.5	…	…	…	…
13	Cinnamon	544.0	634.7	657.3	1088.0	1768.0	1359.7	884.0	1020.0	748.0	782.0	884.0	1088.0	…
14	Cloves	136.0	85.0	76.0	93.5	119.0	102.0	68.0	85.0	102.0	102.0	119.0	129.2	…
15	Conger eel	60.0	65.9	50.8	65.9	56.3	51.0	45.1	…	51.0	46.6	56.5	73.4	58.8
16	Dogfish	…	1054.0	850.0	884.0	850.0	731.0	918.0	816.0	850.0	816.0	816.0	833.0	826.8
17	Eggs	54.0	49.5	43.5	55.4	57.0	54.4	49.5	52.9	54.0	58.9	57.0	57.0	52.7
18	Filberts	583.6	616.1	616.1	…	826.8	952.0	816.0	816.0	680.0	680.0	799.0	969.0	826.8
19	Fish, dried	1224.0	1207.0	1096.5	1088.0	1011.5	986.0	986.0	977.5	1122.0	1020.0	1122.0	1246.7	1020.0
20	Hens	1558.4	1121.3	1113.2	1001.8	1055.7	1436.0	1148.8	1451.1	1121.3	1471.7	1541.8	1632.0	1088.0
21	Honey	144.0	137.0	111.7	128.0	128.0	121.8	126.6	127.9	124.8	133.0	165.8	152.0	136.0
22	Horseshoes	33.3	34.0	34.0	34.0	34.0	34.0	34.0	34.0	34.0	34.0	34.0	34.0	…
23	Incense	…	374.0	306.0	306.0	385.3	317.3	408.0	340.0	430.7	317.3	238.0	340.0	408.0
24	Kid	…	…	48.8	34.0	28.0	…	30.5	…	36.6	32.0	34.0	34.0	…
25	Lambs	758.0	646.4	595.0	642.1	681.3	518.5	587.9	608.3	731.0	839.4	783.4	782.0	748.0
26	Lard	76.5	42.5	39.0	39.2	46.8	34.0	40.0	41.3	68.0	60.0	56.0	50.4	56.0
27	Lentils	…	76.5	68.0	68.0	…	51.0	59.5	68.0	68.0	…	83.0	72.3	…
28	Linen	136.0	87.7	76.0	102.0	102.0	102.0	58.1	…	…	87.8	136.0	119.0	…
29	Marmalade, quince	161.5	153.0	147.3	144.0	141.7	152.0	76.5	118.0	170.0	…	144.0	161.5	221.0
30	Mustard	102.0	153.0	132.0	…	136.0	…	…	…	127.5	…	…	…	…
31	Mutton	26.3	25.7	24.7	27.7	27.7	25.7	28.7	26.9	27.3	30.7	28.3	32.0	38.0
32	Nails, large	34.0	25.0	36.0	…	42.0	36.0	32.5	32.0	34.0	32.0	28.8	34.7	…

		1638	1639	1640	1641	1642	1643	1644	1645	1646	1647	1648	1649	1650
33	Olive oil	892.5	865.9	892.5	1093.7	1586.7	807.7	855.7	884.0	936.8	881.3	987.0	1144.7	986.0
34	Olives	85.0	123.2	114.1	110.2	...	...	88.8	63.4	76.1	...	80.8	54.9	...
35	Oranges	123.3	66.3	87.7	62.1	74.4	...	118.4	89.3	93.1	93.1	139.7	103.2	90.2
36	Paper, writing	974.7	748.0	782.0	906.6	901.0	1020.0	833.0	816.0	1031.3	1020.0	1105.0	1190.0	884.0
37	Pears	165.0	100.0	100.9	...	80.0	170.0	71.3	138.4	130.0	90.0	...	116.7	140.0
38	Pepper	346.0	408.0	612.0	340.0	476.0	476.0	408.0	340.0	...	408.0	340.0	289.0	204.0
39	Perch	17.0	17.0	17.0	17.0	24.0	100.0	17.0	...	17.0	...	25.0	15.0	...
40	Pins, common	136.0	85.0	170.0	...	204.0	...	119.0	...	119.0	...	170.0	...	...
41	Plums	130.0	80.0	90.0	...	80.0	120.0	60.0	135.0	80.0	55.0	80.0	80.0	80.0
42	Pork, salt	52.5	47.0	45.5	...	39.0	39.0	47.5	...	48.0	46.0	48.0	52.0	59.0
43	Pumpkin, candied	153.8	152.0	...	...	...	...	272.0	...	153.2	...	...	220.0	...
44	Quail	58.3	56.7	51.0	46.8	40.4	...	34.0	...	68.0	68.0	...	66.0	68.0
45	Raisins	238.0	238.6	263.5	231.5	284.8	338.0	338.0	323.0	297.5	297.5	336.0	340.0	408.0
46	Rice	935.0	1062.5	888.7	906.7	1114.6	1065.9	900.1	943.5	952.0	1061.5	918.0	1260.6	1271.6
47	Rye	272.0	272.0	223.1	221.0	277.5	272.0	272.0	272.0	272.0	272.0	318.2	272.0	272.0
48	Saffron	187.0	...	168.4	180.0	140.0	...	80.1	81.4	204.0	204.0	204.0	201.8	195.7
49	Salmon	...	51.0	43.3	...	61.8	155.2	146.7	38.6	...	...	51.0	77.3	46.4
50	Sardines	152.9	162.5	91.9	216.0	198.4	...	...	145.5	187.4	202.0	190.0	193.9	191.1
51	Sea bream	51.0	...	...	...	...	51.0	51.0	51.0	49.5	...	56.0	60.0	...
52	Sheepskins	28.4	41.1	60.7	90.3	74.5	76.4	90.3	...	101.6	68.0	89.7	53.4	...
53	Sloes	160.0	55.0	...	...	80.0	130.0	45.0	...	60.0	62.5	100.0	60.0	...
54	Soap	1113.8	1062.9	1145.6	1208.8	1618.7	1103.2	969.0	1190.0	1190.0	1103.2	1321.7	1436.3	1317.5
55	Sugar	3317.8	3502.0	3264.0	3290.1	3577.1	3332.0	2915.5	2683.5	3787.5	3833.6	4318.8	4505.0	5525.0
56	Sweetmeats	170.0	178.5	174.0	...	144.0	144.0	144.5	153.0	178.5	...	198.3	235.2	238.0
57	Trout	51.0	36.5	36.2	34.0	45.5	42.5	35.7	36.1	48.0	43.0	42.5	51.1	51.0
58	Twine	84.0	102.0	94.0	...	96.0	96.0	63.8	82.9	112.0	80.0	126.0	124.7	113.7
59	Vinegar	46.0	...	68.0	97.8	340.0	195.5	238.0	208.3	170.0	175.7	178.5	238.0	170.0
60	Wax, white	212.5	213.0	216.0	233.8	308.8	256.4	230.6	221.0	221.0	223.6	230.6	256.9	252.9
61	Wax, yellow	186.7	193.8	194.1	190.7	242.2	211.8	187.3	181.3	187.0	193.4	204.0	237.0	221.0
62	Wheat	552.5	380.4	342.1	306.0	412.3	597.1	573.8	435.6	509.3	519.9	490.7	414.4	433.5
63	Wine	226.8	384.0	394.0	526.9	288.0	278.7	430.0	236.6	224.0	355.5	289.2	473.3	396.0
64	Wool	408.0	459.0	476.0	620.5	1224.0	486.7	448.5	532.7	578.0	595.0	...	680.0	544.0

D. VALENCIA (IN DINERS)

		1601	1602	1603	1604	1605	1606	1607	1608
1	Ashes	19.7	20.2	20.1	20.3	20.3	19.2	18.4	19.6
2	Bedticks	...	240.0	184.2	175.5	172.5	184.0	156.0	216.0
3	Borage	84.0	102.0	91.9	...	92.0	85.9	72.0	...
4	Bran	349.3	366.4	...	...	256.2	336.0	280.0	340.6
5	Bricks	920.0	943.7	900.0	...	1200.0	...	1116.7	1080.0
6	Brooms	36.0	31.9	33.3	35.8	30.0	24.8	21.0	...
7	Carob beans ..	...	51.8	78.0	56.4	36.0	40.0	...	40.4
8	Charcoal	206.0	201.8	219.7	210.6	208.6	192.5	201.1	180.2
9	Cheese	...	160.0	160.0	127.7	...	...	...	165.0
10	Chickens, spring	32.1	28.1	27.2	30.7	31.0	25.5	28.2	29.3
11	Codfish, dried	6.0	5.0	6.8	6.0	5.7	...	5.2	6.0
12	Eels	...	8.3	6.8	6.8	...	...	...	7.8
13	Eggs	30.5	26.7	28.3	31.1	28.8	32.3	30.1	31.2
14	Firewood	37.8	34.0	34.3	38.6	32.9	31.2	30.0	28.7
15	Flax	26.3	23.9	23.0	25.7	20.5	20.0	23.0	23.0
16	Grits, barley .	...	80.0	80.0	80.0	...	...	...	80.0
17	Grits, wheat ..	...	78.8	80.0	80.0	...	...	...	80.0
18	Hemp	101.7	100.0	100.0	60.0	60.0	60.0	60.0	...
19	Hens	87.0	78.2	80.9	82.7	80.8	72.0	81.6	77.9
20	Honey	1669.0	2112.0	1871.5	1502.6	1370.3	1169.4	1417.9	1359.4
21	Horseshoes ...	12.0	13.0	12.0	...	12.0	12.0	12.0	12.0
22	Lard	37.5	30.0	32.7	24.5	23.0	27.0	24.0	20.0
23	Lime	123.0	108.0	111.0	126.0	132.0	124.0	...	120.0
24	Linen	60.0	69.0	60.0	58.0	72.0	...	42.0	50.0
25	Meal, mixed ..	172.5	180.0	180.0	180.0	180.0	180.0	144.0	...
26	Mutton	54.0	51.0	48.0	49.5	47.0	41.0	38.0	35.0
27	Olive oil	325.1	436.2	488.3	307.3	371.3	441.0	408.5	402.0
28	Pepper	...	...	...	7.6	...	...	...	...
29	Plaster of Paris	108.0	108.0	111.8	144.0	144.0	127.5	119.4	111.0
30	Pork, salt	52.0	50.0	49.0	51.0	51.0	...	...	...
31	Pumpkins, candied	161.0	111.2	105.0	126.8	115.0	96.0	96.0	...
32	Quinces	20.1	17.9	29.3	24.0	19.9	20.0	...	...
33	Raisins	126.3	133.1	163.3	117.5	168.4	109.4	116.2	107.6
34	Rice	1809.3	...	2317.7	2139.2	2096.0	2341.5	2132.0	1838.3
35	Saffron	1334.0	960.0	...	644.0	690.0	609.5	...	...
36	Salt	...	390.7	364.2	360.0	360.0	360.0	402.0	360.0
37	Sandals, hempen	220.5	238.5	240.0	240.0	240.0	208.0	210.0	202.0
38	Sardines	...	65.9	93.0	82.3	...	...	...	...
39	Saucers	184.0	168.0	161.0	161.0	156.0	155.8	168.0	...
40	Shoes	98.0	92.0	102.0	...	92.0	94.0	92.0	92.0
41	Shrouds	20.0	20.0	20.0	20.3	20.0	21.5	19.9	20.0
42	Silk, raw	1000.0	943.0	782.0	736.0	759.0	644.0	552.0	862.5
43	Soap	309.8	327.4	393.0	294.0	288.3	274.5	295.4	308.7
44	Sugar	64.6	78.0	60.0	40.0	44.8	44.2	35.0	44.5
45	Tuna fish	...	12.0	...	8.3	...	9.2	...	8.5
46	Turpentine ...	18.0	12.0	8.0	16.0	12.0	9.0	7.3	11.5
47	Twine	...	...	...	...	...	21.0	18.0	...
48	Vermicelli	...	...	...	...	...	...	...	...
49	Vinegar	30.0	36.0	36.0	42.0	39.6	54.0	33.0	...
50	Wax, yellow ..	72.0	84.0	72.0	62.0	60.0	54.0	69.0	63.5
51	Wheat	1828.6	1347.2	1920.0	1462.5	1820.3	1512.0	2043.5	1738.6
52	Wine	49.9	65.9	73.6	84.4	76.8	67.5	47.5	37.6

D. VALENCIA (IN DINERS) — CONTINUED

		1609	1610	1611	1612	1613	1614	1615	1616
1	Ashes	25.4	46.3	42.0	40.0	38.2	37.5	36.0	35.3
2	Bedticks	184.0	184.0	184.0	188.7	184.0	172.0	...	216.0
3	Borage	92.0	92.0	92.0	...	73.6	44.9	99.5	...
4	Bran	312.0	360.7	334.7	306.6	289.4	302.8	298.7	338.3
5	Bricks	920.0	964.9	960.0	963.0	960.0	960.0	960.0	960.0
6	Brooms	28.0	50.0	41.6	34.7	34.8	36.0	44.4	39.8
7	Carob beans	...	...	...	39.0	...	...	...	...
8	Charcoal	216.3	232.6	230.0	230.0	229.1	228.8	216.0	224.2
9	Cheese	132.0	180.0	180.0	140.0	151.5	151.8	142.5	160.0
10	Chickens, spring	31.6	25.3	33.1	30.3	23.6	...	24.1	34.9
11	Codfish, dried	4.9	...	...	5.0	6.6	5.3	6.0	6.0
12	Eels	4.3	...	...	5.7	6.8	5.8	6.0	5.4
13	Eggs	27.6	30.7	28.7	29.0	29.7	31.1	34.6	30.3
14	Firewood	29.9	41.4	38.1	40.0	38.4	35.0	31.2	31.3
15	Flax	22.0	19.0	17.4	17.2	15.5	23.0	17.5	17.5
16	Grits, barley	80.0	...	...	80.0	80.0	80.0	83.3	90.0
17	Grits, wheat	80.0	...	...	80.0	80.0	80.0	76.0	70.0
18	Hemp	113.3	105.8	78.8	...	95.0	100.0	105.0	100.0
19	Hens	66.5	61.4	76.3	79.8	83.3	89.0	...	...
20	Honey	1444.2	1349.1	1288.0	982.3	976.6	1333.8	1362.9	1196.0
21	Horseshoes	...	12.0	12.0	12.0	12.0	12.0	12.0	12.0
22	Lard	20.0	18.0	15.0	24.0	26.0	26.7	31.7	25.0
23	Lime	120.0	120.0	121.5	120.0	120.0	120.0	120.0	120.0
24	Linen	53.0	53.0	...	64.0	...	60.0	48.0	63.7
25	Meal, mixed	150.0	180.0	180.0	160.0	181.3	180.0	180.0	180.0
26	Mutton	37.0	40.0	40.6	42.0	43.0	44.0	44.0	43.0
27	Olive oil	320.4	373.5	311.3	330.5	303.4	379.9	291.8	351.6
28	Pepper	...	8.0	7.5	7.0	...	...	7.0	...
29	Plaster of Paris	103.5	103.1	102.0	108.5	102.4	103.5	102.0	102.0
30	Pork, salt	...	51.0	51.0	42.0	54.6	52.0	48.3	46.0
31	Pumpkins, candied	92.0	91.5	103.5	...	...	...	96.0	120.0
32	Quinces	15.0	11.9	9.9	22.4	11.4	7.7	12.1	11.0
33	Raisins	106.8	123.1	105.0	142.2	138.7	165.1	199.7	...
34	Rice	1813.7	1773.8	1551.5	2032.4	2256.8	2195.5	1940.0	1875.0
35	Saffron	...	...	...	...	...	...	536.0	720.0
36	Salt	360.0	360.0	360.0	360.0	360.0	360.0	360.0	360.0
37	Sandals, hempen	204.0	204.0	207.0	210.0	210.0	201.0	198.0	198.0
38	Sardines	75.0	...	...	90.0	80.0	63.4	82.7	78.0
39	Saucers	...	168.0	168.0	...	168.0	168.0	168.0	168.0
40	Shoes	117.0	99.9	108.0	108.0	108.0	108.0	...	108.0
41	Shrouds	20.0	20.0	20.0	20.0	20.0	20.0	20.0	20.2
42	Silk, raw	943.0	931.8	828.0	862.5	831.8	782.0	575.0	618.0
43	Soap	276.6	309.9	282.6	271.6	244.5	270.6	287.6	287.5
44	Sugar	45.6	41.1	41.0	...	39.4	36.9	38.9	41.1
45	Tuna fish	7.0	...	...	10.5	8.0	8.0	8.0	8.0
46	Turpentine	...	9.4	10.3	12.0	9.9	8.2	7.8	7.3
47	Twine	20.0	...	20.9	19.0	18.0	...	18.0	30.0
48	Vermicelli	...	12.0	12.0	...	...	8.0	11.5	...
49	Vinegar	...	12.0	12.0	24.0	30.0	32.0	42.0	28.7
50	Wax, yellow	68.0	81.2	81.0	69.0	66.0	68.0	70.0	87.0
51	Wheat	1698.6	1581.0	1479.0	1560.0	1621.5	1900.0	1530.0	1500.0
52	Wine	56.6	63.2	63.1	68.0	59.0	77.5	53.5	59.3

D. VALENCIA (IN DINERS) — Continued

		1617	1618	1619	1620	1621	1622	1623	1624
1	Ashes	35.8	35.4	34.5	30.0	31.3	31.9	36.9	35.5
2	Bedticks	240.0	204.0	204.0	204.0	...	...	...	...
3	Borage	84.0	77.0	96.0	96.0	...	96.0	96.0	96.0
4	Bran	273.0	200.0	270.8	219.4	288.0	...	297.3	336.0
5	Bricks	960.0	960.0	960.0	960.0	960.0	960.0	960.0	960.0
6	Brooms	34.1	35.3	38.8	35.4	34.9	36.8	38.2	39.0
7	Carob beans	56.0	...	38.0	54.0	36.0	40.0	40.0	50.0
8	Charcoal	221.8	220.9	230.0	230.8	228.9	223.1	224.0	220.0
9	Cheese	160.0	...	...	170.0	...	170.0	210.0	...
10	Chickens, spring	36.5	36.6	31.1	38.3	35.7	31.3	36.4	36.1
11	Codfish, dried	5.1	6.0	5.7	5.2	7.0	6.0	8.5	8.0
12	Eels	7.2	7.9	5.8	6.8	9.9	7.6	8.5	8.2
13	Eggs	28.5	28.6	28.6	29.7	30.0	30.3	30.9	28.6
14	Firewood	33.5	33.2	34.8	36.9	37.1	39.7	36.2	41.0
15	Flax	17.4	17.3	17.4	17.0	17.0	17.5	19.3	17.3
16	Grits, barley	90.0	90.0	80.0	90.0	80.0	79.5	100.0	...
17	Grits, wheat	100.0	83.3	86.7	80.0	80.0	79.0	100.0	...
18	Hemp	100.0	120.0	...	100.0	100.0	100.0	97.5	100.0
19	Hens	84.0	75.4	77.2	82.2	76.5	72.9	80.4	80.5
20	Honey	1146.0	1150.5	1470.0	1096.5	1061.3	1102.6	1379.0	1307.0
21	Horseshoes	12.0	12.0	12.0	12.0	12.0	12.0	12.0	12.0
22	Lard	27.0	30.0	28.2	30.0	29.5	32.3	28.3	28.0
23	Lime	120.0	120.0	120.0	120.0	120.0	120.0	120.0	120.0
24	Linen	48.0	45.9	45.0	48.0	53.3	...	57.0	50.0
25	Meal, mixed	210.0	240.0	228.0	191.0	162.0	225.0	192.0	192.0
26	Mutton	39.0	38.0	38.0	37.0	40.0	41.0	42.0	40.0
27	Olive oil	423.8	482.0	375.0	281.8	363.7	321.5	408.0	354.0
28	Pepper	...	...	13.0	...	7.5	7.5	7.7	8.0
29	Plaster of Paris	102.0	100.5	96.0	96.0	104.3	102.0	102.0	101.0
30	Pork, salt	...	...	...	54.6	52.0	52.7	58.8	56.0
31	Pumpkins, candied	...	96.0	...	126.0	98.5	92.7	74.0	...
32	Quinces	...	29.0	22.1	11.7	10.3	14.5	15.8	9.9
33	Raisins	...	165.0	...	123.6	215.9	...	...	...
34	Rice	2094.0	2097.0	2025.8	2181.0	2127.2	2125.5	2131.0	2067.8
35	Saffron	600.0	516.0	480.0	...	864.0	833.8	864.0	624.0
36	Salt	360.0	360.0	360.0	364.5	360.0	360.0	360.0	360.0
37	Sandals, hempen	196.0	204.0	210.7	204.0	207.0	203.5	204.0	204.0
38	Sardines	82.3	71.2	88.9	60.0	65.9	85.0	88.3	80.0
39	Saucers	168.0	168.0	168.0	168.0	...	168.0	154.0	156.0
40	Shoes	...	108.0	105.0	103.7	108.0	96.0	104.0	106.0
41	Shrouds	20.3	20.8	21.0	21.0	21.0	21.0	21.0	20.5
42	Silk, raw	744.0	870.0	840.0	894.0	912.0	966.0	816.0	...
43	Soap	322.1	358.5	312.7	262.5	284.5	274.3	318.6	309.9
44	Sugar	41.1	41.0	40.7	39.2	38.2	38.5	31.8	29.7
45	Tuna fish	8.5	8.0	12.7	10.9	9.5	8.1	8.8	8.9
46	Turpentine	7.0	8.7	9.5	10.3	9.8	8.7	12.0	...
47	Twine	30.0	...	18.0	18.0	18.0	17.7	18.0	21.5
48	Vermicelli	15.0	...	...	...	10.5	11.0	11.3	10.0
49	Vinegar	30.0	35.0	24.0	35.0	24.0	21.6	24.0	18.0
50	Wax, yellow	66.0	64.0	66.0	68.0	63.0	60.0	72.0	72.0
51	Wheat	1878.0	1755.0	1656.0	1272.0	1371.8	1756.5	1993.5	1521.0
52	Wine	70.1	78.1	56.2	51.2	57.4	40.3	48.8	49.5

D. VALENCIA (IN DINERS) — CONTINUED

		1625	1626	1627	1628	1629	1630	1631	1632
1	Ashes	32.5	31.1	27.9	26.6	29.6	29.1	27.5	27.8
2	Bedticks	...	...	...	...	...	240.0	...	...
3	Borage	96.0	109.1	96.0	96.0	98.4	...	96.0	84.0
4	Bran	329.7	347.0	428.9	372.0	277.6	288.0	...	...
5	Bricks	960.0	960.0	961.9	956.0	960.0	960.0	967.5	960.0
6	Brooms	35.0	34.3	35.3	32.8	40.6	40.7	33.9	36.0
7	Carob beans	42.0	...	55.0	47.0	...	48.0	...	36.0
8	Charcoal	230.0	236.3	238.0	240.0	234.4	230.0	230.0	240.5
9	Cheese	150.0	180.0	170.0	...	...	160.0	196.7	180.0
10	Chickens, spring	32.8	36.9	34.3	37.9	43.3	41.0	39.8	37.1
11	Codfish, dried	6.9	8.0	6.8	6.5	8.0	8.0	7.9	9.0
12	Eels	5.7	6.4	7.1	6.9	8.1	7.2	8.1	11.5
13	Eggs	27.0	30.1	30.8	30.5	37.8	30.9	35.5	36.1
14	Firewood	36.4	35.3	37.2	40.5	48.0	54.0	41.0	45.0
15	Flax	17.4	17.6	17.3	17.0	17.0	18.5	19.0	19.3
16	Grits, barley	80.0	80.0	80.0	95.0	90.0	110.0	115.0	110.8
17	Grits, wheat	80.0	80.0	90.0	116.3	100.0	120.0	134.2	126.7
18	Hemp	100.0	105.0	93.3	90.0	75.0	41.7	...	...
19	Hens	70.2	74.6	79.1	86.8	98.5	99.8	86.7	89.1
20	Honey	1284.8	1098.5	1477.5	2071.5	1923.0	1279.5	1424.0	1327.3
21	Horseshoes	12.0	12.0	12.0	12.0	12.0	12.0	...	12.0
22	Lard	...	36.0	...	...	...	...	27.5	41.7
23	Lime	120.0	116.7	120.0	120.0	120.0	120.0	120.0	120.0
24	Linen	48.0	56.0	59.0	...	48.0	66.0	55.3	55.0
25	Meal, mixed	192.0	198.7	192.0	192.0	198.0	194.0	216.0	192.0
26	Mutton	44.0	48.0	48.0	48.0	48.0	48.0	48.0	48.0
27	Olive oil	285.0	381.8	360.0	427.9	371.0	451.9	529.3	529.3
28	Pepper	...	...	...	7.0	...	5.2	5.5	...
29	Plaster of Paris	100.5	102.0	102.0	102.0	105.0	102.0	97.9	96.0
30	Pork, salt	54.0	54.0	51.0	49.4	50.4	48.0	50.0	56.0
31	Pumpkins, candied	72.0	...	128.0	110.4	192.0	120.0	110.4	108.0
32	Quinces	17.3	15.5	16.0	11.9	17.4	14.9	14.2	13.9
33	Raisins	114.3	...	113.3	114.3	...	189.0	...	206.4
34	Rice	2384.0	2325.8	2467.5	2382.8	2320.8	2522.3	2445.0	2457.5
35	Saffron	816.0	720.0	720.0	...	...	655.2	696.0	476.5
36	Salt	360.0	369.0	432.0	414.0	432.0	432.0	442.5	445.5
37	Sandals, hempen	204.0	204.0	204.0	198.0	198.0	210.0	216.0	216.0
38	Sardines	70.0	70.0	80.0	79.0	75.0	85.0	60.0	111.7
39	Saucers	156.0	156.0	168.0	...	180.0	180.0	180.0	180.0
40	Shoes	108.0	102.0	108.0	109.5	108.0	121.0	118.1	104.0
41	Shrouds	20.9	21.0	21.0	21.0	21.0	21.0	21.0	21.0
42	Silk, raw	672.0	816.0	816.0	720.0	684.0	708.0	672.0	828.0
43	Soap	278.0	289.5	310.1	352.5	380.8	418.3	368.3	361.3
44	Sugar	46.9	51.1	47.2	53.9	53.2	48.0	53.8	52.5
45	Tuna fish	8.9	8.4	9.9	10.0	9.3	...	10.9	12.0
46	Turpentine	8.0	...	11.0	10.0	12.0	...	8.2	...
47	Twine	19.0	18.0	18.0	...	17.0	23.5	...	28.0
48	Vermicelli	10.5	11.0	12.0	12.0	11.7	13.2	13.5	13.5
49	Vinegar	27.0	30.0	39.6	34.0	44.7	45.0	45.0	48.0
50	Wax, yellow	66.0	66.0	66.0	75.0	102.0	72.0	72.0	76.0
51	Wheat	1592.0	1714.5	1522.0	1896.0	2160.0	2240.0	2700.0	2271.0
52	Wine	46.2	58.4	58.8	66.0	53.5	66.6	69.2	59.8

D. VALENCIA (IN DINERS) — Continued

	1633	1634	1635	1636	1637	1638	1639	1640	1641
1 Ashes	28.0	31.0	33.0	32.0	32.0	32.0	32.0	31.5	32.3
2 Bedticks	228.0	...	...	...	...	210.9	...	...	246.0
3 Borage	96.0	96.0	102.7	96.0	...	96.0	...	...	...
4 Bran	...	...	...	336.0	264.0	...	336.0	...	360.0
5 Bricks	960.0	960.0	990.0	1020.0	1080.0	990.0	990.0	992.5	1050.0
6 Brooms	34.8	40.6	40.5	40.5	39.5	36.0	40.5	42.0	41.3
7 Carob beans	...	41.0	22.0	51.0	55.1	24.0	26.0	...	...
8 Charcoal	257.6	258.0	258.0	258.0	258.0	258.0	258.0	256.1	257.3
9 Cheese	180.0	180.0	...	...	...	...	...	205.0	205.0
10 Chickens, spring	36.8	33.9	29.1	47.7	45.0	36.4	37.5	38.5	40.0
11 Codfish, dried	10.0	9.9	8.0	10.0	10.0	10.0	10.0	10.0	9.5
12 Eels	10.6	...	9.0	10.6	...	...	7.1	7.7	9.4
13 Eggs	35.9	31.5	32.1	32.3	34.4	33.3	30.4	30.4	37.5
14 Firewood	46.3	48.0	47.5	41.0	46.1	46.9	40.8	40.7	43.5
15 Flax	19.3	19.0	18.3	20.4	23.0	21.0	18.4	18.0	18.0
16 Grits, barley	105.0	...	99.3	104.3	103.0	108.0	90.0	87.5	100.0
17 Grits, wheat	120.0	...	106.7	117.5	110.6	103.3	77.5	90.0	105.0
18 Hemp	...	60.0	125.0	119.0	81.3	90.0	60.0	150.0	182.5
19 Hens	96.5	85.2	81.9	84.2	91.5	89.0	80.2	80.1	93.2
20 Honey	1599.0	1201.0	1055.0	1318.5	1035.0	1273.0	1363.0	1405.5	1291.5
21 Horseshoes	...	12.0	12.0	12.0	12.0	12.0	12.0	12.0	14.0
22 Lard	45.1	...	...	...	48.0	33.0	...	...	...
23 Lime	120.0	120.0	126.0	124.0	138.0	126.0	136.5	138.0	138.0
24 Linen	62.0	62.0	57.0	78.0	66.0	...	69.0	59.5	54.0
25 Meal, mixed	240.0	210.0	210.0	253.0	214.7	210.0	217.0	230.0	270.0
26 Mutton	...	...	48.0	47.0	57.6	53.0	49.0	48.0	48.0
27 Olive oil	376.5	410.9	385.5	456.8	428.8	326.5	313.0	309.0	408.0
28 Pepper	5.5	6.5	8.6	7.8	10.0	9.9	8.9	17.0	13.1
29 Plaster of Paris	100.5	108.0	116.0	110.3	144.0	127.5	132.0	120.8	132.0
30 Pork, salt	49.0	48.0	54.0	52.0	60.0	63.0	...	54.0	60.0
31 Pumpkins, candied	120.0	120.0	120.0	96.0	96.0	103.5	96.0	96.0	120.0
32 Quinces	23.7	28.7	32.9	41.9	35.5	15.7	19.9	29.8	19.9
33 Raisins	...	162.0	...	...	...	...	...	...	...
34 Rice	2349.5	2613.3	2595.8	2686.0	2984.5	2858.3	2175.0	1998.0	1917.0
35 Saffron	724.6	...	1200.0	1161.4	1044.3	768.0	1101.9	1072.1	977.8
36 Salt	446.0	436.5	439.5	444.0	444.0	444.0	444.0	444.0	444.0
37 Sandals, hempen	216.0	216.0	216.0	216.0	216.0	210.0	210.0	216.0	212.0
38 Sardines	100.0	...	90.0	99.0	114.0	91.5	105.0	97.5	98.0
39 Saucers	180.0	180.0	180.0	180.0	180.0	180.0	180.0	180.0	180.0
40 Shoes	...	...	108.0	144.0	150.0	148.0	138.0	126.0	120.0
41 Shrouds	21.0	23.0	23.0	23.0	23.0	23.0	22.8	22.0	22.0
42 Silk, raw	840.0	852.0	744.0	864.0	696.0	672.0	576.0	...	480.0
43 Soap	332.6	298.0	304.4	321.0	313.0	289.1	290.0	265.5	304.2
44 Sugar	54.4	55.2	65.3	67.9	59.4	61.5	55.5	54.3	50.1
45 Tuna fish	13.0	12.7	12.7	11.5	12.0	12.0	12.0	10.8	14.0
46 Turpentine	...	...	...	11.5	11.3	11.7	...	11.2	10.0
47 Twine	...	24.0	18.0	18.0	20.0	21.0	20.0	20.0	18.0
48 Vermicelli	...	...	...	13.0	...	13.0	12.0	9.5	10.7
49 Vinegar	49.1	48.0	...	...	28.5	36.0	32.0	26.5	30.0
50 Wax, yellow	82.0	78.0	69.0	60.0	...	60.0	75.0	72.0	87.0
51 Wheat	1964.5	1828.5	1935.5	2473.5	2522.0	2341.3	1796.0	1791.0	2087.0
52 Wine	54.6	58.7	65.3	58.4	57.2	67.9	61.5	43.7	46.4

D. VALENCIA (IN DINERS) — Continued

		1642	1643	1644	1645	1646	1647	1648	1649	1650
1	Ashes	32.0	32.0	30.6	26.0	26.0	23.0	20.0	20.0	20.0
2	Bedticks	233.3	224.0	228.4	210.9	...	215.3	...	192.0	192.0
3	Borage	89.9	...	...	...	...	...	...	...	...
4	Bran	...	360.0	...	360.0	...	...	336.0	360.0	...
5	Bricks	1020.0	990.0	1065.0	1040.0	1080.0	1050.0	1064.0	1044.0	1080.0
6	Brooms	36.0	36.0	36.0	36.5	37.8	39.0	42.0	45.7	46.0
7	Carob beans	...	...	63.0	...	74.0	71.0	34.0	46.8	38.0
8	Charcoal	258.0	258.0	258.0	258.0	258.0	258.0	254.3	269.7	295.0
9	Cheese	200.0	...	198.5	...	...	...	...	220.0	200.0
10	Chickens, spring	39.9	32.9	35.9	32.7	35.0	40.5	37.8	38.0	32.4
11	Codfish, dried	10.0	9.0	12.8	9.0	4.9	...	...	...	...
12	Eels	7.7	6.3	9.3	...	...	...	...	...	...
13	Eggs	33.7	32.9	35.3	33.7	32.9	35.8	37.0	34.1	32.3
14	Firewood	34.8	37.3	32.8	51.0	53.9	46.2	47.7	56.3	56.7
15	Flax	18.0	19.3	18.0	18.0	18.0	18.5	18.0	...	18.0
16	Grits, barley	100.0	110.0	111.0	...	...	...	150.0	...	102.5
17	Grits, wheat	82.5	110.0	100.9	...	...	130.0	130.0	...	130.0
18	Hemp	180.0	180.0	180.0	180.0	...	...	...	...	...
19	Hens	90.0	76.1	77.9	78.7	78.2	89.1	90.2	99.0	82.9
20	Honey	1137.0	1285.5	1380.0	1703.8	1634.3	1616.0	1594.0	1536.0	1245.0
21	Horseshoes	...	15.0	15.0	15.0	15.0	15.0	15.0	...	15.0
22	Lard	41.7	41.7	60.0	...	...	48.0	33.5	...	33.5
23	Lime	132.0	127.5	132.0	132.0	132.0	132.0	132.0	138.0	144.0
24	Linen	54.0	...	...	61.0	62.0	68.0	54.0	50.0	64.5
25	Meal, mixed	257.3	240.0	240.0	...	...	...	...	...	...
26	Mutton	48.0	48.0	...	...	...	...	...	52.0	59.0
27	Olive oil	384.0	415.0	367.3	428.5	380.1	501.0	526.9	344.4	277.3
28	Pepper	...	7.3	7.0	6.9	...	6.7	...	6.0	5.1
29	Plaster of Paris	129.0	120.0	120.0	129.0	132.0	132.0	132.0	132.0	132.0
30	Pork, salt	64.0	...	60.0	...	...	...	...	...	...
31	Pumpkins, candied	88.0	81.0	96.0	96.0	96.0	96.0	96.0	96.0	96.0
32	Quinces	20.6	23.2	27.3	13.7	...	14.7	15.0	11.0	25.4
33	Raisins	...	...	...	...	92.7	...	...	...	...
34	Rice	2184.0	2607.5	2250.0	2100.0	2202.0	2295.5	2321.3	2380.0	2318.3
35	Saffron	...	576.0	552.0	480.0	...	...	1429.4	810.0	818.0
36	Salt	444.0	444.0	444.0	444.0	444.0	628.0	444.0	444.0	444.0
37	Sandals, hempen	210.0	204.0	204.0	204.0	204.0	204.0	204.0	204.0	204.0
38	Sardines	103.0	115.3	...	130.0	...	...	...	...	...
39	Saucers	180.0	180.0	180.0	180.0	180.0	180.0	180.0	180.0	180.0
40	Shoes	138.0	138.0	...	144.0	138.0	141.0	138.0	144.0	...
41	Shrouds	23.8	24.0	23.0	22.0	22.0	22.0	22.0	22.0	22.0
42	Silk, raw	576.0	417.6	636.0	720.0	696.0	600.0	405.5	...	588.0
43	Soap	327.9	322.0	307.1	333.5	323.9	332.3	362.0	335.3	302.5
44	Sugar	45.6	48.4	46.6	44.7	56.1	58.2	71.3	76.7	72.5
45	Tuna fish	11.3	12.0	14.0	14.4	...	...	...	...	18.0
46	Turpentine	...	...	12.0	...	...	...	...	...	...
47	Twine	20.0	22.0	20.0	18.0	...	21.3	22.0	...	22.7
48	Vermicelli	10.0	11.0	12.0	...	...	14.0	16.0	...	12.5
49	Vinegar	29.4	59.0	56.6	42.0	30.0	...	24.6	40.0	58.9
50	Wax, yellow	64.0	56.0	64.0	67.0	70.5	68.0	102.0	86.0	65.3
51	Wheat	1761.8	1524.0	2414.0	2310.0	2385.0	2826.0	2268.0	2159.5	2143.5
52	Wine	54.1	74.5	117.3	64.0	51.0	68.8	63.4	75.5	74.0

APPENDIX VI

INDEX NUMBERS OF GRAIN PRICES

Base = 1571-1580

	Andalusia	New Castile	Old Castile-León	Valencia
1501	...	...	...	...
1502	...	...	...	...
1503	...	...	...	...
1504	...	37.05	...	...
1505	...	43.15	...	48.66
1506	...	74.65	...	46.77
1507	...	65.92	...	...
1508	...	44.74	44.44	44.55
1509	...	21.68	...	...
1510	...	33.43	24.22	...
1511	...	33.78	27.19	...
1512	...	24.20	...	36.20
1513	...	41.61	31.85	36.81
1514	...	37.94	...	35.82
1515	...	44.99	...	35.82
1516	...	37.25	...	33.79
1517	...	29.41	...	38.75
1518	...	...	24.99	36.91
1519	...	39.53	28.83	36.34
1520	...	32.49	29.03	...
1521	...	...	37.84	...
1522	...	...	46.85	...
1523	...	43.95	41.73	44.69
1524	...	48.56	37.73	42.95
1525	...	...	39.78	40.26
1526	...	58.92	42.24	40.68
1527	...	...	63.39	45.73
1528	...	...	59.80	44.89
1529	...	...	68.81	51.92
1530	...	...	73.73	...
1531	...	52.28	...	54.28
1532	...	42.61	...	48.19
1533	...	...	53.61	...
1534	...	62.55	39.73	50.59
1535	...	41.02	30.26	45.07
1536	...	51.09	44.54	48.71
1537	...	31.74	38.25	41.44
1538	...	31.74	40.91	...
1539	...	55.80	70.96	...
1540	...	...	62.77	...
1541	...	54.66	48.33	45.02
1542	...	78.47	58.06	52.91
1543	...	51.09	59.55	50.74
1544	...	54.06	45.36	48.75
1545	...	...	59.75	56.64
1546	...	...	82.02	73.53
1547	...	91.36	53.81	61.21

INDEX NUMBERS OF GRAIN PRICES — Continued

	Andalusia	New Castile	Old Castile-León	Valencia
1548	...	84.07	54.43	...
1549	...	...	66.61	...
1550	...	58.63	48.90	60.18
1551	...	...	44.3	60.6
1552	...	...	50.1	...
1553	...	...	51.2	...
1554	61.2	42.1	54.1	61.0
1555	112.2	...	69.8	64.7
1556	...	...	81.3	...
1557	125.3	85.3	104.1	114.0
1558	55.8	...	91.2	78.8
1559	49.2	...	76.0	74.4
1560	...	89.1	80.2	...
1561	65.0	105.1	79.4	...
1562	95.1	143.4	88.5	...
1563	57.6	66.6	84.5	...
1564	54.6	71.4	79.2	...
1565	...	68.9	85.8	...
1566	...	84.9	89.2	...
1567	72.2	102.4	90.8	80.5
1568	...	102.5	57.1	79.4
1569	89.4	79.0	...	...
1570	...	...	...	...
1571	...	...	...	...
1572	...	99.5	...	...
1573	83.9	80.5	...	...
1574	...	76.1	...	...
1575	...	89.5	...	...
1576	...	104.1	...	...
1577	...	103.8	...	...
1578	...	110.2	...	109.4
1579	...	118.3	...	...
1580	...	107.0	...	...
1581	...	...	...	...
1582	135.0	120.6	...	...
1583	...	179.2	108.1	...
1584	165.0	132.1	111.8	...
1585	79.9	121.2	115.4	...
1586	...	...	111.0	96.1
1587	107.4	97.2	111.0	...
1588	150.8	113.0	120.6	107.4
1589	197.3	151.4	110.5	110.3
1590	...	...	109.8	110.2
1591	140.8	128.9	128.6	117.1
1592	144.0	105.7	147.7	134.5
1593	157.5	133.7	131.8	...
1594	126.6	173.9	138.9	...
1595	125.6	113.2	135.0	...
1596	136.7	114.1	130.3	112.0
1597	...	124.9	142.3	122.8
1598	228.2	155.5	147.1	...
1599	194.4	191.0	150.1	...

INDEX NUMBERS OF GRAIN PRICES — Continued

	Andalusia	New Castile	Old Castile-León	Valencia
1600	126.2	172.2	147.1	...
1601	115.55	...	127.81	...
1602	95.79	131.87	121.20	116.98
1603	188.76	126.98	121.34	140.60
1604	196.67	145.30	128.93	124.85
1605	222.08	...	145.94	...
1606	154.14	270.66	175.05	...
1607	139.64	283.68	173.78	...
1608	148.11	...	164.36	125.98
1609	139.46	184.98	144.68	124.43
1610	138.52	141.43	121.76	...
1611	117.25	120.68	96.45	...
1612	115.18	162.19	93.78	125.27
1613	136.26	137.36	108.97	131.46
1614	123.65	170.74	136.66	137.65
1615	107.84	210.01	163.80	124.29
1616	175.59	240.33	160.99	125.70
1617	165.80	352.54	153.54	140.18
1618	147.55	203.50	111.21	137.09
1619	141.34	...	107.56	127.66
1620	152.82	143.47	141.44	125.98
1621	...	166.67	144.82	122.32
1622	179.73	155.88	144.68	132.16
1623	141.34	219.98	139.90	149.32
1624	141.53	...	118.67	...
1625	203.07	...	93.78	133.29
1626	218.69	...	115.85	135.40
1627	250.68	204.92	147.77	133.29
1628	216.99	248.47	164.22	149.32
1629	166.56	226.29	163.10	152.27
1630	174.65	235.45	173.50	169.28
1631	162.23	288.97	183.06	182.36
1632	181.05	210.42	164.64	169.14
1633	149.05	192.10	170.69	155.78
1634	135.88	...	153.96	...
1635	173.52	184.37	161.13	157.05
1636	283.24	205.13	163.96	175.61
1637	247.67	...	162.67	182.36
1638	170.51	209.81	179.83	177.72
1639	128.16	...	152.97	139.76
1640	107.27	183.56	124.57	134.69
1641	160.72	258.85	125.42	147.49
1642	282.30	322.95	158.60	144.40
1643	232.80	185.39	173.92	152.13
1644	217.37	220.78	168.44	164.08
1645	159.03	269.67	152.41	156.07
1646	187.26	330.69	163.66	162.11
1647	317.68	285.31	171.39	182.50
1648	289.08	335.16	165.77	187.14
1649	208.53	297.31	166.05	158.60
1650	332.36	472.73	171.25	158.46

APPENDIX VII

Money Wages

THE purpose of the following tables, which form an insignificant portion of the data upon which the index numbers rest, is to illustrate absolute wage levels. Since the quotations will mean most when compared with commodity prices in their respective regions, the original monetary units have been conserved. The wage rates for Andalusia, New Castile, and Old Castile are expressed in *maravedis* and those for Valencia in *diners*. For methods of reducing quotations to terms of a fixed weight of fine silver see Appendix II.

In the column marked "Region," A = Andalusia, N = New Castile, O = Old Castile-León, and V = Valencia; and in the "Unit" column, d = day, y = year, and al = *alna*. The alna was equivalent to 91 centimeters, and the piece-rate quotations represent linen 4½ *palmos* (approximately 1.02 meters) wide.

In addition to their monetary rewards the workers whose wages are quoted by the year in the following tables ordinarily received an allowance of meat, bread, and wine, or monetary commutations of these items, and either lodging or a dwelling.[1] The basket emptiers, cart loaders, and laborers for Old Castile in 1501–1550 were given sufficient wine and bread for the noon meal. So far as I have been able to determine, all other workers listed by the day received only money wages.

---

[1] *Vide supra*, pp. 267–268.

TABLE A

Unit	Region		1501	1502	1503	1504	1505	1506
d	O	Basket emptier	...	...	25.0	...	...	17.0
y	N	Bookkeeper	...	...	...	...	...	...
d	V	Carpenter, journeyman	...	48.0	48.0	48.0	48.0	...
d	O	Cart loader	...	20.0	34.0	...	...	25.0
y	O	Cook, female	...	...	...	...	1224.0	1224.0
d	O	Laborer	...	22.5	31.1	...	...	27.4
y	O	Maid servant	...	1224.0	1224.0	1224.0	1224.0	1224.0
d	V	Mason, journeyman	...	48.0	48.0	48.0	46.0	...
d	V	Mason, master	...	60.0	60.0	60.0	60.0	60.0
d	V	Mason's helper	...	30.0	30.0	30.0	30.0	30.0
y	O	Nurse	...	1224.0	1224.0	1224.0	1224.0	1224.0
y	V	Sacristan	1080.0	1080.0	1080.0	1080.0	1080.0	1080.0
d	V	Stonecutter, journeyman	...	48.0	48.0	48.0	48.0	48.0
al	V	Weaver, linen	5.3	5.4	5.5	5.0	5.0	5.0
y	V	Wet nurse	1440.0	2400.0	...	...	...	...

Unit	Region		1507	1508	1509	1510	1511	1512
d	O	Basket emptier	...	...	...	17.0	...	22.0
y	N	Bookkeeper	...	...	...	1000.0	1000.0	1000.0
d	V	Carpenter, journeyman	...	39.0	48.0	...	48.0	48.0
d	O	Cart loader	...	...	...	34.0	...	34.0
y	O	Cook, female	1224.0	1224.0	1224.0	1224.0	...	...
d	O	Laborer	...	...	...	29.5	...	26.0
y	O	Maid servant	1224.0	1224.0	1224.0	1224.0	1224.0	1224.0
d	V	Mason, journeyman	...	48.0	48.0	48.0	48.0	48.0
d	V	Mason, master	...	60.0	60.0	60.0	60.0	60.0
d	V	Mason's helper	...	30.0	30.0	30.0	30.0	30.0
y	O	Nurse	1224.0	1224.0	1224.0	1224.0	1224.0	1224.0
y	V	Sacristan	1080.0	1080.0	1080.0	1080.0	1080.0	1080.0
d	V	Stonecutter, journeyman	...	48.0	46.0	48.0	48.0	...
al	V	Weaver, linen	5.0	4.5	5.0	5.0	5.0	5.0
y	V	Wet nurse	...	...	...	2198.5	2048.0	2160.0

Unit	Region		1513	1514	1515	1516	1517	1518
d	O	Basket emptier	...	...	...	...	...	17.0
y	N	Bookkeeper	1000.0	1000.0	1000.0	1000.0	1000.0	1000.0
d	V	Carpenter, journeyman	48.0	48.0	47.0	...	45.8	46.3
d	O	Cart loader	...	...	...	...	...	28.0
y	O	Cook, female	...	...	...	...	...	...
d	O	Laborer	...	...	...	...	...	36.0
y	O	Maid servant	1224.0	1224.0	1224.0	1224.0	1224.0	1224.0
d	V	Mason, journeyman	...	48.0	48.0	48.0	47.0	48.0
d	V	Mason, master	...	60.0	60.0	60.0	58.5	60.0
d	V	Mason's helper	...	30.0	30.0	30.0	31.5	32.0
y	O	Nurse	1224.0	1224.0	1224.0	1224.0	1224.0	1224.0
y	V	Sacristan	1080.0	...	1200.0	1200.0	1200.0	1200.0
d	V	Stonecutter, journeyman	...	48.0	48.0	...	47.3	48.0
al	V	Weaver, linen	5.0	5.0	5.3	4.8	4.8	4.9
y	V	Wet nurse	2160.0	2160.0	2160.0	2160.0	2160.0	2160.0

TABLE A — CONTINUED

Unit	Region		1519	1520	1521	1522	1523	1524
d	O	Basket emptier	25.0	25.0	20.0	...	28.0	25.0
y	N	Bookkeeper	1000.0	1000.0	1000.0	1000.0	1000.0	1000.0
d	V	Carpenter, journeyman	48.0	48.0	48.0	48.0	50.0	...
d	O	Cart loader	34.0	34.0	34.0	...	34.0	34.0
y	O	Cook, female	...	1632.0	1632.0	1632.0	1632.0	1632.0
d	O	Laborer	26.8	35.4	29.0	...	37.8	38.0
y	O	Maid servant	1224.0	1632.0	1632.0	1632.0	1632.0	1632.0
d	V	Mason, journeyman	40.0	42.8	48.0	48.0	43.0	48.0
d	V	Mason, master	60.0	60.0	56.0	60.0	60.0	60.0
d	V	Mason's helper	30.0	30.0	30.0	30.0	30.0	30.0
y	O	Nurse	1224.0	1224.0	1632.0	1632.0	1632.0	1632.0
y	V	Sacristan	1200.0	1200.0	1200.0	1200.0	1200.0	1200.0
d	V	Stonecutter, journeyman ...	47.0	48.0	48.0	...	48.0	48.0
al	V	Weaver, linen	5.0	5.0	5.5	5.6	5.3	4.9
y	V	Wet nurse	2160.0	2160.0	2160.0	2160.0	2160.0	2160.0

Unit	Region		1525	1526	1527	1528	1529	1530
d	O	Basket emptier	...	...	25.0	25.0	...	17.0
y	N	Bookkeeper	1000.0	1000.0	1000.0	1000.0	1000.0	1000.0
d	V	Carpenter, journeyman	48.0	...	...	48.0	48.0	...
d	O	Cart loader	...	...	34.0	34.0	...	30.0
y	O	Cook, female	1632.0	1632.0	1632.0	1632.0	...	...
d	O	Laborer	...	...	34.0	28.0	...	17.5
y	O	Maid servant	1632.0	1632.0	1632.0	1632.0	...	1224.0
d	V	Mason, journeyman	48.0	48.0	48.0	48.0	43.1	36.0
d	V	Mason, master	60.0	54.0	60.0	60.0	52.0	...
d	V	Mason's helper	30.0	30.0	30.0	30.0	30.0	30.0
y	O	Nurse	1632.0	1632.0	1632.0	1632.0	...	...
y	V	Sacristan	1200.0	1200.0	1200.0	1200.0	1200.0	1200.0
d	V	Stonecutter, journeyman ...	48.0	48.0	48.0	48.0	48.0	...
al	V	Weaver, linen	5.3	6.0	5.3	4.5	5.3	5.0
y	V	Wet nurse	2160.0	2160.0	2160.0	2160.0	2160.0	2160.0

Unit	Region		1531	1532	1533	1534	1535
d	O	Basket emptier	...	22.0	25.0	25.0	22.0
y	N	Bookkeeper	1000.0	1000.0	1000.0	1000.0	1000.0
d	V	Carpenter, journeyman	48.0	48.0	48.0	48.0	48.0
d	O	Cart loader	...	34.0	34.0	34.0	34.0
y	O	Cook, female	1428.0	1632.0	1632.0	1632.0	1632.0
d	O	Laborer.....................	...	35.0	35.2	31.9	35.1
y	O	Maid servant	1428.0	1632.0	1632.0	1632.0	1632.0
d	V	Mason, journeyman	...	48.0	48.0	48.0	48.0
d	V	Mason, master	...	60.0	60.0	60.0	60.0
d	V	Mason's helper	...	30.0	30.8	30.0	30.0
y	O	Nurse	1428.0	1632.0	1632.0	1632.0	1632.0
y	V	Sacristan	1200.0	1200.0	1200.0	1200.0	1200.0
d	V	Stonecutter, journeyman	...	48.0	48.0	48.0	48.0
al	V	Weaver, linen	5.6	...	6.0	5.6	5.8
y	V	Wet nurse	2160.0	2160.0	2160.0	2160.0	2160.0

TABLE A — Continued

Unit	Region		1536	1537	1538	1539	1540
d	O	Basket emptier	24.0	29.5	25.0	...	...
y	N	Bookkeeper	1000.0	1000.0	1000.0	1000.0	1500.0
d	V	Carpenter, journeyman	48.0	48.0	48.0	48.0	48.0
d	O	Cart loader	34.0	34.0	34.0	...	...
y	O	Cook, female	1632.0	1632.0	1632.0	1632.0	1632.0
d	O	Laborer	28.0	41.0	33.8	...	...
y	O	Maid servant	1632.0	1632.0	1632.0	1632.0	1632.0
d	V	Mason, journeyman	48.0	48.0	48.0	48.0	48.0
d	V	Mason, master	60.0	60.0	60.0	60.0	60.0
d	V	Mason's helper	30.0	30.7	30.0	30.0	30.0
y	O	Nurse	1632.0	1632.0	1224.0	...	...
y	V	Sacristan	1200.0	1200.0	1200.0	1200.0	1200.0
d	V	Stonecutter, journeyman	49.5	48.0	48.0	48.4	48.0
al	V	Weaver, linen	5.5	6.0	5.2	6.0	5.7
y	V	Wet nurse	2160.0	2160.0	2160.0	2160.0	2160.0

Unit	Region		1541	1542	1543	1544	1545
d	O	Basket emptier	24.0	25.0	25.0	25.0	25.0
y	N	Bookkeeper	1500.0	1500.0	1500.0	1500.0	1500.0
d	V	Carpenter, journeyman	44.0	48.0	48.0	48.0	48.0
d	O	Cart loader	34.0	34.0	34.0	34.0	41.5
y	O	Cook, female	1632.0	1632.0	2040.0	2040.0	2040.0
d	O	Laborer	31.0	35.8	30.6	41.0	40.8
y	O	Maid servant	1632.0	1632.0	2040.0	2040.0	2040.0
d	V	Mason, journeyman	48.0	48.0	48.0	46.9	46.0
d	V	Mason, master	60.0	60.0	60.0	56.0	57.0
d	V	Mason's helper	30.0	30.0	30.0	31.5	31.5
y	O	Nurse	1632.0	1632.0	2040.0	2040.0	2040.0
y	V	Sacristan	1200.0	1200.0	1200.0	1200.0	1200.0
d	V	Stonecutter, journeyman	48.0	49.0	48.0	48.0	48.0
al	V	Weaver, linen	5.3	6.0	5.1	5.3	5.1
y	V	Wet nurse	2160.0	2160.0	2160.0	2160.0	2160.0

Unit	Region		1546	1547	1548	1549	1550
d	O	Basket emptier	25.0	25.0	24.0	25.0	30.0
y	N	Bookkeeper	1500.0	1500.0	1500.0	1500.0	1500.0
d	V	Carpenter, journeyman	48.0	48.0	...	48.0	48.0
d	O	Cart loader	42.5	40.0	44.0	60.0	68.0
y	O	Cook, female	2040.0	2040.0	2040.0	2040.0	2040.0
d	O	Laborer	40.5	33.8	36.5	39.3	53.4
y	O	Maid servant	2040.0	2040.0	2040.0	2040.0	2040.0
d	V	Mason, journeyman	48.0	48.0	48.0	48.0	48.0
d	V	Mason, master	57.0	58.5	60.0	60.0	60.0
d	V	Mason's helper	30.0	30.4	30.0	31.5	30.0
y	O	Nurse	2040.0	2040.0	2040.0	2040.0	2040.0
y	V	Sacristan	1200.0	1200.0	1200.0	1200.0	1200.0
d	V	Stonecutter, journeyman	48.0	48.0	48.0	48.0	50.3
al	V	Weaver, linen	5.0	5.0	5.2	6.0	6.8
y	V	Wet nurse	2160.0	2160.0	2160.0	2160.0	2160.0

TABLE B

Unit	Region		1551	1552	1553	1554	1555	1556
d	V	Carpenter, journeyman	48.0	...	48.0	48.0	48.0	...
d	V	Carpenter, master	60.0	...	60.0	60.0	60.0	...
y	O	Cook, female	2040.0	2040.0	2040.0	2040.0	2040.0	2040.0
y	V	Cook, hospital	2016.0	2016.0	2016.0	...	...	2880.0
y	O	Gardener	750.0	...	...	...	...	...
d	N	Laborer	34.0	...	34.0	40.0	40.0	34.0
y	O	Laundress	2040.0	2040.0	2040.0	2040.0	2040.0	2040.0
d	V	Mason, journeyman	48.0	48.0	48.0	48.0	54.0	48.0
d	V	Mason, master	60.0	60.0	60.0	60.0	60.0	60.0
d	V	Mason's helper	30.0	31.5	34.5	36.0	36.0	36.0
y	A	Miller	...	...	...	...	...	...
y	O	Nurse	2040.0	2040.0	2040.0	2040.0	2040.0	2040.0
d	V	Stonecutter, master	60.0	60.0	60.0	...	60.0	60.0
y	A	Wardrobe keeper	2856.0	2856.0	2856.0	2856.0	4500.0	4500.0
al	V	Weaver, linen	6.5	7.0	7.0	7.0	7.0	7.0

Unit	Region		1557	1558	1559	1560	1561	1562
d	V	Carpenter, journeyman	54.0	48.0	54.0	54.0	60.0	60.0
d	V	Carpenter, master	60.0	60.0	60.0	60.0	72.0	69.0
y	O	Cook, female	2040.0	2040.0	2040.0	2040.0	2040.0	2040.0
y	V	Cook, hospital	3600.0	3600.0	3600.0	3600.0	2592.0	2016.0
y	O	Gardener	...	...	...	2992.0	2244.0	2244.0
d	N	Laborer	40.0	40.0	38.0	44.0	60.0	...
y	O	Laundress	2040.0	2040.0	2040.0	2040.0	2040.0	2040.0
d	V	Mason, journeyman	47.6	48.0	49.5	49.1	48.0	53.2
d	V	Mason, master	60.0	60.0	60.0	57.0	60.0	61.5
d	V	Mason's helper	35.6	36.0	36.0	36.0	36.0	37.5
y	A	Miller	...	...	...	...	...	...
y	O	Nurse	2040.0	2040.0	2040.0	2040.0	2040.0	2040.0
d	V	Stonecutter, master	60.0	60.0	60.0	60.0	72.0	...
y	A	Wardrobe keeper	4500.0	4500.0	4500.0	4500.0	4500.0	4500.0
al	V	Weaver, linen	7.3	7.0	7.3	7.3	8.5	8.0

Unit	Region		1563	1564	1565	1566	1567	1568
d	V	Carpenter, journeyman	60.0	54.0	60.0	58.5	58.0	60.0
d	V	Carpenter, master	68.0	60.0	72.0	72.0	72.0	72.0
y	O	Cook, female	2040.0	2040.0	2040.0	2040.0	2040.0	2040.0
y	V	Cook, hospital	3600.0	3600.0	3600.0	3600.0	3312.0	2760.0
y	O	Gardener	2244.0	...	...	2613.0	...	...
d	N	Laborer	60.0	60.0	68.0	72.0	68.0	68.0
y	O	Laundress	2040.0	2040.0	2040.0	2040.0	2040.0	2040.0
d	V	Mason, journeyman	55.5	56.3	60.0	60.0	60.0	60.0
d	V	Mason, master	64.5	60.0	60.0	60.0	60.0	60.0
d	V	Mason's helper	42.0	41.5	42.0	42.0	42.0	44.0
y	A	Miller	6000.0	6120.0	6120.0	6732.0	6732.0	6732.0
y	O	Nurse	2040.0	2040.0	2040.0	2040.0	2040.0	2040.0
d	V	Stonecutter, master	72.0	66.0	72.0	66.0	72.0	72.0
y	A	Wardrobe keeper	4500.0	4500.0	4500.0	4500.0	4500.0	4500.0
al	V	Weaver, linen	8.2	8.4	8.8	8.9	9.0	9.2

TABLE B — Continued

Unit	Region		1569	1570	1571	1572	1573	1574
d	V	Carpenter, journeyman	60.0	60.0	54.0	60.0	...	60.0
d	V	Carpenter, master	72.0	72.0	72.0	69.0	72.0	72.0
y	O	Cook, female	2040.0	2040.0	2040.0	2040.0	2040.0	2040.0
y	V	Cook, hospital	2400.0	...	3456.0	3840.0	3840.0	3840.0
y	O	Gardener	...	2150.0	2250.0	2250.0	2250.0	2250.0
d	N	Laborer	60.0	68.0	68.0	66.5	68.0	68.0
y	O	Laundress	2040.0	2040.0	2040.0	2040.0	2040.0	2040.0
d	V	Mason, journeyman	60.0	...	54.0	...	57.0	55.5
d	V	Mason, master	66.0	67.5	66.0	68.5	66.0	72.0
d	V	Mason's helper	46.0	46.0	45.5	45.5	45.5	45.5
y	A	Miller	6732.0	6732.0	6732.0	6732.0	6732.0	...
y	O	Nurse	2040.0	2040.0	2040.0	2040.0	2040.0	2040.0
d	V	Stonecutter, master	72.0	74.0	72.0	72.0	80.0	72.0
y	A	Wardrobe keeper	4500.0	4500.0	4500.0	4500.0	4500.0	4500.0
al	V	Weaver, linen	9.6	9.8	8.8	9.3	9.0	9.0

Unit	Region		1575	1576	1577	1578	1579	1580
d	V	Carpenter, journeyman	60.0	60.0	60.0	60.0	64.0	66.0
d	V	Carpenter, master	66.0	64.5	66.0	66.0	72.0	72.0
y	O	Cook, female	2040.0	2040.0	2040.0	2040.0	2040.0	2040.0
y	V	Cook, hospital	3840.0	3840.0	3840.0	3840.0	3840.0	3840.0
y	O	Gardener	2250.0	2250.0	2250.0	2250.0	3000.0	...
d	N	Laborer	...	...	76.5	68.0	60.0	60.0
y	O	Laundress	2040.0	2040.0	2040.0	2040.0	2040.0	2040.0
d	V	Mason, journeyman	...	60.0	60.0	62.3	64.5	66.0
d	V	Mason, master	70.0	66.0	66.0	67.5	72.0	72.0
d	V	Mason's helper	46.0	46.0	46.0	46.5	52.1	48.0
y	A	Miller	...	6636.0	...	...	...	6732.0
y	O	Nurse	2040.0	2040.0	2040.0	2040.0	2040.0	2040.0
d	V	Stonecutter, master	...	72.0	72.0	72.0	72.0	...
y	A	Wardrobe keeper	4500.0	4500.0	4500.0	4500.0	4500.0	4500.0
al	V	Weaver, linen	8.6	9.6	9.8	...	...	10.0

Unit	Region		1581	1582	1583	1584	1585
d	V	Carpenter, journeyman	66.0	66.0	66.0	67.0	66.0
d	V	Carpenter, master	72.0	72.0	72.0	72.0	72.0
y	O	Cook, female	2040.0	2040.0	2040.0	2856.0	2856.0
y	V	Cook, hospital	3840.0	3840.0	3840.0	3840.0	3840.0
y	O	Gardener	3740.0	3740.0	3740.0	3750.0	3740.0
d	N	Laborer	85.0	85.0	76.5	76.5	85.0
y	O	Laundress	2040.0	2040.0	2040.0	2856.0	2856.0
d	V	Mason, journeyman	66.0	66.0	66.0	75.0	70.5
d	V	Mason, master	72.0	72.0	72.0	78.0	78.0
d	V	Mason's helper	49.5	54.0	54.0	58.5	58.5
y	A	Miller	6732.0	6732.0	6732.0	6732.0	6732.0
y	O	Nurse	2040.0	2040.0	2040.0	2856.0	2856.0
d	V	Stonecutter, master	72.0	72.0	73.5	72.0	72.0
y	A	Wardrobe keeper	4500.0	4500.0	4500.0	4500.0	4500.0
al	V	Weaver, linen	10.0	10.0	10.0	11.5	12.0

TABLE B — Continued

Unit	Region		1586	1587	1588	1589	1590
d	V	Carpenter, journeyman	66.0	72.0	72.0	72.0	72.0
d	V	Carpenter, master	84.0	84.0	...	84.0	84.0
y	O	Cook, female	2856.0	2856.0	2856.0	2856.0	2856.0
y	V	Cook, hospital	3840.0	3840.0	3840.0	3840.0	3840.0
y	O	Gardener	3740.0	3740.0	3740.0	3740.0	3740.0
d	N	Laborer	76.5	76.5	85.0	85.0	85.0
y	O	Laundress	2856.0	2856.0	2856.0	2856.0	2856.0
d	V	Mason, journeyman	72.0	72.0	72.0	78.0	72.0
d	V	Mason, master	84.0	84.0	84.0	84.0	84.0
d	V	Mason's helper	48.2	56.8	58.3	60.0	60.0
y	A	Miller	6732.0	6732.0	6732.0	6732.0	6732.0
y	O	Nurse	2856.0	2856.0	2856.0	2856.0	2856.0
d	V	Stonecutter, master	84.0	84.0	84.0	84.0	84.0
y	A	Wardrobe keeper	4500.0	4500.0	4500.0	4500.0	4500.0
al	V	Weaver, linen	11.5	12.0	12.0	12.0	12.0

Unit	Region		1591	1592	1593	1594	1595
d	V	Carpenter, journeyman	...	72.0	78.0	78.0	72.0
d	V	Carpenter, master	...	84.0	84.0	...	84.0
y	O	Cook, female	2856.0	2856.0	2856.0	2856.0	2856.0
y	V	Cook, hospital	3840.0	3840.0	3840.0	3840.0	3840.0
y	O	Gardener	3740.0	3740.0	3740.0	3740.0	3740.0
d	N	Laborer	76.5	85.0	85.0	85.0	85.0
y	O	Laundress	2856.0	2856.0	2856.0	2856.0	2856.0
d	V	Mason, journeyman	72.0	78.0	78.0	78.0	72.0
d	V	Mason, master	84.0	84.0	84.0	84.0	84.0
d	V	Mason's helper	60.0	60.0	60.0	60.0	60.0
y	A	Miller	6732.0	6732.0	6732.0	6732.0	6732.0
y	O	Nurse	2856.0	2856.0	2856.0	2856.0	2856.0
d	V	Stonecutter, master	84.0	84.0	...	...	84.0
y	A	Wardrobe keeper	4500.0	4500.0	4500.0	4500.0	4500.0
al	V	Weaver, linen	12.0	12.0	12.0	12.0	12.0

Unit	Region		1596	1597	1598	1599	1600
d	V	Carpenter, journeyman	72.0	...	...	72.0	72.0
d	V	Carpenter, master	84.0	84.0	...	84.0	84.0
y	O	Cook, female	2856.0	2856.0	2856.0	2856.0	2856.0
y	V	Cook, hospital	4800.0	4800.0	4800.0	4800.0	4800.0
y	O	Gardener	3740.0	3740.0	3740.0	3740.0	...
d	N	Laborer	85.0	85.0	85.0	93.0	85.0
y	O	Laundress	2856.0	2856.0	2856.0	2856.0	2856.0
d	V	Mason, journeyman	72.0	72.0	72.0	72.0	72.0
d	V	Mason, master	84.0	84.0	84.0	84.0	84.0
d	V	Mason's helper	60.0	60.0	60.0	60.0	60.0
y	A	Miller	6732.0	6732.0	6732.0	6732.0	6732.0
y	O	Nurse	2856.0	2856.0	2856.0	2856.0	2856.0
d	V	Stonecutter, master	...	...	84.0	84.0	...
y	A	Wardrobe keeper	4500.0	4500.0	4500.0	4500.0	4500.0
al	V	Weaver, linen	12.0	12.0	12.0	12.0	12.0

TABLE C

Unit	Region		1601	1602	1603	1604	1605	1606
d	A	Carpenter, journeyman	221.0	238.0	238.0	272.0	294.7	272.0
d	N	Carpenter, master	170.0	186.0	204.0	204.0	204.0	...
y	O	Cook, female	2856.0	4080.0	4080.0	4080.0	4080.0	4080.0
y	V	Cook, hospital	4800.0	4800.0	4800.0	4800.0	4800.0	4800.0
y	N	Doorman	2250.0	2250.0	3264.0	2448.0	2448.0	2448.0
y	A	Drayman	6528.0	6528.0	6528.0	6528.0	6528.0	6528.0
y	A	Gardener	6732.0	8976.0	9000.0	9000.0	9000.0	9000.0
d	A	Laborer	128.0	140.2	136.0	130.3	110.5	127.5
y	O	Laundress	2856.0	4080.0	4080.0	4080.0	4896.0	4896.0
y	N	Maid servant	2856.0	2856.0	2856.0	2856.0	2856.0	2856.0
d	A	Mason, master	272.0	272.0	272.0	272.0	204.0	272.0
d	V	Mason's helper	...	60.0	60.0	60.0	60.0	60.0
y	O	Nurse	3060.0	3672.0	3672.0	3672.0	3672.0	3672.0
y	A	Steward	8160.0	8160.0	8160.0	8160.0	8160.0	8160.0
al	V	Weaver, linen	12.5	12.3	12.0	12.0	12.0	12.0

Unit	Region		1607	1608	1609	1610	1611	1612
d	A	Carpenter, journeyman	272.0	238.0	263.5	...	238.0	204.0
d	N	Carpenter, master	238.0	238.0	238.0	...	238.0	238.0
y	O	Cook, female	4080.0	4080.0	4080.0	4080.0	4080.0	4080.0
y	V	Cook, hospital	4800.0	4800.0	4800.0	4800.0	4800.0	4800.0
y	N	Doorman	2448.0	2448.0	2448.0	2448.0	2448.0	2448.0
y	A	Drayman	6528.0	6528.0	6528.0	6528.0	6528.0	6528.0
y	A	Gardener	9000.0	8976.0	9000.0	9000.0	9000.0	9000.0
d	A	Laborer	123.2	119.0	119.0	...	133.9	...
y	O	Laundress	4896.0	4896.0	4896.0	4896.0	4896.0	4896.0
y	N	Maid servant	2856.0	3264.0	3264.0	3264.0	3264.0	3264.0
d	A	Mason, master	238.0	246.5	272.0	...	272.0	272.0
d	V	Mason's helper	60.0	72.0	72.0	72.0	69.0	...
y	O	Nurse	3672.0	3672.0	3672.0	3672.0	3672.0	3672.0
y	A	Steward	8160.0	8160.0	8160.0	8160.0	8160.0	8160.0
al	V	Weaver, linen	11.7	12.0	12.0	12.0	12.5	12.3

Unit	Region		1613	1614	1615	1616	1617	1618
d	A	Carpenter, journeyman	...	213.4	...	238.0	...	238.0
d	N	Carpenter, master	238.0	238.0	238.0	...	204.0	204.0
y	O	Cook, female	4080.0	4080.0	4080.0	4080.0	4080.0	4080.0
y	V	Cook, hospital	4800.0	4800.0	4800.0	4800.0	4800.0	4800.0
y	N	Doorman	2448.0	2448.0	2448.0	2448.0	2448.0	...
y	A	Drayman	6528.0	6528.0	6528.0	6528.0	6528.0	6528.0
y	A	Gardener	9000.0	9000.0	9000.0	9000.0	9000.0	9000.0
d	A	Laborer	127.5	136.0	...	136.0	117.0	135.7
y	O	Laundress	4896.0	4896.0	4896.0	4896.0	4896.0	4896.0
y	N	Maid servant	3264.0	3264.0	3264.0	3264.0	3264.0	...
d	A	Mason, master	272.0	272.0	...	272.0	272.0	272.0
d	V	Mason's helper	...	60.0	...	72.0	69.0	72.0
y	O	Nurse	3672.0	3672.0	3672.0	3672.0	3672.0	3672.0
y	A	Steward	8160.0	8160.0	8160.0	8160.0	8160.0	8160.0
al	V	Weaver, linen	11.9	12.0	12.3	12.0	12.0	12.0

TABLE C — Continued

Unit	Region		1619	1620	1621	1622	1623	1624
d	A	Carpenter, journeyman	...	238.0	...	...	204.0	204.0
d	N	Carpenter, master	...	238.0	238.0	238.0	238.0	...
y	O	Cook, female	4080.0	4080.0	4080.0	4080.0	4080.0	4080.0
y	V	Cook, hospital	4800.0	4800.0	4800.0	4800.0	4800.0	4800.0
y	N	Doorman	...	...	...	3264.0	3264.0	3264.0
y	A	Drayman	6528.0	6528.0	6528.0	6528.0	6528.0	6750.0
y	A	Gardener	9000.0	9000.0	9000.0	9000.0	9000.0	9000.0
d	A	Laborer	123.5	136.0	...	...	136.0	138.3
y	O	Laundress	4896.0	4896.0	4896.0	4896.0	4896.0	4896.0
y	N	Maid servant	...	...	...	4080.0	4080.0	4080.0
d	A	Mason, master	272.0	272.0	...	272.0	272.0	272.0
d	V	Mason's helper	72.0	66.0	66.0	...	72.0	72.0
y	O	Nurse	3672.0	3672.0	3672.0	3672.0	3672.0	3672.0
y	A	Steward	8160.0	8160.0	8160.0	8160.0	8160.0	8160.0
al	V	Weaver, linen	12.0	12.0	12.0	12.0	11.7	12.0

Unit	Region		1625	1626	1627	1628	1629	1630
d	A	Carpenter, journeyman	204.0	240.0	272.0	238.0	272.0	...
d	N	Carpenter, master	238.0	...	272.0	272.0	273.0	...
y	O	Cook, female	4080.0	4080.0	4080.0	4080.0	4080.0	4080.0
y	V	Cook, hospital	4800.0	4800.0	4800.0	4800.0	4800.0	4800.0
y	N	Doorman	3264.0	3264.0	3264.0	3264.0	3264.0	3264.0
y	A	Drayman	6750.0	6750.0	6750.0	6750.0	6750.0	6750.0
y	A	Gardener	9000.0	9000.0	9000.0	9000.0	9000.0	9000.0
d	A	Laborer	136.0	144.5	153.0	136.0	...	153.0
y	O	Laundress	4896.0	4896.0	4896.0	4896.0	4896.0	...
y	N	Maid servant	4080.0	4080.0	4080.0	4080.0	4080.0	4080.0
d	A	Mason, master	...	289.0	306.0	272.0	272.0	...
d	V	Mason's helper	72.0	72.0	...	72.0	72.0	72.0
y	O	Nurse	3672.0	3672.0	3672.0	3672.0	3672.0	3672.0
y	A	Steward	8160.0	8160.0	8160.0	8160.0	8160.0	8160.0
al	V	Weaver, linen	12.0	12.0	12.0	12.0	12.0	12.3

Unit	Region		1631	1632	1633	1634	1635
d	A	Carpenter, journeyman	...	260.7	272.0	238.0	...
d	N	Carpenter, master	...	374.0	238.0	272.0	...
y	O	Cook, female	4080.0	4080.0	4080.0	4080.0	4080.0
y	V	Cook, hospital	4800.0	4800.0	4800.0	4800.0	4800.0
y	N	Doorman	3264.0	3264.0	3264.0	3264.0	3264.0
y	A	Drayman	6750.0	6750.0	6750.0	6750.0	6750.0
y	A	Gardener	9000.0	9000.0	9000.0	9000.0	9000.0
d	A	Laborer	153.0	144.5	136.0	157.3	144.5
y	O	Laundress	4080.0	4080.0	4080.0	4080.0	4080.0
y	N	Maid servant	4080.0	4080.0	4080.0	4080.0	4080.0
d	A	Mason, master	...	272.0	283.3	340.0	283.3
d	V	Mason's helper	72.0	72.0	72.0	72.0	72.0
y	O	Nurse	3672.0	3672.0	3672.0	3672.0	3672.0
y	A	Steward	8160.0	8160.0	8160.0	8160.0	8160.0
al	V	Weaver, linen	12.9	13.0	13.0	13.0	13.0

TABLE C — CONTINUED

Unit	Region		1636	1637	1638	1639	1640
d	A	Carpenter, journeyman	238.0	226.7	...	...	...
d	N	Carpenter, master	...	...	306.0	272.0	...
y	O	Cook, female	4080.0	4080.0	4080.0	4080.0	4080.0
y	V	Cook, hospital	4800.0	4800.0	4800.0	4800.0	4800.0
y	N	Doorman	3264.0	3264.0	3264.0	3264.0	3264.0
y	A	Drayman	6750.0	6750.0	6750.0	6750.0	6750.0
y	A	Gardener	9000.0	9000.0	9000.0	9000.0	9000.0
d	A	Laborer	140.2	...	147.3	148.7	153.0
y	O	Laundress	4080.0	4080.0	4080.0	4080.0	4080.0
y	N	Maid servant	4080.0	4080.0	4080.0	4080.0	4080.0
d	A	Mason, master	306.0	238.0	255.0	323.8	283.3
d	V	Mason's helper	72.0	72.0	72.0	...	...
y	O	Nurse	3672.0	3672.0	3672.0	3672.0	3672.0
y	A	Steward	8160.0	8160.0	8160.0	8160.0	8160.0
al	V	Weaver, linen	12.7	12.0	13.0	13.0	13.0

Unit	Region		1641	1642	1643	1644	1645
d	A	Carpenter, journeyman	238.0	238.0	238.0	...	...
d	N	Carpenter, master	...	...	272.0	...	238.0
y	O	Cook, female	4080.0	4080.0	4080.0	4080.0	4080.0
y	V	Cook, hospital	4800.0	4800.0	4800.0	5184.0	5184.0
y	N	Doorman	3264.0	3264.0	3264.0	3264.0	3264.0
y	A	Drayman	6750.0	6750.0	6750.0	6750.0	6750.0
y	A	Gardener	9000.0	9000.0	9000.0	9000.0	9000.0
d	A	Laborer	140.7	183.7	170.0	154.2	161.5
y	O	Laundress	4080.0	4080.0	4080.0	4080.0	4080.0
y	N	Maid servant	4080.0	4080.0	4080.0	4080.0	4080.0
d	A	Mason, master	...	289.0	...	283.3	323.8
d	V	Mason's helper	...	...	...	...	...
y	O	Nurse	3672.0	3672.0	3611.5	3672.0	3672.0
y	A	Steward	8160.0	8160.0	8160.0	8160.0	8160.0
al	V	Weaver, linen	14.0	13.7	13.4	13.0	12.0

Unit	Region		1646	1647	1648	1649	1650
d	A	Carpenter, journeyman	272.0	272.0	297.5	...	340.0
d	N	Carpenter, master	...	272.0	...	...	272.0
y	O	Cook, female	4080.0	4080.0	4080.0	4080.0	4080.0
y	V	Cook, hospital	5184.0	4320.0	4320.0	4320.0	4320.0
y	N	Doorman	3264.0	3264.0	3264.0	3264.0	3264.0
y	A	Drayman	6750.0	6750.0	6750.0	6750.0	6750.0
y	A	Gardener	9000.0	9000.0	9000.0	9000.0	9000.0
d	A	Laborer	153.0	170.0	170.0	170.0	249.3
y	O	Laundress	4080.0	4080.0	4080.0	4080.0	4080.0
y	N	Maid servant	4080.0	4080.0	3264.0	3264.0	3264.0
d	A	Mason, master	306.0	...	...	306.0	...
d	V	Mason's helper	...	...	...	...	...
y	O	Nurse	3672.0	3672.0	3672.0	3672.0	3672.0
y	A	Steward	8160.0	8160.0	8160.0	8160.0	...
al	V	Weaver, linen	12.0	12.0	12.0	12.0	12.0

APPENDIX VIII

Composite Index Numbers of Silver Prices, 1501–1650

Year	Index number	Year	Index number	Year	Index number
1501	33.26	1551	69.40	1601	143.55
1502	36.41	1552	71.32	1602	138.40
1503	37.34	1553	70.24	1603	138.70
1504	38.15	1554	71.77	1604	140.38
1505	40.60	1555	71.02	1605	142.20
1506	46.89	1556	72.28	1606	137.52
1507	46.42	1557	79.74	1607	133.59
1508	44.78	1558	80.92	1608	134.07
1509	39.33	1559	77.86	1609	127.68
1510	38.76	1560	79.09	1610	130.57
1511	39.95	1561	86.83	1611	125.72
1512	37.92	1562	91.49	1612	125.35
1513	39.41	1563	89.66	1613	126.55
1514	40.48	1564	88.67	1614	131.22
1515	41.16	1565	92.38	1615	127.86
1516	40.55	1566	90.29	1616	133.75
1517	40.26	1567	90.91	1617	135.02
1518	43.46	1568	92.44	1618	133.74
1519	43.24	1569	90.18	1619	127.86
1520	42.06	1570	93.84	1620	129.94
1521	46.48	1571	97.53	1621	129.09
1522	50.51	1572	97.32	1622	129.57
1523	48.84	1573	99.07	1623	126.91
1524	49.24	1574	98.29	1624	129.01
1525	50.39	1575	103.71	1625	124.21
1526	49.83	1576	95.65	1626	119.48
1527	53.12	1577	94.00	1627	127.36
1528	51.20	1578	97.84	1628	129.86
1529	53.49	1579	107.77	1629	145.80
1530	56.78	1580	102.77	1630	136.77
1531	57.06	1581	103.95	1631	135.21
1532	54.99	1582	106.57	1632	139.77
1533	51.36	1583	108.51	1633	132.79
1534	53.81	1584	110.36	1634	128.43
1535	48.95	1585	111.35	1635	126.81
1536	53.94	1586	106.62	1636	131.74
1537	53.21	1587	111.30	1637	136.93
1538	57.05	1588	107.62	1638	133.70
1539	56.41	1589	113.09	1639	126.24
1540	58.20	1590	113.97	1640	121.46
1541	56.02	1591	112.73	1641	116.53
1542	60.49	1592	117.12	1642	101.45
1543	61.15	1593	113.43	1643	140.51
1544	60.09	1594	114.24	1644	138.63
1545	59.49	1595	114.08	1645	132.91
1546	64.75	1596	116.61	1646	133.06
1547	62.64	1597	123.75	1647	134.97
1548	66.32	1598	132.55	1648	138.93
1549	70.63	1599	134.92	1649	139.87
1550	69.05	1600	137.23	1650	143.22

INDEX

INDEX